UNDERSTANDING
and COUNSELING
Persons with Alcohol, Drug, and Behavioral Addictions

UNDERSTANDING *and* COUNSELING

Persons with Alcohol, Drug, and Behavioral Addictions

Counseling for Recovery and Prevention
Using Psychology and Religion

Revised and Enlarged Edition

HOWARD CLINEBELL PhD

Abingdon Press
Nashville

UNDERSTANDING AND COUNSELING PERSONS WITH ALCOHOL, DRUG, AND
BEHAVIORAL ADDICTIONS

This book is printed on recycled, acid-free paper.

Library of Congress Cataloging-in-Publication Data

Clinebell, Howard John, 1922-
　Understanding and counseling persons with alcohol, drug, and behavioral addictions : counseling for recovery and prevention using psychology and religion / Howard Clinebell.—Rev. and enl. ed.
　　p.　cm.
　Rev. ed. of: Understanding and counseling the alcoholic through religion and psychology. Rev. and enl. ed. c1968.
　Includes bibliographical references.
　ISBN 0-687-02564-8 (pbk. : acid-free paper)
　1. Substance abuse—Psychological aspects.　2. Substance abuse—Religious aspects. 3. Compulsive behavior.　4. Compulsive behavior—Religious aspects.　5. Addicts—Counseling of. I. Clinebell, Howard John, 1922-　Understanding and counseling the alcoholic through religion and psychology.　II. Title.
RC564.C545　1998
616.86—dc21　　　　　　　　　　　　　　　　　　　　　　　　　98-12348
　　　　　　　　　　　　　　　　　　　　　　　　　　　　　　　　CIP

99 00 01 02 03 04 05 06 07—10 9 8 7 6 5 4 3 2

MANUFACTURED IN THE UNITED STATES OF AMERICA

To those whose insights and struggles
helped shape this book

BILL WILSON
MARTY MANN
HARRY TIEBOUT
PAUL TILLICH
DAVID ROBERTS
E. MANSELL PATTISON
and seventy-nine recovering alcoholics

"Drug and alcohol abuse is America's number one health problem, the number one crime problem, the number one homeless problem, the number one youth problem, including youth violence."
—*Joseph A. Califano Jr., Former U.S. Secretary of Health, Education, and Welfare, now president of the Center on Addiction and Substance Abuse, Columbia University*[1]

Contents

Appreciation: Looking Back with Heartfelt Thanks

Although most books of any depth are written by one person, in the creative process the authors integrate the ideas of those with whom they have touched minds. It does my soul good, therefore, to explain the book's dedication while rearticulating my gratitude for the eye-opening insights of the countless people who touched my life with both head and heart understanding of addictive problems and recovery. Many of those who contributed to my understanding during the protracted pregnancy, birthing, and rebirthing of this book have graduated to heaven.

As I look back over a half century of my interest in alcoholics and the drug addicted, it is clear that one person stands out among those who fed the creative processes in my mind and heart. That person was Bill Wilson, cofounder of Alcoholics Anonymous. I am more keenly aware today than I was then of how profoundly I was influenced by several brief but energizing contacts with this remarkable man—truly, a major spiritual pioneer in the twentieth century. In the late-1940s, Norman B., a nationally known radio commentator and A.A. member, had a home near where I was serving a congregation as a young pastor on Long Island, New York. When I told him that I was considering doing research for a doctoral dissertation at Columbia University and Union Theological Seminary on a comparative study of five religious approaches to alcoholism, he asked if I would like to meet "Bill." I responded, "Bill who?" A few days later Norman drove me to Manhattan where I had an extended, unforgettable conversation with Bill Wilson over lunch. The humility, warmth, and down-to-earth insights of the lanky Vermonter I met that day impressed me deeply. Among the many things that Bill shared, one statement continued to intrigue and puzzle me for years: *"Before A.A. we were trying to drink God out of a bottle."* Searching for understanding of that statement became the central quest of my research on addictions. Bill expressed refreshing openness to the research about A.A. that I was hoping to do. In fact, he offered to arrange in-depth interviews with a wide variety of recovering alcoholics for one phase of my doctoral study. After completing an early draft of the dissertation chapter on A.A., I sent it to him to review. He gave me valuable feedback and corrected several historical inaccuracies. I recall one telephone conversation in which he said with characteristic humility: "My part in the whole thing is a hell of a lot overrated. Actually A.A. had several founders, people who contributed indispensable things to it—people like William James, Carl Jung, Dr. Silkworth."[1] When the first edition of this book was published in 1956, the first person to whom I sent a copy, after my parents, was Bill, expressing my heartfelt thanks for all his help. His generous affirmation of the book made me feel both humbled and elated beyond my fondest hopes. The more than five years of research, analysis, and writing invested in this project clearly had been abundantly worthwhile.

It warms my heart to remember with gratitude others who contributed to my understanding of addictions and thereby to this book. At Bill's request, Bob H., then head of the New York A.A. intergroup organization, lined up interviews of alcoholics and gave valuable help in checking my perceptions of what I thought I was learning from them. Marty Mann, the brilliant pioneer founder of the National Council on Alcoholism, gave me encouragement and guidance at many points in rewriting the dissertation as a book, and later in doing the first revision of the book. Harry Tiebout, a Connecticut psychiatrist who had served as psychotherapist for several of the founding members of A.A., pioneered in understanding the crucial concept of surrender in recovery. When he read the first edition of the book, he wrote confronting me sharply for my lack of emphasis on that key concept. I subsequently drove to his home and had an extended conversation in which he helped me understand more about surrender as a key concept in recovery. It was only later that I came to realize that I had not grasped this initially because I had not yet suffered enough from things that I could not control or change, and therefore had not been forced by life to experience surrender. I am thankful to my late friend, E. Mansell Pattison, who, from his perspective in community psychiatry, first opened my eyes to the possibility that there were alternative ways to understand and treat alcoholism.

Theologian-philosopher Paul Tillich, a key mentor and member of my dissertation committee at Union Theological Seminary, helped guide my reflections on the spiritual roots of alcoholism. I chuckle when I remember one occasion when we were discussing some of my research findings on spirituality and alcohol. Tillich expressed his utter mystification concerning those denominations in America that have substituted grape juice for wine in celebrating the sacrament of Communion. He declared with feeling, "To me, good wine is sacred!" It was his affirmation and his encouragement to rewrite the dissertation for a nonacademic readership that led to the publication of this my first book, which also decisively changed the direction of my professional life. It began a chain reaction of opening doorways that led me from pastoring congregations into a teaching and writing ministry. I am grateful to David Roberts of Union Theological Seminary, also on my dissertation committee, for opening a wide window of understanding of the complex dynamics of suffering, psychotherapy, and religion. His tragic premature death hit me as if I were losing a member of my own family.[2]

I also need again to express thanks to the faculty of the 1949 Yale University Summer School of Alcohol Studies, particularly Selden D. Bacon and E. M. "Bunky" Jellinek, who opened my eyes to many aspects of addictions. Furthermore, I am grateful for what I learned from the faculty of the William Alanson White Institute of Psychiatry, Psychoanalysis, and Psychology. Their intellectual stimulation in seminars over two years deepened my grasp of many aspects of human dynamics, psychotherapy, and addiction. Harry Stack Sullivan, Erich Fromm, and Frieda Fromm Reichman were particularly influential in this learning process. I feel both personal and professional appreciation for the extended exploration of my own inner life guided by my first therapist during my training analysis at that Institute. (His name really was Harry Bone.) Horace Friess, professor in the Department of Religious Studies at Columbia University, chaired my doctoral committee. He gave me scholarly guidance and friendly encouragement through my years of graduate study and research, modeling what I came to value more as I began to teach and supervise Ph.D. students myself.

A number of people have my special gratitude for what they contributed to this rewritten edition. Our daughter, Susan, contributed in a superb way by typing the earlier revision onto a computer disk, making the process of rewriting much easier. Dorothy Owens, then a Ph.D. candidate at Vanderbilt University Divinity School, did valuable research for me as my graduate assistant when I was teaching there in 1995. Dr. Anderson Spickard, Jr. Professor of Medicine and Medical Director of the Vanderbilt University Institute for the Treatment of Addiction, also has my appreciation for his feedback on the drug addiction chapter. The book he coauthored with Barbara Thompson, *Dying for a Drink: What You Should Know About Alcoholism*, is one of the most helpful resources for church people.[3] Dr. Jim W. West, outpatient medical director at the Betty Ford Center in Rancho Mirage, California, also gave invaluable feedback on the drug addiction chapter. Roger Fontanini shared his learnings from his own recovery and his volunteer service at the Betty Ford Addiction Center. Robin Crawford, Bob Albers, and Bridget Clare McKeever, three Claremont graduates who did their dissertation research on addictions, each gave me helpful feedback during the process of rewriting this book, as did Jim Rhoads from his extensive career as a pastoral counselor of addicted persons.

A large group of generous contributors to this volume must remain anonymous. They are the countless alcoholics with whom I talked and from whom I learned at scores of A.A. meetings and at other religious treatments for alcoholism during my intensive study of religious approaches to the problem. I am particularly grateful to the seventy-nine recovering alcoholics who supplied detailed information concerning nearly every aspect of their lives as they were interviewed during sessions that averaged three hours in length. These interviews covered the following areas: early home life; educational, vocational, and marital background; prealcoholic drinking and the developmental patterns of their addictions; experiences in A.A. or other approaches; and self-understanding. Data from these rich interviews supplied much of the material for the A.A. chapter and considerable material for several other chapters. Whatever degree of authenticity and insight concerning alcoholism and A.A. the book has is due in considerable measure to the self-revelation of these A.A. members. As I picture the numerous homeless alcoholics with whom I talked over several days on Skid Row in New York City, I feel both sadness and gratitude. Along with persons involved in the ministries of the Bowery Rescue Mission and the Salvation Army's Harbor Light Mission there, these men taught me much about their agonizing struggles with the triple entrapment of homelessness, addiction, and often mental illness. I am grateful to Captain John Cheydleur, director of the Salvation Army's regional social services department, for providing updated information concerning their program and the current situation on Skid Row.

Many of the insights that have come to me from A.A. and other approaches to addictions have proved unexpectedly to be gifts with applications far beyond this one area of caring and counseling. In fact, I am now aware that these insights have illuminated many of the issues with which I have struggled through the years in the wider field of counseling and psychotherapy. For these extended learnings, I am very thankful.

What has pleased me more than anything else about this book is the way its insights and methods have received affirmation from persons who know the rocky, hazardous road of addiction and recovery personally. These have been persons whose sanity and even survival had been preserved by Twelve Step and other recovery programs.

Our lives are touched by certain people who profoundly influence the directions of our life journeys. To my family—Charlotte and our then small children, John, Donald, and Susan—it's a joy to express again my heartfelt thanks for all that they contributed to the writing of this book by their presence and love. During my years of concentrated graduate study that eventually resulted in this book, they had a husband and father who was often preoccupied and overloaded with other pressing concerns. As anyone who has been through such a demanding process knows too well, all those in one's intimate circle of caring make sacrifices during those times.

Introduction to the Second Revised Edition

This book is for those who want help in understanding and dealing constructively with persons suffering from alcoholism and other drug addictions, as well as those struggling with obsessive-compulsive behavior patterns often called "process addictions" or "behavioral addictions." All addictions are complex psychosocial-spiritual illnesses. Chemical addictions add further complexity by including physiological and perhaps genetic factors. Addictions constitute one of the most widespread and costly, as well as pressing and perplexing, problems in contemporary societies. The book aims at helping persons who have the opportunity to counsel with addicted persons and their families, as well as those who are struggling with such diseases. It also seeks to provide accurate, up to date information that can be used in the vital preventive education in congregations, other religious organizations, and in a variety of secular settings.

I am pleased that an editor of academic books at Abingdon Press encouraged me to do yet another revision of this book, saying that it has become something of a classic in the field. It is difficult for me to believe that over four decades have passed since the first edition was published in 1956, and that it has been some three decades since the first revised edition of this book was published. The fact that much of the basic content of these editions is still relevant to the changing field of addictions, makes me both glad and sad. I am glad because it affirms that some of the basic information and methods in the book have stood the test of time and are still useful, but sad because I wish that more dramatic breakthroughs had occurred that would have opened up new doors of hope and help, making more of what I wrote years ago obsolete. The hope-full and door-opening developments that have occurred are incorporated in this edition. But the heart of the original edition and even more so the first revision remains because it still reflects the current understanding of the art of addiction counseling and prevention.

This latest edition is much more than a revision. In many ways it is a new book. Most of the book has been rewritten and several chapters have been added. My objective was to update the book in light of current knowledge, and to make it relevant to the significant situation in the field of addictive problems in today's turbulent and increasingly addictive society. Here's an overview of what you'll find in this edition:

Part I lays a foundation of basic information for understanding the nature and multiple causes of addictions. Such an understanding is essential for either effective counseling or prevention. Action of any kind in this field that lacks a foundation of accurate information tends to be misdirected, even counterproductive. Two new chapters deal with persons caught in other addictions including gambling, sex, work, and religion, and those who are especially vulnerable to addictions—youth, women, oppressed minorities, gays and lesbians, and older adults.

Part II describes three religious approaches to addictions and evaluates their strengths and limitations. A new chapter focuses on explicitly Christian approaches and on those shaped by a feminist perspective. This section can enable readers to learn from religious approaches that have focused their healing efforts most directly on addictions. Chapter 9 is a discussion of how to understand the psychosocial dynamics of religious approaches in general. This discussion sheds some light on why religious approaches are among the most effective paths to recovery ever devised. Chapter 10 explores the complex ethical issues in addictions and recovery. Such issues are often seen as thorny ones by professionals in the addiction field. To those not familiar with the discipline of psychology of religion, let me say that chapters 9 and 10, and in fact the whole book, draw on that science. It uses psychological and sociological understandings to illuminate and critique religious beliefs and practices by individuals and group.

Part III applies the understandings of Parts I and II to the practical work of counseling-for-recovery with addicted persons and their families. The final chapter describes how to develop alcoholism and drug prevention programs in congregations, schools, and other people-helping agencies. An annotated bibliography and a guide to referral resource groups have been added to earlier editions.

It should be noted that in case illustrations in this book that are taken either from my own clinical practice or from others, I have altered identifying information or created reality-based composite cases to protect the precious bond of confidentiality.

Using This Book in Teaching About Addictions

Here are some guidelines for effective use of the book in study groups and courses in various settings including congregations, colleges, universities, theological seminaries, and in continuing education courses for clergy and addiction counselors:

1. Always begin by discovering how much participants already know and what their main needs and interests are in the field of addictions. I find that having persons write out what they expect and hope for from a

class, and what their background is in the field facilitates this process. In addition, it facilitates the learning to ask each participant to write down for themselves and the instructor their learning objectives and describing what they will do to best use the course as an opportunity to move toward their objectives. Then, after participants have identified their major learning objectives, it is wise to negotiate with the class an understanding of the main issues and topics on which the class will focus, and what you will offer in the learning process. This process is called creating a group learning contract. Having such a contract in writing increases the probability that more participants will use the experience to maximize their own learning.

2. When this book is used either as a text or as collateral reading, it is important to also interface discussion of key concepts with frequent experiential components. For example, I have found that having students attend an open meeting of Alcoholics Anonymous is an excellent way of capturing their interest in the problem and increasing both their head and their heart understanding of alcohol addiction and the recovery process in A.A. It also enhances learning to have seasoned members of self-help groups as A.A., Al-Anon, Narcotics Anonymous, or Co-Dependents Anonymous, as well as professionals in comprehensive treatment facilities, share their experiences with the class as well as field questions. When discussing theories and methods of counseling addicted persons (Part III), it is vitally important for the instructor to give live demonstrations of counseling methods, using either an addicted person in the class or by role-playing. It is also crucial for maximum learning to provide coaching as participants have an opportunity to try out in reality practice sessions (role taking) the skills they are learning.

3. Be aware that in almost every class there will be one or often more persons who are struggling with their own addictions or with the problem of how to relate to a friend or family member caught in the gradually strangling tentacles of an addiction. Over the years I have offered seminars and workshops on addictions, I have been impressed with how many of those who come are motivated by their personal as much as their professional needs. So, be sure to provide opportunities for lots of group sharing and also one-on-one conversations with you outside of the class sessions. Asking students to tell or write their own story of encounters with addictions in themselves and others is a fruitful approach to providing opportunities to bring their hidden agendas into the sunlight of open discussion, individually or in the group.

4. Familiarize yourself both with community resources and with the lit-

erature of the field so that you can be a competent guide as the learners seek trails in what is for them unexplored terrain.

5. Be aware that addictions are not isolated areas of human bondage and pain. We live in an addictive society. To understand the addictive process in depth is to enhance your understanding of the deeper problems of many people in our society in this age of psychochemistry and proliferating drugs. This book and the insights it seeks to communicate can be a window into many areas of human pain and bondage that do not seem directly related to addictions.

When the first edition of this book was published in 1956, I expressed my hope in the preface that it "would be of sufficient value to individuals who were facing the perplexing problems of helping alcoholics that it would justify the investment of countless hours and insights by the many individuals whose help made the book possible." In the first revision, published twelve years later, I was pleased to be able to report that positive feedback from many alcoholics and their families, from clergy, counselors, and teachers in North America and other countries, suggested that it had proved to be useful. Now, nearly three decades after that, as I relaunch this radically rewritten edition, I do so with the fervent wish that the book will have a rebirth of usefulness. I hope and pray that it will be a useful tool to both professionals and family members struggling to treat and/or prevent not only alcoholism, but also the epidemic of other addictions in our society. May it be so for you!

Howard Clinebell
Santa Barbara, California

Foreword by Marty Mann (1968 Edition)

That Howard Clinebell has unusual understanding of the alcoholic and his [sic] problems becomes crystal clear as one reads this book. First published in 1956, it quickly won a place for itself as one of the best books in the field. Revising and enlarging this work has vastly increased its usefulness, to the point that people working in the field can ill afford to be without it; and people who become interested and want to learn will find it "must" reading.

For Howard Clinebell, now professor of pastoral counseling and psychology at the School of Theology, Claremont, California, does not limit his book to the special areas he knows so well. He has provided a broad and well-informed survey of our current knowledge about the disease of alcoholism and its victims, and followed this with many practical suggestions on how to help alcoholics. His interest embraces education and its role both in bringing the alcoholic to treatment and in prevention. Finally, he has included much of the history of the whole alcoholism movement.

Dr. Clinebell's background and vocation naturally ensure that the role of religion in both the treatment and prevention of alcoholism shall have full attention. Many may be unaware of just how important a role this has been, and still is today. While ministers will benefit especially from a study of this book, others who work with alcoholics—doctors, psychologists, nurses, social workers, counselors, and employers, as well as families and friends—should find their effectiveness greatly enhanced if they will take advantage of Dr. Clinebell's expertise as expressed here.

Perhaps most important is the attitude that pervades the book. Howard Clinebell clearly *likes* alcoholics. He does not confuse the condition of illness with the person who has it. His concern is always for that person and his potential as a human being, once he can be freed from the entangling web of his terrible compulsion. This, in my opinion, is the reason Dr. Clinebell has been able to help so many alcoholics to recover.

It is my hope that his readers will imbibe at least some of his understanding, compassion, and caring. If they do, countless sick alcoholics will have a chance to get well.

—Marty Mann, Founder-Consultant
National Council on Alcoholism

PART I
Understanding the Problems of
Chemical and Behavioral Addictions

CHAPTER 1

Who Are Alcoholics and Drug-Addicted Persons?
Some Working Definitions

I expect that almost everyone reading this book has known at least one person whose life has been shattered by the spiraling abuse of alcohol, and many will also have known a person dependent on other consciousness-changing drugs. For few problems are as widespread as those of alcoholism, drug dependence, and multiple addictions to alcohol, drugs, and nicotine. Addictions may have touched one's immediate family, or an employee, fellow worker, friend, distant relative, or someone in one's neighborhood or congregation. It is a rare person or family whose life is not impacted, directly or indirectly, by alcohol and drug problems. In Western industrialized countries and increasingly in developing countries, drug and alcohol dependence is rampant.

Public attention often is awakened by gripping news stories of well-known people's struggles with alcohol and drugs. Prominent American writers Ernest Hemingway, William Faulkner, and F. Scott Fitzgerald were all alcoholics. In recent years, the media has carried the stories about the addiction struggles of former first lady Betty Ford, baseball superhero Mickey Mantle, actress Elizabeth Taylor, singer Johnny Cash, and Kitty Dukakis, wife of former governor and presidential candidate Michael Dukakis. It seems likely that people gain the courage to face their own chemical dependency when the famous come out of the addiction closet.

Clergy, counselors, physicians, nurses, psychotherapists, social workers, teachers, and work supervisors who try to help people in personal and family troubles are well acquainted with problems of chemical dependence. As I reflect on my own professional experience, I am struck by the variety of such encounters. I think, for example, of Mr. K., who stopped after choir practice to chat and during the conversation worked around to unburdening his soul of the grim story of his wife's recent spree. Or of Mrs. L., who phoned to ask if I could help persuade her alcoholic husband to see a psychiatrist. Or Bill, a member of the youth group, who came to tell of the trouble his family had been having with an alcoholic uncle who, though abstinent in A.A., continued to be difficult to live with. Or Joe, a promising young man of twenty-nine, who realized that his drinking was out of hand and, in desperation, appealed for help. Then there was Mr. B, a stranger in work clothes who came to the parsonage door with a convincing story about needing a loan to redeem his tools that he had been forced to pawn during a prolonged illness. On investigation, his story proved to be a clever alcoholic ruse. Or I think of Mr. P., a business executive and church member, who, after many years of periodic binges had been happily sober in A.A. for several years. Or Mr. L., a talented artist and frequent patron of the city hospital's alcoholic ward, who could not admit that he was an alcoholic. Or Mac, a member of another religious faith, who used to knock on my door every few weeks asking for a "loan." (I had made the mistake of being a "good minister" and also following the course of least resistance by giving him a small sum on the first occasion.) Each time Mac came, he looked more like death—toward which he was slipping with tragic alacrity. I remember Bert, a youth from a dysfunctional family, who often arrived at senior youth meetings with alcohol on his breath. After a party, he was arrested at the scene of a near fatal accident and charged with driving under the influence, having failed a breath test at the scene. And of Sally whose parents came to discuss their fear that she was using marijuana regularly. I think of Mrs. R., a parishioner who I felt sure was having serious trouble with alcohol, but who was expert at hiding the fact from everyone, including herself. I remember Peter, a lawyer and church leader ,whose hidden addiction to cocaine and then heroin resulted in behavior that was increasingly strange. Any experienced minister, counselor, physician, or social worker could duplicate such a list.

As I think of the addicted persons who have crossed my path, I remember the times I have felt utterly helpless in the face of their problems, the times I have failed, and the feelings of frustration accompanying these failures. But I also recall the satisfaction when I have been able to make small but significant contributions toward encouraging addicted people or their families to take steps on the rocky uphill road of recovery.

Few problems have been so baffling in nature as alcoholism and drug dependence. For many years, objective data about these illnesses were in short supply. A considerable part of what had been written had been propagandistic with only a flimsy foundation of objective facts. Many of the so-called cures were relatively ineffective. In some cases they were outright deceptions involving despicable exploitation of human misery. Hopelessness often has hung like a gloomy cloud over the whole field of addictions, both alcohol and drug addiction.

Alcoholism and drug addictions still are baffling problems. But both treatment and research developments in recent years offer some new hope. No health problem has been studied more extensively than alcoholism and drug dependence. Many scientific disciplines, spanning the physiological, psychological, and sociological disciplines, have focused their research explorations on these problems, bringing new understanding. Most important of all, from the standpoint of addicted persons and their families, is the hope engendered by the remarkable success of Twelve Step recovery programs.

There is no area of human suffering in which healthy religion has given a more convincing demonstration of its healing, growth-nurturing power than in problems of addictions. For much of the twentieth century it has been recognized that authentic spirituality offers hopeful resources for dealing with addictions. In his classic sermons on temperance published in 1827, Lyman Beecher[1] made it clear that some sort of religious experience was the best hope for the alcoholic. Even those who had no professional interest in religion often shared this view. Around 1930, the director of a large chemical company in America sought help for his alcoholism from the internationally known psychiatrist Carl Gustav Jung in Zürich. Jung went over his case very carefully and then told him that nothing but a religious conversion could give him any lasting help. The man returned to America where he received help in the Oxford Group movement. He told a friend named Bill Wilson what Jung had said. This influenced Bill's thinking in the years before 1935 when he became cofounder of the group that has given the widest and most convincing evidence of the healing effectiveness of religion—Alcoholics Anonymous. This group has reclaimed from the scrap heap of society more "hopeless" alcoholics than any other approach in the long history of humankind's struggles with addictions.

The goal of this volume will be to explore the ways in which religious resources can be used most effectively in dealing with alcoholism and other drug dependencies. It also sheds light on the role of religious resources in dealing with other problems of human bondage and lack of freedom including behavorial addictions to gambling, work, sex, consumerism, and religion. Here is a clarification of some key concepts in this book.

Defining Terms

Obsessive-Compulsive. Those who suffer from psychologically obsessive patterns have repetitive, anxious thoughts that increasingly dominate their mental processes and feed their compulsive behaviors. Like a broken record, these thoughts and feelings come into their minds again and again in spite of their unsuccessful struggles to interrupt the distressing pattern of thinking, feeling, and acting. *Compulsive* and *compulsion* are terms describing repetitive, out-of-control behavior that often accompanies obsessive thinking. In addictions, the focus of both the obsessive thinking and compulsive behavior is on the substance or the process being abused. The hallmark of obsessive-compulsive patterns is the diminishing freedom to interrupt them by choice.

Addiction. In traditional psychiatric usage, the term *addiction* is limited to obsessive-compulsive abuse of substances like alcohol and drugs. These are sometimes called *true addictions*. The body-mind organism of those addicted to such consciousness-changing substances has adapted to the presence of the substance. This produces five criteria that are useful in diagnosing addictions:[2]

(1) *Tissue tolerance* means that increasing amounts of the substance are required to produce the desired effects, and withdrawal symptoms (like severe hangovers) are experienced when the substance is no longer taken;

(2) *Increasing dependence* on the substance, both psychological and physiological;

(3) *Obsessive thinking* about and craving for the substance;

(4) *Loss of control* in using the substance; and

(5) *Continued usage* in spite of negative consequences.

Here, I follow the prevalent generic usage in much current writing that extends the term *addiction* beyond its original psychophysiological meaning to describe any obsessive-compulsive behavior in which there is some loss of voluntary control so that the victims seriously damage one or more important areas of their lives. Psychologist Anne Wilson Schaef has written extensively popularizing this enlarged definition. She distinguishes two basic types of addictions—*substance addictions* and *process addictions*. (I prefer the term "behavorial addiction" for process addictions.) Substance addictions that are epidemic in our society include those involving alcohol; legal drugs (both prescribed and over-the-counter); illegal or street drugs (including prescription drugs that are produced and sold illegally); nicotine; caffeine; and food. Process or behavioral addictions include excessive and destructive uses of work, sex, gambling, shopping, codependent relationships, religion, and acquiring money and power. Such activity addictions could be described more precisely as destructive patterns of obsessive thinking and compulsive behavior, in which human activities are used like drugs in vain attempts to satisfy deep inner conflicts and emotional hungers. As is true of substance addictions, such behavioral patterns tend to become increasingly harmful to victims' overall values, living, and well-being.

Alcoholism.[3] The compulsive-addictive uses of alcohol are recognized as an illness by both the World Health Organization of the United Nations and the American Medical Association. The primary behavior characteristics of this illness are craving for the psychophysiological effects of alcohol and continuing excessive use of alcoholic beverages in ways that are harmful to the users and many others. It also is characterized by diminishing freedom to interrupt the pattern by conscious intention. Alcoholism is a progressive, chronic, and potentially fatal disease if it goes unrecognized and untreated.

Alcohol addiction is roughly synonymous with *alcoholism* (Gamma, Delta, or Epsilon types as described below). In some cases, it is a useful term because it communicates a sense of the intensity of the compulsion involved. *Chronic alcoholism* usually refers to the advanced stages of the illness. It is during these stages that physiological and psychiatric complications most frequently occur. These complications are the physical and psychological diseases resulting from the prolonged excessive use of alcohol and include polyneuropathy, pellagra, cirrhosis of the liver, Korsakoff's psychosis, delirium tremens, acute alcoholic hallucinosis, and others. An alcoholic who is afflicted needs immediate medical attention and often hospitalization.

Drug Addiction. Any prolonged use of consciousness-changing drugs that are harmful to oneself and/or others, characterized by increasing loss of freedom to terminate the use volitionally. This loss of freedom seems to be caused by complex psychophysiological changes in the total body-mind organism. *Chemical dependency* is a another term for drug addiction. Alcoholism, technically speaking, is a drug addiction because alcohol is a consciousness-changing drug.

Problem Drinking and **Drug Abuse.** These involve continued heavy use of alcohol or other drugs that are harmful to oneself or others and does not have the characteristics that identify chemical addictions, namely gradual loss of volitional control of the amount and occasions of use, increased tolerance—meaning more of the substance is required to produce the desired effects, and withdrawal symptoms showing that the body has adapted biochemically to its presence. (Problem drinkers were described by Jellinek as Alpha alcoholics, contrasted with Gamma, Delta, and Epsilon types of alcoholics who are physiologically addicted.) Many problem drinkers do not respond to A.A. or other addiction treatment methods because they are not addicted. Instead, their heavy drinking is the result of habituation and self-medication of pain coming from sources such as a disintegrating marriage, a severe loss, frustration of a cherished dream, or psychological depression. It may be that those excessive drinkers who recover the ability to drink in moderation are nonaddicted problem drinkers rather than alcoholics who are physiologically addicted.

Multiple Substance Abuse Disorders. This refers to the complex problem of addictions to two or more drugs, usually including alcohol. *Polyabuse, polyaddictions,* and *multiple addictions* are synonyms. The vast majority of alcoholics today also are hooked on other drugs. Many switch or combine drugs to get more buzz, depending on what is available. An actor and exabuser who began using drugs at fifteen states: "I was a garbage-can addict. I wasn't choosy. I took pills, drank like a fish, used hallucinogens, did cocaine. I would carry a small aspirin box which contained all the pills I needed, according to how I wanted to feel."[4]

Cross addiction means that if persons are dependent on one psychoactive substance they are at high risk to develop dependence on any other addictive substance.

Dual Diagnosis. This is a medical term used to describe chemical dependency that coexists with a variety of major psychiatric illnesses, each complicating the other.[5] The psychiatric problems may be thought disorders, mood disorders, anxiety illnesses, rage disorders, and characterological disorders. Most substance abuse treatment centers recognize that both of the diseases must be treated simultaneously. Most know that it is unwise to prescribe potentially addictive drugs to treat the mental illness, unless the patients are very closely monitored. Mental illness symptoms often fade or disappear when people are successfully treated for their chemical addictions and stop drinking or using. But with many people whose psychiatric disorder preceded the onset of their addiction(s), ongoing sobriety is usually exceedingly difficult to achieve. If short-term sobriety is achieved, the underlying psychological and interpersonal problems often become visible to others.

Dry Drunk. This is behavior involving *alcoholic thinking* by an addicted person who is not using chemicals but is experiencing serious problems in coping with reality without them. It often includes intolerance, judgmentalism, irrational and grandiose thinking, and a defensive lifestyle.

Surrender. A letting go of defensive denial by addicted persons, thus becoming open to receiving needed help. Usually occurs after confronting a crisis when the person hits bottom.

Codependents. These are caregiving persons who are dependent on addicted people's dependence. They organize their lives around "helping" the addicted by attempting to control them, protecting them from the painful consequences of their actions, and taking responsibility for their destructive behavior. *Enabling* is the term used to describe the behavior of codependent family members, friends, employers, or helping professionals, including clergy, who unwittingly enable addicted persons to continue their self-other damaging behavior. *Letting go* or *release* are terms used to describe giving up enabling behaviors including all the futile, frustrating efforts to control the addicted person's drinking or drug use.

Intervention. This is a carefully planned caring-confrontation of chemically dependent people in which those closest to them present concrete examples of their destructive behavior, statements of strong concern about what will happen if they continue, encouragement to seek help, and information about available resources.

Recognizing the Problem

Whatever the problem, effective treatment depends on accurate recognition and diagnosis. For this reason, the first concern of those who want to help alcoholics or drug addicts is to recognize and understand the problem. Some time ago I attended a dinner and was seated beside a guest who plied me with questions concerning alcoholism. During the conversation she raised this problem: "I am concerned about a friend who seems to me to be drinking too much. How can I tell whether or not he is an alcoholic?" In answering her query, I pointed out that it is often difficult if not impossible to be absolutely certain that a given person is afflicted with alcoholism. But I also shared a useful rule of thumb that often gives valid clues: Does the person's drinking and/or use of other drugs interfere in destructive ways, frequently or continuously, with one or more important areas of his or her life—meaning family life, job, finances, physical or mental health, social relations, or spirituality? If so, the person is probably on the slippery slope of becoming a full-blown alcoholic and/or drug addict. Some A.A. members simplify this working definition by stating: "If your drinking has caused you serious problems and you are still drinking, you are an alcoholic." This points to the essential nature of alcoholism and drug addiction, the characteristics that distinguish these from other kinds of alcohol or drug use. If drinkers who are not addicted find that their drinking and/or drug use is interfering with things that are really important to them, they will recognize this and reduce or cease their consumption. In contrast, alcoholics and drug addicts usually will not recognize the cause-effect relation between their drinking or use and the troubles in their family or work relationships. Instead, they may blame their heavy drinking or use on the painful difficulties in these other areas. The psychological defense of denial will keep them from seeing the key role of mind-altering chemicals in contributing to if not causing their psychological pain and interpersonal and job problems. They are blind to reality because alcohol and drugs have become increasingly important to them. To recognize these as among the causes of their problems in living would threaten the center around which they are increasingly structuring their lives.

Furthermore, if they have moved beyond controlled use into compulsive-additive use, they will probably not be able to reduce their consumption for any extended period. This will be true even if they suspect that the addictive substances may be contributing to their troubles. For psychophysiological reasons that are not understood fully, they have lost the power of choice when or how much they drink or use drugs. The phrase "driven to drink" (or "driven to drugs") can be accurately applied to them. They are driven by addictive-compulsive forces within their mind-body-spirit organism that are somewhat beyond their control. The inner compulsions often are reinforced by enablers, crises, and external pressures. Once they begin to drink or use, they often will not be able to stop for very long until their supply is exhausted or they pass out. Alcoholics and drug addicts, then, are persons for whom one drink or one fix or shot frequently triggers a chain reaction leading to a binge. It should be noted that some alcoholics and drug addicts are able to exercise some control over their use for a time, which reinforces their denial that they really are in trouble with their favorite consciousness-altering chemicals.

There are other danger signs that may be useful in recognizing incipient alcoholism or drug dependence. Anyone who uses alcohol or drugs as a persistent means of interpersonal adjustment (to allow him or herself to be more aggressive, or sexual, or less shy, for example) is probably in danger. Such a person may be nearing or entering the intangible zone that separates drinking and drug use that is controlled and nonpathological from that which is compulsive-addictive and uncontrolled. Furthermore, anyone whose drinking and/or drug use is in clear defiance of the accepted standards of the main groups from which they derive their sense of belonging is engaging in dangerous usage that may indicate the onset of addictions. Sneaking drinks or using drugs alone are examples of such behavior. Users who hide their behavior show that the desired effects of these favorite chemicals is more important to them than the acceptance of the primary reference group from which they derive caring and confirmation of their identity. They are willing to risk rejection by their in-group in order to satisfy their psychophysical-spiritual craving for the effects of the substance or activity.

Frequent drunkenness or being spaced out on drugs would seem to be the most obvious indication of addiction. But, with reference to alcoholism, a word of caution is in order. All alcoholism is attended by drunkenness, but not all drunkenness—even frequent drunkenness—is indicative of alcoholism. Alcoholism and drunkenness are not synonymous. For example, what is called *rough recreational drinking* was much more common during the American frontier days than it is today. Almost every weekend, many men would come together to get and often stay roaring drunk. This was the accepted social pattern among some frontier groups. Although there was a great deal of drunkenness, there was probably less alcoholism than there is today. Drinking on some college and university campuses today also includes rough recreational drinking that produces frequent drunkenness, often attended by aggressive and destructive behavior. This is indicative of problem drinking when it interferes with students' functioning in important areas of their lives. Persons who have heightened vulnerability to alcoholism or drug addiction, for whatever reasons, are more likely to become afflicted with these addictions in a social group that encourages frequent heavy drug use or drunkenness.

Although addicted persons, because of their denial, often are the last ones to recognize their problem, there are ways to recognize addictions. The literature of A.A. suggests:

> We do not like to pronounce any individual an alcoholic, but you can quickly diagnose yourself. Step over to the nearest barroom and try some controlled drinking. Try to drink and stop abruptly. Try it more than once. It will not take long for you to decide, if you are honest with yourself about it. It may be worth a bad case of jitters if you get a full knowledge of your condition.[6]

For this experiment to be reasonably conclusive, persons should be able to stop after one or two drinks for at least a month.

The late Robert V. Seliger, a psychiatrist who worked extensively with alcoholics, developed a well-known "Twenty Questions" checklist.[7] I have reworded his questions to apply to people in serious trouble with either alcohol or other drugs.

Are You an Alcoholic or Drug Addict?
1. Do you lose time from work due to drinking [or drug use]?
2. Is drinking [or drug use] making your home life unhappy?
3. Do you drink [or use drugs] because you are shy with other people?
4. Is drinking [or drug use] affecting your reputation?
5. Have you ever felt remorse after drinking [or drug use]?

6. Have you gotten into financial difficulties as a result of drinking [or drug use]?
7. Do you turn to less desirable companions and an inferior social environment when drinking [or using drugs]?
8. Does your drinking [or drug use] make you careless of your family's welfare?
9. Has your ambition and motivation to succeed decreased since heavy drinking [or drug use]?
10. Do you crave a drink [or a fix] at a definite time daily?
11. Do you want a drink [or use drugs] the next morning?
12. Does drinking [or drug use] cause you to have difficulty sleeping [or do you use these substances because of sleep problems]?
13. Has your efficiency decreased since drinking [and/or drug use]?
14. Is drinking [or drug use] jeopardizing your job or business?
15. Do you drink [or use drugs] to escape from worries or troubles?
16. Do you drink [or use drugs] alone?
17. Have you ever had a complete loss of memory (a "blackout") as a result of drinking [or drugs]?
18. Has your physician ever treated you for drinking [or drug use]?
19. Do you drink [or use] to build up your self-confidence [or diminish anxiety and other painful feelings]?
20. Have you ever been to a hospital or institution on account of drinking [and/or drug use]?

Affirmative answers to even a few of these questions constitute a warning that persons may already by on the slippery slope of addiction.

There are two obvious weaknesses to any such scheme of self-recognition. Because alcoholics and the drug addict usually protect themselves from the truth by denial and rationalization, they may not answer the questions honestly. They will not recognize that their favorite chemical is among the causes of troubles like those listed in these questions. They perceive their chemicals mainly as solutions to their painful problems, not causes of them. The other weakness is that such a diagnostic list is sometimes used to block self-recognition. I remember a client whose family and friends had recognized for years that she had a serious drinking problem. But, when she was pushed to go to A.A. and also to see a pastoral psychotherapist, she rationalized that she was not an alcoholic because she never drank in the morning.

Types of Alcoholics and Drug Addicts

An important reason why alcoholism and drug addictions are often difficult to recognize is that a baffling variety of types and degrees of these disorders exist. Using any generalization as an infallible touchstone can lead one astray in dealing with addicted individuals. Some sample case histories taken from the author's counseling experiences will highlight this point. Names and other identifying data have been altered to preserve anonymity, but the essentials are unchanged.

Sidney L. was born in a midwestern city forty-seven years ago. His father was mean-tempered and harshly authoritarian. His mother died when Sidney was sixteen. He left school in the seventh grade and worked at a series of unskilled jobs. He began drinking at fourteen; his drinking was abnormal from the beginning. He began to drink in the mornings when he was twenty-three. In a few years, he had become the neighborhood drunk and was spending a substantial share of his time "on the bum" living on Skid Rows around the country. At thirty he was sent to a state hospital for his alcoholism. Between then and the age of forty-three he was in the state hospital eleven times. Between hospitalizations he lived in Salvation Army homes, missions, and public parks. He drank whatever was available, including rubbing alcohol and "smoke" (wood alcohol). He deteriorated physically, mentally, and morally, and suffered alcoholic hallucinations. At forty-three he was pronounced a "hopeless chronic alcoholic—a menace to himself and society." He says, "I was living the life of oblivion. I had to beg to live. I was as helpless as a one-year-old baby." He wanted to die but did not have the nerve to take his own life. "But when I met Sid he had been sober for several years in A.A. and his life had been transformed."

Addicts of his type are called *low-bottom* alcoholics, indicating that they have reached a low point of personal and social disintegration. In many people's minds, low-bottom alcoholics are the stereotype of what all alcoholics are like. Actually, they represent less than one out of ten alcoholics. The vast majority of drinking alcoholics are still able, however tenuously, to hold jobs and live with their families. Such alcoholics are "dragging their anchors," as an A.A. member who enjoys sailing put it. They are less adequate as parents and spouses, as well as less efficient in their work than they otherwise would be. They usually have above average absenteeism and are depressed, tired, and generally run-down. Alcoholics who become open to help at this level of minimal social disintegration are called *high-bottom* or *high-high bottom* alcoholics. Such alcoholics are the most difficult to recognize simply because alcohol has not cut them off from normal social interaction, even though it is giving them increasing trouble. It has been estimated that as many as eight out of ten alcoholics are still hidden in offices, factories, and homes in large and small communities all over the country. Unfortunately, many alcoholics and drug addicts remain hidden until the final stages of their sickness when their bodies, minds, and spirits have been irreparably devastated by their illness.

> William B., forty-five, illustrates the high-bottom type of alcoholic. He was born in a small town in a western state. His parents both hated liquor and would not allow it in the house. William was valedictorian of his high school class and graduated Phi Beta Kappa from college. He had the first drink when he was a senior in college. He drank very little during law school. Following graduation his drinking consisted of an occasional social cocktail. When he was thirty-three he began daily social drinking, following the example of an admired senior partner. He liked the boost alcohol gave to his self-confidence. Gradually his drinking increased in volume. By William's early forties, he often felt caught in a "squirrel-cage" of drinking throughout the day. His remorse was intense because he was using money he could ill afford to spend on alcohol. In spite of his heavy drinking, he did not experience severe hangovers and did not miss a single day at work because of drinking. He did reach the point, however, at which he could hardly force himself to work. He would sit in his office and think about liquor. He became desperate when liquor began to lose its effect. At this point he contacted A.A. and had been sober for eight months when I interviewed him. He had not lost his job, his home, or his wife; yet he had been drinking addictively for two years before he came into A.A.

Both Sidney and William were *steady alcoholics* in that they drank heavily nearly every day. In contrast, the *periodic alcoholic* is one who is abstinent for periods ranging from a few days to several months between the times when a wave of craving hits and he or she goes on a bender. The case of Henry P., a low-bottom alcoholic, is illustrative of the periodic alcoholic. Periodics probably appear most frequently among high-bottom alcoholics, however.

Henry P. began drinking at fifteen and, by the time he was eighteen, he was having trouble controlling the length of his alcohol bouts. He left high school after his junior year to take a job. By the age of twenty he had worked his way up to an executive position that he held until twenty-seven, when he was fired because of his drinking. Of his drinking pattern he says, "I would be dry for a couple of months, then a terrible urge would come over me like a wave and I'd disappear for weeks on a bender. I'd come home finally with all my money gone." One drink never interested him. His disintegration was rapid in all departments of his life. By the age of thirty-nine, he was homeless and living in doorways on a Skid Row. He was jailed repeatedly; twice he tried to end his life. Finally a judge suggested he go to A.A. At the time of our interview he had established a successful business, having been sober for four years, after twenty years as a low-bottom, periodic alcoholic.

It is axiomatic among students of alcoholism and drug addiction that these sicknesses can happen to anyone, regardless of age, sex, race, ethnic group, occupation, education, social or national background, or sexual preference. It is worth noting that there was an age range from twenty-eight to seventy among the alcoholics interviewed intensively for this book. In recent decades, alcohol and drug dependence has increased dramatically among adolescents and even preadolescent children.

An A.A. pamphlet entitled "Do You Think You're Different?" has brief statements by a series of women and men. They are identified variously as black, seventy-nine years old, gay, atheist, Indian, fifteen years old, clergyman, lesbian, Jewish, movie star, low bottom, high bottom, agnostic. The concluding summary is entitled, "Now We Are All Special Together."[8]

There are almost endless variations in the patterns by which an addictions develops. Some alcoholics, for example, embark on their addiction after extended periods of controlled or social drinking, often at a time of personal crisis.

The case of Mary P., age forty-four, illustrates this type. She was born in a southern state. There was a great deal of conflict between her parents. Her father died when she was twelve. She describes her mother as "very nervous and neurotic—a cold, straight-laced person who didn't like people." Mary was an only child who had few friends her own age. Often she got her way by means of temper tantrums. At seventeen she left home, "to get away from mother," and went to a large city to work. At twenty she married a man twelve years her senior who proved to be an alcoholic. That marriage lasted four years. She had begun drinking at the age of nineteen to give herself courage for social situations. When Mary was about thirty-five, she suffered a shocking disappointment in love. After fifteen years of social drinking, she began to drink excessively, alone, and often in the morning. After a while, she began to hallucinate and even attempted to jump from a window when the ambulance arrived to take her to the city hospital. Of her drinking she says, "It was escapism—the realities were too unpleasant." At the time of the interview, Mary had been sober for nearly three years in A.A.

Many alcoholics embark on their pathological drinking from what seems like a relatively adequate psychological adjustment. About an equal number were quite obviously disturbed persons before their addiction. Those who begin addictive drinking early in life, or with no period of social drinking, are often of the latter type. Take Rita K., age twenty-eight, for example. She was born in an eastern city. Her father was a weak sort of man who was nagged and dominated by his wife. Of her father Rita says, "He never really cared about me." Her mother is described as "a destructive bitch who was opposed to spanking but who nagged instead." Rita still feels sick inside when she thinks of her mother telling her at age eight that she was egocentric and silly. Later her mother predicted that she was going to become a prostitute. Rita was extremely shy and unhappy during her erratic childhood. She suffered from terrible guilt concerning masturbation. For days she went without saying more than a few words to anyone. She recalls, "I couldn't get along with anyone." After college she held a series of jobs, following which she enlisted in the army. Six months later she was given a medical discharge with a diagnosis of schizophrenia. There seems to be considerable doubt about the accuracy of the diagnosis. She went to a series of psychiatrists and was "diagnosed as everything." Rita began to drink when she was fifteen, when she found she was able to flirt after a few drinks. Before she was sixteen, she was getting drunk at every opportunity. She recalls, "I always liked to get drunk; it was the only purpose of drinking for me. My drinking was a problem to me from the start." At the time of the interview, Rita had been sober for about four months. Concerning her drinking, she said, "Drinking is not my only problem, but it's my first one now." She has come to the crucial insight that she must learn to live without alcohol if she is to be able to work on her psychological problems. Like Henry P., Rita is a periodic alcoholic.

Of the various classifications of alcoholics, the best-known typology is that devised by the late E. M. Jellinek, grandfather of scientific alcoholism research. Acquaintance with this typology will help alert counselors to the multiple forms in which the illness can occur. Jellinek began with a broad operational definition: Alcoholism is "any use of alcoholic beverages that causes any damage to the individual or society or both." He then went on to identify five prevalent types:[9]

Alpha alcoholism is a purely psychological dependence on alcohol to relieve pain—emotional or bodily. Drinking damages interpersonal relationships, but there is no loss of control or other evidence of physiological addiction. Some in the addiction field, including myself, prefer to use *problem drinking* rather than alcoholism in describing this nonaddicted excessive drinking, since there is apparently no loss of the ability to control the intake of alcohol. Clergy often encounter such problem drinking in those marital difficulties in which excessive (but noncompulsive) drinking both reflects and intensifies the pain in the relationships. If the marital conflict can be reduced, this type of drinking usually diminishes and comes within nondestructive limits.

Beta alcoholism is characterized by such nutritional deficiency diseases as gastritis, cirrhosis of the liver, and polyneuropathy, without loss of control, withdrawal, or other signs of physiological addiction. It tends to occur in certain hard drinking social groups in which there also are poor nutritional habits. Damage is primarily physiological, with reduced life expectancy, reduced earning capacity, and reduced family stability resulting. The pastor may encounter this problem in social and economically disadvantaged groups. The nutritional deficiency diseases may also occur in the three following types of alcoholism.

Gamma alcoholism, the type from which the vast majority of American alcoholics suffer, is synonymous with *steady alcoholism*. Like the Delta and Epsilon types, it involves a true physiological addiction, loss of control, craving, increased tissue tolerance to alcohol, and withdrawal symptoms are present. It is the most destructive type, progressively impairing all areas of the person's functioning, including his or her health. It has been estimated that 85 percent of A.A. members are Gamma alcoholics.[10]

Delta alcoholism, often called *plateau alcoholism*, is identified by the need to maintain a certain minimum level of inebriation much of the time, rather than consistently seeking the maximum impact of alcohol on the central nervous system, as the Gamma alcoholic tends to do. This type is found among Skid Row alcoholics who may ration their supply in order to distribute its effects over a longer time. It also is prevalent among French alcoholics, and it is probably much more common than has been suspected among women alcoholics in the U.S. Characteristically, the person nips on alcohol a considerable part of the day, maintains an all-day "glow," but may seldom become obviously intoxicated. Because of this and the fact that, unlike Gamma alcoholism, social disintegration tends to occur subtly and gradually, Delta alcoholics are often able to hide their problem for many years.

Epsilon alcoholism is the *periodic* form of the problem, in which the person is usually abstinent between binges. Although relatively little is known scientifically about this type, it is probable that it occurs in persons subject to bipolar or manic-depressive mood swings. The individual may begin a binge when he feels the skid into painful depression beginning.

As Jellinek recognized, there is nothing absolute about this (or any) typology. The same individual may slip from one type into another, e.g., from Alpha or Beta into Gamma, or from Epsilon into Gamma. There may be other types or patterns of alcoholism not yet identified. The value of this typology for the counselors is that of emphasizing the variety of alcoholisms and identifying several types that they may encounter in their work. There are comparable types of drug addicted and polyaddicted.

The word *alcoholic* will be used in this book to refer only to the three addictive types—steady, plateau, and periodic (Gamma, Delta, and Epsilon)—in which loss of control is a crucial factor that must be faced in counseling. The special problems of counseling with *problem drinkers* (Alpha alcoholics) will be discussed briefly under prevention.

How Alcoholism and Drug Addictions Develop

Why is it essential to know about the developmental patterns of addictions? This knowledge lets counselors recognize these diseases at various stages. Early detection and treatment are as vital in this field as in other serious sickness. Therefore, knowledge of the early symptoms can be a valuable asset. Also, to realize how religion may help addicted persons and their families, it is important to understand the developmental process of these illnesses. What experiences have they been through, and how do they feel when they finally seek help from a clergyperson, a congregation, or spiritually centered group like A.A.? It is worth repeating for emphasis that no two alcoholics are alike and that all generalizations, therefore, are risky. But there is a certain pattern of experiences that is characteristic of many, although not all, alcoholics and drug addicts.

It will be useful, therefore, to trace how addictions develop. The classic systematic study of this process was done by the late E. M. Jellinek, as reported in "Phases in the Drinking History of Alcoholics: Analysis of a Survey Conducted by the *Grapevine,* Official Organ of Alcoholics Anonymous."[11] Here is a summary of Jellinek's findings concerning thirty-four kinds of characteristic alcoholic behavior. Many drug addicts and multi-addicted persons have comparable experiences.

The Addictive Pattern

Here is the sequence of characteristic alcoholic behaviors (with the number of those reporting in Jellinek's sample of 98 alcoholics):

1.	Getting drunk	98
2.	Blackouts	89
3.	Sneaking drinks	89
4.	Weekend drunks	74
5.	Loss of control	95
6.	Extravagant behavior	77
7.	Rationalization of drinking	81
8.	Losing friends because of drinking	63
9.	Morning drinks	91
10.	Indifference to quality of liquor	84
11.	Losing work time because of drinking	90
12.	Midweek drunks	78
13.	Family disapproval	95
14.	Losing job advancements	56
15.	Going on water wagon	80
16.	Losing job	56
17.	Daytime drunks	85
18.	Solitary drinking	87
19.	Antisocial behavior	60
20.	Binges	89
21.	Remorse	91
22.	Protecting liquor supply	77
23.	Tremors	90
24.	Changing drinking pattern	73
25.	Irrational fears	72
26.	Resentment	69
27.	Seeking psychiatric advice	53
28.	Using sedative	60

29. Feeling religious need	60
30. Seeking medical advice	80
31. Hospitalization for excessive drinking	60
32. Admitting to self inability to control	98
33. Admitting to other one's inability to control	91
34. Reaching lowest point or hit bottom	97

In Jellinek's study the average age when persons hit bottom was just over forty. For many alcoholics and polyaddicted persons today, this occurs much earlier. What is missing from this classic study is attention to the ways in which the use of other drugs is intermingled with alcohol to complicate the development of addictive lifestyles.

It is important for those interested in helping alcoholics to keep these characteristic alcoholic behaviors in mind, remembering that no single form of behavior except getting drunk applied to all the alcoholics reporting. Because these thirty-four forms of behavior commonly occur among alcoholics, they constitute a useful guide, not only in identifying individual alcoholics, but also in understanding how far they have moved on the grim addictive journey. The sequence and average age of first occurrence varies tremendously from one alcoholic to another. With this in mind, the list will be used, supplemented by case history material known to the author, to trace the drinking history of a hypothetical alcoholic, "Mr. X."

The Case of Mr. X

X begins drinking in his very early teens, when he becomes a part of a peer group that regularly drinks alcohol (mainly beer) together. (Only a small percent of alcoholics begin as solitary drinkers.) Not long after his first drink, he gets very drunk during a group party. If his need for the effects of alcohol are relatively intense, he may become intoxicated on the occasion of his first drink. One alcoholic of this type said, "I never liked the taste of liquor; I would get in the half-world of alcohol and want to stay there, even in the early years."

X represents the majority of alcoholics who become addicted following a period of what appears to be "normal" drinking. His drinking, however, is dangerous to himself and others as soon as he gets a driver's license because he often drinks before driving. Long before alcohol gives him other obvious problems, X's drinking is abnormal. Alcohol is a social lubricant, and he needs a lot of lubrication. When he drinks, X only knows that he feels good: more adequate and self-confident, less alone and anxious, and more of a man. Someday, in retrospect, he may say with one of the interviewees, "My drinking was alcoholic from the beginning because it meant too much to me." This was a danger signal that he could not recognize then.

The major psychological symptom of the early stages of addiction is a growing dependence on the substance. X is gradually using alcohol more and more as a means of interpersonal adjustment, experiencing its pampering effects. He begins to feel that he is not at his best unless he is "fortified." He drinks at the slightest provocation—when he feels glad, sad or mad; when he has a success or failure in his work; or to help him sleep, combat the tired feeling (which is increasingly present). He organizes his life more and more around his drinking times during the day. To enhance the self-medication effects of alcohol, he may begin to use marijuana, cocaine, or other street drugs, in addition to alcohol.

X has good competitive resources and a strong success drive. In spite of his increasingly heavy drinking, he does passable work in school and later in his job. Occasionally, when something irritates him, he gets very drunk. But he is still able to control the occasions and in general the duration of his drunkenness. He has not yet moved very far into the zone that separates controlled from uncontrollable drinking, but he is moving step by step toward the full-blown disease of alcoholism.

X's tolerance for alcohol is increasing. He must drink more to get the same effect. His use of street drugs increases, as alcohol gives him less of the mood-changing effects he seeks. In his mid- to late-twenties, after a period of particularly heavy consumption, a frightening symptom appears. He "pulls a blank," awakening the morning after a party with an awful hangover and with no memory of what happened after a certain point the night before. His friends assure him that he did not pass out and that his behavior was about as usual. This temporary amnesia disturbs X, and he vows with himself to "take it easy on the hard stuff." It is believed that the occurrence of a blackout may indicate that a new process—probably a physiological or biochemical one—has begun. Blackouts occur approximately three times as commonly among prealcoholics as among drinkers who do not eventually become alcoholics.

There are other omens in X's behavior of moving along the path of developing alcoholism. As his drinking begins to hurt his relationship with his wife of a few years, he sneaks drinks. At parties he slips out to the kitchen for an extra one. Before going to a party, he has a couple of quick ones just to be sure he has enough. He gulps drinks. Everyone else drinks too slowly for him. He often carries a secret supply. He becomes defensive if his spouse criticizes him for drinking too much and lying about his drinking. He also lies to himself to hide the fact that his drinking is not the same as that of his wife and friends. After an embarrassing episode he feels some remorse and promises himself to go "on the wagon" when the pressure of his work lets up.

One day X drops into his favorite tavern after work for his usual two drinks during the happy hour. Against his conscious intentions he gets very drunk and continues to drink long after he had planned to go home. He has to be taken there by a friend and proceeds to pass out just inside the front door, to the consternation and anger of his spouse. Along with her, X is baffled by his lack of control. But he rationalizes that he has been under special strain lately.

Before long X is consistently drinking more than he intends. About the same time, X's Friday night drunks often expand to include the entire weekend. He has lost control. (It is noteworthy that loss of control usually occurs so gradually as to be imperceptible.) He has lost control of the amount he drinks and the drugs he uses trying to get some of the diminishing effects of alcohol. He is losing control of the duration of excessive drinking, and before long he loses control of when he drinks. His craving for the anesthetic effects of alcohol and drugs continues to increase gradually. Once he begins to self-medicate with them, he often cannot stop. This significant fact determines the course of his addiction. He probably could still stop at this point if he were aware of his need for help and could find it. But X rationalizes each experience of excess, convincing himself, through spurious reasoning, that external circumstances cause his excess and that he can stop when he really wants to. Lacking awareness of the nature of his problem, X starts on the search for the magic secret of controlled use of his substances. Trying to learn this missing formula becomes an obsession, a frantic, futile search that leads in one direction for addicted people—downward.

In the case of X, there is no major crisis in his life that precipitates the onset of uncontrolled drinking. He represents the majority of addicts for whom no reason is apparent for gradually crossing into uncontrolled and uncontrollable drinking. It probably is simply that inner pressures and biochemical changes have gradually accumulated until they surpass the critical level—a kind of tilt point. Whatever the cause, X is now drinking compulsively. But he still is blind to his condition because he defends himself from the truth by increasingly elaborate alibis and self-deception. He is caught in the talons of obsessive thinking coupled with compulsive behavior that sabotages the rational, volitional capacities of his mind. He continues to convince himself that his excessive drinking is caused by external circumstances, musing to himself, *A wife who nags like mine would drive anyone to drink.* And he continues to believe that he can control his behavior when he really wants to by using a little more willpower.

In the early years of his drinking, alcohol had been a neurotic solution to X's feelings of inadequacy, inner emptiness, and fear. Now the solution has become a deadly dimension of his problems. He is drinking and using to overcome the pain and chaos caused by previous drinking and drug use. This marks the beginning of the full-blown addiction. A vicious cycle is established. X regards his trouble as a matter of weak willpower, and thinks of himself as a moral jellyfish and a failure as a man. The guilt and shame about his alcoholic behavior brings added guilt and pain, together with wondering if he has lost his mind. So X increases his consumption of his favorite chemical painkillers.

The vicious cycle of addiction also operates on the physiological level. One dismal morning, his hangover is so severe that he feels he can't navigate. His nerves are playing "Chopsticks," and there are drums pounding in his head. Through the fog comes the dim memory of hearing, "Only the hair of the dog that bit you can cure a bad hangover." When his wife is in another room, he pours himself a double shot and gulps it as he sits on the edge of the bed. He manages to keep it down, and by the time he has finished his first cigarette, things begin to look better. He has found a quick, but disastrous, cure for all hangovers. He is now using alcohol as a self-prescribed medicine to cure the symptoms of previous excessive drinking. His morning drink becomes frequent, a sure sign that X is in deep, deep trouble.

Many alcoholics become disorganized in one area but maintain tenuous stability in other areas of their lives. For example, they may continue to hold their jobs even though their domestic life is completely disrupted, a fact that may confuse persons attempting to recognize and help alcoholics. X represents a more common pattern. His addiction spreads like a cancer, gradually disrupting many if not all departments of his life. His inner life has already been hit by the spiraling fears, guilts, shame, rage, and resentments. This inner chaos is now reflected in his home life. His inconsistent, irrational, egocentric behavior gives rise to round after round of heated quarrels, sprees, and promises to do better, ad infinitum. Of the author's male interviewees, sixty-five percent had been divorced at least once. In numerous other cases, the spouse remained, in spite of everything, as a masochistic leaning post for the male alcoholic, with a codependent relationship that made it less likely that the alcoholic would hit bottom and accept help.

X's vocational life is shaken some time after his family relationships are in shambles. He loses times from work because of severe hangovers and occasional binges. Even when he is there physically, he often is half absent mentally. As a result he is bypassed when promotions are available. This gives him added reason to drink and use. Finally X's boss has had it with his inadequate performance. X quits in righteous indignation, just before he is fired, in what his manager says is about to happen because of the company's downsizing. X responds by getting roaring drunk.

Alcoholism also strikes X's social life. Well-meaning friends plead: "You've got everything to live for. Why don't you cut down for the kids' sake?" or "Can't you see what you're doing to yourself? Try sticking to beer." The more he drinks, the less he cares about his friends, particularly those who don't drink heavily. When he hits several friends for a "loan" they gradually disappear. Then X has his first bitter taste of the penal treatment for alcoholism. He lands in jail for drunken and disorderly conduct outside a bar. He is pushed around by the police. Unfortunately, the judge before whom he appears does not do what a growing number do, refer alcoholics to A.A. or a treatment facilities rather than giving more jail time. The humiliation of all his experiences—at home, on the job, with his friends, with the law—adds fuel to the flame of X's motive for drinking. He now drinks whenever he can get alcohol and adds sleeping pills or other drugs, trying to anesthetize the awful sense of failure, guilt, shame, resentment, and isolation resulting from his drinking behavior. He is trapped in the vicious cycle, the "squirrel cage" of addiction. His binges lengthen as his compulsion impels him with greater force so that he is intoxicated at the times that are least socially acceptable. What has happened to X? His excessive drinking, a symptom of inner pain, has gone berserk creating another disease entity. This *runaway symptom*[12] must be halted if X is to be salvaged.

After this point, X's disintegration moves rapidly. His long-suffering wife takes the traumatized kids and goes to live with her parents. X organizes his life totally around his addiction. He becomes increasingly indifferent to the quality of what he drinks, shoots, or pops in his mouth. He ends up in the hospital emergency room when he passes out on the street from the synergistic depression of his central nervous system from combining barbiturates and alcohol. He shows the social isolation typical of many alcoholics, with more and more solitary or "lone wolf" drinking. Antisocial acts—aggressive, often malicious behaviors—are another symptom of social isolation. As the inhibiting power of social sanctions evaporates, X withdraws from normal society and responds in antisocial ways when he is drunk, criticized, or frustrated. He is striking back at a rejecting society, as well as securing punishment that his overwhelming guilt and shame makes him crave subconsciously. Each painful experience drives him deeper into his isolation and thickens his defensive shell of alcoholic alibis and grandiosity. Living in his chemically created private world encased in this shell makes him more and more inaccessible to help.

More frequent binges provide abundant opportunities for brooding and self-pity. Binges now may last as long as he can get liquor or pills and keep these in his stomach. The onset of frequent and longer binges is the beginning of the acute phase of addiction. Each bender brings a horror-filled hangover. Of this, Marty Mann says, "The widely experienced hangover of the nonalcoholic drinker is but a pale approximation of the epic horror known to the alcoholic . . . an all-encompassing onslaught on himself."[13] One recovering alcoholic described such a hangover: "You feel like you're falling apart. Your whole body cries out for alcohol. You shake and shake." It's important to remember that during or following such hangovers, alcoholics' defenses may be beaten down enough by the experience to render them temporarily open to their need for help.

Following a particularly painful hangover, X tries a series of self-help plans. He goes on the wagon and manages to remain abstinent for several weeks, but he is filled with self-pity and is socially unbearable. He's like a speaker at an A.A. meeting who recalled, "My wife said to me, 'You've been dry for three months but you're the same s.o.b. you've always been.'" X's time on the water wagon ends with a humpty-dumpty crash and a long spree. Then he tries changing his pattern of drinking to find the secret of control. He decides that it must be the fourth drink that causes him to lose control, or certain kinds of alcohol that cause him trouble. He changes his brand or drinks only with his left hand. When all experiments fail, he may try changing his geographic location. "After all," he rationalizes, "wouldn't living in a horrible city like this make anybody want to get drunk?" So he moves to the country and gets drunk in the village saloon.

By his early thirties, X is beset with nameless fears. Blackouts occur on nearly every drunk. On one bender he finds himself in a cheap hotel in a city eight hundred miles from home, with no recollection of how he got there. He has long since begun to show the personality change that is so typical that some have labeled it the "alcoholic syndrome." Before his addiction, X had been known as a good-natured fellow, honest, and reasonably unselfish. Now he is mean and selfish, watching the dire effects of his drinking on himself and others with apparent indifference. Freud once wrote, in *Totem and Taboo*, "Neurotics live in a special world in which only the 'neurotic standard of currency' counts." This is also true of many alcoholics and drug addicts. X begins to live in a world where extramural values like honesty have less and less meaning. He will lie and steal, even from close friends, if he still has any, to achieve one value—his pearls of great price—alcohol and drugs. Before his family left, X invested amazing ingenuity in protecting his supply, hiding bottles on ropes out the window and in the water closet of the toilet. If cheap beverage alcohol is denied him, he may drink dangerous liquids like rubbing alcohol. Drinking is no longer an option with him; he lives to drink and must drink to live.

X now is desperate enough to seek help. He begins to pray. His bargaining prayers are variations on this theme: "Get me out of this jam, and I'll never drink (or use) again." Along with X's other relationships, his relation to organized religion has long since disintegrated. If he is a Protestant, he probably began to get away from his church about the time he started having blackouts. If he is a Catholic, this avoidance behavior occurred somewhat later. In his desperation, X may become a religious "taster," trying several churches with a vague awareness that religion may help. He goes to see several clergy—to try to placate his family, get a "loan," or because he feels a genuine religious need. He probably goes to a minister who does not know him, although this depends on the nature of his previous relationships with clergy and the church.

At about the same age X seeks religious help, he may also try psychological and medical help. He lies to the physician about alcohol and drugs. The doctor warns him that his liver is showing dangerous symptoms and he must give up drinking. This warning may produce a brief sobriety, or he may walk out of the doctor's office into the nearest bar. In his late thirties, after a protracted binge, X has his first in-patient hospitalization for alcoholism and drug detoxification. If the hospital has an enlightened addiction treatment program, he will receive medication to ease the pain of withdrawal and vitamin therapy, to make up for the acute deficiency caused by prolonged "drinking his meals." Hopefully, he may be visited by members of A.A. who have a working relationship with the hospital administration or he may attend in-hospital meetings of A.A. that are vital elements of effective treatment programs. If the hospital merely dries him out and treats his physical condition without giving attention to the underlying addiction, X probably will be drunk within a few hours or days after his release. As the months stagger by, X lands in a series of treatment facilities. Forty-one of the author's male interviewees

(69 percent) had been hospitalized; six of these men had been in thirty times or more.

The failure of each attempt to get help plunges X deeper into the dismal morass of advanced alcoholism. He drinks around the clock and uses prescribed drugs like tranquilizers and antidepressants to supplement alcohol's waning effects. Moments of even partial sobriety are filled with irrational fears mixed with overwhelming guilt and shame. One alcoholic said, "I was a facade with a puddle of fear behind." X loses all sense of time. The need for alcohol and drugs provides the only continuity in his life. Withdrawal brings all the tortures of hell. The pleasant sedative effect of his early drinking is now gone. As one alcoholic puts it, "I just tipped back the bottle and skidded into oblivion." Because alcohol no longer produces what he craves, when he can get them he uses more and more drugs (such as barbiturates, tranquilizers, pot, and cocaine) to reduce the pain of chaotic reality. By now he is addicted to various drugs as well as alcohol. Even if a potentially fatal overdose of barbiturates and alcohol is avoided, addiction to barbiturates is extremely difficult to break and the withdrawal symptoms are painful, even deadly.

As his reality becomes increasingly grim, X's battered ego requires longer flights into the reality-denying world of alcoholic and drug fantasy. His prealcoholic inferiority feelings are now grounded in reality. He is not only unemployed, he has also become practically unemployable. Fears of the future form a vicious alliance with sickening shame about his past. His inner conflicts have grown to almost complete paralysis. Even little tasks like tying his shoelaces become impossible without a drink. Two hands may be required to get the glass of whiskey to his lips. He may hide himself in cheap hotels, drinking until he is taken to the city hospital in an alcoholic delirium.

By this time X is a physical wreck. He looks many years older than his chronological age. His face is bloated, his eyeballs yellow. His endocrine and metabolic system are acutely disturbed. His steps are uncertain and his hands tremble. There is a vacant expression in his eyes. However, the extent of physical disturbance that some alcoholics can hide even in the advanced stages of the illness is often amazing. X's alibi or rationalization system, by which he has so long defended his fragile self-esteem, crumbles. He stands before the humiliating truth that he is trapped and powerless. Reality has forced him to face what has been painfully obvious to others for a long time. He is licked and he knows it.

In spite of all this it sometimes takes another year or more for people like X to admit to others that their lives are unmanageable because they cannot control their abused substances. Then X hits bottom and surrenders. This is a matter of emotional bankruptcy and does not necessarily involve the depth of social disintegration described in this composite case. When X hits bottom, for the first time he becomes really open to outside help. What brought X to his bottom? Perhaps a specific and crushing humiliation. Or the fact that liquor and drugs—his gods—have betrayed him by losing their initial, sought-after effects. Or some physical illness may tip the scales in his psychic economy so that the pain of drinking becomes greater than his fear and anxiety about not drinking. In many cases there are no obvious causes. Whatever the cause, the feeling most commonly described is, "I am sick and tired of being sick and tired" or "I am sick of myself and want to die." After coming to this life-or-death fork in his path, X must find help or risk going under. Or, he may go on for several years teetering on the brink of self-destruction.

Some alcoholics and drug addicts who come to ministers and other counselors seeking help have gone through a low-bottom, living hell like X's. Many others hit bottom long before they have descended to a comparable level of physical, mental, ethical, social, and spiritual disintegration. Often such high-bottom alcoholics have managed to stay hidden for years. They continue to hold jobs and live with their families in spite of crippling addictions. Some alcoholics who seek help have paused for years at one stage or another of the developmental pattern. Others have gone through the stages described with great rapidity. Some have had entirely different developmental patterns. But if their drinking and/or drug use seriously damages one or more significant areas of their lives and they keep on drinking and or using, they probably are addicted.

The Staggering Costs of Alcoholism and Drug Addictions

Of all addictive chemicals, alcohol is associated with more human tragedies and costs than all the other drugs combined (with the exception of nicotine). It has been estimated that the total cost of alcohol abuse in America is $86 billion each year. Such an astronomical figure is so mind-boggling as to have little real meaning. So, consider a few concrete indicators of the human costs of alcohol abuse and addictions, remembering that these are only the tip of the iceberg of what all of us pay for these problems. The executive director of the Institute for Preventive Medicine, Dr. Don R. Powell, states that of the ten leading causes of death in the United States, alcohol is a contributing factor to six of them.[14] A Gallup poll revealed that one third of all American families are affected, directly or indirectly, by alcohol problems of some type.[15] One study found that more than one in ten babies born in the United States are affected by their mother's alcohol or drug use during pregnancy and/or in their infancy.[16]

Let's look more closely at the cost of our society's favorite legal and domesticated drug—alcohol. How large is the American problem of alcoholism?[17] No one really knows precisely how many people are alcoholics or nonaddicted problem drinkers, or polyaddicted. I recall E. M. Jellinek's sage observation at the Yale Summer School of Alcohol Studies when he said, in effect, that counting alcoholics is something like counting black cows in a distant pasture on a dark night. All statistics in this area are really "guesstimates" based on various less-than-exact measurement formulae—e.g., hospitalization or deaths because of alcohol and drug-related illnesses and accidents.

The National Institute on Alcohol Abuse and Alcoholism estimated (in 1990) that there were 10.5 million U.S. adults who exhibit some of the symptoms of alcoholism (e.g., physical dependence on alcohol, tolerance, and withdrawal symptoms). An additional 7.5 million were problem drinkers. They abuse alcohol in ways that cause impaired health or social functioning but do not show symptoms of physical addiction. The slippery distinction between alcoholics and problem drinkers relies on ascertaining "impaired control over regulating drinking," a concept that is difficult to define and measure. In any case, 17 million human beings is more than the combined population of New York City and Chicago.[18] The great challenge to all caring people is that the vast majority of these troubled persons are still drinking and/or using, in spite of the proliferating network of effective treatment programs and Twelve Step recovery groups.

What are the measurable costs of alcohol abuse and addictions? Nearly half of all fatal traffic accidents are alcohol related. As most parents of teens know and fear, a disproportionately high percentage of those who die in these tragic deaths are adolescents. Such alcohol-related traffic accidents are now the leading cause of death in that age group. Such accidents kill about as many people as are killed by homicides in our gun-loving society. Alcohol-related accidents and illnesses combined make these the second leading cause of premature deaths in this country, surpassed only by tobacco. Although drunk driving arrests have had an encouraging downward trend in automobile fatalities in recent years, they still are around 100,000. Almost half the pedestrians struck and killed by automobiles have alcohol blood levels indicating that they were intoxicated. It is estimated that at some time in their lives, four out of ten Americans will be involved in an alcohol-related traffic accident.[19]

Half or more offenders convicted of violent crimes such as manslaughter, assault, murder, attempted murder, rape, and sexual assault used alcohol immediately before their crime. According to the U.S. Department of Justice, 1.7 million people are victims of alcohol-related crimes each year. The costs of medical care and lost earnings involved is estimated at $58 billion. Over four thousand people die in such crimes each year.[20]

Informed estimates of all alcohol-related problems put the cost to our nation at nearly $90 billion plus $28 billion more from the use of illicit drugs. (Statistics and estimates are from the National Clearing House for Drug Information.) According to the *Journal of the American Medical Association*, alcohol-related hospitalizations of older Americans in a recent year cost taxpayers some $230 million (paid mainly by Medicare and Medicaid). Such illnesses and accidents of seniors happen more often than heart attacks, a leading killer of middle aged and older adults.[21] It is striking to note that alcoholism is at least five times as prevalent as cancer. What the late Carl Menninger stated some years ago, unfortunately is still true today: "Alcoholics in the United States constitute our largest single mental health problem. Nothing looms as large on the horizon. . . . It is a problem which is taking a tremendous mental, social, and physical toll."[22]

Consider how much of our society's overall economic health is diminished by having millions of men and women out of fully productive relationship with the national economy. This fiscal crippling happens most often during people's potentially most productive years. Still-employed alcoholics are estimated to cost industry hundreds of millions of dollars annually from their increased absenteeism, accident rates, insurance costs, and general inefficiency.

Let us return to the nonquantifiable, intangible costs from alcohol addiction. Severe untreated alcoholism takes a decade or more off the life expectancy of victims. It also tends to make alcoholics' later years a half-life/half-death time by crushing the possibilities for constructive living. The human costs of all this, though impossible to measure, are astronomical. And the pain and destructiveness are certainly not limited to alcoholics or problem drinkers themselves. Beyond the estimated 17 million alcoholics and problem drinkers are the millions of family members devastated by the family illness. Picture a circle of chaos and tragedy, averaging three or four people, surrounding each alcoholic and drug addict. This circle is populated by all those whose own wellness is diminished by the problem. For example, fetal alcohol syndrome, caused by mothers' drinking during pregnancy afflicts tens of thousands of children with incurable mental handicaps. (This tragedy was personalized by an award winning book, *The Broken Cord*, in which a Native American anthropology professor, Michael Dorris, shared the heartache from his adopted son's affliction.)

To the alcohol-caused suffering of families must be added that of the millions of victims of alcohol-related accidents. All this leads to the sobering awareness that the enormous psychological damage suffered by children of addicts is impossible to measure. In one large northern U.S. city, alcohol and drug abuse by parents was a factor in 80 percent of cases of children found by child welfare professionals in filthy, unheated apartments with little or no food.

Cultural impoverishment caused by addictions are enormous. For all the artists who believe they are more creative when a little drunk or stoned, there are dozens who drink, smoke, or shoot their poems, symphonies, novels, paintings, dances, dramas.

Behind the familiar lyrics of Stephen Foster, "All the world is sad and dreary, everywhere I roam," is the pathos of an alcoholic's inner world. Their author died in the alcoholic ward of New York's Bellevue City Hospital at the age of thirty-eight. In his pocket was a torn piece of paper with the words for a song, "Dear friends and gentle hearts," a lyric that might have been loved like "Jeanie with the Light Brown Hair."

In a different area, sports icon Mickey Mantle, whose liver collapsed at age fifty-six, after four decades of alcohol abuse, sadly regretted that he couldn't remember the great moments of his remarkable achievement in baseball, because his mind was a blur. The grim stories of alcoholism and drug addiction are replete with such might-have-beens.[23] It is high time that caring people in all religious traditions, responded to help enable this immense, wasted, God-given potential to be used for the well-being of not only addicted people, but also the whole human family!

CHAPTER 2

Multiple Causes of Addictions, Multiple Levels of Prevention

Both the ethical and the therapeutic approaches to the problem of alcoholism must be based on an understanding of alcohol, drinking, and the physiology and psychology of the human being. Many of those who attempt to control alcoholism are like those who attempted to control lightning without knowledge of electricity.

—Selden D. Bacon, Yale sociologist who pioneered
alcoholism research

The three-pound organ is where the drama of alcoholism and drug addiction takes place. Like a symphony orchestra, the neurological circuits, the neurotransmitters, and the receptors are all highly tuned and respond to each incoming chemical in different but oh so glorious ways. But, this is also the place of gloom where the music dies down when addictive drugs and alcohol have run their course.

—James W. West, M.D., Medical Director,
Betty Ford Outpatient Center

Bacon's astute observation, based on many years of addiction research, is well worth heeding today. Accurate knowledge from all the relevant sciences is the only solid foundation on which to develop reality-based approaches to any complex personal or social problem, particularly one so befogged by misinformation and half-truths as that of addictions. To plan effective strategies for either preventing addictions or helping victims move toward recovery, it is crucial to have empirical understanding of the multiple and interacting causes involved in both chemical and behavioral addictions. Toward this objective, this chapter presents an overview of the clusters of factors that current evidence suggests are among the causes of addictions. As these causal clusters are described, preventive strategies will be explored.

What are the causes of chemical and behavior addictions? No one knows definitively. To a significant degree, these are *cryptogenic* diseases, human dysfunctions for which the basic causes are still partially hidden. Furthermore, it should be remembered that different types of addictions in different individuals are rooted in somewhat different causes. But, thanks to the findings of hundreds of scientific research projects over the past half century, a great deal is known today. It behooves clergy and other counselors to take full advantage of the available knowledge to form working hypotheses to guide their approaches to these problems. All such guiding hypotheses should be used tentatively, keeping in mind that tomorrow's discoveries in the field may reveal that some of today's conceptions, even "certainties," are not valid.

Multidiscipline scientific studies searching for a single cause of alcoholism have been extensive over more than half a century. Yet no single or simple cause of addictions has been determined. Instead, the main thrust of research findings indicate forcefully that alcoholism and other chemical addictions are complex illnesses in which a variety of interacting factors play significant roles. The late Carney Landis, a research psychologist, declared: "If there is any human disorder which can be truly said to be of multiple etiology, it is alcoholism in all its diverse forms."[1] I would add that, at the present stage of partial knowledge, the same is true of other addictions.

The most cogent understanding of what causes chemical addictions is that they develop in particular individuals when two or more of five types of causative factors converge in them. Here then are the five clusters of causative factors:

1. *The biochemical properties of alcohol, nicotine, and other drugs or addictive substances that cause them to be inherently more or less addictive for users.*

2. *Physiological causes that seem to make some people's bodies more vulnerable to addictions than other's.* Recent studies suggest that it is increasingly likely that physiological factors in chemical addictions include *genetic vulnerability* among members of certain families with high rates of addiction.

The determining factors that cause behavioral addictions to develop when they converge in individuals are the following three.

3. *Psychological trauma or deprivation that cause deeply wounded individuals and family systems who experience high anxiety, shame, and alienation, as well as low self-other esteem and general well-being.* These factors cause them to be hypervulnerable to becoming addicted if addictive substances are used or addictive behaviors begun.

4. *Sociological and cultural causes that seem to be a major determinant of the strikingly different rates of chemical and behavioral addictions in different social contexts—meaning in different families, socioeducational classes, genders, religious or ethnic groups and cultures.*

5. Religious, existential, or philosophical dynamics that increase vulnerability to being caught in an addictive process. Some belief and value systems, by which individuals and groups attempt to create meaning and purpose in their lives, are pathogenic or sickness causing. Dangerous drinking and drug use leading to addictions are among the personal and societal problems that such spiritual deficiencies and ethical pathologies create. As a result, those who suffer from pathogenic religious lives tend to develop elevated rates of various addictions.

Factors from these five clusters of causes seem to influence the development of the addictive process in each of its three overlapping stages:

(A) Predisposing factors that make some individuals vulnerable to alcoholism and/or other addictions before they begin the activity.

(B) Factors that influence or determine the unconscious selection of particular addictions as symptoms of underlying pathology, rather than the countless other types of symptoms that vulnerable people develop. Of course, the choice or selection is not intentionally or consciously made.

(C) Factors that make full-blown addictions self-perpetuating, after a certain point-of-no-return in the addictive process. The factors in this dimension of the process illuminate the reasons why most addicted persons do not accept help earlier in the development of their sickness. These factors also may shed light on why the vast majority of chemically addicted people cannot use their substances in controlled fashion, even after they have achieved stable sobriety.

We now look more closely at the predisposing factors that make some people very vulnerable to addictions. Why is it that, among the millions of people in our country who drink alcohol, occasionally use recreational drugs, or engage in enjoyable behaviors like having sex or eating, the vast majority do not become addicted? This question leads inevitably to the search for some Achilles' heel that renders a significant minority addiction-vulnerable. There must be some physiological and/or psychological "soil of addiction" in certain persons that causes them to be receptive to the seeds of addiction.

Two kinds of addiction patterns tend to raise questions about the existence of a predisposing soil of vulnerability. One is the sudden onset of addictive drinking after years of controlled social drinking. Sandra R. drank socially for twenty years during which alcohol posed no apparent problem for her. Then, when the shattering news came that her oldest son had been killed, her drinking became pathological. Long after the devastating pain of her awful grief had lessened, she continued to shut herself in her room with her bottle. To the casual observer, her addictive drinking was caused by what probably is the most painful trauma human beings can experience. This obviously was a crucial precipitant, but the one-cause explanation ignores the countless other parents who were social drinkers, lost children tragically, and did not become addicted. It is clarifying, in the sudden or short-term onset of addictions, to distinguish between *underlying causes* and *precipitating crises*. Crises precipitate the onset of addictions in those who have the soil of addiction that is receptive to making addictive responses to crises.

Oliver M. is an example of the second type of confusing case. In the midst of a successful business career, he began to drink addictively. He was known to his friends to be, as one of them put it, "as normal as the next guy." His load of responsibilities and worries seemed no heavier than that of his nonalcoholic business associates. Only by looking behind the scenes of Oliver's life can one make sense out of his behavior. Here one discovers two significant factors. One is the ability of many people to carry terrific loads of stress, conflicts, grief, and inner chaos over long periods of time and yet present an adjusted life to others and even to their conscious selves that hides their inner storms. The second factor is the wide discrepancy between our culture's definition of success and normal—which in our "Babbitt" culture is often a sort of standardized neurosis—and truly integrated mental, emotional, and spiritual health. Henry David Thoreau was thinking of the successful farmers of Concord when he made his most quoted observation, "The mass of men lead lives of quiet desperation."[2] (Obviously, Thoreau could have added the mass of women to his statement.) Often our human desperation is so quiet and so hidden in the cellar of the psyche that even sufferers are aware of only vague unhappiness, depression, amorphous boredom, or discontent. In the light of this, it is valid to say that normal people can become addicted.

The evidence supports the view that alcoholism and drug dependence come in people, their relationships, and societies, not in bottles, pills, or needles. But, as we will see, these chemicals do have biochemical properties that make them more or less attractive to those who have some vulnerability to using them addictively. Those with high vulnerability can become addicted or at least psychologically habituated more readily, even to substances with relatively low degrees of addictiveness. We must look within people, their families, and the wider social context of their lives to find the causes that create heightened vulnerability.

A shrinking minority of those in the addiction field deny that any special vulnerability or soil of addiction exists. According to this school of thought, the process by which one becomes addicted is simple. A person begins to drink or use drugs in compliance with social pressures. Each occasion leads to another of increasing intensity as one comes under the sway of the habit-forming properties of these chemicals. The majority of drinkers and users have not yet become addicted because they haven't yet consumed enough of the substance for long enough. One alcoholic expressed this viewpoint when he said to me, "The only reason I know why I became alcoholic was that I drank too damn much whiskey."

This conception of the cause of addictions describes what happens to some drinkers and users—namely those who become addicted. It is descriptive, but not explanatory. As an oversimplification it leads to the false assumption that addictive substances per se are all that is needed to produce addictions. It does not answer the question posed by the life stories of two well-known American musicians. Stephen Foster died, as described in the last chapter, at the age of thirty-eight. He looked like an old man burned out prematurely by advanced-stage alcoholism. In contrast, his contemporary, Dan Emmett, author of "Dixie," drank a controlled amount nearly every day of his adult life and lived, still drinking, to the age of eighty-four. Both musicians were amply exposed to the habit-forming properties of alcohol. Why is it that people like Emmett drink or use drugs most of their lives without losing control, whereas others like Foster become addicted at a relatively early age?

The cogency of the belief that addictions are the simple result of drinking and drug use is challenged seriously by comparing drinking and alcoholism rates among different religious and ethnic groups in various cultures and subcultures. Surveys have shown that abstaining from all use of alcohol is practiced by around a third of Protestants but only 10 percent or less of Jews. If alcohol were the exclusive or even the dominant cause of alcoholism, members of the Jewish faith could be expected to have a very high rate of alcoholism. Yet studies have shown that Jewish rates of both problem drinking and alcohol addiction are much lower than that of any other religious or ethnic group in the country, with the exception of Americans of Chinese descent.

The late Carroll A. Wise, a pioneer theory builder and teacher of pastoral counseling, was on target when he stated: "Fundamentally, the alcoholic is not sick because he drinks but . . . he drinks because he is sick, and then becomes doubly sick."[3] The more inner pain addicts experience, the more they tend to drink and/or use drugs, and the more they use these painkillers, the more pain they experience as they become ever sicker.

Correlating Prevention with the Causes of Addictions

A thoughtful consideration of today's epidemic of multiple addictions makes it clear that prevention is the only long-range, reality-based solution. In spite of all that educational and treatment institutions, including government agencies, are doing in the area of addictions, our Western societies are not even holding their own. Instead they are slipping further and further behind. Individuals and family systems are being entrapped in chemical and behavior addictions on a wholesale scale while all the excellent treatment programs are reaching only a fraction of the victims on a retail basis, one by one.

This situation is reminiscent of the image that Toyohiko Kagawa, the great Japanese Christian who chose to live and work in miserable urban ghettos, once used in discussing the many broken lives produced there. He suggested that the strategy being tried was like building numerous rescue stations at the bottom of a dangerous cliff without also erecting a fence at the top to prevent countless others from being shattered by fatal falls. In our addictive society, many more people are falling over the cliff of addictions than are helped to recover by the widespread and often effective network of Twelve Step groups and other treatment resources. This is occurring in spite of the extensive preventive efforts by government agencies in the so-called war on drugs, and the alcohol and drug education programs in public schools, congregations, and Councils on Drug and Alcohol Education.

Somehow we *must* build fences to prevent countless youth and adults, and even children, from falling over the cliff of addictions. The challenge is to discover what types of fences are most effective in preventing the wide variety of chemical and behavioral addictions. The answer is that prevention must aim at reducing the causal factors in each of the five clusters listed above. It also must function at each of the three levels of the addictive process, as follows:

First, prevention must occur at the grass roots by decreasing people's vulnerability to all types of addictions. This involves changing the soil of addictions so that they will be less receptive to the seeds of addictions.

Second, prevention must also occur through influencing symptom selection, so that vulnerable people with highly receptive soils of addiction within themselves will be less likely to engage in the kind of drinking or drug use that plants the seeds of disastrous addictions in their lives.

Third, prevention must also take place through early detection and treatment so that those who are losing their footing at the top of the cliff will grasp helping hands to prevent them from falling into full-blown addictions. Or to change the image, prevention through earlier treatment means enabling those sliding down the slippery slope of addictions to grab hold of help sooner, thus preventing their destruction at the bottom.

Examining the five clusters of causes as they function on these three levels of the addictive process is now in order. The major research findings on causes of vulnerability can be divided into those focusing on physiological, psychological, and sociocultural factors. Actually, contributing causes from each of these three often are involved and must be addressed in both treatment and prevention of chemical addictions. Let's first examine physiological factors that may make people more or less vulnerable to chemical addictions.

Physiological Causes of Vulnerability to Addictions

The idea that alcoholics suffer from a physical allergy to alcohol was suggested to Bill Wilson by physician William Silkworth in 1937. This concept became a useful principle in the belief system and literature of A.A. There seem to be physiological factors among the causes of all chemical addictions. Alcoholics probably are not allergic to alcohol in a literal, medical sense, comparable to allergies that some people have to certain foods or pollens. But they certainly have a psychosocial allergy to alcohol in that they cannot drink without disastrous consequences in many areas of their lives.

The figurative use of "alcoholics have an allergy to alcohol" (or other addictive substances) is an effective way of communicating to addicts and their families that they have an illness with crucial physiological components. The analogy between alcoholism and diabetes—both incurable but highly treatable illnesses—is another useful communication tool in both counseling and education. Whether or not these illnesses prove to be literally comparable physiologically, both are illnesses that can be devastating and even fatal if untreated.

Highly suggestive evidence has emerged that the metabolism of some alcoholics shows significant differences from that of many moderate drinkers and abstainers. Disturbances of the pituitary-adrenal-gonadal triad of endocrine glands are present in many alcoholics. However, as various researchers have pointed out, the pathological changes in metabolic and endocrine systems that are observed in some alcoholics may not be indicators of a predrinking soil of addiction in them. Rather than being predisposing biochemical factors present before excessive drinking began, these physiological changes may be the result of years of "drinking their meals." As we will see, there probably are biochemical changes among the factors that cause most victims of severe chemical addiction to lose the ability to return to controlled use of their additive substances. Jim Rhoads, a pastoral psychotherapist with considerable expertise in addictions has declared, "The more that is discovered about the addictive brain, the more the disease concept of addictions makes sense."[4]

From a standpoint of the brain's complex and orderly functioning, it is appropriate to say that alcohol and drugs hi-jack the brain. Drugs change the brain quickly and radically, causing the intense release of dopamine, the body's pleasure transmitters. Prolonged use of drugs seems to reduce the brain's ability to produce dopamine without drugs. This probably explains the dynamics of powerful craving for alcohol or drugs by addicts.

Closely linked with the issue of physiological vulnerability factors in alcoholism and other substance addictions is the genetic-hereditary vulnerability that may predispose some to addictions. Investigators have long noted that the incidence of alcoholism and other chemical dependencies among children of alcoholics is far higher than among the adult population at large. Of the seventy-nine alcoholics interviewed in depth by the author, fifty reported having alcoholics somewhere on their family tree. Twenty-seven reported alcoholic parents. A broad overview study that examined surveys embracing over four thousand alcoholics found that 52 percent had an alcoholic parent. There is no doubt that children of alcoholics are particularly vulnerable to alcoholism and other addictions.

Does this mean that vulnerability to chemical addictions is genetic? In the 1968 revision of this book, I cited a revealing study by Anne Roe of adult children of alcoholic parents who had been separated from their parents and reared by nonalcoholic foster parents. When they were twenty-one or over, they were compared with a control group of children born of nonalcoholic parents also raised in nonalcoholic foster homes. Roe concluded:

> As regards their present adjustment, there are no significant differences between the groups, and there are as many seriously maladjusted among the normal-parentage group as there are among the alcoholic-parentage group. The children of alcoholic parentage ... cannot be said to have turned out as expected on the basis of any hypothesis of hereditary taint.[5]

In light of that study, I concluded that the transmission of alcoholism from parents to children would seem to be a question of social learning rather than heredity. Obviously the emotionally depriving, chaotic atmosphere of addicted family systems produces high rates of all forms of psychosocial pathology.

In the decades since Roe's research, comparable studies have arrived at contradictory conclusions. A Danish study reported on 5,483 children of alcoholic parents adopted at an early age and raised in nonalcoholic homes. It found that sons of alcoholics were more than three times more likely to become alcoholics in adult life than were adopted sons of nonalcoholics parents. A Swedish study and an American study arrived at about the same conclusion.[6] A similar study of adoptees in the U.S. found that 22.8 percent of sons who had alcoholic biological fathers and 28.1 percent of those whose alcoholic biological mothers were alcohol abusers in their adult lives.

Findings of numerous research studies on genetic, biochemical, neurological, and brain electrochemical factors in addictions during the last two decades have provided increasing evidence that physiological and genetic factors are among the causes that make certain people vulnerable, if not predisposed to chemical addictions. A volume that is particularly relevant is *Alcohol and the Addictive Brain, New Hope for Alcoholics from Biogenetic Research.*[7] It was written by Kenneth Blum, an authority on psychopharmacology and substance abuse, and James E. Payne, executive director of the National Foundation of Addictive Disease. They hold that a genetic predisposition exists for addiction to alcohol and also other psychoactive drugs like morphine and cocaine. The determining factors are biogenetic and biochemical, but psychosocial factors seem to trigger, worsen, or, in some cases, alleviate the genetic deficiency that produces the craving. This deficiency causes a malfunction of the reward centers of the brain involving the neurotransmitters and the enzymes that control them. Addictions involve a genetic imbalance in the brain's natural production of neurotransmitters that are critical to our sense of well-being. The craving produced by this imbalance is temporarily satisfied by drinking or drug use. If further research confirms this theory, and a defective gene eventually is identified and repaired, the predisposition to addictions will not be transmitted from one generation to the next, according to these authors. In the meantime, they recommend nutritional and pharmacological treatments that help offset the imbalance caused by the deficiency.

Kenneth Blum and James E. Payne, along with four other researchers, have summarized the findings of many technical studies of the "Neurogenetics of Compulsive Disease." They conclude:

> If our findings are correct, they constitute a powerful argument in favor of the disease concept of alcoholism and the importance of the genetic factor. . . . We hope that our findings will remove much of the stigma, enabling more indivduals to accept their craving as a symptom of an illness, and make it easier for them to seek treatment and affiliation with self-help Twelve Step programs. They envision the development of a diagnostic tool such as a blood test, that will identify children at risk in alcoholic families.[8]

Psychological Causes of Vulnerability to Addictions

How do scientists who have carried out intensive studies of alcoholism and other chemical addictions understand the psychosocial factors among the causes of vulnerability to additions? Jellinek conducted pioneering research on the disease concept of alcoholism at Yale University and later at the United Nation's World Health Organization and gave this clear answer:

> Repetition alone won't produce addiction. It only comes when there is a motive for repeating. Alcohol is not habit-forming in the sense that a drug like morphine is. Rather than calling alcohol a habit-forming drug, it is more accurate to say that *it is a substance that lends itself to those who form compulsive habits easily.* The alcoholic reaction is atypical, not universal. It is the reaction of a minority of people, not a property of alcohol.[9]

It is now well-established that alcohol is a drug with biochemical properties that make it attractive to those who form obsessive-compulsive behavior habits readily and therefore are very vulnerable to addictions.[10] Evidence that predisposing psychological vulnerability to chemical addictions exists depends on longitudinal evidence that people who become addicted were deeply wounded psychologically before they began to drink or use drugs.[11] Did they suffer from painful psychological disturbances causing anxiety and inner conflicts that enhanced the desire for mind-numbing or ecstasy-giving chemicals? The findings of my research interviews shed light on the childhood experiences of those seventy-nine alcoholics in the period before they began to drink and, in some cases, also use drugs.[12]

Identifying Children's Psychological Needs

Before summarizing these findings, it is useful to point out that children have certain psychological needs or hungers analogous to their nutritional needs. To the extent that these hungers are satisfied, they grow strong, healthy personalities, able to live satisfying lives within themselves and with others. To the extent that severe emotional malnutrition exists in childhood, personality stunting, immaturity, and interpersonal dysfunction result. As with physical starvation, deprivation of adequate emotional food is most damaging in the earliest years of life. It is then that personalities are being shaped, growth is the most rapid, and the foundation of future health or illness is laid down.[13]

I have long appreciated the way that child psychologist Dorothy Walters Baruch summarized the emotional foods that every infant, child, and adult must have to grow and stay psychologically healthy. She said that people need real down-to-earth, sincere affection, and loving, "The kind that carries conviction through body-warmth, through touch, through the good mellow ring of the voice, through the fond look that says as clearly as words, 'I love you because you are you.' " Everyone needs the sure knowledge of being wanted, of belonging, and being united with others in a larger whole, rather than isolated and alone. Every human being needs the nourishment of sensual pleasure, of colors, of balanced forms, and of beauty, as well as harmonious sounds and the hearty enjoyment of taste, smell, and touch, and the awareness that the pleasurable sexual sensations can be right and fine. Everyone needs to feel capable of achievement, that they can do things that meet life's demands and gain the recognition of others. And, very important, all of us humans need acceptance, understanding, and sharing thoughts and feeling honestly with other people.[14]

One of my mentors, David Roberts, wrote these wise words in his classic, *Psychotherapy and a Christian View of Man [sic]*: "The child's foremost need is an adequate supply of wise love. By 'wise' I mean steady and natural, instead of sporadic and forced; unsentimental and geared to growing autonomy instead of plaintive and smothering."[15] In my experience as a therapist-teacher, if children get enough "wise love," love that is as free and accessible, and as important as the air they breathe, they will become healthy, loving, self-reliant people who will not need to use pain-deadening chemicals as personality crutches. Four destructive parental patterns were identified in the childhood homes of alcoholic interviews: heavy-handed authoritarianism, success-worship, moralism, and overt rejection. Each of these impairs parent's ability to give their children an abundant supply of wise love and to satisfy their other emotional-spiritual hungers described by Baruch. In this way, these parental deficiencies contribute to other factors in the soil of addiction.

Of my seventy-six alcoholic interviewees who described their families of origin,[16] seventy-one identified high degrees of feelings, attitudes, and practices that deprive children of adequate satisfaction of their basic emotional needs—the hungers of the heart. Of these seventy-one homes, forty-four were grossly so; the remaining twenty-seven showed fewer or better disguised inadequacies, and would probably be described as "normal" homes by casual observers. In only five of the seventy-six families was no apparent inadequacy found.

Among the disturbed family systems, twenty-seven cases of parental alcoholism produced acute need-deprivation in children and other family members. Just over half of those interviewed reported families broken by divorce, emotional divorce (i.e., constant strife and alienation), or the death of a parent. In addition, four reported having a psychotic parent. In one case the father was an alcoholic and the mother a drug addict. Even if one makes generous allowances, as one must do, for distortions in the data due to memory blindspots in interviewees, a striking impression persists: *Most of these recovering alcoholics came from disturbed families of origin.*

Among interviewees, the most frequent destructive parental characteristic was what psychoanalyst Erich Fromm described as "irrational authoritarianism," meaning authority that is based mainly on superior power. Three-fourths of the alcoholics described this in one or both parents. In fathers this was usually a heavy-handed, dominating, and controlling form. In mothers it most often took the more indirect form of dominance through overprotection and "loving" manipulation. A frequent pattern was sons with emotionally remote fathers, who formed unhealthy, "sticky" closeness with an overprotective mother. Authoritarianism denies fulfillment of children's need for autonomy with love by making acceptance contingent on obedience. It often breeds deep inferiority feelings by denying fulfillment of the need for gradually increasing self-direction and autonomy. Some parental authoritarianism was expressed in overt sadism and emotional rejection, as in these cases: Tom R. recalled: "Father had a killing temper . . . practically killed me when he got mad. I didn't know him very well . . . didn't like him . . . I lost interest in things early in life." Frank P. remembers: "My dad was a big shot in town. I was just someone who happened to come along. There was fear of the head of the house . . . strict discipline . . . he often hit us with his big mit."

If these interviews were replicated today, many of the same parent-child patterns would be evident, although authoritarianism probably would be far less common. Instead, a dominant theme would be a lack of loving parental authority expressed in firm limit-setting and caring discipline. This deprivation of children's needs tends to produce different psychopathologies than authoritarianism. These include destructive acting out of impulses, antisocial behavior, and defects in the development of healthy consciences—all problems that are common among addicts today.

Just as authoritarian parents make love contingent on obedience, success-worshiping parents make it contingent on children's ability to feed parental egos. They do this by their "successes" as these are defined by parents. Of the seventy-nine interviewees who provided usable information on this, thirty-three reported homes in which success-worship was a dominant dynamic. This took various forms. Excessive ambition for children in terms of financial achievement, power positions, or educational attainment were common. The fact that only four of the thirty-three were females points out that the cult of success-worship exerts far greater pressure on boys than on girls. Cultural expectations for girls from traditional families push them, but in different directions—for example, toward gratifying parental needs to have them be beautiful and successful in fulfilling traditional female roles.

However success is defined, its worship deprives children of needed self-direction by saddling them with parent-chosen goals. Because the goals often are derived from the parents' own unrealized dreams, they usually are perfectionistic, unattainable, and out of touch with the realities of children's own gifts, wishes, and dreams. Most children tend to internalize such parents' exaggerated goals for them and become their own slave drivers. Some rebel against parental expectations in self-defeating behaviors that often includes drinking and drugs. In either case, they suffer from chronic anger, low self-esteem, painful rejection of their own unique dreams and gifts, and shame caused by never measuring up.

The childhood of alcoholic Frederick N., age fifty-four, illustrates how overprotection and success-worship are often intertwined, reinforcing each other. He describes his parents in glowing terms. "My father was a very successful banker, a Phi Beta Kappa in college. He often called my attention to how successful my grandfather had been. I was closer to him than my mother. She was a very unusual person—widely traveled and cosmopolitan. She was the family disciplinarian, but there were few spankings because I was a 'good boy.'" Concerning his childhood he says: "I was an only child and the only link in both sides of the family chain. Consequently I was closely guarded. . . . My parents wanted me to win scholarships and study to become a great doctor. Instead, I became the prime disappointment of their lives. Goals and standards were set for me. They made all the decisions. I lost heart very early because I couldn't measure up. Everything became distasteful to me. I did only what was necessary."

Fred began to drink at the age of twelve with a group of boys. His parents got him out of repeated drinking jams in college, thus making it easier for him to continue irresponsible drinking. Finally he dropped out of college and got a job in a mill, a crushing blow to his parents' dreams. Concerning twenty years of binges he recalls, "My deep inadequacy was lost in alcohol. I could feel I was anybody when I was drinking." Speaking out of insight gained in extensive psychotherapy, Fred could say in retrospect, "Had I been allowed to find my own level, I wouldn't have had the terrific sense of disappointment as early as twenty-one. No matter what I did it was so far short of what they had in mind for me, it didn't seem like an achievement."

Moralism describes the behavior of parents who project narrow, life-constricting ethical demands on children and make acceptance contingent on conforming to their demands. This generates deep feelings of guilt and shame, feelings that often focus on sexual impulses and hostile feelings. This causes children to grow up emotionally crippled by being unable to enjoy sex and express normal aggression. Some parents are rigidly moral in relating to their children because of their own unforgiven, unhealed guilt and shame, or gaps in their own consciences. They project impossibly perfectionistic standards on their children, making them feel that they must struggle to earn the all-important love of the parent by being impossibly good. Because the parental standards are perfectionistic, children who internalize these standards never really feel accepted as they are—imperfect persons—by themselves, others, and God. They often cannot accept their normal bodily drives and their normal negative, sexual, or assertive feelings.

Twenty-nine of the seventy-nine alcoholics interviewed described their parents as puritanical and moralistic. Roger L., in his late thirties, illustrates the destructive impact of moralism combined with authoritarianism:

> My father was very stern. I was deathly afraid of him. If I did something that was wrong, he wouldn't talk to me, just beat me. My mother was very much like my father—I never got much love from her. She had a feeling that she shouldn't get too close to me. She was a very righteous person, very moral. My terrific standards come from this, I think.

He recalls his childhood:

> I was shy and aloof, never comfortable with people. I was very weak and never wanted to fight with other boys. My father beat me for walking away from fights. He beat me for petty stealing. Never praised me. Would say, "Why can't you be like other boys?" I had three sisters and one brother. I was the black sheep—very dull in school—deathly afraid of reciting. I was beaten for not being a good student. I took a business course in college because my father wanted me to follow him; I really wanted to be a surgeon—a great surgeon. Always wanted to be something great.

Both Roger's parents were adamantly against alcohol. He began to drink at eighteen and got drunk the first time. He dropped out of college because of drinking. He says, "I had no period of social drinking. It was no fun. I used it to escape from my problems from the beginning." He worked for a time as a salesman. "I drank to sell. Couldn't sell anything without alcohol in me—afraid of people in general—never able to hold a job for long because of my drinking." After a discharge without honor from the army because of drinking, Roger lived on various Skid Rows for several years. Just prior to his discharge he had married a woman seven years older than himself. He says, "I was looking for the maternal care I had missed." Roger's guilt about sexual matters proved too strong, and they were divorced after six months.

Although he has been sober for three years in A.A., Roger still can't forgive himself for sexual deviations during his drinking. The success-worship and puritanical attitudes he had internalized from his parents are reflected in statements such as: "I push myself entirely too much—makes me unhappy. I condemn myself when I do wrong, feel I'm cutting myself off from God. My standards are too high. Always concerned about whether I'm doing right. If I can't be almost perfect I don't expect anything good to happen to me." Roger's rejection by his parents involved extreme authoritarianism, moralism, and success-worship. In many of those interviewed, the parental deficiencies were not so obvious.

How much evidence was there in the interviews that, as in Roger's case, parents' problems produced painful psychological maladjustments in addicts' lives before they began drinking? Here again, the findings were striking. Of the seventy-seven cases in which relevant data were available, only ten lacked evidence of disturbed childhoods. Behavior difficulties, low self-esteem, and unhappy childhood memories were a constant refrain in the interviews. Here are some sample recollections from five different male alcoholics. One recalled, "I was three years behind in school—life a hell on earth, no kid's life." Another: "I had few playmates. There was no love in our home. My big desire was to get away." Another: "I lived in a shell as a kid, felt different and confused." Another: "I was alone as a boy. I was left-handed, and my father forced me to use my right. I stuttered terribly, and the nuns made fun of me." Another: "I never got along with people."

A painful lack of self-esteem during childhood was very common among interviewees. Seven out of ten said that they had "inferiority complexes," were "very shy," or felt "lonely." These samples give the tone of the recollections. One said, "I was shy, fearful—had nightmares of a big snake." Another recalled, "I was timid as far back as I can remember—thought of myself as 'nasty self.' Always expected to fail." A third recalled: "I had no close friends—felt alone and inferior. Never had any self-confidence."

Evidence from numerous broader-scale psychological studies supports the view that many alcoholics and drug addicts were emotionally disturbed long before they begin drinking and using. The soil of addiction was made receptive by the pain and buried conflicts from their early lives. Several studies using psychological tests have shown that, although many chemically addicted persons are able to function with remarkable social adequacy when they achieve sobriety, they often make this adjustment in spite of deep, unresolved inner conflicts.

A knowledge of the psychological attributes that are very common among addicts can guide anyone who wishes to counsel with them. These problems tend to intensify when people are caught in the swirling chaos of active addictions. They are complicated by the psychological and interpersonal consequences of prolonged excessive drinking and/or drug use. But they were present in many addicts before active addictions began, and unresolved psychological problems often continue after people stop drinking and/or using. Although most of my interviewees had been sober in A.A. or other recovery programs for significant periods, many reported continuing painful inner problems.[17] Referring to his severe anxiety, self-rejection, and shame, a male alcoholic reported, "I feel like there's a rattlesnake in me breeding venom." A man who had been sober in A.A. for several years said wistfully, "I keep hoping that I will feel as good sober as I did drunk." When people are forced to give up the masking effects of alcohol and drugs to go on living, they often become even more aware of underlying pain. This may make their continuing recovery problematic unless they have effective psychotherapy that helps them diminish their inner conflicts and pain.

Let's now review the psychological problems that are prevalent among addicts. *Emotional immaturity* is a phrase one hears in many Twelve Step meetings. Two symptoms of this are adolescent-like ambivalence toward authority and authority figures, and conflict between dependence and independence. Addicts often form a very dependent relationship (in counseling, for example) and then resent their own dependency as well as those depended on. This conflict often is projected onto marital relationships of addicts who marry dominant partners who overprotect them to absurd degrees. The addicts then express their resentment of their own dependency in ways that turn marriages into civil wars.

Low frustration tolerance is another characteristic of many addicted persons that makes counseling for recovery challenging. They have learned to use alcohol and drugs to escape from frustration. A Rorschach study concluded: "Statistically, the most significant and most consistent trait is the alcoholic's incapacity to stand strain or tension."[18] Learning to tolerate frustration is achieved by children maturing in secure, emotionally nurturing families. Recovering addicts must learn how to do this without chemical comforters if they are to have continuing sobriety.

Another common psychological attribute in addicts is *grandiosity*. It is evident in the defiant, self-inflating behavior during active addictions when people, as one alcoholic put it, seems to "organize the universe around the perpendicular pronoun." It helps counselors to remember that addicts' outwardly grandiose, self-enamored behavior is protective armor hiding underlying self-rejection and lack of ego strength. Because of crippled self-esteem, addicted people tend to be hypersensitive to criticism and will misinterpret the behavior of others as rejection. Low self-esteem gives rise to painful anxiety in interpersonal relationships, the need to put others down, and the search for even temporary feelings of self-importance.

The late Harry Tiebout, a psychiatrist to whom numerous founding members of A.A. turned for help when they became depressed *after* achieving sobriety, explored the process of releasing or surrendering the grandiosity that he called the "king complex." Until this positive surrender occurs, many addicts are not open to help. To maintain grandiose self-images, addicts must shut themselves off from interpersonal reality by what Tiebout called "the alcoholic shell." Until this shell is shattered by reality, addicts do not hit bottom. Establishing effective therapeutic relationships with them is difficult if not impossible. To lose this defensive shell and accept their need for help involves losing their "idealized image" (to use psychiatrist Karen Horney's apt phrase), a defensive self-image that enables them to feel at least shakey, temporary well-being rather than self-loathing.

It is crucial to remember that many female addicts suffer from severe self-esteem vacuums, in childhood and later, inflicted by the widespread sexism of our culture. In subtle and overt ways, they are treated as less competent, weaker, and less worthwhile than males, and they are not encouraged as much as males to develop their God-given assets, strengths, and competencies. Many women addicts do not need to "surrender" idealized self-images because sexist forces in their personal and social contexts prevent them from developing this defensive shell. But like their male counterparts, they need self-esteem repair and enhancement so that they become aware of their irreducible worth as persons and are strengthened by experiences of growing competence.

The rigid ego defenses of addicts (and others) are both costly and eventually ineffective. It was Saint Augustine, a person of immense insight, who observed that "Pride is known by its despondency as well as its arrogance." The shell of idealized self-images may give people temporary protection from low self-esteem and the normal discomforts of interpersonal life, but it also cuts them off from vital satisfactions. One alcoholic, viewing in retrospect his grandiose isolation, said, "I felt so far removed from common garden-variety people that there wasn't any place for me." More than four out of every ten of my interviewees reported feelings of isolation and loneliness, most of them throughout their lives. A typical comment was, "I can't feel warm toward people."

Perfectionism, a prevalent problem in addicted persons, is actually a form of self-punishment. Inevitable failures to reach unrealistic goals are followed by self-punishing shame and guilt, also common problems among alcoholics and other addicts. An articulate alcoholic wrote in his anonymous autobiography: "I was crucified on the bitter angle that guilt cuts across the rigid upright of every American's puritanism."[19]

However, I offer this caution with reference to guilt. It is important to know that a significant percentage of chemically addicted people come from the clinical group described in traditional psychiatric terms as psychopathic personalities, sociopathic personalities, or those with character disorders. They have crippled consciences that make them unable to experience guilt or responsibility as do those with normal consciences. In A.A. they are called *phonies.* These unfortunate people can give trusting, inexperienced, unaware counselors great trouble. This is because they use all their "smarts" to con others, including clergy and counselors, for their own purposes, often very successfully.

High anxiety, low self-esteem, and shame are frequent effects of parental alcoholism. A female alcoholic recalled: "My father was a periodic alcoholic. This was a disgrace in our little town. . . . He felt he was lord and master. We were all afraid of him. . . . Mother thought sex was a terrible thing." The community's ostracism, the father's alcoholic authoritarianism, and the mother's puritanism combined to cause a little girl to grow up feeling "self-conscious and inferior. . . . I was different. I lived in a shell."

In his insightful exploration of shame, pastoral theologian/psychologist Robert H. Albers describes how many church families with addicts attempt to protect themselves against shame:

It has been my experience in the field of chemical dependency that people within the faith community often exercise the defending strategy of withdrawal and isolation when it comes to dealing with the shame of addiction and/or abuse in the family system . . . the whole family which is afflicted, utilize denial, diversion, and distancing to deal with the problem. This can be observed already in children who avoid interaction with other children for fear that the family secret will somehow be disclosed. The rule is if we don't talk, don't feel, and don't act, the shame will remain hidden as a secret of the family.[20]

Many psychological studies of alcoholics and other addicts conclude that severe psychological maladjustment often is an important part of the soil of addiction. However, the assumption that all addicts have major vulnerability because of such personality disorders has been challenged by cross-cultural studies. Jellinek observed that generalizations about alcoholics are often based on biased samples—those who seek psychiatric help *because* they have serious personality disorders. He reports that many alcohol addicts with only minor personality problems have been seen, especially in wine-producing countries. He concludes: "The contention that neurosis is a sine qua non of alcoholism cannot be accepted."[21] But the evidence is clear that the vast majority of American alcoholics and other addicts did suffer from significant personality problems that helped to prepare the soil so that the seed of addiction readily took root when they began to drink or use drugs.

One will not understand alcohol and drugs as *problems* until one also sees them as *solutions*. For many addicted persons, alcohol and drugs serve as magical, though eventually tragic, solutions to problems in living. Their inner conflicts and anxieties cause intense psychic pain. Alcohol and drugs are cheap, easily obtainable painkillers. (Remember that alcohol is in the general category of anesthetics according to physiologists.) Cross-cultural anthropologist Donald Horton says, after a study of many so-called primitive cultures, "The primary function of alcoholic beverages in all societies is the reduction of anxiety."[22]

Various cruel but revealing experiments on animals have shown that alcohol reduces awareness of pain produced by neurotic conflicts. The classic experiment was conducted by J. H. Masserman and K. S. Yum who induced neuroses in cats by creating a conflict between their fear of pain and intense hunger for food. The animals became thoroughly neurotic, as do humans suffering comparable conflicts. The neurotic cats lost all interest in normal cat satisfactions, until they were given an injection of alcohol. They were suddenly able to perform normally because their neurotic conflict had been anesthetized. Soon they became addicted to spiked milk that they had ignored completely before their neuroses. Only when the neurosis was alleviated by reconditioning (the cat equivalent of learning theory therapy), were their feline addictions broken.[23]

Alcohol and certain other drugs also "solve" the problem of addicts' blocked emotional growth by enabling them temporarily to regress psychologically to a level at which they feel comfortable. Sober adult life demands too much for immature individuals, so they slip back via the Bacchus-trail to a level where the demands are minimal. Alcohol solves low frustration tolerance by allowing them an easy escape hatch in frustrating situations. Alcohol also serves as a quick, temporary solution to guilt, shame, low self-esteem, isolation, and perfectionism by depressing self-criticism. The judging conscience is dulled in them, as in most people, by alcohol. Prolonged substance abuse brings social censure that registers as punishment with masochistic addicts, thus helping them atone for guilt feelings. For addicts with rigid, puritanical consciences, drugs allow behavior otherwise forbidden by their consciences. Drugs reduce the burden of repressed feelings by relaxing the mechanism of repression. A male alcoholic recalls, "The only time I had a temper was when I reached a certain point in a drunk." At other times he had pushed his hostile feelings out of consciousness by means of repression. Drugs "solve" addicts' conflicts concerning authority by allowing them to rebel against those upon whom they are actually becoming increasingly dependent.

Addicts' nagging inferiority feelings are temporarily relieved by alcohol or other drugs. For a time they can feel perfectly successful. As one alcoholic interviewee put it, "With a pint you can feel like you're president." Thus perfectionism is satisfied in the grandiose, illusory world of psychochemicals. The widespread use of alcohol as a social lubricant is an indication of its power to "solve" problems of interpersonal anxiety and conflicts. It allows people to anesthetize their self-alienation temporarily and thereby to feel closer and more accepted by others. For many isolated males in our society, including those afflicted by homophobia, alcohol facilitates pseudocloseness with other men, while enabling them to feel more adequate as macho males by "drinking like a man."

We humans belong to the most sexual of all species. It is not surprising, therefore, that sexuality influences all aspects of our lives, including the use and abuse of consciousness-changing chemicals like alcohol and recreational drugs. Alcohol and drugs provide temporary answers to some sexual problems by lowering inhibitions as well as body and sexual anxieties. A popular male method of seducing women is to ply them with alcohol or inhibition-lowering drugs, making them easier targets. Alcohol could be described as "sexual courage in a bottle" for men who suffer from macho-failures and testosterone-driven sexual anxieties.

The widespread psychological woundedness of many addicts is reflected in the sexual problems that exist before, during, and often after their active addictions. Many women addicts and female adult children of addicts suffered from girlhood sexual violations and violence. It has been estimated that seven out of ten incest survivors are chemically dependent,[24] illustrating how post-traumatic stress disorders are among the precipitating causes of substance addictions. The traumatic impact of incest has some similarity to the violent trauma of rape. But incest can be even more devastating to victims because of the profound betrayal by someone in their trusted circle of "loved ones." If the repressed shame and rage from incest and other sexual trauma and violence are not treated, stable recovery often is difficult if not impossible for the victims. In counseling with recovering addicts of both genders, it is important to remember that preaddiction sexual problems that worsen during addictions often are not solved by sobriety alone. Referral is needed to a competent relationship therapist who also is a trained sex therapist.

There is a double tragedy in using chemical solutions for problems of living. The solutions are illusory, in the long term. They also are pseudo-solutions that can be maintained only as long as the chemicals are ingested. They carry seeds of their own destruction that eventually intensify the very problems for which they gave temporary answers. But, however tragic and transitory, chemical comforters provide almost effortless answers for desperately hurting human beings who have not found better answers.

Alienation and Grief: Causes of Addictions

The life journeys of many humans are replete with times of painful inner emptiness and meaninglessness. These times are caused by agonizing crises, losses, and life transitions that feel like psychological and interpersonal amputations in which important parts of our identity and of our way of getting our basic heart hunger satisfied are cut off. The frequency of these times of loss-generated pain increases as people grow older. Many people have not learned an essential skill for maintaining wellness—to live with emptiness until it is at least partially filled. When the ache of emptiness becomes long term or chronic, those who lack these basic survival learnings often succumb to the alluring temptation to try to fill the inner void with food, alcohol, drugs, work, sex, magical religion, or some other potentially addictive substance or activity.

Those who grow up in psychologically and spiritually toxic families suffer chronic grief, loneliness, and damaged capacity to trust. This makes them hypervulnerable to misusing different substances and activities addictively in vain attempts to feel connected and trustful. A clergyman with a high level of awareness of his inner world tells of the adult consequences of growing up in an alcoholic family system with an addicted father. He describes the hole he feels at his center and says that he has found nothing that really fills this inner void, neither a satisfying marriage partner, considerable success in his work, or even the meaningful relationship he has with God.

Unhealed and infected wounds of the spirit from alienation and grief are among the most prevalent psychological-spiritual causes of addictions. While he directed an addiction unit in a state mental health facility, a pastoral psychotherapist estimated that at least one out of every five patients suffered from one or often several unhealed grief wounds. Until there was some healing of these wounds in a grief recovery group, he said, Twelve Step programs and other recovery methods were seldom effective. In my counseling experience, the percentage is even higher.

Addicts struggling to find their own path to recovery have told me that they have a variety of grief wounds resulting from their addictions. These include:

- A sense of all that they have lost in unlived and wasted years during their addictions;
- Often the loss of their family, job, opportunities, and self-other respect;
- The loss of what one man called his "best friend," meaning alcohol and drugs, and the satisfactions they formerly brought. Addicts' best friends, their bottles, pills, or syringes have betrayed and deserted them;
- The loss of feeling disempowered as a man or shamed as a woman, because of uncontrollable drinking or drug use, and the behavior that results;
- The loss of the conviction that one is able to be in charge of one's life;
- The loss of the way they had structured time around drinking and drugs;
- The loss of the substance that was used to get close to others;
- The loss of the drinking or drug-using subculture composed of "my kind of people."

In counseling with addicted people in recovery, it is essential to explore their loss experiences with them and then help them do their healing "grief work." Until they experience some healing of their wounds, their recovery may be shaky. For this reason, providing easily available grief recovery groups and classes can help reduce slips during recovery. Grief-healing counseling and groups can also help prevent addictions.

Earth Alienation and Addictions

Another long-neglected and profound alienation that is often found among the psychological causes of addictions and that parallels and reinforces other painful alienations is what I call *ecoalienation.* This means the lack of any deep sense of nurturing bonding with the living earth, the wonderful network of living creatures called the biosphere. This is at the root of many forms of human psychopathology, including some addictions. Over the last four centuries, with urbanization, industrialization, the high-tech revolution, and with our deep mind-body-spirit dualisms in philosophy and theology, we Western industrialized humans have largely forgotten that we are profoundly interdependent with all other living beings. In the last century, Western developmental theories generated mainly by male therapists in cities have lacked this crucial awareness. I have explored this earth-grounded understanding of our species and of therapy and teaching in *Ecotherapy: Healing Ourselves, Healing the Earth.*[25] The basic theories and methods described are relevant to understanding, healing, and preventing many addictions.

Earth alienation interacts with and feeds alienation from our bodies, other people, and God. Millions of people lack awareness of our deep human connection with the earth on which we are totally dependent for our survival and well-being. Abusing products of the earth like food and wine are among the destructive consequences of frustrated searching for connectedness with the biosphere that we are in as it is in us. All this lends great intensity to helping ourselves and others find connectedness with the earth and with the transcendent or spiritual dimension in God's creation.

Several addiction recovery programs for adolescents have demonstrated the healing value of using what I call ecotherapy. Believing that helping people get out of themselves is a major goal of therapy, one such program takes teens into the desert on horses. Another uses rock climbing to help them develop trust, teamwork, and self-transcendence. After such experiences, the teens are given an opportunity to reflect on what they have experienced and share what they have learned. A therapist in one of these programs reports that some adolescents have gained a whole new perspective on their lives and on their addictive problems.

Albert J. LaChance is a poet, therapist, and environmentalist who has been in a Twelve Step recovery program for more than a decade. He has authored *Greenspirit, Twelve Steps in Ecological Spirituality: An Individual, Cultural, and Planetary Therapy.*[26] He believes, as do I, that the environmental crisis and what may be the terminal illness of our planet is rooted in addictive human lifestyles. These addictions include consumerism, overeating, materialism, overpopulating, squandering energy, and the capitalistic glorification of these practices—all of which are plundering the earth and spending our children's fair share of the earth's resources. He holds that we are in the denial phase of these earth-destroying addictions. He then applies the Twelve Step recovery principles and classical spiritual disciplines to recovery from these interconnected addictions.

Prevention of Psychological Vulnerability

Primary prevention of the psychological causes of addictions must begin where human personality is formed, deformed, and can be transformed. It must begin where the soil of children's personalities develops—in families and in family-nurturing institutions, especially schools and congregations. Personality that is either receptive or resistant to the seeds of addictions is homemade. In families, society's most influential teachers—parents—have their greatest opportunities to reduce vulnerability to all types of human problems including addictions. Therefore primary prevention must focus on nurturing healthy children who have the inner strengths, self-esteem, and joy in living to resist trying to satisfy their emotional and spiritual needs with chemicals or with the addictive use of satisfying behaviors. This is the bottom-line defense that people of all ages need for living nonaddictively in our addictive society. Whatever is done in families, schools, and congregations to nurture mental, emotional, spiritual, and relational wellness will help reduce addictions at their very roots. Prevention on this basic level obviously is part of a much larger strategy for preventing many forms of personal and social pathology.

Wholistic primary prevention involves nurturing healthy children in all seven dimensions of their lives—mind, body, spirit, relationships, work, play, and in their relationships with the world (meaning both society and the natural environment). Nurturing people throughout their lives, in all these dimensions, is a basic mission of wholeness-oriented religion and of congregations that are seeking to enable people to develop what the New Testament calls "life in all its fullness."[27]

Teachers and religious leaders have significant roles in this grassroots prevention. How? They can help reduce vulnerability to addictions by equipping parents to raise psychologically and spiritually healthy children. Parents and other teachers can help children and teens grow healthy, resilient personalities by providing an abundant supply of nutritious emotional and spiritual food. They also can teach young people—by modeling behavior that is supported by accurate alcohol and drug education—how to satisfy their emotional, spiritual, and interpersonal hungers in healthy, nonchemical, and nonaddictive ways. Effective alcohol and drug education in homes, schools, and congregations clearly is crucially important as a means of providing the basic knowledge necessary for informed prevention on all levels.

Because children and youth in addicted family systems are at paraticularly high risk of eventually becoming addicted or otherwise disturbed, these parents and families must be special targets of primary prevention. All that is done to enable addicted parents and their children and youth to recover from their family illness, and find healing and grow toward greater wholeness, will contribute substantially to the prevention of future addictions. Making individual, marriage, and family psychotherapy readily available for people in recovery and their families who need this help can be an important way to help them find the healing and growth that will help prevent addictions in the next generation.

Some will say that such whole-person, primary prevention of addictions is too broad and even utopian as an objective when seen from the perspective of the more immediate ways to prevent addictions on secondary and tertiary levels. There is some truth to such critiques. Concern for primary prevention should not diminish multilevel preventive action. Individual, family, and community-wide alcohol and drug education should enable teens and adults to make wise choices about the use or nonuse of potentially addictive chemicals, and help them avoid using those that are highly addictive. Such education should alert families with any history of addictions to the fact that they probably are at high risk because of what may be a genetic predisposition. When confronted by the reality of high rates of addiction among youth and adult offspring of addicts, some such people take appropriate preventive steps—for example, avoiding the use or at least the abuse of dangerous drugs like alcohol, tobacco, and cocaine.

Pharmacological Addictiveness

A crucial factor to consider among the multiple causes of chemical addictions is the degree of addictiveness in the biochemical-pharmacological properties of different substances. In both preventive education and counseling for recovery with individuals hooked on various chemicals, it is important to have knowledge of the wide range of addictive properties in different substances. The range is on a continuum—from marijuana's relatively low degree of physiological addictiveness (although it often is psychologically habituating) to alcohol's medium level addictivenss, to the high degrees of addictiveness of cocaine, methamphetamines (uppers), and nicotine. In understanding the multiple causes of alcoholism, for example, alcohol's considerable addictiveness is one crucial variable. More about relative addictiveness will be found in chapter 3.

Preventive education that addresses the issue of levels of addictiveness should highlight the following:

- The high risk factors in many widely used legal drugs including nicotine, alcohol, tranquilizers, and barbiturates;
- Avoiding the use of drugs with a significant degree of addictiveness, particularly by children and youth. Their emotional vulnerability is heightened by normal emotional immaturity and growth struggles in a chaotic, violent society;
- Avoiding the use of drugs with addictive potential by people who know that they are in an elevated risk group;
- The special dangers of using potentially addictive chemicals because the process of addiction is sneaky so that victims usually aren't aware they are hooked until they can't escape on their own;
- The importance of appropriate legal controls so that highly addictive substances like nicotine are regulated as drugs, and seductive advertising and selling to minors are illegal.

Causes Influencing Choice of Addictions as Symptoms

Why is it that of all the maladjusted persons who drink or use drugs, only certain ones become addicted? Answers are in the baffling area of *symptom selection* about which little is certain. It is clear that selection by vulnerable individuals of particular symptoms occurs below the level of consciousness and probably is the result of the convergence of several factors in them. *Secondary prevention* involves steering people who are addiction-vulnerable away from developing addictions. The key factors that influence the selection of particular addictions as symptoms of underlying physiological and/or psychological pathology seem to be primarily sociocultural context forces. Let's examine these now.

Among the sociological causes of addictions are a wide variety of attitudes, behaviors, social sanctions, and pressures, including drinking and drug-use customs, factors that influence gender, culture, ethnicity, class, and religious affiliation in radically differing ways. These factors influence all levels of the addictive process including predisposing vulnerability, symptom selection, and perpetuating the process once it begins. They influence the types, prevalence, responses to treatment, and prevention of addictions in those diverse social contexts. The impact of these sociocultural causes of addictions is illustrated dramatically by the wide range of rates of alcoholism and other addictions in different cultural contexts.

Comparative addiction rates are difficult to measure across cultures because of wide variations in the way vital statistics are recorded, but educated estimates of alcoholism rates in many countries point to wide differences. Women in all countries have lower rates of chemical addictions than do men. Certain countries like France, Italy, Austria, and Ireland have relatively high alcoholism rates whereas other countries like Canada, Israel, Sweden, the Netherlands, and England have relatively low rates. The North American rate, along with Japan and Belgium, is somewhere between the two extremes. It is noteworthy that France has an alcoholism rate twice that of Italy, even though both countries produce and consume lots of wine.

A classic and still illuminating study of the correlation between drinking practices and alcoholism rates in twenty-five different countries was made by Jellinek when he was the primary research scientist at the United Nation's World Health Organization. The findings clarify the interrelationships between individual psychological causes and some highly significant sociocultural causes. The following diagram delineates its major conclusions:[28]

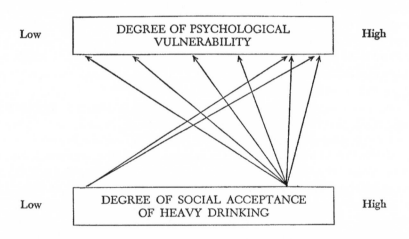

Explanation of diagram: The top bar graph represents the degrees of psychological disturbance in individuals producing varying degrees of vulnerability to alcohol addiction. Grossly disturbed persons would be on the high (right) end of the continuum whereas those who are relatively mentally healthy would be on the low (left) end. The lower bar represents the degree of acceptance of heavy drinking as normal behavior in a particular culture or subculture. The high end represents societies or groups in which heavy drinking is viewed as normal—the low end those in which normal behavior is seen as including only abstinence or extreme moderation (for example, Orthodox Jews, Muslims, and certain Protestant groups that promote abstinence).

The arrows indicate that in social contexts where there is nonacceptance of heavy drinking, persons who become alcoholics tend to be drawn from those suffering from high degrees of psychological disturbance. In contrast, in social contexts cultures where heavy drinking is seen as normal behavior, some persons from all degrees of psychological vulnerability become alcoholics (although many more from the high end of this vulnerability).

This study is very important for understanding both the causes and prevention of alcoholism and other drug addictions. Only those with high physiological and/or psychological vulnerability to addiction are likely to become addicted if they live in societies, or belong to ethnic groups, social classes, or occupational groups that do not accept heavy drinking, drug use, or drunkenness. However, they may become addicted if their psychological pain (and vulnerability) motivate them to defy the social sanctions of their social context. Conversely, those who live in cultures or belong to ethnic groups, social classes, or occupational groups where heavy drinking or drug use is regarded as normal behavior, are more likely to become addicted whether they suffer from major or only minor vulnerability.[29] Thus, chemical addictions can be prevented at their societal grass roots by creating social conditions and practices and education that change social attitudes and practices encouraging heavy drinking, drug use, and drunkenness.

We have seen how addictions often are rooted in personality problems. In her brilliant discussion of inner conflicts, psychoanalyst Karen Horney wrote: "The kind, scope, and intensity of such conflicts are largely determined by the civilization in which we live."[30] The health or pathology of the social context in which babies are born is channeled to them via the parenting persons in their early lives, and thus made available for them to internalize in forming their identity. Which harmful or beneficent aspects of a culture parents transmit to children is determined by the impact of the culture on them as parents. Every culture tends to develop its "configuration."[31] These are patterns of attitudes and practices that control individual and group behavior and produce a nucleus of personality shared by most members of the culture. A health-nurturing culture's basic configuration tends to create emotionally mature and secure individuals who develop many of their God-given potentialities. A sickness-breeding culture's configuration tends to produce patterns of child rearing, family life, interpersonal relations, social, and economic life that cause painful frustration and emotional warping in its members. Healthy cultures produce generally low vulnerability for addictions. Unhealthy cultures lay the groundwork for psychosocial maladjustments of all kinds, including high levels of vulnerability to addictions.

Western societies have many unhealthy attitudes and practices that tend to cause addictions of all types to proliferate. Psychologist Anne Wilson Schaef, in *When Society Becomes an Addict*, declares:

> The system in which we live is an addictive system. It has all the characteristics and exhibits all the processes of the individual alcoholic or addict. To say the society is an addictive system is not to condemn the society, just as an intervention with an alcoholic does not condemn the alcoholic. In fact, those of us who work with addicts know that the most caring thing to do is not to embrace the denial and to confront the disease. This is the only possibility the addict has to recover. Just as with the addict, one has to say that the society *has* a disease. It is not itself the disease. If it admits *having* the disease, it has the option of recovery. This awareness that society has an addictive disease is what is missing from other explanations of treatments of the problems we are facing today.[32]

Schaef understands sexism to be the central cause of addictions in women. Her major thesis is that the "white male system" of power and domination *is* our addictive system causing people to move onto "the path of nonliving."[33] A female client, struggling with nicotine and relationship addictions, observed: "You know, Anne, all these addictions we have been looking at—alcohol, drugs, nicotine, food, relationships, sex, and so on—are all secondary addictions." She explained that she meant that they are all derived from our society's primary addiction to powerlessness and nonliving. When asked for an example, the client told of growing up in a fundamentalist Christian church:

> Her home and her church were the primary formative institutions in her childhood. In both places, whenever she was "alive"—happy, noisy, full of energy, excited, exuberant, sexual—she was labeled a "bad girl." But whenever she was "dead" or nonliving—quiet, sick, depressed, and showing none of the other signs of "life"—she was a

labeled a "good girl." . . . To be accepted by her world, she had to be personally powerless and not alive.[34]

Schaef holds that all addictions are programmed by our society to make us unaware of participating in our own unaliveness.[35] Recovery from addictions, including codependency, involves becoming aware of the deadening impact of our society and choosing not to die inwardly, but rather to live fully. In doing therapy with those seeking recovery, Schaef encourages them to challenge the underlying addictive society. To recover, addicted and codependent women must choose not to support the white male dominance and power system, but instead to discover their own power and competence. In a prophetic spirit, she lifts up this hope for changing the social roots of addictions:

> The good news is that, like the individual alcoholic/addict, the Addictive System can recover. Before this can happen . . . we must admit that the society we care about has a disease and can recover from that disease. We must also be willing to do the necessary work toward recovery. This is a long process that eventually requires a shift to a new system, one I call the Living Process System.[36]

There are important and often neglected truths in Schaef's social-context, growth-oriented position, even though some would critique it as a single-cause understanding of addictions. She shows accurately how addictions are rooted in the life-robbing forces in our society—particularly the macho values of domination, conquest, and power over others. From my perspective, she articulates essential goals of whole-persons-in-society approaches to addiction counseling. These include enabling addicts to let go of defining themselves as victims, to come alive by growing away from the deadening effects of society to find their inner power and competence, and to use these in working with others to change the societal causes of addictions. I would add this to Schaef's perspective: Men as well as women addicts are hurt by macho-distorted social values. Coming alive to one's inner power, competence, and inherent value as a precious person is as important for most male addicts as for females. The recovery path to this healing and growth, however, is somewhat different for men who are in a one-up social position than for women who are in a one-down social position.

Alice Walker has shown how oppressed groups are hit with particular cruelty by their social contexts and how this causes addictions. She grew up in a family of Georgia sharecroppers with eight children, the victims of the crushing social oppression of racism, classism, and demeaning poverty. She writes about how her sanity as a girl was saved by the intimate nurturing she found in the natural world around where she lived. In an interview focusing on her hope-oriented collection of essays, *Anything We Love Can be Saved*, she used a powerful image to describe the traumatizing, addiction-spawning impact of Western civilization on oppressed people's free spirits. She also highlights the healing, energizing power of bonding with the wild things of the earth:

> You can indoctrinate people over centuries, and you can have them eventually give up and give in to whatever you are saying. But the spirit itself is ancient, and its roots are not tricked. This is why many people take drugs, watch television, and are addicted to all kinds of things. They are trying to drown out this little pagan spirit that is a tiny seed buried under a big slab of concrete, which is Western civilization. But they know that the little seed is there. They know it is very different from the concrete. But they have no idea of how to tear up the concrete—and they are afraid to. They are afraid to look at the God they have been indoctrinated to serve. They also don't know what will happen to them if they free themselves.[37]

Significantly, the interviewer entitled her report, "Freeing the Spirit."[38] Walker's autobiographical insights shed light on the ecological as well as social roots of addictions for oppressed groups including native peoples.

Another societal cause of chemical addictions is the easy availability and relatively low cost of alcohol and other drugs. The importance of availability is illustrated by alcoholism statistics during the so-called Nobel Experiment. Prohibition created more problems than it solved, but it is significant that there was a substantial drop in chronic alcoholism rates during the decade of the 1920s. Bearing in mind that alcoholism rates are the product of excessive drinking several years before rates are estimated, this drop probably is the result of the much diminished accessibility of liquor between 1915-20. During those years, more and more states introduced prohibition causing the per capita rate of alcohol consumption to go down substantially. Because the bootleg system was not yet well organized, though it became so later, the supply of booze was down in these years. A probable consequence was that numerous vulnerable potential alcoholics did not become addicted during that time. Today, in contrast, people with underlying vulnerability have endless opportunities to solve their problems with alcohol or drugs. These chemicals are easily available, cheap to purchase, and in fact, they are thrust at us from many segments of society.

Another powerful social factor that encourages chemical addictions is the glamorizing of dangerous, consciousness-changing chemicals in advertising, films, popular media, music, and on the Internet. This makes them seductively attractive to vulnerable children, youth, and adults. Alcohol and nicotine—both glamorized in this way—maintain their front-runner status as the most widely used addictive drugs among both youth and adults.[39] The more addictive substances are glamorized in a particular social context, the more people will use them, and the more will use them in dangerous, excessive quantities. As use and abuse increase, more vulnerable people are drawn down into addictions.

The vast majority of young people do not have opportunities to make free choices about using or not using alcohol and tobacco. On every side drinking and smoking are presented as a part of gracious and fashionable living. Their choices are made under pressure from this commercial propaganda that reinforces their normal desire to enjoy life and be accepted. The high pressure, seductive advertising of products that produce endless tragedy for a high percentage of those who use them as manufacturers recommend, is ethically obscene.[40]

In light of this, education for prevention should include consciousness raising to increase learners' awareness of the seductive social pressures that encourage people of all ages, especially emotionally immature children and youth, to use risky chemicals. It also should include coaching young people in the skills required to resist these manipulative pressures. Effective drug education in peer support groups is a valuable way to help vulnerable adolescents defend themselves against peer pressures to drink and use drugs, against the well-financed advertising/marketing machines that glamorize drinking and smoking, and against the international drug cartels that recruit teenagers to push illegal street drugs on which they become addicted and get their peers hooked.

An extremely important societal dynamic that encourages the choice of chemical addictions as destructive symptoms is the absence of unified social attitudes about what constitutes appropriate alcohol use, and social sanctions that control drinking and drug use and make drunkenness unacceptable. An oft-cited example of the crucial importance of such unified social controls is the traditionally lower rate of alcohol addiction among Jews than among Protestant and Roman Catholic Christians. This is true in spite of the fact that a considerably higher percentage of Jews use alcohol than do those in the other two major faith groups. Even though alcoholism rates among Jewish people have risen significantly in recent years, and Jews have their full share of neuroses, psychoses, and addictions to other drugs, their overall alcoholism rate continues to be well below the rates for other religious groups. The fact that Jews come from a wide range of national backgrounds makes physiological or genetic explanation untenable.

The high rate of alcoholism among Americans of Irish descent is often contrasted with the low rate among Jews. One Irish interviewee quipped to me, "You don't have to be Irish to be an alcoholic, but it helps." Studies of the Irish culture suggest that there are numerous practices and pressures within it that encourage the heavy use of alcohol by males as a way to handle life stresses. The lack of social controls on drinking and drunkenness offer the most convincing explanation of the Irish rate, just as the presence of strong social controls explain the lower Jewish rate. Developmental psychologists hold that attitudes and behavior patterns learned in early childhood in the context of families tend to have the strongest controlling influence on adult behavior. One study of Jewish children between ages five and seven, found that 91 percent of them had been introduced to alcoholic beverages in the context of their families, and that most of them considered it just another food to like or dislike. In short, during their most formative years, most Jewish children acquire strong inner controls guiding appropriate uses of alcohol.

Mainstream Jewish culture has no sanctions against drinking but very strong sanctions against drunkenness.[41] This is reflected in an old Yiddish saying, "A drunk is a Gentile." Traditionally, alcohol use by Jews has been integrated with the strong social and often the religious network of the Jewish community. Because of their century-spanning history of discrimination and persecution, ingroup bonds among Jews tend to be very intense. This makes the controlling power of the group on individuals strong. For Jews who retain their traditional ties with their religious community, the use of wine is closely associated with sacred rituals, including the Sabbath observance in homes. It is alluded to as "the word of God" and the "commandment of the Lord." Because of this, to use wine in excess is to abuse something sacred. My original research interviews included only one Jewish alcoholic. He told of the awful shame and sense of alienation from his family and friends he experienced at thirty-two when he began to defy family and group sanctions by sneaking drinks and drinking alone.

Significantly, changes in recent years show what occurs when unified social controls on drunkenness erode in a culture. The traditional controls that have prevented most Jews from developing alcoholism have weakened in recent decades. Alcohol addiction rates have risen as more Jews have become secularized and integrated into American society's mainstream, adopting its prevalent drinking attitudes and practices. JACS, an acronym for Jewish Alcoholics, Chemically Dependent Persons, and Significant Others, is a national volunteer organization. It provides spiritual and communal support for addicted Jews and their families, serves as a resource center and information exchange, and conducts community educational outreach. It supports Twelve Step programs but is not a substitute for them. JACS groups provide opportunities for members to explore Jewish themes and discuss their emotional, spiritual, and cultural experiences. The Jewish Federation, Jewish Family Service, and JACS have cooperated in providing educational workshops and psychological services for addicted Jews. They are helping Jewish leaders to let go of what they call the "comforting myth" that Jews do not touch hard drugs or become alcoholics.

Rabbi Query M. Oltzky and Stuart A. Copans, medical director of an adolescent alcohol and drug treatment program in Vermont, have coauthored *Twelve Jewish Steps to Recovery: A Personal Guide to Turning from Alcoholism and Other Addictions*. They provide rich Jewish resources for each of the steps. In a moving introduction to this book, the rabbi in whose temple the first temple-housed A.A. group was held, declares:

> As a liberal rabbi and a liberal Jew, I find that the encounter with Jewish alcoholics and alcoholism and the Twelve Step program of A.A. has proven essential to my growth and becoming. . . . I never left a counseling session untouched by God's presence. I have stood before the Holy Ark many times as Jewish alcoholics have prayed or confessed or let go. I have wept with them, I have been angry with them, I have been enriched spiritually to the very depth of my being.[42]

In contrast with the traditional Jewish cultural context, mainstream Western society has no community sanctions, unified attitudes, or social controls on drunkenness. At a certain stage of intoxication, men still have entertainment value for some people. This makes drunkenness socially acceptable, even rewarded in those cultural circles. Such dangerous attitudes tend to encourage the choice of alcoholism as a symptom by those who are vulnerable. Men who often become intoxicated still lose much less social standing than women who are known to drink to excess. This explains in part why more men than women use alcohol, drink heavily, and become addicted. In recent years, female alcoholism and other addictions have risen significantly. Women are catching up but the addiction gender gap still exists.

The widespread ethnic, religious, and social class diversity of American life produces a wide spectrum of conflicting attitudes and values concerning drinking and drug use. In spite of the cultural homogenizing influence of television and social mobility in recent decades, ethnic, religious, and social class differences in drinking attitudes and patterns constitute significant variables in the development of pathological drinking behavior and in rates of addiction.[43]

In our society's crazy quilt pattern of contradictory attitudes, values, and behaviors regarding alcohol and drugs, young people need guidance in making constructive decisions about their use. In this turbulent sea of attitudinal crosscurrents, dangerous attitudes encourage using alcohol and other drugs as ways of being accepted, get high, or relieve inner tensions. In any culture, such attitudes set up vulnerable people for addictions.

Society's confusing and contradictory attitudes concerning alcohol are reflected but also intensified by the conflicting attitudes among and within churches on these ethical issues. Think of the attitudinal chasm separating an upper-class Episcopal church with its occasional "sherry parties" after services from churches that regard any drinking as sinful. Some religious groups still do not agree that alcoholism is an illness. Most denominations do agree that drunkenness is wrong, but some believe that drinking per se is the primary or sole cause and that total abstinence is the only needed solution to drunkenness. Many individual members of denominations that hold to the abstinence position reject their church's policy and some suffer painful guilt feelings when they drink.

Prevention of the Sociocultural Causes of Addictions

Effective approaches to the prevention of the sociocultural causes of chemical addictions, including those highlighted by Schaef and Walker, should focus on two strategies: *First, encouraging people to work together for change of the widespread and dangerous attitudes, customs, and practices that push vulnerable people toward destructive addictions.* These social forces breed addictions like a stagnant swamp breeds mosquitoes. A candid look at America's drinking patterns reveals a measure of truth in the quip, "If alcoholism is a sickness, a lot of people are trying to catch it." *The second strategy is to teach individuals and families how best to defend themselves against these social forces during the uphill struggle to correct them on a broad societal basis.*

Prevention should address each of the causes discussed above. Reducing the easy availability of alcohol can be done by raising taxes and thus increasing the cost. This strategy has the additional advantage of generating revenues to help cover the enormous costs of alcohol-related problems now paid for mainly from public coffers. Rigorously controlling the quantity and location of places where alcohol is sold can also help reduce easy availability. Careful public policy controls on advertising can help reduce the glamorized marketing of legal drugs like alcohol and tobacco products. Everyone concerned about the well-being of our society, particularly its children and youth, should join forces to push government officials on all levels to take health-protecting actions such as these. All people of religious commitment should be proactive in influencing the educational, political, and public policy decisions needed to deglamorize addictive legal drugs and make them less available. Whatever the differences among religious groups about social drinking, there should be unanimity that builds widespread social sanctions regarding drunkenness, drinking and driving, and smoking, and general recognition that these are hazardous to personal and social well-being and therefore ethically wrong.

Causes Perpetuating Addictions and Preventing Early Treatment

Chemical addictions, as we have seen, are progressive diseases that usually become steadily more destructive the longer they continue. If teens and adults in the early stages of this process are motivated to interrupt their own downhill slide, the most costly advanced stages of their illnesses obviously will be prevented. This is *tertiary prevention*. It is possible but difficult because of the forces that tend to make addictions self-perpetuating and cause the vast majority of addicts to become firmly entrapped so that they cannot extricate themselves without help for which they don't become open until they are in the advanced stages of their illnesses.

If brain research and/or genetic research identify physiological and neurological anomalies that predispose certain people to addictions, definitive answers may become available to the self-perpetuating characteristics of addictions.[44] As we have seen, certain metabolic and endocrine changes often are present in the later stages of alcohol addictions—changes that probably play key roles in perpetuating addictions. Perhaps psychophysiological imprinting or irreversible biochemical changes produce the intense craving that causes one drink or drug fix to trigger a brain-mind chain reaction that perpetuates binges. During protracted binges, agonizing physiological withdrawal symptoms occur when ingesting the chemicals is stopped. The only way to avoid this pain is to keep on drinking and/or using drugs.

Whatever the physiological factors, people who are thoroughly addicted to chemicals or destructive behaviors seem to be driven by powerful, unconscious psychological compulsions. When they cross from nonaddictive problem drinking, drug use, or behavior into addiction, powerful subconscious drives seem to diminish their ability to control their behavior. Because of the nature of compulsive thought processes, addicts tend to rationalize their behavior seeing it as normal. This makes it difficult if not impossible for them to recognize their addictions for what they really are—grossly abnormal.

By the time addicts reach full-blown addiction, their dependence on their chemical "solution" is so consuming that often they cannot even imagine any other solution for themselves. They have organized their lives around obtaining and using their substance. Becoming abstinent would not be a matter of giving up a pleasant satisfaction; it would be giving up the center of their living. This dynamic causes addicts to cling to their failing pseudosolutions long after they are exacting a terrible price from them and their families.

Attitudes toward alcoholism and drug addictions that persist in our culture also help drive some addicts ever deeper into their morass, away from treatment rather than toward it. In spite of growing understanding of addictions as genuine illnesses that require treatment, some people hold tenaciously to deeper feeling that addicts are sick—*but not really.* Infected with such attitudes, addicts continue to see their problem in moralistic, willpower terms, long after experience should have demonstrated that willpower alone has not cured the problem. Believing that their problem is essentially one of weak willpower makes their defensive rationalization system work overtime. They must blame external circumstances for their addictive-compulsive behavior and convince themselves that they can stop when they really want to. These dynamics cause many addicts to reach tragic spiritual, mental, and moral bankruptcy before they accept help in utter despair.

Clergy often witness the personal tragedies flowing from uninterrupted addictions. Fortunately, such professionals have important roles in implementing strategies by which these protracted suicidal journeys may be interrupted sooner rather than later. One method is to intervene with problem users who are habituated to drink and/or use drugs in dangerous or harmful ways, but have not yet crossed through the zone into physical addictions. Preventive education makes some vulnerable people and their families aware of the early symptoms of addictions. They also need counseling help in letting go of denial and rationalization so that they will apply their knowledge to their own situation. Other approaches to interrupting addictions sooner include encouraging families to come out of hiding so that they can receive help sooner, and relate to their addicted members in ways that may hasten their also becoming open to help. Counseling methods to facilitate enabling both addicts and their families to come out of hiding are detailed in chapters 12 and 13.

Nonaddictive Excessive Drinking and Drug Use

Counselors should be aware that many people who drink and use recreational drugs in excessive, problem-causing ways are not yet addicted. Instead they are problem drinkers or problem users who are increasingly dependent on their favorite chemicals but not yet physiologically addicted. (They were labeled Alpha alcoholics in Jellinek's typology, in contrast to Gamma, Delta, and Epsilon types who are physiologically addicted.) Problem drinkers/users are in a category between controlled social users and addicts. Their problematic chemical use may be caused by heavy peer-group pressures or by habitually employing chemical comforters to deaden psychological pain. This pain may come from traumatic grief, disintegrating marriages, death of cherished dreams, agonizing depressions, or an overload of everyday frustrations and disappointments. Their overuse of psychochemical solutions often worsens their pain, thus producing an addiction-like vicious cycle of pain, increasing use, increasing pain. Furthermore, their chances of eventually becoming physiologically addicted are high if they continue excessive intake. If the negative consequences of excessive use motivates them to reduce their intake before psychological or biochemical changes cause them to lose control, and their pain is reduced, they *may* learn how to use their chemicals in nonproblematic moderation.

Distinguishing problem drinkers/users from those who are thoroughly addicted is difficult in practice because the transition is usually gradual from one to the other condition. Both groups overuse substances in ways that produce serious problems for themselves and others. Nonaddicted problem users can be recognized as those who do not have symptoms of physiological addiction such as severe withdrawal effects, blackouts, and increased body tissue tolerance so that more of a substance is required to produce the sought-after effect. The nonaddicted substance abusers who are helped by A.A., N.A., and other addiction treatment approaches often are labeled high bottom. Others do not respond to these programs because they cannot accept with their assumptions or identify with the experiences of the addicted people recovering in them. If the evaluation of substance abusing clients does not reveal symptoms of physiological addictions as well as major psychosocial deterioration, and they do not respond to Twelve Step groups, they probably are problem alcohol and/or drug users.

How can such people be helped to control their substance abuse or, if they cannot do this, stop their destructive drinking and drug use? If they are using alcohol or drugs as a self-prescribed anesthetic for pain other than that caused by excessive use, they need counseling help to diminish that pain. Clergy and other counselors first should help them identify the sources of their pain and then either provide counseling or steer them to the specialized psychotherapy they need. I can recall several problem drinkers who changed from excessive to moderate drinking when grief counseling or grief healing groups brought healing of their inner pain. In troubled family relationships involving problem users, effective marriage and family therapy may reduce conflict-generated pain and increase relationship satisfactions so that they move from excessive to occasional moderate use or abstinence. If people are physiologically addicted, efforts to help them reduce pain such as that caused by grief frequently is sabotaged by them. Their continued excessive use is driven by their addiction-caused craving, chaos, and pain. If they are not physiologically addicted, counseling that heals their pain often is effective in reducing their problem-causing uses of chemicals.

Fortunately, several innovative educational programs aimed at helping problem drinkers have emerged in recent years based on pioneering research begun two decades ago at the Addiction Research Foundation of Toronto. DrinkChoice is one such program. A brief, cognitively oriented program begun in Santa Barbara, California, it is designed to teach nonaddicted problem drinkers how to choose one of two objectives—to moderate their problem-causing drinking or to quit altogether, if that is their choice or they cannot moderate their intake. The goal is to help clients change their relationship with alcohol by examining their attitudes and behavior toward drinking. It is staffed by professional counselors at least one of whom is a member of A.A. Clients who come for "training" are first helped to determine whether they are nonaddicted excessive users or severely addicted physiologically. This is done by using diagnostic tools such as the classic "Twenty Questions" from Johns Hopkins, and by discovering how much, how often, for how long, and for what reasons they drink. If clients are discovered to be severely addicted, they are referred to A.A. or other appropriate treatment programs. But if they are identified as problem drinkers, they are eligible for the DrinkChoice's training. After a free telephone consultation, this program consists of four fifty-minute individual training sessions, face-to-face or by telephone, or five ninety-minute group sessions in which clients are trained in using methods in a workbook they receive. The basic fee also covers three follow-up sessions—at three months, six months, and one year—to assess and support clients' progress. Approximately 80 percent of clients who are evaluated as "successful" by the staff choose moderate drinking while the others quit completely.[45]

Religious and Existential Causes of Addictions

There is another crucial cluster of causes that often must be addressed in either preventive efforts or counseling addicts for recovery. These are the powerful and often-hidden spiritual, religious, and ethical disturbances—the existential vacuums—that often play crucial roles in the addictive process. A functional understanding of these deeper causes and of the distinctive contributions of religious approaches to recovery depends on insights into the dynamics of this spiritual dimension of addicts' lives. Causes in this area are ignored or misunderstood by many otherwise competent, secular professionals in the addiction field who are not trained in understanding religious behavior and beliefs using the psychosocial sciences. For this reason, the religious or spiritual dynamics in addictions and in recovery have not received the full, rigorous study they merit. Because these dynamics are so important for clergy and other counselors, they will be explored in depth in chapter 10.

Suffice it to say here that the religious causes involve attempting to satisfy spiritual needs by chemical means. Clergy have the central role in preventing addictions and counseling with addicts and their families around their spiritual issues. Primary prevention of addictions and full recovery from them often require people to learn healthy, nonchemical ways to satisfy their inescapable spiritual or existential hungers. To facilitate this crucial learning for healthy spiritual growth is the most important, as well as the most unique contribution clergy can make in the whole field of addictions.

Vera Sezhina, a perceptive Russian psychologist, has observed that Americans who "have everything" are like empty cups who need to be filled up again and again.

They try to fill their emptiness by buying new toys which they forget in a few days. They go from one thing to another, addictively trying to fill it with sexual intimacy, alcohol, drugs, sports, work, marriages, travel, therapies, play, television, and spiritual practices from the East and West. Nothing fills their empty cup for long.[46]

Why is this true for many Americans as well as people in other affluent countries? I would say that it is because their cup that should be running over with good things in their lives, has a hidden hole in it. This hole is a deep wound in their sense of belonging and connectedness with a trusted, loving human community and with a trusted, loving higher Power.

Having surveyed the complex causes of addictions and their important implications for preventive strategies, the next few chapters will explore understanding drug and behavioral addictions and those at heightened risk.

CHAPTER 3

Understanding Drug Dependence

Drug dependence[1] and addictions are escalating epidemics in our addictive society. All substances that are capable of giving even a small taste of euphoria or blunting the cutting edge of painful reality lend themselves to overuse, abuse, and addictions. As we have seen, alcohol is humankind's most ancient and still favorite chemical-comforting drug, manufactured and used in almost all cultures. Only one mood-changing drug is used by more people on planet earth—caffeine. But today's drug scene is more complicated and hazardous because of the availability of a plethora of new as well as old mind-altering chemicals, both legal and illegal. Many of these produce biochemical and/or psychological effects that make them psychologically habituating and/or physiologically addictive. The social context of the explosion of drug problems today is the era of psychochemistry in which we are living. An unprecedented array of new consciousness-changing drugs, many of which are potentially addictive, are continually developed by pharmaceutical companies and advertised aggressively as the "solution" to most human problems. This motivates an ever-widening search for chemical euphoria, comfort, and escape from the personal pain, boredom, injustice, and tragedies that are part of the fabric of human life.

Drugs in four categories contribute to the current epidemic. These are illegal street drugs such as cocaine, heroin, marijuana, LSD, and the so-called designer drugs; drugs such as amphetamines that often are over prescribed as well as manufactured in illegal labs and sold widely on the streets; many other potentially addictive prescription drugs; and a variety of over-the-counter addictive drugs including nicotine. The fifth major cluster of substance abuse problems that will be discussed in this chapter are the addictive uses or self-deprivation of food.

Understanding today's drug scene is crucial to both preventive education and effective treatment of chemical dependencies. The vast majority of addicted people are hooked on more than one substance. Many alcoholics, for example, also are addicted to one or more other drugs. This often complicates their medical treatment and recovery. Recovery from nicotine addiction provides an example of this. The respected *University of California Berkeley Wellness Letter* reports: "If you're trying to quit smoking or remain a former smoker, watch out when you drink alcohol. Researchers have long known that drinkers tend to smoke more, and that drinking often serves as a cue to smoke, but a new study at Purdue University has shown that, in smokers, alcohol actually increases the craving to smoke."[2]

Reflecting on both their personal and professional experiences, a group of recovering physicians in A.A. illuminates the complex problems encountered by addicted people who mix alcohol and pills:

> Once alcoholics are under the influence of either drugs or alcohol, they are in trouble. Many have started using pills thinking they have found the perfect substitute for alcohol. However, the progression of pill-taking is often the same as that of drinking. Both usually end in a real binge. But in the case of drugs, there may be severe reactions, including convulsions from overdosage. Even death is not uncommon. So alcoholics should never delude themselves about drugs. But they often do. As the late Dr. E. M. Jellinek said about barbiturates: "The alcoholic who uses barbiturates is eating his alcohol instead of drinking it."[3]

The Nature and Seriousness of the Problem

Given the prevalence of drug dependence, it is no wonder that clergy, as well as other caregivers and counselors, frequently encounter drug abuse. The following situations illustrate the variety of such encounters by clergy: The worried parents of a youth group member seeks pastoral guidance concerning his experimentation with pot and, they fear, other drugs. Family members of an older senile woman express concern because her situation is deteriorating while she takes a variety of drugs that have been over prescribed. In addition, she occasionally forgets to take essential medications. A middle-aged parishioner, long dependent on tranquilizers and despairing about her collapsing marriage, commits suicide from an overdose of vodka and tranquilizers. A counselee reveals that he is hooked on a pain-deadening drug, Demerol, which he began taking after major surgery. A successful businessman is hospitalized with a toxic psychosis resulting from a protracted, hidden addiction to tranquilizers and alcohol. A troubled physician with ready access to prescribed drugs loses his license to practice because of his professional incompetence caused by frequent drug-induced mental fog.

The term *drug problems*, as used in the past, has usually referred to illicit street drugs. They still constitute a major problem among all social classes in our pluralistic country, where it is estimated that six million Americans are addicted to illegal drugs. But the hidden epidemic of addictions to legal drugs—prescribed and over-the-counter—is the "polite" addiction epidemic that probably injures and kills more people than do all illegal drugs. If, as is appropriate, alcohol and nicotine are counted among legal drugs, the number of addicted persons and the toll in human suffering far surpasses that derived from illegal drugs.[4] (Each year, some 115,000 people die from alcohol abuse, 450,000 from tobacco, compared to only 30,000 from all illegal drugs.)

It is important to bear in mind that drug dependence often is an iceberg problem with only the tip of the problem showing. To a greater extent even than with alcoholics, many drug problems are hidden below the surface. Drug problems are easier to hide for longer that alcoholism. (As someone has remarked, "You can't smell drugs.") Even those closest to victims often are unaware that drug dependence is a serious problem for loved ones. The truth comes out only when the dire consequences of advanced stage addictions reveal them, often in shocking ways. The hiddenness of drug problems is increased by the fact that many addicted people and their families feel intense motivation to play a favorite game in polite society, including congregations. This game is called "Let's Pretend"—-that things are fine with us even when we are going through hell. To the degree that clergypersons are perceived as moral authority figures, the need to play this destructive game with them, hiding socially stigmatized struggles, is increased. It is important, therefore, to be very alert when working closely with troubled people, watching for what may be subtle clues of drug problems intermingled with and complicating other problems in living.

A recent study revealed that Americans believe that drug abuse—more than crime or family breakdown—is the greatest threat facing children. An astute editorial in a church-related periodical articulated the nagging concern of many people: "Our greatest fear as parents and grandparents is that our children might be harmed or killed in today's violent, drug-driven world . . . the continued rise in drug use and the violence that accompanies it both scares and angers. Even innocent people often die in drug-related, drive-by shootings."[5] Two disturbing events in the news triggered this poignant editorial. One was the drug-related, gangland-type shooting of a rap star, age twenty-five, "Gangsta" Tupac (Two-pac) Shakur, a favorite of many teens. The other was an alarming survey reporting that drug use among youth ages twelve to seventeen had sky-rocketed in recent years.

As the finishing touches were being put on this chapter, four college women died in a tragic accident in the community where I live. The car one of them was driving plunged off a mountain road and was crushed as it tumbled into the deep canyon. The young women had been partying and had blood alcohol levels more than twice the legal limit for driving. Two also had cocaine in their blood. During the same period, a week was designated as "Alcohol and Other Drug-Related Birth Defects Awareness Week." The public was reminded that the leading cause of preventable mental retardation is fetal alcohol syndrome, and that neonatal crack and alcohol addictions often produce severe developmental and emotional impairment in children. Babies whose mothers used alcohol or street drugs heavily during pregnancy often are born addicted. Such children frequently have diminished ability to learn or control their behavior, and need lifelong medical treatment. What is more, child abuse, incest, and chronic violence between parents are common manifestations of alcohol and drug addicted parents.

The problem of drug abuse, like many other health problems, is complicated by the AIDS crisis. There are between 500,000 and one million chronic intravenous drug abusers in the USA. Twenty-five percent of these are HIV positive. It is also true that 80 percent of children born with AIDS have intravenous drug using parents.[6]

Narcotics and other illegally sold drugs have long been big business that criminal cartels have controlled and exploited for multimillion dollar profits. In Los Angeles, hundreds of Hispanic gang members are selling drugs on the streets as part of a widespread distribution system controlled by the ruthlessly violent Mexican Mafia. Many mafia members are in American prisons where they continue to control and make immense profits from street drug sales. The U.S. has the highest incarceration rate of any country in the world, mainly because of the get-tough-on-drug-offenders program started in the mid-1980s. Half of all inmates in federal prisons are there for drug-related crimes. Many are themselves addicted and only a tiny percentage of them receive any drug treatment or rehabilitation in prison or when they are released. This is in spite of the fact that treatment of drug offenders is estimated to cost about $10,000 a year, compared to $25,000 annually to keep them locked up.

One serious aspect of the new drug problem is the illegal manufacture and street sale of amphetamines, barbiturates, tranquilizers, and hallucinogenic drugs. The abuse of methamphetamine (uppers) is a major and growing drug problem, particularly in Southwestern United States, where it rivals the crack cocaine epidemic. Mexican drug cartels smuggle many tons across the borders, having processed it from raw materials supplied by Chinese chemical exporters. Drug dealers sell it on the streets as speed, ice, crank, or simply meth, often making thousands of dollars quickly while maintaining their own supply. In addition, large quantities of methamphetamines are produced locally in hidden processing labs. In one recent year, nearly eight hundred such operations were discovered and destroyed in raids by California drug authorities. Many of the most bizarre crimes against children and others are perpetrated by youth and young adults under the influence of this drug.

In the past, addictions to hard drugs such as opium derivatives flourished mostly among economically disadvantaged and minority groups, mainly in large cities, as well as among some artists and counterculture devotees. But now, drug abuse is proliferating among middle- and upper-class people in many American communities, in suburbia and exurbia, as well as in the heart of cities where the disadvantaged suffer from the social decay around them. Drug problems still are most prevalent in large cities, particularly those that serve as ports of entry for the drug trade. But the pandemic is striking all parts of the country, in villages and county seat towns, as well as major cities. Furthermore, the new drug problem strikes all age groups from children to seniors. Use of "happiness drugs" like marijuana is very common on college campuses and among high school and even junior-high youth and younger. In a recent year, a national survey of grammar school children revealed that 18 percent of eighth graders had tried pot and that one out of every four had tried some illegal drug during the past year.[7] Anyone who becomes knowledgeable about the drug problem in their communities discovers that it is much more common and closer to home that they had suspected.

Types of Drug Users and Abusers

Several overlapping groups can be distinguished among drug-using people:

Recreational users: Many younger people dabble with dangerous drugs for a time, mainly as pleasure seekers looking for ways to get high. Most do not become addicted, but those who are particularly vulnerable to dependency on drugs, for whatever reason, do get hooked.

Rebellious users: Adolescents often experiment with dangerous street drugs as they struggle for peer acceptance and to discover their identity. In contrast with youth who are maladjusted and symptomatic users, they tend to do their drugs in peer groups. Often this is one temporary expression of their struggle for self-definition as they distance themselves from parental norms and other adult expectations and identify with their peer group. Only a small percentage of the many youth who experiment with marijuana or other street drugs either become addicted or go on to hard drugs.

Maladjusted users: These are the countless people who, though not severely dysfunctional psychologically, experience chronic unhappiness, relationship conflicts, loneliness, and a sense of deep guilt, shame, or failure. Such people often begin using drugs as chemical comforters, anxiety-diminishers, or crutches in troubled relationships and lives. In many cases their psychological dependence on the drugs becomes physiological addiction, and they progressively substitute chemical satisfactions for those obtained from constructive relationships or from using their personality resources.

Symptomatic users: These are persons whose abuse clearly is symptomatic of profoundly disturbed personalities. Such people have painful symptoms of psychological disturbances that require treatment. Many are polyaddicted and move from one addictive substance to another.

Accidentally addicted: These are persons who are not particularly disturbed psychologically, but who become physically dependent on drugs prescribed for valid medical reasons to control pain, or carelessly over prescribed by physicians. Such people demonstrate that those whose anxiety and stress level is well within normal limits can become hooked on highly addictive pain-controlling or anxiety-reducing drugs. In drugs such as narcotics and barbiturates, fear of the pain of withdrawal strengthens resistance to discontinuing the drugs. Once people are addicted, the negative consequences of taking the drugs are counterbalanced by the chemical satisfactions they continue to derive, making escape from the addictive cycle increasingly difficult.

Social desperation users: Some oppressed people use dangerous drugs heavily for the same reasons that many alcoholics begin drinking heavily—to try to forget their painful social, economic, and racial oppression. Their use of drugs does not help them cope constructively with their despair or help to change the social problems that make heavy drinking and drug use so attractive. In fact, it makes their total situation worse. An astute observer of crack cocaine's devastation of countless African American ghetto youth, resulting in addictions, drive-by shootings, and prison for some, commented: "Crack is just Jim Crow in a pipe." The ministry of a certain Roman Catholic priest is with men and women who are poor Mexican American farm laborers. He reports that many of them started to use stimulating drugs to gain energy to work more hours at their low paying, menial jobs. Many also drink heavily to forget their miserable circumstances. When they crash, they go through the state narcotics treatment program that includes Narcotics Anonymous and A.A.

Types of Drugs Used Addictively

Here is an overview of drugs that often are involved in addictions. (For more in-depth information about particular drugs and about methods of treating addictions, see *The Facts About Drug Use: Coping with Drugs and Alcohol in Your Family, at Work, in Your Community* by Barry Stimmel, M.D. and the editors of Consumer Reports Books.)[8] The action of mood-altering drugs on the brain and central nervous system is used by researchers and medical professionals to classify them. But the most useful classification of these drugs for the public is one based on the actual effects experienced when taking the drugs. While the terms change constantly, here is a listing.[9]

Central Nervous System Depressants

All these drugs slow down or sedate the excitable brain tissues and affect the brain centers controlling coordination, speech, vision, and judgment. These drugs produce diminished tension, anxiety, and pain. They may induce sleep, and if taken in sufficient quantities, stupor, coma, and even death. Included are alcoholic beverages; the antianxiety, tranquilizers, and sleeping medications.

Tranquilizers are a growing cluster of nonbarbiturates, nonnarcotic sedatives that began to be available in the early-1950s. Because of their ability to suppress anxiety, irrational fears, and tensions, and to produce a sense of well-being, even euphoria in some people, they are invaluable in treating many stress-induced, psychoneurotic and psychotic symptoms. These drugs are classified as major or minor based on their uses, not on their potency. The minor tranquilizers, which are most often misused for self-medication, include Librium, Valium, Xanax, Ativan, Restori, Tranxene, Dalmane, Halcion, Klonopin, Doriden and Serax.[10] These tranquilizers are prescribed for millions of Americans, including nearly twice as many women as men. The chemical characteristics of minor tranquilizers make them conducive to abuse and dependence. Problems occur when people pop a pill or reach for a tranquilizer instead of attempting to deal with the issues in their inner lives, relationships, work, or world that cause their tension, conflict, and anxiety.

When tranquilizers were first developed, it was believed that they were the new wonder drug, the answer to the addictive problems posed by barbiturates. But subsequent experience has shown that all tranquilizers are addictive for vulnerable people. These certainly include such familiar ones as Librium, Xanox, and Valium. The effects of heavy, chronic use are similar to those of alcohol and barbiturates. They produce thinking difficulties and reduce muscular coordination, thus contributing to traffic accidents and interfering with work effectiveness. A wide variety of bizarre reactions have been reported following heavy doses and withdrawal, including hallucinations and seizures. They tend like barbiturates to multiply the effects of alcohol (and vice versa), so that even relatively small doses add unpredictably to the total effects. Tranquilizer abuse and dependency has become a major public health problem. Careless prescribing and prescriptions given unknowingly by several physicians to the same patients, allow many people to acquire an assortment of tranquilizers. Some use these for self-medication as well as sharing with friends.

Another category of central nervous system depressants are *barbiturates*[11]—known on the street as downers or barbs. There are many different ones including secobarbital or reds, (Seconal Sodium) or red devils, amobarbital [e.g., (Amytal)], blue heavens, (Phenobarbital), e.g., (Luminal) or purple hearts, (Nembutal) or yellow jackets, (Tuinal) or rainbows, and a combination of amobarbital and secobarbital. Prescribed mainly as sedative-hypnotics (sleeping pills), they are highly addictive with all the major characteristics of addiction-increased tissue tolerance, both psychological and physiological dependence, and withdrawal symptoms when the intake is reduced drastically or cut off. These symptoms can be very severe including convulsions, disorientation, temporary psychoses, and even death. Most medical experts agree that withdrawal from barbiturates is more dangerous than from morphine drugs and should be supervised by a physician. The symptoms of excessive barbiturate use are similar to alcohol intoxication—slurred speech, staggering, impaired judgment and motor skills, and emotional volatility.

These drugs are prescribed because they are faster acting than tranquilizers, but they are prescribed much less for several reasons. They tend to be more addictive, the gap between therapeutic and lethal doses is much narrower than with tranquilizers, and when combined with alcohol they have a superadditive effect. Barbiturism (barbiturate addiction) is not as common as in pretranquilizer times, because of this and because street addicts know that to drink on top of taking any barbiturate is too dangerous because of the superadditive effect.

The tragic case of Karen Ann Quinlan is still the prototype of alcohol-barbiturate deaths. In 1975 she went into a coma from mixing alcohol and barbiturates and remained comatose for seven years before she eventually died. When it was clear that there was no chance of her coming out of the coma, her parents fought a nationally publicized court battle to be allowed to disconnect her from the life-support system and bring her home for her last days. Everyone in the addiction medicine field, as well as most sophisticated street addicts, and social drinkers who take their regular nembutal capsule at bedtime after a night of partying, has some idea about this tragedy.

Other drugs in the depressant category include anesthetics such as nitrous oxide (used by dentists) and cannabinoids (marijuana and hashish).

Central Nervous System Stimulants

These drugs, of which amphetamines, cocaine, and nicotine are prime examples, stimulate the central nervous system causing the release of energy, excitement, feelings of euphoria, and sleeplessness. Their energy-releasing effects are much like the body's own adrenaline. Amphetamines are widely prescribed in medical practice to lessen mild depression, suppress the appetite (as diet pills for weight reduction), reduce fatigue, and control narcolepsy (going to sleep involuntarily, often at inappropriate times). They all speed up the function of excitable brain tissues resulting in energized muscles, increased heart rate and blood pressure, and decreased appetite. They are used by truck drivers to stay awake on long hauls and by students when they are cramming for exams. The drugs increase physical activity and enhance confidence, optimism, and euphoria. For this reason they have acquired the reputation of happiness pills among teenagers. The characteristics make them seductively attractive to anyone who is depressed—the very people most likely to become dependent. In addition to their legal sources, they are also manufactured inexpensively in illegal bootleg operations and made widely available on the drug black market. Among the *amphetamines*—known as uppers on the street—and amphetamine-like stimulant drugs, are speed, (Benzedrine) or bennies, (Dexedrine) or copilots, methylphenidates such as (Ritalin), (Diphetamine) or footballs, (Benzedrex), (Tuamine), (Desyphed), (Methedrine), and (Hexedrine), and deliriants such as airplane glue, nail polish remover, and gasoline.

Inhalants are used by some children and youth to get high by inhaling the fumes. These are the drugs of choice for many youth. They are not illegal to buy, possess, or sell, and all have legitimate uses. Although many teens regard them as harmless, they can cause brain damage and even death.

All amphetamines including speed (injectable methamphetamine), ice or glass (methamphetamine smoked), crystal meth (injected metham-phetamine), crank (amphetamine taken nasally) are highly addictive. These substances have produced a major drug problem particularly in the western states. Along with cocaine, amphetamines are regarded by drug experts as a major challenge in the drug addiction scene. Large doses of amphetamines and cocaine occasionally result in acute delirium, psy-choses including paranoia and hallucinations, as well as violent behavior and suicides. It is estimated that women use twice as many ampheta-mines and other stimulants as men, and half again as many tranquilizers.

In contrast to barbiturates and opiates, amphetamines seem to produce less physiological withdrawal effects, except when used in very large amounts. However, the psychological dependence on their euphoric effects produces a powerful craving that seems to be rooted in brain func-tion. Heavy users characteristically develop a tolerance for the drugs so that they must progressively increase the dosage to feel good. Some reach the stage where they take a hundred pills or more a day. Although fatal doses can occur, the most common danger is that these drugs mask fatigue causing the body to use energy far beyond a safe point. Unaware of their fatigue, people may collapse from total exhaustion or, before this, have their judgment distorted and consciousness blurred. They may have to be hospitalized to recover from their exhaustion. Numerous fatal auto accidents have resulted from the illegal use of amphetamines. Large, pro-longed doses sometimes produce side effects such as suspiciousness, hal-lucinations, suicidal impulses, and explosions of hostile aggressiveness.

A widely used illegal stimulant drug is *cocaine,* also known as snow, coke, and "C." Many users become hooked on the buzz of cocaine highs. Extracted from the leaves of the *Erythroxylon* coca bush that grows on the eastern slopes of the Andes in Peru, Bolivia, Columbia, and other coun-tries, it is very addictive. Hundreds of tons of cocaine are smuggled across the U.S. borders each year. The profits of the cocaine cartels in Columbia are estimated to be two billion dollars, greater than those of Texaco. Cocaine is usually sold as a white crystalline powder that is inhaled or snorted. It can also be injected. It is an intense stimulant of the central and sympathetic nervous systems, with short-term effects more intense than those produced by amphetamines. Unlike the latter, cocaine is also a local anesthetic. Currently cocaine is a popular drug of choice for many middle class, upwardly striving young adults.

Crack cocaine—also known as rock or crack—is a distilled form of cocaine mixed with baking soda to make it hard. It is much more potent and addic-tive than undistilled powder cocaine, and is the drug of choice of many urban youth. The fact that the penalties for possessing crack are much more severe than for powder cocaine results from the racism in our judicial system. Freebase is a purified form of cocaine made by applying solvents to ordinary cocaine. The effect is brief, very intense euphoria. Coca paste is a crude coca preparation that is usually smoked on tobacco cigarettes.

Caffeine—stimulates the central nervous system and all portions of the brain making it an extremely popular drug. This drug is clearly addictive. A vast majority of teens and adults in the world consume caffeine each day. Many are caffeine dependent. This is demonstrated by uncomfortable symptoms like headaches and lethargy when they are unable to have their regular morning fix of caffeine in coffee, tea, or sodas. A surgeon at the Mayo Clinic in Scottsdale, Arizona has reduced the withdrawal headaches of caffeine-addicted patients by giving them a shot in the intravenous lines soon after surgery. Research findings on health problems associated with the use of caffeine seem to indicate that, for most people, caffeine produces a relatively benign addiction. But heavy use by some people seems to play a role in symptoms like heartbeat irregularities and insomnia. But the fact that many people are able to reduce and control their intake of caffeine shows that its addictive properties are not nearly as strong as nicotine and many other drugs.

Narcotics or Opiates

These highly addictive drugs decrease pain by attaching themselves to receptors in certain brain areas. They generally have a tranquilizing and sedative effect, but physical agitation caused by withdrawal and psychological panic related to anticipation of withdrawal symptoms, may produce antisocial behavior during drug craving. Included are opiates derived from the juice of the seed pod of the Asian poppy *Papaver somniferum*—opium, codeine, morphine, and heroin—also known on the street as "H"; synthetic opiates or morphine substitutes such as methadone (Dolophine), meperidine (Demerol), Percodan, oxycodone, Dilaudid, Darvon, Primadol, and Lomoti. Some of these are legal prescription drugs. Others, such as heroin, are illegal street drugs. Highly potent forms of heroin have become available on the streets in recent years, resulting in numerous deaths from overdoses.

Psychedelics or Hallucinogens

These so-called consciousness-expanding drugs produce distortions of thoughts, sensations, and perceptions of oneself and of external reality, thereby inducing radically altered states of consciousness including visionlike states. Being spaced out in this way is attractive to some people who find their ordinary perception of reality boring, depressing, or painful. On the down side, these drugs are unpredictable in their effects. In vulnerable people they may bring feelings of extreme anxiety, hallucinations, and occasionally may precipitate psychotic episodes. Although they are less physiologically addictive than many other drugs, they can be psychologically habituating. The frequent use by teens and young adults or marijuana sometimes results in what is called *amotivational syndrome* characterized by passivity and lack of ambition, resulting in poor school and work performance.

Several hallucinogens are derived from plants. Mescaline or peyote is derived from a certain cactus and has been used for centuries in religious rites by some Native American tribes in the Southwest. (Their right to use the drug in this religious context has been upheld by the courts.) Psilocybin is a drug found in a sacred mushroom that grows in Mexico. It is used by certain tribes in their religious ceremonies.

Marijuana--also known as pot, weed, grass, tea, and MaryJane—is another natural hallucinogen. It comes from the flowering tops and leaves of the female Indian hemp plant. It is used today by millions of people in many parts of the world as it has been for centuries. As a chemical reality-softener, it is second only to alcohol in popularity worldwide. Feelings of lightness, hilarity, sociability, and the dissolving of emotional restraints, along with distortions of space and time, are common. Its effects usually are regarded by users as generally pleasurable, like mild alcohol intoxication. The supply of this drug that is now available is several times more potent than what was available in the sixties and seventies. Hallucinogenic effects are more prominent when large doses are smoked or eaten. Although an occasional user becomes quarrelsome, there is little evidence to support the belief that it incites antisocial or sexual offenses. Addictive symptoms like physiological dependence, tolerance, and withdrawal do seem to occur in heavy users and many chronic users become psychologically habituated. Significant dangers include loss of judgment and faulty space-time sense that results in accidents and the amotivational syndrome mentioned above.

Marijuana is popular among college students and its use is increasing among high school and even junior high students. Some young people who use it regularly are spaced out so much that their functioning in school and work is erratic and unpredictable. Marijuana is reported to have some effectiveness in diminishing the side effects of AIDS medications and chemotherapy treatment for cancer. The organized effort to make it legal for medicinal purposes has resulted in it becoming so in two states. There is some justification for its reputation as a gateway drug leading to heroin and cocaine. The Center for Alcohol and Substance Abuse at Columbia University reports that children who have used nicotine, alcohol, and marijuana are eighty times more likely to move on to cocaine than those who have not used the gateway drugs.

LSD-25 is short for d-lysergic acid diethylamide—also known as acid. This is a potent and potentially dangerous hallucinogen that can be synthesized by anyone with a basic knowledge of chemistry. It produces drastic changes in perception of reality, self-awareness, and communication. Bootleg LSD is readily available through street drug channels. Psychotic-like, nightmarish experiences occasionally occur, as well as those described as mystically elevating, consciousness-expanding, and even rapturous. LSD-25 has been known to produce temporary and occasionally long-term psychoses with terrifying auditory and visual hallucinations, panic attacks, flashbacks, deep depression, and suicidal impulses. Such symptoms can occur with the first use, and may recur long after taking LSD has ceased. Although the drug apparently is not physiologically addictive, there is evidence that repeated use can result in long-term personality changes characterized by less concern about ordinary reality and responsibility. In some cases, first-time use can cause long-term psychological problems.

Designer Drugs

Beginning in the '80s a new group of drugs became available. These are look-alike drugs that are synthesized illegally in clandestine laboratories. Designer drugs have become a major cause of both addictions and overdose deaths. They resemble highly potent doses of amphetamines or narcotics in their psychophysiological impacts, but they are designed to differ chemically. This enables them to skirt the laws that would make them illegal and make them difficult to detect in urine and blood tests. These drugs tend to be extremely potent and the changes in chemical structure often produce unanticipated toxic effects that are sometimes fatal. Because they are relatively easy to produce they are very profitable. Among the street names of these drugs are ecstasy (a hallucinogen), China white (a narcotic), Eve or love (a hallucinogen), MPPP (a narcotic), and ice (a stimulant derived from methamphetamine in smokable form). There are numerous designer amphetamine variants, including the so-called alphabet drugs. These include DMA, PMA, PCP, TMA, MMDA, DOM, and STP, drugs with hallucinogenic effects.

PCP—which stands for Phenyclidine hydrochloride, also known as angel dust or hog—is a designer drug that first appeared on the street as the "peace pill" in the late-1960s. It is a white, crystalline powder, soluble in water or alcohol. As a street drug it is smoked in a joint with marijuana or dried parsley. It is difficult to classify because different doses produce varied and unpredictable effects, resembling a stimulant, an anesthetic, an analgesic, or a hallucinogen.

Performance-Enhancing Drugs

The manner in which drug addictions and sports addictions interact is illustrated dramatically by the use of illegal performance-enhancing drugs by some atheletes. They use steroids and growth harmones to increase muscular strength, stimulants to enhance their energy, and narcotics to mask their pain. Steroids are abused by professional atheletes, as well as some adolescents and young adults (of both genders, but particularly males), who are preoccupied, even obsessed with body image, athletic strength, and increased muscle mass. These drugs are easily obtained illegally via mail order and black market sources, and from some body building gyms. Side effects of prolonged use may include liver, heart, and blood disorders. Cocaine has a reputation in some circles as a sexual performance-enhancing drug.

Combining Drugs

Various combinations of drugs are used by drug-dependent people to counteract the side effects of one drug or synergistically increase the effect of other drugs. For example, many cocaine addicts use alcohol to cope with the side effect of cocaine. Drugs often combined include heroin and cocaine (called speedball);[12] cocaine and alcohol or marijuana; cocaine and PCP; methadone (used to treat heroine addiction) and alcohol; and cocaine, tranquilizers, and alcohol. The drugs that stimulate the central nervous system are usually involved among a variety of drugs. Poly-dependent people may move from one drug to another or take several at the same time. They may combine the use of alcohol, barbiturates, and amphetamines, and, in some cases, marijuana, hallucinogens, and opiates. A friend who is in recovery tells of using cocaine to enable him to drink more when alcohol began to lose its desired effects. Those addicted to alcohol, barbiturates, and opiates often use amphetamines to ease hangovers or try to restore themselves to a functional state after prolonged use of central nervous system depressants. A common pattern followed by the polydependent is to start the day with an amphetamine in order to counteract hangovers from alcohol, tranquilizers, and barbiturates, take a tranquilizer at midday to reduce tension, and then use tranquilizers, barbiturates, and alcohol to get to sleep. Such multiple dependence is self-perpetuating and progressive, leading deeper into the addictive process.[13]

Nicotine

Nicotine is an extremely popular stimulant drug derived from the leaf of the tobacco plant. (It acts on two areas of the brain producing a strong stimulant, neurotransmitter at one area and dopamine, the "reward" neurotransmitter, at the other.) Compulsive use of tobacco in its various forms constitutes the most widespread addiction (other than to caffeine) in the Western world. This addiction is by far the most costly and destructive of human health and well-being around the planet. Annual deaths worldwide are more than three million a year (over eight thousand a day). If present trends continue, the annual nicotine death toll is projected to climb to ten million early in the twenty-first century. One-fifth of the people alive in developed countries today will eventually die of smoking-related causes according to a recent British study. The transnational American tobacco companies, having had the health hazards of smoking revealed in this country, and the advertising of their products somewhat curtailed, are now focusing much of their promotion in developing countries.

Smoking tobacco is the number one cause of premature, preventable deaths in America. Smoking kills more people each year than die from alcoholism, other drugs, auto accidents, and AIDS combined. Eighty percent of lung cancers and 30 percent of all cancers are caused by smoking. The U.S. Centers for Disease Control and Prevention estimates that seven minutes are subtracted from a smoker's life for each cigarette smoked adding up to a staggering five million years of potential life expectancy lost by American smokers each year.[14]

The forty-six million who continue smoking average twenty-five cigarettes a day. This translates into seventy thousand nicotine hits a year for each smoker. New research has revealed that a large cigar contains about 40 times as much nicotine as one cigarette. Smoking a cigar exposes one to almost as much nicotine as smoking a whole pack of cigarettes in one day. This increases greatly the risk of cancer of the mouth, throat, and esophagus, even if one does not inhale. Health care costs from smoking-related illnesses total some fifty billion dollars a year, over half of which is paid by Medicare for patients over sixty-five. In recent years there has been a dramatic increase in smoking by women and teens. Every day, approximately three thousand young people begin smoking. There is no such person as an "underage smoker" because there is no healthy age to smoke. The vast majority of adults addicted to nicotine began smoking as children or youth. (The use of terms like "presmokers" and "learners" in an internal memo by a tobacco executive that was leaked to the press, reveals the motivation of this drug industry. An internal Philip Morris document dated 1981, released January 29, 1989: "Today's teenager is tomorrow's potential customer.") Lung cancer, not breast cancer, is the number one cancer killer of women. Tobacco-related deaths of women are expected soon to reach and exceed those of men. There is growing evidence that environmental tobacco smoke, or secondhand smoke—has the same serious illness consequences—lung cancer and heart disease—for those who live or work with smokers, including their children. A ten year study of thirty-two thousand nonsmoking women found that women who regularly breathe secondhand smoke have twice the risk of heart disease compared with those not so exposed.

These statistics are personalized by prominent Americans like Al Gore, who struggled to maintain his composure on television when he told of watching his sister, Nancy, die of tobacco-related lung cancer. (Neighbors of the Gore's farm in Tennessee have said that they stopped growing tobacco after Nancy's death.) Jimmy Carter, in a 1992 speech, told of how his father, mother, both sisters and his brother, all smokers, died of cancer.

Nicotine is several times more physiologically addictive than alcohol. It is a mood-changing stimulant drug producing "upper" effects similar, though not as intense as cocaine and amphetamines. Nicotine has all the characteristics that identify an addictive drug—tissue tolerance, withdrawal, and intense nicotine-seeking behavior when one is deprived of tobacco. Tobacco products of all types are do-it-yourself drug delivery devices. Chain smokers are administering their drug fix almost nonstop. The painful withdrawal symptoms experienced when they do not smoke for even a relatively brief time, and the high failure rate among those who try to stop smoking permanently, are evidence of tobacco's high biochemical addictiveness that is about equal to cocaine.

A former U.S. Secretary of Health, Education and Welfare, Louis W. Sullivan, described tobacco as "the only legal product that when used as intended causes death."[15] Until recently, the chief executives of America's seven largest cigarette companies were telling a congressional hearing that tobacco is not a drug, cigarettes are not addictive, and smoking does not cause cancer. They offered "evidence" to support their denials, provided by scientists hired by these companies. The absurdities of public policies regarding tobacco is illustrated by the continuation of tax-funded tobacco farm subsidies, and until recently, the relatively weak controls on the three billion dollar advertising of cigarettes.

The encouraging news in all this is that the tobacco companies have recently been forced by the attorney generals of most states to admit that their products are addictive and the cause of serious health problems. Furthermore, some forty million people have stopped smoking since the mid-1950s, cutting the percentage of American smokers in half![16] There are smoking cessation programs in many hospitals and in most university and community health services. Some church agencies also sponsor stop smoking programs. Given the extreme tenacity of nicotine addictions, it is absolutely astounding that so many people have succeeded in interrupting their addiction on their own, cold turkey, or gradually. Some used nicotine patches that help some people taper off gradually. But most succeeded without the help of hypnotherapy, reconditioning, or the other therapeutic resources now available in stop smoking programs!

In case you know a smoker who wants to live longer, here is some very good news. Studies show that it is never too late to quit; smokers between sixty-five and seventy-four are more than two times as likely as their non-smoking counterparts to die from cardiovascular diseases or cancer, and eight to ten times more likely to die of lung cancer or other cancers directly related to smoking. But within a few years of quitting they lessen their risk of dying to equal that of nonsmokers.[17]

It is important to remember several things about the ethical complexities of the tobacco industry. The vast majority of those who make their living by growing, processing, or selling these products are good people who are between a rock and a hard place. If they let themselves become aware of the major health dangers associated with tobacco their livelihoods, and perhaps their way of life, will be in jeopardy. The same may be true of those who own shares in tobacco companies, and of the states who derive more income from tobacco taxes than the high public health costs of tobacco-related illnesses. Enlightened public policy decisions must provide ways of helping reduce the economic suffering of these people during the transition to a time when tobacco addictions will be much less tempting.

The Causes and Dynamics of Drug Addictions

Many of the insights about the causation and dynamics of addictions in chapter 2 are relevant here because the substance addictive processes have characteristics in common, regardless of what substances are used. Addiction to any drug results from the convergence of a variety of dynamic factors in the total psychological, physiological, spiritual, interpersonal, social, and natural contexts of victims' lives. A clinician who specializes in treating addictions describes their multiple etiology as follows: "Most likely, substance abuse and dependence results from a combination of factors, including biochemical, genetic, familial, environmental, and cultural ones, as well as personality dynamics."[18]

A major variable in all addictions that is a crucial consideration in understanding drug addictions is the relative strength of the addictive properties of the substances. If people use substances that are highly addictive biochemically—like morphine, cocaine, and nicotine—the probability of becoming hooked is great, even if the users are relatively healthy psychologically, spiritually, and interpersonally. An expert in addictions has identified other variables that are involved in the ways people respond to a particular occasion of using drugs: "The effects of any drug depends on the amount taken at one time, the past drug experience of the user, the circumstances in which the drug is taken (the place, the feelings and activities of the user, the presence of other people, the simultaneous use of alcohol or other drugs), and the manner in which the drug is taken.[19]

Physiological factors are particularly important in drug addictions. Intensive research by neuroscientists in the '90s has illuminated some of the deep mysteries in the human brain.[20] Of particular importance here is that most addictive drugs, including nicotine, cocaine, and heroin, trigger the same brain mechanism releasing a surge of chemicals that give the user a high. These chemicals include dopamine, a biochemical neurotransmitter that transmits a pleasurable chemical surge via the synapses connecting brain cells. This lasts for only a limited period, and, when it drops off, the user experiences a craving for more. The director of the National Institute on Drug Abuse, Alan Leshner, explains that "If we can make a chemical that will block the dopamine surge, the addict will lose interest in taking the drug." The hope is that relatively safe medications can be developed to block the craving, comparable to use of an addictive drug like methadone in treating heroin addicts. To this end, some twenty-six chemical compounds are being studied in chemical trials with laboratory animals.[21]

It is important to look more closely at the sociocultural factors that tend to foster drug dependency in many people. As we saw in the case of alcohol addiction, the more people's psychological and sociological "soil of addiction" makes them receptive to the reality-blunting ecstasy-giving effects of drugs, the more likely that they will become addicted if they use them. The psychosocial factors are essentially the same as those that foster widespread alcoholism. For many people in our society, including some in congregations, life is like one long surgical operation without benefit of anesthesia. Consequently, they have ample psychological reasons to crave the blessed oblivion that consciousness-changing, mood-altering drugs may bring for a time. Their drugs of choice can be understood as self-administered anesthetics.

Many of the social context factors that breed drug dependence were discussed earlier. Ours is a period of rapid, mind-boggling social change and unprecedented transitions in the world, with profound anxieties stemming from massive uprooting of millions of people from a sense of community. In this kind of society and world, the easy availability of a plethora of reality-softening drugs makes their use very attractive and their abuse by many people predictable. One of the reasons many people turned to religion rather than drugs in earlier times was because many of the plentiful, easily obtained, relatively inexpensive drugs of our day did not yet exist. This confronts religious people and groups with unprecedented challenges as well as opportunities. We are called to face the spiritual and ethical meanings of the drug dependence epidemic and to respond by developing spiritual and interpersonal ways to cope with pain and change, and by learning to enjoy nonchemical satisfactions and spiritual highs in our daily lives.

Treatment of Drug Dependency

Based on his long experience as the medical director of an addiction treatment program, Anderson Spickard declares:

> The similarities between alcohol and drug addictions are greater than the differences. The differences are primarily in physical effects, diagnostic tests, and medical management of withdrawal. The means of treatment, as well as the spiritual principles involved, are generally the same for all additive substances.[22]

The generic principles and methods of counseling with persons addicted to alcohol and other drugs are described in chapters 11 through 14. Suffice it here to emphasize that clergy and other nonmedical professionals should involve those addicted to highly addictive drugs with treatment programs where detoxification, and a full range of medical treatment resources are available.[23] One example of such resources is methadone, a synthetic narcotic developed during World War II as a painkiller. Because it successfully blocks the effects of heroin, prescribing methadone as a substitute can lead to a better prognosis for rehabilitation in some heroin addicts. It enables them to use individual and group counseling more productively, and educational and vocational training in treatment programs.[24] Maltrexone blocks the optoid rector in the brain, thus nullifying the effect of opium products such as heroin, morphine, and codeine (trade name Revio). Another treatment resource is acupuncture. It alleviates withdrawal symptoms and reduces the craving for heroin, cocaine, and alcohol during rehabilitation. Over 250 acupuncture programs in diverse treatment settings have been established worldwide. Herbert Benson and others have found that TM (transcendental meditation) and other forms of deeply relaxing and quieting meditation help some young drug abusers become motivated to stop.

Inpatient treatment in a drug-free, supportive environment improves the prognosis of most drug addicts. After their detoxification, most drug addicts need long-term rehabilitation and reorientation of their lives without their substances. As with alcoholics, therapy or counseling usually are not effective until some period of abstinence has been achieved. Because chronic substance abusers have learned to substitute chemicals for human contacts, a crucial foundation for treatment is the establishment of a nonthreatening relationship with a caring and consistent individual. As this occurs, group counseling and relearning activities often are the treatments of choice. Such groups provide peer support but also experience-based confrontations by peers with the consequences of both their attitudes and behavior.

As is true of alcoholics, Twelve Step groups are a crucial aspect of treatment for many drug addicts. Groups like Narcotics Anonymous, Pills Anonymous, and Cocaine Anonymous have proved helpful for many. In a comparable way, Nar-Anon and Co-Anon can provide valuable help for adult family members of narcotics and cocaine-dependent people. For adolescent family members, Narateen or Alateen groups can be helpful. Other Twelve Step resources for drug addicts and their families are Women for Sobriety, Rational Recovery, Double Trouble/Recovery Groups for the dual diagnosed, and Codependency Anonymous (Coda) groups. For more information about particular clinical approaches to drug addictions see Shulamith Lala Ashenberg Straussner's book, *Clinical Work with Substance-Abusing Clients.*

What Churches Can Do to Prevent Drug Addiction

As an important part of their ministry of healing and wholeness, religious organizations can make significant contributions to help reduce drug use and prevent drug addictions. They can do this by: (1) presenting rigorously factual, age-appropriate education for children, youth, and adults about the realistic risks of using tobacco and other drugs, and do this in the context of a positive wellness ethic; (2) sponsoring or cosponsoring stop-smoking programs as an integral part of their spiritually centered health programs; (3) making referrals to the competent drug treatment and prevention services in the community; (4) encouraging people to satisfy their needs by adopting spiritually-centered behavior, instead of the quick comfort of chemicals, tobacco, and other drugs; (5) making abstinence from using drugs, including nicotine, the ethical norm of a religious lifestyle; (6) exploring the moral contradictions and public policy dilemmas of government support for growing tobacco and the marketing of tobacco products for huge profits (Of all the teens that begin smoking, half will become nicotine addicted.); (7) including in a congregation's prophetic ministry support for legislation aimed at curbing smoking, particularly by children and youth, and controlling the seductive and misleading advertising by the tobacco industry in this country and in poor, developing countries; and (8) helping to influence government officials to transform the strategy and goals of the so-called war on drugs.

It is more than a decade since President Reagan declared the war on drugs and millions have been invested in waging it. Yet more drugs are crossing our international borders than when it began. In some ways this war is comparable to Prohibition's war on alcohol. One difference is that this one is even more difficult to win because profits derived from illegal drugs are much more enormous than from illegal beverage alcohol. Bill Moyers stated in a recent TV series on addictions that the war on drugs has become the Vietnam of our day. It costs billions and over half of this is used in futile attempts to keep drugs from being smuggled across the country's borders. As long as the predominant emphasis is on limiting the flow of drugs into our country and jailing anyone selling more than a certain amount of illegal drugs, the battle will continue to be lost. Instead, effective strategies must be implemented to shrink the enormous demand for illegal drugs in our country. The emphasis must be on increasing preventive education, rehabilitating the drug dependent, reducing social pressures on those who are particularly vulnerable to drug abuse, and developing values and spiritual strengths that will enable people to live satisfying, drug-free lives in our drug-saturated society. Religious organizations can and should play key roles in such a multifaceted preventive approach.

Conventional wisdom holds that drug education is the key to reducing abuse and addictions. Although education obviously is vitally important, it is clear that something deeper also is needed. A striking example of this is that addiction rates among physicians and nurses, who are among the best educated professional groups in this field, are as high as the general public. The indispensable missing ingredients are in the arena in which many religious leaders have expertise. These are spiritual aliveness and commitment to life-loving values. When people learn how to turn on to life—to celebrate with joy and thankfulness the good gifts of being alive and aware—the lure of turning on chemically becomes less seductive.

Understanding Food Addictions

Although food is not a drug, millions of people use it like a drug so that it becomes a destructive substance addiction. Both dieting and obesity are severe health problems. Fifty-eight million Americans are obese, defined as 20 percent over their ideal weight. Obesity is the second leading cause of preventable death in this country, with 300,000 people dying from obesity-related causes including heart attacks, hypertension, strokes, and diabetes. Only smoking kills more people. On any given day, sixty-five million Americans—50 percent of American women and 25 percent of men—are involved in often vain attempts to lose weight by dieting. More than 50 percent of fourth grade girls and almost 75 percent of high school girls are dieting. The weight loss mega-industry is paid more than thirty-five million each year, mainly by women.[25] Millions of women are trying to make their bodies conform to an utterly unrealistic body image.

Eating disorders are very widespread and destructive problems in our society. The various addictive uses of food all involve compulsive eating and/or dieting, intertwined with obsessing about food and self-rejecting obsessing about the weight and appearance of one's body. Among the most common eating disorders in affluent countries like America are compulsive overeating, chronic yo-yo dieting (repetitive losing weight and gaining it back), and being junk food junkies. Such troubled eaters compulsively gobble large quantities of unhealthy, fast foods loaded with fat, salt, toxic additives, sugar, and refined, nutritionally deficient carbohydrates. Furthermore, the drivenness of their eating robs them of the gastronomic pleasures that are available in eating with awareness. From a health perspective, excessive eating, especially of unhealthy foods, means that food addicts are literally "digging their graves with their forks and spoons."[26]

Two especially dangerous eating disorders are *anorexia nervosa* and *bulimia*. The first involves compulsive dieting and chronic feelings of being too fat even when one is emaciated. Bulimia involves alternating between food binges and compulsive dieting often accompanied by intentional vomiting and severe use of laxatives and diuretics to get rid of the unwanted food. Up to one-third of college women habitually do this. It is estimated that more than 150,000 sufferers from anorexia nervosa die from self-starvation each year.

Here is how Mary Louise Bringle, a professor of religious studies, describes her struggle with bulimia. She tells how she was ridden with self-loathing and guilt after the food binges, and would attempt to undo them by rigorous fasting for an equal period, by abusing laxatives and diuretics, and by running in sweltering summer heat for ten to twenty miles. She describes her awful aloneness in these words:

> I was involved in a painful cycle of compulsive eating and compulsive dieting. For a period of days or weeks I would ingest huge, frantic quantities of food (whole bags of cookies or half-gallons of ice cream at a single sitting)....I thought I was the only person in the world to engage in such bizarre behavior. I was too embarrassed and ashamed.[27]

What Causes Eating Disorders?

As is true of other addictions, these addictions usually result from the convergence in certain individuals of several causative factors. Examining family and cultural attitudes and practices, as these are selectively screened and transmitted subconsciously through parents to their children, can identify key etiologic factors. Food addictions stem from the many meanings of food that are learned in childhood. Both food and loving care are essential for survival. Deprivation of either is most damaging in early life. It is no wonder, therefore, that eating and feeding others can become substitutes for receiving and giving love, rather than expressions of that essential love.

Disorders of eating are rooted in the food and eating attitudes, practices, and symbolic rituals that victims learned in their childhood family systems. They seem to proliferate in relationships where the dynamics of security, power, esteem, and accepting love are confusingly intertwined with eating or not eating food. Where these essential emotional foods, especially accepting love, are missing or in short supply, physical food becomes an inadequate substitute for the missing emotional food. Eating disorders proliferate in such family systems, as victims seek to self-medicate emotional pain, low self-esteem, sexual guilt and shame, body hatred, spiritual emptiness, and lack of meaning in their lives. It is important to remember that the addictions are not to food per se, but to using food to try to meet nonfood hungers. An apt way of describing destructive eating is: "Gluttony is an emotional escape, a sign something is eating us."[28]

The cultural causes of eating disorders are also crucial. Members of both sexes struggle with compulsive eating and obesity. Beer bellies are plentiful even among young and middle-aged men. But the two most severe eating disorders—anorexia and bulimia—afflict adolescent girls and women disproportionately. Much of the pain that many females try to dull by cycling back and forth between binge eating and destructive dieting flows from socially-programmed rejection of their body-self identity. In a revealing survey sponsored by *Ms Magazine,* 65.4 percent of women who responded said, "I would like myself better if I were thinner"; 40.5 percent reported that they "often diet"; 69.6 percent said they overeat when bored, 55.5 percent when depressed, 51.2 percent when lonely, and 47.5 percent when anxious. All this is from the relatively liberated readers of *Ms.*

Compulsive-obsessive eating disorders are deeply rooted in our society's sexist attitudes about both female and male bodies. Cultural thinness stereotypes for females and macho, big muscle stereotypes for males engender chronic disgust with real-life body images. Cultural biases against women who are not thin (called *weightism* in a recently updated dictionary) is reinforced by ubiquitous television, film, advertising, and printed media images. This cultural propaganda helps prepare the receptive soil for eating disorders, especially anorexia and bulimia.[29] The sexist male problem of viewing women first as sex objects often is internalized by women themselves. Living in this context, self-hatred of their bodies proliferates, intertwined with sexual addictions and dysfunctions, and food disorders.[30]

Like other addictions, the root causes of eating disorders include unsatisfied spiritual hungers. An insightful member of the Sisters of Saint Joseph, a Roman Catholic order, writes candidly about her struggles with compulsive eating. In light of her experience, she affirms psychiatrist Gerald G. May's view that addictions of any type are "forms of idolatry ... characterized by increased tolerance, withdrawal symptoms, self-deception, loss of willpower and distortion of attention."[31] She then describes how recovery made her painfully aware of the way she had used food in an attempt to fill an inner void: "As I experienced the letting go of surplus food and the energy usurped by the addictive god, I was uncomfortable with the hole it left."[32] This emptiness can be filled most constructively by an enlivening relationship with the divine Spirit who gives transcending meaning to the everydayness of living.

How Can Those Suffering from Eating Disorders Best Be Helped?

The place to begin is to communicate accurate information about food-related problems, including the hopeful knowledge that they are treatable illnesses. This should be one part of a congregation's overall wellness education program when healthy nutrition is discussed or when addictive disorders are presented with empathy and understanding. Countless individuals and families need to know that many others suffer as they do, that recovery is possible, and what resources are available.

The most widely available, effective, and cost-free programs are the Twelve Step groups called Overeaters Anonymous. OA was founded in 1960 by Rozanne S. in Los Angeles. It now has chapters throughout North America and in over forty other countries. Unlike the many commercial weight loss programs, it does not recommend diets or exercise plans. Instead it adapts A.A.'s Twelve Steps and Twelve Traditions to enable recovering overeaters to interrupt their addictions by accepting their powerlessness over compulsive eating, open themselves to the help of a Higher Power and the group rewarded support, clear up the ethical debris in their lives by a rigorous moral inventory, experience a spiritual awakening, and carry the message of hope to other food addicts.

If OA's help is not enough for food addicts to find the recovery road, referrals should be made to treatment programs with professionals trained to deal with various addictions including compulsive eating or self-starving. Sufferers from anorexia nervosa and bulimia should be referred to a professional treatment program specializing in such problems. Most inpatient treatment programs include individual psychotherapy, medical nutritional guidance, educational and therapeutic groups, as well as conjoint family sessions to deal with the addicted family's dynamics.

Mary Louise Bringle, drawing on learnings during her recovery of over fifteen years, offers a series of wise pastoral strategies designed to help persons with eating disorders. They include recognizing that food problems afflict countless people, especially women, and are both serious and treatable; in caregiving, don't hesitate to ask people about their relationship with food; understand that the way people feed or misfeed themselves affects their spirituality profoundly; reject the "beauty myth" and learn to see beauty in all the diverse shapes of people's bodies; increase nonperfectionist acceptance as well as forgiveness in attitudes toward our bodies; enjoy receiving pleasure and nurture from others, which is what is yearned for when food is abused; avoid attempting to fill with food the emptiness of physical or emotional hunger, or loneliness or fear; learn to trust life's rhythms with their ups and downs, their satisfactions and pain, without trying to use food to medicate the problems away.[33]

I would add another strategy to this excellent list: Get in touch with the incredible miracle of transformation involved in eating food. Become aware of the way that food—the good gift of God's good earth—is transformed by our body-mind-spirit selves into love and laughter, work and play, prayer and worship, sex and sensual pleasure, creativity, and adventure, and all the other activities made possible by food's captured sunlight and health-nurturing nutrition. Learn to eat with gratitude and awareness of this continuing miracle. Remember all this and be thankful![34]

Food, Tobacco, and Alcohol Addictions in Global Perspective

The complex spiritual and ethical issues involved in addictions will be explored in chapters 9 and 10. Suffice it here to point to the perplexing ethical issues that are raised when one thinks of the wider social context of food abuse and other addictions. People of religious dedication are citizens of God's whole planet. So let's take a brief look at food, alcohol, and tobacco problems in other countries.

Remember our society's terrible waste of food along with other natural resources, its billion dollar obsession with dieting, Proctor and Gambles's investment of $250 million to develop a nonfat fat substitute so that we can have our cake and eat it too. Consider these facts while also remembering that 850 million people go to bed hungry every night in developing countries and in the large pockets of poverty in our rich country. Remember the forty thousand children who will die today, somewhere in the world, because of malnutrition and diseases related to it.

Here are some global perspectives on tobacco problems. The World Watch Institute, in the 1997 edition of its definitive *State of the World,* reports that tobacco-caused illnesses are expected to overtake all infectious diseases as the number one health threat on a global basis. Poor developing countries promise to be particularly hard hit for two reasons—increasing numbers of people are smoking, growing, and manufacturing tobacco products and producing an increasing percentage of their revenues by both taxes and sales. Almost 1,000 people will eventually die for every 1,000 tons of tobacco produced. While Western investors and foreign investors encourage them to increase their markets, these governments find their sustainable economic development threatened because they cannot find afford to pay for the health costs that result.

The United Nations World Health Organization reports that a total of 1.1 billion people smoke worldwide, which is almost one out of every five inhabitants of the earth. The annual estimated costs of tobacco-caused illnesses in healthcare and lost productivity is put at $200 billion. These costs are expected to soar as tobacco use increases worldwide, particularly among adolescents and young adults. About one-third of all smokers will die prematurely from these illnesses. Each of them will lose around twenty-two years of their normal life expectancy in their countries. An estimated 300 million smokers live in industrial nations, while 800 million are in developing countries. An epidemiologist at a cancer research center at Oxford University has estimated that by 2025, annual deaths from tobacco will reach 10 million, making this the leading cause of death around the world.[35]

As cigarette sales have declined in the United States, the transnational tobacco megacorporations have increasingly targeted developing countries. These ads are particularly effective in these countries where cigarette sales are reported to have skyrocketed. Viewed on a global scale the liquor companies spend about $2 billion dollars each year on advertising, much of it targeted at vulnerable new drinkers among youth, women, and those in developing countries.

Alcohol produces a huge number of deaths worldwide. In 1993 (the latest year for which such data are available), alcohol abuse resulted in the death of an estimated 1.2 million people. Four-fifths of these deaths followed years of drinking producing severe health crises especially liver damage. But many of those who died were nondrinkers killed by alcohol-related homicide and other violent crimes and accidents as well as domestic violence. In what seems like a gross understatement, the *State of the World* report concluded, "Worldwide, alcohol consumption represents a global health and safety issue."[36]

It should be noted that global alcohol consumption is often underestimated by as much as one-third. This is because home brewing is very prevalent in developing countries and the brew made is often more potent and also more dangerous than alcohol available commercially. For example, women in some African villages turn to home brewing to get some income for their families. They often sell the alcohol to their husbands to keep them from spending money on it outside their homes. This brings some income to buy family necessities, but it also encourages men to continue drinking heavily.[37]

Unfortunately, some governments—for example, those in China, the Czech Republic, and Mexico—hold that alcohol production is economically beneficial. They promote production and consumption actively. Countries that rely on alcohol for economic development are like alcoholics who refuse to believe they have a problem with drinking. They are in denial about the risks and costs of dependency on this product for the economic health of their countries. Worldwide, according to the WHO and the Harvard School of Public Health, alcohol causes nearly three times the disabilities and illnesses that tobacco does. Beyond all this looms the ethical problem of the use for making alcohol of millions of tons of grain that could feed countless hungry children and adults.

Think of the costs of illegal drugs in the United States (with a greater drug appetite than any other country on earth) in terms of what the money involved could do to ameliorate social problems or enhance the well-being of needy people at home or abroad. A study released in 1997 by the Office of National Drug Control Policy revealed that U.S. citizens spent $57.3 billion on illegal drugs in 1995, even though drug use had dropped in the previous decade ($38 billion of this was spent on cocaine, $9.6 billion on heroin, $7 billion on marijuana, and $2.7 billion on other illegal drugs). This money would pay for a college education for a million youth or for a year's child care for fourteen million youngsters in the United States. Or it probably would more than cover the cost of immunization for all the countless children around the world who die because they have not had this life-saving protection.[38] Certainly religious leaders and others who care about people are challenged to help heal these social evils producing enormous pain.

CHAPTER 4

Behavioral or Process Addictions: Understanding and Helping

Addiction taps into the most fundamental human processes. Whether the need to be high, to be sexual, to eat, or even to work—the addictive process can turn creative, life-giving energy into a destructive, demoralizing compulsivity. The central loss is the addict's values and relationships.
—Patrick Carnes, *The Sexual Addiction*

This chapter will explore behavioral or process addictions, also called *activity addictions*. It will describe their nature, dynamics, and some treatment options. These problems, which are associated with daily living, could be described more precisely as destructive patterns of obsessive thinking coupled with compulsive behavior. Most people who are addicted to substances also suffer from one or more of these nonchemical addictions. Conversely, those afflicted with behavioral addictions often suffer from one or more substance addictions. Obsessive-compulsive behavior patterns usually involve common human activities that nonaddicted people can take or leave, or choose to do in moderation. Victims of obsessive-compulsive behavior are caught in increasingly all-consuming fixations on certain activities that gradually take more and more of their attention and energy as these fixations control larger and larger areas of their lives. Their mental health, intimate relationships, and fiscal viability are diminished as their addictions gain increasing power over their lives.

In our addiction-spawning society, almost any human activity that people may find satisfying, exciting, numbing or distracting from the anxieties of everyday life can become the focus of obsessive thinking and compulsive action. Obsessive-compulsive patterns proliferate in the lives of millions of people causing them to lose voluntary control in certain areas. The most widespread and destructive activity addictions include those centering on the misuse of work, sex, gambling, shopping, codependent relationships, sports, religion, money, and power. But evidence of addictions to a wide variety of other activities have appeared in the popular media—for example, addictions to traveling, collecting certain items, chain letters, and being a pack rat. An unlikely and humorous food addiction was reported by the *British Journal of Medicine*. Three patients ate so many carrots that their skin turned yellow. They had withdrawal symptoms when they interrupted their carrot addiction on their doctors' orders.[1]

It is noteworthy that irrational hoarding (one of my addictions) has acquired a DSM psychiatric diagnostic label that defined it as "The inability to discard worn out or worthless objects even when they have no sentimental value." A "world-class pack rat" reported to a mental health counselor: "I don't understand why, but when I have to throw something away, even dead flowers, I feel my old abandonment fears and I also feel very lonely." Psychoanalyst Erich Fromm described the "hoarding orientation" as one of four basic unproductive ways that people cope with their anxieties in Western societies. Most pack rats rationalize their addiction by suggesting they may need an article at a later date. Having to get rid of things upsets them emotionally and may produce psychophysiological symptoms of distress. But the chaos and clutter created by accumulating piles and boxes often causes painful conflicts in pack rats' relationships.[2]

A dramatic example of a person addicted to traveling is a twenty-six-year-old man named Chris English. He is reported to have flown some 750,000 miles in the last decade. If he doesn't fly at least three times a week, distressing withdrawal symptoms hit him. "I get the shakes. I suffer cold sweats," he says. He doesn't care about where he flies and often does not leave an airport to look at a city to which he has flown. He has worked out a complicated system to get the most mileage for the least amount of money, fitting his trips into a flexible work schedule. His parents and friends, who at first worried about his compulsion, apparently have accepted it.[3]

To prevent people from becoming addicted to chain letters, science writer Eugene Emery has created what he hopes will be "a black hole of chain letters." His goal is to stamp out the danger of falling into this trap baited by those who exploit people's greed and superstitious fears of breaking the chain. He invites recipients to send such letters to "Chain Letters Anonymous,"[4] and even offers to take on the fears of negative consequences that keep people hooked.

Dynamics of Behavioral Addictions

The forces driving these addictions become so powerful that victims often do not (and probably cannot) interrupt them in spite of their becoming increasingly destructive to their overall values and well-being. The dynamics and causes of different behavioral addictions, like those of substance addictions, are complex and only partially understood. Addictions to different activities seem to involve somewhat unique dynamics. However, it is possible to generalize about certain common characteristics involved in these addictions paralleling those of substance addictions.

The lives of many activity addicts become increasingly unmanageable. Most are in denial, refusing to believe that their compulsive activity is really a problem. They rationalize in elaborate ways to prove to themselves that their behavior is rational and necessary. They become increasingly self-absorbed, crisis-prone, and spiritually impoverished as other values are ignored in their lives. Behavioral addictions are reinforced by distorted values and addictive patterns in our society that many children absorb in their early lives as they internalize these from their parents, teachers, religious leaders, and the media, especially television.

From the perspective of depth psychology, addictive activities are repeated almost endlessly in vain attempts to satisfy deep inner conflicts and emotional hungers of which victims are dimly aware or utterly unaware. In general, addictive behaviors seem to be efforts to deal with threatening feelings of angst, both neurotic and existential. In seeking to understand the "repetition compulsions" that he observed in some of his neurotic patients' behavior, Freud proposed a theory that such patterns are driven from an unconscious level as a way of defending oneself against the emerging into consciousness of unacceptable impulses and repressed memories. If their repetitive activities are interrupted, addicted people report experiencing waves of feeling ranging from relatively mild discomfort to overwhelming anxiety. Consequently, they may go to great lengths to avoid having to interrupt the behaviors.

Sports Addictions

Many health benefits can be derived from participating nonfanatically in sports. Countless people of all ages love their games and play for joy, renewal, friendly competition, and strengthening of their body-mind-spirit selves. But many sports spectators and some hard-driving, highly competitive participants, live out the concept from which "fan" is abbreviated— fanatic. They are addicted to their favorite team, sport, or players, as shown by their compulsive irrationality during sporting events. Enjoying occasional performances of their favorite team (on television or live) is a healthy minivacation from everyday life for millions of people. For a brief time they can forget their anxieties, problems, frustrations, failures, and the pressures of life. Some devoted sports watchers apparently enjoy sports highs. These are pseudospiritual experiences of a type that psychologist Abraham Maslow called "peak experiences." But to those who suffer from sports addictions, compulsive watching of sports is their drug of choice that may squeeze out other interests and values in their lives. It is their means of denying reality rather than having an occasional minivacation from it. They experience increasing cravings as in other addictive processes. The longed for sports highs become a dominant longing for them.

Sports fanaticism generates what resembles passionate religious devotion. Superfans could be described as sports worshipers. Altercations resembling religious wars that include fist fights and even riots have occurred among fans and players when those on one side feel that their team was robbed by umpires' or referees' calls. Consider this dramatic example of the prevalence and power of sports addictions as well as the skewed values of many people in our country: In 1997, nearly twice as many people watched football's annual TV extravaganza on Superbowl Sunday as had voted in the national election for president and congress two months before.

Violent sports seem to be particularly addictive, especially to many men. Vince Lombardi, the renowned Green Bay Packers football coach, once observed, "Football isn't a contact sport. It's a collision sport." Superbowl frenzy is a dramatic example of the grip that violent sports has on millions of people in our society. Sports violence has a seductive attraction reflected in the violent football yells that high school and college students learn and yell at the top of their lungs. The powerful lure of violence is also reflected in the frenzy aroused by the highly-rewarded, intentional brutality of a very primitive sport—professional boxing. Fans often seem to become ecstatic when their superhero batters and bloodies the opponent and then knocks him unconscious on the mat. This is a contemporary expression of the spectacles in ancient Rome where gladiators killed one another and lions ate Christians as the spectators cheered in glee. The lawyer for Mike Tyson stated, after Tyson bit off part of an opponent's ear during a fight, "I don't believe that when you put two people in a ring, tell them to commit battery against each other and pay them $65 million to do that, that you can have a situation where a crime is charged against him."

A protracted debate among psychologists continues about whether sports violence, viewed live and by millions on television, has a positive or a negative influence on levels of violence in our society. Defenders of sports violence hold that spectators' vicarious identification with this violence drains off their potentially destructive aggressive impulses harmlessly. Those who oppose socially rewarded sports violence hold that the vicarious identification gives tacit permission to spectators to act out their own aggressive impulses. Among the evidence cited to support this position is that phone calls to domestic violence hotlines soar on Superbowl Sunday. (A parallel debate among psychologists focuses on how the level of youth violence is influenced by television programs that are loaded with violence.) My view on this crucial issue sides with those who regard sports and television violence as significant causes of increased violence in a society already oversaturated with it.

Many women are joining men as avid sports fans, particularly as more and more skilled women compete on television. But sports violence certainly reinforces the macho misunderstanding of male strength that is widespread and destructive in our culture. This distorted view of male strength has a negative effect on women who are struggling to claim their own power against male sexism and are fighting for equal respect and opportunities to use their God-given intelligence, creativity, and leadership gifts. If you have doubts about the macho-supporting message of violent sports worshiping, talk to any man who has enough courage to admit to other men that he is not a sports fan. Anorexia means having no appetite. As a longtime sports anorexiac,[5] I have experienced the cool responses of some men who seem to be questioning one's maleness if one does not "talk the talk" of a knowledgeable and enthusiastic sports fan.

SpoilSports is a national club and support group for nonfans. The thirty-year-old male cofounder says, "Tell another guy you're not a sports fan, and he looks at you like you're wearing a party dress from Wal Mart!" Started in 1994, SpoilSports publishes a newsletter that has included helpful articles on "Deprogramming Techniques for Sports Fanatics," "Superbowl Sabotage Tricks," and "How to Appear Sports Literate (When You Really Don't Want to Be) in Order to Blend in and Gain Trust from Unsuspecting Sports Junkies." A newsletter feature aims at preventing two-feet-in-mouth comments like, "Why sure I like the Bears, boss. They're a hockey team, right?"[6]

As a marriage and family counselor, I have witnessed the destructive effect on family wellness when one spouse (usually the husband) becomes fanatically involved, almost every evening and weekend, in viewing of television sports events in which the other spouse's interest is minimal or nonexistent. A cartoon shows a husband saying to his wife, during an ad break on television, "Anything you want to say before the end of the football season." A sports humorist reported during a prolonged strike of professional baseball teams, "Some wives really worry about the strike—they're afraid it will be settled." Another humorist commented, "Professional baseball is very valuable. Without it, kids wouldn't know what millionaires look like."

Work Addiction[7]

Art Buchwald, the humorous columnist, once wrote a tongue-in-cheek piece entitled: "If There Is a Cure for Work Addiction, It Doesn't Work." He quoted psychiatrist Nelson Bradley who stated:

> A work addict shows all the characteristics of an alcoholic or narcotic addict. He has a driven craving for work, develops an increasing tolerance for it, and suffers withdrawal symptoms without it. Like other addictions, this often results in medical and social problems, including bad family relationships with depressed wives and children.[8]

After commenting that this view is bunk, Buchwald describes a hilarious weekend vacation during which, at his wife's insistence, he tried to break his addiction to working at writing.

Diane Fassel, a management consultant and author of *Working Ourselves to Death: The High Cost of Workaholism and the Rewards of Recovery*, cites convincing evidence that extreme

> ... workaholism is a killer stalking our society.... The effect of workaholism is a growing compulsiveness about work. The obsession grows completely out of bounds and, in the process, workaholics ... are alienated from their own bodies, from their own feelings, from their creativity, and from family and friends. They have been taken over by the compulsion to work and are slaves to it. They no longer own their lives. They are truly the walking dead.[9]

Fassel observes that not all work addicts are employed. They can be unemployed, underemployed, or retired. The same life-damaging behavior patterns characterize the rushaholics, careaholics, and busyaholics—any person who is driven to do too much running around like a headless chicken. She distinguishes four types of workaholics, all of them out of control: compulsive workers, binge workers, closet workers (who try to hide their excessive working), and work anorexics who are addicted to avoiding work.[10]

A crucial fact to which Fassel points is that work addiction is difficult to identify and treat in our society because it is the cleanest, most respected, and rewarded addiction. Even though it is a deadly disease, our competitive society rewards it with praise and promotions, making it what she calls "the pain others applaud," and "a lifeboat guaranteed to sink." The social attitudes transmitted by the institutions of our society (including schools, churches, and businesses), tend to encourage work addictions. They make it difficult for victims, even for those who literally are "killing themselves by their work," to hit bottom, recognize their work patterns as problematic, and accept their need for help.

How Can Work Addiction Be Identified?

The proportion of affirmative answers to several of the following diagnostic questions suggest one's degree of work addiction:

1. Do you frequently work on weekends and on family or public holidays?

2. Does the pressure of your work prevent you from taking regular days off or vacations?

3. Did one or both of your parents set an example for you of overworking with high stress, drivenness, and absence of joy in work?

4. Does your involvement in your work cause problems for your spouse or children?

5. Do you on occasion hide from others the fact that you are working?

6. Does your work contribute to health problems rather than make you feel more alive and well?

7. Do you frequently pass up enjoyable activities with others (like parties or sex) because you "need to work"?

8. Do you often take work with you when you go on pleasure trips?

9. Do you keep a cellular phone (or two) within easy reach when you take a bath, or make love, or "relax as hard as you can"?

10. Do you feel insecure or a little depressed when you don't have work to do?

11. Do you make sure you have one or more other work projects waiting to do when you finish a project?

12. Do you feel guilty after you take time off or a vacation and perhaps atone by overworking?

13. Do you keep "to do" lists that have lots more on them than you can accomplish in the available time?

14. Do you often try to do two or more things at the same time when working?

15. Do you hover on the brink of burnout or experience early-stage burnout at times?

16. Is your work life running you, rather than vice versa?
17. Are you usually running trying to catch up?[11]

In my experience, it is important to distinguish hard working, happy, productive people from compulsive work addicts for whom work is a fix like smoking is for a nicotine addict. The former usually love many things in addition to their work as life-enhancing parts of their total existence. They balance their work with play, rest, and relating to people. They enjoy their work and often work in playful ways that lessen their stress and increase their creativity. The wall between their work and play is low or nonexistent. They have a sense of purpose and mission in their work. They don't get depressed or anxious when they are not working, or guilty when they take time off to rest, play, or enjoy relationships. Although they often work very hard, they usually do not suffer burnout.

In contrast, severe workaholics tend to be relatively inefficient and therefore unproductive because they are working frantically but without zest or creativity. They do this because they are trying to satisfy inner hungers that cannot be satisfied constructively by working. They are type A persons who are driven by the myth that they can find real self-esteem by achievements. Their identity is formed around doing rather than being. Workaholics tend to play stressfully, pushing themselves to work at playing. They are attracted to highly competitive play seeking to win whatever the cost. Vacations and minivacations on weekends leave them exhausted, not refreshed. Their implicit feeling when weekends are over is TGIM (Thank God It's Monday). The problem with the distinction between compulsive work addicts and healthy hard workers is that many people, including the author, have both compulsive and creative work patterns intertwined in their work lives.

A productive way to understand the dynamics of this addiction is to use the parent-adult-child schema of personality created by Transactional Analysis. The playful "natural child" sides of workaholics' personalities is controlled in heavy-handed ways by the "punitive parent" within them. This robs them of playfulness, spontaneity, and creativity, transforming the natural child into what is called the "adapted child" in TA theory. The inner parent voice demands perfectionistically that they keep working in the hope that they eventually will feel accepted by their inner parent. Of course, like all perfectionism, work addiction is a double bind. Even if they succeed in doing more and more, and reaching important goals, the longed-for feelings of self-other acceptance automatically stays beyond their reach, because their successes are never enough.

In theological terms, work addictions indicate that a demanding Calvinist work ethic is at the center of one's identity and life. Work addicts are in the cul de sac of seeking to achieve a sense of acceptance and well-being by their work achievements. Grace is absent from workaholics' attitudes toward themselves, their work, and their worth. As the apostle Paul discovered on the road to Damascus, only a lively experience of God's grace can enable persons "to accept themselves as being accepted" (to use Paul Tillich's term). A transforming experience of grace is what many people find in Twelve Step recovery programs—including Workaholics Anonymous and Overachievers Anonymous.

Summary of Some Recovery Strategies for Workaholics

For those with severe work addictions:

- Planning and implementing interventions for those in denial, by family, friends, clergy, and health professionals, in which those with severe work addictions are confronted with the negative health and family consequences of their working pattern, by those who care about them, may help them face reality and become open to help.
- Getting involved in a Twelve Step recovery group focused on work addictions, like those just mentioned, may hasten victims' self-identification and use of these spiritually energized recovery programs.
- Investing in counseling or psychotherapy with a pastoral counselor or other competent therapist often helps heal the inner wounds that motivate self-damaging work patterns.

For people with less severe work addictions:

- Learning to listen to, love, and care for their body-mind-spirit selves may help interrupt the addictive process.
- Learning to laugh at the absurd expectations they put on themselves by their exaggerated schedules and "to do" lists.
- Intentionally taking three or four healthy minivacations each day— brief (ten to fifteen minutes), renewing change of pace activities like briskly walking around the block, meditating or praying, breathing and stretching, listening to favorite music, chatting with a friend, telling and laughing at a joke, relating to a favorite tree or house plant, petting a dog, and so forth.
- Encouraging the inner child to laugh and play several times a day including brief play breaks during work.
- Knowing if their work schedule is overgrown, they should mow it, (Wayne Oates' apt recommendation).

- Revising priorities to stop majoring in minors and giving more time to the people and goals that are most important to them.
- Asking for God's help in slowing down, and then doing the things that are the most likely to enable this prayer to be answered.

Shopping Addiction

Consumerism is one of the fastest growing and most destructive addictions in our society. Being "thingaholics" is damaging to both the addicts and to a healthy natural environment. Many factors in our society make this a seductive and potentially destructive solution to painful feelings of inner emptiness, lack of purpose, and anxiety from personal and/or societal problems. A variety of social pressures contribute to this addiction. These include television and the multimillion dollar advertising business aimed at motivating (or manipulating) people to buy, buy, buy; megashopping malls; self-centered narcissism empowered by affluence; a lack of spiritual meaning and higher purposes in living than buying and wasting consumer goods; and the "technoaddiction" we have to technology and its products.[12] Huge shopping malls have become the cathedrals of our society for millions of worshiping shopaholics. Thousands of teens spend much of their free time in malls. But older people are also addicted. Ann Landers tells of a ninety-year-old Wisconsin woman who died peacefully while shopping at a local mall. Her relatives suggested that she be buried in her "Shop 'Til You Drop!" sweatshirt. Bumper stickers like the following point to our society's love affair with shopping, consuming, and wasting—"This car stops at all garage sales"; "When the going gets tough, the tough go shopping."

Our consumerism in an affluent, throw-away society is threatening to exhaust our planet's limited resources. Al Gore shed brilliant light on humankind's addiction to things in *Earth in the Balance: Ecology and the Human Spirit*. He holds with valid psychological insight that such addictions distract people from "having to experience directly whatever they are trying to avoid. Anyone who is unusually fearful of something—intimacy, failure, loneliness—is potentially vulnerable to addiction, because psychic pain causes a feverish hunger for distraction."

Gore continues:

Our civilization is holding ever more tightly to its habit of consuming larger and larger quantities every year of coal, oil, fresh air and water, trees, topsoil, and the thousands of substances we rip from the crust of the earth, transforming them into not just the sustenance and shelter we need but much more that we don't need: huge quantities of pollution, products for which we spend billions on advertising to convince ourselves we want, massive surpluses of products that depress prices while the products themselves go to waste, and diversions and distractions of every kind. We seem increasingly eager to lose ourselves in the . . . . rituals of production and consumption, but the price we pay is the loss of our spiritual lives. . . .

Evidence of this spiritual loss abounds. . . . The three leading causes of death among adolescents are drug- and alcohol-related accidents, suicide, and homicide. Shopping is now recognized as a recreational activity. The accumulation of material goods is at an all time high, but so is the number of people who feel an emptiness in their lives.[13]

Plumbing deeper into this devastating addiction, ecopsychologists Allen D. Kanner and Mary E. Gomes observe that the consumption habits of our culture have

. . . a vast fantasy life that now rivals dreams as paths to insights about the irrational depths of everyday life—the mesmerizing power of the media and advertising industry stimulates these fantasies to grow into a vast collection of projected desires, fears, and aspirations.[14]

They see this as a part of the narcissistic wounding of the American psyche by the advertising industry and predict that "the American addiction to unbridled consumption only promises to get worse." Seeking to cure depression and find happiness via shopping and consumerism is to walk on a Catch-22 path. Like all idolatries, consumerism ends up betraying the worshipers who become more depressed and unhappy when their materialistic god fails them and is revealed as a destructive demon.

There is growing evidence that our addiction to things is a major contributor to the most serious health threat of all times. What is at stake is whether the earth we leave to all the children of the human family (and the children of all other species) will be a toxic wasteland or a healthful place where they can live healthy lives. My book, *Ecotherapy: Healing Ourselves, Healing the Earth* spells out in detail what earth-caring, earth-literate people can do to help save our threatened planet—God's wonderful creation—and with it, save ourselves and give a priceless gift to all future generations.[15]

Frederick G. Levine has elaborated on the conviction that "we're all addicted to overconsuming and polluting our environment and ourselves to the edge of oblivion." He holds that "Western culture is as addicted to eating up the planet as the most desperate junkie is to his needle."[16] To enable our culture to recover from what he calls "suicide on the installment plan," Albert LaChance has developed a Twelve Step recovery program for our culture's collective addiction to comfort, materialism, consumerism, overeating, and ease-of-travel. His book, *Greenspirit: The Twelve Steps of Ecological Spirituality* [17] describes an innovative program that seeks to reawaken people to themselves, to humanity, to all species, to the planet, and to the universe, and to enable them to practice ecological spirituality in all aspects of their lives.

Addictive Gambling

Gambling fever has swept across America in recent years with the proliferation of legal gambling and a dramatic increase in public acceptance of gambling. It is estimated that between $300 and $400 billion is bet each year. State lotteries, casinos, paramutual and riverboat gambling, gambling offered by over three hundred Native American tribes, bingo games by charitable and religious organizations, and betting on sports events has made gambling a major industry in this country. Lured by the promise of more jobs, increased receipts from gambling's "painless taxation," and tourism, a vast majority of states have lotteries. In the mid-1990s, $2.5 billion was wagered illegally on a NCAA men's basketball tournament and $3.5 billion on a football Superbowl. Over 60 percent of Americans say that they have gambled, and it is likely that gambling will become even more easily available on the media superhighway.

Millions of people seem to be able to gamble recreationally without becoming addicted. But, as in the case of alcohol and other drugs, predicting who cannot do so usually is not possible until after their addiction has progressed to a destructive level. The compulsive grip of gambling on some people's lives is illustrated by a couple who were arrested in Connecticut for leaving their nine-year-old son asleep in a car while they spent the night gambling at a casino. When the boy was found by authorities the temperature in the car was 22 degrees Farenheit.[18]

Teenage gambling has become an epidemic. In a Texas study, 79 percent of adolescents said they had gambled, with 66 percent having done so in the last year. Of those who gambled weekly, 78 percent said that they had also used alcohol and 34 percent illicit drugs. Adolescent gamblers are twice as likely as adults to get hooked. The best estimates put the total amount gambled annually by teens between $500,000 and $1 million, and the number already addicted something over one million. To support their addiction, some teens, resort to selling drugs, theft, and even prostitution. The suicide rate among adolescent problem gamblers is two times that of others in their age group. Unlike drugs and alcohol, most teens are not informed about the potential dangers of gambling. It is clear that innovative programs of preventive education for teens are urgently needed.

At the other end of the age continuum, gambling by the elderly is growing rapidly as the population ages. Studies in Rhode Island and Florida, states with large elderly populations, revealed that many are on fixed and limited incomes. Gambling money often comes from pensions or social security. If seniors become compulsive gamblers and gamble away their retirement savings, they have no way to recover financially. Gambling to escape loneliness, the loss of a spouse, or frustrating illnesses is common. Lotteries have been the most popular form of senior gambling but there is evidence that casinos are attracting an increasing older population.

Capitalist countries have the world's largest legal gambling operations at the center of their economies. These nations' stock markets, real estate, commodities futures, and transnational currency transactions make Las Vegas look like a small time gambling operation. Billions are won and lost by individuals and investment corporations as these legal megagamblers try to outguess one another concerning the fluctuations of all these markets. This, the U.S.'s largest gambling casino, was spotlighted by the media frenzy when it was learned that first lady Hillary Clinton had turned an investment of a few thousand dollars in cattle futures into a huge profit while her husband was a governor. The international stock market gambling network was revealed recently when the sharp fall of one (Hong Kong) triggered wild roller coaster falls and rises in all the other stock markets.

With gambling soaring among all age groups, the number of those who become hooked has also risen sharply. Many of the addicted are the poor who are least able to afford the huge losses that often result from this compulsion. Among middle-class males, much white-collar crime is committed by pathological gamblers trying to repay huge debts. On the theme of multiple addictions, it is noteworthy that thousands of calls to Gamblers Anonymous hotlines are made by desperate family members around sports extravaganzas such as Superbowl Sunday and fiercely competitive college and professional sports playoffs. Sports addiction and pathological gambling often become intertwined in mutually reinforcing ways. Various studies have shown that more than a third of those receiving inpatient treatment for pathological gambling are also addicted to alcohol or drugs.

The full social costs of this rising wave of compulsive gambling are not yet known, but it is clear that costs are soaring. Many gambling addicts squander their life savings and the equity in their homes, often in a day or two of gambling, when they think they are on a roll. Some use money that was not theirs, borrowing large sums expecting to repay it with winnings that do not materialize. Suicides by those who cannot pay gambling debts are rising. Organized crime syndicates still succeed in muscling in on some gambling operations, especially illegal ones, although the legal gambling industry has worked hard to prevent these infiltrations by organized gambling cartels that often also push street drugs.[19]

Many compulsive gamblers describe a mind-body tension that builds up in them prior to gambling, followed by a high level of pleasure associated with the relief of tension and the exciting high of gambling. I remember a young adult client who was a compulsive gambler. He reported that the high he got during gambling in Las Vegas was much like a sexual orgasm. It is not surprising that many addicted gamblers lose interest in the pleasures of sex and eating when the tension-laden impulse to gamble builds up in them.

How Can Pathological Gamblers Be Distinguished from Nonaddicted, Recreational Gamblers?

The American Psychiatric diagnosis of pathological gambling specifies that at least four of the following nine indicators apply to a person: (1) frequent preoccupation with gambling or with obtaining money to gamble; (2) frequent gambling of larger amounts of money or over a longer period of time than intended; (3) a need to increase the size or frequency of bets to achieve the desired excitement; (4) restlessness or irritability if unable to gamble; (5) repeated loss of money by gambling and returning another day to win back losses (chasing); (6) repeated efforts to reduce or stop gambling; (7) frequent gambling when expected to meet social or occupational obligations; (8) sacrifice of some important social, occupational, or recreational activity in order to gamble; and (9) continuation of gambling despite inability to pay mounting debts, or despite significant social, occupational, or legal problems that the person knows to be exacerbated by gambling.

Gamblers Anonymous's twenty questions for identifying addictive gambling include these queries for self-diagnosis: Has gambling ever made your home life unhappy? Did gambling affect your reputation? Have you ever felt remorse after gambling? Did gambling cause a decrease in your ambition or efficiency? After a win did you have a strong urge to return and win more? Did you often gamble until your last dollar was gone? Did you ever borrow to finance gambling? Have you ever sold anything to finance gambling? Have you ever committed or considered committing an illegal act to finance gambling? Did gambling make you careless of the welfare of yourself and your family? Have you ever gambled to escape worry and trouble? Do arguments, disappointments, or frustrations create within you an urge to gamble? Did you ever have an urge to celebrate any good fortune by a few hours of gambling? Have you ever considered self-destruction as a result of your gambling?

How Can Gambling Addictions Be Treated?

The motto of the National Council on Problem Gambling reads, "Compulsive gambling is a treatable disorder." Many victims have interrupted their gambling addiction, but recovery in our gambling-saturated society usually is an uphill battle involving several slips backward. This is particularly true of people who are polyaddicted. Most specialists in the field, like most alcoholism specialists, follow the disease model including the belief that the only feasible goal of therapy is total abstinence from all gambling. They believe that a recovering pathological gambler never recover fully or are cured. Only a very small minority of therapists believe that controlled gambling is possible for pathological gamblers.

Treatment of gambling addictions parallels that of alcoholism and drug addictions in many respects, except, of course, for the necessity of treating the physiological effects of prolonged substance abuse. Hitting bottom is an essential prerequisite for treatment. Often this occurs only after families are shattered, and gamblers are buried under towering debts and serious legal, even criminal problems. Before that, trying to rescue gambling addicts by lending them money or protecting them from the grim consequences of their behavior only feeds their denial and postpones their collision with disaster. When that occurs, they may hit bottom, face their reality, and becoming receptive to help.

Gamblers Anonymous (G.A.) is the most widely available and effective approach. It was started in Los Angeles by two recovering alcoholics in A.A. whose wives had divorced them. In 1957, they decided to use the A.A. program of group meetings, Twelve Steps, and total abstinence in a desperate effort to control their irresistible impulses to gamble. Chapters spread throughout the United States, and after a few years family members formed Gam-Anon groups that are similar to Alanon. There are now over eight hundred chapters of G.A. in this country. In 1972, the Board of Trustees of G.A. invited their spiritual director, Monsignor Joseph A. Dunne, to establish what became the National Council on Problem Gambling. Headquartered in New York City, it sponsors a national hotline, produces educational resources, acts as a clearinghouse for information, and holds clinics for mental health professionals, many of whom are not informed about how to respond when compulsive gamblers or, as is more often the case, their families come for help.

In addition to G.A., some comprehensive, thirty day in-patient rehabilitation programs for pathological gamblers are available. Many of these use multidiscipline treatment teams that integrate psychological assessment, medical and psychiatric treatment with group psychotherapy and, in most cases, participation in Gamblers Anonymous.

Sex and Love Addictions

As I write, I see in my mind the handsome face of a highly effective clergyman. As a powerful preacher, a caring pastor, and a creative initiator of innovative church programs, he was loved and respected by his large congregation and by the community. Then, a hidden and devastating side of the man was revealed. A woman parishioner and leader in the congregation had the courage to break her shame-ridden silence. She revealed that she and the pastor had been having sex for several years. Her revelation gave six other women parishioners the courage to voice similar allegations. The minister left in disgrace with his wife (who chose to stay with him). His whole congregation was traumatized in collective betrayal and grief. He surrendered his clerical credentials just before his denomination convened a judicatory trial.

Our human species is the most sexually active of all the animal species (rivaled only by the Bonobo apes). In light of the intensity and ubiquitous nature of sexual interest and desire, it is not surprising that human sexuality lends itself to a wide variety of expressions as well as distortions. Men and women suffering from sexual addictions are estimated to number in the millions in our society. They may be heterosexual, homosexual, or bisexual, and of any age, ethnic, social, or religious background. These addicts suffer from a tragic compulsion that causes them to engage in repetitive and often risky sexual behavior that they feel powerless to control. They think obsessively about sex. Finding the particular sexual experiences they crave is a constant, consuming preoccupation.

Many sex addicts are terrified of emotionally intimate relationships. Out of their deep loneliness, spiritual emptiness, and longing for love, they seek to connect with people in superficial, impersonal, repetitive, and obsessive-compulsive ways. Among these are exhibitionism, voyeurism, shallow affairs with strangers, sex with prostitutes, pedophilia, and masturbating while listening to strangers' voices on the phone.

As in all addictions, the key to sexual addictions is some degree of power-lessness to choose. Sex addicts become slaves to their sexual fantasies and impulses and use sexual highs and their search for them like alcoholics and drug addicts use their magical substances. Sexual highs become an anes-thetizing drug, a painkiller that lets them escape, however fleetingly, from the agony of their lonely lives. As their addiction deepens, their self-con-tempt and hopelessness become more and more overwhelming. Defenses of their self-esteem like denial ("Just one more time won't hurt") and ratio-nalizations ("Things have been tough and I deserve this sexual relief"), become increasingly difficult to maintain. Driven to illegal sexual behavior such as repeated exhibitionism or pedophilia, many suffer disgrace when they are arrested, stand trial, and are imprisoned.

Sex addicts who feel driven to have multiple sexual contacts, frequent-ly with strangers, exposes themselves to extremely high risks of infection by sexually transmitted diseases including AIDS. When they are polyad-dicted, their excessive use of alcohol and drugs elevates their risk of dan-gerous, even fatal sexually transmitted infections. Their judgment is impaired and their inhibitions lowered when they mix heavy drinking and drugs with promiscuous sexual behavior.

Two specialists in sexual addictions, Ralph Earle and Gregory Crow, highlight the dynamics of this addiction:

> Anyone who has ever had an orgasm recognizes the enormous power of sex. The incredible rush of sexual pleasure during orgasm is indeed intoxicating—and not just for the addict. But a person who is not addicted to sex, no matter how much or how often he or she enjoys sex, can have fun doing other things as well, while the sex addict frequently finds little gratification in anything else. For the sex addict, the quest to duplicate this sexual euphoria over and over becomes an obsession. Neglecting or sacrificing jobs, spouse and family, friends, and personal well-being, a sex addict ritualistically sets out to recapture a sexual high again and again.[20]

It is important to remember that sex is not at the heart of sexual addic-tions. What such addictions really are about is using sex to escape from loneliness, guilt, shame, fear of real intimacy, and insecurity about one's maleness or femaleness. Sexual addictions involve desperate, self-destructive uses of God's wonderful gift of human sexuality in failing, self-sabotaging attempts to deal with overwhelming feelings.

In *Sacred Pleasure: Sex, Myth, and the Politics of the Body,* cultural historian

Riane Eisler illuminates the societal context of today's sexual addictions by showing their dynamic similarities with the sexual orgies of men of power in ancient Rome:

> But for all their idealization of the power of the phallus, if we look at the compulsive sexual excesses of Romans, we see that what they reflect is actually a sexual powerlessness: the powerlessness to feel real sexual and emotional fulfillment. For what we are today learning about sexually obsessive and compulsive behaviors is that they generally stem from an inability to fully experience bodily sensations and a full range of emotions ... a dominator psychosexual armoring that effectively blocks the full experiencing of bodily and emotional sensations. It is this same sexual armoring that in our time continues to drive men to ever more sexual conquests, to the "excitement" of warfare, and to all the other frantic compulsions that fuel both war and the war of the sexes.[21]

Eisler shows how the dominator/dominated way of structuring male-female and other relationships fuels the orgies of sex and violence in contemporary society and its media as well as the pornographic industry. One up-one down relationships suppress, distort, and stunt full sexual pleasure in both women and men, cutting it off from fulfilling and loving relationships. The Christian church has been a major force in maintaining hierarchical relationships that cut sexuality off from nature, pleasure, and the erotic, replacing the wonders of sex, birth, and rebirth at the center of life with suffering, punishment, and death.

A key factor in sexual additions is the power dynamic. History, both recent and remote, is replete with examples of males (including presidents) with political, military, athletic, financial, or religious power, who had a kind of harem mentality, expressed with multiple sexual partners. Since the woman's movement gave increased courage and mutual support to women, more have begun to confront perpetrators of sexual harrassment. Some sexually attractive women have used their beauty seductively to gain a sense of power over men, especially powerful men, to offset feelings of powerlessness in our sexist society.

Like all addictions, sexual addictions have spiritual components among their dynamics. Sexual experiences and highs become the victims' ultimate concern, their god, their bottom-line object of devotion. For many addicts, this deity replaces whatever relationship they had with religion and God. They feel as if they were surviving in a spiritual wasteland.

Their childhood religious training often gives their guilt, shame, and self-depression a theological intensity. They live with chronic, spiritual lostness and depression, their private "dark night of the soul."

Here are questions that are useful in identifying sexual addictions:

- Do you sense that sexual thought and/or behaviors are causing problems in your life?
- Have sexual thoughts interfered with your ability to function at school or work?
- Do you fantasize about sex, or masturbate, or engage in sexual activity with another person in order to escape, deny, or numb your feelings or cope with problems?
- Do you spend more money than you can afford on sexual activities?
- Do you risk legal problems in order to be sexual?
- Do you put yourself in danger by your sexual practices?
- Has an important relationship in your life ended because of your inability to stop being sexual outside that relationship?

If you have answered yes to three or more questions, it may indicate a sexual addiction.

The usual goal of treatment for sexual addictions is comparable to that of food addictions. Rather than total abstinence from sex, the goal is learning how to enjoy sex choicefully as one part of life rather than as an all-consuming obsession. Two pathways that enable some victims to escape from these addictions are used in treatment. One is psychotherapy by a competent therapist trained in sexual therapy and skilled in helping people deal with the underlying psychological, interpersonal, and spiritual causes of sexual addictions. Many sex addicts are also addicted to alcohol, drugs, food, work, or rigid religion. Dealing with other addictions concurrently may be essential to recovery.

Many sexually addicted people are also addicted in codependent ways to parents, spouses, lovers, or authority people (like clergy or physicians). The identifying characteristics of these so-called love addictions are: spending exorbitant amounts of time obsessing about the person; assigning more worth to the person than to oneself (or putting oneself down in order to keep the other on a pedestal); and suffering harmful consequences from the relationship or from one's obsessing about and overvaluing the person, and yet not changing or terminating the relationship.

Sexual addictions are family problems that usually affect everyone in a family. Patterns of sexual dysfunction often seem to be passed along from one generation to the next. Many addicts, especially those who were sexually wounded in their childhood or youth, internalize the sexually dysfunctional attitudes, inhibitions, and behaviors of their parents and/or other significant adults. Oftentimes their sexual and gender identities are deeply distorted because of sexual violence and abuse. This violence includes rape, molestation, and the ultimate betrayal of incest by a parent or other adult who had been trusted and loved. Healing these still-infected wounds from these life- and sex-shattering experiences is an essential component of treatment.

The most widely available paths out of sexual addictions are the several Twelve Step recovery programs begun by A.A. members who also suffered from this addiction. These groups include Sex Addicts Anonymous, Sex and Love Addicts Anonymous (SLAA), Sexaholics Anonymous, Survivors of Incest Anonymous, and, for family members, Codependents of Sex Addicts and S-Anon. Each of these has somewhat unique emphases, although all of them make the Twelve Step program central in their approach. SLAA includes addictive love and sexual relationships, and tends to attract more women. The first step is reworded as: "We came to admit that we were powerless over lust, that our lives had become unmanageable."

Addiction to Pathogenic Religion and Values

Shortly before she died, a dear friend named Erma Pixley shared this priceless insight gained during her lifelong commitment to spiritually centered wholeness: "Religion can be either a set of wings with which our souls can fly or a lead weight about our necks."[22] Countless experiences over my years as a teacher and psychotherapist have convinced me that she was on target. People's personal faith and values, and the institutions that generate these, can be a clear, clean, bubbling, refreshing spring of healing and wholeness, or a poisoned well causing mental, physical, spiritual, and relational illnesses. Those who drink from the poisoned well often believe erroneously that they are receiving the water of life, when actually they are drinking the water causing sicknesses.

Some Characteristics of Sickness-Causing, Addictive Religion

1. *Beliefs and values prescribed by religious authority figures who teach that their way is the only path or at least the far superior path to salvation and spiritual wellness.* Such closed belief systems are attractive because they serve as a kind of anxiety-allaying security blanket for those that accept them. Followers are enjoined not to exercise freedom to think for themselves about issues of religious or ethical truth. They are encouraged to be "true

believers" who do not challenge the official party-line beliefs and values.

2. A rigid, literalistic understanding of sacred writings that regard every word as equally inspired. This robs scriptures of their poetic power and ability to communicate the living truths of God. Those who accept this view miss the opportunity to love God more fully with their minds by using them to distinguish the precious eternal truths in sacred writings from many uninspired passages and stories. The latter simply reflect cultural attitudes and beliefs during the many diverse times and social contexts in which these writings originated.

3. Followers are discouraged from owning their honest doubts and using them as a point of departure to grow spiritually. When people ignore their doubts they become locked into increasingly rigid beliefs and ethical guidelines. They are stuck with immature hangover beliefs and values left over from childhood. These values become less and less relevant to the believers' adult lives. They thus are deprived of the freedom to grow their faith and values and to keep these relevant to their growing evolving adult experiences and thoughts.

4. Authoritarian religious leaders who are experts at arousing guilt, fear, and shame in followers by manipulative messages that control feelings to keep their followers in line. The leaders offer followers the "only answer" to guilt, fear, and shame—on "the only true path to salvation"—which means their own understanding of spiritual, ethical, and biblical truths.

5. Compulsive participation in religious rituals and practices including church attendance. People lose the inner freedom to choose to not participate without intense feelings of guilt and shame. Their spiritual life is dominated by compulsivity as they lose what the New Testament calls "freedom in Christ."

6. Thinking and talking obsessively about religious beliefs, values, and other religious matters. They tend to believe that it is their God-appointed mission to try to convert those they encounter to the party line of their belief and value systems.

7. Self-righteousness and defensive superiority feelings toward people in other faiths. Interpersonal religious barriers are created rather than bridges of mutual understanding when people participate in exclusivistic religious groups. Collaboration on important social issues such as justice, peace, and the environment becomes impossible. As is painfully evident in our pluralistic society and world, such divisive parochialism causes violence and discrimination to proliferate among followers of different faith traditions.

8. An emphasis on sinfulness and what is not right in people and society. This is seldom balanced by recognizing the other truths about us humans—the numerous things that are good and right and strong. These positive characteristics can be the firm foundation on which to develop ways of correcting the destructive aspects and enhancing the strengths already present in individuals and society. In theological terms, the dominant Fall-Redemption theology is not balanced by a strong, life-affirming creation theology emphasizing the basic goodness of life and people and the potentials for continuing growth in using God's good gifts more fully.

9. Moralistic and judgmental attitudes toward sexual and aggressive impulses. Acceptance of bodily energies and impulses as gifts of God to be used responsibly is lacking. Furthermore, the prevalent body-spirit dualism splits basic human unity artificially. Things of the spirit are seen as good and things of the body as bad. This view blocks a health-engendering understanding that embodied spirituality is at the center of the Christian good news. It also keeps those who hold to such dualistic views from recognizing that the health of our bodies, minds, and spirits are deeply interdependent.

10. Beliefs and practices designed to keep women subservient to men and "in their place." Biblical passages (such as Ephesians 5:22), reflecting the male-dominated first-century culture in which they originated, rather than the abiding truths of healthy religion, are used to justify and reinforce sexist patterns in church and society. As a result, both genders are locked into traditional roles that deprive both women and men of full opportunities to develop their God-given potentialities.

How can those locked in rigid and spiritually diminishing belief and value systems be helped? How can they learn to use their relationship with the divine Spirit not as a prop for their shaky self-esteem, but as a transcending source of energy for living whole, productive, socially responsible lives? Fortunately, the basic principles of A.A.'s Twelve Steps can be adapted and used in transforming ways. A Twlede Step recovery network called Fundamentalist Anonymous has been created by victims of religious addictions to help themselves and others find freedom from the oppression of religious addictions.

Leo Booth, who describes himself as "a recovering priest," has explored religious addictions in depth in his book *When God Becomes a Drug: Breaking the Chains of Religious Addition and Abuse.*[23] He writes about "dysfunctional relationships with God" that produce religious addictions in families and in religions:

> Religious addicts use the "things" of God—rituals, dogma, and scriptural texts—to reinforce the dysfunctional message that all

humans are evil, stupid, or incapable of merit. Thus, far from enhancing spiritual development, religious addiction stunts or paralyzes spiritual growth and creates barriers to a healthy relationship with God.[24]

Clergy and other counselors should learn counseling methods designed to help heal the spiritual and ethical wounds at the roots of addictive religion. By using these methods, they may be instruments in helping nurture higher levels of spiritual and ethical wholeness in the lives of those who trust their lives to their caring competence. Booth's insights concerning recovery from religious addictions can be useful in helping people find self-liberation. In addition, the textbook I authored, *Basic Types of Pastoral Care and Counseling*, presents a wide variety of spiritual and ethical healing and growth methods.[25] Chapter 5 describes ways of "Facilitating Spiritual Wholeness: The Heart of Pastoral Care and Counseling," and chapter 6 describes approaches to "Counseling on Ethical, Value, and Meaning Issues."

Television, Computer, and Internet Addictions

A high-tech addictive wave is claiming more and more victims as the marvels of the electronic and communication revolution increase at mind-boggling alacrity and become more widely available and at a lower cost. People who become addicted to the amazing communication tools of our time lose control and cannot keep their use within reasonable limits. Their obsessive-compulsive behavior causes serious harm to themselves and to their intimate relationships.

Television, particularly with cable and satellite connections, makes countless channels and viewing options available at one's fingertips. The vast majority of American homes, rich and poor, have one or more television sets. In many one-parent families, the main babysitter is the television. Even in developing countries that I have visited, many television antenna are seen on shacks of the poor. In our country, high quality educational programs are available on a few channels, particularly on public, noncommercial ones. But much of television's total offerings are cultural garbage that tend to diminish the intellectual wholeness of millions of individuals and families.

In a volume revised in 1985, *The Plug-In Drug*, Marie Winn documents many of the adverse effects of television.[26] The average child watches television for twenty-five hours a week. By the time young people graduate from high school, they have watched fifteen thousand hours of television, on the average, compared with spending only eleven thousand hours in classes. Evidence is accumulating that television provides a false, alternative reality, a virtual reality for children and adults. This reduces the time and motivation of children to learn from the real world through creative play, reading, and interacting with peers, parents, and nature. It encourages passive spectatoritis and creates the false expectation that life should be continuously entertaining. The nonstop murders and mayhem, along with increasingly explicit sexual scenes on television, probably make society seem even more violent and sexually obsessed than it actually is. Furthermore, there is evidence that viewing this plethora of violence and sex may encourage violent and sexual acting-out on the part of some vulnerable youth, particularly those from psychologically wounding backgrounds. I recall the murder trial of a fifteen-year-old. "Involuntary, subliminal television intoxication" was used (unsuccessfully) by the defense lawyers.

Many children watch television inertly for long periods, unaware of their surroundings. Often they seem to be hypnotized or at least tranquilized by the plug-in drug, eating their meals while watching television. They are exposed to million dollar manipulation by Madison Avenue as they view countless seductive advertisements designed to shape their wants and, through them, both their own and their parents' purchases.

Medical studies show that a lack of adequate aerobic exercise contributes to many life-threatening diseases. In America, lack of exercise probably causes several hundred thousand preventable deaths each year. For adults and children, excessive television watching encourages the couch-potato lifestyle. For those who overdose on television, their main exercise during long hours is to walk a few steps during commercial breaks to grab high fat, high calorie junk food, and high sugar or alcoholic beverages. This behavior pattern contributes to the plethora of junk food junkies whose wellness is diminished by what they eat and drink while passively watching escapist television.

Television is changing family communication patterns in profound and problematic ways. Television-addicted families must learn to communicate in hundred-second segments—the time it takes for stations to identify themselves and present three commercials. Frequently, families whose television sets break down and they choose not to have repaired often report that they spend more time reading, talking, playing together, and being outdoors. Furthermore, educational studies reveal that the average attention span of children is shrinking year by year as concentration is limited to the length of sound bites. Unless new visual and auditory stimuli are introduced after a few minutes in school, as happens on television, they lose interest. It is estimated that some 60 percent of adults, after they finish their schooling, never read books. As someone has put it, "Television eats books." In reflecting on the profound impact of television on all areas of our lives, a knowledgeable commentator observed, "It's OK to introduce new ideas on television—as long as it doesn't take more than five or six seconds to explain them."

The Internet, E-mail, and World Wide Web are creating vast new opportunities for electronic communication but also addictions. On-line junkies stay hooked on their computer screens for hours ignoring other people and activities. Psychologists are trying to understand the symptoms and their consequences, but there is no doubt that these are genuine, rapidly growing addictions. Kimberly S. Young, a psychologist who heads the Center for On-line Addictions in Rochester, New York, has surveyed hundreds of Internet users as part of her research. She reports that the very small percentage who become addicted

> spend more time with their computer than with people, give up other activities and complain of fatigue, back pain or neck aches from sitting in front of the machine. They become compulsive, logging on every time they walk by the computer or checking E-mail twenty or thirty times a day. Like alcoholics and drug users, on-line addicts usually deny that they have a problem—even as their marriage, job, or school career crumbles.[27]

A clinical psychologist who studies people and technology says, "There's something to be said for checking electronic mail, but when you do it before having a conversation with your wife, or spending time in a chat room (on the Internet) rather than playing with your kids, you've got a problem."[28] A sixty-year-old woman in Washington State is reported to spend ten to thirteen hours a day alone on-line with her computer that is in her bedroom. She often stays on-line until about 3 a.m. She no longer prepares meals or does housework.[29]

College and university academic and social life is changing rapidly because of electronic communication via computer networks and modems. College officials are wondering how a sense of community can be developed when students spend more and more time in their rooms communicating via their computers. The use of student union buildings as gathering places is declining as students spend more time in their computer-wired dorm rooms. The five thousand students and three thousand faculty and staff at Dartmouth receive about 250,000 E-mail messages a day, an average of thirty messages a person.[30] Situations like this throughout our addictive society make the proliferation of electronic addictions among young people almost inevitable.

It requires several hours a day for a Southern California man who is hooked on the World Wide Web to keep in touch with his fifty electronic pen pals living from Singapore to Khabarovsk, Russia. He has switched to the swing shift on his job to have more time on-line. Those who spend lots of time talking in Internet chat rooms with on-line friends may believe that they have an active social life. But this electronic interaction usually enables people only to touch others but not establish deeper relationships. Although this is easier than mixing face-to-face with people it also makes it possible to have superficial contact with many people quickly, but not to know them in any depth.[31] The often-bewailed loss of a sense of community in our society is increased by the availability of electronic devices that make all this possible.

The avalanche of information easily available electronically has produced a new clinical syndrome—*information fatigue overload.*[32] Distinguishing information from true wisdom is increasingly problematic when spiritually starved people are targets of a nonstop barrage of information. There are now 320 million Web sites on the worldwide Internet.

A dramatic and tragic example of the way high-tech sophistication and computerized manipulation of information can coexist with psychospiritual insanity was the mass suicide by thirty-nine members of the Heaven's Gate cult who chose to leave their bodily "containers" in Rancho Sante Fe California.

The good news is that the positive possibilities of enhancing humankind's overall well-being by the creative uses of television, computers, and all the other electronic communication marvels, are almost beyond imagination. The widespread use of these tools in schools is beginning to actualize some of these exciting possibilities. What is the challenge in the electronic communication revolution to those in all the major faith traditions and others who care about human values and health? It is to take the initiative in developing and testing better ways to enable individuals, families, and social institutions to use these marvelous machines as instruments for human well-being, education, enjoyment, and the arts. The only alternative is to let the machines, by default, diminish the wellness of the human family because they are being used addictively in depersonalizing ways. The choice is at our fingertips—today!

In terms of their underlying psychological and spiritual dynamics, all the behavioral addictions discussed in this chapter have much in common with one another and with substance addictions. Each addiction is a detorted expression of a profound spiritual hunger for an integrating commitment to an object of devotion that will gives lives purposeful unity. When people seek to satisfy this spiritual need by either an activity or a chemical substance, they are hypervulnerable to becoming painfully addicted to the behavior or substance.

[Note: The addresses of groups treating some of these addictions are listed at the end of the annotated bibliography.]

CHAPTER 5

Understanding and Helping Those at Special Risk of Addictions

This chapter deals with the sociocultural factors that make members of numerous groups in our society unusually vulnerable to addictions. These groups include youth, seniors, minorities, health professionals, women, gay men, and lesbians. In all of these groups, oppressive cultural attitudes and practices cause them to face special risks.

An astute psychotherapist who read an early draft of this chapter observed, "It seems as though the only people in our society who are not at special risk are middle-class, mentally healthy white males." To correct the impression, it is important to reemphasize that many white males are not exempt from heightened vulnerability to addictions. Middle-class males scrambling to stay upwardly mobile are particularly prone to becoming addicted in our competitive, win-lose society. The chronic pressure of failure anxieties and fear of slipping down in the pecking order, plus the general pressures on males in our culture of changing male-female roles, are contributing causes of addictions among many successful males. The same is true of those females who have become "honorary males" by making it to high positions by their ability to compete successful in male power games and male-dominated professions. It is well to remember that in our violent, addictive society, no one is really immune to the dangers of chemical abuse and addictions!

Addicted Adolescents

The death of Teresa Jane McGovern, daughter of former U.S. Senator and presidential candidate George McGovern, made many people aware of the tragic reality of adolescent alcohol abuse. At age forty-five, she stumbled out of a bar in Madison, Wisconsin, in December 1994, passed out, fell in deep snow and froze to death before she was found. Terry Jane had struggled from her teens with alcoholism and depression. Her parents had done everything they knew to enable her to get on the path to recovery. In spite of being in and out of many treatment facilities (beginning at age ninteen), her life ended prematurely in her middle years. In his book *Terry*, written after her death, McGovern remembers "My lovable little girl who had given me ten thousand laughs, countless moments of affection and joy, and yes, years of anxiety and disappointment."[1]

Popular media columnists receive many letters like this one to Ann Landers:

Dear Ann: Like the guy who wrote to you from jail, I also screwed up my life with drugs. Although I never went to jail, I was burned out on life and wanted to die. I am now in a recovery home and feel like a worthwhile human being. I am seventeen and have been clean for ten months, thanks to the Twelve Step recovery program. Life looks great now, and I'm going to make it. Heather.[2]

There is alarming evidence that problem drinking among adolescents is a significant and growing problem. The average age of first use of alcohol and drugs keeps declining, setting the stage for a sharp rise in alcohol, drug, and multiple addictions among older teens and young adults. Epidemiologists at the National Institute on Alcohol Abuse and Alcoholism surveyed 43,000 people and discovered that the younger children or teenagers begin to drink alcohol, the more likely they are to become alcoholics. A nationwide study found that the average age of first using illegal drugs was thirteen. Ever since A.A.'s beginning in 1935, the average age of members has been declining. There are now many members who are in their late teens or early twenties. The illusion that they were "too young to be alcoholics" evaporated as more and more young people go to A.A. and recover. The A.A. pamphlet "Young People and A.A." includes the moving autobiographical stories of those who joined in their teens and early twenties.

In Phoenix, Unity High (nicknamed Sobriety High) is a program for teenage recovering addicts who don't want to struggle with the pressures of a regular high school. Recovering students tell of being offered alcohol and drugs almost every day by other students when they returned for a short time to high school. They tell of kids who wave bags of crystal (methamphetamine) in front of them in the halls or cutting lines of cocaine on desktops. They got tired of having to repeat, "No, dude, I'm sober."[3]

Beer is the drug of choice of the vast majority of youth who drink or use during high school and college years. Pot runs a very distant second. A national survey of six thousand youth regarding their use of alcohol and drugs found that 36 percent of seventh graders, 49 percent of ninth graders, and 60 percent of eleventh graders, said they had consumed beer in the last six months. On many college and university campuses heavy beer consumption is almost the norm. Alcohol abuse is the number one killer of teenagers, even though DWI (Driving While Intoxicated) arrests of teens have declined in the last few years thanks to public education on the dangers of mixing alcohol and driving. Drivers between fifteen and twenty are grossly over represented in fatal accidents involving alcohol. The healthcare costs of teen drinking and driving are enormous.

Because of the near hysteria surrounding street drug use by adolescents in our society, alcohol education has declined as drug education has increased. Many parents breathe a sigh of relief when a teen child comes home intoxicated on alcohol. They feel, "at least it wasn't drugs." Evidence exists that alcohol and pot can be gateway drugs for some vulnerable youth, opening the way to hard street drugs. An A.A. survey of members under thirty found that 58 percent of men and 60 percent of women had been addicted to other drugs as well as alcohol (compared to 31 percent of the overall A.A. membership).

Hillary Rodham Clinton in her insightful book, *It Takes a Village: And Other Lessons Children Teach Us,* illuminates the reasons why some youth do and some do not engage in risky behavior including alcohol and drugs.[4] She quotes the findings of the Center on Addiction and Substance Abuse (CASA) at Columbia University. It conducts an annual survey of attitudes of American adults and teens toward alcohol, cigarettes, marijuana, cocaine, heroin, and other illegal drugs, with the goal of alerting adults to what they can do to help protect children. She quotes the chairman of CASA, Joseph A. Califano, Jr., who points to what is at stake:

> Make no mistake about it. If our children get through adolescence, ages ten to twenty, without using drugs, without smoking, without abusing alcohol, they are virtually certain never to do so.

Hillary Clinton cited several factors that increase the risk of teen substance abuse. These risk factors include: having a parent who abuses drugs or alcohol; parents' casual attitudes toward minor's use of cigarettes, marijuana, and alcohol; dropping out of school; low self-esteem and lack of optimism; parents who are not really involved in their children's lives and who do not give them firm guidance on these issues; and the glamorizing of drugs and alcohol in the media and advertising.

About her husband's experience with his half-brother, she writes:

> If this knowledge had been available years ago, Bill and his mother might have been aware that Roger, who for years witnessed his

father's alcoholism and experienced its destructive consequences, was a prime candidate for alcohol and drug abuse. One reason my husband is adamant about curbing smoking among teens—and adults, for that matter—is the fact that he learned firsthand, in his own family, about the slippery slope that begins with the use of one addictive substance and leads to other destructive behaviors and attitudes.[5]

The use of alcohol and other drugs by adolescents is particularly problematic for a variety of reasons, in addition to the deadly threat of automobile accidents. Youth are in the difficult struggles to work out their identity. They are searching for constructive answers to questions like "Who am I really?"; "What am I worth?"; "What are the values that I can freely choose?"; and "What do I want to do with my life?" During this crucial period of development, using chemicals instead of personality resources can block or postpone crucial personality growth. By age twenty, 60 percent of females and 86 percent of males are sexually active. One teen out of sixteen has had one or more STDs (sexually transmitted disease). Alcohol and drug use increases unsafe sex, raising the risk of an STD, including AIDS. Behavior patterns established during teen years often persist into adulthood. For example, the vast majority of adults who are addicted to nicotine began smoking in grammar school or high school.

For parents and professionals who work with youth, here are some warning signs that may point to alcohol and/or drug use and abuse:

- Sharp drops in school performance and increasing truancy;
- Sudden changes in mood, personality, activities, and friends;
- Sharp decrease in motivation;
- Unexplained depression, hostility, or defensiveness toward adults;
- Raiding parents' liquor supply;
- Signs of hangover such as nausea, headache, puffy eyes;
- Chronic "spaciness" and blank stares.

It is important to remember that many of these symptoms can point to other underlying psychological, physical, or family problems rather than alcohol and drug use and abuse. Mental illnesses often have their onset in adolescence. Heavy drinking and drug use may be symptoms of severe depression. In such cases, the possibility of suicide attempts should be evaluated by a health professional trained in suicide prevention. As in the case of adults, teens sometime use of alcohol and drugs as responses to painful losses and crises including the chronic family crisis of parental alcoholism and/or violence. Teen drinking and drug use can be rebellion against adult authority figures, or imitation of adult behavior around them, or a rite of passage to adulthood.

What Types of Help Are Designed for Adolescents?

A.A. and N.A. groups for teens are available in some places. If these don't help, there are both inpatient and outpatient adolescent treatment programs that should be considered. These programs, after initial assessments to determine what type of treatment is needed, usually include group therapy with other teens, medical services, Twelve Step groups, family sessions, a firm "no use" policy that is enforced, and an aftercare plan. Outpatient programs are much less expensive. Unless a dual diagnosis is present (with both substance abuse and psychiatric problems), an outpatient program is the logical first treatment alternative to try if Twelve Step groups alone are not enough.

Unlike most adult addicts who hit bottom and seek help for themselves, the majority of teens are brought to treatment angry and intensely resistant by parents, or sent by courts after they are arrested for alcohol or drug-related offenses. Parents often ask treatment programs to "transform an unruly, disobedient, and self-destructive teenager into a drug-free youngster who listens to them." Parents must be helped to accept that treatment programs are not obedience schools for teens and their only feasible goals are to get young people off drugs and alcohol; create a new belief system inside them about using these substances; and help them learn how to be strong in implementing these new beliefs. Achieving these goals is difficult but possible. In some cases teens are helped to awaken enlightened self-interest. Some are helped when other members of their family system also change their side of the family interactions.[6]

Addicted Seniors

Alcoholism, addiction to prescribed and over-the-counter drugs, and polyaddictions among people over sixty constitute a hidden health epidemic in America. With baby boomers retiring and the average age of the population continuing to rise steadily (with an increased life expectancy of twenty-eight years during the twentieth century), the problem is almost certain to grow worse before it gets better. Alcohol is the drug of choice among seniors. The American Medical Association estimates that there are some three million American problem drinkers over sixty. It points out that alcohol is a factor in much more than half of the hospitalizations of older people, a greater number than are hospitalized for all heart attacks. In a recent year, Medicare paid over $233 million for alcohol-related illnesses and hospitalizations. To make things worse, it is estimated that five million seniors suffer from having wrong or conflicting medications prescribed by physicians, resulting in hospitalizations or death in some cases.

Many medications taken frequently by seniors interact with alcohol in ways that change and make unpredictable the effect of prescriptions, sometimes with disastrous results. Alcohol has a mutually reinforcing effect with almost half of the most frequently used drugs. Drinking alcohol while taking barbiturates, sedatives, and antianxiety drugs can be deadly. The AMA has issued guidelines for physicians, the majority of whom have ignored alcohol in the past as one cause of senior patients' health problems.

Older adults are more vulnerable to alcoholism and drug addictions because of changes in body chemistry associated with aging. Physicians who do research in the area of addictions have discovered that as people grow older, alcohol and other drugs remain in their bodies longer because their metabolism slows down. This increases the risk of drug overdose, alcohol intoxication, or negative interaction between alcohol and prescription drugs. If they also develop memory problems, they may forget to take essential medications, take these too frequently, or mix medications, and alcohol in dangerous ways. Also, the symptoms of alcoholism often are confused with those many people inaccurately consider a normal part of aging—for example, forgetfulness, unsteady walking, disorientation, frequent falls, and sloppy appearance.

Identification of alcoholism and drug dependence of seniors by family members often is difficult for several reasons. Most seniors are out of the mainstream and no longer working for pay in jobs where their problem would be more likely to be noticed. Many live alone and/or drink in secret. The public stereotype persists that alcoholism and drug dependency are mainly problems of youth, young adults, and middle-aged adults. If older people show symptoms of heavy drinking, it often is accepted either because they are respected or because people believe that they probably don't have very long to live and should be allowed to enjoy their remaining years. This unfortunate societal attitude ignores the fact that overuse will produce, not happiness, but even greater health problems, depression, and despair.

The tendency of most heavy drinkers to minimize or deny the consequences of their drinking and underestimate how much they drink is even greater among some seniors. Heavy use often increases memory problems and causes forgetfulness about taking essential medication. Alcoholism is viewed moralistically by more seniors than younger people. This makes it very difficult for them to accept the reality that *they* are addicted. Many seniors view alcohol as a convenient, inexpensive method of self-medication. They believe that it is necessary to drink to anesthetize the pain from arthritis and other common and painful problems of seniors, and to try to treat chronic depression and insomnia.

The social context of aging in America is a crucial contributor to drug and alcohol abuse by seniors. Many drink to forget their feelings of powerlessness, loneliness, multiple griefs, and wounded self-esteem that so often results from forced retirement and the widespread ageism and sexism in our society. A mental health geriatric nurse, Louise Currey, who works with substance abusers declares: "Seniors are stigmatized population anyway. If you have a substance abuser who is a woman, and old, that's a triple whammy. Add poverty and isolation and the outlook is bleak indeed." [7]

The *Johns Hopkins Medical Letter for Health After Fifty* suggests that these four questions can help seniors with self-diagnosis of problem drinking:
1. Have you ever felt you should cut down on your drinking?
2. Have people annoyed you by criticizing your drinking?
3. Have you felt bad or guilty about your drinking?
4. Have you ever had a drink first thing in the morning to steady your nerves or to get rid of a hangover?[8]

Answering two or more of these questions affirmatively indicates that, as the *Medical Letter* states, "you should consider decreasing your intake."[9] Unfortunately, this recommendation is seriously flawed because it can be implemented only by nonalcoholics who still retain some power of choice about their drinking. It would have been better if a sentence like this had been added: "If you find that you are not able to decrease your drinking, it is strongly recommended that you phone the local chapter of A.A. or addiction hotline." About a third of A.A. members are over fifty. In some places, new A.A. groups have been formed to target the schedules and special needs of senior alcoholics. A valuable A.A. pamphlet for encouraging seniors to try A.A. is "Time to Start Living: Stories of Those Who Came to A.A. in Their Later Years."

The director of the Smithers Rehabilitation Center for alcoholics in New York City suggests these guidelines when talking to an older adult about a drinking problem:

> Be direct and treat the person as an adult capable of making decisions. Avoid judgment—don't add to the person's sense of shame

and guilt. Point out the damaging effects of the person's drinking on the family, especially grandchildren. Don't use pejorative words like "addict" or "alcoholic." Avoid a confrontational style, maintain a gentle and loving attitude and focus on the person's positive attributes. Don't discuss the problem when the person is drinking.[10]

Family and close friends of seniors (or others) who are abusing alcohol and drugs can express their love by planning and then doing an *intervention* with them. This strategy involves a firm but very caring confrontation with addicted persons aimed at motivating them to accept treatment. (How to do this will be described in chapter 12.) A geriatric nurse emphasizes that the leverage used with many seniors to persuade them to accept help is different from that used for younger people. Young and middle-aged adults who are targets of interventions often are motivated when spouses, children, and other important people in their lives confront them with concrete examples of their self- and other-destructive behavior, together with serious threats that they will lose their marriage, family, or job unless they get help and change their drinking behavior. The elderly have other fears including loss of independence, their residence, or their life. They are more likely to be motivated by a statement such as, "You might have ten years left. Do you want to spend them incapacitated or productively?"

Because so many older adults are very involved in their churches, congregations have important roles both in preventing senior addictions and in encouraging addicted seniors to go to A.A. or other treatment programs. One effective congregational approach is to provide a variety of interesting, intergenerational classes and small sharing groups aimed at enabling older people to cope nonchemically with the accelerating crises and losses in the second half of life. Another approach is to include in a congregation's educational program information on drugs and alcohol and the special hazards that they pose for seniors. Older members of A.A. often can help other seniors accept that help. In my experience, it is more often the families of seniors with serious drug and alcohol problems who ask for help than the addicted seniors themselves. Family members can benefit by being referred to Al-Anon, whether or not seniors are ready to accept help.

Oppressed Minority Addicts

Those trapped in the culture of poverty and members of oppressed ethnic minorities often suffer from wounded self-esteem as well as economic and social discrimination. Despair from society's rejection often causes oppressed minorities and the poor to become substance abusers, especially of alcohol. Much of the excessive drinking by victims of oppression has been described as "social desperation drinking" by addiction specialists. This despair-driven problem drinking and use of drugs frequently produces greater despair, greater rejection, and greater violence among those trying to cope with their pain and despair in chemical ways. Thus an addictive vicious cycle is established from which it is very difficult for those so trapped to extricate themselves. Recent immigrants to America, especially older immigrants, may be vulnerable to addiction because they are struggling to carry the load of culture shock, language shock, white racism, and vocational and financial problems that many experience.

There are major differences in the rates and types of addictions suffered by those in various countries and by ethnic and cultural groups within countries. Take Asians, for example. The residential director of the Asian American Drug Abuse Program in Los Angeles, Al Mizuno, reports that "by the time they call us, the problem is out of control."[11] Traditional Asian cultural values such as not bringing shame to the family and not losing face in the community cause parents to go to any lengths in vain attempts to cure their addicted youth and young adults by giving them money and buying them material things. Everything possible is done to ensure that no one outside the family knows about the problem. Asian American families often carry the heavy stereotype of being perceived as the model minority among other minorities. Those who do not fit this stereotype are seen as terrible failures who threaten to betray their extended families causing the whole family system to lose face. For this reason, only when members in close-knit families have failed completely and are in utter desperation will they reach out for help.

Al Mizuno wisely recommends to parents and other family members that they use tough love in responding to their addicted members—for example, by not giving them money or gifts and not bailing them out if they are arrested for stealing to get their drugs. It is extremely difficult for adults to confront addicted members because of cultural taboos against expressing feelings, even in the family. Tough love is difficult because of Asian cultural pressures to maintain a united front and not reveal shameful behavior to the outside society.

Numerous crosscultural studies by anthropologists have found extremely high rates of alcoholism among different tribes of Native Americans, as well as among other indigenous people. Federal statistics reveal that deaths among Native Americans, attributed to excessive drinking, are declining but they are still five times more frequent than the national average. The suicide rate among Native Americans is 85 percent higher than the national average, due in part to alcoholism, drug addiction, and hopelessness caused by economic and racial oppression.

A variety of factors have been identified as contributing to the high vulnerability of Native Americans to alcohol abuse and addiction. Unlike many other cultures, Native Americans historically have lacked social sanctions against inappropriate uses of alcohol. This was due in part because they had not encountered alcohol until Europeans introduced them to distilled liquor.[12] What Native Americans then called firewater (whiskey) was used by some whites as a chemical bribe to manipulate and pacify them.

Not far from where we live in Santa Barbara stands the "Queen of the Missions." I experience a wave of sadness when I drive past it, see the crowds of tourists flocking there, and remember its history. Two centuries ago, the Chumash tribes of Native Americans, who still live in this region of California, were being converted by the Franciscan missionaries who came with the Spanish soldiers. The tribe was persuaded to move from the offshore islands and traditional sites on shore to live crowded together near where the mission was to be built. The ostensible motive of the missionaries was to "Christianize" them, but they also were used to provide the enormous manual labor needed to construct the mission, its water supply, and other buildings. Their earth-grounded culture was treated as pagan and seen by their spiritual conquerors as grossly inferior to civilized European culture. Many died of European diseases to which they had no genetic immunity. Over time most of the survivors lost their language, their ecologically grounded spirituality, and their rich, artistic, and peaceful cultural lifestyle. They had been robbed of their cultural identity. Only with the "red is beautiful" awareness movement of the last few decades has a systemic effort been made by some Chumash to remember and reclaim their language, unique culture, and self-esteem as a people.

It is impossible to understand the high rates of addictions of native people around the world apart from the tragic effect of countless comparable, hope-extinguishing scenarios. Tribes all over North America, as well as in other countries, have been traumatized—robbed of their land, their collective self-esteem, their traditional lifestyles, and their spiritual and cultural identities. A Native American leader who tried to help addicts in Detroit declared: "We found they were totally out of touch, lost, no identity. They got their identity when they got together and drank."[13]

The cultural oppression that still ravages individual Native Americans and their communities is highly conducive to addictive behavior. Drinking is a self-destructive personal and social protest against what has been inflicted on them as a people. Heavy drinking and drugs provide a means of forgetting, for a brief time, the spiritual agony of the collective cultural holocaust they have suffered. One historic factor in the prevalence of alcoholism is the widespread practice of removing children from their families to boarding schools. This often produced a loss of a sense of family and Native American identity, so that when they returned they no longer fit in the Indian community and could not adjust or be accepted in the white community. Many Native Americans move from reservations to large cities hoping for a better life there. Instead, they often live in poverty, dependent on public agencies and welfare. They barely exist economically with few job skills or other tools needed to cope constructively with the demands of urban life. In a study of over five hundred Native American living in Los Angeles, alcoholism was identified as the major problem. Over half the men reported blackouts and fights while drinking. Two-thirds had a history of arrests, two-thirds of which were alcohol-related, e.g., driving under the influence and public drinking.

However, there are some small rays of light and hope in the generally dismal picture of Native American alcohol and drug abuse. One is the formation of the National Indian A.A. Conference. A recovering Native American who attended a recent convention in South Dakota told of his lift at the banquet with the "spiritual miracle" of over a thousand "sober Indians" from tribes around North America. Here is an Native American version of the Twelve Steps as modified by recovering alcoholics on a reservation in Wisconsin. The modifications reflect their Ojibwe cultural and spiritual heritage:

1. We admit we are powerless over alcohol, and that our Indian way of life had become unmanageable.

2. Came to believe that the power of the pipe is greater than ourselves and can restore us to our Culture and Heritage.

3. Made a decision to turn our will and our lives over to the care of the Great Spirit, through the sacred Pipe.

4. Made a searching and fearless moral inventory of who we are, and understand the symbolic means of the four great directions.

5. Acknowledge to the Great Spirit, to ourselves and the Indian Brotherhood, our struggles against the tide and its Manifest Destiny.

6. Be entirely ready to have Manitou remove all these defects of an alien culture.

7. Humbly ask Manitou to remove all these defects of an alien culture.

8. Made a list of all the harm that comes to our people from alcohol, and become willing to make amends to them all.

9. Made direct amends to our people that struggle against the alcoholic disease whenever possible, except when to do so would injure them or others.

10. Continue to take a personal searching and fearless moral inventory of who we are, and when we sell out, promptly admit it.

11. Seek through prayer and meditation to improve our conscious contact with equality and Brotherhood of all the Earth's creatures and the Great Balancing Harmony of the total Universe.

12. Having the Universal understanding and wisdom of the heart, mind, and spirit of all people, carry this message to Indian alcoholics and practice these principles in all Indian affairs.[14]

Another ray of light and hope is the development of effective alcohol and drug treatment programs sponsored by tribes and staffed in part by Native American counselors and mental health professionals who themselves have found sanity and sobriety in recovery programs. These tribal programs usually are based on the Twelve Steps of A.A., but certain unique elements often prove indispensable for Native Americans to achieve ongoing sobriety. These elements are the traditional spiritual and healing methods of Native Americans, including drumming and smoking the sacred pipe, that are part of what they call the "Indian Way."

Enoch Jackson, a Native American member of the staff of the Puyallup Tribe's intertribal addiction treatment center in Tacoma, Washington, described how indigenous healing wisdom and methods are used in addition to the other treatment resources, including required attendance at two A.A. meetings a week. For those in treatment who have lost what he called an essential "spiritual path," because of the disease of alcoholism, he regularly uses the smudging ceremony.[15] This is a ritual of cleansing involving rubbing smoke from smoldering sage over the recipient's body and "letting the smoke go up in all four directions to the Great Spirit who is everywhere." After the smudging, another traditional method called the "talking circle" is used. In this, a special stick called a "talking stick" is passed around the circle. While each person holds it, they have an opportunity to talk while others listen. Enoch says that this sharing (that sounds to me like a kind of group therapy) helps to heal people's minds, bodies, and spirits.

Twice a week at the Puyallup Center, the sweat lodge ceremony is offered to those in treatment. From having experienced a sweat lodge at the Native American Theological School in Tempe, Arizona, I have a sense that this powerful, earth-based spiritual ceremony must be deeply meaningful to many Native Americans searching for their lost identity and a deepening relationship with a Higher Power in their recovery process.[16]

Addicted Physicians and Other Health Care Professionals

As I write, I remember with sadness a client in her midthirties I saw years ago in an eastern state. She was a nurse and the wife of an alcoholic physician who had a large, lucrative practice. He had a reputation as one of the most caring and effective doctors in his community. It astonished me that he had been able to continue his successful practice even though his thinking processes and sense of professional responsibility were increasingly impaired by his excessive drinking.

When, at my suggestion, his wife persuaded him to see me for one exploratory session, it became clear to me and to her that he was in the advanced stages of alcoholism (and, as I now suspect, drug addiction). But he was trapped behind his massive wall of denial that was reinforced almost every day by the worshipful attitudes of his grateful patients. My attempt to refer him to a physicians A.A. group failed utterly. Eventually the man terminated the protracted suicide of his addiction very suddenly when he tried to drive home in his sports car on a rainy night from a local tavern very intoxicated and at excessive speed. The police report of his fatal crash gave his wife the tragic details. He had died instantly when his sports car flipped over several times on a narrow road causing his neck to be broken and his whole body to be shattered. Along with other addicted persons for whom my efforts to motivate them to accept help failed, this man personalizes for me the astronomical costs of addictions. His family lost a father and husband, his church lost a devoted member, and our whole community lost a health professional who might have brought healing to countless others if he had been open to recognizing and accepting treatment for his fatal illness.

Doctors and doctors-in-training often are at high risk to become polyaddicted because drugs are so easily accessible to them. Persons with the powerful letters "M.D." after their signature and a medical license can write themselves prescriptions for whatever drugs they want. To the degree that they have internalized the godlike transference image that our health-miracle worshiping society projects on them, they have great difficulty diagnosing their own drug dependency because the denial of addictions is reinforced by their wonder-working self-image.

A national survey of over nine thousand physicians revealed that one out of nine admitted using self-prescribed sleeping pills, one out of six used self-prescribed opiates such as Darvon or Percodan, and one out of ten drank alcohol on a daily basis.[17] In a study of addicted nurses, alcohol was found to be the most common substance abused by them, with alcohol plus other drugs such as Demerol also common. The Committee for Physicians Health (also known as the Impaired Physicians Program of the New York Medical Society) has treated over one thousand physicians since its inception some years ago (45 percent were referred by colleagues, 30 percent by themselves, only 5 percent by their hospitals, and about 7 percent by their families). In a California physicians rehabilitation program, most addicted physicians were polydrug abusers. Their drugs of choice, in descending order of frequency, were alcohol, narcotics, and cocaine.

Over the years, physicians in A.A. have organized a large national network of recovering health professionals. Many of these men and women fly their own planes to large national conventions of their network. The medical director of an alcohol and drug rehabilitation center has pointed out that chemically impaired health professionals are increasingly likely to experience earlier identification of their problem, have others do an intervention, and receive appropriate treatment so that they can continue to practice good medicine. The recovery rate of physicians (and airline pilots) addicted to alcohol and/or drugs is around 80 percent, the highest in the treatment field. As one psychiatrist puts it, "It's because they have something big to lose—their license."[18]

Addicted Gay Men and Lesbians

Why is it that a disproportionate number of lesbians and gay men are addicted to alcohol and other drugs? Homosexuals suffer from the same types of personal and relationship problems and body chemistry experienced by those who are heterosexual. But, they often carry an added burden of social pressures, rejections, and self-esteem damage because of widespread unfortunate judgmental attitudes toward their homosexuality. Among the stresses that contribute significantly to their vulnerability to become addicted to alcohol and other drugs is the frequent need to hide their homosexuality and intimate relationships, both important dimensions of their personal identity. Many still live with the real fears of losing jobs and rejection by their family, community, and congregation if they choose to come out of the closet. For gays, including many who are in long-term committed relationships, the AIDS pandemic adds the cumulative grief from frequent deaths of dear friends and lovers. For those not in committed relationships who have multiple sex partners, there is the constant fear of contracting the HIV virus and eventually the incurable disease AIDS. All these pressures tend to exacerbate the emotional suffering that is among the complex causes of addictions.

There are three hopeful developments within gay and lesbian communities. One is that the AIDS tragedy has generated networks of mutual caring and support among both gay people and their families. Another is that there now are special, well-attended A.A. meetings where addicted gays and lesbians can give one another understanding and support in coping constructively with the special problems generated by their sexual orientation.[19] A third hopeful development is the new treatment, with several drugs used together, that is lengthening life expectancy with AIDS patients significantly.

Addicted Women

Any understanding of female addictions is fundamentally flawed if it ignores the impact of women living in a patriarchal, male-controlled society where most women have less power and prestige and fewer opportunities to use their full gifts than do most men. This sexist societal context generates some distinct dynamics in addiction patterns and their causes, as well as different experiences in treatment programs including A.A. Famed anthropologist Margaret Mead once wrote:

> In the modern American world, women live under different frustrations and face very different pressures. It should be obvious, then, that the situation in which women become vulnerable to the disease of alcoholism are in large measure peculiar to women and that they have special needs that must be met if they are to find their way back to normal, healthy living.[20]

Mead continues:

> I believe women can help other women who are troubled and getting into difficulties with alcohol. . . . Women, knowing best what women's frustrations and loneliness are, can talk straightforwardly with each other and help work out some better solutions.[21]

Mead's observations shed light on why some addicted women do not find traditional religious approaches to their recovery effective. An insightful novel entitled *Tales of Burning Love* by Louise Erdrich tells the story of the painful struggles of an alcoholic woman. Erdrich recalls:

Then straight bourbon got involved. Seeing Dr. Hakula, I went into a twelve step program and got in touch with my higher power. Then my higher power fizzled on me and my lower power came back strong.[22]

Fortunately, efforts to understand addicted women and develop recovery programs attuned to their special needs have received increased attention in recent years. Research has increased, paralleling the rising numbers of women needing help for addictions. The percentage of women in A.A. has risen steadily, and their average age declined since its founding. Now just over one-third of members are women, of whom over 40 percent are under age thirty.[23] These changes reflect two social trends—a rise in the number of hidden women alcoholics who have gained courage to come out, and a major increase in the number of women who use alcohol and drugs, especially prescription drugs, exposing more to the risk of addictions. These increases began after World War II and have risen sharply as more women join the male competitive rat race, learn to "drink like men," and become victims of what formerly were mainly male stress illnesses. Society's sexism breeds pervasive feelings of inferiority, isolation, low self-worth, and loneliness among many women, making them vulnerable to both psychological depression and abuse of mood-altering chemicals.

What Are the Significant Differences Between Male and Female Alcoholics?

An enzyme called alcohol dehydrogenase (ADH) may be among the physiological causes of alcoholism. It metabolizes some alcohol in most drinkers' stomachs before it enters their blood stream. Some studies suggest that women have less ADH in their stomachs so that they become more intoxicated than men of the same body weight with equivalent amount of alcohol. This inability to neutralize some of the alcohol in their stomachs means that women are more susceptible to alcohol-related diseases such as cirrhosis of the liver and high blood pressure. A study in France revealed that liver cirrhosis increased in women who consumed two or three drinks a day at the same rate as in men who had four to five drinks.

Women who drink heavily run two health risks not experienced by men. A study of eighty-six thousand female nurses, published in the *New England Journal of Medicine* in 1995, reported that those who had more than three drinks a week had a significantly greater risk of breast cancer. Because alcohol can cross the blood-brain barrier from mother to a fetus, the almost 70 percent of women who consume some alcohol during their pregnancies risk causing their babies to suffer fetal alcohol syndrome. Use of alcohol by the mother during pregnancy is the leading cause of mental retardation. There is no safe level of alcohol use during pregnancy and the heavier and longer the use, the greater the harmful effect on the fetus. Women who drink addictively during pregnancy put their infants at major risk. The harmful effects of binge drinking on fetuses may not show up until much later in the child's life. Mothers who use cocaine during pregnancy are responsible for the increasing number of cocaine-addicted infants being born. There is a consensus among physicians that if a women is pregnant, thinking of, or at risk of getting pregnant, the only wise decision is not to drink or use street drugs at all.[24]

Some studies have suggested that women who become addicted tend to be more disturbed psychologically than men. However, if this is true, it may not be because of their having greater psychopathology before becoming addicted. Instead, their heightened disturbance may result from the fact that women tend to continue the increasing psychosocial and physical deterioration of their addictions longer before they seek help. Their reluctance to seek outside help results in part from the greater social stigma for women than men of being seen as drunks. Many women with alcohol and drug problems do not seek help because of their fear of losing custody of their children. It probably is true that the onset of alcoholism tends to occur somewhat later for women than men, but women's addictions often develop more rapidly.

Another difference among women alcoholics is that having an alcoholic parent, sibling, or spouse is more common than among male alcoholics. Still another difference is that the vast majority of women remain with alcoholic husbands, whereas the exact opposite is true of men who have alcoholic wives. It may also be true that more women join in their husband's addictive behaviors and become addicted themselves, than vice versa.

In one study, twice as many women as men could identify a specific life crisis such as divorce, death of a parent, or an unhappy love affair that seemed to precipitate excessive drinking. Because physicians prescribe mood-altering drugs much more often to women than men, and because drug dependence usually can be hidden more easily and longer than alcoholism, polyaddictions involving both prescribed drugs and alcohol, seem to be more prevalent among female than male alcoholics. Though the gap between the number of women and men who drink alone at home has narrowed as more and more women work and drink outside their homes with other women as well as with men, it probably is still true that a greater proportion of women alcoholics do solitary drinking, especially single women who live alone.

Psychologist Anne Wilson Schaef, whose theories were discussed earlier in chapter 2, provides some help in understanding the sociocultural causes of women's addictions. You will recall that she holds that what she calls the "white male system" controls and defines traditional women's and men's identity, and also defines how institutions function in our society. This hierarchical system is the generic cause of addictions in both genders. In her discussion of codependence, an addictive relationship pattern suffered by many more women than men, Schaef sheds light on addictive family systems and the societal causes of women's chemical addictions.

Psychologist Charlotte Davis Kasl has substantiated the special issues and needs of addicted women. Kasl describes herself as "a feminist, Quaker, psychologist, healer, peace and justice activist, and a woman on my own spiritual journey." In *Women, Sex, and Addiction: A Search for Love and Power* and a subsequent volume *Many Roads, One Journey: Moving Beyond the Twelve Steps*,[25] she explores in depth both sexism and the special therapeutic needs of addicted women. She identifies the social roots of both addictions and codependency in the sexism, racism, classism, and poverty of our hierarchical and patriarchal society.

Kasl also provides an insightful critique of the traditional male orientation of the Twelve Steps including their religious belief system. This traditional bias makes these approaches less than fully adequate as a path to liberation and empowerment for many women. She offers an alternative path to recovery that she regards as more responsive to the needs of many women than traditional Twelve Step programs. (See chapter 8.)

Having examined a variety of groups who are at special risk of developing addictions, we can now identify some important implications. The most important implication is that both treatment and preventive education programs will be more effective if crucial social context factors are taken into account in designing these approaches. Programs that ignore these factors, responding to addictions as though victims lived in a social vacuum, will be much less effective. Preventing addictions among groups at high risk obviously is often difficult but also very important. Because millions of persons in these hypervulnerable groups are members of congregations, imaginative approaches are needed to prevent addictions from developing and to treat them as quickly as possible when they do develop.

PART II
Exploring Some Religious Approaches to Addictions

CHAPTER 6

How Religion Helps Low-Bottom Alcoholics and Drug Addicts

A street of homeless, forgotten people can be found in all large cities in North America and most such cities around the world. In some places these streets are called Skid Row, the term used in this chapter. These are catch-basins that collect many rejects of our social system. Hope has died for many of the street people who live there. In such blighted areas one finds a variety of low-bottom alcoholics, drug addicts, homeless mentally ill persons, exprisoners unable to find employment, poor single mothers and two-parent families with children, and runaway and throwaway teens and children. In recent years, with huge gaps being torn in the U.S. government's economic and mental health safety nets, homelessness has mushroomed to epidemic dimensions all over this country.[1] Some cities have responded (with a nonsolution) by passing an ordinance forbidding "urban camping," a cruel euphemism for sleeping on the streets.

When I spent several days unshaven and in old clothes on the Bowery, New York's Skid Row, in the early 1950s, most of the homeless with whom I talked and attended rescue mission services were low-bottom male alcoholics. In recent years the situation has changed radically, although excessive drinking and drug abuse (of the social desperation type), are still among the causes contributing to much homelessness. Cities have used urban redevelopment in an effort to put Skid Rows out of existence. The result has been to create many smaller Skid Rows in those cities. When I did my research on the Bowery, women were rarely seen there. Today, the scope of homelessness has spread widely—it includes both genders, is geographically more diverse, and the types of problems the homeless suffer are more complex. Many more impoverished women and even some parents with children are now among the homeless. Homeless people can be found living in old cars, under bridges, and in public shelters usually located in the inner city. The majority of homeless alcoholics are polyaddicted, with cocaine (especially crack cocaine) and heroin being favorite drugs. Some use alcohol when they can't get cocaine. Some are homeless for relatively short periods—until they get a job or gain more public assistance that enables them to rent a place to live. The director of a network of rescue missions estimates that about one-third of the thousands of people living in their facilities around the country are veterans. Many are psychiatric casualities from the tragic war in Vietnam.

John Cheydleur, a knowledgeable Salvation Army leader with expertise on addictions, points out that a few decades ago most of the men they served were alcoholics who walked in off the street to get a bowl of soup and a place to sleep.[2] The average age was substantially older than today. Many who came had worked for pay and lived with their families before they became addicted and homeless. They often had more education and had learned more about how to cope with adult responsibilities than is true today. Younger crack addicts often become addicted in their midteens causing their psychosocial development to be fixated at that age. Now, in their twenties, they are homeless and addicted. Many come to the Salvation Army Adult Rehabilitation Centers or Harbor Light Missions from detoxification centers after being taken there by the police for crimes like robbery to support their addiction. Unlike some older addicts today, as well as in the past, they have little education, fewer job skills, and more often lack families to which they might return. All this has caused the Salvation Army, as well as progressive rescue missions, to modify their approaches to respond to their changing needs.

Overcrowding in state mental hospitals around this country was slashed drastically in the 1980s when the major tranquilizers transformed the treatment of some mental illnesses. Hundreds of thousands of mentally ill patients were released with the public expectation that they would receive outpatient treatment. But because the mental health safety net was subsequently downsized drastically, countless victims of mental illnesses have joined the homeless population wandering on the streets. Some estimates place the mentally ill at 40 percent of all homeless people. In our affluent country, this avoidable tragedy is compounded because most homeless mentally ill persons receive no sustained treatment by outpatient mental health facilities.

To picture the historical context of alcoholism and homelessness, the following is a description of the Bowery on New York's lower East Side as it was when I did part of my doctoral research on religious approaches to alcoholism there. I will describe it in the present tense. It is a run-down street, no longer canopied by the metallic arms of the Third Avenue elevated train but still lined with noisy dives, cheap flophouses, pawnshops, used clothing stores, and rescue missions. In warehouse doorways ragged, vermin-infested men lie in alcoholic oblivion. A huddle of disheveled individuals talk raucously as they pass about a bottle of

Sneaky Pete—a cheap wine fortified with rubbing alcohol. Human dere-licts wander aimlessly up and down the street milling together like swarming insects. Two, in the belligerent stage of drunkenness, shout curses and exchange blows. A crowd gathers to watch. Every few feet panhandlers ply their trade, begging from all likely prospects who are better dressed. In Dead Man's Alley a "squeeze" is in progress—Sterno is being warmed over a fire of newspapers before squeezing it through a sock to make a drink called Pink Lady. As one watches the scene, the words of a young alcoholic come to mind. Out of the pain and pathos of his own tragic experiences, he described the Bowery (and by implication, other Skid Rows, then and today) as "this dirty, dead trail of a thousand broken dreams in a thousand broken minds and bodies."[3]

The outstanding, and now considered classic research on homelessness was done by sociologist Robert Straus who studied 203 homeless men who came to the Salvation Army social center in New Haven, Connecti-cut. Many of his findings are still relevant for older and chronically home-less alcoholic men.[4] Unfortunately, the several studies of homeless men have not been paralleled by comparable studies of homeless women. Straus found that the typical chronically homeless man left his parents' home at an early age, often following the death of a parent or a serious conflict. Early emotional instability and deficient socialization are charac-teristic. He stopped his education between the seventh and eight grades. He has usually either never married or is widowed or divorced. He is con-stantly on the move, going from one Skid Row to another and rarely stay-ing in one place more than a few months. Denominationally he is either Catholic or Protestant, almost never Jewish. Concerning attitudes toward religion, Straus reports that "Nearly all of the men spoke of their religion in the past tense. They felt that they had lost touch with their faith and expressed little interest in church attendance." Many of them are chroni-cally unemployed and unemployable. Others work sporadically and/or seasonally at various unskilled jobs for minimum pay. For the rest of the year they are "on the bum."

Are low-bottom chemically dependent persons homeless because they are addicted, or are they addicted because they are homeless? Sometimes the answer is one or the other, but more often it is both. Straus found that heavy drinking preceded and seemed to be a contributing cause of home-lessness in two-thirds of the men. In the other third, heavy drinking fol-lowed and seemed to result from the painful condition of homelessness. He concludes: "Drinking seemed to be one of the several causes or one of the several results of homelessness."

It is important to remember that chronic homelessness often is a pathological sociopsychological problem in itself, that homelessness and chemical dependence often arise from some of the same causes, and that each condition tends to enhance the other. For the person whose ability to relate meaningfully to others has been impaired by severe early emotional deprivation, alcohol and drugs, but also homelessness, are ways of escaping the pressures of adult interpersonal living with which they are unable to cope. Living closely with others is too demanding for many such undersocialized people, whereas homelessness is a lifestyle that demands relatively little except learning survival skills. Because homelessness removes not only the responsibilities but also the satisfactions of living closely with others, chronically homeless persons, drifting and rootless, have little or no motivation for abstaining from drugs and alcohol. The more they become divorced from normal life, the more they must resort to chemical pseudosatisfactions. Thus the vicious spiral of homelessness and addiction is established.

Another classic study was made of 187 revolving-door alcoholics—low-bottom alcoholics who are constantly in and out of jail as a result of repeated drunkenness-related arrests. Here is a summary of what was discovered about such persons:

> Our study has shown him to be the product of a limited social environment and a man who never attained more than a minimum of integration in society. He is and has always been at the bottom of the social and economic ladder; he is isolated, uprooted, unattached, disorganized, demoralized, and homeless, and it is in this context that he drinks to excess. . . . He is the least respected member of the community. . . . He never attained, or has lost, the necessary respect and sense of human dignity on which any successful program of treatment and rehabilitation must be based. He is captive in a sequence of lack or loss of self-esteem, producing behavior which causes him to be further disesteemed. Unless this cycle is partially reversed, we doubt that any positive results can be attained.[5]

Today, many knowledgeable people share a similar pessimistic view because of the added number of mentally ill and former prisoners who have joined the homeless.

The Skid Row existence provides a kind of solution or at least survival adjustment for many of the chronically homeless who live there. Alcohol and drugs are major ingredients in this solution. Heavy drinking is regarded as normal, and the few abstainers are viewed with suspicion.

Many of Straus's interviewees said that alcohol provided them with congenial companions and, in their present situation, let them forget their lack of possessions and status. Alcohol also can serve as an alibi. When confronted by criticism or remorse, they state that they are afflicted by the unfortunate drink or drug habit.

The fellowship of Skid Row, facilitated by alcohol and drugs, is another ingredient in this solution. This is a special kind of fellowship in which one can participate or withdraw at any time. The Bowery has its unwritten code, its street slang, and when I was there, its newspaper—*The Bowery News: The Voice of Society's Basement.* Little ad hoc groups of men band together for the purpose of obtaining a constant supply of alcohol and drugs. This urgent common need is the bond that unites them for a short time.

When I began to understand the many ways in which consciousness-changing chemicals are means of survival for some homeless men, it became clear why a majority of those with whom I talked said they had no desire to stop. This does not mean that Skid Row inhabitants necessarily are satisfied with their lot. Those who are there temporarily, because of the availability of free or inexpensive food and housing, have not incorporated being homeless into their identity. They seem to hate being there. But even many of the chronically homeless are not satisfied. Again and again those with whom I talked expressed dissatisfaction. One man advised me: "Listen, Slim, don't hit this street like I did." A seaman said, "I'm just waiting until I can get off this binge and back on a ship." Even though most are not satisfied with their solution, it is the only one that they see open to them, at least for the present. For some who have adjusted to chronic homelessness, their dissatisfactions are outweighed by the rewards of chemical solutions.

Other factors also make Skid Row the solution of choice. The flophouse, known colloquially as the scratch house, makes the Bowery the cheapest place in the city to get shelter from cold and rain. But for chronic alcoholics, if a choice between a flop and a bottle of cheap booze is necessary, the flop usually rates a poor second. Sleeping indoors is a luxury, alcohol is a necessity. The ambulance from the city hospital is another part of the Bowery solution. The city hospital or detoxification centers are to Skid Row alcoholics what private, expensive clinics are to financially solvent alcoholics. When injured by street violence or suffering from alcoholic delirium, the Bowery alcoholic is taken to the city hospital. When released, his first stop may be the nearest gin mill. The "dead wagon" from the city morgue makes regular rounds on Skid Rows. After a freezing night it goes about its grim business of collecting the newspaper-covered remains of those too drunk to find shelter.

For many of the low-bottom, chronically chemically dependent on Skid Rows, the possibility of rehabilitation is minimal if not nonexistent. Many have gone far beyond the bottom described earlier. The downward spiral of progressive addictions has swirled through years of physical and mental deterioration resulting in one or more diseases of chronic alcoholism such a polyneuropathy and cirrhosis of the liver. For these persons, what is desperately needed is humane custodial care. Fortunately, studies have revealed that many Skid Row addicts are not in the final stages of their drinking and drugging careers. Some have just arrived and, as noted, others are there only temporarily. The possibility of helping these persons obviously is much greater than is the case of seriously deteriorated addicts. Some of this group are younger and potentially employable if they learn how to stay sober and live more responsibly, even though they probably are unskilled occupationally. They are not beyond the possibility of restoration to a socially constructive life.[6]

It is with the various kinds of homeless people who still are about 70 percent males that over two hundred rescue missions and more than one hundred Salvation Army centers on Skid Rows across the country do their ministry. They are a constructive part of the Skid Row solution. At the very least they offer some food and clothing, opportunity for delousing, and a warm place to sleep in winter. Beyond this, they hold up the promise of release from addictions through rehabilitation, as well as their versions of spiritual healing and salvation.

The following description of the Bowery Mission is presented both to show the historical context and to describe major aspects of such programs that continue to be used to help low-bottom, homeless addicts today. It is well to remember that rescue missions vary greatly. Some are more enlightened by contemporary knowledge concerning addictions and are not as rigid in their fundamentalist belief systems as the one described here.

The Rescue Mission Approach to Addictions

A raw wind is whipping up the street in front of the Bowery Rescue Mission. Here is a five-story stone building on which a large neon sign blazes forth the name of the mission. Smaller signs read: "A Friend to the Friendless"; "Free Facilities in the Basement, Clothing, Washing, Mending, Shaving, Shower Bath, Fumigation"; "Gospel Meeting Every Night, 7:30." If one enters the chapel, one immediately notices the characteristic blend of alcohol and body odor. The organ plays old hymns. The chapel is nearly full. Here and there a man scratches vigorously as others doze in alcoholic slumber. Behind the back pew is an array of paper sacks and bundles tied in dirty newspaper. The worshipers have deposited their worldly possessions for the duration of the service. Over the pulpit at the front is a dark blue banner with bright yellow and red letters that proclaim, "Jesus Saves." One looks at the faces of broken and defeated men. Eyes seem to stare in cold, bloodshot cynicism.

The organist has stopped playing. The evangelist begins to pray asking God to reveal the proper hymn with which to begin the service. The prayer ended, the hymn "Nearer the Cross" is announced. Singing by the congregation is spotty. Another gospel song follows. Then a young woman evangelist testifies in song with the selection "It Is Well with My Soul." After a heartfelt rendition of the song she asks rhetorically, "How about your soul, friend? Is it well with your soul?" The leader of the service steps to the pulpit and says, "The important thing is to stop trying to do things in your own strength and let Christ take full possession of your life. Christ, he's the best friend we have." The congregation then sings, "What a Friend We Have in Jesus." The leader tells how he was saved from a life of gambling, alcohol, and sin. Several more recent converts, now a part of the staff, then testify. The leader then invites testimonies from anyone who wishes to tell what Christ has done for him. A sprinkling of short testimonies comes from the audience. One grateful man stands near the back and says, "I thank God that I can say through the blessed blood of our Lord Jesus that I'm sure I'll meet my dear mother in heaven."

After the testimonies the leader begins his fundamentalist sermon including the following:

> I feel led to discuss the two highways—the broad road that leads to hell and destruction and the narrow highway that leads to heaven and eternal life. We get on the highway of righteousness only by the Lord Jesus, the way of the cross. He is our guide who takes us by the hand. Christ bridged the great gulf separating the two highways and therefore can snatch you from the highway of destruction over to the highway leading to heaven. Come to Jesus and say, "Lord, I'm a sinner," and he'll get you across the great chasm. I beg you, heed the word of God. Some of you are waiting to die, but it's not over then! The way of destruction goes directly into hell! *(A passionate tremor appears in the speaker's voice.)* Put your sins under his blood. I have no

fear when I die. My loving Savior will meet me and take care of me. Can you say, if the Lord calls you today, "Goodbye, world; I'm glad to leave the world and go to be with Jesus"? Can you say that and know that you will?

The message is followed by the altar call. The congregation is led in prayer. While heads are bowed, those who wish intercessory prayer on their behalf are asked to "slip up their hands." The leader encourages response by recognizing the hands that go up, "There's one in the back." "I see your hand over on the side, brother." Then a hymn, "Almost Persuaded," is sung. Between each stanza the invitation to come forward and be saved is repeated. The wonderful blessings of "answering God's invitation" are presented with increasing vigor and volume as are the awful consequences of refusing. The preacher tells about a former crony on the Bowery who postponed coming to the altar one night too many, was hit by a truck, and "went to a Christless grave!" Pointing at his audience, he asks, "Are you ready for heaven?" When "Almost Persuaded" is exhausted, "Jesus Is Calling," another invitation hymn, is announced. The leader described the death of his mother, perhaps awakening old feelings in some of the targets of his appeals. While this is going on, former converts canvass the audience, fishing for converts—the "almost persuaded."

Those who go forward have a worker who kneels beside them to help "pray them through." The worker tells them how Christ saved and cleansed him and helps the penitent to say a prayer, however short or faltering. If the procedure is successful, according to one worker, the penitent experiences a powerful emotional experience of forgiveness, release, and exaltation. The altar call, or invitation, usually lasts about fifteen minutes, but it may go on longer if a substantial number have not been converted.

The essence of the rescue mission approach to alcoholism and drug addictions is contained in one word—salvation. Salvation, as understood by mission thinking, consists of the kind of religious experience described above. To produce this experience is the ultimate goal of all mission activities. These activities may be divided into two categories: (1) the religious services including gospel meetings such as described and smaller prayer meetings; and (2) the work of guidance, and physical and social help aimed at relieving suffering and, it is hoped, leading to rehabilitation.

The gospel meeting is the heart of the mission program. In order to receive food or shelter in some missions, recipients must first attend the religious services. After the service at the Bowery Mission, I joined with the others who filed downstairs silently for supper consisting of soup and bread. After supper those who could be accommodated were given cots on which to sleep. (I left for my home.) Before I left, I was told that the next morning those who stayed could shave and shower and have breakfast. Then the converts of the previous evening would be interviewed briefly by a mission worker, himself a recovered alcoholic. A few questions about the convert's employment record and intentions would be asked. If converts seem to offer possibilities of permanent recovery, they are assigned to a bed and locker in one of the dormitories. Before they sleep there they must be fumigated. They may be invited to stay at the mission until they can get back on their feet, but they are free to leave if they wish. If they need used clothing and medical attention from the part-time clinic maintained at the mission, they receive these.

If the convert decides to stay at the mission, it becomes his home for a while. He may be assigned work around the mission and, when he is recovered enough, is sent out on small jobs obtained by the mission's employment service. He is expected to attend regular Bible study, prayer, and gospel meetings. After a short time he will be asked to testify at a meeting. Members of the mission staff are available for guidance on practical problems and directive counseling on personal issues. In this way, it is hoped that the conversion experiences will be solidified and strengthened. After several weeks of testing, converts may be transferred from the mission itself to the Home Uptown, a house where about twenty converts who seem to be making the grade are allowed to go. Here they have a room of their own and a closet for clothes. More important, they now have an address that has no stigma attached. They are off the Bowery. From here they seek employment, often helped by the mission. If it is feasible, mission staff members try to facilitate a reconciliation between converts and their families. The goal of mission therapy is to save people's souls but also to help them move out of homelessness as well as addictions. This is based on the realistic recognition that as long as addicts stay on Skid Row, unless they stay and work at the missions, their chances of long-term recovery are small.

Some rescue missions maintain fellowship groups for former alcoholics. Alcoholics Victorious, founded at the Chicago Christian Industrial League, now has chapters in rescue missions in various cities. The groups hold weekly meetings at which members give testimonies, discuss personal problems, and help one another. Like the closed meetings of A.A. and N.A., only addicts can belong. The program of Alcoholics Victorious will be discussed in chapter 8.

The Dynamics of Mission Therapy

How do rescue missions function in terms of their dynamics? Much of the analysis that follows also applies to any fundamentalist revival meeting. Gospel meetings and mission evangelical programs can be analyzed in terms of four stages: *crisis, preparation, surrender-acceptance,* and *consolidation.* It is necessary to prepare the individual for the powerful emotional crisis experiences that sometimes produce long-term and even permanent sobriety. There are several reasons for this. The mission clientele is composed largely of people who have little desire to stop drinking. For non-homeless alcohol and drug addicts, severe crises are "bottoms" during which they are relatively open to help. For many homeless addicts, life is one long crisis. They have, so to speak, used up their "bottoms" without finding help. Their psychological condition is in the realm beyond remorse and hope. It is necessary to revive these long-repressed emotions if a crisis is to be induced.

Preparation is also necessary because as studies have shown, most of them look with contempt on the very missions from which they receive food, clothing, and shelter. Religious services are something to be endured in order to get a much needed flop or a bowl of soup. Unless this negative attitude can be transcended, it is unlikely that these addicted people will respond in the way desired by the mission.

Group singing of old hymns and gospel choruses is important in preparing some for conversion. Studies in the psychology of music have shown that rapid, loud, rhythmic group singing of songs that stress the repetition of a few simple ideas tends to produce lowered inhibition and enhances suggestibility, a sense of closeness, emotionality, and a tendency toward impulsive action. Under the influence of a rapidly moving revival atmosphere, punctuated by the singing of the simple, emotional lyrics and rhythmic music of what may be old, familiar hymns and gospel choruses, the defensive shell of some may be gradually softened and they begin to feel more a part of what is going on. Then, too, the singing of old salvation hymns may awaken in some long-forgotten emotional associations from their prehomeless life. A convert recalled: "I didn't think much of the services at first. But when they sang, 'Jesus, Savior, pilot me over life's tempestuous sea,' it struck a spark somewhere. We used to sing that at home around the piano."

Personal testimonies also are a powerful form of preparation. The testifiers describe themselves as having lived on Skid Row and tell of their sins and degradation. This may help some derelict identify with them and then, in spite of themselves, begin to listen to what is being said. There is a strong element of positive suggestion in the participation of testifiers scattered (probably by staff members) throughout the audience. This participation helps mold some within the aggregation of individuals who enter the chapel into a unified pliable group. What is more, the testimonies may awaken a glimmer of hope in a few hopeless listeners— "Maybe there's a chance I can do it too."

Those in the mission pew are assailed by a barrage of emotionally charged illustrations and ideas that serve to reactivate slumbering fears and guilts. Frequent mention of home and mother may awaken memories of life prior to their homeless state. Lurid threats of eternal punishment, with personal illustrations of those who died unsaved, are sprinkled through mission sermons and interviews. One mission superintendent quoted the counsel he had given to an unconverted man: "I told him, 'Unless you accept the Lord, you're on your way to hell! You'll burn! You're still a little green, but you'll burn, not just smolder.' Jesus said you must be born again—not may but must!"

The foundation of most mission thinking and speaking is what could be called the *moralistic assumption*. This is the conviction that both chemical dependency and homelessness are the result of one thing—sin—for which addicts are responsible. Addictions are sinful habits acquired by the sin of using alcohol and drugs. Homelessness results from the addictions. Although there are numerous exceptions in more enlightened missions, this conception has stood largely unshaken from the days of Jerry McAuley, the "father of the rescue mission."[7] A revealing encounter with A.A. ideology was described to the author by one mission employee: "A fellow from A.A. came in claiming that alcoholism isn't a sin but a sickness. I opened God's Word to 1 Corinthians 6:10 and Galatians 5:21 and proved to him that it was listed by God as a sin along with murder and stealing."

By proclaiming the moralistic assumption with passion, mission evangelists make head-on attacks on low-bottom addicts' defenses. By stimulating guilts and fears under the influence of group emotion, they may be able in some cases to crack the defensive alibi systems. When this happens, individuals are exposed to their raw feelings of self-contempt and self-rejection. They are made to feel as miserable, hopeless, and helpless as possible, while their bodies are wracked with the impact of prolonged inebriety, withdrawal symptoms, terrible diet, and illnesses from sleeping in doorways. The rescue technique thus aims at creating a "bottom," an emotional crisis in which they may temporarily be a little more open to help. Into this physical pain, emotional chaos, and spiritual gloom, a shining hope is projected. There is a way out! Sinners can do nothing for themselves, but there is an all-powerful savior who cares. All that persons must do is repent and accept this wonderful savior's promises and salvation will be theirs. The pressure of opposites is created by presenting eternal punishment and eternal beatitude side-by-side with the hope of producing the desired response.

Effective therapy for homeless alcoholics must provide substitute rewards for abstinence at least as great as the rewards of excessive drinking and and drugging that do not require greater effort than drinking requires. Salvation, as understood by mission ideologies, measures up on both scores. It requires only a decision to repent. God through Christ does the rest. It is quick, relatively effortless, and carries the rewarding offers of acceptance and dependency, of hope and physical help. For some lonely, wretched, emotionally starved addicts, this kind of womblike dependency carries great appeal.

A transforming religious experience of "being saved" is itself a dynamic reward. If listeners have been caught up in the rhythmic singing, the testimonies, the fervent prayers, the appeals to fear, to guilt, to memory, to hope, to dependency—in short, if they have felt the lift and lure of forgiveness in a pulsating religious group where the collective group psychology prevails, they have found a substitute value for alcohol. Religious ecstasy provides an alternative path to feelings of transcendence, expansiveness and larger life that in the very distant past may have been brought by alcohol and drugs.

The altar call is a masterpiece of juxtaposing negative and positive suggestions. The various psychological-spiritual threats of the evening are recapitulated. Then follows the opportunity for a series of positive responses in which persons are urged to move from a small to a larger and larger "yes." The first is merely raising a hand when heads are bowed to request prayer. This intercessory prayer in itself has a powerful influence in that it focuses the feeling of divine attention and caring on each individual. Then the leader may ask for those who want to be saved to raise their hands. As hands go up, he repeats the nest egg stimulus of "Thank you. Yes, brother. Three more back there." The third positive response is that of going forward. A hymn suggesting this response is sung (e.g., "Just as I am . . . I come, I come"), while all stand. The fact that everyone is standing makes it easier to get started to the front. The resistance of those who are wavering may be worn down by repetition and by personal invitations from those who are fishing for converts.

When persons go forward and do so with a glimmer of sincerity, they have already taken a tremendous step. For this action means that they are motivated strongly enough to defy the opinion of their cronies who look with scorn on those who "take a dive for Jesus." Even more difficult, they must relax their own defenses for the moment and be at least a little open to receiving help. The individual attention of the worker who helps "pray them through," plus the act of praying themselves for help from God, may bring them to a conversion experience. It is impossible to describe fully the powerful religious experience that may take place in converts. Those who attempt to put it into words tell of sudden release from guilt, of inner cleanness, of wonderful elation. They tell of feeling back home after years of spiritual wandering. Some tell of sudden release from the craving for alcohol. After his conversion Jerry McAuley told of feeling that "life was all new."

It seems probable that it is the emotional intensity of such an experience combined with intense fear and guilt, plus hope that generates the crises and the offer of supernatural help that produces the surrender. The conversion experience may well be psychologically analogous to the following: Children who have been rebelling against parental authority find the estrangement unbearable; they rush back into parents' arms. The parent figures embrace them, and the inner child feels a wonderful euphoria. They are accepted by the authority upon whom they are dependent. In the mission setting, parent figures will take care of them as long as they are obedient to parental demands. Drug-dependent people who experience transforming conversions are no longer fighting authority. They feel accepted and are soon invited to also represent the authority of God as they move into testifying and perhaps eventually becoming mission workers.

The mission structure provides an environment in which the conversion experience may be consolidated. The dependence on an Almighty Power is buttressed and symbolized by concrete dependence on the mission workers and on the physical surroundings. Food and shelter are tangible evidences of the mission's parental care. For shaky new converts the mission organization provides opportunities to become a part of the in-group where they are both accepted and needed. It is through continuing experiences in the religious groups that their initial religious experiences are consolidated. They learn the mission language, belief system, and methods. They thus become members of an exclusive fellowship, the "saved" as distinguished from the great unwashed. Continued membership depends on compliance with its moral demands. One of the demands is abstinence, understood as a by-product of salvation.

If born-again converts stay converted, they turn away from worldly vices. Abstinence is rewarded by God through God's group. Social controls are reestablished or learned for the first time. Being among the saved, converts come to believe they are uniquely empowered to save others. Because of the ambivalence toward authority of many chemically dependent persons, the shift from helped to helper is important for the consolidation and continuance of their rehabilitation experience. In addition, the new role provides outlets for unresolved hostilities and aggression by turning these energies against sin and helping save sinners. Converts now have a group-approved channel for their aggressive feelings and energies.

How Effective Is the Mission Therapy Approach?

The assumption throughout this book is that no analysis of religious approaches to addictions can be complete if it leaves out the creative power of the divine Spirit. I believe that all healing, whatever its mode, depends on this power. This power is equally available to all religious and nonreligious approaches to addictions. Yet some are much more effective than others. The question then is this: Why are religious approaches more or less open channels for the healing forces that are available in the universe? More specifically, how effective is a given approach in utilizing religious resources to produce and maintain sobriety?

The incomplete evidence that is available suggests that mission approaches are effective in producing initial sobriety for some by arresting the *runaway symptom* aspect of addictions. Given the uphill struggles that homeless addicts have in achieving sobriety, it is impressive if even a very small percentage of those exposed to this treatment achieve periods of sobriety. In its yearly report, the Bowery Mission reports several thousands of *professed conversions*. Implied in the word *professed* is the recognition that not all conversions are sincere. One of the alcoholics I interviewed in depth told of drawing matchsticks to see who was going to be saved so that the meeting would end and the meager meal be served. Then there are the "mission stiffs," those who survive for years by exploiting one mission after another, becoming very skillful in going through the motions of conversion. Even if one makes generous deductions for these phony conversions, there probably is still a sizable group that responds sincerely to mission approaches. This supposition is supported by those who have had extensive firsthand experience with missions. For example, a member of A.A. whose attitude toward missions was sharply critical admitted, "A hell of a lot are sobered up at such places."

When one considers the total number who attend mission meetings, the percentage of conversions is probably very low. Obviously many homeless alcoholics do not respond to mission-structured therapy. The use of food and shelter as bait to get the alcoholic into the religious services, and the general tone of those services, probably enhances the resentment of religious institutions for many, making it more difficult to reach them with other religious help. Further, in many cases mission moralism seems to stimulate addicts' hostility and defensiveness rather than their sense of responsibility. Instead of cracking their defenses, the steamroller attack merely makes their defenses more rigid. The attitude of general resentment toward missions, which exists among many Skid Row people, is in part a reaction to the battering of their ego defenses and self-esteem to which they must expose themselves to get the mission's much needed food and shelter.

The mainstream mission understanding of addictions and homelessness are grossly inadequate, overlooking nearly all that contemporary scientific and therapeutic understanding has to tell about these two phenomena. Their naive moralism can be maintained only by ignoring that inebriety is as much a symptom as a cause of the disturbed life of the addicted; that chemical addictions are complex diseases involving physical, cultural, and sociopsychological as well as moral and spiritual factors; and that homelessness in itself is often a complex symptom of psychological and family problems, not the simple product of excessive drinking and drug use.

This fundamentalist conception of the human situation—the nature of sin, free will, salvation, and responsibility—as it relates to addictions is philosophically, theologically, and psychologically inadequate. If depth psychology has demonstrated anything, it has shown that human behavior, and mental and physical illnesses are never simply a matter of freely choosing between simple alternatives. Every act is conditioned by early life experiences that shaped the personality. Untrammeled free will, in the sense that it is used in much mission thought, does not exist. The concept is especially inapplicable to addictive-compulsive illnesses. The more driven persons are, the more their actions are controlled by inner compulsions, the less freedom of choice they have in the areas of their addictions. The mission's treatment of their problems as simple moral dereliction must drive many alcoholics away from help by conveying a complete lack of understanding.

To the degree that missions have an exclusivistic attitude and practice, their level of effectiveness is reduced. If any group believes that theirs is the only valid approach to addictions, they deprive those they serve of the therapeutic resources available in networking with other treatments including Twelve Steps and medical resources. In problems as complex as substance addictions and homelessness, this myopic view is particularly unfortunate. It is important to point out however, that more enlightened rescue missions do make the resources of medicine and A.A. available as part of their programs.

What percentage of alcoholics who achieve initial sobriety are able to achieve long-term recovery through this approach? It is impossible to cite reliable statistical evidence, for, as one mission staff member put it when I inquired, "God keeps the records." Any mission can produce a group of individuals who are known to have remained abstinent over many years, including those who became staff members. But no one knows what percentage of the daily converts remain abstinent for a week, a month, a year, or five years. But all indications suggest that the percentage of long-term abstinence may be low.

A basic reason why mission-induced sobriety is often impermanent is that low-bottom homeless alcoholics are extremely difficult to help by any means. Beyond this, however, it is undoubtedly true that, in many cases, this approach does not deal with basic causes. Symptoms are shuffled and compulsive religion replaces compulsive drinking. Some converts give one the impression that their solution is decidedly brittle and that they must keep very busy saving others or their own solution is likely to collapse. Too much fear and repression of negative feelings is employed. Too little resolution of underlying problems seems to result from the experience, even though significant surface changes obviously occur.

The emotionalism of the rigid mission approach carries potential weaknesses as well as strengths. The clue to this is expressed in an alcoholic's autobiography in which he writes of "sprees of salvation."[8] For some, the mission experience is an emotional binge. Unless follow-up procedures are successful in sustaining peak experiences or bringing people down gradually, spiritual hangovers are apt to result. Out from under the influence of charismatic leaders and the surge of group emotion, some individuals cool sufficiently to rue their actions and resent the manner in which they were manipulated. Further, as Bill W. learned after the "hot flash" that began his sobriety, the primary emphasis on sudden, dramatic religious experiences leads to an underemphasis on the less dramatic but essential process of personal, spiritual, and interpersonal growth following the conversion.

Another barrier to permanent sobriety inheres in what might be called the *diminishing returns of authoritarianism.* Recall that a pivotal conflict in many addicts is between their need for and resentment of dependency.

Straus found that most of those he interviewed both valued the security of the Skid Row institution and felt hostile toward it. This is the inner struggle. As the initial euphoria of the conversion experience and acceptance by authority figures and God dims, the old conflicts exert pressure. The essence of mission therapy is dependence—on God and on the mission. As the need to defy authority grows, the chemically dependent may revert to their habitual defiance devices—alcohol and drugs. The authoritarianism of the mission approach was symbolized by one mission superintendent who said he paid his workers only a paltry amount each week because "that is all they can handle." Such benevolent authoritarianism is galling to anyone, especially those who are hypersensitive to domination and manipulation. Evangelistic aggressive manipulation may be a product of spiritually coated hostility and the unresolved repressed conflicts of the authority figures. On some level, this is conveyed to prospective converts, to the detriment of their sobriety, particularly longer-term sobriety. Resentment against mission evangelists also is derived from the perception of potential converts that they are seen only as opportunities to save more souls.[9]

A substantial percentage of converts who do achieve longer-term sobriety are never reassimilated into normal community living. Some remain institutionalized, living at the mission and doing its work. They have capitulated to permanently dependent relationships. The fundamental tenet of benevolent authoritarianism, "Do what I say and I'll take care of you," makes weaning from immature dependency difficult. Others slip back into the maelstrom of Skid Row. If converts are to succeed in leaving the mission and making the difficult transition out of long-term homelessness, the bridging environment of a half-way facility is essential. Fortunately, many missions have such facilities.

On the positive side it is well to remember that the healing power of God *is* mediated through the mission approach in some cases. It *does* help some addicts to long-term sobriety including a lesser number who become reassimilated into society. The philosophy of most missions recognizes accurately that healing for low-bottom chemically dependent persons must minister to their physical, vocational, as well as their spiritual needs; must involve profound personal reorientation; and must, if it is to be complete, return them to society. Whether they achieve these goals in many cases or not, the goals are valid. Even if a conversion involves the substitution of compulsive religion for compulsive drinking and drugging, there are real gains for individuals and society. Furthermore, by providing physical necessities, missions help ameliorate the grim lot of many homeless people, including some who never get sober.

It seems probable that in some cases emotionally intense conversion experiences produce at least a partial reorganization of personality conflicts. In 1930 L. Cody Marsh conducted an interesting experiment in group therapy with psychotics at Kings Park Mental Hospital on Long Island. His aim was to provide the "psychological equivalent of the revival on a secular level." He conducted therapeutic classes in which there was spirited group singing, rituals, inspirational lectures, and testimonials by patients who were making outstanding progress. After considerable experimentation, Marsh came to the conclusion that such group experiences had many positive results. Patients were motivated toward recovery and had a helpful release of their emotions. There is undoubtedly an element of this kind of group healing involved in the mission experiences of some homeless addicts. It is also well to remember that various missions differ in their approaches. Some are much more enlightened than others.

Repeated efforts have shown that homeless, low-bottom alcoholics and drug addicts are almost inaccessible to the usual outpatient treatment programs. Long-term inpatient treatment programs are necessary for them to recover. Such programs for those without health insurance are extremely scarce. In light of all this it is appropriate to be thankful for the degree to which the missions are successful in ameliorating the multiple tragedies of Skid Row.

The Salvation Army Approach to Addictions

The long history of the Salvation Army (SA or Sally, as it is known on some Skid Rows) has demonstrated persistent concern with the practical application of religious resources to help victims of social chaos, oppression, and addictions. From the beginning, there has been an ongoing commitment to help "the least, the last, and the lost" with "soup, soap, and salvation." This down-to-earth orientation led the Army from its inception into the field of alcoholism. Firsthand experiences in the squalor of London slums made the founders, William and Evangeline Booth, and their fellow Salvationists keenly sensitive to the problem. Booth agonized over the tragic plight of England's half million alcoholics. Their "effective deliverance" was the keystone of his earliest program of social reform as outlined in his magnum opus *In Darkest England and the Way Out.*[10]

Booth was far ahead of his time in understanding alcoholism as a disease, at least in some cases. In 1890 he wrote:

After a time the longing for drink becomes a mania. Life seems as insupportable without alcohol as without food. It is a disease often inherited, always developed by indulgence, but as clearly a disease as ophthalmia or stone.[11]

Booth was aware that there is a physical component in the disease and wrote of "treating the passion as a disease, as we should any other physical affection, bringing to bear upon it every agency, hygienic and otherwise, calculated to effect a cure."[12] Alcoholism has always been regarded by the Salvation Army as involving sin, but not in the naive sense of being simply the result of sinful failure of the individual alcoholic. Booth, in fact, spoke of alcohol as the only comfort of the downtrodden and regarded the saloon as "a natural outgrowth of our social conditions." Society, he pointed out, "greased the slope down which these poor creatures slide to perdition," and society therefore should take responsibility for helping them.

It is noteworthy that psychologist-philosopher William James, in his classic *Varieties of Religious Experience*, paid tribute to William Booth's genuine personal concern for society's rejects:

> General Booth . . . considers that the first vital step in saving outcasts consists in making them feel that some decent human being cares enough for them to take an interest in the question whether they are to rise or to sink.[13]

Through the years since its founding, the Sally has continued to evolve its ministry to addicted persons by experimenting with a wide variety of innovative strategies for helping them. In the early days "Drunkards' Rescue Brigades" were formed that went into the streets trying to help alcoholics. For a while, "Inebriates' Homes" and "Inebriates Colonies" were established. A unique experiment in mass outreach for alcoholics was tried in New York just before World War I. On a designated "Boozers' Day" as many as 1,200 alcoholics were rounded up in Skid Row areas and transported on double-decker buses to a great hall where they were exposed to a gospel meeting on a grand scale. In 1914 the converts of these meetings banded themselves into a fraternal organization devoted to the reclamation of drunkards, known by the intriguing name of United Order of Ex-Boozers. Today the SA has some 8,000 beds at 179 centers treating alcoholism and drug problems. Other than Twelve Step programs, this probably is the single largest religious program in the country that treats addictions.

On the surface, the program, clientele, and dynamics of the SA low-bottom addiction facilities have numerous similarities to those of rescue missions. The programs center on the salvation meeting, which seems to have much in common with the evangelistic meetings of the rescue mission, except that the tone and spirit usually are much more open and less judgmental. The programs of physical help and rehabilitation also have many parallels, and the dynamics of conversion experiences seem to be similar.

But, in spite of numerous apparent parallels with rescue missions, today's SA addiction programs are different in a variety of constructive ways. At the root of these differences is the enlightened understanding of the complexities of addictions by key SA leadership. Most higher officers seem to have an informed understanding of addictions and the needs, behavior, and rehabilitation of low-bottom addicts. Over the years, many SA officers have attended the well-known Summer Schools of Alcohol and Drug Studies. Those I have met evidenced both deep concern for addicted persons and broad knowledge about their problems.

Captain John R. Cheydleur, the SA social services leader who briefed me on their addiction programs, said that alcoholism is viewed as "a physical disease (like diabetes) but a disease with a spiritual cure." He said that the widely accepted SA view is that "A.A.'s understanding of alcoholism is probably true." Most SA leaders are comfortable with the psychiatric distinction between nonaddicted problem drinking and alcohol addiction. He pointed out that "drunkenness is a sin but alcoholism is a disease." Concerning the view that drunkenness is a sin, he noted that most Christian theology teaches that everyone is a sinner in one way or another. He said that the heart of SA's approach is spiritual because "people who get and stay well over time have a spiritual center."[14]

Other strengths are quite evident in the SA addiction programs at what are now called Adult Rehabilitation Centers (ARC) or Harbor Light Centers. The ARCs do not have treatment programs but rather focus on spiritual and practical aspects of rehabilitation, whereas the Harbor Light Centers do include treatment of the addictions. The fact that most if not all such SA centers have A.A. and N.A. groups as one integral part of their programs is an important strength of their programs.[15] The fact that the SA networks with hospitals and detoxification centers in two-way referrals enhances their effectiveness greatly. When addicts go to one of their facilities in need of detoxification or mental health treatments, staff members arrange to get them to the needed public facilities. After they receive this treatment, they often are referred back to the SA.

Another SA strength is that of the 112 Adult Rehabilitation Centers in the U.S., a dozen now include special women's programs and more are being added to meet the needs of the increasing number of women addicts. Still another strength is that most of the rehab staff are state certified alcoholism counselors (the standard credential now), whether they are officers with graduate degrees or firmly recovered substance abusers (about 50 percent each). Another SA achievement is that addiction rehab programs are designed to help the addict move through planned phases in ninety-day or six-month programs. The SA has developed a variety of related rehab resources including families-in-crisis services for domestic violence victims. Auxiliary programs like this have been possible because of the vision of key SA leaders and because 70 percent of their clients are sober and clean (meaning drug free) when they begin rehabilitation, having just been through detoxification.

Another strength of SA addiction programs is the wide recognition that converts in the rehabilitation process need a supportive fellowship group after leaving a facility. Many converts return to the SA centers regularly after they are reestablished in their communities. They assist the officers in conducting religious services and hold fellowship meetings for ongoing mutual support. Converts often continue to regard the center where they were "saved" as their spiritual home. The SA also provides facilities for converts who need to live in a transition setting as a bridge to help them move away from heavy dependence on the SA program and back into their community.

The ARCs are residential facilities that provide shelter, food, and structured work therapy for the male and female residents. During a given year thousands are served by the many ARC and Harbor Light Centers in this country. None of these facilities are labeled services for chemical-dependent persons because SA leaders have discovered that better results are obtained when they have more general labels. The shops in the ARCs engage in repairing large quantities of used clothing and furniture, the sale of which in SA Thrift Stores is a major source of income for their entire network of programs. Both ARCs and the Harbor Light Centers conduct regular religious services that follow the familiar Protestant revival meeting pattern. Residents at such centers may attend a gospel meeting one evening and an A.A. meeting the next.

Unlike rescue missions that usually are freestanding entities, the SA facilities for the homeless are a part of a wide network of installations and services. Their many therapeutic resources are all available for helping addicts who need them. The SA has a remarkable ministry in ninety-one countries around the world and is served by three million "soldiers". In the United States it has some 10,000 centers with various kinds of ministries carried on by 5,200 officers and 32,000 workers. They minister to the hungry, homeless, elderly, families, as well as to thousands of drug and alcohol abusers. The Family Service Departments, usually staffed by officers trained as social workers, do a great deal to help the families of addicted persons bring together the casework techniques with the spiritual resources. The officers in charge of a Skid Row facility often refer converted alcoholics to these family services, which provide counseling and otherwise assist in the recovery and reconciliation of the family.

The success of the SA approach is enhanced by its well-developed structures for consolidating conversion experiences. One aspect of this is its military structure. Studies conducted around World War II showed that some men who were problem drinkers before and after the war had little trouble during their period of military service. Apparently they found security and a sense of belonging in the authority-centered, hierarchical military structure. The Salvation Army's structure seems to serve a comparable function for some converts. The converts become a part of a worldwide military organization engaged in an all out war against sin and human suffering, including that associated with alcohol and drug abuse. They are made to feel uniquely equipped to save others and are given a challenging mission that is comparable to the Twelfth Step work in A.A. As soldiers or officers they must be absolutely obedient to their superiors. The organization provides for all their physical needs. The security in such a system has strong appeal, especially to dependent persons. Further, wherever a Salvationist goes, he is a part of an in-group that requires both obedience and abstinence from alcohol and drugs.

Another important SA strength, in contrast to some other religious approaches to chemical dependence, is that women have a strong and respected place among the leadership. The many women officers must be a major asset to the increasing numbers of chemically dependent women as well as dependent men who come for help. Empowering women leaders goes back to the Army's roots and the cofounder Catharine Booth. And from 1986 to 1993, the general overseeing the entire Salvation Army was a dynamic woman named Eva Burrows.

Unlike the less structured follow-up procedure of some rescue missions in the early 1940s, the Salvation Army has put its recovery principles into this series of nine Christ-centered steps paralleling some of the important Twelve Steps of A.A.-modeled recovery programs:

1. The alcoholic must realize that he is unable to control his addiction and that his life is completely disorganized.
2. He must acknowledge that only God, his Creator, can re-create him as a decent man.

3. He must let God through Jesus Christ rule his life and resolve to live according to His will.
4. He must realize that alcohol addiction is only a symptom of basic defects in his thinking and living, and that the proper use of every talent he possesses is impaired by his enslavement.
5. He should make public confession to God and man of past wrong-doing and be willing to ask God for guidance in the future.
6. He should make restitution to all whom he has willfully and knowingly wronged.
7. He should realize that he is human and subject to error, and that no advance is made by covering up a mistake; he should admit failure and profit by experience.
8. Since, through prayer and forgiveness, he has found God, he must continue prayerful contact with God and seek constantly to know His will.
9. Because The Salvation Army believes that the personal touch and example are the most vital forces in applying the principles of Christianity, he should be made to work continuously not only for his own salvation but to help effect the salvation of others like himself.[16]

An outstanding strength of the SA approach is their open, eclectic spirit—as contrasted with the exclusivistic spirit of some rescue missions. The healing resources of social work, psychology, psychiatry, medicine, and Twelve Step programs of various kinds are available when needed to complement their Christian evangelistic orientation. Many in the Army's leadership believe that an effective approach must be a team job. In keeping with its broader spirit, this leadership in general recognizes abstinence as an essential goal of therapy. This is in contrast with those leaders in some missions who considered salvation as the only significant goal. One such mission leader said that it might be better for a man to stay drunk if he is going to hell anyway.

How Effective Is the Salvation Army Approach?

In my judgment, the Salvation Army, together with some more enlightened rescue missions, represent evangelistic addiction therapy at its best. It is difficult to give an overall evaluation of an organization as large and as varied as the SA. In spite of its authority-centered, military, hierarchical structure, there are striking differences of approach from one facility to another depending on the officers in charge and the staff. There is convincing evidence that some facilities have remarkable success in getting and keeping countless formerly homeless, low-bottom addicts sober and living constructive lives.[17]

The late Cap'n Tom Crocker illustrates the power of the Salvation Army's approach when embodied in a talented officer. As a young man Crocker was doing well as a clerk in a Detroit court until his drinking got the best of him and he began to "borrow" funds entrusted to him by the court. Fired in disgrace, he was soon on Detroit's Skid Row where he spent eight horrible years. Finally, in the desperation of alcoholic delirium, he stumbled into a Salvation Army Rescue Corps and was soundly converted.

When he went to work in that facility, his talent for helping alcoholics soon became apparent. After a time the same judge who had fired him invited him to help as a court consultant for alcoholics. Some years later, Crocker moved to direct the Harbor Light Corps on West Madison Street in Chicago. The judge of a municipal court invited him to help as he had in Detroit. Each morning at court the alcoholics who seemed to have the best chance of making a comeback were called out and turned over to Captain Crocker. They were taken to the Corps where he would address them in this way:

> Remember you don't have to stay here. If you want to live like bums, I'm not going to stop you. Another thing, nobody has to do any phony praying to get help. I was on the street myself once, so I know a phony when I see one. But if you really want to lick Skid Row, I have the answer. We'll help you get a job and teach you how to use a fighting faith in God. But you'll have to supply the guts.[18]

The men who chose to do so were allowed to stay at the Harbor Light where they were exposed to conversion therapy and rehabilitation. The Chicago judge said of Crocker's work: "Right from the start he did a wonderful job." Of the 3,048 alcoholics that he accepted in one six-month period, 789 experienced conversion. Considering that many were low-bottom alcoholics, this proportion is strikingly high. Even more significant is that 331 of the 789 converts returned to their homes.

Charismatic leaders like Crocker are probably uniquely successful with addicted people. But it is clear that many other officers and centers also achieve considerable success. Consider this example of the healing power of the SA, particularly when it collaborates with A.A. One of my interviewees, Bob B., age fifty-five, attributed his rehabilitation to a combination of influences. He had been a machinist and stationary engineer and had been drinking excessively for nearly twenty-five years. He spent eight years in various institutions taking "cures." He went to Cleveland and placed himself under the care of the Salvation Army Social Service

Center. The officers at the center tried various therapeutic approaches, but still he could not stop drinking. They offered to introduce him to members of A.A., but he refused flatly.

Finally after another severe crisis and a terrible spree, he returned to the center completely licked. "For God's sake get me an A.A. man," he said. Within an hour he was in a hospital with a strong A.A. program for detoxification. After four days he was returned to the center. When he was able, the officers contacted an industrial plant and arranged for him to start work. At the time of my interview, Bob had been sober for over two years, was active in an A.A. group in the plant where he works, and attends a Cleveland church. He returns to the center at least once a month to do personal work with the men there.[19]

Despite its success, there are some weaknesses in SA thought and therapy that probably lessen its effectiveness with certain victims of addictions. There apparently is some degree of sin-sickness and puritanical moralism among some rank-and-file Salvationists. Although the authority-centered solution (in terms of organization and philosophy) helps some low-bottom alcoholics, it has a significant limitation. Some addicts resent the benevolent authority-centered structure of the Army and what they may experience as theologically disguised power abuses of some officers. One interviewee, a convert in the SA who later joined A.A., was sharply critical of the SA. He compared it to the authoritarianism of some Roman Catholic leaders. When William Booth's *In Darkest England* was published, declaring that "society needs mothering," T. H. Huxley wrote a series of protest letters to the *London Times*. He pointed to the dangers of "blind and unhesitating obedience to unlimited authority" and showed that mothering adults does not contribute to their maturity and growth. One need only recall Erich Fromm's *Escape from Freedom* to be reminded that an authoritarian religious or political system may be seductively attractive to anxious people and yet not be psychologically constructive. This does not apply to the SA as a whole. But some segments of its leadership may unwittingly use the Army system to encourage dependence instead of independence and conformity to the system instead of individual autonomy. Huxley's point that mothering adults is hardly the road to emotional and spiritual maturity, merits reflection. But, on the other hand, addicts who are deeply emotionally crippled may need the tight security of the SA system to stay sober and survive.

In spite of its limitation, the Salvation Army's extensive, worldwide, evolving program is still the most enlightened and the most effective evangelical approach for low-bottom, homeless addicts as well as some nonaddicted, chronically homeless people. Whatever its weaknesses, the Sally has been helping alcoholics for a much longer time than any other religious organization. For most of the twentieth century, it has devoted itself to homeless alcoholics while the vast majority of mainstream Christians, except for rescue mission leaders, considered them hopeless or not worth helping, or both. Concerning the SA's work, this tribute by the late Yale sociologist and alcoholism expert, Selden Bacon, is still relevant today: "It has been criticized justifiably but nobody else is doing the job on Skid Row or has been doing it for the past fifty years."

One must respect the Army for its devotion to low-bottom alcoholics, its willingness, in the words of its founder, to "net the sewers for Christ." Without a doubt, a great host of rehabilitated alcoholics and drug addicts are giving thanks that in the Salvation Army's book there are no incurables. "A man may be down, but he's never out" because "the word 'hopeless' isn't in God's dictionary!"[20] This is the Army's dauntless faith.

What We Can Learn from These Approaches

By way of summary, here are some practical guidelines that can be distilled from these approaches:

1. Some low-bottom, homeless, chemically dependent people *can* be helped by religious means. The belief that all are hopeless is not valid.

2. Evangelistically oriented approaches can induce powerful conversion experiences that do help some alcoholics and drug-dependent people, many of whom would not respond to less emotional approaches.

3. Evangelistic approaches tend to be much more effective if they encourage participants to become actively involved in Twelve Step programs, in addition to what they offer.

4. Because of its general psychological and theological enlightenment, the Salvation Army probably is more effective than many rescue missions, although there are missions that also are enlightened and effective.

5. If religious approaches to low-bottom addictions are to be effective, they must convey empowering experiences of acceptance to replace their paralyzing experiences of feeling rejected by people, society, and God. Evangelistic approaches can be channels for this transforming experience of grace to reach the lives of some addicts.

6. Residential "whole person" rehabilitation programs, offering physical, vocational, as well as spiritual help frequently prove to be essential for long-term recovery by low-bottom addicts.

7. Intense religious and group dependency satisfactions are often needed to replace the immediate satisfactions that alcohol and drugs give some people.

8. Putting converts to work helping other homeless addicts can be important for their own continuing sobriety. In helping low-bottom, homeless addicts, those who have been through similar experiences on the street have a distinct advantage.

9. The social pathology of chronic homelessness as well as that of addictions must be addressed in holistic treatment programs for low-bottom addicts.

Needed: Other Resources for Low-Bottom Addicts

The thousands of low-bottom chemically dependent people living on the streets in our affluent country constitute an often-ignored national tragedy. If these homeless are to be reached, a variety of innovative programs, both religious and secular, must be created and tested for effectiveness. A high percentage of those with low-bottom addictions obviously do not respond to the programs offered by Christian evangelistic approaches such as rescue missions and the Salvation Army. In light of this, there is an urgent need for secular treatments for homeless addicts to be developed. Fortunately, a variety of other approaches is being tried, including the use of temporary institutionalization, outpatient and day treatment programs. Critical components in such programs, according to Barbara C. Wallace, professor of health education at Teachers College, Columbia University, are:

> On-site counseling, random or routine urine testing (for drugs) on a frequent basis, and ideally on a daily basis; regular Twelve Step-program group meetings on the program site, as well as active encouragement to utilize outside meetings and to secure a sponsor ... group therapy, relapse-prevention groups, exercise groups, AIDS-prevention groups, parenting skills groups, and Treatment Center representatives' groups.[21]

It is clear that treatment centers with all these facets are very expensive. They are in short supply in part because of this, but also because of judgmental public attitudes and low levels of interest in helping homeless addicts.

It is fortunate that A.A. has a fine track record in helping thousands of low-bottom alcoholics and the polyaddicted find survival, sobriety, and sanity. There are many A.A. meetings in municipal lodging houses, rehabilitation centers, halfway houses, rescue missions, and SA centers focusing on low-bottom homeless addicts. In some communities halfway houses have been organized and directed by the members of A.A. groups. The

A.A. traditions do not permit official affiliation with any institution including these but the crucial fact is that their treatment is A.A. oriented. Such facilities constitute a kind of A.A. alternative to evangelical Skid Row programs.

How can clergy, congregations, and individuals who desire to help the homeless get involved? The National Alliance to End Homelessness can provide resources including a paper entitled, "What You Can Do to Help the Homeless." There are several explicitly Christian approaches focusing on helping alcoholics and drug-dependent people, including low-bottom addicts. These will be discussed in chapter 8.

CHAPTER 7

Alcoholics Anonymous: Still Our Greatest Resource

A.A., this fellowship, has been for me like the sun—radiating every corner of my life. I am overwhelmed by the rewards it has brought to me from my very first day until this one. The personal joys that it has brought to me and my family are without number, and the great adventures that I have enjoyed through these years of sharing and learning and enjoying sobriety through love and service with all of you are treasures without price. . . . My cup continues to run over. I shall continue to be with you in the Fellowship of the spirit, and we will surely meet again as we trudge the road of happy destiny.
—C.L.B., a friend with forty years of sobriety speaking at an A.A. convention

If I were asked to give the most striking conclusion from the intensive study that underlies this book and my subsequent experiences with alcoholics over the years, I would have no hesitation in responding with this: "In all the long, dark, dismal history of the problem of alcoholism, the brightest ray of hope and help is Alcoholics Anonymous!" This conclusion has two important corollaries: First, A.A. and the many Twelve Step recovery programs that have come from it are the most effective and widely available referral resources available today. Second, it behooves everyone concerned with helping victims of alcoholism and drug addictions to become thoroughly familiar with A.A., and other Twelve Step groups like Al-Anon, N.A. (Narcotics Anonymous), and Overeaters Anonymous.

Because of A.A., more than a million alcoholics, a vast majority of whom had been labeled hopeless by their families, friends, doctors, and clergy, are today living constructive, happy lives without alcohol. The existence of all these miracle stories is evidence enough that here is something of momentous significance for both healing and spirituality. The Twelve Step programs are not the complete answer to the problems of addiction nor do they claim to be. Like all approaches to human problems, Twelve Step programs have some inadequacies. Everything considered, however, A.A. and other similar groups offer the best referral resources for these reasons:

1. They are easily available in almost every community in our country and in most other countries.

2. They are free, supported by the voluntary contributions of recovering members.

3. Their effectiveness in enabling addicted people to walk the road of recovery is greater than any other approach, religious or nonreligious.

4. In addition to helping countless grateful people to interrupt the addictive cycle and find the road to survival, sanity, and sobriety, these step-by-step programs are often remarkably transforming, gifting members with new ways of life.

Psychiatrist M. Scott Peck gives this superlative evaluation of A.A. in *Further Along the Road Less Traveled:*

> I believe the greatest positive event of the twentieth century occurred in Akron, Ohio. . . . when Bill W. and Dr. Bob convened the first Alcoholics Anonymous meeting. It was not only the beginning of the self-help movement and the beginning of the integration of science and spirituality at a grass-roots level, but also the beginning of the community movement . . . which is going to be the salvation not only of alcoholics and addicts but of us all.[1]

An insightful minister I know appropriately describes A.A. as "a modern chapter in the book of the Acts!" He means that it is a wonder-full expression of the healing, creative, empowering work of God's Spirit in our times. Whether or not one resonates with these affirming descriptions, it is impossible to deny that A.A., past and present, provides a thrilling spiritual story. It is the story of how a group of men and women who had been consigned to society's scrapheap banded together, joined hearts and hands, and conquered an unconquerable craving, becoming an inspiration to countless people around the world.

How A.A. Began and Grew

Throughout the A.A. story, two names stand out—Bill Wilson and Dr. Bob Smith—its cofounders. I remember Bill as a lanky, homespun Vermonter. He was born in East Dorset, Vermont, in 1895. His father was owner-operator of a marble quarry.[2] When Bill was ten, his parents divorced and he went to live with his grandparents in the same town. His schooling, which had started in "a one-room schoolhouse with a chunk stove" was continued at a boarding school in Manchester and then at Burr and Burton Seminary and Military College in Norwich. World War I interrupted his college career in his junior year and he married Lois Burham just before he went overseas.

While in the army Bill began to drink. In describing the reason for his previous abstinence he says, "I had been warned . . . too many people had died of it." Like many who come out of the military experience, he faced a difficult adjustment. As he puts it, "I had been an officer and thought I was pretty good. I came out and all I could get was a clerk's job with the New York Central Railroad. I was such a damn poor clerk that I got fired at the end of a year." After a while he got a job as an investigator for a security company on Wall Street. He completed a night school course at Brooklyn Law College but never received the diploma because he was intoxicated and did not attend the graduation. In retrospect he comments whimsically, "Wasn't that just like a drunk?"

By the late twenties Bill and Lois had saved some money. Bill began to dabble in stocks with considerable success. Meanwhile his drinking was increasing steadily. When the crash came in 1929, Bill found himself $60,000 in debt. He then drank himself out of an opportunity for a comeback. By 1932 he was in bad shape physically, and his wife went to work to support them. From 1932 to 1934 he went downhill at an awful rate. At the end of a series of hospitalizations, a medical specialist in alcoholism, Dr. William D. Silkworth, confided to Lois that her husband was hopeless. He explained that Bill's attempt to adjust his neurosis by means of alcohol had led to an obsession that condemned him to go on drinking and, further, he had a physical sensitivity—an allergy—to alcohol that guaranteed that he would go insane or die, perhaps within a year. (Many years later, after A.A. was well established, Bill pointed out that the concept of the fatal power of the disease provided by Silkworth became in A.A. a powerful deflationary tool that shattered the ego at depth and opened egotistical alcoholics for conversion.)

Meanwhile an alcoholic named Rowland Hazard, the influential director of a large chemical company, had been desperately seeking help from the internationally renowned Swiss psychoanalyst, Carl Gustav Jung, in Zurich. He told Hazard that nothing but a religious conversion could save him from insanity or death caused by his addiction. Determined to find this solution, he returned to America, and came under the influence of the Oxford Group movement and Samuel M. Shoemaker, the charismatic rector of the Calgary Episcopal Church in New York.

The Oxford Group movement was a small group religious movement in the early decades of the twentieth century. It was started by a Lutheran clergyman, Frank Buchman, but was strongest in Episcopal churches.

Its evangelistic goal was to change people's lives by its spiritual philosophy and small group program.[3] While teaching in China, Shoemaker had met Buchman, under whose influence he experienced a personal conversion that transformed his entire life and career. He was "changed," to use Oxford Group language. Rowland and another Oxford member in Shoemaker's church went to see an alcoholic named Ebby Thacher, to whom they were able to pass on the group's philosophy and experience. Hazard and Thacher became a part of the Oxford Group meeting in Shoemaker's church.

Bill, having received what amounted to a death sentence from his doctor, maintained three months of fear-inspired sobriety. As is true of almost all such sobriety, it was limited in duration. Then one day, as Bill sat half drunk in the kitchen of his Brooklyn home, Ebby Thacher, whom he had known for a long time, paid him a visit. Ten years later Bill could say, "It was perhaps right there on that very day that the Alcoholics Anonymous commenced to take shape."[4] Bill noticed immediately that there was something different about his friend, so he asked, "Ebby, what's got into you?" Ebby replied, "Well, I've got religion." This came as a shock to Bill since he had thought Ebby, like himself, to be a confirmed agnostic. Knowing Bill's prejudices, Ebby went on to say, "Well, Bill, I don't know that I'd call it religion exactly, but call it what you may, it works." This aroused Bill's curiosity. He insisted that Ebby explain. So Ebby told of his encounter with the Oxford Group:

> Some people came and got hold of me. They said, "Ebby, you've tried medicine, you've tried religion, you've tried change of environment . . . and none of these things has been able to cure you of your liquor. Now here is an idea for you. . . . Why don't you make a thorough appraisal of yourself? Stop finding fault with other people. . . . When have you been selfish, dishonest . . . intolerant? Perhaps those are the things that underlie this alcoholism. And after you have made such an appraisal of yourself, why don't you sit down and talk it out with someone in full and quit this accursed business of living alone? . . . Why don't you take stock of all the people . . . you have hurt—all the people who annoy you, who disturb you? Why don't you go to them and make amends; set things right and talk things out, and get down these strains that exist between you and them? . . . Why don't you try the kind of giving that demands no reward? . . . Seek out someone in need and forget your own troubles by becoming interested in his.[5]

Ebby told Bill how he asked the Oxford Group where religion came into the picture. They replied:

> Ebby, it is our experience that no one can carry out such a program . . . on pure self-sufficiency. One must have help. Now we are willing to help you . . . but we think you ought to call upon a power greater than yourself, for your dilemma is well-nigh insurmountable. So, call on God as you understand God.[6]

Many of the principles that later became central in A.A. were inherent in the Oxford Group approach to Ebby. He was careful not to force any of his views on Bill. He just said that he was leaving with him the ideas that had helped him with the hope that they might help his friend.

In spite of Ebby's permissive approach, Bill was irritated by this blow to his pet philosophy of self-sufficiency. So he continued to drink. But he couldn't help turning Ebby's words over in his mind. At last, in his desperation, the question hit him: "Well, how much better off am I than a cancer patient? But a small percentage of those people recover and the same is true of alcoholics." Bill became willing to do anything that might help him get rid of the obsession that had condemned him to death. He was at his bottom and was open to help.

In order to get the alcohol out of his system so that he could think the whole thing through, Bill had himself admitted to Towns Hospital in New York City. When Ebby came to visit him, Bill's first thought was, "I guess this is the day he is going to try to save me. Look out." (Incidentally, this is the way many alcoholics feel when approached by those with religious ideas.) But Ebby skillfully evaded Bill's defenses, talking only in general terms until Bill himself asked him to review his story. After Ebby left the hospital that day, what is known semifacetiously in A.A. as Bill's "hot flash" occurred.

Here is Bill's description:

> When he was gone, I fell into a black depression. This crushed the last of my obstinacy. I resolved to try my friend's formula, for I saw that the dying could be open-minded. Immediately on this decision, I was hit by a psychic event of great magnitude. I suppose theologians would call it a conversion experience. First came an ecstasy, then a deep peace of mind, and then an indescribable sense of freedom and release. My problem had been taken from me. The sense of a Power greater than myself at work was overwhelming, and I was

instantly consumed with a desire to bring a like release to other alcoholics. It had all seemed so simple—and yet so deeply mysterious. The spark that was to become Alcoholics Anonymous had been struck.[7]

Bill called the physician, Dr. Silkworth, to his bed and tried to tell him what had happened. The doctor said he had heard of such experiences but had never seen one. Bill asked, "Have I gone crazy?" to which Silkworth responded, "No, boy, you're not crazy. Whatever it is, you'd better hold on to it. It's much better than what you had just a few hours ago." Bill later recalled:

In the wake of my spiritual experience there came a vision of a society of alcoholics, each identifying with, and transmitting his experience to the next—chain style. If each sufferer were to carry the news of the scientific hopelessness of alcoholism to each new prospect, he might be able to lay every newcomer wide open to a transforming spiritual experience. This concept proved to be the foundation of such success as Alcoholics Anonymous has since achieved.[8]

When Bill came out of the hospital, he felt extremely grateful to the Oxford Group. Although he had been an agnostic (or perhaps an atheist) before his "hot flash" and his recovery in the Oxford Group, he attended the Group meetings at Calgary and got acquainted with the dynamic rector Sam Shoemaker.[9] He worked intensely with alcoholics at the Calvary Mission telling them about his life-changing religious experiences and trying to inspire it in them. The Calvary Mission, an expression of the Oxford Group's impetus in Shoemaker's church, was a rescue mission serving low-bottom alcoholics. Bill and Lois worked tirelessly day and night. Often their Brooklyn home was filled with alcoholics in various stages of sobriety. Sam Shoemaker encouraged them in this work and Silkworth also continued to encourage Bill in his efforts and provided him with numerous alcoholics with whom to work. In spite of all their efforts, at the end of six months, Bill had sobered only one person by his evangelistic method—himself. But a cardinal A.A. principle was growing from his failures. He had learned, as he put it, "that working with other alcoholics was a powerful factor in sustaining my own recovery."[10]

In May 1935 during the depth of the Great Depression and six months after his conversion, Bill was still unemployed. He went to Akron, Ohio pursuing what seemed like a promising job opportunity. But he was deci-

sively defeated in a proxy fight and his hopes of heading a company totally collapsed. He didn't have enough money for the train fare back to New
York or to pay his bill at the Mayflower Hotel. Overwhelmed by the failure, Bill had one comforting thought: *With a fifth of gin, I could be a mil-
lionaire—at least for a while.* He wondered how God could be so mean to
him after all the good he had done for God. Suddenly he realized that he
might get drunk again unless he found another alcoholic with whom to
talk. From the church directory in the hotel lobby, Bill (who had always
been intrigued by unusual names), chose a minister named Walter Tunks,
rector of Saint Paul's Episcopal Church. Over the phone Bill told him of
his urgent need to work with another alcoholic. Tunks gave him the
names of ten Oxford Group members who were in a group that met in his
church, suggesting that they might know of alcoholics. The first nine calls
proved to be of no avail, but on the tenth he was greeted by a warm southern voice, a nonalcoholic Oxford Group member named Henrietta Seiber-
ling. Bill told her, "I'm from the Oxford Group in New York and I'm a rum
hound." She and others in the local group had been hoping for someone
who could talk with Dr. Bob Smith from firsthand experience of recovery.
Smith, a still-drinking alcoholic who belonged to the group, was known
as a good surgeon when he was sober. She insisted to Bill that she understood how he felt and that he should come to her home. She arranged for
him to meet Dr. Bob and his wife, Anne, who came to her home for dinner the next day. This was Mother's Day, May 12, 1935—a major turning
point in the whole history of recovery from addictions.

Dr. Bob had had a long series of terrifying bouts with alcohol, had been
hospitalized repeatedly, and was losing his medical practice. In 1933 he
had begun attending Oxford Group meetings, desperately seeking help,
and was counseled by two prominent ministers who were active in the
movement. For two years he did everything they and the other group
members suggested. He read the Bible daily, prayed intensely, and attended
church regularly. In spite of everything, his drinking increased.

When the tipsy Dr. Bob appeared at Henrietta's door, she discreetly
whisked him and Bill off to the library. Dr. Bob's first words were,
"Mighty glad to meet you, Bill. But it happens I can't stay long, five or ten
minutes at the outside." Bill laughed and observed, "Guess you're pretty
thirsty, aren't you?" Dr. Bob replied, "Well, maybe you do understand this
drinking business after all." Out of Bill's desperation the A.A. principle of
enlightened self-interest was taking shape. He explained to Dr. Bob how
much he needed him if he was to stay sober. Bill showed Dr. Bob the missing ingredient in his solution—that "faith without works is dead." The

two men talked nonstop for six hours—until 1:30 A.M. the next day. This illustrates another cardinal principle of A.A.: An alcoholic has a valuable natural advantage in establishing rapport with another alcoholic. Except for one brief slip at a medical convention, Dr. Bob never drank again. In a real sense, the fellowship of A.A. was born that day. Dr. Bob later recalled their momentous meeting:

> Here was a man . . . who had been cured by the very means I had been trying to employ . . . the spiritual approach. Of far more importance was the fact that he was the first human with whom I had talked who knew what he was talking about in regard to alcoholism from actual experience. In other words, he talked my language.[11]

To maintain their own sobriety, the two men knew that they quickly must find another alcoholic to help. Their first attempt, with an alcoholic suggested by a neighboring minister, was unsuccessful. (Fifteen years later this "unsuccessful" prospect, now a successful A.A. member, appeared at the funeral of Dr. Bob.) Then they tried a prominent Akron lawyer, Bob D., who had lost nearly everything due to his alcoholism. They found him in a city hospital chained to a bed. They explained the medical nature of his sickness and told of their own drinking and recoveries. The man on the bed shook his head, "Guess you've been through the mills, boys, but you never were half as bad off as I am. For me it's too late. I don't dare to go out of here. Alcohol has me, it's no use." (This feeling of being worse than anyone else is common among alcoholics.) Bill and Dr. Bob made no attempt to argue away the man's hopelessness. But they returned to the hospital the next day.

When they entered the man's room, he cried to his wife who was visiting him:

> Here they are. They understand. After they left yesterday I couldn't get what they told me out of my mind. I laid awake all night. Then hope came. If they could find release, so might I. I became willing to get honest with myself, to square my wrongdoings, to help other alcoholics. The minute I did this I began to feel different. I knew I was going to get well.[12]

This man rose from his bed never to drink again. He became A.A. number three. What was to become A.A. grew in the Akron Oxford Group. A woman named Ethel Macy got sober and became the first female A.A. member.

Let me share a personal anecdote here. In late 1996, during a speaking engagement in Akron, I had the privilege of visiting the home of Dr. Bob and his wife, Anne. A two-story frame house at 855 Ardmore Avenue in Akron, it has become a kind of A.A. shrine that was restored and is now staffed by grateful A.A. members. Visitors from far and wide now come to get in touch with the place where it all started. Having known Bill, it was a moving experience for me to remember that he had stayed there for six months after his first meeting with Dr. Bob. I found a spiritual lift as I drank a cup of strong coffee prepared by an A.A. volunteer in the kitchen, knowing that the cofounders had consumed gallons of coffee there as they struggled to hammer out what became the working principles of A.A. I stood in the two upstairs rooms where Bob and Bill brought many agonizing alcoholics for detoxification and then sharing sparks of hope with them by telling their own stories. I recalled that Bob's and Anne's home doubled as a halfway house for many of the earliest members of what would become A.A., including those who took the program to Cleveland, Chicago, Detroit, and other cities. As I looked at Anne's Bible in the living room, I wished that it could talk and tell what it had witnessed and helped inspire.

After staying with the Smiths, and working with Dr. Bob trying to help others to find sobriety, Bill returned to New York in the fall of 1935. There he began to apply the approaches he and Dr. Bob had developed, bringing many alcoholics to his and Lois's home. Marty Mann became the first female member in New York. For a time, the unnamed movement was connected with its parent, the Oxford Group. But in Cleveland, it was discovered that Jews and Roman Catholics who needed help would not attend as long as it was connected with that movement. There and then in Akron and New York, the little recovery movement became an independent entity.

A.A. had learned much from the Oxford Group movement in New York and in Akron, including the essence of what became the Twelve Steps. Most important, they had learned the power of nonprofessional, religiously oriented groups where people help one another with common problems. A.A. also learned what not to do in trying to help alcoholics. The aggressive evangelism and focusing on public figures that was coming to characterize Oxford groups had to be eliminated from any program that would be effective with alcoholics. The modifications and changes of the Oxford ideology were made on a trial and error basis by the early members of what came to be called A.A. The modifications probably proved to be at least as important for the eventual success of A.A. as the original

Oxford ideas with which it started. These modifications allowed A.A. to be tailored to the special psychological needs of alcoholics.

According to A.A. member Dick B., who has done the most extensive in-depth historical research and writing on A.A.'s origins, Sam Shoemaker was a primary conduit for incorporating Oxford Group ideas into the A.A. way of life and its methodology for helping alcoholics. Bill asked Shoemaker, who had become his spiritual mentor, to write out the emerging procedures in simple language that everyone could understand. Fortunately, Sam responded that it should be done by an alcoholic. So Bill, with input from Dr. Bob, wrote out the Twelve Steps, adapting many of the key ideas of the Oxford Group to the specific needs of alcoholics. Dr. Bob, with his wife, Anne, had a long, deep commitment to Bible study, daily devotional practices, and Christian growth. His push to keep it simple, offset Bill's tendencies toward being somewhat grandiose in his thinking about the developing program. Dr. Bob was concerned that A.A. might "louse it up with Freudian complexes that are interesting to the scientific mind, but have very little to do with our actual A.A. work."[13] In his farewell address to an A.A. convention, Dr. Bob expressed his keep-it-simple theme: "Our Twelve Steps, when simmered down to the last, resolve themselves into the words 'love' and 'service.'"[14]

In the fall of 1937, Bill visited Dr. Bob and the two began counting noses. They were amazed to be able to count forty alcoholics who had been dry for a significant time. Suddenly the awareness dawned on them that something new, perhaps something great, had been started. They saw that, "God had lighted a torch and shown alcoholics how to pass it from one to another." From that moment plans for spreading the good news to the thousands of alcoholics who could be helped began to take shape.

The growth of the movement was slow at first. By the end of the fourth year, there were one hundred members. It was decided by the early members that a book would be published that would share the collective experiences of these members in their efforts to help other alcoholics. The April 1939 completion of the "Big Book"—as it affectionately became known in A.A.—marked a milestone in the growth of the movement. *The Way Out*, their first choice for a title, turned out to be the title of twelve other books, so they decided to call their new book *Alcoholics Anonymous*. In this way the little fellowship of recovering alcoholics acquired its name.

Sales were so slow at first that a deputy sheriff appeared one day at the Newark office of A.A. to dispossess them because they could not pay the printing debt. A grateful member mortgaged his business to lend A.A. the needed money. The group's fortunes improved rapidly in the fall of 1939 when *Liberty* magazine and the *Cleveland Plain Dealer* each published an article about A.A. Inquiries poured in from distant places. The movement was spreading like a chain letter. In 1940 it reached such places as Chicago, Detroit, Little Rock, Houston, Los Angeles, and San Francisco, by way of the book and by members moving to new cities. In 1941 an article by Jack Alexander, entitled "Alcoholics Anonymous: Freed Slaves of Drink, Now They Free Others," appeared in the *Saturday Evening Post*. The little handful of drunks watched with mingled joy and amazement as thousands flocked in seeking help.

Since then A.A. has grown exponentially. Beginning with two people in 1935, the estimated total membership in 1996 was just over 1,900,000 in some 95,000 groups, including more than 5,000 groups in Canada, and 37,000 groups overseas, with an estimated 670,000 members. In addition to these A.A. members, hundreds of thousands of family members belong to corollary Twelve Step groups. The largest of these is probably Al-Anon, the group for family members of alcoholics. It was started by Lois Wilson in 1951 after working with wives of A.A. members from the beginning years. There are more than 20,000 Al-Anon groups in the U.S. and Canada and some 10,000 in about 100 other countries. Total membership is estimated to be over 500,000. Other A.A.-related Twelve Step groups include Alateens and Children of Alcoholics, for adolescent and children living in alcoholic families, and Adult Children of Alcoholics groups.

A.A. has become a remarkable worldwide, multicultural network in over 140 other countries. In many of these countries there are A.A. groups in prisons, hospitals, and rehabilitation centers. A.A.'s Big Book has been translated into thirty-one languages in addition to English. Other books and pamphlets have been translated into many foreign languages. I remember Bill Wilson wondering if A.A.'s program would help alcoholics raised in cultures that were very different from the Western culture. Clearly that query has been answered with a resounding "yes" from around the world. As I write this, I relive a memorable experience of only two years ago in Seoul, Korea where I had the joy of speaking, through an interpreter, to several hundred Korean A.A. members and their spouses at their national roundup.

I also have vivid memories of the Thirtieth Anniversary International Convention in Toronto, Canada, in July, 1965.[15] More than 10,000 grateful A.A. members and spouses from many countries crowded the huge Cow Palace for the plenary meetings. Amid profound thanksgiving and rejoicing for A.A.'s startling effectiveness with "lost cause" alcoholics, there was a persistent note of determination that this success would not lead to complacency. When Bill and Lois Wilson were introducted, there was thunderous applause and repeated standing ovations. In his talk, Bill reminded the convention, "When we remember that in the thirty years of A.A.'s existence we have reached less than 10 percent of those who might have been willing to approach us, we begin to get an idea of the immensity of our task and the responsibilities with which we will always be confronted." He also reemphasized the need for cooperation with all who work on the alcoholism problem, including the more than 100 agencies (in the U.S. and Canada) then engaged in rehabilitation, research, and alcohol education.

Administratively each local A.A. group is autonomous. Three overall structures have been created to function as service bodies, not as a government for A.A. The General Service Board acts as custodian of the Twelve Steps and Twelve Traditions. The General Service Conference, composed of state and provincial delegates, meets yearly as A.A.'s policy-making body. It provides a representative group to "take the place of Dr. Bob and Bill," and is responsible for the General Service Office, keeping the General Service Board firmly anchored to the movement it serves, and ensuring the continuity of services to members and groups.

The A.A. General Service Office in New York City implements the decisions of the Board and Conference. It also acts as a clearinghouse for A.A. groups, distributes literature, answers letters of inquiry from all over the world, advises members about group problems, and provides other services to members and groups around the world. The Twelve Steps and Twelve Traditions are embraced by most of the membership, but not enforced by any of the three bodies. They have no enforcement powers.

In 1950, Dr. Bob died from cancer, after fifteen years of sobriety. During the decade before his death, he had brought medical help and the A.A. message to some 5,000 alcoholics. He helped establish the first alcoholic hospital ward in the country with eight beds at Saint Thomas Hospital in Akron. Sister Mary Ignatia, a remarkable Roman Catholic staff member there, worked alongside him. She continued the work, making medical help and A.A.'s message of hope and recovery available to 10,000 after Dr. Bob's death.

Bill Wilson died in 1971, thirty-six years after his dramatic spiritual experience that brought him permanent sobriety. Earlier that year he had given his last talk at the international convention in Miami, attended by 11,000 A.A. members. Throughout his years in A.A., Bill was the main person who formulated A.A.'s wisdom in written form. Especially in his latter years he devoted much of his time to writing for A.A. His books have become respected commentaries in A.A. circles especially illuminating A.A.'s bible—the Big Book.[16]

In the decades since the deaths of Bill Wilson and Bob Smith, the remarkable movement that they birthed has continued to flourish and grow, though at a somewhat slower rate. One indication of its growth is that in 1973 the one millionth copy of the Big Book was presented to President Richard Nixon. In the twenty-two years between that milestone and 1995, thirteen million additional copies were sold. As A.A. has grown, the robust sense of global responsibility on the part of many A.A.'s has been focused on doing everything possible to reach the millions of still-suffering alcoholics around the world who meet the single requirement for membership—the desire to stop drinking.

How and Why A.A. Works

The evidence from my seventy-nine research interviews with A.A. members and contacts with others as clients in the subsequent years has convinced me that there is no such thing as a blanket answer to the questions of how and why A.A. works. For A.A. is a permissive organization, and each person who comes to it works out his or her own program. But it is possible to describe certain common principles and experiences that summarize the growth sequence of many recovering alcoholics in A.A.. To do this I will create a hypothetical alcoholic named Joe, a composite of the experience of many different alcoholics. As you read, remember that A.A. members follow a wide variety of different recovery paths.

Joe might have come in contact with A.A. in one of several ways. For example, a concerned friend or business associate who is sober in A.A. or knows someone who is, might have suggested he try A.A. Or his doctor or minister might have recommended it to him when Joe's denial was temporarily shaken by a crisis and he asked their advice. But let us say that his wife, Karen, is the person who made the initial contact. She has had about all she can take of Joe's drinking, that for several years has been making life almost unbearable for her and their two grammar school children. After each drunken episode triggered another family crisis, Joe responded with a plethora of promises that he had learned his lesson and he would make sure "it never happened again." Now he gets very drunk and verbally violent almost every night. It is clear to Karen that all his promises and good intentions have produced no diminishing of his excessive drinking.

In desperation, Karen remembers a magazine article about A.A. that recommended checking the phone directory to get the local number. She finds and dials the number, and a seasoned A.A. volunteer at the central inter-group office answers. Karen pours out her pain about Joe's drinking and asks if they can "do something to get Joe to stop drinking the way he does." The volunteer on the phone inquires whether Joe sees his drinking as a problem, and whether he would be willing to talk with someone in A.A. who would share his recovery story and find out if Joe wants help. Let's say that Karen replies, "No way, but the Lord knows he needs it! He'd be mad as hell if he knew I was talking to you!" The member on the phone explains that A.A.'s approach usually works only when an alcoholic has some desire for help, and that to talk to Joe now would only antagonize him and make him angrier at Karen for calling A.A. Instead, he suggests that Karen talk by phone with a woman in Al-Anon, the Twelve Step program for family members of alcoholics. He explains that such a person, having experienced in her own family something like what Karen is going through, may give her some useful information about the nature of Joe's alcoholism. When Karen responds, "He isn't an alcoholic, he just drinks too much," the A.A. volunteer says, "At least he's doing some problem drinking that's painful to you and your kids." He points out that if she is willing to talk with Al-Anon members, the women there might suggest certain things that Karen can do to make things better for her and her children, and perhaps even make it more likely that Joe will eventually become open to going to A.A. If Karen agrees, the A.A. volunteer will give her the first name and phone number of a woman with a similar background who will be glad to talk with her if she calls. Or, he'll ask Karen if she would prefer the Al-Anon member to phone her, and if so, when.

Let's say that Joe is aware that he might need help with his drinking and tells Karen that he is willing to talk with someone from A.A. A pair of Twelfth-steppers will call on him at home. When they come, they introduce themselves, and depending on Joe's condition and response, one of them probably will share something about his own painful struggles with alcohol—for example, his drinking pattern, the jobs he lost, the trouble he caused, the anger, the hopelessness, and the loneliness he felt. The other A.A. member may tell a bit of his story, depending on how Joe responds to the first account.

As often happens, Joe senses that these fellows know what they're talking about. The communication bridge that one alcoholic is able to establish with another is being constructed. This is another key to the effectiveness of A.A. and other Twelve Step groups. The Twelfth-steppers' candid accounts of their drinking experiences may cause Joe to open up a bit. He is still suspicious, but he advances a cautious question about "the program" that they have mentioned. "How much does it cost?" The men explain that there are no dues or fees, that expenses are covered by passing the hat at meetings, and that most of the work is done by volunteers like themselves who do it to keep sober. "Sobriety insurance" they call it.

This sounds strange to Joe, but as he gradually grasps what they are saying, he realizes that he may be helping them by allowing them to help him. Thus he does not feel the heavy burden, which might eventually become unbearable to his alcoholic ego, of being entirely the recipient in a one-way helper-helped relation. Thus, from the beginning, A.A. allows Joe the opportunity to feel a little useful and not entirely dependent.

The men go on to explain that there are no pledges and no "musts" in the A.A. program that is only a "suggested program." Even longtime members only agree with themselves to stay sober a day at a time. This, they explain, is the "twenty-four hour plan." In plain English this means, as one recovering alcoholic put it, "Tomorrow I may go on the damnedest bender you ever heard of but I'm not going to have a drink today." They explain that anybody can stay sober for twenty-four hours if that person really wants to. The twenty-four hour plan is one of several practical tools that A.A. will provide Joe to help him through what may be difficult struggles during the first days and even weeks of tenuous sobriety. These tools help in breaking the addictive cycle—drinking to anesthetize the effects of previous drinking—and are another reason for A.A.'s considerable effectiveness.

As to joining, the A.A. members assure Joe that everyone who admits that alcohol has them licked and wants help is a member. They go on to tell Joe more about how they discovered, after years of trying to handle alcohol, that alcohol was handling them. Their lives had become unmanageable because their bodies didn't react to alcohol like the body of a normal drinker. Because they had an allergy to alcohol, their schemes to "drink like a gentleman" were doomed to failure. Further, they discovered that it was the first drink that set them off on a binge. By presenting alcoholism to Joe as a problem that is at least in part a physical sickness for which there is no known cure, they achieve several things that contribute to A.A.'s effectiveness. The staggering guilt-shame load that had paralyzed Joe's psychic energies is diminished quickly. They reduce his guilt and shame by showing him that, because he has a disease, changing his drinking behavior is not primarily a matter of willpower, as he had assumed. His fear that he is going crazy is also lessened because Joe has the first rational explanation for his bizarre and out of control behavior. In this way, his psychic energies are released from the "squirrel cage of alcoholic thinking" and are made available for his active participation in recovery. By pointing out that his sickness involves physical causes, they avoid the moralism and neurotic guilt that, unfortunately, still often tend to cling to mental and emotional illnesses in our culture. By emphasizing the fact that there is no cure for the illness, they stress its seriousness. But they also point out that the A.A. program has allowed them to live healthy lives with their illness—"like insulin, a healthy diet, and exercise do for diabetics."

The presence of two well-dressed men who talk his language and seem to understand the horror of his alcoholic world begin to penetrate Joe's isolation and he lets himself have a little hope that "if they did it, perhaps I can too." Because they are there to help themselves by helping him, and because they do not lecture or try to sell him anything, Joe gradually relaxes his defensiveness. Since they each have staggered through similar dark valleys, the A.A. members can anticipate and recognize his fears and suspicions, his alibis, and his defenses. Joe senses that here are two men he cannot fool. He begins to feel a little less alone.

Throughout all their conversation with Joe, the A.A. members are careful not to say to Joe that he is an alcoholic. They know that there is only one person whose decision about that can make the slightest difference—Joe himself. If they told him their diagnosis of his problem they might prevent him coming to the crucial decision that alcohol really has him licked. But, by sharing their own "drunkaloges" and stories of their experiences on the recovery road, they plant two sets of seeds—accurate knowledge about his addiction and beginning understanding of A.A.'s methods and program of recovery.

If Joe shows even mild interest in what they are saying, the men will offer to take him to an A.A. meeting. If he has reacted negatively or shows that he obviously has not had enough in his struggle with alcohol, the A.A. members will leave with the hope that they have planted some seed that will stimulate his desire for help at some later date. (Among those I interviewed there was often a time gap ranging from one month to five years between the first contact with A.A. and the beginning of real participation.) Whatever Joe's responses, the Twelfth-steppers probably would jot down their first names and phone numbers on a card and give it to him with the suggestion that he call them any time he wants to talk more or feels like taking a drink. This is another of the simple tools that the A.A. members leave with Joe. If he has decided to quit drinking, having them as close as his telephone may help him make it through the periods when he longs for one more drink. But Joe must use this tool himself, like the other tools, if they are to be effective. Thus the initiative is kept with him.

If he eventually succeeds in the A.A. program he will know that it is *his* success. Before the A.A.'s go, they may leave a copy of the Big Book or a small pamphlet with basic information about A.A.'s understanding of alcoholism and its recovery program.

If Joe is obviously in serious physical condition, especially if he has been mixing alcohol with dangerous drugs, the Twelfth-steppers probably will recommend to him and his wife that he would be wise to spend a few days in a hospital so that he can receive detoxification treatment, vitamin therapy, and a healthy nutritional diet. A.A. itself does not own any therapeutic facility, nor is it affiliated with any, but it cooperates fully with hospitals and detoxification and treatment centers. Such facilities usually have a number of A.A. volunteers who commit themselves to regular availability for Twelfth Step work in their institutions. These include general hospitals and mental hospitals and correctional facilities. Most facilities specializing in addiction treatment include staff counselors who are stable A.A. members who also have had training in working with the addicted. Effective treatment programs usually have frequent in-house A.A. meetings, attendance that is either an expected or strongly recommended part of their programs.

There are three common patterns of addiction hospital treatment. One involves hospitals that have separate alcoholic and drug addiction wards. More hospitals assign alcoholics to general medical wards and rooms just as they would any other sick person. This second pattern is based on research that has shown that, with modern detoxification methods and tranquilizers, alcoholics cause no greater disturbance than any other group of seriously ill patients. The advantage of the all-alcoholic ward is that the entire atmosphere can become saturated with A.A.'s spirit of hope, particularly if some of the nurses and paraprofessional staff members are A.A. members. The third pattern consists of outpatient and day treatment programs related to hospitals. In all these patterns, the volunteer services of A.A. members are invaluable parts of the treatment program. With the doctor's encouragement and the patient's agreement, A.A. members make frequent visits and conduct A.A. meetings, surround hospitalized alcoholics with acceptance, and begin to build a relational bridge between them and the A.A. program. Equally important, they continue to offer support and help during the shaky days after patients leave the hospital. Several of the interviewees attributed their successful beginnings in A.A. to the fact that they had had such hospitalization.

The term "sponsor" came into wide use as a result of certain hospital programs that admitted alcoholics only if they were sponsored by A.A.

members. It soon became apparent that the principle of having experienced, stable members designated to partner with new members during their early days in A.A. and beyond tended to enhance recovery rates. So the idea was applied by A.A. groups to new members in general, who were encouraged to choose as their sponsor someone with whom they hit it off and felt confident. I have encountered numerous A.A. members who said that their sponsor was their best friend and the most important person in their recovery and new A.A. lifestyle. When sponsors have slips or die, the ripple effect among those they sponsor tends to be strong.

To return to Joe, let us say that he has especially good feelings of connection with one of the men—we'll call him Harry—who called on him. Eventually Joe asks Harry to be his sponsor. Harry accepts and after this they talk almost every day in person or by phone, particularly at the beginning of Joe's recovery. Harry may phone Joe frequently, perhaps each morning, just to say hello, ask how he's doing, and remind him, "One day at a time." At the beginning, he introduces Joe to other A.A. friends, helping him build a support group of abstinent friends.

As soon as Joe is feeling a little better, Harry takes him and his wife, Karen, to an open meeting of a local A.A. group. Closed meetings are only for those who have accepted that they are alcoholics. Open meetings also welcome nonalcoholic relatives, friends, and anyone else who is interested.[17]

This meeting was held in the parish house of a church rented by the A.A. group at a nominal rate. Warm and lively camaraderie pervades the atmosphere in the hall. There is spirited conversation and laughter as those present mix informally. It is obvious that these people enjoy being together. As Harry enters with Joe and his wife, they are surrounded by other A.A. members, a couple of whom have already been to see Joe. Joe is still somewhat shaky, but he is impressed with their interest in him as a newcomer and by their general appearance. These people look successful and happy. Joe wonders, "Can these folks be alcoholics? Maybe they'll bring the drunks in later." He feels relieved that none of his old drinking buddies is there. He is also relieved that no one seems to notice that his hand still trembles when he reaches out to shake theirs or that he can't carry on much of a conversation yet. The men and women he meets seem to represent a cross section of occupations—a plumber, a dentist, a stevedore, an artist, a corporation lawyer, and a homemaker. As has been said, "A.A.'s membership is as diverse and exclusive as a classified telephone directory."[18]

A little after 8:30 P.M. the chairman of the groups raps a gavel, calling the meeting to order. Conversation subsides as members move to take their seats. Joe glances around. There are a little over one hundred present, about a third of whom are women. Ages range from the white-haired grandfatherly man to several young people in their late twenties. On the walls of the room are several placards: "Easy Does It," "First Things First," "Live and Let Live," "One Day at a Time," "There But for the Grace of God." Joe, who feels down on life in general, including religion, winces internally at the last one. The chairman begins to speak with energy and enthusiasm:

> Hi, my name is George and I'm an alcoholic! (The whole crowd responds vociferously, "Hi, George!") This is the regular Friday night open meeting of the East Brooklyn group of Alcoholics Anonymous. I would like to welcome all of you, especially the newcomers. Our A.A. magazine, *The Grapevine,* says on its masthead: "Alcoholics Anonymous is a fellowship of men and women who share their experience, strength, and hope with each other that they may solve their common problem and help others to recover from alcoholism. The only requirement for membership is an honest desire to stop drinking. A.A. has no dues or fees. It is not allied with any sect, denomination, politics, organization, or institution; does not wish to engage in any controversy, neither endorses nor opposes any cause. Our primary purpose is to stay sober and help other alcoholics achieve sobriety." That pretty well says it for my money. We're fortunate in having a group of speakers from the Uptown Group Number 2 with us. It's a pleasure to welcome them and to present Bob G., who will lead tonight's meeting. (Applause as the leader comes forward from the audience.)

Bob takes the speaker's stand:

> My name is Bob G., and I'm an alcoholic! (Enthusiastic response, "Hi, Bob!") It's good to be here tonight. As the chairman said, this is a fellowship. We're all here because this is the best way we know of helping ourselves stay sober.

The leader for the evening continues for a few minutes, telling a little more about A.A. and about his own drinking story. He concludes his opening remarks:

> I want to say a word to the newcomers. Only as we strive to help

213

you, can A.A. continue or any of us stay sober. The only thing we ask is that you keep an open mind. We're going to hear from three speakers tonight. If you don't hear something that rings a bell with your experience, keep coming back to meetings. And I must add that anything that I or any speaker says represents our own opinions, not the opinion of A.A. in general. With this I'll give you my first speaker, Jake W.

Jake says:

My name is Jake W., and I am an alcoholic. (Response: "Hi, Jake!") After twenty-two years of drinking, I actually quit. I still can't believe that I'm sober. My wife kept criticizing my drinking—she didn't understand that the reason I was drinking so much was because of her nagging. *(Laughter.)* So of course I had to figure out how to get the liquor in without her knowledge. I would put a couple of bottles in my coat and stalk past her—when you're half loaded nobody sees anything—*(laughter)* and hide them in the hamper. Usually, when I tried to get the bottles out of the hamper quietly, I got the bottles but the hamper came with them. *(Laughter.)* One time after a particularly bad bout, my wife said to me, "Why don't you make me the happiest woman alive?" I said, "How?" She replied, "Drop dead!" *(Laughter.)* Finally my wife kicked me out. I had said to her, "This house is half mine, let's divide it." We did. She took the inside and I took the outside. *(Laughter.)*

So I took a furnished room and got a job in a hospital—admissions desk on the maternity ward. *(Laughter.)* I soon discovered that in Jewish hospitals the fathers of new baby boys throw a party. So I could freeload on good Jewish wine regularly. Finally it got bad, so I quit just before they fired me. My family had given me up long before. I was getting so bad I was scared of myself. Lying in a cheap furnished room drinking, dreading the time when the liquor would give out or I wouldn't be able to keep it down on my stomach. I finally called up the only brother who'd still speak to me and asked him to come down. He protested but finally came and got me in the county hospital for dryng out. While I was there a social service worker asked me if I'd heard about A.A. I said, "What's that?" He gave me an A.A. pamphlet to read. I actually read it when I started to feel better. On Sunday some A.A. boys came to visit me, and I saw the light for the first time. I went to A.A. with them. It felt like the thing I'd been looking for. At that time, most A.A.'s were low-bottom. They'd been on the Bowery, been in all sorts of places I had never been in—like bobby hatches. As I listened to their stories over a few weeks, I began to feel a little superior—like at least I'm not as bad as these guys. *(Laughter.)* Sound familiar, anybody? *(More laughter.)* Of course I didn't get around to taking my inventory and really looking at my own record honestly.

After four months I said to myself one day, "Maybe with all my knowledge of A.A., I could take a couple of beers." The first night I had six. *(Laughter.)* I woke up the next morning feeling fine, but I was scared to death of what would happen if I got drunk. The third night of my experiment I got drunk, my papa threw me the hell out of staying with him, and I was back in the furnished room. For the next five years I was on the bum. I would sit in a cheap gin mill telling drunks they should go to A.A.—just the thing for them. *(Laughter.)* I lost job after job. One year it took two envelopes to send in my income tax slips, I had so damn many of them. *(Laughter.)*

I lost all hope and resigned myself to the alcoholic death I knew I was close to. Then two men came to see me. I knew before they spoke that they were from A.A. I was never so glad to see anyone in my life. That was May, twenty-three years ago. No drinks since then. I poured the liquor I had tied to the bed springs down the drain when those men left. I was really through!

A.A. doesn't fail! We fail it. It works, if we will work it. To the newcomer I want to say two things. First, the most important thing in A.A. is to get active in the work and get to know people here. The more people you know, the better time you'll have and the easier to stay sober. Second, it's easier to stay sober than to get sober. I owe everything to A.A! If it wasn't for A.A., I'd probably be dead by this time. Instead, I've got my home back together again and I'm holding down a job and enjoying life—without booze. I hadn't had anything much to do with the "Man upstairs" during my drinking. Now, when I talk to him, I say "thank you for A.A." *(Rousing applause and some cheers.)*

Following Jake's speech, the leader interjects some of his own experiences, confirming some things Jake has said. After mentioning that alcoholism is no respecter of age, color, or sex, he introduces his second speaker, an attractive woman who looks about forty. She begins in the usual A.A. way: "Hello, I'm Judy and I'm an alcoholic!" Response: "Hi Judy!" She tells about how she was able to help her kid brother get into A.A. and

N.A. because he was on crack as well as alcohol. She wouldn't go herself, even after she was in terrible trouble,

> ... because I couldn't imagine that anything could help me and besides I was the one who helped other members of my family including my brother and a cousin who was a pill head. I got so bad I couldn't comb my hair. ... I drank by myself behind closed doors. I couldn't tell where sleep ended and blackouts began. I started to use some goof balls (sleeping pills) when alcohol quit doing much for me.

Then Judy described how, with no hope but as a last resort before killing herself with an overdose, she decided to try A.A.. With the exception of one brief slip after three months, she had been sober for two years and ten months. Judy then discusses the Fourth Step—the moral inventory—describing how it helped her. She concludes her talk with these words:

> To the newcomers I'd like to say, don't be discouraged if you don't get it right away. You can do it if you put a little of the effort into the program which you formerly put into getting and hiding liquor. I have a lot to be thankful for—to A.A., my sponsor, and the Higher Power. One is the fact that before A.A. when I woke up, I used to say, "Good God, it's morning!" Now I can say, "Good morning, God!" (*Applause.*)

After the second speaker, the visiting group's leader turns the rostrum over to the secretary of the local group who makes announcements concerning future meetings and says: "There are no dues or fees in A.A., but we do have expenses, so we'll now pass the hat." During the collection there is a buzz of conversation. Some stand and stretch and refill their coffee cup from the large and frequently replenished coffee maker on a rear table. Since many A.A. members are heavy smokers, and this is not designated a nonsmoking meeting, the air in the room is a blue haze by now.

After a few minutes the leader introduces the third speaker, one of the older members from the visiting group and a popular speaker on the A.A. meeting circuit.[19] He mentions his own drinking experiences briefly and sprinkled with lots of jokes at his expense. Then he spends most of his time telling how several Steps have helped him, introduced with this moving story:

We A.A.s are like a man who has bought a farm with the sole thought of raising wheat. And raise wheat the farm does—the finest of wheat. But as the farmer goes about the task of raising wheat, he finds the most beautiful flowers springing up in odd corners and he notices for the first time a grove of stately trees. And as time goes by, he strikes oil in this acre and gold in that; here he finds coal, and there he finds silver, and now he comes upon a healing spring. And the end is not yet. Each day he comes upon new comforts, new beauty, new riches; each day he rises to new adventures; each day's discovery sets him atingle for the next one.

Does my allegory sound farfetched—just some words strung together to make a speech? Let's take inventory—an old A.A. custom. Everything in A.A. stems from the Twelve Steps Recovery Program. Let's look at the Twelve Steps, not to discuss them and what they mean, but solely to see what they give us over and above sobriety.

In the First Step we admitted that alcohol had made our lives unmanageable. With that admission comes the first peace we have known in years. Why? Because for years a battle had been raging inside us—our mind and our conscience on one side, this strange and savage appetite on the other. Now the battle is over.

In the Second and Third Steps we came to believe that a Higher Power could help us and we placed our will and our lives in his hands. And what do we get? A resurgence of faith and hope. A great gift, indeed, to us who have lived in despair. The Fourth and Fifth Steps led us to take inventory of our lives and to tell others the exact nature of our wrongs. The devil of remorse that had long plagued us has gone. The burden of evil that bent our shoulders and weighted our limbs has gone.

And so we break with the past. So we become new people. That's not a figure of speech. The seven remaining Steps make that just as real as the platform I stand upon. In the Sixth and Seven Steps, we made restitution to ourselves by casting off the shoddy, sodden garments of the drunkard—and clothed ourselves in tolerance, in humility, in honesty, and charity. In the Eighth and Ninth Steps, we made restitution to others. Those four Steps help us to get rid of those alcoholic lenses that were before our eyes—the ones that caused us to see not the decent, kindly folk about us but grotesque and distorted figures—demons in a land of nightmare.

Perhaps the greatest gift of all the Steps, next only to sobriety, is contained in the next two—the Steps of daily inventory, the daily seeking of closer union with God. And so to the Twelfth Step. It told us that we'd have a spiritual experience. Some of us were a little doubtful about that. We realize now that it's impossible to make a real effort to fulfill the other Steps without having a spiritual experience. The Twelfth Step told us, too, to carry this message to other alcoholics. No one in this audience, I don't care what his life has been, has ever savored a satisfaction so complete, so unalloyed, as that which comes to one who is the instrument by which an alcoholic enters into and is redeemed by A.A. Yes, there are reasons—a hundred times the number of those I have cited—for joining A.A., over and above and beyond achieving just plain sobriety. *(Enthusiastic applause for the inspiring talk.)*

When the third speaker finishes, the leader thanks the local group for the privilege of "carrying the message," and says, "Now let's stand and close the meeting in the usual way." The group then repeats the Lord's Prayer in staccato phrases. This comes as a jolt to Joe who has been pleasantly surprised up to this point by the lack of much religion in the meeting. The smoking, the laughter, the occasional "damn" during the talks had made him feel more comfortable and a little less anxious and edgy.

Feeling socially awkward, Joe starts to make an excuse to leave soon, but before he and Karen can do anything, they are ushered by Harry and several other friendly members to a table where coffee and doughnuts are waiting. Harry makes sure that his "baby" gets comfortably acquainted with some group stalwarts who drift over to the table. Among others, Joe meets a fellow who works at his trade. They begin to talk shop and before long have exchanged telephone numbers. Joe's A.A. circle already is starting to grow. Conversation, mostly about A.A. activities and alcoholism, fills the room in waves. Twelfth Step work is going on over coffee cups. After about a half hour some begin to leave, including Harry and Joe. (Many stay longer.)

Let's analyze what has happened to Joe. He has begun to become a part of an emotionally meaningful group that can provide him with a supportive web of relationships within which he can learn to apply the working principles of A.A. It is an attractive group. Most alcoholics have associated "cures" with the unpleasant. In contrast, here is a group that is enjoying sobriety. It gives Joe's ego a lift by making him feel important as a newcomer. He is no longer an outcast. These people actually want him in their group! During the course of Joe's drinking he has become generally desocialized. Here is a group that can reverse the process and serve as a doorway to the land of the living. It can do this because it is, sociologically speaking, an in-group whose close ties of fellowship provide the environment for relearning healthy living. The intensity of the fellowship has been compared by one A.A. speaker to that shared by those who have been through a battlefield experience together. This attractive in-group is open only to alcoholics. Joe's inner reluctance to keep accepting that alcohol has him licked is counterbalanced by the fact that this admission is his ticket of entrance to the group. His chief liability has thus become a valuable asset. Equally important, here are people who speak with complete candor and lack of guilt about their common sickness. Joe feels a great relief. He thinks, "Since they don't blame themselves for their alcoholism, they won't blame me for mine." It is by reversing the punitive attitudes toward addictions that still linger in our culture that A.A. is able to provide a solution to the problem.

Already Joe's isolation is beginning to break down. He realizes that he is not alone and is not uniquely cursed. He senses that his starved longing to belong may find sustenance at last. He has seen a room full of examples of those who do not even regard it as a curse. He has seen a hundred examples of proof that the A.A. program works. He also has begun to identify with some of the drinking experiences of the speakers. The rewards of the man-buying-a-farm story seem very attractive, though also very remote to him.

The A.A. group can help Joe because it is anonymous and nonexploitative. Anonymity quiets his anticipatory anxieties that someone will find out he's an alcoholic. (Actually everyone who knows Joe has long been acquainted with the fact.) Anonymity nurtures humility and counteracts temptations by members to exploit the group for personal ego desires. It also casts a clandestine atmosphere around the movement, giving it a certain added appeal, especially for members who are in the gang stage of psychosocial development. A.A.'s lack of fees and its basis on the principle of alcoholics helping other alcoholics in order to help themselves, means that Joe need not fear either financial or emotional exploitation. All this helps him identify with the group. The more he feels a sense of belonging to and emotional satisfactions from the group, the more the group will be able to influence his attitude and behavior along group-approved lines. This is an unconscious process by which normal social controls, which have had little meaning to Joe in the advanced stages of his addiction, are relearned. The A.A. group provides an interpersonal environment where abstinence from drinking is rewarded by group acceptance. This helps keep Joe sober, particularly during his early months in A.A.

When they reach their house after the A.A. meeting, Harry is invited in for another cup of coffee. While Joe fixes it, he queries Harry about the signs on the walls of the meeting hall. Harry explains:

> Those are the A.A. mottoes, Joe. They're more tools that A.A. gives us to use, if we want to, in staying sober. For example *"Easy Does It"* means different things to different A.A. members, but it's good advice for most of us, who need to take life in our stride rather than letting everything get us bent out of shape in our feelings. Before A.A. when we'd get mad, sad, or hurt, we'd go and get drunk. The motto helps remind us of the cost of getting upset and, when we do, the high cost of getting drunk. For newcomers, "Easy Does It" may suggest that our problems have been piling up over the years and we can't expect them to be solved magically overnight.
>
> This is where *"First Things First"* comes in. When we come into A.A., we have a pile of problems. We discover that it pays not to forget that staying sober is always our number one problem! We can gradually solve all the other problems that can be solved, but only if we stay sober. *"Live and Let Live"* reminds us to keep our damn noses out of other people's business. If they decide to get drunk, that's their business. If they want to believe an elephant is their Higher Power, that's up to them too. We alkies are short on tolerance before we hit A.A. We often got mixed up in other people's business, got hurt and pissed off, and then got drunk. This motto helps keep us from judging each other. *"But for the Grace of God"* simply reminds us that we're not different or better then the next drunk—just luckier. It helps in Twelfth Step work to remember this and to remember that you're just one drink from a drunk yourself.

Joe points out to Harry that he's afraid he can't "go for the God business." Harry reassures him:

> That's OK. A lot of us felt that way when we came in. Take what you can use from the A.A. program and forget the rest, at least for now. Your Higher Power can be whatever suits you—nature, science, the A.A. group—why, I have one friend in A.A. whose first Higher Power was a Fifth Avenue bus that almost knocked him down. He stayed sober, and gradually his ideas began to change.

By its general permissiveness concerning theology, A.A. is able to help countless alcoholics whose painful experiences in churches have created huge prejudices against organized religions. This spiritual woundedness would probably keep them from getting help from overtly religious approaches. It is fortunate for folks like Joe that A.A. calls itself a "spiritual" rather than a religious approach, and is permissive about how people find the spiritual help they need.

Joe brings the coffee, and the conversation continues. The question of the Twelve Steps comes up. Harry takes the worn copy of the Big Book, which he has loaned to Joe and opens it up to the pages where the Steps are listed and their workings explained. He points out that the "we" refers to the early members who pooled their experiences as the Steps were being written down. Joe takes the book and glances over the Steps.

THE TWELVE STEPS OF ALCOHOLICS ANONYMOUS

1. We admitted we were powerless over alcohol—that our lives had become unmanageable.
2. Came to believe that a Power greater than ourselves could restore us to sanity.
3. Made a decision to turn our will and our lives over to the care of God *as we understood Him.*
4. Made a searching and fearless moral inventory of ourselves.
5. Admitted to God, to ourselves and to another human being the exact nature of our wrongs.
6. Were entirely ready to have God remove all these defects of character.
7. Humbly asked Him to remove our shortcomings.
8. Made a list of all persons we had harmed, and became willing to make amends to them all.
9. Made direct amends to such people wherever possible, except when to do so would injure them or others.
10. Continued to take personal inventory and when we were wrong promptly admitted it.
11. Sought through prayer and meditation to improve our conscious contact with God, *as we understood Him,* praying only for knowledge of His will for us and the power to carry that out.
12. Having had a spiritual awakening as the result of these steps, we tried to carry this message to alcoholics, and to practice these principles in all our affairs.

Joe gulps and says, "It's a big order for a guy like me." Harry responds:

> Yeah, it's a big order for all of us, and nobody is ever able to follow the program fully. Just remember that the Steps are only suggested. Take them cafeteria style. Use what you can. Don't worry about the others. When you have taken the First Step and admitted your problem, you are a part of A.A.

Thus Harry again demonstrates the permissive and accepting atmosphere of A.A. In subsequent conversations and A.A. experiences Joe will gradually absorb the philosophy implied in these steps.

Before Harry says goodnight, he learns that Joe and Karen used to play bridge before Joe's drinking interfered with their social life. So he invites them to play with a group of A.A. members who meet once a week in various homes. Here is another expression of the A.A. fellowship. Harry also arranges to take Joe to a "beginner's meeting," at which a member with several years' sobriety will lead a study of the Twelve Steps, as well as discuss problems raised by the newcomers. In addition, he makes a date with Joe to attend the closed meeting of the local group two nights later. Harry knows that he must keep Joe immersed in A.A. if he is to maintain his sobriety during the first difficult days and weeks.

There are no passwords, esoteric practices, or secret cures involved in a closed meeting. The fact that persons are there means that they admit that they have a drinking problem that they want to learn how to overcome. Closed meetings usually are smaller than open meetings. They almost all involve extensive opportunities for active participation by those present. There may be a panel of members who field questions from the group. Sometimes an individual chairperson may facilitate sharing issues and experiences around one of the Steps, or there may simply be a sharing of ideas concerning concrete sobriety problems raised by anyone present. Here are some questions raised at one closed meeting that I was given special permission to attend when my interest in understanding A.A. was explained to the group by an A.A. friend of mine:

> Will someone give me some help on the Eighth and Ninth Steps? How can I achieve more tolerance? Is it necessary for members to attend meetings in their own home town? Is it possible to achieve the power of sobriety without the spiritual side of A.A.? Can a person have such an aversion to alcohol that he will not be tolerant in Twelfth Step work? How can I expect A.A. to help me when other

groups have failed? Can someone give me some tips on a Twelfth Step situation that is giving me trouble?

Each of these issues was discussed roundly by the group, often with helpful results, according to several questioners.

Closed meetings may have these values for Joe and other newcomers. They give him a chance to talk in a smaller, all-alcoholic group that is less threatening than larger open meetings. He feels freer to talk, if he wants to do so, because he knows that he is among those who understand. Closed meetings provide Joe with opportunities to make new friends within A.A. Being a part of a group from which nonalcoholics are excluded gives Joe's very battered self-esteem a boost. He probably will get some good suggestions for coping with sobriety problems with which he is struggling.

Another resource that Joe may find helpful are the clubs for A.A. members set up by some members on their own, completely independent of A.A. Most of these are supported by voluntary contributions, although some, unlike A.A. itself, have dues. Until Joe finds a job, he may spend part of most days at a club in his city drinking coffee and chatting with A.A. friends who drop in. This, like A.A. fellowship in general, serves as a substitute for the fellowship of the tavern and is an important help in keeping Joe sober.

Karen is invited by Harry's wife to attend an Al-Anon Family Group meeting. Here she finds understanding and help in a group of wives and a few husbands and parents or siblings of alcoholics who are struggling to deal constructively with their own problems in living by applying A.A. principles. Karen makes friends as well as gets useful advice from others who have been through many of the same problems she is facing in a family system skewed by alcoholism. She learns how to take better care of her own and her children's needs while Joe seeks to learn ways of satisfying his own needs in nonalcohol ways. (More about this in the chapter on counseling with family members.)

During the first few weeks, Joe is "as conscious of alcohol as a toothache." He still obsesses about it a lot of the time. But he holds on desperately to his newborn sobriety. Sometimes he wonders if it is worth it; then he remembers the horror of the last binge and the last few years of his drinking. For a while, he breaks the twenty-four hour plan into sixty-minute periods, saying, "I'll not take a drink for this hour!" This, and the desire not to let Harry down, are what keep him from the first drink. Gradually his obsessing and craving subside.

After Joe has a month or so of sobriety under his belt, Harry invites him to go along on a Twelfth Step call. To please Harry he agrees, in spite of the swarm of butterflies in his stomach. To his surprise, he discovers that telling a little of his story to the alcoholic gives him the lift of making him feel more useful. He gets a taste of the awareness that his alcoholism has prepared him in a unique way to help other alcoholics. As Harry put it before they arrived at the prospect's house, "Your story will probably do this guy some good since you are closer to what he's going through now than I am." Seeing someone else in the throes of a hangover refreshes Joe's memory of his own recent miserable condition. This helps him stay sober.

Joe is in the "honeymoon" or "pink cloud" stage. The first long hours have lengthened into days, the days into weeks. He has had a checkup by his physicians at the suggestion of Harry. He is feeling much better physically and getting to enjoy his new found sobriety and friendships. His Higher Power is the A.A. group. He hasn't paid much attention to the Twelve Steps. Everything looks rosy to Joe.

After about three months of sobriety, the elation may begin to dim. Joe begins to think of good reasons why he can't attend several meetings a week. He doesn't see Harry nearly as often either. Then one day, when he steps into a bar "just to make a phone call," the idea hits him that surely one drink won't hurt him since he's feeling so much better. So he tries an experiment. Sure enough, nothing happens. He continues to nibble, avoiding most meetings, Harry, and other A.A. friends. After a few days, he goes off the deep end. The binge lasts for several days during which he experiences worse remorse than he has ever known before. He feels that he has betrayed Harry and other A.A. friends.

For a while after his slip, Joe continues to avoid Harry. Finally he screws up his courage, phones Harry, and goes to a meeting, expecting the worst. To his surprise nobody looks askance at him or treats him with condescension. When he tells Harry about his slip, his sponsor smiles and dismisses it with, "Could have happened to anybody, and often does, Joe. Welcome back!" His group's response to Joe is simply, "Glad to see you back."

His slip causes Joe to take stock. With the aid of Harry's counsel, he sees that prior to the slip he had admitted intellectually but not accepted emotionally "in his guts" that he, Joe Blank, is an alcoholic. The slip is a great persuader in his case, enabling him to accept the truth about himself at a deeper level. He has now really taken the first step. In so doing he has surrendered some of his alcoholic grandiosity about himself. He feels less defensive because this ego image has been a burden. The burden is now reduced, and Joe is open to help from the A.A. program in a new way. It is not true that all alcoholics must have slips in order to achieve sobriety.

Over a third of my interviewees had achieved what appeared to be reasonable sobriety without any slips.

Joe realizes that up to now he has practically ignored the Twelve Steps. So he begins to read the Big Book and work on the "fearless and searching moral inventory" described in Steps Four through Ten. These Steps, Harry tells him, really go together and are important "to keep you sober, not to get you that way." They do this by clearing up some guilt-arousing memories of alcoholic behavior with the experience of forgiveness of oneself and often by others.

The theory is as follows. Because of alcoholics' psychophysical response to alcohol, one drink may set off a chain reaction of drinking, leading eventually to a drunken episode. Since this allergic response is incurable, the key issue is to avoid taking the first drink. This is a central purpose of the A.A. program that it accomplishes this in a variety of ways, many of which have already been described. It reprograms members with the idea behind the A.A. slogan—"It's the First Drink That Does It"—until it becomes almost a conditioned reflex. This helps counteract the rationalization process that leads back to the first drink. A.A. helps members call on the help of whatever Higher Power they can believe in, to help withstand obsessive-compulsive temptations. It teaches them to attend meetings frequently and keep talking to other members, as well as reaching out seeking to help other alcoholics. And very important, it helps them reduce the internal and interpersonal pressures that push them toward taking the first drink. This is the purpose of the moral inventory Steps Four through Ten.

The word "moral" is a stumblingblock for Joe at first until Harry explains that it simply means those feelings and messy actions, past and present, that tend to make alcoholics hit the bottle again. So Joe makes a list of the various people he has hurt by his drinking, starting with Karen and their children. He talks the whole list over with his trusted friend, Harry, discussing feelings and events he hasn't dared verbalize before. This brings feelings of relief and release to his spirit. He feels that a load has been lifted, which gives him courage enough to make some direct amends where they are obviously in order. When this difficult process is completed, Joe feels that he can look the world in the eye for the first time in years. By straightening out many of his past moral messes, he reduces both his guilt about the past and his anxiety about the future. All this helps him maintain sobriety with more serenity. Harry reminds him that regular personal inventories are important to keeping sober.

Here we see A.A.'s handling of the problem of responsibility. Alcoholics' guilt is reduced by recognizing that they have a disease with a physiological dimension. Yet, A.A. prevents them from using this as an alibi by pointing to the factors that keep the disease from being controlled by them. This is their "alcoholic thinking"—selfishness, fear, resentment, lack of humility—matters for which they are responsible. Thus, though Joe is not responsible for having an alcoholic disease, he is responsible for doing what it takes to change his alcoholic thinking, feelings, and behaviors.

When Joe has achieved three months of sobriety with no slips, he is asked to speak at an A.A. meeting. He discovers that telling his story to the group has a remarkable effect. He is pleased when the audience laughs at some of his drinking escapades. He finishes on a note of gratitude to his sponsor and other A.A. friends who have "saved my life." The warm applause gives him a lift. After the meeting, members of the group gather round to congratulate him. Somehow he feels that now he really belongs to this fellowship. He has declared publicly that he is an alcoholic. To a group of people who care about him and vice versa, he has told his story—a story he could not even admit to himself a few months before. There is a sense of release in this, as there is satisfaction in the thought that his talk may have helped some newcomer to find the doorway to A.A.

At one meeting Joe hears a speaker tell her story and read the "Twelve A.A. Promises" from the Big Book.[20] (They come after Step Nine, making amends to those one has harmed.) Joe listened intently as she read, becoming aware that he is already experiencing the fulfillment of some of these promises:

> We are going to know a new freedom and a new happiness. We will not regret the past nor wish to shut the door on it. We will comprehend the word serenity and we will know peace. No matter how far down the scale we have gone, we will see how our experience can benefit others. That feeling of uselessness and self-pity will disappear. We will lose interest in selfish things and gain interest in our fellows. Self-seeking will disappear away. Our whole attitude and outlook upon life will change. Fear of people and of economic insecurity will leave us. We will intuitively know how to handle situations which used to baffle us. We will suddenly realize that God is doing for us what we could not do for ourselves.
>
> Are these extravagant promises? We think not. They are being fulfilled among us—sometimes quickly, sometimes slowly. They will always materialize if we work for them.

As a result of his own moral inventory and other experiences in A.A., Joe's attitude toward the "spiritual angle" gradually changes. Like the majority of A.A. members, his type of spiritual awakening was described by William James as the "educational variety," rather than the "hot flash" type that Bill Wilson had, and some people experience in evangelistic approaches to addictions. He begins to join with the others in saying the Lord's Prayer at the close of meetings. He notices, as he said to Karen, "The folks who seem to get the most out of the program are those who develop the spiritual angle." One day it strikes him that he is sober and enjoying it! This seems like nothing short of miraculous. There must be some Higher Power to effect such a miracle. He finds that he is getting increasing satisfactions from Twelfth Step work and Karen notices that he has become less self-centered. So he begins to try praying on his own. Although he still doesn't use the word "God," Joe begins to mention the "Man Upstairs" in his talks and conversations. He is surprised that, over many months, he begins to feel conscious contact with his Higher Power.

What has happened to Joe? He has cleaned up the debris of his past and has become accepted in the nurturing network of A.A. As all this happens, his bitterness and hostility toward life gradually changes to more accepting attitudes. This naturally begins to affect his religious life. He and Karen have come to depend increasingly on the A.A. and Al-Anon groups for many of their interpersonal satisfactions, and therefore are more and more influenced by group attitudes and values.

Behind the theological permissiveness of A.A., which is real and very significant, the Higher Power one encounters in A.A. literature and in most A.A. stories is a personal God with whom one can communicate, who is interested in individuals, and who will help those who try to live in harmony with his will as they come to understand this. In terms of group psychology, this essentially mainstream theological belief system exerts a kind of a ideological gravitational pull on those whose new identity is linked with the group. From a social psychology of religion perspective, changes in people's belief systems in a certain direction tend to take place within a group, most of whose members are dedicated to that understanding of religious ideas and values.

In terms of the psychology of alcoholism, this principle is significant for the spiritual dimension of Joe's recovery. He has made three important "acceptances" or "surrenders." Each of these reflects the dominant ideology of A.A. and is an important step away from the lonely self-isolation of addiction. Each represents the relaxing of his grandiose ego-image or self-concept which, like many male alcoholics, has been both his defense and his curse. First, he has accepted that he is an alcoholic and cannot control his drinking. Second, he has accepted the help of the group, and it serves as his Higher Power for a time. Now he has accepted a Higher Power who is found in but is also beyond the group. In terms of his inner dynamics, he has let go of fighting authority and authority symbols.

There seems to be a high correlation between length of sobriety and acceptance of the mainstream theology of A.A.'s Big Book that is reflected in the beliefs of the majority of its members. As a part of the research underlying this book, I divided my interviewees in terms of their God concepts. These ranged from atheist, to agnostic, to traditional beliefs. Those persons in the atheist and agnostic categories, though several had been associated with A.A. for considerable periods of time had with one exception relatively unstable and brief periods of sobriety. As one A.A. said in commenting on this fact, "They're still fighting."

A more relaxed and personal relationship with one's Higher Power serves several important functions that facilitate staying sober. It gives a sense of "at homeness" in the universe that helps satisfy the longing to belong to something that is larger than oneself—a deep spiritual human hunger. It gives the vital energy and resources of faith to recovering people for use in meeting the problems of learning a more life-affirming, non-alcoholic life-style. What is most important, such a nurturing spiritual relationship helps allay the ultimate, life-death anxiety that is triggered by all perplexing human problems, especially a problem like alcoholism.

As Joe's sobriety becomes more stable over several years, some of his A.A. behavior patterns may gradually change. He will no longer feel the necessity of attending so many meetings and engaging in so much Twelfth Step work as in the first year or two in A.A. He will attend a meeting or two a week mainly because he enjoys the fellowship and knows staying immersed in it will enliven his life as well as ensure that he will not have a slip. After a time, he will begin to venture outside the social circle of A.A. This is an indication of his increased self-esteem and the consequent diminishing of his need for the psychological protection of an all-alcoholic group. The majority of his friends will still be in A.A., however. He may join in church activities. (The Big Book encourages this.) If he does this, it may indicate both his expanding interpersonal circle and his growing interest in spiritual values. If he and Karen join a church, they will very likely be a great asset to it.

As Joe's self-esteem and sobriety become stronger, he probably will have increasing interest in exploring the spiritual aspects of the A.A. program. When he tells his story, he will put less emphasis on his drinking history and more on his spiritual growth struggles and discoveries. If, as happens to more than a few A.A. members, Joe becomes depressed as his alcohol-caused problems are resolved and his sobriety lengthens, he may seek professional counseling from a pastoral counselor or psychotherapist. What is probably happening to trigger his depression is that underlying personality problems, long hidden beneath an accumulation of alcohol-related problems, have reasserted themselves and need to be resolved. In any case, as long as he does not drink or use drugs, whatever his personality problems, they will no longer be complicated and exacerbated by his active addiction. He is better able to cope with everyday reality-based problems, with or without professional counseling assistance.

Let us leave our friend Joe now, remembering that there is no such individual as a typical A.A. member. Just as each person's alcoholism develops differently, so each person's A.A. experience is somewhat unique. A longtime member of A.A. who read this chapter commented that Joe's alcoholism is probably further along the developmental progression of this addiction than the average, younger newcomer to A.A. today. It also is well to remember that Joe's developmental pattern in A.A., though reflecting the experiences of many male A.A. members, may not reflect the experiences of many females who try A.A. and do not find it to be the path to sobriety.

How Effective Is A.A.?

The issue of A.A.'s effectiveness will be divided into three categories: (1) its effectiveness in breaking the addictive cycle and producing initial sobriety; (2) its effectiveness in producing long-term sobriety; and (3) its effectiveness in transforming addiction-prone personality dynamics, rather than substituting obsessive-compulsive participation in A.A. meetings and work for obsessive-compulsive drinking and drug use. In fairness, it should be reemphasized that A.A. itself does not aim at changing underlying personality problems. Sobriety alone is its central goal.

The fact that A.A. has grown from two recovering alcoholics to nearly two million members in its first six decades is ipso facto evidence that it is very effective in producing both initial as well as long-term sobriety, at least with many alcoholics. In the early years of A.A., Bill Wilson gave some widely quoted estimates based on his observations:

> Of those alcoholics who wish to get well and are emotionally capable of trying our method, 50 percent recover immediately, 25 percent after a few backslides. The remainder are improved if they continue active in A.A. Of the total who approach us, it is probable that only

25 percent become A.A. members on the first contact. Carrying a certain amount of indoctrination, the remainder depart for the time being. Eventually two out of three will return to make good. . . . A list of seventy-five of our early failures today discloses that seventy returned to A.A. after one to ten years. We did not bring them back. They came of their own accord.[21]

These gestimates reflect the situation in the early years of A.A. when mainly more highly motivated alcoholics were seeking help. Since that time many younger alcoholics and those in earlier stages of the illness have approached A.A. Often they are halfhearted and not motivated by having reached their bottom, or they are sent there by courts as an alternative to being sent to jail. Consequently, the percentage of estimated recoveries undoubtedly has declined substantially. No one really knows how much it has declined or what percentage of all those who now make some gesture toward A.A. eventually become members and recover. Furthermore, there is evidence that "about one third of all heavy drinkers, including those diagnosed as alcoholics, improve over time without any treatment. The 'maturing out' is even higher among drinkers who belong to the higher socioeconomc classes and those who have relatively stable personal and social lives."[22] It also is possible, as researcher Herbert Fingarette holds, that those who stay with A.A. and become abstinent tend to be those who, for whatever reasons, accept A.A.'s basic belief system about both alcoholism and religion, and do not represent the broader population of alcoholics who are not in A.A.[23]

But even if one makes generous deductions for probable inaccuracies in membership estimates, a possibility that is readily admitted by A.A. leaders, the overall picture is one of remarkable effectiveness—compared with other religious as well as nonreligious approaches—in helping countless alcoholics achieve both initial and long-term sobriety. There is no denying that A.A. sobriety is often of long duration.[24] I know personally, and have well-documented evidence about members who have been continuously abstinent for twenty, thirty, and forty years or more. Also, even those many A.A. members who have slips, including frequent ones, most often return and stay sober for extended periods of time, many for the remainder of their lives. Such recoveries after slips are plentiful because people can return quickly without experiencing rejection or judgment on top of their own guilt for having slipped.

A.A. has demonstrated great effectiveness in breaking the addictive cycle and producing initial sobriety because:

1. It tends to wait until alcoholics are at least somewhat receptive to help. This means that alcoholics have suffered enough through their drinking so that the pain outweighs the pleasure (or anesthetic satisfaction) of drinking. A.A. rightly recognizes that alcoholics' own desire for sobriety is an indispensable ingredient in any plan of help. It is successful because it relies mainly on attraction as the means of bringing new members. The fact that it is an attractive fellowship enhances its effectiveness. Essential ingredients in this attractiveness are A.A.'s lack of moralizing, its group warmth, caring, and acceptance, its humor, and its subtle do-it-yourself approach to spirituality.

2. A.A. immediately relieves the stresses of the advanced stages of alcoholism. Inexperienced psychotherapists may (foolishly) seek to go directly to the underlying causes of the addiction and many evangelistic approaches are immediately concerned about the general condition of the soul. A.A., on the other hand, concentrates on halting the runaway symptom by helping alcoholics stop drinking, avoid the first drink, and diminish the pain and problems resulting from the excessive drinking itself.

3. A.A. provides new members with certain sobriety tools such as the twenty-four hour plan, attitude-shaping slogans such as "One Day at a Time," and the continuing availability of other members, including sponsors. It teaches them to use these tools to avoid taking the first drink when the craving hits them. This is in contrast with the evangelistic approaches that seek to produce initial sobriety by intense religious conversion experiences. Because many alcoholics have strong aversions to anything religious, the A.A. method appeals to many who do not and perhaps cannot respond to overtly religious approaches.

4. A.A. immediately reduces many of the stresses of guilt, shame, and fear by providing alcoholics with a new way of thinking about their problem. The A.A. concept of alcoholism as a physical allergy coupled with a mental obsession renders alcoholics' self-destructive behavior intelligible to themselves and their families, and greatly reduces the fear, shame, and guilt that were supplying them with the added desire for the "blessed oblivion" of alcohol and other drugs.

5. A.A. immediately surrounds newcomers with an accepting fellowship of individuals who have been through similar experiences and therefore can establish rapport relatively quickly when professional counselors have failed. It is this fellowship's caring, support, and nonjudgmental confrontation with reality about addictions that carry them through the first difficult days of recovery. The fact that the fellowship is focused on the new member by an individual sponsor for most members (about 78

percent) is very important. Sponsors often become a much needed, caring, and honest parent figure for new A.A. "babies." Such dependent and dependable relationships allow the course of social regression, which alcoholics often have followed, to be reversed. The sponsors and the A.A. in-group thus may serve as a kind of substitute family, at least for a while. In this way, A.A. uses supportive group healing rather than religious healing to undergird initial sobriety and re-learning.

6. A.A.'s positive and collaborative relationships with hospitals, doctors, and detoxification centers allows newcomers who need these medical modalities to have the medical therapies that are often so important in establishing initial sobriety. Since most holistic treatment programs include frequent attendance at inhouse A.A. meetings, alcoholics in treatment are exposed to A.A. and are strongly encouraged to become ongoing members of this fellowship.[25]

A.A. has demonstrated great effectiveness in producing long-term sobriety because:

1. In contrast with the rescue missions and Salvation Army, A.A. deals with a much smaller proportion of those whose alcoholism is complicated by the difficult problems of homelessness and socioeconomic deprivation, both of which make for poor prognoses.

2. A.A. depends neither on religious lift (as evidenced, for example, by the lack of group singing), nor on "hot flash" types of religious experience, and thus makes for a more stable sobriety on the part of many alcoholics. As we saw earlier, religious ecstasy is apt to produce an emotional hangover, which diminishes the likelihood of long-term sobriety. In A.A., members are free to find their own meaningful religious beliefs. The spiritual awakening most frequently takes places gradually, as a result of changes occurring as the Twelve Steps are utilized. Spiritual awakening is utilized more often for maintaining than producing initial sobriety. Also, A.A. avoids theological conflicts by its permissive attitude toward theological concepts, its explicit refusal to "engage in any controversy" and "neither endorses nor opposes any causes." It accepts alcoholics at whatever places they have reached in the ups and downs of their religious life and allows their religious formulations to grow in whatever directions their own spiritual struggles draw them. "God as we understand him, Higher Power, and Power greater than ourselves" become vehicles for expressing beliefs in just about anything an A.A. member wants to call God. Because the "spiritual angle" is so subtle, it can "slip up on a person," as one A.A. member put it. It thus does an end run around the defensiveness toward religion that

many addicted persons feel because they have been wounded by religious leaders or institutions.

3. A.A. provides numerous substitute satisfactions to replace those of alcohol and drugs. Enjoyable and caring support in the fellowship overcomes loneliness, a great enemy of prolonged sobriety. In addition, there is an abundance of oral satisfactions—smoking (in most meetings), non-stop talking, and oceans of coffee—to replace the orality of alcoholism with group-approved oral satisfactions.

4. A.A. keeps alcoholics involved in helping "those who have not heard the message," a dynamic that is similar to the religious evangelism that gives believers an empowering sense of mission. This outreach zeal also provides a needed sense of special usefulness. Becoming a sponsor imposes a responsibility on persons to set a good example for their "babies." This motivates sponsors in the direction of their own continued sobriety. It also helps them feel genuinely important to a suffering human being, thus continuing to boost their self-esteem as they give what may be lifesaving help to those they sponsor.

5. A.A. provides a series of suggested Steps, and thus provides a continuing program of psychological and spiritual growth. This is essential, especially after the first enthusiasm of belonging has dimmed. It is significant that the seven moral inventory Steps (out of the Twelve Steps) are devoted to healing the negative feelings like guilt and shame, cleaning up the ethical debris, and healing the interpersonal conflicts caused by addictive behavior. In many alcoholics, if these sources of painful inner conflicts are not reduced, the desire to self-medicate with alcohol and/or drugs returns with intensity.

6. A.A. brings the pressure of responsibility to bear on alcoholics when they are better able to handle it. In the early phases of recovery, they find help in the belief in a physical component in their addictions. As they acquire more stable sobriety, they are confronted by the necessity of taking responsibility for changing those attitudes and feelings or "alcoholic thinking," that motivates them to obsess about alcohol and drinking. Eventually, they take on some responsibility for another alcoholic when they begin to do Twelfth Step work. In doing this, responsibility often is rewarded richly by the power of being able to give vital help to another suffering alcoholic.

7. A.A. strengthens real self-esteem, as distinguished from alcoholic grandiosity. It does this by respecting members' right to keep the initiative with themselves throughout the process, by making them feel deeply accepted in a group, by respecting their rights as adults to think and do

what they will (including getting drunk), and by giving them a sense of unique usefulness in helping other alcoholics. The spiritual nurture of self-worth is provided by encouraging a growing relationship with a Higher Power in whom they can believe and who often is understood as loving and respecting them. As A.A. members increase their genuine self-acceptance, their need for defensive grandiosity decreases. Like medieval armor, defensive grandiosity is a terrible weight as well as provides some protection only until it is pierced.

8. A.A. is nonauthoritarian in both organization and philosophy. Each group is autonomous in all matters that affect only that group. National and international bodies are considered as coordinating and service groups for A.A. as a whole, as well as for A.A. groups and individuals living away from groups. This decentralized democracy tends to distribute the sense of responsibility to each member and reduces the inherent frustrations of authoritarian or hierarchical organizations. It even diminishes intragroup power struggles. It does not eliminate these for a simple reason: It is made up of human beings. Healthy group life within A.A. is more likely because of these factors. Being part of healthy in-groups enhances the prospects for sustained sobriety. That A.A. and other Twelve Steps groups are self-help programs in which there are no outside authorities is very significant in the light of the tendency of some addicts to be compliant and/or defiant toward authority.

9. A.A. can provide continuing group support in most places in North America and in countless places around the world. A.A. is so widely distributed that wherever members go they are likely to find a group. If they do not, they are encouraged to start a group with helpful consultation from the staff of A.A.'s International Service Organization.

Some social scientists have wondered about A.A.'s long-range viability as society experiences more rapid and radical changes. At this point it seems unlikely that A.A. will meet the fate of a group like the Washingtonian movement, the first organized attempt in America by alcoholics to help other alcoholics on a large scale. This movement began in the 1840s in Baltimore. At the beginning of the Washingtonian movement, attention was focused sharply on helping alcoholics. By means of mass meetings, testimonials, pledges, and material assistance, they succeeded in helping a large number find sobriety. The movement rose meteorically, spreading from city to city. Unfortunately it did not follow two guidelines that a century later were to become axioms in A.A.—admitting only alcoholics to membership and limiting the purpose only to helping alcoholics achieve sobriety. Soon the movement was inextricably mixed with the so-called temperance movement. (Actually, temperance meant abstinence.) It attracted countless nonalcoholics whose agendas were not focused mainly on helping alcoholics. This sealed its doom. It was thoroughly absorbed into the temperance movement and, having largely lost its distinctive task of helping alcoholics, declined and died out within a few years. (However, I visited a Washingtonian hospital in the Boston area during my intensive research. This may be the only surviving remnant of what began as a pioneering and successful program of helping alcoholics use religious resources for recovery.)

A.A. has an excellent chance of survival and continued growth because it has avoided the fatal mistakes of the Washingtonian movement and has protected itself against many of the perils of institutionalism and the dangers of becoming sidetracked into other causes. It has done this by the adoption at the International Convention in 1950, of "A.A.'s Twelve Traditions" based on the problems and experiences of many groups in the early years. These traditions are officially recognized within the movement and are generally observed—so much so that A.A. has refused to accept several sizable bequests left by grateful members. The deep respect for and observance of these traditions is the primary reason why the long-range well-being of this healing movement seems very probable. The complete traditions, along with an in-depth discussion of them and the Twelve Steps, is found in the book by Bill W., *Twelve Steps and Twelve Traditions.* Here they are as they appear in A.A.'s Big Book:

THE TWELVE TRADITIONS OF ALCOHOLICS ANONYMOUS

1. Our common welfare should come first; personal recovery depends upon A.A. unity.
2. For our group purpose, there is but one ultimate authority—a loving God as He may express Himself in our group conscience, Our leaders are but trusted servants; they do not govern.
3. The only requirement for A.A. membership is a desire to stop drinking.
4. Each group should be autonomous except in matters affecting other groups or A.A. as a whole.
5. Each group has but one primary purpose—to carry its message to the alcoholic who still suffers.
6. An A.A. group ought never endorse, finance, or lend the A.A. name to any related facility or outside enterprise, lest problems of money, property, and prestige divert us from our primary purpose.
7. Every A.A. group ought to be fully self-supporting, declining outside contributions.
8. Alcoholics Anonymous should remain forever non-professional, but our service centers may employ special workers.
9. A.A., as such, ought never be organized; but we may create service boards or committees directly responsible to those they serve.
10. Alcoholics Anonymous has no opinion on outside issues; hence the A.A. name ought never be drawn into public controversy.
11. Our public relations policy is based on attraction rather than promotion; we need always maintain personal anonymity at the level of press, radio, and films.
12. Anonymity is the spiritual foundation of all our traditions, ever reminding us to place principles before personalities.

The Twelve Steps and Twelve Traditions are reprinted with permission of Alcoholics Anonymous World Services, Inc. Permission to reprint the Twelve Steps and Twelve Traditions does not mean that A.A. has reviewed or approved the contents of this publication, nor that A.A. agrees with the views expressed herein. A.A. is a program of recovery from alcoholism only—use of the Twelve Steps and Twelve Traditions in connection with programs and activities which are patterned after AA, but which address other problems, or in any other non-A.A. context, does not imply otherwise. Additionally, although A.A. is a spiritual program, it is not a religious program. Hence, A.A. is not allied with any sect, denomination or specific spiritual belief.

We turn now to the third criterion of A.A.'s effectiveness.

A.A.'s effectiveness in healing addiction-prone personality dynamics

How often is A.A. effective in resolving psychological problems that often are at the roots of alcoholism? Are members who remain sober really new persons, in the psychological and spiritual meaning of this term, or have they achieved more effective ways of controlling unresolved inner conflicts? As far as A.A. is concerned, such questions are not of interest, because the sole object is sobriety. But those who are concerned about personality, health, and the roles of religious dynamics in enabling sobriety must ask these questions. Even partial answers may throw light on the nature of addictions and recovery. They may also illuminate the dynamic functions of religious belief systems and group practices in sickness and health.

Data from my interviews and subsequent clinical impressions, suggest that sweeping generalizations in answer to these questions are not possible. In some cases, A.A.'s solutions seemed rigid and repressive, as if the persons involved were having to exercise strenuous controls to keep from slipping. For example, when asked how they now handle their hostile feelings, one alcoholic responded: "I feel all bound up—all under control. I want to say, 'to hell with it all.'" Another said, "Anger is something I must absolutely avoid!" On the other hand, some of the alcoholics with whom I have worked, particularly those who had been sober for several years, seemed relatively relaxed and noncompulsive about "the program" to which they were committed. For example, "I don't keep resentment inside me. I go to talk it over with the person"; or "Before, if my wife and I had a fight, I'd go out and slam the door and get drunk. Now I just go out and slam the door." The manner in which a religious approach to problems deals with the so-called negative feelings such as anger, constitutes a useful barometer for measuring the degree of repressiveness involved.

One reason why A.A. has certain repressive tendencies is its concept of human personality. The A.A. perspective, as set forth in its literature, does not take full cognizance that personality factors such as selfishness, resentment, and hostility, which may be controlled rather than resolved through the A.A. program, are often symptoms of deeper problems of inferiority feelings, insecurity, and inner conflicts. It is true that anger, as A.A. holds, often does produce slips in alcoholics. It also can have other destructive effects, depending on how it is expressed. Anger produces destructive effects, not because it is an inherently destructive or unhealthy feeling. Appropriate anger is actually a constructive emotion. Anger makes for slips, at least in part, because it is considered bad by many people's conscience, causing them to feel guilty and expect rejection or retaliation. It can also be destructive because it damages intimate relationships when it is expressed in ways that produce escalating fights and mutual alienation.

For many adults, because of their early conditioning, anger is unacceptable to their self-concept and/or associated with alienation between their parents. It therefore produces severe guilt feelings, anxiety, and fear of rejection or abandonment. It may be that these frightening feelings from early conditioning, together with painful interpersonal conflicts associated with anger in their present lives, cause alcoholics to have slips after expressing or being the target of anger. Some individual A.A. members do recognize the symptomatic nature of much selfishness and many negative feelings like anger. Nevertheless, there is an understandable resistance to emphasize this awareness within A.A. circles because, as one member put it, "this psychologizing would frighten away many alcoholics who can come to A.A. and find help in its present form."

However, if powerful feelings like anger and resentment are repressed by "sitting on the lid harder," rather than redirected in constructive channels, or if the basic causes of such feelings, both within and between people are not resolved, sobriety tends to be precarious. Even if deeply repressed people stay sober, other symptoms of the unacceptable feelings may appear. In many cases these symptoms are relatively harmless and considerably less objectionable than active alcoholism. Substitute compulsions seen in A.A. are examples of this, for example, compulsive meeting attendance or frantic, Type A Twelfth Step work. But the substitute symptoms often are not harmless. Continuing to smoke after sobriety can be a lethal addiction. Depression is often repressed anger turned inward on oneself. Severe episodes of depression and nervous breakdowns following long periods of sobriety in A.A. are not that uncommon.

A frequent assumption by spouses of A.A. members is that severe marital problems will be a thing of the past after sobriety. Although dramatic improvement in intimate relationships usually follows sobriety, underlying problems that were hidden by the chaos in addictive families frequently become evident. Some alcoholics become irritable and unpleasant "dry drunks" after they are sober. Their spouses *almost* wish they were drinking again. While the *almost* must be emphasized, dry drunks' behavior and severe depression may be much more than failure of recovering alcoholics to "work the program" more fully, as A.A. members often assume. They probably are indicative of powerful unsolved and repressed feelings and inner conflicts.[26]

But several issues must be pointed out on the other side of the picture. If one compares A.A. with dynamic psychotherapy, it is valid to label it "repressive inspirational," as one psychoanalytically oriented critic has done. But such in-depth psychotherapy has not proved effective in treating most addictions including alcoholism. And, if one compares A.A. to most evangelistic religious approaches to addictions, it is relatively unrepressive. Furthermore, A.A. is accurate in regarding sobriety as very valuable in itself. A.A. does not see solving deeper personality problems as its job. And, as long as alcoholics are drinking they are going nowhere even though their motors are racing, because their personality resources are out of gear. To stay sober is an essential prerequisite to the solution of any deeper personality problems. By enabling them to stay sober by means of its social-spiritual therapy and Twelve Step program, A.A. makes it possible for many recovering alcoholics (including dual diagnosis addicts), to benefit from counseling and psychotherapy.

Furthermore, if A.A. members do stay sober and use the program fully, many of the personality and interpersonal problems *caused* by prolonged excessive drinking are resolved in remarkable fashion. When they stop drinking, become accepted in the A.A. group, and "work the program," they often become much healthier people who live healthy and socially productive lives. Even though A.A.'s self-limited objective is sobriety, I have witnessed tremendous personal and spiritual growth in members who continue working in the program. In recent years, the emphasis on continuing emotional growth seems to be increasing as more and more members have achieved very long-term sobriety.

Most, if not all methods of healing use some positive and negative controls on behavior. Compared to many other religious approaches to alcoholism, A.A. has fewer negative and far more positive controls. Being nonauthority centered, it does not use manipulative power games or create irrational fears to motivate sobriety. Fear of losing some status in one's home group by having a slip and fear of the disastrous consequences of continuing to drink, are both reality-based, appropriate fears. The major motivators in A.A. are positive—for example, the simple joys of nondrinking lifestyles; the satisfactions of being helpful, perhaps even a lifesaver, to a drinking alcoholic; and the valuable reward of being esteemed in the group. It is because the groups satisfy so many of alcoholics' needs and desires nonchemically and nurturingly, that they are able to help shape attitudes, feelings, and behavior that support both sobriety and improved mental health.

A.A. rightly recognizes that there must be a fundamental reorientation of alcoholics' personality if they are to enjoy long-term sobriety. In this sense, personality change and sobriety are mutually interdependent. As one recovering alcoholic put the matter, "I don't know if I'm sober because I'm happy or happy because I'm sober." A.A. emphasizes the importance of self-understanding (Steps Four and Ten). In my experience, many members show that they have gained considerable self-understanding through this phase of the Twelve Step growth process. Within the supportive relationship of A.A., these individuals had been able to do, often to a considerable extent, what some nonalcoholics are able to do in effective psychotherapeutic relationships. They feel secure enough to relax their defenses, take honest looks at painful aspects of themselves, and make some constructive changes.

Individual or group counseling or psychotherapy is frequently needed in addition to A.A. in order to produce permanent, noncompulsive sobriety. This is not to suggest that most addicted persons need psychiatric treatment, although those with dual diagnoses certainly do. Rather it is to indicate that recovering people in whom repressed levels of conflicts continue to produce painful disturbances and repeated slips can often experience invaluable help from psychotherapy. Such help complements and strengthens A.A.-generated sobriety and personality reeducation.

This view is in accord with much A.A. thinking. Many A.A. members, including some of the founding members, have sought psychotherapeutic help once they were sober. When I first talked with Bill Wilson, nearly a half-century ago, he learned of my interest in pastoral counseling and psychotherapy. His response was to say that the Fourth Step provides a natural entree for A.A. members who need and want counseling help. He obviously regarded counseling and psychotherapy as potentially valuable extensions of this personal inventory process. The "Alcoholics Anonymous 1992 Membership Survey" discovered that, after coming to the program, 56 percent of members received some type of treatment or counseling. Of those who did, 87 percent said it played an important part in their recovery.[27]

Alcoholism, like all other complex human problems, could be likened to a building of several stories, above and below ground. A.A. is admirably equipped to bring healing on the runaway symptom levels. It can halt the self-feeding addictive cycle and repair some or even much of the personality damage resulting from the addiction. But once people have been sober for a considerable time, whatever their underlying personality problems are, they may need the added healing of psychotherapy. This is where counseling or psychotherapy can complement the A.A. program in very valuable ways. The ongoing supportive therapy of A.A. can give indispensable group support and resocialization during the healing process. Psychotherapy can enable those in recovery to resolve any deeper psychological conflicts and thus enhance their relationships in their families, in A.A., and beyond.

In order for this to happen counselors and psychotherapists must have an appreciative understanding of A.A. and of how religious dynamics function in recovery. When counselors and therapists are effective in referring alcoholic clients to A.A. and in being available to help alcoholics maintain sobriety, the power of collaborative partnerships is demonstrated. What takes place illustrates the life-enhancing, even lifesaving power that becomes available to hurting people when mutual understanding, respect, and collaboration occur between these two major healing streams in today's society.

What has been demonstrated repeatedly during A.A.'s first six decades is the life-changing power of its program, principles, and methods. The wisdom of the Twelve Steps was drawn from the Bible, as understood in the Oxford Group movement. The wisdom of A.A. has proved to be healing wisdom for countless people suffering from an incredible variety of different human problems. It is a tribute to A.A.'s founders that the Twelve Steps have been adapted and proved to be helpful for many in groups in addition to those related directly to A.A.— including Al-Anon, Alateens, Children of Alcoholics (COA), Co-Dependents Anonymous, and Adult Children of Alcoholics (ACA). The General Service Office of A.A. reports that over two hundred groups have received permission to adapt the Twelve Steps (which are covered by a copyright), to other human problems. It has been estimated that, across America, there are 500,000 such groups attended by some 15 million people. The list of other Twelve Step groups include the following: Narcotics Anonymous (N.A.), Nar-Anon (for family members), Cocaine Anonymous, Emotions Anonymous (for those with painful emotional problems), Divorcees Anonymous, Gamblers Anonymous, Gam-Anon (for family members), Debtors Anonymous, Fundamentalists Anonymous, Overeaters Anonymous (OA), O-Anon (for family members of OA), Workaholics Anonymous, Shoplifters Anonymous, Compulsive Shoppers Anonymous, Batterers Anonymous, Kleptomaniacs Anonymous, Schizophrenics Anonymous, Depressives Anonymous, Incest Survivors Anonymous, Cross Dressers Anonymous, Sexaholics Anonymous, Problems Anonymous, Prostitutes Anonymous, Impotents Anonymous, and

Messies Anonymous. Frank Reissman is the executive director of the National Self-Help Clearinghouse in New York City, which keeps track of self-help groups and movements. On the light side, he reports that he has heard of a Twelve Step support group for those who get hooked on going to too many support group meetings.[28]

The development of critical alternatives to A.A. suggests that this amazing movement, like all healing movements, religious and otherwise, has its weaknesses and limitations. Some of these will be discussed in the next chapter. Here I would like to reemphasize that A.A., by itself and in its present form, is a tremendously hopeful and helpful program. One grateful alcoholic expressed a view that is echoed by hundreds of thousands of alcoholics today: "For me, A.A. was the birth of hope!" Among the reasons why it has been so, explored in this chapter, perhaps the bottom line reason is that it enables addicts to experience acceptance by life, by God, by other people, and most important, by themselves. A.A. is a wide, deep channel for the healing, empowering grace for addicted people who have a great need to experience such grace. Many religious organizations would be more true to their professed message if they learned from A.A. the transforming power of accepting the unaccepted in our society.

One of the precious rewards that A.A. has given to our society is to make widely known a healing gem known as the "Serenity Prayer." After having been attributed to nearly every saint and seer in history, especially Saint Francis of Assisi, it finally was traced to Reinhold Niebuhr, one of my mentors at Union Theological Seminary in New York City. He used it as the end of a longer prayer around 1932, probably in the chapel at Union. An early A.A. member saw it in an obituary that appeared in the *New York Times.* Liking it, he showed it to Bill Wilson who felt that it suited the needs of recovering alcoholics precisely. It was printed and passed around among A.A. members (without its author being noted). Soon it became an integral part of the movement. Now it is framed and placed on the walls, as well as in the hearts of the members and repeated at the close of meetings of many kinds of Twelve Step recovery groups throughout the world.[29]

This familiar prayer expresses a healthy, healing philosophy for dealing with all manner of life's difficult issues, in sickness and in shadows. To use an old Quaker phrase, it "speaks to the condition" not only of the addicted and those of us who desire to help them, but of millions of others in the human family who are coping with the agonies and ecstasies of life:

> God grant me the serenity
> To accept things I cannot change,
> Courage to change the things I can,
> And wisdom to know the difference.

Ruth Fox, who was a psychiatrist with superb expertise in helping addicted persons, once made the therapeutic observation that, if her patients acquired the ability through psychotherapy to live by the principles of this brief prayer, she would regard their therapy as successful. My experiences, both personally and as a pastoral psychotherapist, confirms Ruth Fox's wisdom concerning the therapeutic value of this prayer's simple but profound message.

CHAPTER 8

Other Paths to Recovery and Beyond

Alcoholics Anonymous and other Twelve Step recovery programs are remarkably effective for many addicted people, but they are not the only spiritual recovery paths that are needed in our society. There are millions of addicted people who have not responded to these approaches for a variety of reasons. It is estimated that only about 20 percent of addicts have any type of treatment. Furthermore, many addicted people who find Twelve Step approaches helpful in achieving the initial stages in the recovery process then experience a desire for more than these programs are designed to offer. They look for a second phase beyond recovery from the addiction per se. Many who have achieved stable recovery in A.A. look for additional paths explicitly devoted to continuing personal and spiritual growth. Other addicted persons look for explicitly Christian approaches that are Christ-centered. It is therefore fortunate that a variety of options have emerged for recovery and beyond. This chapter will overview some of these programs.

Women for Sobriety

After a twenty-eight year struggle with alcohol abuse and depression, and following frustrating experiences in A.A., Jean Kirkpatrick began Women for Sobriety (WFS) in 1976. This was the first women-created, women-centered alternative. She recalls how her nerves were grated at A.A. meetings by males who dominated them, bragged about their lurid drinking tales, and kept displaying their male chauvinism by calling her "gal." As a result, she found that her desire to go out and get drunk increased with each meeting she attended.[1]

Kirkpatrick developed WFS through trial and error, at first to help herself. In contrast to A.A.'s limited focus only on gaining sobriety and belief in surrender to an external Higher Power, her approach focuses on women's overall healthcare and empowerment. It encourages them to smoke less, eat nutritious food, meditate, and give themselves and their bodies lots of loving care. WFS is now a loosely knit international program of mutual self-help groups of women. They meet regularly to share their struggles and successes in developing and implementing a "New

Life" based on what is called an "Acceptance" philosophy of living. The group policy excludes coffee, smoking, and sugary foods at the meetings. Women are strengthened by being encouraged to identify with their health, their power, their love, and with one another.

The nature and principles of this program are evident in the thirteen basic "Statements of Acceptance," which members are encouraged to use in whatever way they choose to meet their needs:

To communicate their general "positive thinking" flavor, here are some of these statements: "I have a drinking problem that once had me." "The past is gone forever." "Negative emotions destroy only me." "Problems bother me only to the degree that I permit them to." "I am what I think." "Love can change the course of my world." "The fundamental object of life is emotional and spiritual growth." "I am a competent woman and have much to give others." An earlier statement, "I am responsible for myself and my sisters" was changed to, "I am responsible for myself and my actions."[2]

Rather than following traditional Christian Fall-Redemption beliefs as A.A. does, Kirkpatrick emphasizes personal spirituality and growth. She believes that men drink for power. Women drink for different reasons— because of frustration, emotional starvation, loneliness, and harassment in society. Women therefore need a different path to recovery—a path involving only women. WFS aims at healing women's shattered self-esteem and lets them release their load of shame and guilt by sharing experiences while they give and receive mutual support and encouragement. It has a positive understanding of human personality and centers on self-affirmations. It clearly seeks to enable women to grow beyond achieving sobriety.

It is noteworthy that some of the therapeutic assumptions implicit in WFS's methods are similar to those developed in cognitive-behavioral therapies such as psychologist Albert Ellis's *rational emotive therapy*. These therapies aim at enabling clients to learn how to reprogram the powerful internal *self-talk* messages that people repeat to themselves. This is done by substituting affirming, esteem-enhancing self-talk for the negative, esteem-diminishing self-talk that often characterizes troubled people including those who are addicted.

An appreciative but balanced evaluation of the strengths and limitations of Kirkpatrick's approach is provided by Charlotte Davis Kasl. She objects, as do I, to the "smiley face" tone of some of the acceptances and the handling of negative emotions as though they are just to be avoided because they can be destructive to oneself.[3] In addition, I have trouble with the lack of explicit methods for overcoming the struggles involved for addicted people in extricating themselves from the tentacles of what has had them hooked. The "smiley face" flavor of WFS seems to suffer from superficial optimism like that of many new thought and new age beliefs. WFS moves away from A.A.'s Fall-Redemption belief system, but unfortunately goes to the other extreme.

How effective is Kirkpatrick's approach in producing recovery in women, either in the short term or the long term? It is not possible to answer with objective evidence at this point. However, cognitive therapy methods have been demonstrated to be effective in enabling some people to reduce their own depression and enhance their self-esteem by reprogramming their depression-reinforcing self-talk. For example, Recovery, Inc., a secular group self-help program founded by Chicago psychiatrist, Abraham Low to help nervous people get well and former mental patients stay well, uses cognitive-behavioral methods effectively. Some addicted persons have found it helpful as a supplement to Twelve Step programs. Recovery, Inc. seems to demonstrate that do-it-yourself cognitive change methods can be effective for some psychologically wounded people, without the coaching of a skilled therapist.[4] My clinical hunch is that WFS is most helpful after the acute crises generated by addictive behavior have been resolved. In any case, the mutual support and sharing in all-women groups undoubtedly provides a valuable, healing dynamic. This may well be the heart of how WFS helps some women.

Moving Beyond Recovery to Discovery

As described in chapter 5, Charlotte Davis Kasl offers illuminating insights concerning the social roots of women's addictions and codependency in sexism and injustices. Her social context perspective goes beyond Kirkpatrick's focus on male sexism by recognizing that racism, classism, and poverty in our hierarchical, patriarchal society are primary causes of addictions in women and also in oppressed minority men. Kasl's empowerment-discovery approach to treatment, like Kirkpatrick's model, is not seen by her as competing with or replacing the Twelve Step recovery approach. Instead, she understands her approach to be a more effective path by which many women and other oppressed people can move beyond sobriety and even recovery as they experience growth and empowerment. Her goals include helping people "move beyond the concept of being an addicted person to that of being a sacred person who is an integral and important part of society at large."[5]

To enable this to happen, therapy for addicted women and minority men, (and also women who seek treatment for mental health problems),

247

must be reconceived to include *empowerment* as a major objective. Empowerment means enabling people to find and use their inner power as persons to live full lives—lives that are creative, passionate, wise, self-aware, and self-protective. Empowerment occurs as women bond with one another and discover how they all have been hurt by society's injustices. In this way they become aware of many of the societal roots of their individual and family problems. Through this bonding process, women gain a sense of their inner strength and collective power. They are empowered to take charge of their own lives in healing ways and to work with others to help correct the sexism and other oppression in the social systems that damage their lives.

Kasl offers an insightful critique of Twelve Step programs by highlighting the problems that many women experience in them. Although she criticizes these traditional recovery programs, she begins by recognizing the important healing resources available in them that have helped countless women as well as men find sobriety. She discusses the Twelve Steps, articulating what she sees as the strengths and limitations of each of them.[6] She also points out that much of the attraction of Twelve Step groups comes from satisfying the need for meaningful rituals in people's lives.

Kasl then identifies some key reasons why many women and some oppressed men do not find the road to empowered recovery in Twelve Step programs. A basic key is that these programs, in keeping with their principle of avoiding controversy, lack any emphasis on the crucial social-cultural context issues in all addictions. Because these issues are among the most significant causes of addictions, particularly for oppressed people, she holds that these approaches "heal only half of persons." The historical key to the male orientation of the steps is that they were created by one hundred middle-class men (and one woman) based on their own ideology, struggles, and recovery. Consequently, they emphasize breaking down the inflated egos that characterize many addicted males. Kasl holds that to apply this surrender model to oppressed women and minorities is a therapeutic error. Their problem is not inflated egos but the very opposite—a lack of ego strength. Making surrender normative for them perpetuates a basic factor that made them and others who are one-down in society very vulnerable to addictions in the first place.

Kasl claims accurately that the A.A. steps themselves reflect a traditional Christian sin-redemption belief system. They see the process of recovery and "being restored to sanity" as dependent on surrendering one's life and will to an external, male Higher Power—"God as one understands *Him*." Kasl holds that the image of women's turning their wills and lives over to a male God "conjures up scenes of women passively and mindlessly turning their wills and their lives over to the care of male doctors, husbands, clergy, teachers, politicians, the military, authority figures, often with devastating results.... The last thing women and minorities need to do is to hand their wills over to others to control them. To do so is the heart of oppression."[7]

The searching moral inventory steps of mainstream Twelve Step recovery programs emphasize the sins and failures, and not the affirmation of their gifts and potential strengths that women have and need to develop. Healing occurs, according to these steps, by confessing "to God, ourselves and another human being the exact nature of our wrongs," and "humbly [asking] Him to remove our shortcomings" and "defects of character." These emphases are contraindicated for women and others who need to feel less socially programed guilt and more self-worth.

In a discussion entitled, "Boundaries and Sexual Exploitation: Or Why Do I Have This Knot in My Gut?" Kasl throws a needed spotlight on the unhealthy dynamics in some Twelve Step groups in their lack of controls on sexual harassment of women. (Only the Twelve Step programs focusing explicitly on sexual addictions have prohibitions of sexual harassment.) She also provides valuable guidance for women (and I would add men) on "Healthy Groups, Dysfunctional Groups: How to Know the Difference."[8]

Kasl then points out some of the strengths of Twelve Step programs—they are nonhierarchical, leaders are regarded as servants, and many of their principles are congruent with acceptance of and empathy for a diverse range of people. Although the theological assumptions implicit in A.A.'s Big Book are close to traditional Christian doctrine, there also is theological permissiveness that respects each member's understanding of the Higher Power. The steps are only "suggestive." However, they often are treated by members as if they were official A.A. doctrines. As a result, there is little or no acceptance of criticism of mainstream A.A. beliefs—a fact that inhibits exploration of alternative beliefs by members.

Instead of A.A.'s traditional Fall-Redemption theology, Kasl proposes an inclusive, passionate, life-loving spirituality with a robust ecological emphasis:

I believe the greatest challenge of the 1990s and early twenty-first century is to learn the art of bridging differences and developing respect for all people, all life. In order to ... keep the world from eventual disaster, we need to get rid of the concept of "the other" and realize we are all in the same boat together. My pollution is your pollution, your pain is my pain. Seeing things from this perspective is a sign of an aware ego. It also reflects the movement back toward a spirituality that is life-loving, creative, and open; one that is sometimes described as feminine, Goddess, or creation-centered spirituality, which is similar to the views held by indigenous peoples such as Native Americans. All these approaches believe that all life is interconnected and sacred. We are not here to transcend life or conquer the earth; rather, we are to merge with each other and our environment and live in harmony, using our resources wisely and unselfishly. . . . A life-loving spirituality fosters creativity, for when our senses are open to take in the natural wonders of the earth, and we live without fear of abuse, our playfulness and creativity are free to grow throughout our lives.[9]

Kasl's "Sixteen Steps for Discovery and Empowerment" communicate clearly the alternative philosophy and working principles of her approach. Designed to enable people "to move beyond recovery to discovery," they highlight the sharp contrasts of her approach with the traditional fall-redemption psychological and theological assumptions of Twelve Step approaches:

1. We affirm we have the power to take charge of our lives and stop being dependent on substances or other people for our self-esteem and security. (*Alternative:* We admit we were out of control/with powerlessness over _____, but have the power to take charge of our lives and stop being dependent on substances or other people for our self-esteem or security.)

2. We come to believe that God/the Goddess/Universe/Great Spirit/Higher Power awakens the healing wisdom within us when we open ourselves to that power.

3. We make a decision to become our authentic Selves and trust the healing power of the truth.

4. We examine our beliefs, addictions, and dependent behavior in the context of living in a hierarchical, patriarchal culture.

5. We share with another person and the Universe all those things inside us for which we feel shame and guilt.

6. We affirm and enjoy our strengths, talents, and creativity, striving not to hide these qualities to protect others' egos.

7. We become willing to let go of shame, guilt, and any behavior that keeps us from loving our Selves and others.

8. We make a list of people we have harmed and people who have harmed us, and take steps to clear our negative energy by making amends and sharing our grievances in a respectful way.

9. We express love and gratitude to others, and increasingly appreciate the wonder of life and the blessings we do have.

10. We continue to trust our reality and daily affirm that we see what we see, we know what we know, and we feel what we feel.

11. We promptly acknowledge our mistakes and make amends when appropriate, but we do not say we are sorry for things we have not done and we do not cover up, analyze, or take responsibility for the shortcomings of others.

12. We seek out situations, jobs, and people that affirm our intelligence, perceptions, and self-worth and avoid situations or people who are hurtful, harmful, or demeaning to us.

13. We take steps to heal our physical bodies, organize our lives, reduce stress, and have fun.

14. We seek to find our inward calling, and develop the will and wisdom to follow it.

15. We accept the ups and downs of life as natural events that can be used as lessons for our growth.

16. We grow in awareness that we are interrelated with all living things, and we contribute to restoring peace and balance on the planet.[10]

Kasl challenges A.A. beliefs that members are always "in recovery," by emphasizing the importance for women to:

> ... not identify ourselves with such labels as codependent and addict, or get stuck in chronic recovery as if we were constantly in need of fixing. The goal is to heal and move on from recovery to discovery. Then we can break through the limitations imposed by hierarchy, work together for a just society, and free our capacity for courage, joy, power and love.[11]

From my perspective, Kasl has made a variety of highly significant contributions to the field of recovery from addictions. She has had the courage and insight to identify some correctable weaknesses in the dominant and most effective approach to recovery—A.A. She has pointed to crucial social context issues at the roots of addictions. She also has developed a psychologically enlightned alternative recovery path that is needed by many women and some addicted men. This is a path along which many addicted women, but also many men, can move beyond recovery to discover and develop their God-given gifts for a full, creative lifestyle.

Based on counseling and teaching experiences with both women and men, I affirm much in the basic philosophy and methodology that Kasl has articulated. But I think of Marty Mann and the hundreds of thousands of other women who celebrate the sanity, sobriety, and socially constructive lives they have developed by way of the Twelve Step path. It is clear that many such women have moved far beyond recovery to empowerment by this path. They have done so, as all people on these paths are encouraged to do, in their own ways using their own resources to develop the gifts that enable them to lead empowered lives. In contrast to the experiences reported by Kirkpatrick and Kasl, A.A.-modeled programs have provided them resources and motivation for continuing growth beyond sobriety.

Women in recovery today have more available opportunities to participate in all-women support and sharing groups within Twelve Step programs than in the past. This probably helps more women discover personal and spiritual empowerment in these programs. Furthermore, the emphasis on spiritual and emotional growth for both genders in Twelve Step groups seems to have increased in recent years as more and more people achieve long-term sobriety and are motivated to continue growing in these directions.

It is important to remember again that millions of addicted persons, including a high percentage of women and minority men, still die trapped in deadly addictions. It is fortunate, indeed, that Jean Kirkpatrick and Charlotte Davis Kasl have had the courage, creativity, and vision to chart alternative recovery-discovery paths. Women and men who stumble when they try to walk the Twelve Step paths now have other routes. Furthermore, numerous women have successfully interrupted their addictions in Twelve Step programs, but have not felt fully at home there interpersonally or spiritually. Many of these women may well find helpful resources in the growth-oriented approaches of Kirkpatrick or Kasl.

I would describe Kasl's growth-nurturing, empowerment approach as the second essential phase of full recovery, the growth dimension that is needed after the initial healing phase. In the first phase, it is wise to use whichever approaches prove to be the best path to stable sobriety for a particular individual. In my experience, Twelve Step approaches are most often this path. But sobriety and recovery become more secure, relaxed, and firmly grounded if people continue their growth intentionally in the second phase. Continuing growth, building on initial healing, is an essential second level objective, not just in addiction counseling, but in all wholistic counseling and therapy.[12]

Challenges to the Disease Concept

As is evident throughout this book, my understanding of alcoholism and other addictions has been influenced profoundly by the disease model and the Twelve Steps philosophy. But it is important to recognize that the whole field of chemical dependency is in ferment that may well produce radical conceptual revisions. Among the indications of this is the development of alternatives to Twelve Step treatments by competent therapists like Kasl, even challenges to the disease model by some in the field. For example, Mark B. Sobell and Linda C. Sobell, psychologists at the Addiction Research Foundation in Toronto, Canada, have developed a secular behavioral therapy treatment for problem drinkers that rejects the disease concept of alcoholism. They have written a treatment manual for practitioners entitled *Problem Drinkers: Guided Self-Change Treatment.*[13]

Here is a summary of their theory of problem drinking and the treatment methods based on it: Research studies have shown that many people with alcohol problems recover on their own, without outside help, and that one session of advice-oriented counseling often produces treatment outcomes comparable to intensive treatments. They hold that "a sizable proportion of individuals with alcohol problems can solve their problems on their own if they are sufficiently motivated and are provided with some guidance and support."[14] They describe a "guided self-management approach" for problem drinkers who do not have signs of physiological addiction. Their approach uses a small number of formal treatment sessions that can be extended as needed. Clients are helped to choose their own treatment goals in order to increase their commitment to changing their drinking behavior. Then, focused alcohol education, in the sessions and by homework reading, aims at enabling clients to understand their own drinking problems and develop problem-solving strategies to avoid future drinking difficulties. Self-monitoring of alcohol consumption and related behaviors like urges, moods, and settings of drinking, are used to enable clients to evaluate their progress and plan self-help strategies.

A research scholar who has developed an alternative to the disease concept is Herbert Fingarette, a faculty member at the University of California at Berkeley. His book, *Heavy Drinking: The Myth of Alcoholism as a Disease,* is the most fully researched challenge of the mainstream of alcoholism education and treatment programs including A.A.[15] Fingarette defines "heavy drinkers" as those for whom drinking has become a central activity around which they organize their lives and identity. He summarizes extensive evidence that the pillars of the classical disease model—spelled out by Jellinek following the beliefs of A.A.'s founders—has not been substantiated by much of the multidiscipline research over numerous decades.

Fingarette cites evidence supporting his view that many people drink very heavily at times, for a wide variety of reasons, and that approximately one-third of heavy drinkers reduce or choose to stop their consumption on their own. He argues that people who stay with A.A. constitute a very biased sample because they are mainly people who accept the spiritually centered way of life philosophy and A.A.'s belief system, including the unchallenged belief that permanent abstinence (usually called sobriety), is the only recovery pathway. In spite of this, A.A. members' experiences and beliefs are assumed to be normative for all problem drinkers, by the general public and most of the alcohol and drug prevention programs. For this reason, the many conflicting experiences of heavy drinkers and the findings of scientific researchers that do not fit this dominant belief system are largely ignored by the mainstream treatment network as well as the general public. He points out that controlled drinking programs for those with drinking problems are widely available and apparently effective in other countries, especially the United Kingdom, Canada, and Norway. These programs (of which the Sobells' is an example) all use behavioral relearning principles, and all emphasize the heavy drinkers' acceptance of responsibility and playing the key role in changing their drinking behavior.

If Fingarette's views are demonstrated to have validity, (as seems probable), and if the methods derived are shown to have wide applicability as self-help approaches (which seems much less likely), sixty plus years of mainstream thinking and the wide networks of preventive education and treatment based on it will have to be radically modified and expanded. But, for the foreseeable future, the working hypotheses that are the most effective in helping addicted persons and their families and in providing effective preventive education are the disease model and the principles derived from it. However, the quality of evidence Fingarette and the Sobells cite points to the importance of staying open to consider radical new understandings of addictions and treatment methods. Those who continue to use the classical disease model, as described in these pages, are wise to keep their minds open to the real possibility that this paradigm eventually will be revised as alternative understandings and methods emerge. Of course, as mentioned earlier, it is possible that many so-called "alcoholics" on whom both the Sobells' and Fingarette's research has focused are problem drinkers and not physiologically addicted alcoholics.

Explicitly Christian Approaches to Recovery

Several Christian addiction-recovery groups or networks have been formed in the last few years. Although they are diverse in their structures, they all use Christian adaptations of A.A.'s Twelve Steps. They all share two defining beliefs—that Jesus Christ is *the* Higher Power and the path to sobriety is finding salvation in Christ. Persons from the conservative or evangelical end of the theological spectrum of Christian denominations in America have taken the initiative in forming these groups and the majority of their present constituents probably are conservative Christians. Some seem much more conservative than others.[16] They usually accept the disease concept of addictions, but some also emphasize that alcoholism involves the sin of drunkenness before the onset of the addiction. They all aim at reaching out to become interdenominational and inclusive in their membership.

National Association for Christian Recovery

In 1990, an individual membership organization called the National Association for Christian Recovery (N.A.C.R.) was established as a result of the initiative of Carman Berry and Pat Pringle. It was the first of a family of ministries sponsored by its parent organization, Christian Recovery International. N.A.C.R. grew rapidly and now reports that it "represents a wide cross-section of denominational backgrounds and a wide diversity of recovery groups."[17] At the end of its first six years, the network reported membership between twelve and fifteen thousand. It publishes a quarterly magazine, *STEPS*, an annual *Directory of Recovery Resources*, as well as sponsors an annual national conference. N.A.C.R. also offers membership in two professional groups it sponsors, the National Clergy Network and the Mental Health Professional Network.

Here is the group's mission statement:

> The N.A.C.R. is a membership organization that seeks to assist people recovering from life-dominating issues—typically addiction, abuse, or trauma. We hope together to encourage the Christian community to become a safer and more supportive environment for people in recovery. The N.A.C.R. seeks to serve hurting Christians from all denominations who are seeking to integrate emotional and spir-

itual wholeness, as well as non-Christians in recovery who are seeking a clearer understanding of God.[18]

One of the founders, Carmen Berry, declares:

> You are not alone. There are other Christians who understand and who have more than simplistic slogans to offer. . . . Joining N.A.C.R. won't make it all better . . . but you won't be so alone. I urge you to join today. The Christian community needs a network like this!

A priest, Father Jack McGinnis, affirms the organization:

> Membership in N.A.C.R. will connect you with some of the most loving and visionary people in the church today. The breadth and depth of wisdom and honesty about recovery found in N.A.C.R. publications is unmatched anywhere.

Overcomers Outreach

Overcomers Outreach[19] (O.O.) is an expanding network of Twelve Step recovery support groups with a Christian evangelical orientation. It was founded by a Christian couple, Bob and Pauline Bartosch. Bob was an insurance executive who suffered through a long struggle with alcoholism, largely hidden from those in the conservative Baptist church in which they were respected members. As their marriage was at the point of nearly being destroyed by his addiction, Bob hit bottom and became open to help. Pauline had a long-hidden addiction to Valium. Both of them found the path to recovery by working the programs in traditional Twelve Step groups. They say that these groups "literally saved our lives."[20]

After gaining stable sobriety, Bob, like many recovering people, wanted to become a counselor of alcoholics. He earned a credential as an alcoholism counselor and then a master's degree in counseling. With his professional credentials, he worked for two years as a counselor in a treatment center. After that he served for five years as director of the Long Beach, California office of the National Council on Alcoholism.

In 1977, the Bartoschs decided to form a small support group in their congregation of people who were struggling with chemical dependencies. Those in the group, like the Bartoschs, found meaning and power in an explicitly Christian understanding of A.A.'s and Al-Anon's Twelve Steps. The group decided to use a concept rooted in the New Testament as their name, calling themselves the "Overcomers." They developed a meeting guideline book entitled *Freed*, which contains the meeting format and study material. Their meetings included praying, personal sharing, and studying biblical passages supporting the Twelve Steps. Those attending discovered that this Christian fellowship was remarkably supportive and spiritually empowering for them. Their numbers grew and word began to reach people with similar needs in other congregations.

In light of the group members' transforming experiences during its first eight years, the Bartoschs, after extensive prayer and consultation, felt called to take a leap of faith. They quit their jobs and launched Overcomers Outreach, Inc. Their objective was to extend the recovery program developed in Overcomers to hurting individuals and families in other congregations, denominations, and institutions. Through their intense dedication and hard work, aided by volunteer group members, and with publicity help from evangelical Christian leaders including psychologist James Dobson, the network grew to around a thousand groups during the next twelve years. At this writing, such groups are functioning in forty-nine states and in thirteen other countries.

O.O. defines itself as a "Christian Twelve Step Recovery Ministry." It does not see itself as a substitute for traditional Twelve Step groups or as a "Christian A.A. group," even though the Steps are one of two pillars of the program. O.O. also is not a substitute for prayer and Bible study groups in churches. Instead, it is a Christ-centered ministry reaching out to all hurting people in churches and other religious organizations who are struggling with alcoholism, drug addictions, eating disorders, compulsive gambling, sex/love addictions, workaholism, nicotine addiction, codependency, and other addictive-compulsive illnesses.

O.O. provides both useful information and support for addiction-plagued persons, many of whom had tried to hide their addictions in the dark, lonely closet of guilt, and fear of rejection by their church friends. Others were reluctant to attend recovery groups in the community but feel more at home in Christ-centered Twelve Step groups meeting in churches. O.O. also offers members of traditional Twelve Step programs

> a fresh look at the "Higher Power" they have been seeking, in the person of Jesus Christ. This experience can pave the way for their return to the church of their choice.[21]

In 1994 what could be described as a kind of O.O. Big Book was published. Compiled by Bob and Pauline Bartosch, it is entitled *Overcomers*

Outreach: A Bridge to Recovery.[22] Included are a minihistory of its origins and development as well as the miracle recovery stories of Bob and Pauline and thirty-one others who had been trapped in a wide variety of addictions. One section, "O.O. Support Groups: A Christ-centered Program of Discovery," summarizes the overall O.O. program and describes a typical meeting. A final chapter, "The Twelve Steps Come A-L-I-V-E in the Scriptures," goes through the A.A. steps, citing passages from the Hebrew Scriptures and the New Testament that relate to each of them. Study of these passages is a central part of O.O. meetings.

O.O.'s "Preamble" is read at every meeting. These paragraphs summarize the network's guiding beliefs:

> Overcomers is a fellowship of men and women who have been affected either directly or indirectly by the abuse of mood-altering chemicals or compulsive behavior. We believe that as we look to a loving God for help, and put into practice those principles for living which He has given in His Word, we find both the strength and freedom we need to live productive and happy lives. We strongly believe that our "Higher Power" is Jesus Christ, our Savior and Lord. Our five-fold purpose, based directly upon the Word of God, is set forth as follows: (1) to provide fellowship in recovery; (2) to be and live reconciled to God and His family; (3) to gain a better understanding of alcohol and mood-altering chemicals and the disease of addiction/compulsion; (4) to be built up and strengthened in our faith in Christ; (5) to render dedicated service to others who are suffering as we once suffered. . . . we do believe that Jesus is the Christ, the resurrected and living Son of God, we hold no corporate view concerning denominational preferences.
>
> We practice the suggested recovery program of Alcoholics Anonymous, Al-Anon, and other Twelve Step groups because we believe these to be the practical application of these life-changing principles which are so clearly set forth in Scriptures. We welcome anyone who has a desire to stay clean and sober; anyone who has a desire to rise above the pain and turmoil engendered by the addiction of a loved one; anyone wishing to break the bondage of compulsive behavior. . . . Attendance at additional Twelve Step groups is encouraged.[23]

As in A.A., persons in need of counseling or medical help are referred to competent professionals. Meetings, led by different group members each week, include sentence prayers, personal problem sharing, and testimonies of successes, along with Twelve Step-focused Bible study. Groups usually develop close family-like relationships. Honest sharing is encouraged by observing the principle of confidentiality. Members are urged to continue attending traditional Twelve Step groups.

O.O. has also developed Christ-centered recovery ministries for adult children of alcoholics, sex addicts, adolescents, and for children ages five to twelve living in alcoholic and/or dysfunctional families. In addition, there are O.O. ministries in hospitals, rescue missions, and in Salvation Army installations. O.O. publishes a quarterly newsletter available to anyone who requests it.

The Twelve Traditions of O.O. are adapted from A.A.'s traditions. They shed light on this movement's basic orientation:

1. Our common welfare should come first. Personal recovery depends upon God's grace and our willingness to get help.

2. For our group purpose there is only one ultimate authority—a loving God as He expresses Himself through His Son Jesus Christ and the Holy Spirit. Our leaders are but trusted servants. They do not govern.

3. The only requirement for O.O. membership is a desire to stop addictive or compulsive behavior.

4. Each group should be autonomous except in matters affecting other groups or O.O. as a whole.

5. The primary purpose of each group is to serve as a "bridge" between traditional Twelve Step groups and the church. We carry the message of Christ's delivering power to individuals and family members both within and without the church who still suffer.

6. An O.O. group uses the Holy Bible along with the Twelve Steps of Alcoholics Anonymous for its tools of recovery. Outside enterprises are prayerfully evaluated lest problems of money, property, and prestige divert us from our primary purpose.

7. Every O.O. group ought to be fully self-supporting, declining outside contributions.

8. O.O. groups should remain forever non-professional, but our Service Centers may employ special workers.

9. Overcomers Outreach, as such, ought never be organized, but group coordinators network with the Central Service Center, seeing that the group is facilitated through adherence to the *Freed* book's "Meeting Format" and rotating leadership.

10. O.O. is, without apology, a Christ-centered recovery group; however, persons of all faiths are welcome. Discussion of religious

doctrine should be avoided; our focus must be upon our mutual recovery.

11. Our public relations policy is based upon attraction rather than promotion; we need to always seek the Holy Spirit's discernment whenever sharing in the media, in order to maintain personal anonymity of all O.O. group members.

12. Jesus Christ is the spiritual foundation of all our traditions, ever reminding us to place principles before personalities. We claim God's promise that His power will set us FREE![24]

Alcoholics Victorious

In 1948, William Seath, director of the Chicago Christian Industrial League, an inner-city gospel mission, started a Christ-centered recovery group program called Alcoholics Victorious (AV). After its first fifty years, it had about 150 groups in various parts of the world. It is a ministry of the International Union of Gospel Missions, a network of some 250 inner city missions. Most of the groups meet in rescue missions but some meet in evangelical churches.

AV accepts the American Medical Association's definition of alcoholism as a disease. The AV coordinator reports that his organization has an appreciation of A.A. and other Twelve Step recovery groups, and that all groups use the Twelve Steps, but "we want a Christ-centered approach to the Higher Power." AV has an extensive outreach program. It coordinates a site on the World Wide Web for a variety of Christian recovery programs. This carries an abundance of information about the widening network of such programs. AV has a newsletter and is a large distributor of books and tapes about Christ-centered recovery groups and programs.[25]

Alcoholics for Christ

In 1976, Bill Keaton and Jim Broome, two men with A.A. experience who also had "accepted the Lord Jesus Christ as savior," started a men's retreat center for alcoholics who "wanted to know more about Jesus." This grew into Alcoholics for Christ, an interdenominational Christian fellowship ministry that focuses on three groups—alcoholics and other substance abusers, their families, and adult children from addictive families. To the query, "Is alcoholism a sin or a disease?" Broome responded, "It's both. The Bible makes it clear that drunkenness is a sin. We choose to sin at the beginning . . . but as we become controlled by addiction, we find ourselves dealing with a disease."[26]

Alcoholics for Christ (AC) has approximately eighty active groups, about half in Michigan where the movement began and has its headquarters. There are also groups in some other American states, and Canada, Germany, and Nigeria. Meetings take place in rescue missions, a few in Salvation Army centers, and in churches, homes, and prisons, including a youth correctional facility. The groups use A.A.'s Twelve Steps and affirm "the great program of Alcoholics Anonymous." Two steps are reworded to express the Christian beliefs: "Came to believe that through Jesus Christ we could be restored to right relationship with God the Father, and subsequent sanity and stability in our lives" and "Made the decision to turn from the things of the past and invite Jesus to be Lord and manager of our lives."[27]

The present national program coordinator encountered Alcoholics for Christ in a Salvation Army addiction treatment center where he accepted Christ. A.C.'s chief goal, according to him, is to enable substance abusers to find "a dedicated relationship to Christ and, as born again believers, receive eternal life and become free from their addictions." A.C. is rooted in very conservative evangelistic Christianity. One respected leader is described as beginning meetings with "Praise God!," to which his wife would add, "Glory Hallelujah!" and the whole group would yell "Thank you, Jesus."

What is the significance of these explicitly Christian recovery programs for the field of addictions? Their evangelical theology and language gives them opportunities to increase enlightened understanding of addictions by many conservative Christians. Such people often regard A.A. as non-Christian since it encourages people to choose their own Higher Power, and as competitors of Christian churches. Explicitly Christian recovery programs have the potential of awakening conservative Christians and congregations to their crucial role in both treatment and preventive education that goes beyond advocating their usual abstinence position. These programs also increase conservative congregations' awareness of their corporate ministry to the hidden addicted individuals and families among their members.

Christian recovery movements probably help diminish futile moralizing about addictions among evangelical Christians and they can help more conservative Christians accept the disease concept and the saving spiritual power of traditional Twelve Step groups. It is to be hoped that these groups will enable more leaders of conservative denominations to see A.A. and other Twelve Step groups as ministry-enhancing allies whose core values are expressions of basic biblical and Christian values.

The vast majority of middle-of-the-road, mainstream Christians probably accept A.A. as a valuable spiritually centered resource for helping addicted persons. They do not feel a need for A.A. theology to be stated in explicitly Christian terms for them to sense that Christ's healing spirit is present. But acceptance of the disease concept and A.A. may be accompanied by a leave-it-to-A.A. mentality. Unfortunately, this ignores the unique opportunities that all congregations and other religious organizations have in helping to heal and prevent our society's epidemic of addictions.

It is conceivable that explicitly Christian Twelve Step groups, particularly Overcomers Outreach, will help more conservative Christians to make two important discoveries. One is that the spirit of the healing Christ often shows up in very unexpected places and people, including Twelve Step recovery groups. The second is the discovery that congregations who develop their own innovative addiction programs designed to communicate their message of hope and help are channels of this healing Spirit.

CHAPTER 9

The Psychosocial Dynamics of Religious Approaches to Alcoholism and Other Drug Addictions

> Roland's craving for alcohol was the equivalent on a low level of the spiritual thirst of our being for wholeness which, expressed in medieval language would be, "the union with God." . . . The only right and legitimate way to such an experience is that it happens to you in reality and it can happen to you when you walk on a path which leads you to a higher understanding. You might be led to that goal by an act of grace or through a personal and honest contact with friends or through a higher education of the mind beyond the confines of mere rationalism. . . . You see, alcohol in Latin is spiritus, and you use the same word for the highest religious experiences as well as the most depraving poison. The helpful formula is "spiritus contra spiritum."[1]

This letter, written by Carl Gustav Jung only two weeks before his death, was to Bill Wilson, the cofounder of A.A. Jung wrote in response to Bill's letter thanking him for opening Roland's eyes to the fact that his recovery was dependent on a transforming religious experience. As we have seen, this message, when Roland passed it along to his drinking friend, Bill, became a major factor in the latter's recovery. Jung's idea expresses this chapter's theme—the dynamic interrelationships between alcohol and religion. Psychology of religion—a scholarly discipline that employs the social and psychological sciences to understand religious beliefs and behaviors—will be used here to explore this interrelationship. The foci will be on illuminating the role of anxiety in addictions, and how *pathogenic* (sickness-causing) religion is a spiritual cause of addictions and how *salugenic* (health-fostering) religion is a crucial resource in recovery for many addicts.

Coping with Anxieties: A Key to Understanding Addictions and Recovery

Three interrelated types of human anxiety are among the causes of many addictions. Examining these can shed light on how unsatisfied spiritual hungers contribute to the process of becoming addicted. The three types of anxiety are *neurotic, historical,* and *existential.* None of these is unique to addicts' experience. All are experienced by everyone to some degree. Anxiety, of whatever type, rises from a threat to the essential security of persons and is therefore an experience of their total personalities. Psychiatrist Harry Stack Sullivan called anxiety a "cosmic" experience, a shaking of the foundation of a person's world and faith. In contrast, fear is a reaction to threats from specific, concrete dangers. Anxiety is a generalized feeling of uncertainty and helplessness. The psychological burden of many, if not most addicts is not just fears. It is also free-floating anxiety of all three types.

Neurotic Anxiety

Much of the anxiety experienced by alcoholics and other addicts is neurotic anxiety resulting from inner conflicts, repressed memories and impulses. For example, children often repress their anger or sexual impulses in an effort to feel acceptable in families where these normal feelings are taboo. They feel anxious, as children and later as adults, whenever hostile feelings or sexual desires threaten to bubble up into their awareness from their unconscious minds. This kind of anxiety functions as a defense mechanism for keeping unacceptable feelings out of conscious awareness. Many people, addicted or not, use consciousness-changing drugs like alcohol to blunt awareness of neurotic anxiety. The appropriate treatment for this type of anxiety is counseling or psychotherapy aimed at reducing or resolving the underlying feelings and conflicts that trigger it.

Historical Anxiety

Neurotic anxiety is intermingled and increased by historical anxiety arising from the psychosocial and spiritual crises of our times of baffling changes. Millions of humans today have had their faith shattered and their philosophical props knocked from under them. Comfortable certainties about themselves, other people, God, and the universe have been threatened or destroyed by the pandemic of violence, including the effect of two world wars and the many subsequent regional and ethnic blood baths. The momentous scientific revolutions wrought by Copernicus, Darwin, Freud, Einstein, and modern astronomy have disturbed many people who have never integrated the meaning of these profound scientific discoveries into their personal theologies or philosophies of life. They find their hold on traditional certainties weakened by the profound influence of scientific revolutions and reductionistic materialism. Some wonder if we are accidental denizens of an insignificant grain of cosmic dust lost in the mechanical emptiness of an exploding universe that will ultimately snuff out all life. Furthermore, many people feel impotent in the face of mass social forces over which they have no control. A tidal wave of historical anxiety rooted in the mixed realities of recent history make meaninglessness a continuing threat to the philosophical security and mental and spiritual well-being of millions of human beings, including many addicts and potential addicts.

Existential Anxiety

This collapse of traditional faith and value systems leaves many people at the mercy of the third type of anxiety—existential or religious anxiety. This anxiety is existential in the sense of being nonpathological and arising out of our awareness of being living-dying creatures. This type of anxiety is a crucial dynamic in everyone's life, including addicts and those of us who try to help them. Only two of the alcoholics I interviewed in my doctoral research labeled themselves as atheists. One described what he called "my cockeyed philosophy of life," saying, "A fellow sleeps to get strong, so he can work to get money to eat and have a place to sleep, so that he can get strong and be able to work to get money, and so on."

In German philosophical literature existential anxiety is called *Urangst* meaning original or ultimate anxiety. The late Paul Tillich described its source clearly in his book of sermons appropriately titled *Shaking of the Foundations*:

> Man's [sic] essential loneliness and seclusion, his insecurity and feeling of strangeness, his temporality and melancholy are qualities which are felt even apart from their transformation by guilt. They are his heritage of finitude.[2]

In his Terry Lectures at Yale, published as *The Courage to Be*, Tillich gave us an insightful discussion of nonpathological, existential anxiety from a theological standpoint.[3] We humans know that we are a part of nature, subject to its powers, to sickness, pain, and death. Yet one of our deepest longings is to transcend nature and death.

Our existential anxiety arises from the awareness of our own mortality and contingency. In *Thus Spake Zarathustra*, philosopher Friedrich Nietzsche wrote:

"Man [sic] is a rope connecting animal and superman."[4] Psychoanalysts, including Rollo May, Karen Horney, and Erich Fromm, probed this anxiety with great insight from their psychotherapuetic perspectives. In his book on the relation of psychoanalysis and religion, Erich Fromm declared:

> Self-awareness, reason and imagination have disrupted the "harmony" which characterizes animal existence. Their emergence has made man [sic] into an anomaly, into the freak of the universe. He is a part of nature, subject to her physical laws and unable to change them, yet he transcends the rest of nature. . . . He is homeless, yet chained to the home he shares with all creatures. . . . Being aware of himself, he realizes his powerlessness and the limitations of his existence. He visualizes his own end: death. Never is he free from the dichotomy of his existence. . . . Reason, man's blessing, is also his curse.[5]

The moral capacity of our species—the ability to feel responsibility and guilt—is a blessing. It is also burden, in being a source of existential guilt, shame, and anxiety. The second creation story in Genesis states this symbolically—the expulsion from Eden was the result of eating the fruit of a tree that made men "like God, knowing good and evil" (Gen. 3:5). Henry David Thoreau pointed to the eternal restlessness of a human's spirit when he said that we are always "searching for some lost Eden."[6] In a similar vein, Fromm says, "Having lost paradise, the unity with nature, he has become the eternal wanderer (Odysseus, Oedipus, Abraham, Faust)."[7]

Existential anxiety also arises from what historian Arnold Toynbee called the "Promethean elan," or the human drive to assert ourselves.[8] Viewing our evolution during a million or more years on this planet, it is evident that we are involved in a perennial struggle to achieve autonomy—to rise above primitive dependence on the herd. We are separate selves with distinctive needs and potentialities and a striving for autonomy. Yet we still need the herd. When we get too far from it, we become anxious and quickly return to find collective security, shelter, and identity.

Existential anxiety is normal in the sense of it being the experience of all human beings. It is unneurotic, yet it probably is at the roots of all other anxiety—neurotic and historical. Humans are crippled by the weight of existential anxiety only when their backs also bear a heavy load of these other anxieties, *and* when they lack the resources of vital faith that alone provides the energy to face, carry, and even transform it. Because of this, existential anxiety is a crucial consideration for understanding the spiritual dynamics of addictions and methods for helping addicted people.

Neurotic, historical, and existential anxiety all tend to reinforce one another. Each contributes to all three levels of the multiple causes of addictions described in chapter 2. They contribute to the soil of addictions, making potential addicts hypervulnerable by intensifying their craving for the anxiety-deadening effects of psychoactive chemicals. On the level of symptom choice—the second level—they operate by creating spiritual, religious, or philosophical hungers that alcohol and drugs provide seductive and immediate pseudosatisfactions. On the third level— factors that help to perpetuate addictions once they are started—all these forms of anxiety contribute by accelerating the self-feeding addictive cycle. The anxieties become increasingly intense as addicts continue to try to satisfy their psychological and spiritual needs by means of alcohol and drugs or obsessive-compulsive behaviors. The more they use substances or behaviors to allay their anxieties, the more hopeless, spiritually empty, and meaningless life seems to them.

The Spiritual Dynamics of Recovery

Any in-depth understanding of chemical dependencies and other addictions must include the recognition that many addicted persons are attempting to meet religious hungers by alcohol, other psychoactive drugs, or addictive behaviors. As one person described himself before A.A., "I had a God-shaped hole in me filled by alcohol." If a religious approach is to be successful, it must supply what another alcoholic called a "spiritual substitute" for alcohol. The ability to provide such a substitute is the chief advantage that religious approaches have over nonreligious approaches. This accounts in large part for the relatively high level of effectiveness of spiritually oriented approaches to addictions.

In this light, consider the tragic story of the male alcoholic who, in utter despair and hopelessness was asked by a psychiatrist, "Who can help you?" He responded:

No person or institution. Only what I do not now possess—a belief, a faith in something outside myself, something stronger, more overwhelming than my weakness—some form of spiritual substitute that yet evades me.[9]

Sad to say, he never found such a substitute. He committed suicide shortly after completing his story.

There are several ways in which religion and alcohol are deeply related in terms of their dynamic function. Because of some religious leaders' intensely negative feelings about the many problems caused by alcohol and drugs, they have tended to overlook that alcohol provides some people with answers of sorts—unfortunate as such answers may be. Both religion and alcohol and drugs give answers to the problems of anxiety, weariness, failure, drudgery, rejection, boredom, and loneliness in our dog-eat-dog society. Thomas Wolfe's writings contain frequent illuminating references to alcoholism. In *Of Time and the River,* one of his characters asks searching questions to which alcohol has been the answer for many:

> Where shall the weary rest? When shall the lonely heart come home? What doors are open to the wanderer? And which of us shall find his father, know his face, and in what time, and in what land? Where? Where the weary heart can abide forever, where the weary of wandering can find peace, where the tumult, the fever and the fret shall be forever stilled.[10]

Alcohol, drug, and other addictions are tragic responses to numerous areas of tragedy in our culture. The insecurity and emotional malnutrition bred by an anxious, violent, competitive society has resulted in many damaged orphans of the spirit. These are people who, because of their fears and inner conflicts, are cut off from trustful, fulfilling relationships both with other human beings and with God. Alcohol and other drugs have always offered something to the weary, the anxious, the despairing, the lonely, the spiritual wanderers. It offers the illusion of unity with one's fellows, temporary deadening of anxiety, the quieting of inner conflicts and turmoil, and a sense that things seem to be a little more right in the world. Its relief is temporary and illusory, but it is easily available to many who have found no other. Substances that can give feelings of self-confidence and the illusion of strength have tremendous appeal to those who feel submerged by powerlessness, shame, disappointment, frustration, and self-rejection.

In the mood of the psalmist, Thomas Wolfe speaks through one of his characters, expressing the feelings of many people who try to satisfy their religious needs by alcohol:

> Immortal drunkenness! What tribute can we ever pay, what song can we ever sing, what swelling praise can be sufficient to express the joy, the gratefulness and the love which we, who have known youth and hunger in America, have owed to alcohol? We are so lost, so lonely, so forsaken in America: immense and savage skies bend over us, and we have no door.[11]

Through the use of alcohol and other drugs, humans have temporarily anesthetized the sufferings caused by social chaos. William Booth, founder of the Salvation Army, apparently had this in mind when he wrote, "Gin is the only Lethe of the miserable." (Lethe, in Greek and Roman mythology, was the river flowing through Hades whose water brought forgetfulness and blessed oblivion to those who drank.) The Wisdom literature in Proverbs 31:7 offers this problematic prescription for alleviating social suffering: "Let them drink and forget their poverty, and remember their misery no more." As the social burdens of urbanization, industrialization, and most recently, hi-tech depersonalized lifestyles have increased, the desire for the escape of alcohol and drugs has grown. Many centuries ago the psalmist blessed God for "plants for people to use, to bring forth food from the earth, and wine to gladden the human heart" (104:14-15). Some people, as I recall E. M. Jellinek once putting it, use wine not to make their hearts glad but to put their souls to sleep.[12] The tragedy of using alcohol to deaden the pain of either severe personal problems or social oppression becomes clear when the painkiller causes even deeper pain, oppression, and self-rejection.

Religion, too, has always had something to say to the weary, the anxious, the lonely, the spiritual wanderer, and the downtrodden. Like alcohol, religion has offered solace and a haven from the burdens of society. As Karl Marx observed in his times, religion often has been used by those in power as an opiate, blinding people to the social injustices that oppress them. On the other hand, at its best, religion has motivated people to fight for justice, freedom, and peace. And religious insights have shown the oppressed the principles by which they could do this most effectively. (Gandhi's inspired leadership of his people to defeat British colonial imperialism nonviolently is a shining illustration of this, as is the ministry of Martin Luther King, Jr.) Prophetic religion has inspired millions of oppressed people to live and even die for these liberating values. In this basic way, it is totally unlike chemical solutions to social suffering.

In discussing existential anxiety, it was suggested that there is a dimension to our species' problems that transcends our individual and social problems. Our very finitude, our awareness of our earth-boundness, our impotence in the face of the forces of nature and death—all these are inescapable to any self-aware human. They impose a burden on our souls as well as on our minds, hearts, and relationships. We humans are the animals who know we will die, but we also have intense desires to transcend our finitude and vulnerability to become something larger, more powerful, to feel infinite. Intoxicating chemicals and addictive behaviors can give some people illusions of transcendence.

In his novel, *Look Homeward Angel: A Story of Buried Life,* Thomas Wolfe describes this power of alcohol to give feelings of grandiosity. Here are the musings of the young man Eugene who is intoxicated for the first time:

> In all the earth there was no other like him, no other fitted to be so sublimely and magnificently drunken. . . . Why, when it was possible to buy a God in a bottle, and drink him off, and become a God oneself, were men not forever drunken?[13]

In discussing religious mysticism during his Gifford lectures, pioneering psychologist and philosopher William James recognized this similarity of function between alcohol and religion:

> The sway of alcohol over mankind is unquestionably due to its power to stimulate the mystical faculties of human nature, usually crushed to earth by the cold facts and dry criticisms of the sober hour. Sobriety diminishes, discriminates, and says no; drunkenness expands, unites and says yes. It is in fact the great exciter of the Yes function in man. It brings its votary from the chill periphery of things to the radiant core. It makes him for the moment one with the truth. Not through mere perversity do men run after it. . . . The drunken consciousness is one bit of the mystical consciousness.[14]

Addictions are attempts to shortcut and outsmart our finitude by the illusion of chemical transcendence.[15]

Because alcohol has the power to give temporary feelings of expansiveness, transcendence, and even ecstasy, it has been regarded in many cultures as something magical, even divine. In Greek mythology, Dionysus, the god of wine, was also the divine representative of the larger life after death. In the ancient Greek, Roman, and Jewish traditions, wine was often used as a symbol of the "fluid of life." For example, the figures of drunken men with containers of wine hung on erect penises were carved on the gravestones in one ancient cemetery. Sexuality and wine were thus joined as symbols of life transcending death. The use of wine that has been blessed, for example, in the Catholic mass and the sacrament of the Lord's Supper in some Protestant churches, and in the Jewish and other traditions, are examples of the manner in which alcohol has symbolized the ecstatic, the mystical, and the transcendent in religions.

In our secular, materialistic culture, the transcendent and ecstatic dimension of life has often been hidden or lost. In this spiritual context, chemicals that can give some people ways to escape from the flatness of daily existence are powerfully alluring. Alcohol and some drugs can give some users temporary feelings of uplift and unity, not only between them and others, but also between them and God. In our world of barriers and walls, the longing for unity and intimate bonding is intense.

More than a century before the United Nations sponsored the unprecedented and planet-saving Earth Summit, and long before our tragic human alienation from the natural world was widely recognized, Friedrich Nietzsche made a remarkable statement. He articulated the way that experiences of the ecstatic can bridge these human-human and human-earth alienations and bring powerful feelings of bonding:

> Under the charm of the Dionysian not only is the union between man and man reaffirmed, but Nature which has become estranged, hostile, or subjugated, celebrates once more her reconciliation with her prodigal son, man. . . . Now all the stubborn, hostile barriers which necessity, caprice or "shameless fashion" have erected between man and man, are broken down. . . . He feels that the veil of Maya has been torn aside and now merely fluttering in tatters before the mysterious Primordial Unity.[16]

Addictions, Religious Experience, and Grace

Paul Tillich illuminated our deep inner alienations as humans from our capacity to love ourselves and experience the love of God: "The depth of our separation lies in just the fact that we are not capable of a great and merciful divine love toward ourselves."[17] For many self-alienated people who are not able to love themselves or others in any depth, psychochemicals like alcohol and drugs bring temporary feelings of self-other bonding. They still the civil wars within and make them feel unified and at peace with themselves, for a brief time. These chemicals also give some a brief taste of being accepted by and acceptable to others, of having it together, or some intimate connectedness with others and of mystical unity with life. Their existential anxiety is quieted by this pseudoreligious sense of oneness with themselves, others, and the divine Spirit.

The tragedy in all this is that so many people are able to find experience of grace, acceptance, and relatedness *only* via addictive chemicals and obsessive-compulsive behavior patterns. That so many have found no other path to satisfy their spiritual-existential needs is profoundly sad.

The situation was aptly described by William James when he wrote about this use of alcohol:

> It is a part of the deeper mystery and tragedy of life that whiffs and gleams of something that we immediately recognize as excellent should be vouchsafed to so many of us only in the fleeting earlier phases of what in its totality is so degrading a poison.[18]

I felt the poignant pathos in the experience of one female alcoholic who recalled: "When I reached a certain point in a drunk, I felt as though I was on the edge of a beautiful land. I kept drinking to try to find it, even though I never did." I realize now the tragedy implicit in Bill Wilson's statement at our first encounter (perhaps paraphrasing Thomas Wolfe): "Before A.A. we were trying to drink God out of a bottle." Countless spiritually starving people are on dead-end searches for God in drugs, alcohol, and addictive behaviors because they have not found God anywhere else. Psychiatrist Gerald G. May, reports:

> After twenty years of listening to the yearnings of people's hearts, I am convinced that all humans have an inborn desire for God. Whether we are consciously religious or not, this desire is our deepest longing and our most precious treasure. It gives us meaning. Some of us have repressed this desire, burying it beneath so many other interests that we are completely unaware of it. Or we may experience it in different ways—as a longing for wholeness, completion, or fulfillment. Regardless of how we describe it, it is a longing for love. This yearning is the essence of the human spirit. It is the origin of our highest hopes and most noble dreams.[19]

Gerald May wrote this in his in-depth exploration of the key role of grace in recovery from the multiple addictions in our secularized society. He understands addictions, as do I, to be idols that replace the divine Spirit at the center of people's lives and devotion. Whether addicted to alcohol, narcotics, nicotine, food, work, power, money, success, relationships, ideas, sex, sports, or rigid religious creeds, they "make idolators of us all, because it forces us to worship these objects of attachment, thereby preventing us from truly, freely loving God and one another."[20] Because addictions truncate freedom and choice and grossly cripple the will, recovery on one's own becomes increasingly difficult as the addictive process sabotages one's best intentions. For this reason, according to May, grace and, one of its fruits, hope are keys to recovery. He points out that grace is a motif in many faith traditions, including the Christian:

> For Christians, grace is the dynamic outpouring of God's loving nature that flows into and through creation in an endless self-offering of healing love, illumination, and reconciliation . . . a gift that is often given in spite of our intentions and errors. At such time, when grace is so clearly given unrequested, uninvited, even undeserved, there can be no authentic response but gratitude and awe.[21]

A historical Christian emphasis, highlighted by Protestantism, has been on "salvation by grace through faith," as the New Testament describes it. This is essentially what both Tillich and May were discussing—a deep, healing, enlivening experience of acceptance and reconciliation, of coming home spiritually. Loving parents accept and love their children, not because of what they do but because they *are* their children. In a comparable way, grace is a transforming experience of God's unconditional, loving acceptance that cannot, and fortunately need not, be earned.

When addicted people have gone through the deep water of suffering and have finally accepted the fact that they are not God, they often become aware of their deep need to trust and depend on God. When this occurs, their hearts often become open to receive God's priceless gift of grace. Someone has described this step in spiritual growth as "resigning as general manager of the universe." Then trust opens the door of their hearts to the healing, empowering love of God. It is when people surrender their grandiosity and feel deeply accepted by God that they can "accept themselves as being accepted," to use Tillich's apt phrase again.

When captives of addictions really hit bottom, their ingenious strategies, their attempts to "figure out how to control this thing on my own," have collapsed in shambles around them. They surrender, admit that they are powerless, and thus become open to help from other people and eventually, through them, for help from God. The gifts of grace and hope usually come as a surprise. These precious, healing gifts may come via an A.A. sponsor, a Twelve Step group, or a caring treatment center counselor, all of whom have been surprised by the gift of grace themselves. At times the gift is channeled via clergy or other counselors who know this transforming gift personally. Whoever they are, such persons become imperfect but open channels for God's healing love to flow into shattered lives. It is through experiencing God's accepting love, incarnated in loving human relationships, that existential anxieties are allayed. Often, for the first time in years, people feel reconnected and the peace of knowing that they really are at home in the universe.

As trust in a Higher Power suddenly or gradually grows, existential anxiety may become what the grandfather of existentialism, Sören Kierkegaard called a "school," that is an opportunity to learn and grow. When this happens, addicts become able to face and integrate their existential anxiety into their fractured human identity. In his classic work, *The Concept of Dread*, Kierkegaard pointed out that in the very experience of facing existential anxiety in a context of some trust, anxious people can be educated to inner certitude or faith. This gives them the

> courage to renounce anxiety without any anxiety, which only faith is capable of—not that it annihilates anxiety, but remains ever young, it is continually developing itself out of the death throes of anxiety.[22]

Like Kierkegaard, Tillich believed that only as existential anxiety is confronted and taken into people's self-identity can it enrich rather than disrupt and diminish their lives. Healthy religious faith and experience help humans transcend anxieties about our finitude. Therefore, religious answers are the only deeply satisfying ones to our species' awareness that we are all living-dying creatures.

Healthy vs. Unhealthy Religion and Ethics

In the ways described above, healthy or salugenic religious beliefs and practices give genuine answers to the spiritual problems for which alcohol and drugs have only chemical pseudo answers. Healthy religion provides awareness of unity, of self-forgiveness, of God's acceptance, and of the larger life.

Here is an overview of our universal, existential needs to which healthy religions alone can bring genuine satisfactions:

- The need for a growing relationship with the divine Spirit of love and justice who becomes our uplifting, energizing center of devotion, with whom we are challenged to become cocreators of a world where all people will have opportunities for developing their full gifts of God;
- The need for regular times of transcending the "everydayness" of life by what psychologist Abraham Maslow called "peak experiences," those moments when we experience getting high and celebrate something eternal in the our temporal lives;
- The need for vital beliefs (that we really believe) to give life some meaning and purpose in the midst of its frustration, losses, and tragedies;

- The need for healthy values, priorities, and life commitments centered on integrity, love, and justice, to guide us into personally and socially responsible lifestyles;
- The need for developing the inner wisdom, creativity, love, and spiritual riches of our core self—known as the soul in traditional religious language;
- The need for spiritual resources to nurture self-esteem, empowerment, hope, trust, courage, and forgiveness (of ourselves and others); and the need for spiritual resources to help heal the soul wounds of despair, distrust, anxiety, boredom, self-rejection, grief, alienation, guilt and shame;
- The need for a loving, caring awareness of our oneness with other people in the human family and with the whole network of living things in the marvel-filled natural world that is God's continuing creation.[23]

In our society, expressions of wholeness-nurturing religion that satisfy these spiritual needs in constructive ways seem in short supply. The grim tragedy of the mass suicide by thirty-nine members of the Heaven's Gate cult is simply the tip of the iceberg of the epidemic of less dramatic pathogenic faith and value systems in our society. When people live in a barren spiritual wasteland, healthy spiritual food that satisfies their deep heart hungers in healthful ways is hard to find. Consequently they often turn to psychospiritual idols and give their ultimate devotion to seductive gods like cult leaders. Or they worship the alluring idols of success, money, and power that cannot really satisfy their spiritual hungers.

When spiritually malnourished or starving people try to use alcohol and/or drugs, or addictive activities like gambling as substitutes for all that healthy religious living could give them, they are worshiping idols that eventually will betray them. When these substances or activities begin to take over the center of people's lives and devotion, they are on the slippery slope of addiction. It is then that health-giving religious resources, usually mediated through spiritually oriented caring people or groups like A.A., may bring healing help. These individuals or groups become channels that supply the nourishing spiritual and interpersonal food that addicted persons often need for their full recovery and spiritual wellness.

Recovery Spirituality Contrasted with Addiction Spirituality

The typical characteristics of the spirituality of those in recovery who are moving toward life transformation contrast sharply with the typical characteristics of addicted persons who are still drinking and/or using. The spirituality of the former tends to be much more salugenic, as they satisfy their spiritual needs in healthier ways. In contrast, the spirituality of those in active addictions tends to be more pathogenic, as they try to satisfy their spiritual needs in unhealthy ways. Here is a list of the typical spiritual attributes of those on the path of effective recovery, and the contrasting spiritual attributes of those still trapped in addictions. The source of health-nurturing spirituality usually flow from a growing relationship with a Higher Power who is loving, accepting, and full of grace, as opposed to a harsh, judging, and punishing one. From their healing, empowering relationships with their Higher Power, the spirituality of those moving ahead in recovery usually is more:

- open, flexible, and growing instead of closed and rigid;
- reality respecting and nonmanipulative of God instead of magical, manipulative, and trying to make God adjust to one's personal desires;
- joyful, uplifting, and celebrative of the good gift of life instead of heavy, burdensome, and deadly dull;
- self-esteem, self-acceptance, and forgiveness fostering instead of fostering guilt, shame, and rejection of oneself, including one's body image and sexual impulses;
- love, humility, and trust inspiring instead of generating anger, fear, and prideful superiority feelings;
- respectfully connecting with others who differ instead of excluding, rejecting, and even attacking of them;
- intimate bonding with the natural world instead of alienated from God's natural creation;
- playful instead of constricted and controlling;
- motivating to envision and implement strategies for creative change instead of preoccupied with self-serving protection of the status quo);
- a love-affair with life instead of experiencing life as boring and mainly a chronic struggle and trial.

In counseling with people on the road to recovery, it is important to bear these characteristics of constructive recovery spirituality in mind so that they can be nurtured in those being counseled. To the extent that those on what often is a rocky recovery road develop such healthy spirituality, their recovery will tend to be more ongoing, stable, and productive of the well-being of themselves and their families.

As we have seen, religious approaches provide spiritual alternatives for alcohol and drugs in a variety of ways. The following chart gives an overview of ways in which the religious groups explored in this book seek to encourage constructive answers to the problems of addicts, in place of the destructive answers of alcohol and drugs. Column I, entitled "The Alcoholic Feels," describes some common emotional distress that many suffer from at the stage of their sickness at which they often seek help from religious groups. Column II, "Alcohol's Solution," describes the unsatisfactory answers that alcohol and drugs give to these problems. Because many of the dynamics of the Rescue Mission and the Salvation Army are quite similar, the solutions that these approaches usually offered are lumped together in Column III. The Emmanuel approach is presented in column IV and A.A.'s solution is presented in column V. (The Emmanuel Movement will be discussed briefly in chapter 15.)

Prevention by Nurturing Healthy Spirituality

Drug and alcohol prevention in religious institutions can be facilitated by helping children, youth, adults, and families nurture healthy spirituality and values to satisfy their religious and ethical needs in nonchemical ways. As we have seen, alcohol and other consciousness-changing drugs have the capacity to temporarily allay the agonizing awareness of the different types of anxiety, particularly existential or religious anxiety. They also have the ability to bring some users pseudomystical experiences of unity and transcendence. Some spiritually hungry people, who long for the numbing of existential anxiety or to transcend their earthbound finitude, use drugs and alcohol as an attempt to participate mystically in the larger life of the Spirit. If their religious life is empty, lifeless, or negative, they may gravitate to alcohol and drugs, or overuse activities, such as sex, gambling, or work, seeking satisfaction of these spiritual longings.

If these individuals are vulnerable to addictions because of psychological, physiological, or cultural factors, their development of addictions can be facilitated by their increasing attempts to satisfy spiritual hungers by the use of chemical or behavioral comforters. But the fleeting superficiality of these pseudospiritual experiences actually enhances their deeper spiritual hungers. As the addictive process deepens, their chemicals or behaviors become increasingly the center of their lives and devotion. A.A. and other spiritually centered recovery programs provide healthier, nonchemical satisfactions of addicts' spiritual hungers to replace the temporary spiritual satisfactions they have found in drinking and using drugs. In summary, congregations can contribute to prevention of addictions by nurturing nonchemical, health-giving spirituality and constructive values.

I THE ALCOHOLIC FEELS	II ALCOHOL'S SOLUTION	III RESCUE MISSION AND SALVATION ARMY SOLUTIONS	IV EMMANUEL'S SOLUTION	V A.A.'S SOLUTION
1. Trapped in the vortex of an addictive spiral.	Anesthetizes pain of this feeling but accelerates velocity of the spiral.	Breaks spiral by powerful emotional experience of "salvation" induced by fear and guilt plus promise of new life.	Uses suggestion and auto-suggestion to break the spiral; medication recommended where necessary. Supportive group experiences.	Provides practical tools (e.g. 24-hour plan) for maintaining sobriety, plus example and support of sober group. Medication recommended where necessary.
2. Depressed.	Gives feeling of elation, followed by worse depression.	Gives feeling of thrill or religious ecstasy.	Encouragement of the therapist, plus the reduction of guilt through analysis.	Group uplift, plus the reduction of the guilt at the root of depression.
3. Isolated, rejected, unacceptable, in a shell, desocialized.	Gives temporary feeling of nearness to people.	Melts shell by powerful emotional experience, plus acceptance by the ingroup of the "saved."	Provides relationship to an accepting person—the therapist—plus some group acceptance, providing the experience of acceptance.	Gives an accepting group in which resocialization and growth in responsibility can take place.
4. Guilt and self-rejection.	Depresses self-critique; allows atonement via self-punishment.	Salvation experience gives sense of forgiveness by supreme Authority plus devices of atonement.	"Sickness" concept of alcoholism, acceptance by therapist, reduction of guilt via insight into one's own psychic life.	"Sickness" concept reduces guilt and releases energies for therapeutic ends. Nonjudgmental group sharing common problem.
5. Nameless fears, awful pain, jitters.	Anesthetizes pain and fears; quiets jitters. May increase fears by releasing repressions.	Fears reduced when alcohol leaves body. Sense of protection by God.	Dependence on an authority figure plus analysis of the roots of fears. Medication for jitters.	Medication for jitters. Safety in group. Understanding of strange alcoholic behavior.
6. Oppressed by a sense of futility, tragedy (in the philosophical sense), and finitude. Ultimate anxiety.	Gives temporary panacea; anesthetizes all anxiety; gives sense of larger life.	Gives a religious experience of larger life, meaningful relationship to the Ultimate here and hereafter, experience of acceptance.	Offers a new sense of relatedness to the whole of creation and awareness of divine potentialities within.	Gradual, growing sense of meaning and relatedness to people. Growing faith and assurance about life, strong experience of acceptance.

7. Inability to meet adult interpersonal demands.	Allows adjustment by regression.	Encourages dependence on the wonderful Power and on authoritarian group.	Dependence on therapist followed (in theory) by independence through insight.	Encourages dependence on group in which one may grow in interpersonal adequacy.
8. Inadequate, weak, inferior.	Gives an illusion of adequacy, superiority by depressing self-critique.	Gives feeling of strength through identification with the saved and with the Supreme Power.	Inferiority feelings reduced as he understands real causes of addiction. Becomes more adequate in interpersonal realm. Identification with therapist; strengthening of self-esteem.	Strength from group identification. His weakness (alcoholism) now seen as sickness and becomes basis of unique usefulness and acceptance by the group. Strengthens self-esteem.
9. Defensively grandiose, magically powerful.	Gives feeling of expansiveness and magically powerful condition.	Gives opportunity to become instruments of divine power. Reduction of guilt reduces need for grandiosity. Partial surrender of grandiosity in salvation experience.	Strengthening of self-esteem plus psychological maturity removes need for grandiosity.	Reduces need for defensive grandiosity. Rewards "humility." Surrender of grandiosity possible in accepting group.
10. Useless.	Makes him feel he is world's benefactor, or not care that he isn't.	Gives a sense of mission to help save others.	Insight allows one to achieve a more constructive role in relation to others.	Gives sense of unique usefulness in helping alcoholics.
11. Tension of repressed aggression and rage.	Melts frozen rage, giving partial release of repressed aggression while defenses are lowered,	Allows release of aggression in group-approved channels—i.e., toward unsaved. More effective repression, strengthened by group and religious sanctions.	Reduction of the inner pressures through therapeutic release; repression of some by suggestive therapy.	Through moral inventory removes many of the precipitants and occasions of anger and frustration. Release by aggressive activity in helping others.
12. Egocentric, selfish, lack of group controls.	Increases egocentricity.	Other-directed activities and interests rewarded by group. Group controls possible because of group satisfactions.	Psychoanalytic reduction of inner conflicts removes a degree of need to be selfish. Patients could become friendly visitors, etc., thus acquiring other-directed interests and activities.	A planned program of other-directed activities (Twelfth Step) designed to keep the individual from egocentric isolation. Enlightened self-interest recognized as legitimate.
13. Pressure from inner conflicts, guilt of unlived life.	Gives the illusion of inner unity, freedom, self-direction.	Pressure continues but somewhat offset by unifying religious devotion.	Character change through self-understanding resulting from psychoanalysis.	Some character change through group therapy, social participation, self-analysis.

Recovery Without Religion

The view that a spiritual dimension is an essential part of any widely effective recovery program is held by the majority of practitioners in the addiction field, including some who have little or no personal interest in religion. But in understanding the dynamic roles of religious beliefs, attitudes, and practices in treatment, it is useful to examine a recovery movement that is explicitly and vigorously nonreligious in its basic philosophy and methodology. James Christopher, a freelance writer and longtime sober alcoholic, is the founder of Secular Sobriety Groups. His book, *How to Stay Sober: Recovery Without Religion*, describes his experiences with and criticisms of A.A., and challenges the A.A. view that long-term sobriety is rarely if ever possible without depending on "God as you understand Him." (The book also gives concrete guidelines for organizing Secular Sobriety Groups at a local level.)

Christopher, who was raised in a Baptist family in Texas, describes himself as an

> . . . agnostic, naturalist, rationalist, skeptic, moderate existentialist, secular humanist, and free thinker, among other things. I find no evidence of God or a supernatural higher power in the natural universe. . . . Although life has no meaning per se, it is up to me to pump meaning into it on a daily basis . . . Gods or goblins have nothing to do with alcoholism, cancer, or any other disease. Agnostics, atheists, deists, secular humanists, and rationalists can achieve sobriety and maintain it without belief in the intervention of a higher power or "personal God."[24]

His philosophy as well as his negative experiences in A.A., when he raised questions about the Higher Power concept, caused him to conclude:

> Being wrapped in the swaddling clothes of cult care can be comforting as long as one doesn't stray from the "protection" of the A.A. party line. Such a departure, I hereby attest, can result in powerful peer pressure, since the group's automatic reaction is to maintain its collective concepts, no matter how irrational these concepts may be in the light of reason. . . . To accept the concept of utilizing a substitute addiction—reliance on a mystical power greater than oneself . . . is, at worst, to involve oneself in an oppressive cultist atmosphere. At best, it is to encourage dependence upon something or someone

other than oneself for sobriety, rendering sobriety conditional.[25]

Christopher remembers that he first convened a Secular Sobriety group in November, 1989 in Los Angeles. People from a wide variety of occupations including social workers, carpenters, nurses, athletes, office clerks, and teachers are now among the members. Some have been sober for many years, proving that it is not necessary "to be mystical to be merry, or go from grog to God" to stay sober. The group keeps its meetings "dogma free" and emphasizes the life-and-death need of alcoholics and other addicts to stay sober regardless of what takes place in their lives that might contribute to slips. He reports that "lives are being saved and made fruitful" with "no gods or gobblins" or belief in a Higher Power, or accepting any party line. They focus on celebrating and supporting alcoholics in achieving and continuing their sobriety, whatever they believe or don't believe.[26]

Some members of SSG find a secularized version of the Twelve Steps helpful as a framework for living, while others have abandoned these steps entirely. These suggested guidelines highlight the basic principles of SSG:

1. To break the cycle of denial and achieve sobriety, we first must acknowledge that we are alcoholics.

2. We reaffirm this truth daily and accept without reservation—one day at a time—the fact that, as sober alcoholics, we cannot and do not drink, no matter what.

3. Since drinking is not an option for us, we take whatever steps are necessary to continue our sobriety priority lifelong.

4. A high quality of life—the good life—can be achieved. However, life is also filled with uncertainties, therefore, we do not drink regardless of feelings, circumstances, or conflicts.

5. We share in confidence with each other our thoughts and feelings as sober alcoholics.

6. Sobriety is our priority and we are each individually responsible for our lives and our sobriety.[27]

The 1996 Southern California regional conference was billed as a celebration of the first decade of SOS (standing for both Secular Organizations for Sobriety, and Save Our Selves) of which individual groups are a part. The topics announced for this conference seemed to suggest a vigorous and varied program. They included "Couples in Recovery," "Multicultural SOS," "SOS Outreach Programs," and "Life Issues and the Courage to Change."

Some substance abusers find the religious dimensions in Twelve Step programs difficult or impossible to accept. Their number includes at least some longtime sober members of A.A. who consider themselves agnostics or atheists. Their Higher Power ranges from the group itself to the marvelous but impersonal life processes. It is not accurate to dismiss the nontheistic views of all such persons as "resistance to taking the Third Step," as is sometimes done by A.A. members. It is more clarifying to recognize that the belief systems with which we humans satisfy our spiritual needs are widely diverse and include a variety of nontheistic philosophies of life. One of the strengths of our pluralistic culture is its valuing of diversity. In any case, for the countless untreated addicts, it is fortunate indeed that Secular Sobriety Groups now offer another recovery option. How widely effective such secular programs will be over time remains to be seen.

The view expressed by Gerald A. Larue, professor emeritus of Archaeology and Biblical Studies at the University of Southern California, in the foreword of Christopher's book, articulates a cogent perspective:

> This book makes an important contribution to prolonging and enhancing the lives of alcoholics, to enriching the lives of their families and loved ones, and to protecting the lives of those who become the victims of alcoholics who drink and drive. Responsible sobriety under personal control is the key.[28]

Larue believes that this approach is effective because it utilizes the human instinctual drive to live, to live well, and to be in control of our lives, and because it provides what we as social creatures need—mutual support of one another's living well.

Summary

Here is a summary of some inherent benefits of salugenic religious approaches for many substance abusers. Substance use that becomes addictive has been understood, at least for some people, as a tragic attempt to satisfy the universal needs of our species for spiritual experiences and meanings. Religious approaches can provide many individuals with a sense of transcending or superhuman help, not only in meeting their daily problems of living, but also in coping constructively with the general frustrations, disappointments, drudgery, and interpersonal conflicts that contribute to the etiology of addictions. The help of a Higher Power is available even when the help of individuals or groups is not, thus complementing the healing help of sponsors and groups.

Because addicted persons often suffer from defensive grandiosity and ambivalence toward authority, religious approaches provide opportunities for them to grow by coming to terms with a Power greater than themselves. This often means that they accept their need for help from beyond themselves.

Religious approaches can provide addicted persons with feelings of being accepted by life. As we have seen, individuals often experience healing acceptance in A.A., first from their sponsors, then from the group, and then from their Higher Power. Increasing self-acceptance often accrues from this progression of acceptances.

An addicted clergyman I know has discovered a vital, joyous personal faith for himself in A.A. He points to connection between God's acceptance and genuine self-acceptance:

> The love of God is the love of self. The real self. And the love of the real self is the love of God. The two cannot be separated. For me, the gulf, the great distance between an all-perfect God in heaven and a sinful self here on earth was completely bridged. Bridged? No, gone![29]

When A.A. members' Higher Power changes from the group to God, it is often an indication of psychological growth in the sense that they now feel accepted by life itself—instead of just by the in-group of other alcoholics. They have become less defensive because they have experienced acceptance. We saw earlier that worshiping success on the part of parents is one dynamic factor among the psychological roots of some addictions. Children feel that they must achieve impossible goals in order to be accepted. In this context, the significance of the religious experience of self-acceptance based on being accepted unconditionally by God is evident.

Religious approaches may provide addicts with a nonchemical means of handling their ultimate anxiety.[30] If it is true that anxiety about death, meaninglessness, and finitude is one significant factor in causing much alcoholism and drug dependence, then religious approaches obviously make much needed contributions to recovery. They do so by providing a sense of relatedness to and participation in the larger life of spirituality. They may provide faith in the trustworthiness of the spiritual universe, helping many people in recovery handle their ultimate anxiety more constructively.

Effective religious approaches to addictions can help many persons to discover purposes in living based on personally meaningful philosophies of life. Organized religious systems are time-tested ways of satisfying what psychoanalyst Erich Fromm called the universal human need for a "system of thought and action shared by a group which gives the individual a frame of orientation and an object of devotion."[31] Thus, religious approaches can strengthen a sense of order, meaning, and other-directedness in living, giving recovering persons a role in what they see as a God-given plan to help others. This supplies another positive reason for not using their addictive chemicals. In a group like A.A., they find the emotional involvement and sense of mission that comes from feeling a part of something that really matters.

A religious orientation can provide recovery groups a unifying commitment to a group-transcending mission, a shared cause in which to focus their devotion beyond the group. This gives group members a stronger sense of cohesiveness. Most people, including recovering addicts, need to feel themselves a part of something that is bigger and more enduring than themselves. The sense of a shared mission in religiously oriented groups can satisfy not only the longing to belong but also the powerful need to belong to something that has abiding significance.

CHAPTER 10

Understanding Ethical Issues in Addiction and Recovery

Two recent accidents near my home brought into sharp focus the complex ethical dilemmas related to alcoholism and drug addictions. Disturbed by these tragedies, a local newspaper columnist wondered why the wrong people die:

> I'm haunted, in this season of warm family togetherness, by the faces of two young, beautiful women, wives and mothers. By all accounts, they led unusually happy, productive lives. But those lives were snuffed out by two irresponsible, self-destructive people whose days were wasted, blurred by alcohol and drugs.[1]

Patricia Ann Higbie was killed, and her two children critically injured, when a forty-three-year-old alcoholic lost control of his speeding stolen car and smashed into her car. A street person, he had been arrested twenty-eight times in the last thirteen years for drunkenness and misdemeanors like possessing marijuana. (This man had tried to flee from the accident and died when a truck hit him.) Kristina Waldman died when a longtime drug user careened across to the wrong side of the road as Kristina was doing her usual morning jog. The driver, who has a $500 a week crack cocaine addiction, was saved by her air bag. She was arrested, convicted, and sentenced to six years in prison, "not a minute of which will help bring Kristina back," as the columnist observed. The columnist concluded by wondering, with many of us: "Shattered lives, wasted lives. When will we learn?"

These tragedies remind us that addictions are costly, destructive diseases to everyone in society, not just to the addicted and their families. Troubling questions are raised by such accidents: Not just when but *what* will we learn? What should society do to prevent or reduce such tragedies? What are the ethical and responsibility issues involved? What are appropriate ways to handle these issues in preventive education, treatment programs, and public policy decisions? There are no facile or fully adequate answers. While many thoughtful people ponder these ethical dilemmas, my studies show that many religious leaders have failed to understand and speak out on these issues. Could this be one reason why organized religious groups have not made more crucial contributions to healing the runaway pandemic of addictions?

I recall some wise words by a leading Roman Catholic authority in the field of alcoholism. Although spoken years ago, they should be an axiom in clergy's approach to alcoholics and drug addicts today. Father John C. Ford, then a college professor of moral and pastoral theology at Weston College in Massachusetts, advised that "One must never approach an alcoholic on the basis of what is usually called morality." Anyone who has dealt insightfully with even one alcoholic or drug addict can affirm the validity of his statement. From the standpoint of therapeutic effectiveness, to moralize with an addicted person is the ultimate in counseling futility. But for clergy and other counselors to have some clarity in their own minds about the ethical issues in substance addictions has numerous practical implications. Whether we are aware of it or not, our relationships with the addicted will be influenced in subtle but crucial ways by our understanding of these ethical questions.

Fortunately, in the last few decades, the social context of prevailing attitudes toward social drinking, drunkenness, and alcoholism seem to have changed significantly, making it somewhat easier to avoid judgmental attitudes toward addicted people. Drinking in controlled moderation is seen as inherently sinful by a smaller percentage of religious people, whereas voluntary excessive drinking seems to be more widely regarded as dangerous and inappropriate. More religious people accept the fact that full-blown chemical addictions are genuine sicknesses in which treatment, not punishment, is the appropriate response. Furthermore, addictions seem less frequently to be lumped in with stigmatized illness.

Studies of clergy attitudes toward addictions show that people in our profession have a wide variety of views, convictions, and questions regarding ethical issues in addictions. This includes many clergy who are well informed with accurate facts about addictions. That this is true is not surprising in light of the fact that issues of ethics and addiction push us to examine our basic orientation concerning morality, sin, punishment, human freedom and trappedness, as well as the tangled, often paradoxical, complexities of human behavior in general. To those who struggle to understand and respond constructively to the ethical complexities of living, it is not satisfying to say that addictions are diseases if this is taken to imply that all ethical issues have thereby been eliminated. For they know that every personal and social problem is also an ethical problem calling for a constructive response.

Sin, Sickness, Alcoholism, and Drug Addictions

Do addictions involve sin and, if so, sin in what sense? And how does sin relate to the basic sickness nature of addictions? It is important to recognize at the outset that the word "sin" has been used with a confusing variety of meanings in the field of ethical theories. Most of the varied conceptions have been applied, now and again, to alcoholism and other substance addictions. Here is an evaluative summary of some of the more frequently mentioned concepts with suggestions concerning how they can be applied appropriately to addictions. Several of these concepts are not mutually exclusive:

1. Addictions are the result of personal sin. At no point are they sicknesses.

This view was encountered in the study of rescue missions. According to this concept, substance addictions begin as the sin of drinking or using drugs, progresses to the greater sin of excessive use (abuse), and ends as a sinful habit. At all stages, addictions result from immoral behavior based on misuse of free will. At no point can they be called a genuine sickness, except perhaps a "sin-sickness." This untenable view is limited mainly to believers in fundamentalist religious traditions who are far to the right on the wide theological spectrum.

Such moralistic concepts are psychologically, sociologically, and theologically naive, ignoring well-established facts about human compulsions and the multiple causes of addictions. They ignore the fact that chronic excessive drinking and drug use very often are symptoms of factors such as childhood emotional crippling, social programming, social and peer pressures, unconscious conflicts, physiological addiction, and, in all likelihood, genetic vulnerability. Focusing on symptoms while ignoring underlying causes is an approach that guarantees failure to be helpful to either the victims or to society's well-being.

It is not within the scope of this book to attempt adjudication of the disagreements among sincere Christians as to whether drinking and using any potentially addictive drug are sins, per se. However, if one chooses to apply the 100 percent personal sin view, it is well to remember that even the early drinking and use by those who eventually become addicted often is part of a total obsessive-compulsive behavioral pattern. Most addicts were compulsive persons, to some degree, even before they became compulsive drinkers and users. Because personal sin requires personal freedom of choice, the sin involved in the early stages of addictions is limited by the degree that persons' freedom is constricted.

2. Addictions begin as personal sin that results in an obsessive-compulsive disease process called addiction.

This is a widely accepted view among clergy from different traditions, especially those who view any use of alcohol or pleasure-giving drugs as sinful. This view was encountered earlier as the dominant position of the Salvation Army. Briefly put, any alcohol or drug use is seen as sinful. Drinking and using drugs excessively is much more sinful, for a variety of reasons, including the fact that those who do so expose themselves to the risk of addictions. Once drinking and drug use have passed a certain point and voluntary control is significantly diminished or lost, it becomes an addictive illness. Victims are no longer fully responsible, since their drinking and using are now done compulsively to some degree, beyond the control of their wills. However, they *are* responsible for having caught the compulsion or disease. In this sense addictions are sin sicknesses.

This view is considerably more adequate than the first. It is more likely to result in effective education, therapy, and public policy because it recognizes that, at least in its advanced stages, addictions are illnesses. But this view, like the first, has the limitation of oversimplifying the causes of alcoholism, ignoring or deemphasizing the complex array of factors that tend to diminish the freedom to choose not to drink or use.

3. Addictions are sicknesses that are caused by the sin of voluntary excessive drinking or drug use.

This view, a variation on the second one, holds that it is drunkenness, the abuse and not the mere use of substances, that constitutes personal sin. This is the official Roman Catholic position. The sin is the sin of excess involved in becoming addicted. However, the Catholic Church recognizes that neurotic compulsion is involved in at least some alcoholics' behavior and holds that "culpability is reduced according to the strength" of their neuroses. This position, together with the previous position, has the practical difficulty of making it necessary to establish a degree of responsibility or to define a line of demarcation beyond which addicted persons are not ethically responsible. With human beings, such a determination is utterly inexact if not impossible.

4. Alcoholism and other substance addictions are sicknesses caused by the convergence of a variety of factors involving both sin and sickness, responsibility and compulsivity.

This is a fair statement of the view of those who regard drinking and using as wrong but who also recognize the sickness caused by various factors that are beyond the control of persons caught in the addictive process. It also approximates the view of A.A. which, though it takes no sides in such matters and does not use the word "sin," does not regard drinking per se as morally wrong. It emphasizes that alcoholics have a psychological compulsion joined with a physical addiction to alcohol. It goes on, however, to express the belief that one is driven to drink by selfishness and its symptoms. Alcoholics are responsible for changing the feelings and attitudes, and the moral failures that contribute to the mental obsession to drink, even though they are not responsible for having what A.A. believes is an atypical physical response to alcohol.

5. Alcoholism and drug dependence involve sin in the sense that they have destructive consequences. These include preventing people from developing their God-given capacities for living fully and productively.

This is comparable to the view that addictions involve sin in the sense expressed in the New Testament as "missing the mark." In a survey I conducted about clergys' attitudes concerning alcoholism, one minister expressed this view: "Alcoholism is sin in that it hinders the person from abundant living and true happiness. It is not a sin insofar as morals are concerned." Another minister declared: "It is a sin in the sense that it detracts from the alcoholic's relationship with God, his family, and his community." These are descriptions of the consequences of alcoholism rather than judgments about the responsibility involved. If sin is defined as anything that harms persons, whatever the cause, then addiction most certainly involves sin.

6. Addictions are illnesses resulting from social sins.

One of the ministers in my study stated this point of view well: "Alcoholism is a sin only in the sense that it is a sin attributed to society, especially a Christian society—that we have been unable to bring about a world free from the tensions and conflicts of the present day. I do not consider it a personal sin." Another put it this way: "It may be a sin, but it is more a symptom or an evidence of a sinful condition in some parts of our society. It is more sinful for Christian and civilized people to not only allow but promote the conditions that cause it."

Whatever one's view of addicted persons' responsibility, the fact that society greases the slope down which they slide certainly is true. The chaos and psychological insecurity of our world, the confusion and conflict of values regarding drinking and drunkenness, and the traumatic experiences to which many children are subjected—these are expressions of which the sicknesses of addictions are a manifestation. I remember a striking illustration that Jellinek once used in discussing the ethical aspects of alcoholism. He observed that if six out of every hundred people who went swimming at a certain beach contracted a disease that had all sorts of destructive effects, it would certainly be regarded as a question of public morals and safety. Our society contributes in many ways to the causes of addictions. It therefore has an inescapable responsibility for both their prevention and treatment.

7. Alcoholism and other addictions involve original sin.

In presenting this traditional theological concept, I am not expressing the untenable position of biblical literalism that holds that human nature is corrupted by the sin of a generic ancestor named Adam. Instead I am attempting to describe the dynamic sociopsychological meaning that is implied in the concept of original sin—a meaning that has been illuminated by the findings of contemporary depth psychology. This is the only sense in which the concept is intelligible, as I understand it.

We all must take into account the genetic and environmental factors, the historical and societal situation into which we happened to be born, the powerful childhood conditioning that occurred before we could exercise power of choice, the continuing social learning from our culture, and the inherent limitations of our finitude or our existential condition as living-dying creatures, if we are to fully understand addictions. Further, an analysis of the human experience leads many of us to the conclusion that all evil cannot be explained as the result of ignorance, as the Socratic tradition has claimed. There often seems to be a certain recalcitrance at the very center of human beings that tends to inhibit doing what we know to be good for ourselves and others. This has been described, in traditional theological language, as the "bondage of the will."[2] In even our best acts, we humans seem to have an inescapable self-centeredness that causes us to deify ourselves, our cultures, religions, institutions, sacred books, the things we make. The alienation from God that results from this idolatry is one of the roots of our existential aloneness and anxiety. By making ourselves the center of our universe, we cut ourselves off from our own fulfillment—a fulfillment that is possible only by the self-transcendence that enables us to establish mutually enhancing relationships with other people, the Creator, and the rest of the natural world, God's creation.

This grandiose self-deification is close to the meaning of original sin. As we have seen in the discussion of the etiologic factors in chapter 2, the freedom of addicted persons often is contructed by the givens in their lives. Whether or not the term "original sin" is used—and its usefulness has certainly been diminished drastically by the manner in which it has been employed by the literalistic fundamentalists—the facts of experience behind the term must be taken into account in understanding the addicted persons and their struggles.

In deciding where one stands on the ethical issues involved in addictions, it would be well to consider combining several of the concepts mentioned above. An adequate view must certainly include the responsibility factors in the definitions of sin described in sections 5, 6, and 7. The concept expressed in section 4 will undoubtedly prove meaningful to some clergy, although the difficulties involved should be faced.

The Problem of Responsibility in Addictions

A more systematic examination of the problem of responsibility, as it is related to addictions, in the light of depth psychology, is now in order. I find it well to heed the reminder of one of my mentors in graduate studies, the late David E. Roberts. In his classic volume *Psychotherapy and a Christian View of Man* he wrote:

> The concept of responsibility has been a source of endless difficulties in psychology, philosophy, and theology. Any one who has pondered the problems of freedom and determinism will probably sympathize with the sentiment which prompted Milton to assign discussion of this topic to some little devils in Satan's legions who liked to bandy it about during moments of relaxation—without getting anywhere.[3]

Depth psychology has made it clear that much human behavior, which had formerly been attributed to free will, inherent human corruption, or mere chance, is actually caused by unconscious forces over which one has no control as long as they remain out of conscious awareness. This does not mean that the human personality is a robot whose behavior is completely determined by internal or external forces. What is meant is that all behavior has psychodynamic causes. The moving forces within the psyche are orderly though often hidden. Most important of all, the self is one of the causes of behavior, to some extent, depending on the degree of one's self-awareness and mental health.

The goal of counseling for spiritual or psychological health is the enhancement of self-directedness, meaning growth in the capacity of a self to be responsible for its own behavior. Relatively self-directing, responsible persons are able to take the givens in their lives—factors that they cannot change—and arrange them to some degree creatively, as a self-determining self. But when people are driven by inner compulsions in certain areas of their lives (such as their use of alcohol and drugs), their ability to be self-determining in those areas is crippled, and they are not able to exercise responsibility in that behavior.

Addicted people tend to be prisoners of their past and victims of their givens. There are many factors—heredity, environment, historical circumstances, childhood conditioning, repressed conflicts, and psychological wounds—that impinge on people's lives as they make significant decisions. The manner in which the self is able to use and shape these factors in their lives is the area of creative possibilities. The more obsessive-compulsive people are, the less creative they can be in arranging the givens in healthier designs. The challenge is to become aware of the unchangeable givens and choose to cope with them and, if possible, use them in constructive and creative ways. (A.A.'s serenity prayer is on this theme.)

There is some degree of self-determination in anyone who is not completely detached from reality, but in many people it is greatly limited. The available evidence concerning the early life and adjustment of many drug and alcohol addicted persons points to serious limitations of their capacity for self-determination in areas where their obsessive-compulsive forces prevail. All this points to the appropriateness of nonjudgmental attitudes toward those who drink and use drugs in addictive ways.

Christian theology has held that all persons are sinners in the sense that they tend to abuse the degree of freedom that they possess. All addicts, of course, share in this attribute of humanity. The important thing to remember is this: The factors that separate addicted sinners from other sinners— that is, the factors that make alcoholics into alcoholics and drug addicts into drug addicts—are factors in which they have relatively limited self-determination. Deeper understanding of addicted persons and the etiology of their sickness leads directly to the feeling expressed by the familiar words used as a motto in A.A., "There, but for the grace of God, go I." This is not spiritual sentimentalism, but the essence of psychological insight as well as the basis for real acceptance and empathy. To reach this point in their feelings toward the addicted often involves considerable self-understanding of one's own addictions that may be more polite or easily hidden. At that point, interest in trying to pin sin on more obviously addicted people evaporates. Interest shifts to helping them grow in their capacity for self-determinism and responsibility. Relating to them can be done without condescension and in more mutually healing ways because it is done with deeper empathy, acceptance, and feeling that we are all in the boat of our human limitations, in a stormy sea.

Objections to the Disease Concept of Addictions

One objection to the sickness concept of alcoholic and drug addiction is that it provides excuses for addicted people to avoid feeling responsible for their sorry condition. This objection has its counterpart in the traditional Augustinian-Pelagian controversy. David E. Roberts wrote:

> Pelagius was an earnest, practically minded moralist who was convinced that men [sic] could promote good ends if they tried hard enough; therefore, he sought to close off the "excuse" that they are compelled to do evil by sinful predispositions.[4]

Turning from the theoretical issue to the practical question: How does growth in the capacity for self-determination and responsibility occur? Psychotherapy and A.A. have given us our clearest answers. Psychotherapy has shown that one does not cure irresponsibility or egocentricity by a direct attack upon them, nor does one produce real self-determination by increasing people's guilt and shame load. The assumption of traditional moralism is that by emphasizing people's personal culpability one would make them more responsible and less immoral. Psychotherapy has demonstrated the basic fallacy of this assumption. By increasing their guilt and shame load people tend to become more self-hating, driven by compulsion, less self-determining, and therefore less capable of being responsible. Direct attacks on irresponsibility and egocentricity usually increase defensiveness and inaccessibility to help. The moralistic approach may cause people to change surface behavior through psychological pressures. This makes it seem to some that they are behaving more morally because they are more compliant to the ethical code of a particular in-group, church, or culture. But, if real morality involves self-determination, they are actually behaving less morally rather than more so. Their concern will tend to be compliance with an external code and not to internal affirmation of basic human values such as love, caring, fairness, justice, and grace-full forgiveness of themselves and others.

Psychotherapy and depth psychology have shown that growth in the capacity for self-determination comes as persons feel less guilty and shameful and more able to accept themselves. In my personal therapy and in working with clients, I have rejoiced when the liberating realization dawns that many of the things for which people have been blaming and punishing themselves, consciously or subconsciously, are actually the result of early experiences over which they had little or no control. At this point acceptance of themselves as sinners and becoming more able to accept others as sinners is linked with becoming more able to accept responsibility for making constructive changes. The discovery in psychotherapy that the core of people's personality is their basic character structure formed in the very early years of life, has helped countless people release themselves from the vicious cycle of guilt, shame, and self-rejection.

It is well to remember that this acceptance-healing process can happen in counseling and psychotherapy because people feel unearned, gracefull acceptance by the therapist and can therefore lower their defenses and face both the negative and positive truth about themselves. Therapists can accept clients to the degree that they have resolved their own punitive self-blame and thereby become able to accept themselves as imperfect, growing human beings. From a theological perspective, the unearned acceptance in a healthy family, friendship, or in a healing relationship like pastoral counseling, provides a channel through which people can experience the healing grace of God's acceptance.

A.A. teaches the same lesson with one important modification. Almost every addicted person I have known (with the exception of those suffering from severe character disorders that involve being crippled in their ability to feel "oughtness") had a heavy load of guilt and shame. Clergy and counselors whose ethical orientations are rigidly moralistic overlook this load because it does not fit the moralistic formula—that guilt and shame are means of producing ethically responsible behavior. They overlook it, too, because addicts usually hide their real feelings behind a defensive wall of denial. A direct attack on this defense only increases their need to defend themselves.

Twelve Step approaches, in contrast, quickly reduce the addicts' guilt-shame load by providing them with two liberating experiences: group acceptance with almost no conditions except admitting that one is an alcoholic who wants help, and the sickness concept of addictions. A.A. communicates, in effect, "You are not responsible for the fact that you have an allergy to alcohol." Then, within its web of accepting interpersonal relationships, A.A. proceeds to utilize the alcoholic's growing capacity for self-acceptance and responsibility by saying in effect, "But you do have a responsibility to face your loss of control over alcohol and to use the program to re-educate your attitudes toward alcohol so that you won't be driven to take the first drink." Note that A.A. waits until the person is sober and feels accepted in the group before encouraging him to face up to the necessity of learning self-protective responses to the craving to drink. This timing is as crucial to effectiveness in A.A., as it is in counseling.

A.A.'s wise approach takes two important things into account. First, in our culture with its long tradition of voluntaristic moralism, it is difficult for people to accept the idea that individuals are not personally responsible for having an addiction, and yet they are responsible to themselves and the people around them for getting help that will enable them to become responsible and choiceful by not drinking or using. Second, in our cultural setting, where many people believe that psychological dynamics are "only in your head," A.A.'s emphasis on the physical component in addictions is more effective in reducing the guilt-shame load and facilitating therapeutic change than emphasizing psychological components.

A.A. has demonstrated repeatedly the importance of waiting until people are sober, clean, and able to accept at least minimal responsibility for themselves, before introducing means of self-change. A.A. also knows the importance of utilizing this minimal capacity for self-determination when it begins to emerge. It insists that people must have some openness to being helped before A.A. can help them, usually they hit at least a minor "bottom." Until then, they are incapable of accepting even the responsibility for accepting help. Counselors and clergy will save themselves a lot of frustration if they remember this, rather than assuming that alcoholic and other addicts could accept help if they really wanted it. Once the minimal capacity for self-determination has emerged, it is crucial that it be utilized in the counseling process. Only as this capacity is exercised and nurtured, will it grow. All this is not to suggest that counselors and family members must simply sit and wait passively until the addicted persons struggle through the agonizing process of reaching their bottom. In a later chapter, methods of "elevating the bottom" by carefully planned interventions will be described.

If it were true that emphasizing the sickness concept of addictions tended to deter the addicted from getting help because they now have an excuse for their behavior, a case could certainly be made against using the concept. Actually, the opposite is true in the vast majority of cases. So long as addicts think of their substance abuse primarily as a lack of willpower and ethical strength, they will tend to go on struggling to reform themselves. This is what some strong beliefs in our culture have taught them to do. If, on the other hand, they begin to understand their trouble as primarily a sickness over which they have diminishing control, they will be more likely to seek the help they must have if they are to recover. This is because there are strong pressures in our society for sick people to get treatment.[5]

Another reason why it is difficult for some religiously oriented people to accept the sickness concept of addictions is because, unlike many physiological diseases to which it is often likened, alcoholism involves the search for pleasure. Some moralistic people feel, "I can accept the sickness concept only if I am convinced that the alcoholics, being sick people, experience unmixed suffering." A former pioneering medical director of the Yale Plan Alcoholism Clinic, Giorgio Lolli, discussed the pleasure problem insightfully in exploring therapeutic success in helping alcoholics.[6] Therapists who have this problem, he says, sooner or later will be confronted by the disturbing realization that alcoholics experience pleasures during some phases of their drinking and that the longing for pleasure is deeply involved in addictions. Lolli writes:

> An even dim awareness of the pleasurable connotations of some phases of the drinking episode cannot fail to stir up anxieties in those therapists whose conscious and even more unconscious life is governed by the principle: "I shall help the sufferer and punish the celebrant."[7]

Although Lolli did not apply this principle specifically to clergy, it often does apply to some in our profession. Clergy often attract counselees who have had above average doses of the pleasure-anxiety that are one of the dubious legacies of the long tradition of Puritanism in our culture. Pleasure-anxiety in many troubled religious people burdens them with heavy guilt and shame when they begin to experience pleasure, especially physically sensual and sexual pleasures. They feel that pleasure for its own sake is self-indulgence and, therefore, very wrong.

Lolli goes on to say:

> The therapist who is unable to accept the pleasurable connotations of alcoholism will seldom be able to affect favorably those whom he should help. Lack of acceptance of this pleasurable connotation often leads the therapist to rejection of the alcoholic. This rejection is rationalized in a variety of ways, the most common of which is expressed in the statement, "The case is hopeless."[8]

Lolli points out that a physician who would be eager to help a tuberculosis patient after his twentieth relapse often labels an alcoholic as hopeless after two or three minor relapses. The rejection implied in the label "hopeless" reactivates the alcoholic's hostilities and hopelessness, thus contributing to the continuation of drinking.

This problem has more general connotations. As Freud observed, the pain-pleasure principle—avoiding pain and seeking pleasure—is involved in motivating all human behavior. In some addictions, particularly those involving pleasurable drugs like cocaine, it is simply more obvious. If the presence of self-gratification prevents problems from being considered true sicknesses, then all neuroses must be eliminated from the category of sickness. Neurotic solutions involve some satisfactions, however warped. If clergy resolve their own inner conflicts about pleasure, they will relate more acceptingly not only to alcoholics but also to people in general, including themselves. Thus, constructive confrontation of the pleasurable aspect of many addictions can be a growth experience for ministers or other counselors. What is more, it may lead to constructive revisions of their thinking concerning many ethical problems that involve the interrelationship of sin and sickness.

A Perspective from History

Many of the objections to the sickness concept of addictions in our day were given convincing answers by persons of ethical awareness in the past. Around the middle of the nineteenth century an idealistic young physician named J. Edward Turner decided to devote his life to the treatment of "inebriety," the term for alcoholism in his day. For sixteen years he worked indefatigably for the establishment of what came to be called the New York State Inebriate Asylum. Turner made over seventy thousand calls on potential subscribers to the work and met with all the stock objections to the treatment of alcoholism as a disease. One farmer declared: "I cannot believe the disease theory of drunkenness. My Bible teaches that the drunkard is a criminal in the sight of God, and he is forever debarred from heaven." A learned professor refused his support on the grounds that: "The enterprise of building asylums for the drunkard would encourage drinking. The moderate drinker would imagine that if he became a drunkard he would go to an asylum and be cured, and hence the fear of becoming such would be entirely removed."

Henry Bellows of Union Theological Seminary in New York City worked actively alongside Turner, along with many other clergy. At the laying of the cornerstone for this pioneering institution on September 24, 1858, Bellows made a memorable statement:

I remark that it can never weaken the sense of moral responsibility, anywhere, privately or publicly, to acknowledge anything that is true; and that there is not the least reason to fear, that to make provision for the rescue of the miserable victims of an hereditary or abnormal appetite for drink will diminish in the least, in those conscious of the power and obligations of self-control, the disposition of the conscience to exercise them. . . . We might as well expect . . . asylums for the deaf and blind, to make possessors of perfect eyes and ears careless of their safety and indifferent to their preservation; or humanity towards the aged and the suffering to promote idleness and improvidence among the young and healthy . . . as to imagine that asylums for inebriates will promote and increase drunkenness.[9]

The Author's Position

I understand addictions as involving genuine sicknesses but also sin in several of the definitions described above. Personal sin is the misuse of whatever degree of personal freedom one has in a particular situation, in ways that hurt oneself, other people, society, or the natural environment. All of us humans are sinners in the sense of misusing our freedom in many ways and on many occasions, in ways that have destructive consequences. I understand full-blown addictive behavior as resulting from a genuine sickness because victims have lost whatever freedom they had, in their preaddiction lives, to use the alcohol or drugs in a controlled fashion. They have lost much of their response-ability—the ability to make choices and therefore be responsible in this dimension of their lives. But what they retain is the potential freedom to recognize their loss of freedom and control in this area and to choose to get whatever help is required to learn how to not use the addictive substances. Suffering the painful consequences of irresponsible drinking and drug use, as happened to the drug-addicted woman who killed Kristina Waldman, may crack the defensive rationalization or alibi system that often blocks addicted people in facing the reality of their behavior.

In the preaddiction period, freedom to make responsible choices about one's use of mood-changing chemicals is a matter of degree. It is limited by the various factors that make some people more vulnerable to addictions. Exercising the ability to stop drinking and using drugs in the early phases of addictions is made more difficult by two things—the ingenious ways in which the ego's defenses of rationalization and denial interfere with self-awareness of changes in one's drinking and drug use behavior and the gradual, often imperceptible process by which addictions usually develop as control slowly diminishes. Addictions literally sneak up on people. But, except for persons suffering from dual diagnoses in which mental illnesses preceded the addictions, those who eventually become addicted had some degree of freedom that was abused by them in the preaddiction phase.

Several other types of sin, in addition to personal sin, have a role in the development of addictions. The fact that alcoholism and drug dependence involve sin in the sense of having many destructive consequences is obvious. Original sin, in its psychosocial meaning, is certainly involved in the transmission of psychological but not genetic vulnerability to addictions from parents to children, generation after generation. Social sin also is abundantly present in the social desperation of drunkenness seen in oppressed peoples and in the many factors in societal contexts that contribute to differential rates of addictions in different cultures and subcultures. The theological definition of sin in the New Testament, from the Greek meaning "missing the mark," certainly is involved in addictions, as is sin that's defined as self-idolatry, meaning self-worshiping narcissism in which we make ourselves our ultimate concern rather than God and God's people and world.

Let's return for another look at the two accidents described earlier in light of this discussion of sin, sickness, and responsibility. Both perpetrators of these fatal tragedies were in the advanced stages of the disease called polyaddictions. Their addictions had strangled their freedom to use their addictive substances responsibly. The addict who was hit by a truck and died was also infected with a complicating form of social pathology—homelessness. Both were living in an addictive and addicted society where social learning had reinforced their dangerous, excessive drinking and drug use. To say all this is not to excuse their life-destroying behavior, but rather to seek an accurate understanding of it. If the responsibility of government agencies to protect the public had been exercised more carefully, the woman, in light of her well-known addictive behavior pattern, would not have been granted a driver's license. Whether or not this would have deterred her from driving is unknown. In terms of her future, the desired scenario would be that the punishment she receives will cause her to hit bottom and become open to accepting the help of A.A. and N.A., both while in the setting of the women's prison and after her release. It is quite possible, unfortunately, that incarceration will only deepen her rage, self-hatred, and alienation from society and thus make it more difficult for her to accept the needed treatment of her addictions.

Dramatic Changes Coming?

The radical new view of alcoholism, not as a disease but as a "central activity in heavy drinkers' way of life," as described by Herbert Fingarette (see chapter 8), clearly has transforming implications for conceptualizing and dealing with the ethical issues in alcohol addiction. Think about the possible ethical influence if this understanding is proved over time to have considerable validity. This will occur if the behavioral approaches, by which problem drinkers (as believed by those who subscribe to this understanding) can change their drinking-centered way of life, are shown to be widely effective. This could help many more problem drinkers and alcoholics who do not find either A.A. or the mainstream disease model treatment center approaches helpful. Certainly the whole debate about ethical and responsibility issues in alcoholism, based on the disease concept, will have to be rethought and the issues reframed. But it is important to point out that the new way of conceptualizing the problem and the behavioral approaches to helping alcoholics derived from this, make personal responsibility for changing and taking action central. As Fingarette writes, "All the newer approaches also emphasize [like current mainstream approaches] that the drinker must accept responsibility and play an active role in bringing about the desired change."[10]

As we have seen, the ethical problems in alcoholism and other addictions, with their complexities, are not easy to define. Clergy and other counselors will have to arrive at their own working hypotheses based on their understanding of the fundamental human problems of sickness, sin, freedom, determinism, and personal responsibility. It is my hope that by pursuing lines of thought such as those suggested in this chapter, readers will come to see some new dimensions of the truth of the classic statement by William James quoted earlier concerning drunkenness: "Not through mere perversity do men run after it." I sometimes recall in my own reflections about the ethical issues in addictions, these wise words by Yale scientist Giorgio Lolli:

> More is unknown than is known about the addictive drinker. What is already known breeds a more tolerant attitude toward him and favors a shift of attention from his objectionable deeds to those unfortunate experiences that determined them. The moral issue is not denied but reinterpreted in the light of medical, psychiatric and sociological facts. This reinterpretation helps considerably in efforts to free the addict from his ties to alcohol.[11]

What Lolli wrote decades ago, is still essentially true today. Such a statement could well guide us in struggling with the ethical problems in alcoholism and other substance addictions.

PART III

Methods of Counseling with Alcoholics and Other Addicted Persons

CHAPTER 11

Preparation for Counseling Alcoholics and Other Addicted Persons

This chapter focuses on major issues on which clergy and other counselors need to be informed in order to effectively counsel chemically addicted persons. Among the major topics are: the need for clergy to be involved in such counseling; how to increase opportunities; realistic goals for this counseling; acquiring essential knowledge; learning about available referral resources; connecting with A.A. and other Twelve Step programs; and understanding the medical and psychotherapeutic approaches.

Is There a Need for Clergy to Do Addiction Counseling?

Twelve Step programs have achieved impressive success in our day. Hundreds of thousands of persons have been helped to freedom from their addictions. There also are several hundred privately sponsored and government programs, many of which offer effective treatment. In addition, multidisciplined scientific studies are increasing understanding of addictions, and countless private and government treatment facilities are available to help addicted persons. When clergy face their frequent frustrations and often meager success rates in the field, it is important to find answers to questions such as these: Is there a real need for clergy to be informed and active in the field of alcoholism and drug addictions? Do addicted people and their families need more clergy to be actively involved? If clergy are needed, in what areas can they function most effectively? The remaining chapters in this book will aim at shedding light on these questions and illuminating current opportunities for clergy and congregations in the complex addiction field.

No one familiar with the runaway epidemics of chemical dependencies and behavioral addictions, with the transgenerational educational opportunities of congregations, and with the counseling and healing skills of many clergy, could reasonably conclude that clergy and congregations are no longer needed in this field. It is at least as true today as it was when this book was in its first incarnation that dealing with alcoholics and the drug dependent people in creative ways is a major challenge and opportunity, and, yes, sometimes a major headache for ministers.

Even brief firsthand experiences in a congregation's ministry today provides evidence that opportunities are available to help alcoholics, other drug addicts, and their families there. Calling them "opportunities" may seem painfully euphemistic when referring to some of the messy encounters clergy have with alcoholics and other addicts. Such encounters occur whether or not clergy want them or are prepared to deal with them, often at the most inconvenient times. But the question is not whether clergy will encounter addicted people, but whether clergy will deal with them in a more or less constructive and healing manner.

Various studies of clergy have revealed that many thousands of chemically addicted persons contact clergy each year asking for some type of help. In addition, ministers come face-to-face with desperate family members seeking help, two or three times as often as their help is sought by addicted persons. Often clergy are not aware of the hidden addictive problems in congregations and those lurking behind more surface level "respectable" issues brought to them. More significant than the sheer number who come is that clergy are often the first persons seen for help, outside the addicts' families. It is clear that clergypersons have an important job to do in this area and that we must be prepared to do it well!

Perhaps you are wondering whether clergy can realistically hope to be effective in counseling with alcoholics and drug addicts, particularly if you have believed the opinion expressed by some A.A. members—particularly newer members—that "only an alcoholic can help an alcoholic." This view has diminished the confidence of some clergy in their ability to help addicted persons except to refer them as quickly as possible to Twelve Step programs or other treatment resources. It also has lessened the sense of responsibility to be actively involved in this helping process. Clergy who are well-informed regarding addictions, according to the findings of my research, make one thing clear. Ministers can be remarkably effective, if they have done their homework in preparing for what is often a very complex and challenging task.

Experience has shown that clergy who are effective in working with addicted persons, and who cultivate ongoing relationships with Twelve Step group members, develop a reputation for success in this area. They often attract a considerable number of alcohol and drug dependent people referred to them by A.A., Al-Anon, physicians, court officials, or other clergy who don't find such counseling satisfying.

The findings of my initial study of informed clergy's effectiveness in counseling with alcoholics have been confirmed repeatedly by subsequent feedback in workshops with clergy.[1] Respondents in the early survey were asked to evaluate their success in dealing with alcoholics. They expressed feelings about the value of this work that ranged from: "I have never found a drunk who wasn't worth my time and attention and it meant a lot to them," to: "As far as my experience goes, it is a discouraging piece of work trying to help people who do not want it." The general feeling was between these extremes, the majority closer to the first—that is, working with alcoholics is often difficult and involves many discouragements, but it also is exceedingly worthwhile. As one minister put it, "Some cases have responded beautifully. In others, I have been able to do exactly nothing." Two thirds of the clergy reported 50 percent or better success in dealing with alcoholics, and almost all of these reported working closely with A.A. and Al-Anon.

There is no valid basis for clergy to feel that they cannot help some alcoholics because they are ministers or are not alcoholics. Tens of thousands of ministers, like those in my study, are helping individual alcoholics and drug addicts find sanity and stable sobriety. They are making significant and continuing contributions, day by day, to helping heal the painful brokenness of many addicted people and their families. From their own experience, they know that the assumption that "only an alcoholic (or drug addict) can help another addicted person" is a fallacious half-truth.

However, realism demands that clergy face both their advantages and limitations in dealing with alcoholics and other addicts. In one study, clergy were asked about both the pluses and minuses of those in their profession. In general, they saw the advantages as far outweighing limitations. The limitations most often mentioned could be divided into two categories: the alcoholic's attitudes toward religion and ministers, on the one hand, and the ministers' attitudes toward alcoholics, on the other. In the first category were alcoholics who feared that clergy would censure them, those who resented religion from having been hurt by rejections from other religious leaders, and those who feel that ministers (who are not alcoholics) cannot really understand their alcoholic experiences. One minister wrote, "Most folks figure the minister has a set attitude toward alcoholics and will therefore not give him [sic] much opportunity except in hopeless cases." In the second category of limitations were mentioned such matters as ministers' tendency to moralize and to "preach at" rather than to "counsel with" alcoholics.

Among the advantages mentioned were the natural entree to families, the fact that many people trust and take their problems to pastors, the confidentiality of counseling relationships with clergy, the fact that no fees are involved, and, most important, that clergy have the spiritual power of their faith and the congregational fellowship available for helping alcoholics. One respondent summarized the feeling that several expressed: "The only important limitation a minister has is the initial hesitancy of the alcoholic to approach a minister. Beyond that, it is an advantage to be a minister, provided you have the right attitude and understanding."

Increasing Opportunities to Help

Studies have shown that there is a wide range in the number of counseling opportunities clergy have, including those with addicted persons. Obviously, if ministers are interested in maximizing their service to the addicted, it is important to know the variables that influence the number of such opportunities. The type of congregation being served is one important factor. For example, pastors of downtown churches usually have considerably more transient alcoholics come to them than do clergy in suburban churches. This is particularly true of inner city clergy who make the mistake of giving money to low-bottom alcoholics. (Clergy often are understandably interested in minimizing rather than maximizing this often frustrating work.) Another key variable influencing the number of opportunities ministers have to help addicts is their relationships with A.A. and Al-Anon. Those who have higher numbers of addiction-related counseling opportunities almost always have good working relationships with A.A. and other Twelve Step groups, often having them meet in their parish halls.

A third but less influential factor seems to be the denomination to which clergy belong. Some alcoholics may shy away from ministers who are associated in the public mind with groups vigorously advocating abstinence. However, there is no doubt that how nonjudgmental and accepting individual clergy are in their public statements and their general approaches to people is much more important than their denominations' stand on drinking and addictions. Furthermore, most people today seem to have little or no knowledge of official denominational positions unless they are in conservative groups that emphasize these issues in frequent public pronouncements.

Certainly, ministers' attitudes and public statements regarding alcohol and alcoholism, drugs and drug addictions, are significant variables that influence the number of addicted persons and their families who seek their help.[2] My original study compared ministers who consider alcoholism primarily a sin with those who consider it a sickness. Those who considered alcoholism primarily or entirely a matter of sickness had seen an average of three times as many alcoholics as those who considered alcoholism primarily or entirely a matter of sin and regarded drinking alcohol as the primary cause of alcoholism. In this study, taking cognizance of contemporary scientific findings and communicating nonjudgmental attitudes toward addictions as sicknesses were clearly associated with greater opportunities to help addicted people.

Today, far fewer leaders and members of denominations advocating abstinence hold to extreme or prohibitionist views that formerly were pushed with passion in these churches. But current evidence still seems to suggest that clergy who accept the sickness concept of chemical addictions and understand their multiple causes have significantly more opportunities to help victims than do those rejecting these views. Whether or not the many hidden addicted persons in congregations are encouraged to come out of hiding and ask for help certainly is influenced by clerical attitudes toward alcoholics and other addicts. Clearly, if ministers communicate moralistic, judgmental attitudes, some addicted persons and their families who might otherwise seek their help, will give them a wide berth. They will fear, with good reason in some cases, that clergy will meet them with subtle, if not overt, rejection rather than empathy, acceptance, and understanding.

The decisive factor does not seem to be clergy's personal convictions regarding the use or nonuse of alcohol, but the spirit in which they present their views. Addicted people, like others who are deeply wounded emotionally, are hypersensitive to what they experience as subtle rejection. Clergy who hold strong abstinence views concerning alcohol and other mood-changing chemicals may have to choose between advocating this vigorously or counseling with more of the addicted persons in their congregations. But, it must be emphasized that some pastors who are outspoken abstinence advocates also carry on effective counseling ministries with alcoholics. The key issue, as indicated earlier, is the general people-accepting attitude and grace-full spirit of clergy.

The vast majority of alcoholics and drug dependent persons in our society are hidden addicts. They are having increasingly serious problems with their favorite "solution" substances. But their addictive behavior can still be hidden or be sufficiently within the bounds of social conformity to allow their problems to be kept as a family secret. The interpersonal chaos caused by their addictions are carefully guarded from the outside world. The hiddenness of so much alcoholism—a situation that probably is even more common for drug addictions—is the most baffling aspect of the addiction problem. It is ironic that in spite of the new helping resources that are now available, the vast majority of addicted persons and their families continue to suffer the ravages of the illness and do not seek treatment. It is important to discover addicted persons within congregations because the earlier help is received in these progressive illnesses, the more personal and social disintegration the addicted persons and their families will be spared. Clergy have strategic potential roles in helping solve the perplexing problem of hidden addictions.

How can ministers encourage addicted people to come out of hiding and trust their painful secret to clergy's caring and skills? As just indicated, clergy attitudes toward addictions and those trapped in them are important. A related factor was described by the late Otis R. Rice, a respected pioneer in pastoral work with alcoholics. He used the apt phrase "remote preparation for counseling of alcoholics." By this he meant the general tone and quality of clergy relationships with their parishioners. Have pastors made their parishioners feel that they are really interested in them as persons and not just as a means of running a church machine? Have they established relationships that made parishioners feel genuine warmth and human caring and the assurance that they will keep shame-laden secrets in total pastoral confidence? Are their general attitudes moralistic, or do their sermons and informal conversations reveal a deeper understanding of human behavior? Are they aware of their own fractured finitude or do they give the misleading impression that they have it made on all the human issues they face? Are they relatively shockproof so that recital of grim facts will not make them anxious or defensively moralistic? Can they be counted on to really listen—particularly to those things that are very painful to share? If so, then hidden addicts and their families will be more likely to risk coming to them for help.

Parish ministers are in a strategic position to attract hidden addicted people out of their dark closet of fear and despair. Here are four strategies for accomplishing this:

1. Educational Seed Planting

A productive way to create greater openness to help is to mention alcoholism and other addictions in a sermon or other public statement, and to do so in an informed, accepting, and hopeful manner. In most worship services and church gatherings it is likely that there are one or more people with some personal pain related to addictions. If they hear an enlightened, hopeful understanding of these problems, close relatives of hidden addicts and, occasionally, even addicts themselves, may decide to confide in the pastor later. In my experience, a brief, understanding mention of the diseases of addictions or an appreciative, hopeful reference to A.A. in a sermon or talk often results in counseling opportunities. If listeners sense that the minister has an informed, hopeful, accepting attitude toward these problems, their hope may be awakened so that they may muster courage to open up about their problems. Public talks that mention the disease concept and early symptoms of addictions frequently open at least a few eyes to the nature of their problem and the need for help.

A second strategy for encouraging hidden addicts to seek pastoral help is developing an imaginative addiction education emphasis for youth and adults in church schools. Such programs plant the seeds of understanding the nature and treatment of alcoholism and other addictions, some of which will take root and flower as preventative understanding. Others will flower in counseling and pastoral care opportunities. (Alcohol and addiction education will be discussed in the concluding chapters.)

2. Pastoral Care and Precounseling

A third strategy is derived from the fact that clergy have regular entrees to a network of families, during their normal, day-to-day pastoral care activities. This aspect of clergy's professional role definition give them important advantages over those in the other healing and helping professions in making earlier discovery of distress in individuals and families. If their emotional radar is tuned to the wavelength of people's pain, ministers often sense that particular people are troubled—perhaps by hidden addictions or non-addicted excessive drinking and drug use. This usually occurs long before the crises becomes full-blown and sufferers are pushed by enough pain to seek help outside the family system.

If pastors notice that particular individuals or family members are showing what may be heavy surface stresses from hidden problems, they should make themselves more psychologically available to them by frequent pastoral care contacts. The process of building relationship bridges over which burdened people can bring their hidden problems to ministers is an essential part of the process that pastoral care pioneer Seward Hiltner once called "precounseling." Clergy in the high church traditions in which hearing confessions is a priestly function, and all pastors to whom people talk informally about their concerns, have opportunities to identify hidden addictions. Whether or not these opportunities are recognized depends on ministers' sensitivity and their skills in helping parishioners move from confessional and pastoral conversation modes into informal counseling relationships.

What are some distress signals that may point to hidden problems including substance or activity addictions? They include disturbed children, veiled spousal antagonism or open family violence, acute or chronic financial problems, repeated job losses for no convincing reasons, drinking or recreational drug use at inappropriate times, guilty avoidance of clergy or embarrassment if they call, and radical changes in church-related behavior such as unexplained withdrawal from regular participation. Such symptoms may be coded cries for help by individuals and families who cannot yet bring themselves to ask for help openly.

Here is an illustration of the bridge building function of pastoral care as a means of creating counseling opportunities with addicted families:

Because he had observed several of the above signs of disturbance, Pastor Martin suspected that one of his parishioners, Mr. L, might be having serious troubles of some kind. Neither Mr. L. nor his family mentioned any difficulties. So, Pastor Martin made it his business to devote more than average attention to Mr. L. and his family. He arranged to have several contacts with the family for various reasons that were actually incidental to his main bridge-building objective. After several pastoral contacts, he received a phone call from Mrs. L. saying that she would like to talk with him about a problem in the women's group of the church. When she came to the pastor's office, Mrs. L. began by discussing this problem. But later in that session, she opened up about her husband's drinking. From what she shared, it was evident that Mr. L. was not ready to admit that alcohol was giving him trouble, and was not interested in talking with the pastor about his drinking. So the minister concentrated on helping Mrs. L., beginning by encouraging her to pour out her painful, pent up feelings, thus gaining some relief from their pressure. Martin then discussed with her the probable nature of Mr L.'s problem and the crucial importance of helping him move toward becoming open to outside treatment. He also suggested that she attend a meeting of the local Al-Anon group, explaining how this might help her. He gave her the names of two women in their congregation who were a part of that group. In responding to her questions, he offered some practical guidance about how she might cope more constructively with the increasing problems in her relationships with her husband and their two children. The pastor let Mrs. L. know that he was available to talk further whenever she felt the need. After responding to her questions, he closed their time together with a supportive prayer.

Later, the pastor used his professional entree to their home. When he called on them, he said nothing about Mr. L.'s drinking. To have done so probably would have defeated his purpose by putting Mr. L. on the defensive and triggering an angry confrontation with his wife after the pastor left. Instead, he concentrated on strengthening the relationship of trust with both of them, hoping that Mr. L. would eventually become open to talk about his problem drinking.

Under what circumstances should clergy take the initiative in raising the issues of excessive drinking or drug use with a parishioner? This will vary, depending on the nature of the pastor-parishioner relationship and circumstances in particular situations. In general, three guidelines should be followed. First, take the initiative only when it is clear that persons have serious abuse problems that they are not willing to bring up on their own. Second, do so when the pastor-parishioner bridge is strong enough not to be fractured by such a confrontation. And third, do so only after a family member or someone else who has revealed the problem, agrees.

It may be essential to risk taking some initiative, even if only the third guideline can be followed, if there is evidence that serious emotional or physical harm is being done to the children or spouse. In such cases, it is usually wise for pastors not to intervene alone. It is better to keep responsibility with the family by helping adult family members plan a structured confrontation called an "intervention," (see chapter 15). Remember that addicted people usually experience even the best intentioned pastoral concern about their drinking or drug use as a threat. Thus, taking the initiative is a calculated risk that may do more harm than good by solidifying victims' anger and resistance to accepting help. For this reason, it is best not to take the initiative, except in emergencies or in cases where pastor-parishioner relationships are unusually strong.

In some cases, addicted persons may give subtle clues that they are on the verge of discussing their problem, but are having trouble breaking the ice. A nonconfrontational observation or question may help. Here are some examples of pastoral openers:

- "I get the feeling that there's something that's worrying you, but it's not easy to talk about it."
- "You seem to have a burden on your mind. Would you like to tell me about it?"
- "You seem to be carrying a load of some kind. Would it help to talk?"

The important thing is to raise issues in such a way that allows the person to reject the question without rejecting the questioner. If addicted people are defensive, this is easier said than done. It often is easy to miscalculate the degree of openness or defensiveness present when deciding whether or not to take the initiative.

3. Crisis Care and Counseling

Many people spontaneously turn to clergy when they are going through deep water of any kind. Among those seeking pastoral help are some whose problems in living are caused or complicated by creeping addictions. These may be hidden even from addicted persons and their families in that they do not yet recognize the out of control quality of their drinking or drug use. Many who are dimly aware that their substance use may be out of control are ashamed to admit this possibility to others. By being sensitive to the possible presence of hidden addictions behind individual, marital, and parent-teen problems, clergy may be able to identify hidden problems and encourage victims to seek appropriate help. Methods that sometimes prove useful in motivating addicted people who are still in denial will be discussed in subsequent chapters.

Reality-Based Goals in Counseling Addicted Persons

What are realistic goals of counseling with alcoholics and other addicts? Much of the frustration in counseling results from counselors' confusion about goals or their striving for unrealistic ones. The ultimate goal of all pastoral counseling, including that involving addictions, is to empower persons to grow toward their God-given potential for full personhood, constructive relationships, joyful spirituality, and productive living including service to a needy world. With addicted persons, an essential subgoal, implicit in this master goal is enabling them to achieve ongoing abstinence or true moderation in the use of the addictive substances or activities. For them, achieving this goal is a prerequisite to moving ahead toward a happier, more constructive life. Recovery involves the reconstruction of one's identity, which is a difficult growth task. Fortunately, people in recovery for a while often make the rewarding discovery that every day without alcohol or drugs lets them take a small step toward becoming the person they really want to be.

Let's look more closely at a crucial, and still moot, issue in this subgoal. The inability of addicted drinkers ever to drink again in controlled fashion was accepted as axiomatic for many years by most people engaged in helping alcoholics. This axiom is expressed by a phrase often heard in A.A., "Once an alcoholic, always an alcoholic!" It is articulated by those doing therapy with alcoholics as: "Alcoholism can be arrested and treated, but not cured." This long-held therapeutic assumption has been challenged repeatedly in recent decades.

The challenge began with the publication in 1962 of a surprising report by a British physician, D. L. Davies, entitled "Normal Drinking in Recovered Alcohol Addicts."[3] He told of seven men, out of a group of ninety-three treated for alcohol addiction, who subsequently had been able to drink normally for periods of seven to eleven years. The short-term treatment consisted of Antabuse and individual discussions with patients during brief hospitalization, plus social work services for their relatives. All those in treatment were advised to refrain from drinking. These seven chose to ignore the advice. Each of the seven, after periods of complete abstinence of up to a year, seemed to resume drinking within the limits regarded as "normal" by their peer groups. None of them had been drunk even once since their treatment. Two of the men, whose excessive drinking prior to their hospitalization was symptomatic of chronic anxiety states, continued to be about as anxious as before, but their abnormal drinking patterns disappeared. However, after presenting his startling evidence, Davies stated: "It is not denied that the majority of alcohol addicts are incapable of achieving 'normal drinking.' All patients should be told to aim at total abstinence."[4]

In 1971, the National Institute on Alcohol Abuse and Alcoholism sponsored a comprehensive treatment program for patients with severe alcoholism in forty-five community centers around the country. A monitoring system required reports on patients six and eighteen months after intake. The Rand Corporation, a respected research center, tallied the results. A remarkable improvement rate of around 70 percent was reported, but, to the utter surprise of many, the vast majority of those evaluated as improved had not become abstainers. They were either drinking at "normal" levels or alternating between periods of drinking and abstention. The reported relapse rate among social drinkers was no greater than among abstainers. Nearly two-thirds had no slips in eighteen months.

Davies's and this subsequent Rand report triggered a critical storm of responses from some experienced experts in the addiction field. The reports were labeled "dangerous" and "irresponsible" because they could encourage alcoholics to drink, with disastrous results. But several suggested that the Davies and Rand studies and other evidence in the alcoholism literature indicated a need to consider revising the widely held axiom that no alcoholic can ever drink again in controlled fashion. The most devastating criticisms attacked the Davies report because of its tiny sample and the Rand report because it was based on sloppy research that failed to meet the minimal standards for scientific studies.[5] A number of social scientists called for more rigorous research on this crucial issue.

Most therapists who had occasionally observed alcoholics who seemed to be able to return to social drinking agreed that the occurrence is exceedingly rare and that no one can predict which clients may have this capacity. Most agreed that total abstinence is the only realistic and humane treatment goal for alcoholics. R. Gordon Bell, a Canadian addiction specialist, stated this view well:

> For every alcohol addict who may succeed in reestablishing a pattern of controlled drinking, perhaps a dozen would kill themselves trying. At this stage of our knowledge and clinical orientation to the complex problems of alcohol addiction, the only policy likely to prolong life consistently and improve human capacity to function in an intelligent manner is one of total abstinence.

He goes on to suggest that is may eventually become possible to identify a small percentage of alcohol addicts who could drink moderately, after a year or two of abstinence and a resolution of their personal and social problems at the roots of their addiction. Until this is possible, all clinical studies should be done with as little publicity as possible. "Otherwise the health and safety of a great many people could be seriously jeopardized."[6]

The abstinence versus moderation controversy has continued unabated to the present. Substantial evidence has emerged in the last three decades confirming the view that problem drinkers, who are not physically addicted, often can learn how to drink in a controlled fashion. It is possible that some physiologically addicted drinkers (alcoholics) can do so as well. In 1972, Mark B. Sobell and Linda C. Sobell, psychologists at the Addiction Research Foundation in Toronto, reported successful results of a carefully designed program of controlled drinking.[7] Their report again triggered criticisms from those who rejected the findings of their research. Later Herbert Fingarette, who rejects the disease concept and builds a case for substituting the concept of "heavy drinker," supported the view that controlled drinking is possible for some heavy drinkers. He declared:

> Despite the objections and criticisms, the literature on the numbers of former heavy drinkers who maintain moderate drinking continues to grow. A recent rigorous study reports that among socially adjusted former heavy drinkers, the majority were social drinkers

rather than abstainers. . . . Most heavy drinkers aged forty and older who show signs of severe physical dependence and acknowledge themselves to be alcoholics tend to do better in programs aimed at abstinence, while heavy drinkers under forty who have moderate physical symptoms may be more successful if they learn to drink moderately rather than aim at abstention.[8]

Fingarette points out that controlled drinking treatment programs for problem drinkers are widely available in countries such as the United Kingdom, Canada, and Norway. For example, in the United Kingdom, three-fourths of addiction clinics offer controlled drinking as one optional goal. In the U.S., the dominance of the disease concept of alcoholism has discouraged the establishment of treatment programs with goals other than abstinence.

From my perspective, the distinction that probably is crucial in clarifying this controversy is between problem drinkers who abuse alcohol but do not show the classic signs of physiological addiction and alcoholics who do exhibit these symptoms. As mentioned in chapter 1, it seems probable that so-called alcoholics who learn to drink in moderation may actually be problem drinkers who are habituated to excessive drinking but are not physically addicted. Unfortunately, in practice there is no simple or safe way to distinguish problem drinkers and addicted alcoholics.

What are the present implications for counselors of this unresolved controversy? As Gordon Bell recommends, until the needed research and careful clinical trials of controlled drinking programs produce definitive answers, it seems prudent for counselors of people whose drinking produces ongoing problems to heed the most widely accepted treatment assumption (in the U.S.)—that total abstinence is the wisest goal. However, it would be fortunate if those who do not achieve the abstinence goal, for whatever reasons, had access to other options such as treatment programs that use learning-theory and behavior therapies aimed at enabling them to learn how to drink in controlled fashion.

It should be remembered that finding the secret of controlled drinking is the frantic and futile desire of many drinking alcoholics. Their attempts to find this magic answer often is their downfall. It would be utter folly, therefore, to suggest to physically addicted drinkers that they might recover their ability to drink socially. Even to imply that rare alcoholics seem to recover this ability is to foster a dangerous, unrealistic hope for most alcoholic counselees who want desperately to believe that they are the rare persons who can recover control. The effect would be to strengthen their resistance to accepting the hard reality that they probably must learn to live without alcohol if they are to live constructive lives, perhaps even to live at all.

The most realistic long-range goals of counseling with alcoholics and other adults, then, is permanent abstinence, a prerequisite to development of their potential for constructive living. Subsumed under this goal are four operational objectives that are overlapping stages of treatment: Helping addicts to (a) accept that their drinking and/or drugging is a problem with which they need help; (b) obtain medical treatment; (c) interrupt the addictive cycle and keep it interrupted by learning to avoid the first drink or drug hit; and (d) continue personal and spiritual growth including rebuilding their lives and relationships without addictive substances. The role of clergy and other counselors varies at each stage of this recovery process as does their uses of community resources. The next two chapters will explore methods for enabling addicted people to move toward these objectives.

Alcoholism and drug addictions are complex illnesses. Treatment, ideally, is a team effort. Ministers who attempt to go it alone usually find their effectiveness at least doubled when they learn to fully use Twelve Step programs and other addiction treatment resources. Some uninformed health professionals, treatment center staff members, and Twelve-Steppers do not think of clergy as potentially valuable members of treatment teams. In spite of such myopia, clergy should think of themselves as team members with valuable roles in facilitating movement toward each of the four sub-objectives.

Most clergy are happy to refer alcoholics and drug addicts to A.A. and agencies specifically designed to meet their problems. They recognize that these resources are tailor made to help addicts interrupt the addictive cycle. With reference to A.A., as the influential preacher Harry Emerson Fosdick once observed, human problems (including alcoholism) are something like stained-glass windows. Those who see and appreciate them from the inside often have unique and valuable understanding of them. Wise clergy usually accept as their starting point a perspective stated clearly by Marty Mann, founder of the National Council on Alcoholism and Drug Dependence:

> The pastor will also have discovered that he [sic], himself, cannot do
> an A.A. job on the alcoholic. He will see with his own eyes at meet-
> ings . . . that the man or woman who has actually been through the
> appalling experience of alcoholism has an edge on him that no sub-
> stitute knowledge can replace. For one thing, the sober A.A. mem-

ber is the embodiment of hope. He is the living promise that it can be done. He makes faith in the possibility of recovery a thing that can be seen and touched and heard—himself.[9]

Most experienced clergy rejoice in the increasing availability of Twelve Step groups and specialized agencies to treat addictions. They know that when they make effective referrals to such programs they often have helped start addicts on their recovery journeys. Like many alcoholics who have found their way to A.A. and life-saving sobriety by the help of clergy, Bob P. recalls with gratitude:

I was at the end of my rope. I used to joke about not going to church, saying that the last time I went was when I got married and I've never forgiven the church for that. But in despair I went to church. After the service I got the minister aside and told him I wanted to stop and couldn't. He said, "I'll get in touch with a fellow who can help you." That's how I got in touch with A.A.

Out of the frustration of repeated failures, some clergy want to shift responsibility quickly to anyone else who might help. There are two dangers in overly abrupt referrals. First, an addicted person might experience this as personal rejection rather than wise referral. And second, if clergy understand referral to mean "Let A.A. do it," they miss opportunities to offer the valuable spiritual growth enabling work for which they are uniquely trained. It is appropriate to think of referrals to specialized agencies as broadening and sharing responsibility, not avoiding it.

Even if clergy are well trained in helping the addicted, the time needed for such involvement often makes solo intervention prohibitive. It also typically involves considerable frustration and other emotional strain and drain. For these reasons most pastors, including those with extensive training in the field, are rightly glad to make maximum use of their community's treatment resources.

Acquiring the Necessary Knowledge Base

In order to counsel addicted persons effectively, clergy need a basic understanding of alcoholism and other addictions, as well as of A.A. and other treatment resources. They need to understand the nature and typical development of the sickness so that they can interpret this to the addicted people and their families. Reading and digesting this volume, the Big Book of A.A., and other key books on both drug and activity addictions can give clergy the foundational understanding that they need. (See the annotated bibliography for key books.)

It is crucial to full effectiveness in their counseling of addicted persons and families to have a good working relationships with local A.A. and Al-Anon groups, and with treatment centers. In a very practical sense, the most valuable preparation for this counseling is close at hand, for it simply involves attending open meetings of A.A. and other Twelve Step groups. No amount of reading about these groups is a real substitute for the experience of observing them in action. Continuing to attend Twelve Step meetings occasionally is a worthwhile investment of a busy pastor's time. To do so lets members know that clergy are supportive of their spiritually centered recovery work . Listening carefully to what is communicated at meetings, verbally and nonverbally, and talking by phone with seasoned A.A. and Al-Anon members, are excellent, experiential ways to learn useful insights about Twelve Step groups, and also about alcoholism, alcoholics, and family dynamics.

Open meetings provide excellent opportunities to get acquainted with long-term members of each gender and various ages. These members become contact people that can be valuable allies and bridge persons for making successful referrals. The coffee cup fellowship times before and after Twelve Step meetings are ideal times for chatting and building rapport with several members. (Group chairpersons or secretaries are good ones to know since they have stable sobriety, knowledge about other group members, and sufficient Twelve Step experience to provide helpful guidance.) Open meetings also provide opportunities to acquire helpful books and pamphlets for giving to counselees and making available in a congregation's literature rack or library.

What about more intensive training in addictions to prepare for this counseling? Many clergy are doing effective counseling with addicted people without the advantages provided by the excellent specialized academic and clinical training in addictions now available. And even clergy who have prepared by specialized training frequently experience frustration and failures in this field. Because much addiction counseling is difficult and demanding, the stronger one's preparation, the greater one's chances of being effective.

Clergy and others who have a strong interest in this area of counseling should consider attending one of numerous interprofessional summer schools focusing on alcohol and drug problems. The curricula of these schools are designed to be useful to teachers, physicians, clergy, social workers, law enforcement and probation officers, industrial leaders, directors of addiction programs, alcoholism counselors, and those interested in addiction education, research, and rehabilitation. Both a three week Summer School of Alcohol and Drug Studies and a one week Advanced School of Alcohol and Drug Studies for professionals are available at Rutgers University summer school. These schools are sponsored by the education and training division of the Rutgers Center of Alcohol Studies, an interdisciplinary program that also includes divisions of research, clinical services, and prevention, as well as publishes the *Quarterly Journal of Studies on Alcohol,* and maintains the Center of Alcohol Studies Library, which is open to the public. (See "Annotated Guide to Further Resources" for the address.)

Learning About Available Referral Resources

One of the most important preparations for effective counseling with alcoholics and other addicts is learning what referral resources are available. The following checklist is designed to suggest important resources for which to look in your community. (You may wish to put a check in front of those resources available in your area, and jot down phone numbers in the margins.)

___ Twelve Step groups including Alcoholics Anonymous, Narcotics Anonymous, Al-Anon, and Alateens: _____
___ My contact persons in these groups: _____
___ Clergy in the community who have more experience in counseling and referring addicted people: _____
___ Physicians who combine expertise and compassion in detoxification methods and a psychiatrist for dual diagnosis addicts: _____
___ Hospital facilities with services for alcoholics, drug addicts, and the polyaddicted, that have working relationships with and respect from stable A.A. members, the staff of the local Council on Alcoholism and Drug Education, or experienced clergy: _____
___ An outpatient alcoholism and addiction treatment program, sponsored by governmental or private agencies, with a good track record of recoveries and a favorable reputation among community clergy and A.A. members who have been helped to sobriety by its program:
___ An inpatient alcoholic rehabilitation program with a favorable reputation and with multifaceted programs, including medical detoxification and psychiatric services, group therapy, A.A., family groups, and a follow-up program: _____
___ Halfway houses for addicts in recovery, and for victims of family vio-

lence, including those sponsored by healthy religious groups and with religiously motivated staffs: _____

___ Pastoral psychotherapists and other mental health professionals who understand addictions and their treatment, and therapists trained in family counseling, meditation, biofeedback, and acupuncture that can be useful in enabling addicts to handle stress in nonchemical ways:

_____

___ Treatment programs for homeless addicts including enlightened Salvation Army installations and/or rescue missions that integrate Twelve Step programs in their treatments: _____

___ The Information Center sponsored by a Local Council on Alcoholism and Drug Dependence: _____

___ Other resources: _____

Very few busy parish clergy will have or make time to acquire firsthand knowledge of many of these resources in advance of needing them to make a referral. Fortunately, the nearest Alcoholic and Drug Information Center can provide quick and comprehensive information about community resources. Also, seasoned Twelve Step members often know a lot about the quality and reputations of local hospitals and addiction treatment programs, which physicians and psychotherapists are most effective in treating addicted patients, and resources where homeless addicts can be housed, fed, and perhaps helped to sobriety. If there is an American Association of Pastoral Counselors approved counseling center nearby, staff members usually can provide reliable information and evaluations of referral resources.

The National Council on Alcoholism and Drug Dependence, (NCADD), started in 1944 by Marty Mann, provides excellent help for anyone (including clergy) concerned about addiction problems. Those fortunate enough to live in one of the 117 communities with local affiliates should use their services, support their work, and encourage parishioners to do so as part of their community service as Christians. The functions of NCADD and its affiliates include providing objective information on alcoholism and other drug dependencies through information sheets, pamphlets, and video tapes; referral for individuals and families seeking treatment; community prevention and education programs; community awareness presentations in schools, businesses, and community organizations; local media advocacy campaigns; advocacy in governments on all levels for alcoholics and other drug dependent people; and working with public and private agencies to increase cooperation on comprehensive alcoholism and drug programs. It also has a national HOPE Line

(1-800-NCA-CALL) that receives over thirty thousand calls each year. The National Council will give callers the location of the nearest affiliate, (1-212-206-6770). Its web site address is: http://www.ncadd.org/index.html.

In addition to the National Council and its affiliates, most states have extensive, tax supported alcoholism and drug programs to which clergy can turn for information about referral resources. These programs facilitate the exchange of information about education, research, and treatment programs, promote constructive legislation, and encourage professionals to deal with addiction problems within their own ranks. They also encourage cooperation among all those engaged in activities involving substance abuse. Some states also provide treatment facilities.

There are many other valuable resources. Several universities, including Columbia, Brown, and Rutgers, sponsor outstanding research and professional training programs on addictions. In addition, several divisions of the U.S. Department of Health and Human Services offer abundant resources in the area of alcohol and drug problems. One of these, the National Clearing House for Alcohol and Drug Information, provides information both by mail and on the Internet.

The problem drinking and drug abuse programs that now are functioning in many industries offer education and treatment for their employees. Fortunately humanitarian and bottom line economic considerations coincide in this area as industrial leaders recognize that it is far less expensive to provide treatment for addicted employees than to ignore the problem and to pay the costs of accidents, inefficiency, absenteeism, strained interemployee relationships, and eventual retraining replacements. These programs are usually coordinated through company's personnel or medical departments. Most have achieved impressive recovery records.

Connecting with Twelve Step Programs

How does one establish contact with the local A.A. and Al-Anon groups? Telephone directories list these in the yellow pages or in the section on community resources. A phone call to the Alcoholics Anonymous number for example, will put one in touch with the intergroup secretary or an experienced A.A. volunteer. The person who answers can give information about meetings, make arrangements for the caller to come to the A.A. office, or give potentially helpful suggestions concerning a particular alcoholic. Most A.A. groups welcome such professional inquiries. If local contacts do not provide all that is needed, one can write or phone the A.A. General Service Office. This office will provide needed information, including the location of the nearest groups. In the unlikely event that there is no group nearby, this office can provide guidance in getting a group started where one is needed.[10]

For many nonalcoholics, including myself, an important fringe benefit of attending an occasional Twelve Step open meeting is the spiritual lift and refreshment this often gives. To acquaint theological students in pastoral counseling courses with Twelve Step recovery groups and to help them feel a little more at ease with addicts and their families, I often have required them to attend an open meeting and write a report on "What I learned and what the church could learn from this group." Here are segments of some reports on their first exposure to A.A.:[11]

> It was one of the most meaningful spiritual experiences I have had. God's love was truly present in this group of people.
>
> . . .
>
> There was a depth of fellowship which I wouldn't mind being a part of.
>
> . . .
>
> To me both the honesty and the acceptance were overwhelming.
>
> . . .
>
> I felt a desire to become a part of their fellowship which I can't because I'm not an alcoholic. Why can't the churches develop this kind of fellowship? Surely more people than alcoholics agonize over the waste of their lives. Some I am sure have descended into hell and have returned.

Pastors who attend Twelve Step group meetings regularly usually discover that recriprocally helpful relationships develop spontaneously with persons there. Members who learn to know and trust clergy may come for pastoral counseling or to ask them to officiate at weddings or funerals.[12] The majority of clergy, in my experience, appreciate A.A.'s strengths and use it as their first place to refer alcoholics. Here are some comments by ministers of mainstream denominations reflecting their gratitude:

> The church could learn something about real fellowship from A.A. It should learn to be a warm, friendly place where alcoholics and others may find acceptance, strength, and self-confidence.
>
> . . .

The church might learn to make allowance for people's failures and never give up on them.

Because A.A. is every counselor's most valuable referral resource, let's look at some criticisms of it that may inhibit clergy's relationship with it. Some conservative clergy are baffled by A.A. members' indifference to whether nonalcoholics do or do not drink. From the standpoint of A.A., there are two reasons for this. First, most A.A.s believe that alcohol, per se, is not the basic cause of their problem. Rather, they hold that it is their unique response to alcohol that is the cause. Second, it is official A.A. policy not to "endorse or oppose any cause" nor to be drawn into public controversy, that might divert them from their "one primary purpose . . . to carry its message to the alcoholic who still suffers." As indicated earlier, the wisdom of this policy has been abundantly demonstrated.

Some Christian clergy object that A.A. does not have Christ in its program. They should remember that its flexible, permissive beliefs are an important reason why it attracts many alcoholics who would shy away from overtly religious teachings. If A.A. is to serve alcoholics of all religious backgrounds, it must avoid becoming identified with any one theological position. This has become more important as the movement has become increasingly international and intercultural in scope. The word "Christ" is not used in A.A., except perhaps in some groups in the Bible Belt section of this country. But it would be difficult to find more Christlike concern and outreach than is found in A.A. at its best. Furthermore, let's be honest with ourselves: most ministers will agree that "God as we understand him" is an apt description of the average church members' actual beliefs as distinguished from the creedal beliefs they repeat, often with little understanding, in worship services.

I have known clergy who objected to the clannishness on the part of some A.A. members and their lack of awareness of A.A.'s limitations. In my experience, these behavior patterns are most common among relative newcomers in A.A. As members become more secure in their sobriety and less defensive, these characteristics tend to diminish or disappear. Also, it is well to remember that the strong sense of belonging to an in-group is an essential part of the healing energy of A.A. The attitude of superiority to professionals sometimes heard in A.A. meetings—"A.A. did it when the doctors, ministers, and shrinks failed"—can be understood and accepted in this light. The fact is that A.A. does help countless addicted people more than health professionals and clergy who work without using A.A. as an ally. However, as indicated earlier, A.A.'s official policies affirm the importance for some members' recovery of various types of professional skills.

Some clergy are critical of bragging about past sins and the swearing A.A. members sometime do in telling their alcoholic stories. What are the dynamics of this behavior? Telling one's story, including one's past escapades, to an empathetic audience, many of whom did similar things in their drinking days, is an invaluable part of the healing process. Describing in public experiences that not too long before were too painful to even admit to themselves is an important method of healing and growth. The healing power of humor also is demonstrated in A.A. meetings. Speakers and other members can now see the ludicrous implications of behavior that before was either denied or only seen as tragically serious and shame producing. Verbalizing alcoholic stories, in their vivid details, is a means of identifying with the group. Occasional "damns!" and "hells!" are valuable ways of communicating something quite important to many members—that this is not a pious or churchy group. Behavior of these types tends to lessen as member's sober tenure in A.A. lengthens. However, the entertainment value of past escapades, and their colorful embellishment, tends to reinforce and perpetuate that behavior.

Clergy sometimes criticize A.A. because some of its members make it their church. As an A.A. member who also is a devoted churchman pointed out: "Many people find so much more acceptance in A.A. than in the church, they make A.A. their church." Most A.A.s who do this have found a measure of transforming faith and vital service within its fellowship. They probably would not be in a church if A.A. did not exist. In many cases they would not even be alive. But my intensive interviews made it clear that A.A. is a bridge back to a church home for many of its members. A.A. policy encourages this. Tens of thousands of clergy can echo with enthusiasm the sentiments of one minister who wrote: "The churches should be grateful to God for the many fine, active members that A.A. has saved and sent into their fellowship."

Understanding Medical and Psychotherapeutic Resources

Clergy need at least minimal, nontechnical understanding of the functions of medical, psychiatric, and psychotherapeutic resources in the recovery process. This knowledge makes it possible to draw on these resources appropriately and interpret them to addicted persons and their families.

Here is an early question that should be answered when working with an addicted person: Does this person need medical or psychiatric help in addition to A.A. and pastoral care? In answering this question it often is necessary to consult with a health professional knowledgeable about addictions who can evaluate the individual's need for these therapies. Reading an overview of current medical treatments for addictions also can be helpful. One such book is Barbara C. Wallace, editor, *The Chemically Dependent: Phases of Treatment and Recovery.*[13]

These treatments can be divided into four categories according to their purposes:

(1) *Medical treatments aimed at detoxification and withdrawal symptoms and restoring physiological balance after protracted alcohol and/or drug binges.* Problems in this area range from agonizing hangovers to delirium tremens and alcoholic hallucinosis. These result from the withdrawal of alcohol and/or drugs from the body after it has adjusted biochemically to compensate for their presence. In a small percentage of cases, withdrawal symptoms can be fatal, unless the person is given medical attention. Painful withdrawal symptoms often drive addicts back to their favorite chemical comforter. If any mood-altering drugs (like tranquilizers) are needed to reduce anxiety, they must be prescribed with extreme caution because addiction prone people often become hooked on such drugs.

(2) *Medical treatments aimed at physical rehabilitation and the restoration of physiological health after prolonged excessive drinking or drug use.* This often is done on an outpatient basis. In some cases it is done by outpatient follow-up after hospitalization for detoxification, which usually requires only a few days. The diseases resulting from severe addictions that must be treated include severe malnutrition, cirrhosis of the liver, and polyneuropathy. Many addicted people in recovery need mega doses of vitamins and minerals and a healthy diet to overcome the devitaminosis and general malnutrition resulting from drinking one's meals for extended periods. Both detoxification and needed follow-up medical treatment enhance the possibility of long-term recoveries significantly.

(3) *Medical or psychological treatment aimed at keeping the addictive cycle broken, and thus maintaining sobriety so that other therapies can be utilized.* The importance of this type of treatment was demonstrated in the case of a middle-aged business executive. After prolonged heavy drinking with periodic binges, he was in wretched condition physically and emotionally. He kept trying to stop drinking and was hospitalized repeatedly to be "boiled out" and given physiological rehabilitation treatment. Each time, after short periods of posthospital sobriety, he began to drink excessively again, thus conitinuing the self-feeding addictive cycle. Finally, Antabuse was prescribed at a treatment center.[14] The period of Antabuse-induced

sobriety interrupted the vicious cycle and made it possible for regular A.A. meetings plus group psychotherapy to play significant roles in his achieving stable sobriety.

A psychological method that is sometimes used to produce a period of abstinence is the *aversion* or *counterconditioning* treatment. This has been used for several decades and is now available at three Schick Shadel Treatment Centers in the United States.[15] Counterconditioning is widely used as one option in treatment programs in several European countries including Great Britain. In Russia it is the chief method available. An aversion to the smell, sight, and taste of alcohol is induced by giving patients their favorite alcoholic drink just before a drug that produces violent nausea and vomiting. After five such episodes, patients become conditioned so that the sight or smell of alcohol triggers nausea. According to this theory, excessive drinking is caused by the unconscious mind's powerful memory that alcohol equals pleasure. The grip of this memory is broken as the notion that alcohol equals being sick is reinforced by immediate discomfort. Patients are encouraged to get positive group support of some kind, adopt a healthy lifestyle, and associate with people who affirm their self-esteem. Since conditioned reflexes tend to weaken as time passes, periodic reinforcement usually is required to maintain the aversion.

Hypnosis is a psychological technique used as an adjunct to psychotherapy to reduce craving, induce aversion to alcohol, (or nicotine and other drugs), and create a positive attitude toward life. Addicted people under hypnosis are given suggestions that they will be indifferent to the substance when they come out of the trance. Hypnotherapists usually teach their patients how to use autohypnosis to reinforce the suggestion.

(4) *Treatments aimed at healing the psychological problems that are among the underlying causes and/or consequences of most addictions.*

Psychotherapy alone has not had an impressive record of success with addictions. This is particularly true of extended, psychoanalytically oriented psychotherapy. Such depth therapies involve long-term, anxiety-laden interactions. With their low frustration tolerance, addicts tend to retreat into their readily accessible chemical anxiety tranquilizers. One A.A. member I interviewed remembered:

> I went to see the psychiatrist when I couldn't stop drinking. I was shaking and in one hell of a shape. He started asking me questions about my childhood. I thought to myself, "The damn fool!" I didn't go back.

Another A.A. member said that, on some occasions, he drank six martinis before visits to his psychiatrist. This negated the possibility of insights and constructive change. Such drinking alcoholics frequently sabotage their own therapy in still other ways—by missing appointments, not paying their bills, and trying (often with self-defeating success) to deceive the therapist. Jellinek was on target when he observed that young therapists who lack experience in working with alcoholics frequently recommend long, intensive psychotherapy when they first see them. But after they have attempted to do such therapy with one or two alcoholics, they usually refer them to the nearest A.A. group.

Yet, once they have stopped drinking and using, addicted persons who still are disturbed by painful inner conflicts often benefit from psychotherapy. This is particularly true of those who feel worse rather than better after several months in sober recovery. Psychotherapy can help them find healing of their anxiety, guilt, anger, resentment, and shame. In my experience, the psychotherapy that is most helpful is the supportive, reality coping, relationship-oriented type rather than in-depth, reconstructive therapy. But the timing of any such therapy is crucial. It usually is effective only after the addictive cycle or runaway symptom is interrupted and recovering persons have been sober for a substantial time. At that point, individual, couple, or family counseling or therapy often is helpful in resolving personality and relationship problems. In choosing a pastoral counselor or psychotherapist to whom to refer addicted people, it is crucial to recommend two or three so that an addicted person can choose the one with whom he or she feels most comfortable. Also, it is crucial to choose therapists who understand addictions and are appreciative of Twelve Step recovery programs.[16]

Frederick N., had been struggling to work the program in A.A. for over four years. He had been plagued by slip after slip. Finally, in desperation, he sought the therapeutic help of a psychiatrist who had a supportive attitude toward A.A. His psychotherapy enabled Frederick N. to resolve some of his painful inner conflicts and feelings. At the time of my interview with him, he had enjoyed his longest period of continuous sobriety. He reported that, through psychotherapy, he finally has "gotten the program in A.A."

Short-term therapy (a few weeks or months) with a pastoral counselor or psychotherapist who is knowledgeable in the area of addictions and Twelve Step groups can be invaluable for some addicts. Such short-term therapy aims not at deep unconscious problems, but at helping people in recovery improve their chances of achieving long-term productive sobriety—things such as accepting that they really are addicted, learning how to resolve or handle disturbing feelings constructively, doing an in-depth moral inventory, and changing their ways of relating so that the old guilt-isolation-shame-anger spiral does not trigger the runaway symptom of a slip. Furthermore, therapy needs to help addicts move ahead on the personal and spiritual growth pathway that leads to a new way of life based on inner strengths and healthy relationships rather than alcohol, drugs, or compulsive activities. Short-term marriage and family therapy can be useful in assisting families in adjusting to the new demands of recovery while making their relationship more mutually fulfilling.

One of the most helpful therapeutic methods in treating some of those with chemical and behavioral addictions is group therapy. I would extend psychiatrist Ruth Fox's evaluation of such therapy with alcoholics to include addictions of all kinds:

> Group therapy is perhaps the most effective type of treatment for the alcoholic aside from A.A. There is almost immediate identification and mutual support, which makes the alcoholic feel quickly accepted. The group represents a nonthreatening, socially rewarding yet challenging atmosphere in which their many problems can be discussed. Problems about drinking, their jobs, and their families come up first, but soon they begin to discuss and show their deeper feelings of anger, resentment, sensitivity, guilt, distrust, loneliness, depression, fear, sense of inferiority, and worthlessness.

Fox goes on to observe that the warm, understanding tolerance of the group atmosphere enables feelings like these to be drained off. Typical alcoholic defense maneuvers such as projection, rationalization, and denial are recognized and discussed understandably in nontechnical terms. Both positive and negative interactions among group members provide opportunities to understand group members' ways of relating outside the group. Many strong and lasting friendships grow up in the group.[17]

If addictions are accompanied by mental illnesses, as in dual diagnosis addicts, it is essential to get victims to a mental health professional who can evaluate their need for psychotropic drugs and for psychiatric hospitalization. Such addicts often do not respond to Twelve Step approaches because of their mental illnesses. However, it is well to remember that the great majority of those with chemical addictions do not also suffer from severe mental illnesses, so psychiatric evaluation and hospitalization are not needed. Hospitalized nonpsychotic addicts in mental hospitals may actually make their recovery more difficult.[18]

High recovery rates often are achieved in programs in which a combination of therapies, tailored to the particular needs of individuals, are available and treatment is defined as a team job. Clergy are fortunate if they live in one of the several hundred places in the United States and Canada where chemical addiction clinics are available for referrals. In such facilities the clinical team consists of various combinations of an internist, a psychiatrist, a nutritionist, a psychologist, a social worker, and recovered addicts. In clinics that have the most enlightened and effective approaches, clinically trained pastoral counselor-chaplains are essential staff members. Each member of the team has special skills to bring to the common task of helping addicted persons and their families recover. Internists are equipped to treat the physiological problems and administer needed medications. Psychologists are trained to do testing by which patients' therapeutic needs can be evaluated, and they also may do individual and group psychotherapy as well as outcome research. Psychiatrists can prescribe medication for drug therapies and treat those who have dual diagnoses. Social workers may be trained to help addicts resolve marital and vocational problems, do group as well as individual therapy, and work with family members. Clinically trained pastoral counselors are equipped to help addicted persons with their spiritual problems as these relate to recovery, and the spiritual angle issues in Twelve Step programs. They usually are trained to do individual, group, and marital counseling. The recovered addicts on the team (who often do much of the work with patients), frequently can reach less motivated patients and serve as bridge persons to help them accept Twelve Step programs. Most clinics probably do not have all these members on their teams because of costs and limited understanding of the need. But the principle of interprofessional teamwork is widely accepted and at the center of the working philosophy of most effective clinics.

To avoid the trap of professional perfectionism, several facts need to be emphasized. Few if any clergy in parishes and even chaplaincies, unless their ministry is in addiction treatment centers, have had all or even much of the preparation described in this chapter. What has been overviewed here is optimal preparation. If clergy have had good general training in pastoral care and counseling, especially clinically supervised education, and if they have basic knowledge about addictions and have developed good working relations with Twelve Step programs, they can be effective in counseling with many addicted people and their families! Now, let's move on to examine the basic methods of counseling for recovery and beyond in the chapters that follow.

CHAPTER 12

Counseling for Recovery and Beyond:
Motivating and Beginning the Process

Learn your theories as well as you can, but put them aside when you touch the miracle of the living soul. Not theories but your own creative individuality alone must decide.
—Carl Gustav Jung, *Psychological Reflections*

The purpose of this chapter is to describe how to begin the process of counseling with addicted persons and their families. It will explore in some depth the most difficult problem in this type of counseling: finding ways to awaken addicts' motivation to receive the help they need for recovery. It also will shed light on these crucial topics: how to establish a counseling relationship; learning the early warning signals of addictions; the dynamics of surrender in the process of recovery; and avoiding clergy (and other counselor) codependency.

The Heart of All Effective Counseling

Before further discussion of particular techniques for helping addicted people and their families recover, it is important to describe the characteristics of the counseling approach that I have found most effective. The heart of any counseling process is a relationship characterized by warmth, genuineness, acceptance, caring, and trust. This quality of relating is described in psychological language as *therapeutic* and in religious language as *redemptive*. Such a relationship is the basic channel for the flow of the helping-healing process, without which technical skills in counseling are ineffective in facilitating either healing or growth. If a therapeutic quality of relationship does exist, healing and growth can occur in spite of weaknesses in counselors' methodology. Such a relationship with addicted persons enables counseling techniques to become potent instruments for the healing that brings recovery and the growth that brings a full, creative life.

Every counseling relationship is a new creation. Each is unique, developing as it does from the interaction of two unique individuals, a counselor and a counselee. This is the meaning of Jung's words cited above. Addressed originally to psychiatrists, they are applicable to all types of caring and counseling relationships including those of clergy. The uniqueness of each relationship causes counseling to be both an art and a science. Counselors' effectiveness depends on their discovery of their own creative style that allows them to connect deeply with others and use themselves as healing and growth facilitators in relationships.

One danger of emphasizing counseling methodologies is that the artistic essence of the helping process may become obscured by overemphasis on technique. To reduce this hazard, it should be made clear that what follows is a description of general principles and methods that have proved useful in counseling with people suffering from chemical addictions and also behavioral addictions. They are only general guidelines. To be most effective, you should use them experimentally, evaluate them critically as you go, and adapt them to reflect your own particular mode of therapeutic relating. It is salutary to remember that different counselors, using a variety of theories and methods, have obtained positive results with countless addicted persons. In other words, there is no one right way of counseling with anyone, including the addicted.

All effective counseling is like playing the piano by ear. It is an art, but a disciplined art in that it is based on generic principles that transcend the infinite variety of differences in counseling theories, counselors, and counselees. In learning to play the piano, there are general principles of harmony, rhythm, and technique that players usually learn by practice. Learning these frees players to utilize the principles and skills as a solid basis for developing their own unique musical expression. As they develop their skills, the music they play becomes increasingly their own. It flows from and through them, expressing a musical individuality as much their own as their fingerprints. In an analogous way, counselors aim at a basic mastery of the principles of their art that will free them to develop their own style of counseling—a style that releases their unique personhood in a trusting, transforming human encounter called counseling.

Establishing a Counseling Relationship

Effective counseling with alcoholics, drug addicts, and their families utilizes the same general principles and methods employed in counseling with anyone else struggling with serious, socially stigmatized problems in living. To discuss these generic principles and techniques in detail is beyond the scope of this book.[1] Instead the task here is to apply the general principles to the special problems of counseling with the addicted, and to do so with particular reference to some of the psychological characteristics that are typical of such persons.

When clergy make contact with problem drinkers, alcoholics, drug dependent people, and their families, the first step is to build a relationship bridge with them. As in other counseling, this is done by in-depth listening and responding to hurting persons with the fullest attention one can give. It is not easy for nonaddicted counselors to understand the inner world of painfully addicted persons, but it is also not impossible. Understanding is acquired by focused, in-depth listening to them and allowing them to become our teachers. Psychiatrist Karl Menninger once observed that "listening is the most important technical tool possessed by the psychiatrist."[2] It is also the most important tool of counseling pastors as well as specialists in pastoral psychotherapy who are usually called pastoral counselors. What has been called "healing listening" or "responsive listening" requires suppressing one's urge to interpret, reassure, ask many questions, or give facile advice.[3] (In this vein, someone has observed that wisdom results from a lifetime of listening when one would prefer to be talking.)

Psychoanalyst Theodor Reik once referred to the art of "listening with the third ear," meaning being aware of feelings, both those that are hidden behind the words and the subtle messages communicated in moods, postures, and facial expressions. Responsive listening means responding to messages picked up by the third ear so that persons know that they really are heard. Communication by effective counselors must transcend the superficial talking and responding in many everyday relationships. Such interaction often consists of parallel monologues that include impatient, inattentive listening dominated by each party wishing the other would stop talking so that they could talk. Listening and responding with empathy, in healing and growth stimulating ways, is a skill that counselors must learn through disciplined practice.

Therapeutic listening seeks both head understanding and heart understanding of addicted peoples' words and their feelings, including the ones that are too painful to trust to words. Such listening enables effective counselors to sense, in part, how addicted persons feel about themselves, others, God, and, particularly what they perceive as their real problems. Precious fragments of counselees' hopes and fears, dreams and nightmares gradually are understood as a counselor begins to see how life looks through the eyes of the burdened person.

Listening and responding with warm empathy serves to establish the first fragile strands of the interpersonal bridge called rapport, over which the counseling process moves back and forth. In this way a therapeutic relationship is established. The good news is that if addicted counselees sense that counselors really want to understand, even though their initial efforts to do so are partial or fumbling, trust and rapport begin to grow. Counselees' awareness that counselors care and are trying to understand, allows a beachhead of mutual understanding to be established. From this starting place, the counselors may move into the dark and often mysterious terrain of addicted persons' inner worlds.

Fortunately, as counselors become familiar with the experiences and feelings shared by many addicted persons, it is easier to pick up and respond to the feelings of particular addicts more accurately. Often counselors can sense what addicted counselees' feelings are before they verbalize them fully. As counselors are able to stay on addicted persons' feeling wavelengths, therapeutic relationships are strengthened. A counselee becomes aware that "this counselor really cares and is trying to understand the strange agony of my inner world which I don't understand fully."

As noted earlier, many seriously addicted people are plagued by low self-esteem, a sense of aloneness, guilt, fear, shame, and anxiety. These painful feelings naturally cause them to keep their defenses high. This increases the problems of establishing vital bridges of understanding rapport with them. It often is necessary to move slowly and carefully in building a connection with addicts. Hidden feelings of guilt and shame make them expect, and sometimes even court, rejection. Like many other hurting people, their emotional antennae are extended. They tend to be hypersensitive to what they perceive as subtle condescension or rejection. This makes it imperative that counselors try to avoid saying or doing anything that could be interpreted as criticism until rapport is established.

Emphasizing the importance of listening does not mean that the counselor should function in a passive manner. Not knowing what a mainly silent counselor is thinking, addicts often project their own self-disparagement onto the counselor causing them to feel judged by the latter's silence. To be effective, counseling relationships need to be warm, caring, empathetic, active. In such relationships, counselors' insights, experience, and skills tend to be effective. It is the human qualities in the counselor that provide the indispensable healing energy that empowers their competencies.

Clergy sometimes face a special challenge in establishing healing relationships. This is because people often perceive them as superego or conscience figures, for example, as professionals who represent the "oughts" and "shoulds" of religion and/or society. Counselees with guilt loads and authority problems may believe that ministers are sitting in judgment when actually they are not. This makes it important for clergy to let clients sense that they are reaching out to them as human beings, not down to them from an elevated spiritual and mental health position. The best way to do this is to relate to counselees in accepting, nonjudgmental, human-to-human ways that don't fit the moralistic stereotype that is projected on clergy by some people. (Like most stereotypes, it is reinforced by those clergy who are moralistic.)

Implementing a horizontal and accepting way of relating, as opposed to a vertical and judgmental way, was well described by Carl G. Jung in a discussion of psychotherapists' effectiveness. In his classic volume, *Modern Man in Search of a Soul*, he writes:

> If the doctor wants to offer guidance to another, or even to accompany him a step on the way, he must be in touch with the other person's psychic life. He is never in touch when he passes judgment. Whether he puts his judgments into words, or keeps them to himself, makes not the slightest difference.[4]

There are various ways of communicating this vital acceptance and, by doing so, avoid raising addicted people's defenses. Responding to painful addiction stories in empathetic, caring, and accepting ways is a key method. As counselees risk telling even a part of their messy stories, they usually are wondering how counselors are feeling about what they are sharing. This makes it important to respond frequently with accurate empathy and acceptance that lets the addicted counselees know that a counselor is feeling with them in their problems. Some counselors suggest using encouraging grunts to let counselees know that they have been heard and to encourage them to keep sharing their stories and feelings. It also is helpful for counselors to give periodic feedback by paraphrasing, in a sentence or two, what they understand clients are meaning and feeling. This communicates counselors' desire to understand and also provides opportunities for counselees to correct misunderstandings. This listening-responding-listening pattern can be a effective way of strengthening addicted counselees' trust.

It is important in all counseling to listen much more than talk, not to barrage clients with questions, particularly during the early relationship building phases of counseling. This respects troubled persons' right to stay as hidden as they feel they need to be.[5] In contrast, asking questions that may seem probing or irrelevant often strikes the addicted as prying into their private inner space.

The use of "we" statements or queries is a method of avoiding seeming to be in a superior position, on the one hand, and also of inviting active collaboration by counselees in resolving their own dilemmas, on the other. The late Otis Rice, a hospital chaplain with skills in counseling with alcoholics, gave these illustrations of "we" approaches: "Now what can we find in the situation?" or "What can we do with the problem you have brought?" The use of "we" lets addicts feel counselors' partnerlike support in coping with their problems. It puts counselors beside them as allies.

Another way of speaking from such a collaborative position is for counselors to share brief, relevant comments or stories from their own lives about their own very human struggles and stumbling. Less threatening than a direct focus on problems in the clients' family relationships, for example, is for counselors to mention comparable issues in their own family. Another alternative, if counselors do not have their family members' permission to share such things, is to describe how "a couple (or person) I know handled a similar problem." It is essential to never use examples identified as other counselees. To do so violates the principle of pastoral confidentiality and makes today's counselees wonder if they will be tomorrow's case examples.

These "we" approaches help prevent anxious counselees from feeling more threatened, on the spot, and defensive. It can be reassuring and supportive for counselors to level with them about some of their own human struggles, as well as some of their solutions to comparable issues that seem to work. In doing this, counselors use what Paul Tillich once called the "principle of mutuality" in pastoral counseling. By this counselors communicate to the counselees that they understand from their own experiences.[6] A vivid example of the power of the "we" or mutuality principle is the way A.A. members usually structure Twelfth Step conversations. They focus first and foremost on their own drinking experiences, problems, and recovery. In this way they communicate hope but also that they are not judging or talking down to the other person.

In the same spirit, Marty Mann once suggested that clergy would be more successful as spiritual mentors of alcoholics if they told about some personal suffering or deep crisis in their own experience, and how they found strength and comfort in their faith. Telling their own story simply and directly, she said, could enable clergy to come down from their "symbolic mountain above the battle and meet the tormented soul of the alcoholic on its own level of suffering." This could help the alcoholic accept comfort and perhaps gain some faith from clergy counselors. She also recommended that pastors who are not alcoholics tell about someone they know who has received help for alcoholism.[7]

In my experience, brief references to one's own problems or struggles lets clients know that their counselor also has problems and is speaking as one who shares foibles and faults with the rest of the human family. It is best to do so briefly, in an "in passing" manner. This lessens the risk that severely disturbed people will resent a comparison of what seems to them to be relatively minor problems with their all-consuming, devastating problems. Mentioning one's own problems briefly does not detract from counselees' main concern—their own pain.

The acceptance climate of addiction counseling relationships is influenced powerfully by whether or not counselors really do accept the sickness concept of addictions. If they do not accept it at both their heart and head levels, they may convey subtle critical, judging feelings in spite of their conscious intentions. By accepting the sickness concept deeply, counselors free their minds from residual feelings that destructive addictions are essentially moral deviations or perverse habits. Furthermore, if they accept that we all share in some of the common sicknesses of our addictive culture, residual feelings of being one up on the obviously addicted will tend to melt like a snowball in the sun.

Addicted people frequently choose to talk with clergy because they desperately want to unburden themselves of terribly heavy feelings, especially guilt and shame. Clergy are more than just the most accessible and inexpensive counseling professional available to the vast majority of people. They also are representatives of the profession to which countless people have gone through the centuries, hoping for relief from guilt and shame. When addicted people pour out their painful feelings, several types of healing often occur. Emotional unburdening takes place, lightening guilt and shame loads enough to free up previously paralyzed energies for use in coping more constructively with reality-based problems. As counselors listen with caring and even partial understanding, the interpersonal bridge of empathy and rapport grows stronger. Having one's agony heard by a respected and accepting religious authority figure can bring deeply meaningful spiritual healing. And, very important, by encouraging the verbal flow of addicts' stories, counselors can acquire much of the relevant information needed to understand the issues and plan counseling strategies. Important information that is not shared spontaneously can be learned by a few direct questions.

Here is how one clergy counselor unwittingly blocked the development of a potentially healing relationship. A young adult alcoholic finally mustered enough courage to talk with a minister about his disintegrating addictive situation. He began by pouring out remorseful self-condemnation. Believing that the man's put downs and castigations of himself were exaggerated, the pastor tried to reassure him. When the man tried to ventilate more feelings of shame and despair, the pastor responded, in effect, that there were extenuating circumstances that made what he had done not as bad as he thought. The minister did not give him the healing gift of hearing him out and letting him know that his feelings were heard and accepted. Instead, the pastor assured him prematurely of God's grace and forgiveness, and then used a prayer that reinforced his error. The young man did not return for the subsequent pastoral counseling session that had been scheduled.

Unfortunately, this minister was not aware that most reassurances do not reassure deeply troubled people. He was ineffective in his role as a facilitator of healing forgiveness. His faith assurances were premature, shortcutting the time tested process by which forgiveness eventually could have become real in the man's experience. According to the wisdom of the Christian tradition, adapted in A.A. to become the moral inventory steps, the man needed to confess fully, have his confession heard by another person and God, and then make appropriate amends. Only then could the healing reconciliation and forgiveness begin to dawn like the sun in his inner life.

Motivation: A Key to Recovery

The most frequent dilemma frustrating those who try to help addicted people is their lack of adequate motivation to find the help they need to recover. A general axiom in all counseling is that people can be helped only with those problems that they regard as problems and with which they want help from the counselor. For this reason, it is important during initial contacts with addicted persons to discover how open they are to help and what type of help they want and expect. If missing or inadequate motivation is not recognized and remedied by counselors, it is unlikely that healing and growth will occur in those relationships. This is true even if counselors and clients go through the motions of extended counseling sessions. If motivation for recovery is inadequate, the prerequisite counseling task is to awaken clients' motivation. The main focus of the remainder of this chapter is on methods for doing this.

Awakening Clients' Motivation

To discover the degree and type of motivations that addicted people bring to counselors, certain questions should be in counselors' minds as they listen to them. If clear answers do not emerge, it is important to ask a few questions like these that are relevant to particular situations:

- From their perspective, is their use of alcohol and drugs causing them problems or do they regard these substances mainly solutions to other problems?
- If they see alcohol and/or drugs as problems in their lives, do they see themselves as needing help with these, or do they believe they can handle them by themselves?
- If they are honest in seeking counseling help, is this motivated by external needs—for example, to pacify their spouse, parents, or boss? Were they nagged or dragged to come for counseling Or is their motivation at least in part internal—for example, to lessen the pain from their drinking and use, and perhaps to enhance their own well-being and satisfactions in living?
- If they have had the same problems for some time, why did they choose to come seeking help now? What has changed to motivate the decision to come now? Have they been hit by a motivating crisis that puts them under acute short-term pressure, but will pass quickly?
- Why have they come to a particular counselor, for example, a minister, instead of a secular counselor or a Twelve Step program?

What are some indications of the strength of motivation for successful treatment? Motivation is weak and prognoses for recovery are poor if addicted people view alcohol or drugs more as solutions than as problems; regard other people as the main causes of their excessive consumption and want help in manipulating them; only desire help in avoiding the painful consequences of their recent addictive behavior; come mainly because they are pressured by a crisis or by another person; or believe that they can quit on their own whenever they decide they really want to do so. Conversely, motivation is adequate and prognoses favorable if they have surrendered and regard their addictive substances as more of a cause than a solution to their problems in living; accept some responsibility for their substance abuses; come on their own because they are desperate and hope to get help; and are beginning to recognize that they have lost control of their drinking or drug use.

In evaluating addicts' motivation, it is important to bear in mind that the motivation of all humans is mixed. Few, if any addicts have unambivalent motivation to stop drinking or using entirely. Instead, they are pulled in opposite directions by inner forces. Many want to reduce their intake because they are afraid of the disastrous consequences of continuing, but at the same time they also are afraid to stop because their addictive substances have become the consuming center of their day-to-day lives. Thus, to ask if addicts are ready to stop using is not a precise way of ascertaining the adequacy of their motivation for recovery. A more reliable indicator is whether they are aware that the pain resulting from alcohol and drugs outweighs the satisfactions derived from their use. If so, their desire to stop probably is stronger than their desire to continue. In practice, this often is not easy to determine except on a trial and error basis.

I find it helpful to think of the motivation of hurting counselees as something like a teeter-totter tipping back and forth. At times the pain and the fear of the probable consequences of continuing heavy consumption outweigh the craving for alcohol's or drugs' anesthetic effects and the fear of life without them. When this occurs, addicts hit bottom and become open to help, at least temporarily. At other times their motivational teeter totter tilts away from being receptive to help. A severe hangover or a painful crisis like a DWI (driving while intoxicated) arrest may cause a "little bottom"—a state of emotional receptivity in which their defenses against recognizing the need for help are temporarily cracked by the physical and/or emotional pain of the experience. It is wise to encourage such persons to get help immediately and not to wait until they feel better. There is quaint wisdom that is related to hitting bottom that is expressed in an old Christian hymn that Wayne Oates quoted in one of his insightful books:

> Come, ye weary, heavy-laden,
> Lost and ruined by the fall;
> If you tarry till you're better,
> You will never come at all.[8]

I remember one alcoholic who was in wretched condition but could not admit that his drinking was a real problem. Again and again he would blame his drinking pattern on his wife's being a frigid woman. It seemed apparent that the frustrations of his poor sex life, and the inadequate interpersonal relationship at the roots of that, were among the frustrations that he tried to anesthetize by his self-destructive drinking. But the fact that he would not consider that his excessive drinking was also an important cause of his marital and sexual problems showed that his motivational teeter-totter had not yet tipped toward openness to help.

In the light of the complexity and mysteries of human motivation, it is wise to modify the familiar statement, "You can't help alcoholics (or other addicts) until they are ready!" This is a misleading half-truth that may be accepted by counselors as the whole truth. If they do, they will miss the opportunity to do everything possible to awaken and mobilize addicts' latent motivation for accepting help. It is much better, therefore, to ask if individuals show any willingness to consider sobriety, if they can be helped to glimpse the potential rewards of recovery, develop even a faint glimmer of hope, and are shown a path to more satisfying lives. Addicted people often are not able to admit their need for help, even to themselves, until and unless they see a small ray of hope that help is possible and that it may be more rewarding for them than their present situation.

During my research on the recovery process, I accompanied an experienced member of A.A., who I will call Henry, on a Twelfth Step call. The person, who I will call John, had just come off a binge described by his wife, who had called A.A., as "a binge to end all binges." He mentioned that he wasn't sure whether he was an alcoholic or just a heavy drinker because he never had taken a morning drink. (Much later he admitted that this usually was because he hadn't made sure the night before that he had hidden a supply for the next day.) Henry's response suggests a useful test of motivation to stop drinking as well as a wise sidestepping of wasting time by discussing a single symptom of alcoholism:

> To discuss whether one is a heavy drinker or an alcoholic can easily become a matter of semantics. The important question is this. Are you satisfied with your life as it's been going for the past year, two years, five years? Take any period you want. If you are, there's no problem. If you aren't satisfied and feel that alcohol is the cause or at least part of the cause of the way your life has been going, then the thing to do is to make a decision that you're going to stop. Then the problem is to make the decision stick, which is where A.A. comes in.

The man turned to telling a little about his painful experience during the recent binge and his resolve not to let it happen again. Henry responded, in effect:

> The problem is to make your present feeling stick—to keep it alive. You're very sincere now, we're assuming that, but how about in three months or six? A.A. is the way you keep the desire alive—keep on remembering that you have a problem with alcohol. After you've

been away from alcohol for a while, you'll probably begin to question whether it's really a problem or not. A.A. helps keep your present desire from drying up.

Toward the end of the visit, Henry said:

You have to remember, John, that nobody really cares if you have a few drinks. It's up to you. If you want to stop drinking, then A.A. can help you. But it's your decision.

Such a statement left the initiative and responsibility with John where it belonged. A.A. recognizes that people must make the initial decision to accept help themselves—however mixed their feelings about it—before any real helping can begin.

In dealing with unmotivated addiction victims, it is important to do what Henry did—recognize and accept their right not to accept help. Of course they can exercise this right, regardless of how counselors feel about it. In some cases, acceptance of their right and freedom not to accept help seems to increase the possibility that they will actually accept help. In symbolic terms, it is as though clergy counselors must respect people's right to go to hell before they can help them move toward heaven.

Helping Enhance Addicts' Motivation

Many addicted people, like the one who received that Twelveth Step call, consult clergy counselors before they are open to facing the truth about their addiction. Even if they try counseling, they usually do not make a real commitment. The same is true of those who come (and especially those who are sent) to A.A., secular addiction counselors, or outpatient treatment centers. It is estimated that at least a third of those who come to such resources do not return after the first session. Deficient motivation is a major cause of dropping out of treatment before recovery. But it is important to remember two things. Some who contact recovery resources with little motivation for sobriety—including those pushed to go to A.A. by a judge as an alternative to jail—eventually get their motivation strengthened so that they achieve sobriety. Because so many addicted people are rejecting or resisting their need for treatment, it is important for counselors to learn motivation-enhancing skills.

I remember a pastor who was baffled by the behavior of a male periodic alcoholic. With the cup of his remorse and good resolutions running over, he often would consult with the minister after his increasingly frequent binges. Each time, the pastor attempted to relate him to A.A. through a recovering member in his church, but the man refused. In spite of his repeated defeats and relapses, he was still sure that he could "lick this thing" by himself. It became apparent to the minister that the man had not yet hit bottom. When he pointed this out to the distressed family, the man's young adult daughter posed the obvious question in its most disturbing form: "Do you mean that we must sit and watch him go down and down and down, and do absolutely nothing?"

Few things in life are more heartrending or frustrating to family members or caring clergy than watching while addicted people engage in what amounts to protracted suicide. Fortunately, it is unnecessary to wait and do nothing. What strategies can clergy and family members use to increase the odds that addicted people will become open to help more quickly?

One strategy is to avoid relating in ways that increase unmotivated addicts' resistance to accepting help. The pastor of a suburban congregation received a phone call from Jane P., the wife of a couple in his church. With her voice shaking and tearful, she asked, "Will you please come over and talk to Robert, pastor? He's having his problem again." She quickly sketched her husband's current drunken crisis. Because the minister saw himself as a good pastor with dedication to helping troubled people, he accepted her plea, knowing that he probably would be getting into a difficult situation. When he arrived at their home, he immediately discovered that it was worse than he had expected. Robert obviously was very drunk and in no mood to talk to the pastor about anything—particularly not about his drinking. He was unrestrained in his anger toward his wife for calling the pastor to "stick your nose in our private business!" The minister felt threatened and responded defensively that he was only trying to help. He left feeling himself to be a miserable failure.

In spite of his intentions to be helpful, this pastor had allowed himself to be drawn into the couple's ongoing power struggle about the husband's drinking and put himself on the wife's side. Robert's resentment probably delayed the time when he would become open to accepting help. If the pastor had not jumped to accept Mary's appeal, he might have been in a position to be of help later when Robert became open to being helped.[9]

The pastor should have asked Jane four crucial questions before deciding how to respond to her urgent appeal: "Is Robert drunk?" "Does he see his drinking as a problem with which he wants help?" "Does he know you are calling me?" and "Does he sometimes get violent when he's drunk?" Knowing that Robert was drunk, didn't see his drinking as a problem, and didn't know Jane was phoning him, the pastor would have known that it would be utterly counterproductive to try to talk with him at that point. If Robert was violent or had had episodes of drunken violence before, the pastor should have helped Jane take whatever action was needed to protect herself and their two children from what could be deadly danger. She might have decided to stay with relatives for a few days or, if Robert became physically violent, call the police.

In light of what he would have discovered by Jane's answers to the four questions, the pastor would have been wise to say to her:

> I want very much to help in any way I can. But trying to talk with Robert now would probably do more harm than good. It would only antagonize him, giving him an added excuse to go on drinking. What would you think about telling him, after he sobers up and feels better, that I will be glad to talk with him about anything he wants to discuss? If he will give me a call, we'll find a mutually convenient time to meet. In the meantime, I want to talk with you later today or tomorrow about how you can cope with your difficult situation. When could you come to my study to talk?

By responding in this way, the minister would have created an opportunity to offer guidance to her, whether or not Robert decided he wanted help. Most people who request help for someone else can themselves benefit from crisis counseling. Often, it is difficult for them to shift gears to think of themselves as the ones who could be helped by counseling rather than the persons about whom they are concerned.

If nonaddicted clergy visit people who are sober and have expressed a desire for help with their substance abuse, here it is a good strategy. Explain to them why it would be helpful to bring along someone who knows the problem firsthand—an A.A. or Al-Anon member. As in making referrals, it is well to find an A.A. or Al-Anon person of the same gender, general age group, and socioeducational background. During addicts' periods of remorse following drunken episodes, stable members of these groups usually sense how best to use the temporary enhanced openness to help. It is unwise to go alone to visit alcoholics, particularly those of the opposite sex, even if they are sober. The danger of their acting out impulsively, in hostile or sexual ways, is even greater if they are drinking. This is an additional reason for having an experienced A.A. member of the alcoholic's gender present wherever or whenever the meeting occurs.

Spouse-motivated and parent-motivated substance abusers are frustratingly familiar to most pastors. It is essential, in such cases, to do everything possible to implement strategies that encourage addicted persons to accept responsibility for their own recovery. Like many other dynamics in counseling, this often is easier said than done. However, its importance cannot be overemphasized. Repeated experience has made something very clear: Those who try to find their recovery path mainly to satisfy someone else, rather than seeking it for their own sake, usually stumble and fall before they have walked more than a few steps on that path. It is essential to try to mobilize addicted people's self-motivation and sense of responsibility.

If counselors or family members attempt to get and keep addicted persons sober, thus assuming responsibility, failure is almost certain for a simple reason. No one can get or keep any other person sober for long. Addicts' dependent side tends to draw the counselor into the trap of assuming responsibility for their sobriety. Some will expect the minister to be a wonder-worker who can, by some magic religious formula, cure them or give them the secret of moderation. It is wise to let addicts know, gently but firmly, that no one, including God, can make them recover unless they are willing to work responsibly at recovery. They must use their own God-given resources, perhaps with help from a counselor, A.A., or medically oriented treatment resources, to work out their own recovery. No one can do it for them or to them.

To keep responsibility with addicted counselees, it is crucial to avoid doing anything that might have the effect of protecting them from the normal painful consequences of their irresponsible behavior. It is seldom if ever constructive to intervene with employers, spouses, or the law, asking for special concessions on their behalf. Most such actions are harmful in that they deprive addicts of the painful experiences that may eventually bring them to the point of openness to help. Such overprotection may appear to be kind but actually is cruel in its long-term effects.

A therapist on the staff of a center treating alcoholics described an alcoholic who had been going on periodic binges for years, using the inpatient center as a drying out place. The man admitted he was licked and needed help only when, through a prearranged plan, the man's wife told him she was leaving if he didn't get help, his employer announced that he was through unless he got help to stop drinking, and the therapist informed him that he would not be accepted as a patient in the future unless he agreed to stay long enough to allow for effective therapy. Up to this point, the man had been shielded from the consequences of his behavior by his relative affluence and the allowances that significant people in his life had been making. It was when they stopped this, and he knew that they meant what they said, that he was forced to face reality.

This was a calculated approach to withdrawing the props that supported an addict's denial of painful reality. It was what is now called an *intervention* (see below). When codependent enablers stopped overprotecting him, he knew that he would be hit by the normal adult consequences of irresponsible drinking behavior. This tipped his inner motivational teeter-totter toward accepting the help offered. In effect, overprotectors sit on the wrong end of the teeter-totter, delaying the person's hitting bottom. By withdrawing dependency shields and allowing them to experience the pain of what one recovering alcoholic called being "clobbered by reality," the concerned people caused his teeter-totter to tilt toward openness to help.

When counseling with alcohol or drug addicts, it is crucial to find out whether they have been nagged or dragged to talk with the minister. I recall an intriguing description by Jellinek of how he approached alcoholics who had been sent or brought by well-meaning spouses or other family members. After inviting the person into his office alone, he immediately directed the conversation to some superficial, irrelevant topic. During this light conversation, he would drop a few seed thoughts about the nature and symptoms of alcoholism. Then, after a while he would say, "Well, I guess you've been in here long enough to satisfy your spouse. You may go now if you wish."

This approach usually has surprise or shock value. But more important, it tends to let counselors stop being perceived as being on the same side of the table with pushy family members. It makes it more difficult for the addicted to keep their hostile, resentful, and defiant feelings toward family members attached to counselors by misperceiving them as allies of the misguided relatives. It also confronts counselees with making the crucial choice—to leave or to stay on their own initiative. Respecting their ability and right to make this choice may boost their self-esteem a little. If they choose to stay, this respect also strengthens their relationship with the counselor. I would recommend using this method when an addicted client remains resistant (actively or passively) during the first interview in spite of the use of the other strategies described in this chapter.

If addicted people come mainly because of third party pressure, the counselor's first task is to try to establish an autonomous relationship with them and separate psychologically from the pressuring persons. Unless this occurs, the addicted person will not claim the counseling as his or her own. As long as their main motivation is to satisfy the others, a therapeutic relationship—the necessary context in which healing and growth may occur—will not develop between them and the counselor.

It can be helpful for a spouse and/or other concerned and caring relative to be present in the initial counseling contact. Their presence provides an opportunity for counselors to gain a feel for the nature of the interaction in that family system. But it is important for counselors also to talk with addicted persons alone at some time during the first session. This helps to build an independent relationship with them and may let counselors learn information that they will not share in family members' presence. Here is an example of how this can be accomplished.

> *Pastor (to the spouse):* "I appreciate knowing how you see things. It's helpful to get your point of view. Now, I think it would be helpful for me to talk privately with your husband (or wife) about the issues. You'll find some magazines in the next room, if you want to read while you wait. I'll let you know when I'd like you to join us again."

Even when the pushing people are not physically present, they often are there psychologically, complicating counselors' efforts to establish a therapeutic relationship. Here is one way of beginning an independent relationship with a person who has been pushed by a family member.

> *Pastor:* "From what they told me, and by the fact that they pushed you to see me, I'm aware that your spouse and family think that you have a problem with alcohol (or drugs). But what I'm most interested in hearing from you is how you see the situation. I can imagine that things look a lot different from your perspective. What seems to be the trouble, as you see it? By the way, whatever you tell me will be kept between the two of us. If I think that sharing something with your family would be helpful, I won't do this unless I get your permission."

This approach communicates that the counselor is not siding with the relatives by accepting their view as the whole picture, and that the addicted person's understanding is important. What is hoped for is that as the counselor listens responsively and with empathy, rapport will grow and a therapeutic relationship will develop, and the person will sense that the counselor is genuinely interested in him or her and in understanding the situation fully so as to be of help.

While it is important that addicted people sense that clergy or other counselors are not on their family's side of the table, it is equally essential to avoid criticizing family members or sharing anything they shared in confidence. Counselors' pastoral responsibility is to not side with either party in a conflict. It is to provide whatever help is possible to those on all sides so that their well-being may be enhanced. Equally important, the recovery of "identified patients" (Virginia Satir's term) will be more stable if their family systems also recover from their codependency, thus freeing everyone to change and grow.

In other words, understanding the helping process from a social systems perspective makes counselors aware that effective help for individuals is much more likely to occur when interpersonal systems are healed and grow healthier. If family confidences are betrayed or counselors' criticisms are quoted (or, as often happens, misquoted) to family members in moments of anger, the possibility of being of any help to the whole family system is virtually destroyed. Furthermore, family members usually get involved, even in ways that are unhelpful, at least in part because they care about addicted family members. If their caring is misguided, it often can be redirected into constructive channels, with the help of Al-Anon or, as we will see below, by an intervention.

During any initial counseling interview, it is important to encourage clients to verbalize fully their honest feelings about being there. This is especially true if addicted people come under pressure or threat, or come fighting their inner resistances to admitting they need help. As negative or conflicted feelings are articulated, counselors should let clients know— by understanding and accepting responses—that their feelings are heard and understood, and their right to all their feelings is respected. Here are examples of statements aimed at helping counselees express negative feelings: "I could understand it if you have some strong feelings about the circumstances that got you here today." "I can imagine that you might feel some resentment at being pushed in to see me."

Counselees whose hidden resentment, anger, or resistance are not brought out and discussed usually stay uncooperative for no obvious reason. Such feelings about being coerced or feelings of weakness for having to ask for help seem to function like logjams blocking the flow of healing interaction in counseling. Such logjams are often dispersed when addicted clients express their feelings and sense that counselors accept them.

From his extensive psychiatric practice with alcoholics, Harry Tiebout once observed that even the most adamantly resisting alcoholic has an Achilles' heel. A therapist's job, he said, is to find that heel, for the place

347

where a troubled counselee can be motivated is also where they are hurting, worried, frustrated, afraid, or want something intensely. The key to reaching troubled counselees, including addicts, who are not receptive to help, is to discover where they are hurting or hoping. If they can begin to understand how their uses of alcohol or drugs are among the causes of their pain, offers of help are more likely to be accepted. Areas of frustration, pain, hopes, and longing usually become evident when people are encouraged to talk openly about their problems in living, and what they want changed to reduce their pain and make life better for them.

This is not to suggest that alcoholics and drug addicts should necessarily be given the type of help for which they ask. Frequently, what they want would, in the long run, work against their recovery—for instance, a loan or gift of money, or intervening with someone to shelter them from the consequences of their behavior. Instead, what counselors should do, as they understand what clients want, is to gradually modify their expectations, if necessary, to make these contribute to their recovery and well-being.

In searching for the Achilles' heels of resisting addicts, counselors should encourage them to tell about their experiences of using their favorite chemical comforters—when they drink or use drugs, with whom, how they feel, and what happens to them when they do. During their active addiction, people frequently lie, particularly in early stages of counseling relationships. They often give inaccurate or incomplete pictures of their drinking and drug use and how they really feel about this. Unless they are dual diagnoses addicts suffering from character disorders that complicate their addiction, they lie to defend themselves from the painful truth and/or from critical responses they expect from the counselor. They may be much more concerned about their drinking and drug use than they are willing to admit. If so, as trust of the counselor grows stronger, they usually reveal more of the truth.

Whether or not counselees give accurate pictures of their drinking and drug use, the discussion provides opportunities for counselors to plant factual seeds of understanding of addictions, and by so doing, perhaps stimulate appropriate concern about their drinking and/or use. This is what I call *educative counseling*, meaning offering relevant information during the process of counseling interaction. A few questions such as the following can be asked when they fit into the flow of pastoral conversations:

1. Do you sometimes find yourself drinking (or using) more than you intend?

2. Before you go to a party, do you sometimes have some drinks, or at the party do you sneak a quick one on the sly when nobody is watching?

3. Do you ever take a fast drink or a pill to help get you through tough social situations?

4. Do you get very defensive when your spouse is critical about your drinking or accuses you of overdoing it at a party?

5. Have you ever "pulled a blank" (had a memory blackout) while drinking or using?

6. Have you lost time or has your efficiency slipped at work because of drinking or recreational drugs?

7. Are the conflicts in your marriage ever complicated by your drinking?

8. Do you sometimes spend money you can't really afford on booze or recreational drugs?

It is important to avoid grilling counselees about such issues, putting them on the defensive. But an occasional question such as these—or others from among the diagnostic questions listed in earlier chapters—can be sprinkled into a discussion of a counselee's alcohol and/or drug experiences at relevant points. Depending on counselees' responses, it may be appropriate to mention that these are among the common symptoms of serious drinking or drug use problems. It also can be pointed out that people headed for chemical abuse troubles usually don't have all these experiences and don't recognize danger signals in those they have.

If individuals are on the slippery slope of losing control over addictive substances, they probably already have had several of the common early symptoms. Even if they lie defensively about having had any of these symptoms, this educative counseling effort usually has not been wasted. What the seed planting often does is increase counselees' knowledge of early warning signs. After counseling sessions, they may ruminate: "I certainly pulled the wool over that minister's eyes! But I wonder if there's anything to what she said about memory lapses." One would hope that some of the educative counseling seeds sown will take root and eventually flower into a willingness to face the truth about their need for help.

Thus, encouraging problem drinkers and early-stage addicts to learn the fundamental facts about their potentially life threatening illness is an essential aspect of addiction counseling. We humans have a remarkable self-protective capacity for repressing, ignoring, and rationalizing painful facts and memories, including those associated with excessive drinking and drug use. As time passes in the recovery process, these memories grow dimmer, making it easier to ignore the need for finding the path to sobriety. As people in recovery begin to feel well and in control of their lives, they may begin to wonder if they must continue to work at the recovery program. If their knowledge of addictive illnesses does not interrupt this psychological trajectory, a slip or relapse is likely.

A useful tool in both addiction education and counseling, is the so-called *valley chart* (see below). Here is how the chart may be used with resistant problem drinkers or drug dependent people in counseling:

> *Pastor (during discussion of the person's drinking pattern):* "It might be helpful for us to take a diagnostic approach to get some clues about whether you might be on the road to bigger problems in this area." (Hands counselee a copy of valley chart.) Down the lefthand side of the valley, you'll find typical symptoms that many people have as this illness develops. Let's have a look at these to see if any of them fit." *Later*: "Look at the road up, on the righthand side of the valley chart. This shows the typical stages of recovery from the illness."

By tracing the rocky road down into advanced-stage addiction, counselors offer some clients a view of where they are and a preview of where they may be headed. It is important to see the ascending road, alongside the descending road, because this tends to kindle hope that recovery is possible by communicating that addictions are treatable. (For a larger form of the chart, contact the National Council on Alcoholism and Drug Dependence.) What is essential is for counselors to be familiar with the warning signs of substance addictions so that they can help clients recognize them if they are present or appear later.

Valley Chart of Alcohol Addiction and Recovery[10]

Emphasizing the physiological components of chemical addictions can help motivate some resistant problem drinkers and users. Drawing an analogy between addictions and diabetes or life-threatening allergic reactions communicates that addictions are not all in the mind and therefore obtaining treatment is essential for recovery. Psychological explanations still carry overtones of moralism and free will in our culture, whereas medical explanations usually escape these overtones. Because most people have an allergy of some kind or know someone who has diabetes, these medical problems can be bridges to understanding and accepting the physiological component in addictive illnesses. Drawing parallels between addictions and diabetes can be a particularly useful communication device.[11] Both alcoholics and those with diabetes have physical illnesses that are incurable but very treatable. Both must learn to live within the limitations imposed by their illness and, to the degree that they accomplish this, both can live relatively healthy and productive lives. Both conditions involve a malfunction of the body-mind organism and, if untreated, become progressively more severe until they are fatal.

In counseling aimed at enhancing motivation to accept treatment, it is important to make it clear that loss of control is often so gradual that it is almost imperceptible to those caught in this process. Also, some counselees still picture alcoholics and drug addicts in low-bottom images, or they believe that all addicted people are psychiatric wrecks. If such hazardous misconceptions are discovered, it is crucial to help the counselee change them by acquiring accurate knowledge about substance abuse and addictions.

In counseling with those who are resistant to admitting they need help, it is important to maintain a warm, caring relationship and to understand the common feelings that make it difficult for many addicts to face their obvious (to those around them) need for learning how to live abstinent lives. Many are deterred by anxiety about the possible loss of their favorite pain deadener if they stop drinking or using. There is anticipatory grief about losing their chemical solution that has worked for them in life crises over many years. Some male addicts fear the blow to both their macho self-image and their acceptance by drinking buddies if they admit that they can no longer "drink like a man." Addicted people for whom drinking or using drugs is a shared ritual of belonging in their jobs or important social groups, naturally fear what stopping might do to those valued relationships. It is important to listen carefully, with understanding and empathy, to powerful feelings such as these. They are inner barriers to admitting their need for help. Therapeutic discussion may enable them to offset these fears with reality-based fears of what will happen if they continue to refuse to get help with their chemical abuse.

Using Caring Confrontation

It is important to protect addicted persons' shaky self-esteem, but this is very different from protecting them from the painful consequences of destructive drinking and drug use. Communicating acceptance of them as persons does not mean approving of their irresponsible behavior that is harmful to both themselves and others. In many cases it is only as the significant people (including clergy) around the addicted become confrontational *because* they are caring, that addicts face the reality of their need to change. It is because overprotecting the addicted enables them to continue avoiding this reality that it has fittingly been called "cruel kindness." Such overprotection often is motivated by caring. But its effects are cruel in that it helps keep the addicted from hitting bottom and becoming open to the help that may save their lives. Counselors should use tough love that insists that people who are sick have an obligation to themselves, as well as their loved ones, to obtain the treatment they need.

This is to say that, if substance abusers continue to avoid the truth about their self-other destructive behavior, speaking the truth in a knowledgeable, nonattacking, and caring way may help. If trust and feelings of acceptance are present in helping relationships, constructive confrontation of this type may open addicts up to some awareness of their need for help. Constructive confrontation, in the New Testament, is described as "speaking the truth in love" (Eph. 4:15). If addicts feel genuine concern and warm caring from clergy counselors or others, they often listen. They may still be defending themselves with denial, so that their immediate response is rejection of counselors' words of warning. But their mental wheels may be set in motion so that they accept the truth sooner than they otherwise would.

Constructive confrontation often includes leveling with people about their obvious warning signs of addiction. If they are defensive, it is wise to understate the case, thus avoiding head-on confrontations that would make their defenses more rigid. Psychiatrist Harry M. Tiebout once illustrated this principle. A defiant alcoholic who consulted him on one occasion described his drinking pattern and then demanded, "Tell me, does that make me an alcoholic?" Rather than giving a direct and easily rejected answer, Tiebout wisely responded, "I suppose that what really matters is your answer to that question. But frankly, I'm glad I'm not in your shoes." Several years later, the man introduced himself after an A.A. meeting at which Tiebout had spoken. He said that he had been sober for some time in A.A. and thanked Tiebout, saying that his brief words had become a key factor in his eventual decision to seek help.

One effective way for counselors to be less threatening in their confrontations is by describing their own self-justifying alibis and struggles related to unhealthy but seductively satisfying behavior. This can be followed by a query such as, "Does this sound familiar as you think about the drinking episodes we have just discussed?" In this way, counselors can empathize with how difficult it is to let go of alibis and face tough truths about oneself. With some addicted persons, this provides a needed nudge toward accepting the truth about themselves. Hard confrontations almost always cause defensive people to become more so. Even a soft confrontation may be ineffective. But if they are nearly ready for accepting treatment as shown by their beginning to question their own alibis, counselors' firm but gentle confrontations may help them face the truth they have been denying. In any case, well-timed and caring confrontations often plant seeds in people's minds, and one never knows which or when some of these will flower into recovery.

A crucial principle related to constructive confrontation must be underscored. Counselors should offer reality-based hope and offers of help in the same time frame in which they hold up their perception of addicts' dangerous reality. It is less difficult for addiction-trapped people to face the grim fact that their lives are in shambles if they know that recovery is possible and effective ways are available by which they may put their broken lives back together and thereby rejoin the human family.

Raising Addicts' Bottom

Various methods described above may help people stuck in denial to face their need for help with addictions. All these are ways of what has been called "elevating the bottom" of such people. This apt phrase was coined by a physician, Daniel J. Feldman, while he was practicing in a hospital-based alcoholism clinic in New York City. He had discovered that it is possible to save some addicts from years of suffering by hastening the time when they hit bottom and become open to help. The factors he identified as essential were discussed above. He called them simply "acceptance" and "bringing reality through." Acceptance, he emphasized, means accepting alcoholics as sick people. Feldman recommended that counselors who cannot accept alcoholics as sick and needing treatment should refer them to someone who can, because counselors' nonacceptance will reinforce alcoholics' resistance to accepting it. In discussing "bringing reality through" (the same as constructive confrontation), Feldman offers wise guidance to counselors: "Keep holding the reality situation before him [sic] in a factual, nonjudgmental way. For example, "I'm not saying that it's good or bad—that's for you to decide—but it's a fact that your employer is just about through with you."[12] As in this example, enlightened self-interest can be utilized in counseling by mentioning concrete ways that persons are damaging their own interests and blocking themselves from reaching goals that are important to them.

The key players who frequently have the greatest influence in determining if and when the addicted become open to help are family members, close friends, work associates, and health professionals. Addictions are interpersonal illnesses that influence the entire social networks within which people receive their vital sense of belonging, caring, esteem, identity, and love. Many addicts have one or more persons in that system of caring who are called "enablers" in addiction treatment jargon. They unwittingly enable the addicted to continue their addictive behavior by misguided efforts to cause them to stop. In trying to help, they actually make the situation worse.

Enablers who are spouses, parents, clergy, or others can interrupt their unhelpful "helping" behavior by doing what Al-Anon calls "release." Releasing, in this context, means letting go of vain efforts to control addicts' behavior or protect them from the painful consequences. Until the enablers release addicted people, efforts by pastors, counselors, self-help groups like A.A., and treatment programs usually fail. The full meaning and methodology of this process will be described in the chapter on counseling with family members.

Understanding Interventions

Interventions are one of the most innovative addiction counseling developments in recent decades. This treatment has been used widely in the addiction field by counselors and treatment centers, often with considerable success. The intervention technique is now being used in the early stages of addiction in some addiction-prevention programs with vulnerable teens who are using drugs, alcohol, and nicotine. The aim is to help motivate obviously addicted persons who will not face their need for treatment. The central method is a joint, well-orchestrated confrontation that ideally involves all the key persons in an addicted person's life. Such high pressure, simultaneous confrontations are more difficult for highly defensive people to ignore or dismiss by rationalizing than the usual series of confrontations by one concerned individual after another. This joint confrontation may crack through their defenses so that they become open to help sooner.

The approach was developed by Episcopal priest Vernon E. Johnson more than two decades ago based on his own recovery experience and extensive expertise in addictions and counseling with alcoholics. A brief description of how interventions are done is found in his *I'll Quit Tomorrow: A Practical Guide to Alcoholism Treatment* and his more detailed account is available in *Intervention: How to Help Someone Who Doesn't Want Help*.[13]

Johnson starts with the premise that the delusional thinking, ego defenses, and blackouts of alcoholics prevent them from taking seriously the repeated criticism of their drinking by spouses and other concerned individuals, or learning from their alcohol-induced crises. By the time these crises become painful enough to cause them to hit bottom and seek help on their own initiative, it is often too late for reversing their personal and social disintegration. Many who do recover have wasted years of potentially productive living in needless suffering. By planning, rehearsing, and then implementing a collective intervention, coached by a skilled counselor, addicted people may become opened to accepting sorely needed treatment.

Here is an overview of the intervention process. Johnson assumes that the sickest "chemically dependent person can accept reality if it is presented to him [sic] in a receivable form."[14] Interventions begin when one or more enablers hear of this technique and find a knowledgeable addiction counselor who guides them throughout the process. The following steps are involved:

1. Key enablers and other influential people in addicted persons' lives are identified, intervention is explained to them, and they are asked if they are willing to be involved. In addition to close family members, interveners include professionals like physicians or clergy who are informed about addictions, and workplace supervisors or bosses. Employers have been found to be especially effective because addicts know that their jobs may be on the line. Two or three interveners has proved to be an effective number, although more may be involved.

2. Those who choose to participate are instructed in basic facts about addictions. The explanation emphasizes the view that addictions are treatable illnesses whose victims have lost their ability to control their use of addictive substances or change by using willpower alone without outside help. The educational counseling component equips enablers with the knowledge needed to correct ineffective, attacking confrontations, and make their joint confrontation reality based.

3. Interveners are coached in formulating carefully written lists of factual episodes involving abnormal drinking or drug use—episodes that they

have observed personally. To be avoided are opinions and generalizations such as "You drink too much." To illustrate, an employer may be prepared to tell the addicted person, "The word is around among your colleagues at the office that you should not be sent clients after lunch. This is because of what happened three times in the last month on these dates." Or a teenage son may be ready to tell his father, "Last Sunday afternoon, I felt terrible when I brought my friend home and you passed out drunk after throwing up on the living room rug!" Or a family physician may be prepared to confront the addicted person with this medical reality: "The blood tests show that your liver problems have gotten much worse in the last six months. As your doctor, I have to tell you that continuing to drink is very dangerous."

4. The interveners in training decide how best to persuade the addicted person to come to the confrontation session without knowing what is planned.

5. With the counselor's coaching, the intervention session is rehearsed by participants with someone role playing the addicted person. It is emphasized that using the things they listed in making their confrontations must be done in a detailed, concrete, caring, nonjudgment way. The united barrage aims at penetrating addicted persons' defenses so that they accept, however grudgingly, the need for treatment. Interveners are cautioned to be prepared to resist the temptation to stop because their target seems to be hurting too much. They must be prepared not to retreat or attack back when the addict responds, as most do, with intense anger and what is hoped are last stand denials.

6. Plans are made to present several available professional treatment options, and the strategy devised aimed at causing the addicted person to accept one of these. In the actual intervention session, the atmosphere must radiate loving and hope. Factual confrontations should be interspersed with warm assurances by the interveners of the love and caring that motivates their interventions. Hope for recovery needs to be articulated clearly as addicted persons are informed of treatment options. When caring hope is offered after the confrontations, denial defenses may give way, at least temporarily. It is then essential to push with firm, collective resolve for the addicted person to decide which help they will accept. The opportunity to decide among options is designed to offer them the dignity as well as the responsibility of making their own decision.

7. Strategy is planned to maximize the probability that addicted persons will implement their decisions quickly after the intervention. They must be convinced that the interveners mean what they say and will not abandon their insistence that they follow through by getting treatment.

As recovery progresses, it is hoped that addicted people will begin to feel, "Thank God they knew enough and cared enough to make me face this problem. I might have died if I'd been allowed to continue."[15] The training to participate in interventions, even if they turn out not to succeed in helping the addicted, can be of significant value to trainees. Families get together and begin to talk more honestly about their family relationships. Frequently interveners gain much for their own well-being from what they learned about addictions and recovery. Family follow-up sessions after inventions tend to increase these benefits. Some family members begin to apply A.A. and other recovery principles to their own lives, having become aware that they have been in denial concerning their own addictive behavior. I remember a clergy couple, both of whom had alcoholic parents, who took training with Vernon Johnson. The intervention with the husband's father was not successful, but the well-being of the couple's individual lives and their marital and family relationships were enhanced by what they had learned.

Interventions utilize the basic dynamics of what I call the growth formula. This formula holds that caring plus confrontation tends to produce constructive change and growth. This means that people are most likely to change and grow when they encounter loving care and honest confrontation with reality in the same relationships. This formula presents the fundamental dynamics of growth-oriented counseling and education in their various forms, including the strategies for elevating addicts' "bottoms" described above. In most such approaches to counseling, caring is emphasized as the vitally important context of all effective confrontation, as it also is in interventions. But the styles and force of confrontation in most other therapeutic approaches is much less head-on, directive, and high pressure than in interventions. In other approaches, the transforming process of tough love or caring confrontation is facilitated by more subtle means of stimulating self-confrontation as caring people, including counselors, lift up reality.

There is a significant risk involved in heavy confrontations like those used in interventions. If targeted addicts reject even high-powered collective confrontation, they are likely to feel even more isolated, angry, despairing, and rejected by their circle of caring people. Clergy who have regular face-to-face contact with addicted family systems are in strategic positions to suggest that family members consider getting professional help to guide them in making an intervention. But because of the risk involved, interventions should be used only with those self-destructive addicts with whom Twelve Step approaches and less extreme forms of family or counselor confrontation have been tried but proved ineffective.

It usually is wise to recommend an intervention only after enablers have become ex-enablers by learning and using methods of tough love (caring confrontation) themselves, perhaps with guidance from a clergy counselor. Ministers who do not have special training in counseling, including addiction counseling, are well advised to help family members find addiction treatment professionals who have good track records as skilled coordinators of effective interventions.

Surrender and Recovery

To understand the psychodynamics of hitting bottom and becoming open to help, whether this occurs on one's own or as a result of caring confrontations, the concept of surrender, as explored by Tiebout, is illuminating. It is particularly relevant to understanding the recovery process of male addicts and women who have learned to excel in male dominated arenas. The phenomenon that Tiebout described in a series of innovative and controversial professional journal articles has been observed by many workers with addicted persons, including myself.[16] In my counseling experience, surrender reoccurs on different levels at progressive stages of recovery. The first and most decisive surrender is the one involved in hitting bottom and becoming open to help. This surrender occurs when addicted people give up the illusion that they can handle their addictive substances. To take Step One of the A.A. or N.A. recovery programs—"We admitted we were powerless over alcohol (drugs), that our lives had become unmanageable"—many addicts must surrender that factor in their self-image that makes them need to feel equal to whatever comes. A spiritual surrender is required by Step Three—"Made a decision to turn our will and our lives over to the care of God as we understood him."

It is important to be aware that many people in Twelve Step programs report that they first took Steps One and Three only because they were totally wiped out and desperate. As one A.A. member put it: "I knew I was at the end of my rope so I tied a small knot with Step One and Three to try to hold on. It wasn't until after I had a couple of huge slips that I realized that I must take those steps wholeheartedly to help me with my spiritual angle."

Tiebout observed accurately that when alcoholics really surrender there is a dramatic shift in their inner life. Their self-deceiving alcoholic thinking is replaced by openness and honesty. They stop fighting life and begin to cooperate with it. Feelings of inner peace, acceptance, and genuine humility replace their guilt, tension, isolation, defiant grandiosity, and self-idolatry. Theologically, surrendering seems to be letting go of a terrible burden—the unsuccessful attempt to play God. It is significant that

Step Eleven states that a "spiritual awakening" occurs as a result of the previous steps—the surrender and moral inventory and restitution steps. This sequence can serve as a guideline in clergys' and other spiritually oriented counselors' work with addicts who are spiritually stymied and depressed. Tiebout stated the matter this way:

> A religious or spiritual awakening is the act of giving up one's reliance on one's omnipotence. The defiant individual no longer defies but accepts help, guidance, and control from the outside. And as the individual relinquishes his negative, aggressive feelings toward himself and toward life, he finds himself overwhelmed by strong positive ones such as love, friendliness, peacefulness.[17]

Surrender, in this context, is not a negative defeat. Rather it is a turning away from an immature, illusory, self-defeating orientation and a positive turning toward a reality-accepting way of feeling about oneself, God, and life's problems. By accepting rather than denying their human brokenness and fractured finitude, addicted people find strength in their weakness, relatedness for support, and strategies for coping constructively with their problems. As Tiebout observed, a life-affirming transformation occurs in their inner lives. In a way somewhat analogous to the change of climate that melted the gigantic sheets of ice and brought a springtime of awakening life at the end of the ice ages, surrender seems to transform the emotional climate of people's inner lives dramatically.

Mark M., (not his real name) age forty, came to his minister because his marriage was on the verge of disintegration. According to his wife, the problem was caused by his excessive drinking, a view that he denied adamantly. Mark made it plain that he wanted no part of A.A. He had "tried that approach," he said, and felt that he was too intelligent to need that kind of help. He declared that he could handle his drinking by himself and that he just wanted a few tips on "how to get the little woman off my back." During his first three weeks of counseling, he maintained this mask of defiant self-sufficiency tinged with superiority feelings, keeping the minister at a distance. His view of the problem was that all would be fine if his wife would nag less and be more appreciative of his good points. Nothing significant was accomplished in counseling, and he continued to come only because he was afraid his wife would leave him if he stopped. His heavy drinking was undiminished.

After a two-week break in the counseling, Mark appeared at the minister's study door for a counseling session with an enlivened look on his face.

This and his other buoyant body language made it clear that a major change had taken place. The minister exclaimed in surprise, "What happened?" Mark responded, "I don't know what did it but I guess I gave up my I-ism." He described a family crisis, during the two-week break from counseling, involving the tragic death of a child. Instead of pulling together with other family members to give one another the mutual support that everyone desperately needed, he had gone on a five-day binge. When he sobered up, intense shame and remorse were burning inside him. This painful self-confrontation apparently caused him to "hit bottom." His smug mask of self-sufficiency and denying his problem while blaming others, was knocked off by the awareness that he had been living what he called "a self-centered lie." His alibis collapsed in a heap around his head, along with his compulsion to "run the show," as he put it. His self-defensive pride crumbled, and he experienced the shame and self-disgust that had been hidden behind his I-ism. When he surrendered, his inner load was dramatically lightened. He began to feel the way he looked when he came to his post-surrender counseling session—more relaxed, self-accepting, upbeat, and grateful for the gift of life than he could have imagined before all this happened.

Mark told the minister that he had gone back to several A.A. meetings after letting go of his I-ism. He said that it was a whole new experience, as though he had not been to A.A. before. He also reported that he was feeling warmer and closer to his wife and children than before. Even the color of the sky and trees, he said, and other things in the natural world seemed more vivid to him.

Mark showed a new openness in counseling, as he began searching for ways that he could help make things better in his marriage. With the counselor's help, he focused on his side of that conflicted relationship and also on his other big concern—how he could keep his I-ism from returning. Reflecting on his excessive drinking, he said, "When my I-ism increased, I drank more, and the more I drank, the stronger it became." Gradually, over several sessions of counseling, he learned to recognize the danger signs of slipping back into I-ism—the egocentric, self-pitying, demanding superiority feelings that he now saw as often preceding his runaway drinking bouts. And, very significant, as Mark's defensive pride was surrendered, he said he felt more solid feelings of self-worth.

How can we understand this surrender experience psychologically and spiritually? The type of I-ism that Mark demonstrated by his behavior before hitting bottom may be derived from the infantile narcissism that is part of normal human development in the early months of life. It is well established that a part of alcohol's general attractiveness is that it facilitates psychological regression. For many alcoholics, it facilitates regression to these early feelings of godlike power, control, and self-sufficiency. (For religious addicts and fanatics, religious belief systems seem to be used for a comparable defensive regression to early life narcissism.) The feelings from this narcissism create a temporary defensive barrier against deeper feelings of powerlessness, fear of death, and meaninglessness.[18] However, any regression to the psychological world of the infancy exposes people to the terrifying giants—the nameless anxieties and amorphous fears of that period of development. As addictions progress and tolerance to the drugs increase, illusions of special power, control, and invulnerability become increasingly difficult to maintain as they are battered by reality-based failures, fears, and shame.

The experience of surrendering in this sense seems to have at least two components. First there is an unconscious renunciation of the path of regression to infantile narcissism—a regression that no longer gives illusory satisfactions to offset its painful fears. Psychologist David A. Stewart, in his insightful book *Thirst for Freedom*, describes the operation of the alcoholic's narcissism as "the little dictator." He sees this as an unconscious psychological complex of magical thinking, inflated pride, fear, and anger, lack of insight, and resistance to facing one's need for any help from others. When surrender occurs, the little dictator is deposed, and the self-damaging defense of narcissism is given up.[19]

The second component in surrender, as I understand it, is a desperate leap toward relationships and living—to fill the aching void left by the now-empty pattern of distancing from people and self-centeredness. This may sound like the leap of faith described by religious mystics in the "dark night of the soul." In a sense it is, but it also is something more. One alcoholic described his experience with this image: "It's a leap of fear. You leap (the chasm) blindly, not knowing what's on the other side. Fear is pushing you, and hope is pulling you." During their heavy drinking and drug use, many addicts saw their world as peopled with depriving parent-authority figures. Having taken the leap toward hope and people, they often discover (in A.A., for example) that trustworthy, nurturing relationships are possible for them. They can participate in the give and not just the take in relationships. For some addicts, this is a strikingly new experience. By leaps of fearful hope and wavering faith toward people, they free themselves from the vicious, self-feeding cycle in which they have been trapped. This is the cycle of spiraling illusions of grandiosity, surrounded by lonely isolation, intense shame, resentment, and tidal waves of existential anxiety. Thus, as one alcoholic described her experience, they "rejoin the human race."

As a direct result of this positive surrender to life-in-relationships, and a growth group setting like A.A., addicted people begin to develop feelings of genuine self-esteem (the opposite of narcissism), rooted in trustful, mutually nurturing relationships. New and effective ways of coping with reality-based problems and anxieties are discovered by them within these relationships. Having let go, for a day at a time, the narcissistically seductive need to play god, they are increasingly immersed and supported by a new in-group that often incarnates and communicates the accepting love of a Higher Power. As this happens, many addicts begin to change their understanding of and relationship with God as they understand their Higher Power. As their spiritual awakening deepens and their trust in their Higher Power increases, these spiritual experiences reinforce their trust in people and their inclination to become more giving in relationships. By remaining in a growing relationship with their Higher Power, they gain the power to retain genuine humility and resist the temptation to regress to narcissistic self-idolatry that leads to excessive drinking or drug use. And, very important, a trustful relatedness to God provides them with effective ways to face and handle their existential anxiety, robbing it of much of its terror and perhaps even making it a stimulus to creative living. As Tillich held, it is only when existential anxiety is confronted and taken into persons' self-identity that it enriches rather than haunts and diminishes living. People who have developed trustful relationships—with themselves, others, nature, and God—become more able to "die living rather than live dying," as a former client of mine once put it.

Yet, the experiences of many in A.A. suggest that those who have surrendered must continue to exercise some vigilance to avoid losing their humility. Humility, in the root sense of accepting one's earthly humanity, is the doorway to meaningful connectedness with ourselves and therefore with other people and God. The underlying pull of infantile narcissism is a human problem that is never eradicated, though its powerful pull back is interrupted by positive surrenders. When deep-seated anxieties are aroused by tragedies, threats to self-esteem or by failure to grow psychologically and spiritually, temptation to regress to old primitive defenses that became curses still is there. This probably is part of the reason why most A.A. members feel the need to continue to "work the program," even after their sobriety has been stabilized for years. As indicated earlier, many also do so because they love being with A.A. friends and in the A.A. atmosphere.

Avoiding the Counselor Codependence Trap

The ambivalence toward authority of many addicted persons is a psychological issue that must be taken into account in counseling. Some people, including addicts, are developmentally fixated in their relationships with authority figures, even though they are relatively mature in other dimensions of their lives. They alternately crave dependence and resent it. Some addicted people project authority-centered transference feelings onto clergy and other counselors. They try to lean heavily on them but they also rebel against them—for example, by having a slip that proves (to them) that the authority figure can't succeed in getting them sober.

If helping professionals fall into the codependent relationship trap offered by addicts from their unresolved authority conflicts, counseling is very difficult if not foredoomed to failure. The key to avoiding being ensnared is to let go of feeling responsible for chemically dependent people's sobriety or lack of it, and therefore not become overly involved in the outcome of counseling relationships. A success drive in counselors, derived from the need to prove oneself, is detrimental to effectiveness in most counseling. It is particularly so in working with alcoholics and other addicts. If they sense that counselors have a sizable stake in their getting sober, they have acquired a weapon to use against them (and themselves) during times of angry resentment of their dependency. Counselors who try too hard and thus reveal that they need to prove themselves by counseling successes, convey a lack of concern and respect for clients in and of themselves. Addicted people with low self-esteem react to such counselors like many low-bottom alcoholics do when mission workers give them the impression that their main interest in them is saving their souls. (An astute counselor of alcoholics called this "collecting spiritual scalps.")

In light of these dynamics, it is best not to take much personal credit for the success of counselees who recover, or feel that it is one's personal defeat when, as is inevitable, some continue on the downward addiction path. How can those with concern for counselees gain this difficult caring yet detached attitude? The primary focus of our concern should be on troubled people as unique and valuable human beings and how to help them help themselves. It should not be on meeting our ego needs to be successful counselors. Gaining this focus is not easy. It requires robust inner sources of self-worth that enable us to enjoy it when we do effective work as facilitators of healing and growth, but not be dominated by craving achievements to buttress shaky feelings of self-worth. Most of us achieve this attitude only to a certain limited degree. I find that it helps to admit to myself that, if addicted persons recover, it really is because they achieved it with the help of God. We counselors, at best, are only imperfect catalytic instruments in this healing process. As a wise counselor with alcoholics once observed to me, "If an alcoholic with whom I've been working gets sober, I try to remember that it may be in spite of what I said or did. It surprises me when I discover again that God sometimes seems to help alcoholics use even my fumbling efforts for their healing."

CHAPTER 13

Counseling for Recovery and Beyond:
Basic Methods

The purpose of this chapter is to describe effective methods for helping addicted people move toward the basic objectives of recovery counseling, after they have become motivated to accept help by recognizing that their substance abuse per se is a serious and treatable problem (as described in chapter 12). It focuses on these topics: the characteristics of an addiction counseling model; using crisis intervention methods; obtaining medical and psychotherapeutic help; interrupting the self-perpetuating addictive cycle and maintaining initial sobriety; healing the psychological, spiritual-ethical wounds contributing to and resulting from the addiction; helping addicts rebuild their lifestyles without addictive substances; nurturing whole person growth; healing spiritual trauma, and facilitating growth toward spiritual wellness; and using religious resources. This chapter will also describe methods designed to help low-bottom addicted persons.

The Basic Counseling Approach for Addicts and Their Families

As a framework for understanding particular techniques for helping addicted people and their families, it is important to understand these basic characteristics of the optimal counseling approach for use in this type of counseling:

1. The approach uses short-term, crisis counseling methods aiming at equipping troubled people to mobilize their own resources to cope constructively with their immediate problems in living, rather than aiming at intrapsychic changes by long-term counseling.

2. In the mode of reality therapy, it focuses directly on helping people learn how to make their behavior more responsible and effective in moving toward constructive goals they have chosen.

3. It focuses on peoples' strengths and successes in living, and their potential resources for handling problems (including addictions), as well as on their weaknesses and failures in coping effectively.

4. It focuses on peoples' feelings only to the extent that this is needed to establish counseling relationships and to reduce clients' emotional overloads blocking constructive coping with their addictions and other problems.

5. It explores past experiences only as this is useful in helping people discover how they handled past problems creatively and avoiding repeating past mistakes, including nonsolutions.

6. It uses tough love—caring plus confrontation—to help people enhance mutual fairness, need-satisfaction, and loving care in their own lives and in their relationships.

7. It has a dual agenda that includes both healing and growth. It seeks to facilitate healing of the brokenness of addictions, but also to nurture growth toward wholeness, defined as the maximum use of people's God-given potentials.

8. It is holistic and systemic in seeking to enable healing and enhance wellness in all dimensions of people's lives and relationships. It responds to individual and family problems with a keen awareness of family systems and the wider social context of institutional systems in which injustice and violence breed widespread addictiveness in our society.

9. As a part of clients' growth, it aims at empowering them to work with others in changing the social and institutional causes of individual problems, including addictions. It thus seeks to avoid causing people merely to adjust to sickness-generating relationships and pathological social systems.

10. It integrates spiritual and value perspectives and resources in all phases of the counseling process, implicitly if not explicitly, seeking to enable people to experience transforming religious power in their struggles to recover and grow.[1]

Those who use this model should begin by gaining a tentative diagnosis of the problem on the basis of which tentative counseling goals and concrete treatment plans are developed.

However one understands recovery, it is clear that it is a process of growing a new way of living. It is a continuing path along which people move rather than a static goal that they achieve. The role of the clergy and congregations vary from person to person and from one stage of recovery to the next.[2]

Using Crisis Intervention Principles with Addicts

In the early stages of counseling for recovery from addictions or codependence, the essential help needed is *solution-oriented crisis counseling.* Several key insights should guide clergy and other counselors in this phase of counseling. The primary initial goal is to help people to mobilize and use their latent psychological, spiritual, and relational resources to handle their immediate crisis constructively. Discovering how a fire started is not necessary in order to put it out, in most cases, meaning that it is usually unnecessary to discover why addicted persons became addicted in order to help them begin their recovery journey. It usually is a mistake in the crisis phase of addiction counseling to search for underlying causes. To make this attempt—while the runaway crises are picking up destructive momentum—is unnecessary and futile, as well as grossly mistimed. It usually accelerates the slide down the slippery slope of excessive drinking and/or drug-use. Instead, what is urgently needed, to the point of being lifesaving in some cases, is steering clients to medical help, Twelve Step programs, or treatment centers so that the addictive cycle will be interrupted, making other steps to recovery possible.

It is important in crisis counseling to recognize that our human personalities are like muscles in the sense that they weaken and eventually atrophy with disuse, and grow stronger with exercise. The practical implication for addiction crisis counseling is clear: Those asking for and needing help must be encouraged and trained to use their own coping resources rather than depending on others (including clergy) or blaming others from a victim's self-pitying perspective. By struggling to cope, they exercise and thus strengthen their own personality muscles. While addicted persons are drinking or using, most of their energy and coping skills are partially immobilized or focused on ensuring the supply of their chemical comforters and avoiding the consequences of their addictive behavior. Facing reality and coping constructively with even small parts of their overwhelming crises gives recovering people hope and energy to cope with other parts. Each part of a crisis that is handled in realistic ways helps equip them to handle the next part using their personality resources instead of chemicals.

As mentioned earlier, alcohol and drug addicts become increasingly like a stick shift car with the engine racing but the clutch disengaged. Their personality is out of gear so they are not going anywhere in the real world. Breaking the addictive cycle of using more of their substance to treat the effects of previous over use puts their personalities back in gear. They can now choose to use their psychological and spiritual resources to handle adult responsibilities and rebuild their fractured lives and relationships. The more they use their own engine to move in these directions, the stronger it becomes. In this way, many addicted people recover and live constructive lives without a need to rebuild their engine (through depth psychotherapy). This is not true of those deeply disturbed persons suffering from dual diagnoses.

The simple principles of William Glasser's "reality therapy" have important affinities with this aspect of the addiction counseling model just outlined. A central emphasis of his approach is on responsible living in the here and now. By responsible he means satisfying one's basic needs for love, self-esteem, and identity within the realities of one's relationships, and doing so without depriving others of the satisfaction of their needs. Glasser's action-oriented therapy consists of establishing a relationship with troubled people, diminishing self-defeating (reality-denying) behavior, and then helping the person "learn to fulfill his needs responsibly in the real world" of human relationships.[3] It involves asking counselees two questions: Is what you are doing getting you what you really want? If not, how will you change your behavior to get what you desire? Glasser's approach actually is quite similar to what A.A. and other Twelve Step programs have been doing to help addicted people for many years.

Obtaining Medical and Psychiatric Help

The second objective of counseling is to get chemically dependent people to a physician who can, if needed, facilitate detoxification and treat the physical consequences of prolonged inebriety, as well as decide whether brief hospitalization is needed. If physicians have psychiatric knowledge, they can identify dual-diagnosis addicts who also suffer from severe underlying psychopathology. Medical treatment is often needed by addicts long before they hit bottom psychologically. Many have repeated hospitalizations before their motivational teeter-totter tilts decisively toward accepting treatment for the addictions per se. In such cases, it is important that addicted people, and especially their families, be informed by a health professional that simply treating the physical effects of excessive drinking and/or drug use, as important and even lifesaving as this can be, does not constitute treatment of the addiction. Some persons erroneously believe that unsuccessful treatment has occurred when actually only the preliminary stage of treatment—drying out and physical rehabilitation—has taken place.

Most alcoholics and other addicts who obviously need medical attention do not resist getting this help because they hope that it will relieve their pain. But it is also prudent for others who are feeling relatively well after achieving initial sobriety to have a checkup to discover if there are less obvious organic problems that need treatment. Clergy's role is to assist addicted people to connect with doctors who accept such patients, know the latest methods of treating addiction-related medical problems, and most important, are appreciative of the roles of both A.A. and pastoral counseling. Physicians who do not understand addictions or appreciate Twelve Step programs can, by their not-so-subtle attitudes and statements, unwittingly push addicted patients away from the help they desperately need. I recall several A.A. members who said that their trusted physician unfortunately told them, in effect, "You are not an alcoholic who needs to go to A.A. You simply drink too much and should cut down." This professional opinion petrified their denial and resistance to seeing their drinking pattern for what it clearly was. On the other hand, because of the godlike authority and status given physicians by many in our society, their accurate explanation of the nature of addictions and firm recommendation that addicts try a Twelve Step program can carry special weight with many addicted people and their families.[4]

What are clergy's roles during the time addicted parishioners are hospitalized and/or just beginning to relate to Twelve Step programs? They should, of course, provide frequent pastoral care contacts, maintaining a supportive relationship by visits and phone calls to both patients and to their family. In addition, if hospital treatment is not focused on addictions and therefore does not have any Twelve Step components, clergy should ask carefully selected A.A. or N.A. members to visit patients in the hospital—with the permission of the patients and their doctors. Al-Anon members can do the same for the spouse and other family members.

If ministers are contacted by alcoholics, polyaddicted people, or their families after addicts have been engaged in prolonged excessive drinking and/or drug use, it is crucial that the minister recommend that the addict gets medical attention as soon as possible. As indicated earlier, withdrawal symptoms such as DTs (delirium tremens) and alcoholic convulsions can be very dangerous, even fatal. The danger is compounded if the person has been combining alcohol with other drugs, especially depressants of the central nervous system such as barbiturates. Each substance tends to enhance the depressing effects of the other. If it is suspected that alcoholics may have been taking drugs without the family's knowledge, the only safe course is do everything possible to make certain they are seen by an addiction-knowledgeable health professional.

Interrupting the Addictive Cycle

When addicted people show even a little acceptance of their need for help with their use of consciousness-changing chemicals, their highest priority recovery task should be explained clearly. This is to learn how to interrupt the craving of the self-feeding addictive cycle—the obsessive-compulsive chain reaction of using more alcohol or drugs to self-medicate the painful effects of excessive drinking and/or use. Early in the process of working with chemically dependent clients, when some trust has been generated with them, it may be helpful to explain why they have an uphill battle. If they are to achieve long-term sanity and sobriety, they must win a difficult body-mind struggle against a physical addiction reinforced by a mental compulsion.

Gordon Bell, a physician who formerly directed a major addiction treatment center had an effective way of confronting alcoholics with the task they faced. He explained to them that their bodies no longer have the ability to handle the chemical (alcohol), which they had been using to cope with stress. He then points to symptoms of the loss of this ability. Next, he emphasized that they must, for health reasons, learn other ways of handling stress, using people methods rather than chemical methods. Finally, he explained that they were caught in a self-perpetuating process that had to be interrupted in two stages. The first is "turning off the physical motor" by getting the alcohol out of their bodies and thus interrupting physical craving, and second, turning off the mental motor, meaning ending the mental craving of obsessive thinking about alcohol and the (conditioned) response of automatically turning to alcohol to handle any stress.[5] In pastoral counseling with alcohol and drug addicts, Bell's way of communicating their task to them can be useful.

The focus of counseling, at this stage, is on the drinking and/or drug use pattern itself and the need to learn how not to take the first drink, pill, or shot. A part of this essential learning consists of identifying and interrupting the rationalization process that precedes the first ingestion. (For instance, "One beer can't possibly hurt me. After all, I've been totally dry for three weeks.") Addicts should be helped to see that although their heavy use of their stress-allaying chemical may have begun as a symptom of other problems and may continue to be aggravated by them, the use pattern itself has become the first problem that must be treated in its own right, if they are to recover. In a useful analogy, Harry M. Tiebout once likened the "runaway symptom" of alcoholics' out-of-control drinking to the dangerously high fever of pneumonia. The fever is a symptom of the underlying infection, but unless it can be lowered, the person may die of the symptom. Treatment of the runaway symptom is essential.

Counseling, at this stage, should focus primarily on helping addicts change their runaway symptom behavior. It should deal with feelings only to the extent that they are blocking the interruption of the vicious cycle. Counselors should not allow themselves to be diverted into long discussions of why clients drink or use excessively. As suggested earlier, searching for causes usually is ill advised because it allows clients to avoid facing their highest priority need—how to keep the addictive cycle from being reactivated. Even if causes in the past are discovered, some clients may use them to avoid responsibility for changing their substance abuse that is damaging themselves and others.

How should counselors respond if counselees make statements like, "If I didn't feel so damn depressed, it would be easier to stay off the bottle"; "If my husband hadn't had an affair and left me . . . "; "If I didn't have such a pressure cooker job . . . "? One might observe that, although there probably is some truth in their statements, their first problem is to stay off alcohol and/or drugs. Their many other problems can become accessible to help only if they learn how to avoid triggering the addictive pattern. Even though addicts feel depressed, are frustrated by their spouses, or abhor their jobs, they don't have to drink or use drugs. Doing so will probably make their other painful problems worse and solving any of them probably won't happen unless they stop drinking and using. (After they have stopped drinking and using, it may be productive to raise questions about whether their stressful situations are caused or worsened by their substance use or abuse.) If counselees continue to view their other problems as more urgent and important than getting and staying sober, it usually indicates that they are still fighting accepting the fact that they are addicted.

A.A. and other Twelve Step programs are the most widely available and effective means of interrupting the addictive cycle and keeping it from becoming reactivated while people pull their lives back together. Hence, clergy should strongly encourage involvement in such groups. The best way to accomplish this, in my experience, is to use the *bridge method of making referrals.* When counselees show even a little receptivity to help, they should be asked: "How would you feel about talking over your situation with someone who has been through the same experience and has found an answer that works for her (or him)?" If addicts agree, a phone call should be made while they are still present to arrange for a three-way talk involving the addict, minister, and an A.A. or N.A. member who can become the bridge person to those groups. (As indicated earlier, the member should be of the same sex, general age, socioeducational group, and vocational background, if possible.)

If the three-person meeting goes well, meaningful communication and the beginning of a positive bond may develop between the Twelve Step member and the counselee. When clergy sense that this is happening, it may be well for them to excuse themselves, thus encouraging the other two to relate as one addicted person to another. The frequent outcome of such meetings is that counselees accept an invitation by Twelve Step group members to accompany them to a meeting.

When recommending any Twelve Step group or treatment program, it is important to ask counselees what they already know about such programs. This gives counselors an opportunity to correct misinformation or help to resolve other inner barriers to successful affiliation by clients. I remember a high-bottom addicted woman who was hooked on both alcohol and tranquilizers. When I asked what she had heard about A.A. and N.A., she responded defensively, "Am I that badly off?" Behind her response was the misconception that Twelve Step groups are designed to help only those in the very advanced stages of addictions. A young adult male alcoholic responded to his minister's suggestion that he try A.A. by mentioning that his alcoholic uncle had stopped excessive drinking on his own. "He just decided to quit hitting the bottle." It came out that there were two messages behind this statement. The young man felt that he should, like his uncle, be able to stop excessive drinking without outside help. He also was expressing his refusal to identify with a group of self-acknowledged alcoholics. If people are still convinced that they can quit solo on the basis of their own willpower, counselors can wish them success, but then remind them that, if it doesn't work, help will be available.

In describing to counselees why it would be wise for them to go to A.A. (or another treatment program), in addition to continuing in counseling, it is well to reemphasize that making the grade to sobriety is a tough, demanding task in which several forms of help often are needed. It is good to also emphasize that the A.A. fellowship and other effective treatment approaches complement each other in important ways, but do not replace the help available in counseling. If obviously addicted people refuse to go to A.A. or other treatment programs, pastoral counseling alone seldom is effective in enabling them to achieve on-going recovery. In such cases, the focus of counseling should be on awakening their motivation to accept the help they need as described in chapter 12.

Counselors should encourage addicted people to attend frequent Twelve Step meetings during the early phase of their recovery, whether or not their initial reactions to the meetings are positive. As they continue to attend, make friends in the group, and listen to recovery success stories, people often begin to soak up the philosophy and belief system. If this happens, they gradually will begin to identify with the Twelve Step group spirit, almost in spite of themselves. The strong sense of belonging that exists in most Twelve Step groups is a powerful magnet. (Indicative of this is that some people make the grade by achieving sobriety, even though they begin attending as an alternative to going to jail.)

As people begin to attend A.A., N.A., or Al-Anon, counselors should inquire regularly about their experiences and ask other key questions such as, "Have you found a sponsor?" If people have negative reactions to the Twelve Step approach or to experiences in a particular group, these often can be resolved in counseling.

Many addicts have dabbled halfheartedly in A.A. or N.A. before they hit bottom. Some seem to get vaccinated against Twelve Step programs by attending meetings under pressure from a court or family member while they are in a highly defensive frame of mind. To help such persons, the counselor should explore the nature of their resistance. Does it reflect the problems of an unhealthy group or unfortunate experiences with particular people in A.A? Or does it reflect reluctance to admit their need for such help? If they simply don't feel at home in one group they should be encouraged to try others until they find a good fit. Depending on the nature of their resistance, counselors can strongly recommend that addicts keep trying the Twelve Step program by going to a healthier group or one that has more members with backgrounds and addictive experiences similar to their own.[6] Another strategy to assist addicts who resist treatment is to use the bridging method again by arranging for them to get acquainted with longtime sober, warm, and accepting members of A.A. who can be relational bridges to feeling at home in their group.[7]

With counselees who refuse to attend Twelve Step meetings or do not find the help they need there, clergy's role is to help them resolve their resistances or find other help. The latter may consist of referral to holistic alcohol and drug treatment programs where other modalities such as individual and group therapy, medical adjuncts such as Antabuse, or psychiatric help are available. Adding one or more of these modalities, in a residential or outpatient facility, may supply the help needed to break the addictive cycle and maintain stable sobriety.

Such referrals are also appropriate for those who are continuing to "work the program" in a Twelve Step group but clearly need additional help. As indicated earlier, dual diagnosis clients suffer from severe underlying personality disturbances that predate their addictions. They use alcohol and other drugs to numb their overwhelming anxiety and inner conflicts. They often require psychiatric and psychotherapuetic treatment, in addition to Twelve Step help, to keep the addictive cycle broken. In some cases, forced abstinence without psychiatric help may cause them to deteriorate psychologically.[8]

Many chemically addicted people have one or more slips, particularly during the first year of their serious efforts to keep the addictive cycle broken. Counselors should handle these in such a way as to make them opportunities for discovering the warning signs that may help them avoid future slips when they are about to happen again. These red flags of impending slips include the rationalization process, the return of alcoholic thinking, the buildup of resentments, staying away from Twelve Step meetings, and not talking regularly with one's sponsor. Addicted counselees often avoid clergy counselors after slips because of guilt feelings and fear of criticism. In some cases, it may be wise for clergy to take the initiative by making a phone call to reestablish contact. Otherwise, the opportunity to encourage clients to use their slips as opportunities for learning and growth may be lost. It is particularly healing for some addicted persons to discover that clergy do not judge or reject them because they stumbled on the path to recovery. One polyaddicted man described his surprise and spiritual lift when his priest responded in a way that caused him to feel "welcome to the club" (of human frailties).

During the early stages of recovery in A.A. or in an alcoholic treatment facility, the primary pastoral role is to be supportive. Responsibility for learning to avoid the first drink, pill, or needle is on the addicts, and their major resources for accomplishing this are Twelve Step groups and/or addiction treatment programs. Their main emotional supporters (often hour by hour), during the first difficult days of struggle to maintain sobriety, are sponsors in Twelve Step groups and/or staff members of treatment centers, particularly those who themselves are recovered addicts.

During this time, clergy should remember that they cannot do what Twelve Step group members and such addiction center staff members can do. The main role of pastors, priests, and rabbis in congregations is to give pastoral care by maintaining caring relationships with both recovering addicts and their families. They also should be available for counseling if requested. Without hovering or prying, clergy should show pastoral interest in what addicts are experiencing in whatever treatment approach they are trying. Occasionally phoning and asking how things are going is an effective and timesaving way of expressing interest after referring them for particular treatment. Attending open meetings of A.A. or Al-Anon with parishioners can be a very affirming pastoral care investment. It can also be a valuable opportunity for clergy to enhance their heart understanding of and connections with these group allies in pastoral caregiving. People in recovery, as they identify more closely with Twelve Steps groups, often lessen their dependence and emotional ties with clergy. This usually indicates growth that clergy should welcome. Such people often eventually move beyond this distancing, as they grow more secure in recovery, and relate to their clergypersons in close but not heavily dependent ways.

Healing Psychological, Spiritual, and Ethical Wounds

When chemically addicted people interrupt the psychophysiological chain reaction called the addictive cycle, they create opportunities for themselves to experience healing of their psychological and spiritual wounds. These are of two types: wounds produced or deepened by self-destructive behavior during their addictions, and wounds from their early lives that are among the multiple causes of addictions in many people.[9]

There are several areas of potential healing in which ministers' counseling skills can be uniquely helpful to recovering alcoholics and drug addicts—*after* they have attained reasonably stable sobriety and begin striving to rebuild their shattered lives. One area is the still festering ethical and relational wounds from drinking and drug-abusing behavior. The most frequent opportunities to help bring healing of these wounds occur for clergy when Twelve Step group members ask them to assist in taking their "moral inventory"—Steps Four through Ten. This makes it possible to help recovering people clean up the mess within themselves of accumulated ethical and relational problems. The skills of a trained pastoral counselor or secular therapist lets those in recovery do their inventory in more psychological depth than usually occurs when doing it with another Twelve Step group member.

Female A.A. member to her female pastor:
"I already talked about these things from my inventory with my sponsor. That helped, but it seems to me that it might be good to discuss them with you, also. There are several things on which I really felt hung up, even after talking about them with my sponsor and confessing all the crap to my Higher Power. The guilt and resentment still bug me. They just won't go away."

Even with little formal training in counseling, most clergy can help in such situations. They can use all that they have learned from hearing confessions (liturgical or in counseling), about enabling people to move from guilt and shame to restitution, forgiveness, and reconciliation. They can help alcoholics and other addicts look below their surface-level transgressions and deal with the deeper sources of resentment, self-pity, guilt, shame, anxiety, and self-rejection. If these festering feelings are not resolved, they will tend to push recovering people toward slips and remissions. As people experience healing of these emotional wounds, the likelihood of their remaining on the recovery pathway improves.

John E. Keller is a seasoned pastoral counselor of alcoholics. He shares some wise guidelines concerning the crucial goals and potential benefits of this dimension of recovery. His recommendations are that clergy talk with A.A. members about their moral and spiritual inventory in positive terms, stressing the values that can be derived from taking an inventory. Keller has identified significant benefits of this approach to counseling. They include: getting to know oneself better; becoming more aware of how one needs to change; recognizing the danger signals that threaten one's sobriety; living more comfortably with oneself and others; and having the door opened for a more personal and meaningful relationship with God.[10]

Helping Twelve Step members with their moral inventories can be a valuable means of engaging them in an ongoing counseling process by which the hard cold lumps of hidden feelings that often resist healing, immobilize growth, and block constructive relationships can be melted. An indispensable part of the inventory process is making amends to persons one has harmed, if this can be done constructively (Steps Eight and Nine). Counselors should encourage this in spite of the pain involved. Otherwise the recovery process may be short-circuited. By taking this action, recovering people assume healthy responsibility for past irresponsibility, guilt and shame are reduced, self-acceptance enhanced, and relationships often improved. As addicted people make lists of those they have harmed, they may be gently reminded of persons they have forgotten. Keller wisely emphasizes: "Essential also is to put himself [sic] on this list and make amends with himself. He may have hurt a lot of people, but no one quite as much as he has hurt himself."[11]

During this Fourth Step counseling, ministers can help counselees learn an important insight that will contribute to their general mental and spiritual healing and wholeness. This is the psychological principle that self-forgiveness and forgiveness of others are always linked, and that the way one makes amends to oneself is to live in those ways that fulfill one's God-given uniqueness and potentialities.

Healing the Wounded Inner Child

Most addicts, codependent people, and the adult children of addicted or codependent parents, seem to share one problem—the unhealed wounds of the little child within them. In my workshops, counseling, and psychotherapeutic practice, I have developed a simple guided imaging method that often helps people focus healing energy on inner wounds from any stage of their past lives. It is a way to bring healing to and make peace with one's painful past. This enables people to reclaim and use the creative energy that has been wasted in repressing and thus ignoring powerful memories or obsessing about past trauma.

To illustrate how this guided imaging method is used and the potential power of inner child healing, here is a description of one of the most dramatic healings in my years of teaching and counseling. It occurred when I used healing memories meditation as a learning device in a seminar at a graduate theological school. I will refer to the young pastor as Sam Johnson, the pseudonym he chose when, at my request, he described his experience of personal transformation in writing. (Sam's description is used here with his permission. He did this with the hope that sharing it might help others.) I first asked class members to focus on childhood or adolescent experiences that still had painful memories around them. Then I invited them to be themselves at the age and place at which the event chosen took place, and to "relive the painful memory, now, letting yourself experience all the feelings that are still there in yourself." Here is Sam's description of his experience:

"I began to remember and then relive the first eight years of my life as a child of a chemically dependent parent. My mother was addicted to prescription drugs. I recalled when I saw her have several convulsions. My father, a physician, had given my older sister and me instructions on what to do when people have convulsions. When I was around six, mother had a convulsion while my father wasn't home. My sister did what we had been instructed and saved her life. She came out of the convulsion and saw both of us in tears.

"Other memories ran through my mind as I relived those years. When I was at school I would find myself in the principal's office crying because I was afraid that my mother would not be alive when I got home. Another memory was when I stood between my parents. My father came home and asked my mother, 'Have you been using today?' She said, 'No!' Then he asked me if she had been using and I said, 'Yes.' There painful memories were deep inside me.

"As the exercise continued, Howard asked us if there was someone we would like to bring to be with our inner child, somebody who might say something that would bring healing. I invited my mother into that room in my childhood home. She held me lovingly and told me, 'The drug addiction was not your fault and I am sorry that you had to go through it.' Then Howard suggested that we go to our childhood home as our adult selves, in our imaginations, and be with our inner child. My adult self, when I invited myself as I am now into the room with me as a little boy, spoke lovingly, telling me, 'Your mother's addiction was not your fault. She had a disease that caused the painful behavior you saw.' Then I held myself in my arms and said, 'Everything will be okay.'

"Third, Howard Clinebell encouraged us to invite a religious figure who is important to us into the room with our inner child. I began to picture Jesus with the little children. Suddenly he was in the room with me as a child. He picked me up and held me tight in his arms. He said that he loved me very much and that my mother's drug addiction and what went on between my parents was not my fault. Then he sat down and placed me on his knee. As we continued to talk, he turned over his hand showing me the nail prints there. He smiled and said, 'Sam, I know the pain that you have been through and I am sorry that you had to go through this. You see these holes in my hands. These tell you that I died on a cross for you and your pain. I love you Sam.'

"Finally, the instructor invited us to bring the person who caused our pain back into the room with the religious figure and us, and 'see if the three of you can play a game and have fun together.' So Jesus, my mother, and I played hide and go seek. Then we took Mason jars and caught fireflies."

After this guided meditation, so that everyone in the seminar could tell something about what they had experienced, we all shared in pairs. We then shared experiences in the whole group, and several class members told of their inner healing. As Sam described his healing in glowing terms, we were all deeply moved. Everyone joined hands as we closed the class with sentence prayers of thanksgiving for what we had experienced as individuals together.

When Sam later described his "transformation" in writing, he recalled:

"Howard Clinebell suggested that we choose among the three parts of the exercise he would describe. In the midst of my emotional roller coaster, I found myself doing all three. I finally received healing for my inner child. This experience was an ultimate source of healing for my life. I had carried the burden in my inner child for twenty years. There were so many unfinished areas in my life because of my parent's drug abuse. I can now rejoice fully that my mother is in recovery celebrating twenty years of sobriety this fall."

It is noteworthy that Sam, like many adult children of addicted and codependent parents, was still deeply wounded. His mother had been off drugs for two decades, and he had had some helpful psychotherapy to deal with other issues. In spite of this, the haunting childhood sense of being responsible for her addiction, and the guilt and shame associated with this were still unhealed.

As I now recall this experience, I rejoice that the divine Spirit of healing moved so powerfully that day, as some might say "even in an academic setting." I wish now that I had done what I would have done if this had occurred in a counseling session—encouraged Sam to share his experience with his wife and with his parents. This might have opened opportunities for healing and growth in those relationships. I suspect that he probably did this on his own.

I invite you to pause in your reading and try this healing exercise now. You may simply follow the steps in Sam's description of his experience, beginning by deeply relaxing your mind and body in order that the images you relive in yourself can be the most beneficial. (If you prefer to be led through this guided meditation with fuller instructions, see pages 289-91 in *Well Being: A Personal Plan for Exploring and Enriching the Seven Dimensions of Life.*[12]

Physician Charles L. Whitfield specializes in therapy for addiction-traumatized patients and adult children of nonaddicted but dysfunctional families. His primary therapeutic goal is to enable these patients to experience healing of their wounded inner child. If you are interested in learning more about the theory and methods of inner child healing, Whitfield describes these more comprehensively in his book *Healing the Child Within: Discovery and Recovery for Adult Children of Dysfunctional Families.*[13]

Growth to Rebuild Life Without Addictive Substances

The healing described so far in this chapter usually overlaps and stimulates the growing that people must do to sustain stable, productive recovery. Their need is to grow healthier whole-person lifestyles, with healthier values, relationships, and thinking, to replace their chemical-centered way of life. To reintegrate their lives without their addictive substances requires learning how to center their lives around values and relationships that are both healthy and satisfying.

Furthermore, they must learn to cope with crises, losses, frustrations, and everyday stresses by using their interpersonal skills and spirituality in place of addictive substances. During their addictions, their favorite chemical served important functions, however costly it had been to their overall well-being. It served to dull anxiety, guilt, and shame; reduce pain and loneliness; find some sense of well-being; give minivacations from harsh reality; and give some lift of euphoria out of flatness and boredom. Long-term sobriety with productive living is dependent on their finding out how to satisfy these needs in more effective nonchemical ways, using constructive relationships with people, the natural world, and their Higher Power.

For persons to rebuild their lifestyle obviously is a long-range, demanding, and continuing process. It involves moving beyond achieving sobriety and "beyond recovery to discovery" (to use Charlotte Davis Kasl's phrase), meaning discovery of how to live life in all its fullness (John 10:10, NEB). To do this often involves finding ways to make their lives count for something worthwhile outside themselves, discovering a sense of meaning and purpose, cultivating a deeper relationship with God, and developing relationships in which they learn to nurture love by mutual nurture of one another's growth toward wholeness.

For many recovering people, Twelve Step programs are invaluable means of stimulating precisely these types of personal and spiritual growth and discovery. As indicated earlier, these self-help/mutual-help programs are designed to facilitate the kinds of continuing growth needed to undergird long-term serenity and sobriety. But, for their whole-person growth, many people in recovery also need the spiritual insights and growth counseling skills of clergy or psychotherapists.

How can clergy best help addicted people find healing and begin to grow in those dimensions of their lives that have been shattered or neglected during their addicted years? An important way is by being readily available to make growth-oriented pastoral counseling and growth nurturing groups available to them. Such counseling and groups can complement in crucial ways the vital help the addicted can receive from Twelve Step groups and/or addiction treatment programs. Pastoral counseling is most effective with addicted people when it incorporates characteristics of the model overviewed at the beginning of this chapter. Crisis counseling, bereavement counseling, marriage and family counseling, and counseling aimed at forgiveness and reconciliation in close relationships can all be useful, depending on the needs of particular recovering individuals and families.

Clergy with advanced clinical and academic training in pastoral psychotherapy who have time available can go beyond the essential short-term crisis and referral counseling described earlier. Their use of psychotherapeutic methods can help addicted people whose deeper conflicts and repressed wounds from childhood still make their hold on sobriety tenuous. To use a familiar California image, earthquakes from their psychological basement shake the houses of such people's psyches so violently that some form of reconstructive psychotherapy is essential for sobriety. Clergy with the training and time to do pastoral psychotherapy can give significant service to such addicted people. However, depth psychotherapy that explores early life trauma and relationships can be very anxiety producing. It should be attempted only after other forms of help have proved inadequate, and if possible, after sobriety has been reasonably stable for an extended period. Psychotherapy with addicted people should always include a robust emphasis on helping people develop responsible skills for handling their present situation effectively. Therapists should prevent the process of exploring the past from becoming for clients a substitute for coping responsibly with the demands of the present.

Nurturing Growth in All of Life's Seven Dimensions

Let's look at the meaning of the whole-person growth that chemically addicted people often need to do for their full recovery. By the time they hit bottom, their lives often are in shambles in many if not all of the seven dimensions of human life. These seven are the major areas in which sickness or health develop: people's bodies, minds, spirits, relationships, work, play, and their interpersonal-institutional and natural environments. Interrupting the addictive cycle is an absolute prerequisite to rebuilding or enriching any of these key areas of living. But sobriety per se does not automatically accomplish this healing and growth. The permanence and productiveness of sobriety depends, to a considerable degree, on the repair and revitalization of those life areas that have been disturbed or impoverished.

The overall aim of growth in these seven dimensions is to enable recovering people to move beyond necessary self-healing to enhanced well-being in all areas of their lives. As they do so, their recovery becomes stronger and they experience more fulfillment, joy, and satisfaction in their everyday lives.

1. *Enhancing the spiritual well-being* of recovering people usually involves helping them mature in their religious lives. This means letting go of the immature values and magical, manipulative beliefs that dominated their

spiritual lives during their addictions. Increasing spiritual health is a key growth dimension in moving beyond recovery to discovery. All aspects of pastoral counseling with addicted people, whatever the other problems, should aim at increasing their spiritual and ethical health. The same is true of all efforts by clergy and congregations to help recovering people experience healing of their spiritual and moral woundedness. This is a central dimension of all humans' total well-being. The psychosocial dynamics of religious approaches to addictions, the basic existential needs, and the contrast between healthy spirituality and that which often characterizes the spiritual life of people during addictions, were explored in chapters 9 and 10. Methods for enabling spiritual healing and growth in counseling and religious education will be discussed below.

2. *Increasing physical well-being* frequently involves coaching people in recovery to practice healthier nutrition; limit, or better, stop their smoking, and reduce drastically their consumption of other toxins; engage in regular big muscle exercise; and get renewing relaxation and adequate rest. The unity of the mind, body, and spirit is increasingly emphasized in contemporary health sciences, as well as in both Christian and Jewish understandings of healing and health. People's bodies are regarded in New Testament terms as temples of the Spirit. Therefore, anyone's self-care for physical fitness is an expression of spiritual discipline, and should be an integral part of a congregation's wellness programs.

3. *Increasing mental well-being* often involves encouraging recovering people to learn how to use their minds to activate their self-protective immune systems; regularly practicing methods of mind-body stress reduction such as meditative prayer; increasing their creative thought processes; and increasing mental fitness by the strenuous, regular exercise of serious as well as enjoyable reading, problem solving, and writing. A congregation's program of lifelong learning opportunities can be an excellent resource for helping people in recovery strengthen their mental well-being. Addiction education should be an integral part of this.

4. *Increasing relational well-being* often involves helping recovering people learn how to nurture maturing love in their families and other close relationships. Addictions are family illnesses that create chaos in family systems. Many recovering people need help in improving communication and conflict resolution skills, and in intentionally satisfying one anothers' emotional needs or heart hungers for loving care, respect, honesty, fairness, adventure, and playfulness. A congregation's program of marriage, family, and singles enrichment can provide opportunities for people in recovery to learn these love-nurturing skills.

5. *Increasing work well-being* often involves helping recovering people rebuild their vocational lives and find a more viable sense of purpose and meaning in their work. Vocational enrichment workshops in congregations can provide needed encouragement, inspiration, and guidance to people in this key growth phase of recovery.

6. *Increasing play well-being* for recovering people involves their learning to enjoy playfulness and humor without depending on alcohol or drugs to liberate their playful inner child. For Christians who are seeking new ways to follow the example of Jesus, it is healthy to remember his love of life as demonstrated at the wedding of Cana, where he first used his miraculous powers to renew the diminishing supply of wine so that a joyous wedding party could continue to celebrate the loving relationship. Workshops in congregations should include a time to be "playshops" too.

7. *Enhancing the well-being of recovering people's relationships with both their natural and social environments* involves several different learning and growth strategies. As indicated in the discussion of the role of ecotherapy in addiction counseling, relationships with the natural environment can be intentionally deepened by encouraging people to enjoy being nurtured by nature and the healing energies in beautiful natural settings. Many people also find their healthy grounding in the natural world enhanced by relating more frequently and in more depth with loved pets, flowers, and plants.

When people's recovery is firm, their well-being can be increased if they are encouraged to study, understand, and then become involved in helping to change some of the injustices and societal sicknesses in their community and world that help to spawn epidemics of addictions. The findings of several recent studies of comparative levels of mental wellness have come to similar conclusions. They have confirmed the validity of the belief in the Jewish and Christian traditions that the wellness of people is enhanced when they reach out to help others. A part of this outreach is to "think globally and act locally" (and vice versa) as they work with others to increase the health of all the institutions that influence everyone's well-being day-by-day. The prophetic witness that Marty Mann implemented in establishing and leading what is now called the National Council of Alcoholism and Drug Dependence is a striking illustration of how one courageous woman reached out to help prevent the illness that she knew from her own experience.

In presenting this overview of growth opportunities for recovering people, I am not suggesting that clergy should try to take primary responsibility for helping them grow in all these areas. (To attempt this would expose clergy to the dangers of work addictions and burnout.) I am convinced, however, that clergy should lead congregations to provide innovative programs of learning and training for spiritually centered fitness in all seven areas of people's lives, throughout their life journeys. Those in recovery in congregations and those who contact clergy for counseling, should be invited and encouraged to become involved in those well-being groups or programs that focus on the particular areas in which they need to grow. If they do this, their progress in moving beyond recovery to discovering better ways to wellness will be accelerated.

A cornucopia of insights, exercises, methods, and resources for nurturing wellness in each of these basic life dimensions is available in *Well Being: A Personal Plan for Exploring and Enriching the Seven Dimensions of Life*. Included are many of the resources that have proved to be most helpful to clients and students, as well as in my own growth through the last four decades of my ministry. A comparable workbook with an explicitly Christian orientation is *Anchoring Your Well Being: Christian Wholeness in a Fractured World*. It is accompanied by a leader's guide, and both are designed as resources for use by individuals and classes in congregations on the seven dimensions model of well being. These resources can be utilized in the continuing growth phase of recovery by counselors. They also can be used by recovering addicts themselves because these books are do-it-yourself manuals and resource treasury that encourages readers, as well as whole congregations, to make and implement self-care-for-wellness plans. Because of the availability of these books, I will not elaborate further here on growth nurturing strategies.

Using Solution-Oriented Counseling

Solution-focused therapy has significant similarities to my growth counseling approach to addictions described in this volume, as well as to Charlotte Davis Kasl's approach to helping addicted women (see chapter 8). This innovative approach was developed by Steve de Shazer and his colleagues at the Brief Family Therapy Center in Milwaukee, Wisconsin, and successfully applied by two colleagues, Insoo Kim Berg and Scott D. Miller. In their *Working with the Problem Drinker: A Solution-Focused Approach*, they suggest a therapeutic option that, in my view, can enrich addiction counselors' helping resources.[14]

The basic principles of this approach, like Kasl's and my approaches, provide a healthy therapeutic balance to pathology-oriented therapies and the Twelve Step philosophy and methodology. Berg and Miller apparently use the principles as the primary therapeutic approach to problem drinkers in general. I regard a growth approach such as this as useful with nonaddicted alcohol abusers and also during the second or growth phase of counseling with addicted alcohol abusers (alcoholics). For the latter, the first phase focuses on healing their brokenness.

The following are some working principles of solution-focused therapy that are relevant to clergy's work with problem drinkers, alcoholics, and behavioral addicts: (1) The clients' strengths, abilities, and resources are highlighted, rather than their deficits and disabilities. Therapy capitalizes on the healthy patterns that already exist in clients. (2) Treatment focuses on discovering clients' answers to their drinking problems. Therapists then encourage them as they seek to implement their solutions, doing the hard work involved, and using their own skills and resources. (3) The main emphasis is on finding here-and-now solutions that work. If one doesn't work, another is tried. (4) The emphasis in this therapy is on the clients' present and future problem solving, not on analyzing the past. (5) The approach treats drinking problems in terms of the family systems involved.

Spiritual Healing and Growth in Recovery

In responding to addictions in their communities, the highest priority opportunity open to clergy and congregations is helping recovering people grow in spiritually centered ways as they rebuild their lifestyles without addictive substances or behaviors. Clergy are the only professionals who have had graduate level training as enablers of spiritual counseling and growth. Their most valuable contributions to the recovery of addicted people are in the areas of these crucial spiritual tasks. When such people seek help with religious and ethical problems, ministers have opportunities to encourage and guide them in developing a vital, spiritual life-center that becomes the unifying, empowering core of their new way of being and becoming.

In terms of the inescapable spiritual or religious needs that all humans possess (see chapter 9), ministers' central task in counseling with recovering people is to help them learn healthy ways to satisfy these needs. By the time they become open to help, their efforts to fulfill these by pseudoreligious means—alcohol, drugs, other addictive substances and obsessive activities—have collapsed. Their spiritual longings can be met in healthful ways only as they do the growth work involved in developing spiritually and ethically vital lives. However this occurs, spiritual-ethical growth is essential for long-term, productive, and joyful recovery.

Clergy have many valuable resources for use in this ministry. These begin with the caring and counseling skills described in this book. In addition, a wide variety of pastoral counseling methods aimed at spiritual and ethical healing and growth are described in two chapters of the textbook, *Basic Types of Pastoral Care and Counseling*.[15] Another unique resource many clergy possess is their training in understanding, diagnosing, and facilitating healing of the common kinds of spiritual and ethical pathologies that characterize addicted people. Well-trained clergy have professional expertise in using the powerful resources of faith, hope, and love to help heal spiritual sicknesses in addictions.

A wealth of spiritual resources for recovering people also is available in many congregations. Such people often discover that their unmet spiritual hungers are satisfied in the small groups, education, worship, spiritual enrichment, and outreach of a growth-oriented faith community. These recovering church members can be valuable resource people in assisting clergy in making referrals, as well as developing an addiction prevention educational program within the congregation. (See chapter 15.)

Let us look more closely at the resources in spiritually healthy congregations. The numerous spiritual nurture and growth experiences in spiritually energized congregations offer resources that help many recovering people continue their spiritual growth journeys beyond what they achieve in Twelve Step groups. These dimensions of a person-centered, congregation's life may bring healing and growth: worship services, religious festivals and sacred rituals such as communion; prayer and Bible study groups; a variety of other study and growth groups; family and singles enrichment events; spiritual direction aimed at teaching healthy spirituality; mutual help in the crises and losses of life; and all the prophetic and outreach opportunities of service- and justice-oriented congregations. All these offer opportunities for people in recovery to learn healthy ways of satisfying basic religious needs, especially their need for renewal of basic trust and their sense of purpose in living. Amidst the wealth of growth opportunities in health-nurturing congregations, clergy should guide people in discovering which of these can satisfy their religious needs and stimulate their spiritual growth most effectively.

Clergy should avoid pushing recovering people to become involved in church groups before they are ready to seek such experiences. Those who have been hurt by and alienated from organized religion usually require time and spiritual growth in a Twelve Step program before they may feel a yearning to find a congregation were they will feel at home.

Many healthy, wholeness-nurturing congregations have a variety of personal and spiritual growth groups, some of which were mentioned briefly above in discussing the seven dimensions of well-being.[16] More and more recovered alcoholics and other chemically dependent people are becoming sober and drug free for very extended periods. It is not surprising that some of them have felt a desire for spiritual learning and growth experiences that build on and transcend the significant growth achieved in Twelve Step programs. This desire represents a superb opportunity for congregations in all faith traditions to provide spiritually centered growth workshops, retreats, and classes for people of various ages in recovery and for their families. Congregations who have offered such groups usually report appreciative responses from those who have found more meaningful, practical, and growth-enabling faith and values.

Spiritual growth and maturity is a key goal of all pastoral counseling with addicted people. Clergy's counseling skills can be used to help those in recovery grow beyond the immature beliefs and values prevalent during addiction to the open, life-affirming beliefs and values that can energize the continuing process of recovery.

Alcoholics sometime tell of praying "until they had calluses on their knees" during their drinking days. Generally these prayers were of the magical, manipulation-of-reality type described earlier. Addicts sometime come to ministers seeking easy, magical solutions to their worsening problems, and are angry because God has not rescued them from the consequences of their irresponsible addictive behavior. Clergy must not reinforce such expectations, of course. Instead, when such addicts become sober, the goal of helping them spiritually is to enable them to surrender their manipulative prayer requests and begin to see that the distortions in their relations with God are directly related to their relationship problems with people in their lives, and that both are distorted by their irresponsible addictive behavior. It is important to remember that addicts' spiritual problems are intertwined with all their other problems.

Clergy can help some recovering persons live the implicit theology of Step Eleven, "Praying only for knowledge of His will for us and the power to carry it out." The profound spiritual significance of this step becomes clear if the will of God is understood as meaning spiritual reality. Praying for this is asking for insight and ability to align one's life with reality rather than expecting, as during the active addiction, that spiritual reality should adapt itself to addicted persons' wishes. Recovering addicts should seek to develop a relationship with God and spiritual reality that may be the polar opposite of what they were seeking during their presobriety days. Doing "spiritual angle" counseling with those struggling to outgrow narcissistic, manipulative spirituality can lead gradually to the discovery of the earthy humility and spiritual empowerment of a more mature faith.

Helping Addicts Gain Healing from Spiritual Trauma

How can clergy counselors help addicted persons who have been hurt spiritually by churches, clergy, or fear-shame theology, and therefore are turned off to anything religious? Such traumatized people may ask for pastoral help because they are blocked and frustrated in their search for meaningful spirituality.

While serving as a chaplain-therapist in a hospital addiction program, Robin Crawford developed an innovative method of counseling with patients who wanted to find meaningful experiences of a Higher Power.[17] The addiction treatment program there included a strong emphasis on the Twelve A.A. Steps. Consequently, troubled patients frequently discussed their spiritual frustrations in the context of Step Two, "Came to believe that a Power greater than ourselves could restore us to sanity," and Step Three, "Made a decision to turn our will and our lives over to the care of God *as we understood him.*" Patients would divulge their painful stories, as they had been encouraged to do in A.A., telling about drunken episodes, sins, failures, and dead dreams. Because they knew Crawford was a minister, some told about their painful religious backgrounds and frustrating spiritual blocks. By hearing their stories, he would establish rapport and often gain a diagnostic impression concerning the pathology of their spiritual lives. Most of them associated things religious with fear, shame, and guilt.

After hearing their "drunkalogues," Crawford reframed the therapeutic conversation in a positive direction by asking them what had been good, strong, and sane in their lives. (He came to call this healthy side of addicted patients' stories their "sane-alogues.") He based this reframing approach on his belief that everyone, including agnostics and those suffering from severe dysfunctions, have had some experiences of health and sanity that they can recover with pastoral guidance. He then suggests that they relive in their imagination a time when they felt the most sane, healthy, and together.

During the debriefing after they had relived these positive, high-energy memories, most discouraged people recognize that they do have more resources for sane living than they had seen before. Crawford inquires what those experiences said to them about God and God's ability to bring them sanity. Some see that what they have just re-experienced could be bridges to relating in healthy ways with their Higher Power who might help "restore them to sanity." If Crawford had started with "God talk" about their religious trauma and God's help with their pain, this probably would have been a therapeutic cul de sac. By their first reliving healthy times in their lives, he enabled them to be affirmed by the knowledge that they have the capacity to live better lives. Some patients recognize these experiences as examples of the divine Spirit's healing and health-giving power. Here are two illustrations of how Crawford used this approach with two patients.

One male patient described himself as a "program failure" because he had slipped back into addictive drinking several times after completing the hospital treatment. He talked with the chaplain-therapist about his lost spirituality and his hopelessness. "I know that the Higher Power thing is what I need, but I just can't get it," he said. Sensing that the man was on the verge of the deep despair of believing that recovery was forever beyond his grasp, Crawford suggested that they pass over the God problem for the time being while the man shared more about himself, including when he felt the most insane. He poured out stories of terror during the Vietnam War and how he had returned from there spiritually empty and addicted, only to have a series of work and marriage failures. He said he now felt emotionally dead.

As he talked, the man mentioned the death of his father in passing. He said he had cried only once. With Crawford's encouragement, he told about that. He had gone camping with his current girlfriend, after his father's funeral. They had camped by a fast flowing creek near a tiny island of granite boulders. He told of being able to cry as he sat alone on one of the rocks, surrounded by rushing water. Asked how that felt, he responded, "It was so good just to let go." Being aware of his festering, unhealed grief wound, the chaplain invited him to simply close his eyes and "sit on that rock again." For long moments, the man was quiet as he relived this powerful memory. When he opened his eyes, he said that it was just like being there again and that he had found the inner peace that had eluded him since his addiction began. The chaplain responded: "It sounds like you have found your Higher Power." The man asked rhetorically, "Is it that simple?" Answering himself, he said, "It *is* that simple. It's really here inside me. I can sit on that rock any time."

Another patient, also a young adult male, had about completed the twenty-eight day treatment program. When he had come to the hospital, he was drunk, completely discouraged, with his life in shambles. Early in the program, the chaplain recalled, "As we surveyed his life, the man lit up (emotionally) as he spoke of a small ranch he once owned. It had a tiny house set back from a rural road. His favorite time of day was walking to the mailbox under an arch of trees lining the road. I invited him to follow that joy, to imagine himself under those trees once again. As he did so, he re-experienced that joy. I suggested that he invite God to take that walk with him, to see what might happen. In the warm emotional environment of a much-loved natural setting, the man found that he was able to experience God's presence quite easily. He discovered that God's presence actually enhanced the feelings of well-being in revisiting that setting." After that, the man made a daily routine of his comforting "walk with God." He confided in the chaplain, "I was afraid of God. On those walks I told him how angry and frightened I had been. I found that God could handle all I had to say. . . . That walk you sent me on was the best thing that happened to me here in the hospital."[18]

These two cases are vivid examples of the effective use of imaging and the healing energy of experiences in nature, when counseling with addicted people. Imaging enables addicts to relive meaningful memories and puts them in touch with the transcending divine Spirit in very down-to-earth experiences. These cases also illustrate the key role of grief in causing addictions and the grief-healing energies of mother-father nature, God's living creation.

Using Religious Resources Effectively

Some clergy ask themselves, "Should I use prayer, scripture, or sacraments in counseling with addicted people, and, if so, how?" Many of those who go to ministers for help expect and want something different than when they consult secular therapists, namely the strength and help of religion. Responding to this need may or may not involve traditional religious resources. It is well to remember that it is sometimes necessary to avoid using what may sound like churchy language and explicitly religious symbols. Avoiding these may help establish counseling relationships that can become religious in the deeper sense of being channels for God's healing power. As mentioned earlier, A.A. members are fond of saying, "The spiritual angle often has to slip up on us alcoholics."

Establishing at least a beginning trustful relationship with addicted people should precede any use of religious tools. As in all pastoral care and counseling, it is wise to use explicitly religious resources only after one knows how clients are likely to feel and what the meaning is likely to be for them. In any case, traditional resources should be used selectively and in moderation. I recall what one alcoholic confided in me after some trust had developed in our relationship. He said that he had resisted coming to talk with me, knowing that I am a minister, because he didn't want to be "prayed over." Clergy who tend always to pray with counselees should restrain themselves until they get to know where the counselees are in their religious struggles.

Whatever clergypersons do or say may register as "religious" in the sense that, to many people, they represent the spiritual dimension of life and the religious community. It is well to adopt the view that all healing, whatever the means, involves the liberating action of God. If prayer, scripture reading, and holy communion or other sacraments seem to hold potential value for particular persons, they should be used. However, it is crucial never to use them to make ourselves feel more useful as clergy when we don't know what else to do. After one has prayed (or used other religious resources), asking the client a simple question can enable the experience to facilitate growth in the counseling process: "What was going through your mind while I was praying?"

In deciding whether or not to include religious resources in counseling, it is helpful to ask oneself whether such use will contribute to the person's recovery and to developing a more mature, reality-based faith. Addicted persons who are searching for a deepening sense of trustful relationship with the divine Spirit sometimes find real help in the use of traditional resources by clergy and, more important, in their own personal devotions.

When one does pray or choose scripture to read, clearly one needs to pick up the problems and feelings of clients. This shows them that their messy issues and feelings, often including feelings of bitter resentment toward God, are acceptable to the clergyperson and to God. In praying, it is important to avoid phrases that might be construed to mean asking for a magical solution. In this way, the idea is communicated implicitly that God helps when we participate responsibly by mobilizing and using our own God-given resources. The "faith without works is dead" theology is a healthy spiritual attitude in counseling with addicted people who may be looking for an easy prayer pill to solve their problems.

Counseling Low-Bottom and Homeless Addicts

Most ministers, especially those with downtown churches or those near a main highway, are often confronted with the perplexing problems of how to respond constructively to low-bottom alcoholic and drug addicts who come unannounced seeking some kind of assistance. The earlier discussion of such addictions and what can be learned from religious approaches (in chapter 6) may provide useful insights concerning how to respond, including where to refer such persons.

It is prudent to remember that low-bottom addicted people frequently come to clergy hoping to make an easy touch. Many of them regard ministers as naively trustful. Of course asking clergy for a loan is not confined to addicts, and it is often difficult to distinguish those with legitimate needs from those for whom any money given will be used to purchase drugs or alcohol. Some alcoholics and other addicts, particularly those suffering from character disorders, are ingenious in concocting stories about why they need money. Protective clergy skepticism born of disillusioning experiences typically results from being manipulated.

The most constructive general guideline concerning giving money to persons who show signs of being addicted and/or con artists, is don't! Such people are often "from out of town." Their stories usually make it sound imperative that they have the gift or loan at once. This is the bait that inexperienced clergy who have church funds to help the needy sometimes take, to their subsequent regret. No matter how convincing and urgent their stories seem, ministers should follow the standard procedure of social agencies—investigate. Say, in effect: "I can't give you anything now because it is the policy of this congregation to always confirm needs before providing any financial assistance to newcomers. You can understand that we sometimes get requests that are not accurate. If you will give me the phone number of someone who will confirm your need, and come back tomorrow, I'll be able to tell you whether or not I can respond to your request." If strangers give valid phone numbers, a phone call after they leave will allow the accuracy of their stories to be checked quickly. If people are not on the level, they usually give phony numbers, think of excuses why they cannot give phone numbers, or they will not return later.

This procedure does not mean missing opportunities to give real help to sick persons because an opportunity usually does not exist. If addicts' only motive is to get money, the odds are extremely high that they are not open to help with their substance abuse. Giving them money may delay the time when they may bottom and become open to help.

Con artists with character disorders, including those who are addicted, sometimes make their living by panhandling. They have hidden contempt for those they exploit. Underneath surface displays of gratitude they sneer at the suckers they have duped and revel in their own superior cleverness in having accomplished this. By giving them money one is contributing to their exploitative orientation, as well as unwittingly pushing them a little further down into the morass of addiction. Panhandlers sometimes inform one another about "easy touch" clergy who give out funds readily.

Even if alcoholics show what appears to be a genuine desire for recovery, it is not wise to give them more than a little financial assistance. A.A. experience has shown that it is better for newcomers to work their way up from the bottom, using their own resources and the guidance and support of other members. If they succeed, it is their victory. Because money is a symbol of power, esteem, and independence in our culture, limiting this type of help tends to lessen the dangers of addicted people becoming overly dependent on clergy. In some cases, this policy may help addicts face the fact that their underlying problem is not their lack of money but staying sober.

If strangers say they are hungry, instead of giving them money, it is better to give them food or a coupon that they can exchange for food at a nearby restaurant. If they need a jacket on a cold day, give them a garment with little pawn value. If they say they need shelter, give them the address of the nearest Salvation Army installation, rescue mission, or public homeless shelter where they can get temporary shelter and probably needed food and clothing. If people seem to have a legitimate and pressing need for a little money (for example, carfare to get to work), invite them to work for it. This tests the legitimacy of the alleged need and also respects their self-esteem.

In evaluating available resources, a phone call or visit to the local Salvation Army center, mission, or shelter can help clergy discover which programs are probably most effective. In making referrals of homeless people who probably are addicted, it is important to choose a facility that includes Twelve Step groups in its programs in addition to offering physical help, counseling, and religious resources.

Unfortunately, however well clergy are prepared to respond, they probably will have only occasional and small successes with low-bottom, addicted people. As described in chapter 6, they often are dealing with people suffering from more than one serious sickness. To addictions is added homelessness, which, if it is chronic, is a complex psychosocial long-standing problem. And many homeless people suffer from dual diagnoses with major mental illnesses intermingled with their chemical addictions.

However, it is salutary to recall the compassionate challenge of Thomas B. Richards, a minister with experience in heading a comprehensive Salvation Army treatment program for homeless addicts. He called cities places "where people are lonely together," adding that "the city minister, busily engaged in church activities and active in all manner of worthy civic causes, may forget the fact that for many, many people a city is a cold, lonely place."[19] He went on to point out that, with their preoccupation with their clergy obligations in a big city, they "may overlook the growing multitude" of those who are friendless and alone on the city streets, in the hospitals, and other institutions within a stone's throw of their churches. Richards suggests that if clergy's basic interests are with people, they will discipline themselves to follow through and check with the helping professionals and agencies to which they try to refer.

Many who struggle full time trying to help low-bottom addicts are overwhelmed by the sheer number of those who need assistance. Other clergy have a healing opportunity to express collegial interest and friendly concern, as well as support to these harried, harassed clergy and other staff members in programs working with low-bottom addicted people. As suggested earlier, clergy and congregations should support the comparatively effective programs that now exist and the innovative programs such as halfway houses that are being developed in some cities. These programs are desperately needed and may bring a little reality-based hope to addicts overwhelmed by hopelessness.

In this and other types of caregiving and counseling with persons trapped in addictions the importance of counselors' frustration tolerance and their not becoming heavily ego-involved in the outcome of counseling with chemically addicted persons must be emphasized. Clergy counselors are fortunate if they have learned to cherish little successes, because such work is often slow and fraught with setbacks, even with A.A.'s valuable help. But, at the same time, even small, occasional successes in addiction counseling can be deeply satisfying. I am thinking of those times when one is aware of having been a very imperfect but nonetheless useful instrument in helping addicts—encouraging them, perhaps, to discover faith and trust, mobilize their resources and move into fresh, constructive chapters in their lives.

CHAPTER 14

Counseling with Families for Recovery:
A Systems Approach to Codependency

The first codependent couple was Adam and Eve. Eve listened to a snake instead of herself, and Adam blamed her for all their problems.

—Jann Mitchell, *Codependent: An Original Jokebook*

I love my father very much. And I have a very loving father. But, in reality, I have two fathers—one sober and one not. My father is an alcoholic. Both of us have tried to ignore his drinking and pretend that it doesn't affect me—that it is just his problem. But, really, it affects our relationship a lot. He is a different person when he is drinking, one I prefer not to be around. And often I feel like I am the parent, constantly worrying about him. And trying to figure out what it will take to make him finally do what he has to do—so he can get on with his life without alcohol. I haven't given up hope that he will change.

—Letter from a woman, age 20

My husband is an alcoholic, but will not ask for help. He thinks he can work it out for himself. He's not doing it, but what can I do? Is there anyone in the world who can help us or will try to? Please, for God's sake, can you help me?

—Letter received by the Al-Anon clearinghouse

Appeals like these are familiar to many clergy. They hear similar cries when desperate wives, husbands, parents, or adult children of severely addicted people ask for help. Such appeals point to open doors of pastoral opportunity—opportunities to be instruments of God's healing. Through the years, the most frequent addiction-related counseling scenarios I have encountered were with family or close friends who sought help for an addicted person who was still in denial.

There are two reasons why clergy in congregational ministries often have many more opportunities to counsel with members of addicted families than they do with addicts themselves. The obvious reason is simply the weight of numbers. There are an average of at least three or four family members in the circle of suffering, chaos, and often tragedy surrounding each addicted person. In the United States there are an estimated 10.5 million (addicted) alcoholics, which translates to at least thirty-five to forty million family members, intimate friends, and work associates who have direct concern for them. Add to these the family and friends of the estimated 7.5 million problem drinkers whose drinking patterns cause them serious problems, even though they do not yet show the hallmarks of biochemical addiction. Add to all these the people close to the several million drug addicts and the enormous burden of human suffering caused by addictions becomes clear.

The other reason why clergy have many more occasions to help family and close friends is because they usually become motivated to seek help several years before addicted persons hit bottom and seek help on their own initiative. It also is true, in my experience, that family members tend to feel somewhat less defensive and deterred by guilt and fear of criticism than do addicts. Because they are less defensive, family members are more likely to seek help before the final stages of their addicts' illness have developed. Working with families of chemically dependent (CD) individuals, therefore, represents the largest single cluster of opportunities for prevention through earlier treatment of addictions.

Here are the major facets of clergy's multiple roles in helping those in the caring circles surrounding chemically dependent persons:

1. Clergy can help hidden family members risk coming out of hiding so that they can be helped, whether or not the addicted persons decide to "come out." The methods for bringing closet addicts out of hiding, described in chapter 12, are also useful with family members.

2. A significant role as well as opportunity is to provide pastoral crisis counseling for the spouse, parents, children, and teens during what often is an extended period before addicted persons become open to help. Anyone who has lived with alcoholics or drug addict knows the overwhelming shame, loneliness, confusion, and despair that often develops in such toxic family systems. Alcoholism and other addictions in a family, as someone has observed, is like having an elephant in the living room that everyone walks around and pretends is not there, even though it takes up enormous valuable space, causes all manner of problems, and is the family secret around which this social system is increasingly organized.

3. Another clergy role is to teach family members how to recognize and change their counterproductive, codependent behavior in relating to addicted family members and to one another. If they are able to do this, their own well-being as individuals and as a family system will be significantly enhanced.

To the extent that families are enabled to increase the health of their interpersonal relations by improving communication and conflict resolution, they will increase the likelihood that their chemically dependent member will become open to help, sooner rather than later. This is the desperate hope that brings most family members to counselors for help. If the constructive changes they make in their family interaction do hasten addicts' becoming open to help, then they have prevented the most destructive advanced stages of addictions.

I recall one clergywoman who described how she had helped motivate a male alcoholic to find sobriety, even though she had no opportunities to see the man himself. She accomplished this by helping the wife and teenage children increase their understanding, and on the basis of this, change their codependent attitudes and behavior toward the husband and father. These changes probably accelerated the man's overcoming his denial and going to A.A. Such indirect access may be all that clergy counselors have, but it is a valuable connection for healing ministry.

4. Helping family members respond constructively during and after their addicted family members' treatment is another significant counseling opportunity that increases the chances of the successful recovery of all those in the family system.

How can clergy and other counselors best prepare for counseling family members? A basic part of preparation is understanding the common interpersonal dynamics within intimate social systems impacted by addicted persons. The goal of this chapter is to overview these dynamics and spell out some practical implications for counseling aimed at recovery and beyond that to discovery. Preparation also can be facilitated by reading books available from Al-Anon and other books cited in this chapter.[1]

In preparing to help family members, it is essential to acquire firsthand understanding of how groups like Al-Anon, Nar-Anon, and Alateen function. For making effective referrals of family members, it is wise to get well acquainted with several members of these Twelve Step groups who have recovered from codependency. The easiest strategy for doing this is to attend several open meetings of these groups. The times and places of nearby meetings of most Twelve Step groups can be learned quickly by calling the number listed in the phone directory.

Understanding Crises in Addicted Family Systems

The often-repeated cliche that "alcoholism is a family disease," can be extended to include all addictions, both substance and behavioral. This is true in several senses. First, as in all intimate social systems, the emotional and relational climate of the whole system influences all those in it. Second, anything that disturbs, diminishes, or enhances any member's well-being inevitably impacts everyone else's degree of wellness. And third, a plethora of sociopsychological studies have shown that mates and children of severely addicted people often are nearly as disturbed, anxious, and in need of help as are the addicted. The whole family system needs guidance and help, not only for recovery for their acute crisis, but also for the growth that needs to follow. The most efficient and effective way of enabling movement toward whole-family recovery is to work directly with the whole family-friend network. If it is not possible to involve everyone, it is important to understand the counseling process with individuals in family systems terms.

The process of chemical dependency (CD) often engulfs an entire family in a creeping nightmare. While she was a research sociologist at a major medical school, Joan K. Jackson did what has become a classical longitudinal study of wives of alcoholics.[2] The stages she identified in the development of the family crisis of alcoholism are still relevant today for many families with male members addicted to alcohol and other drugs. However, the developmental sequence in families with addicted wives and mothers often is radically different than families with male addicts like those explored in Jackson's research. This is because of differences in female and male roles and because husbands often refuse to tolerate addictive behavior (like lying, deceit, and irresponsible drinking or drug use) much sooner than wives. They tend to leave addicted wives after a shorter time. When they do, and children are left with addicted mothers, the impact on their mental well-being can be even more devastating.

Here are the stages Jackson discovered when the husband is addicted:

Stage 1: Sporadic incidents of excessive drinking (or drug use) begin and place increasing strains on the marital relationship.

Stage 2: Social isolation of the family begins as incidents of excessive use increase. This increasing isolation magnifies the impact of toxic family interaction. Thoughts and behavior become increasingly centered on drinking and drug use. Husband-wife relating deteriorates and conflicts increase. The wife tries desperately to control her husband's behavior, but everything she does seems to make it worse. She begins to feel self-pity and to lose her self-confidence as her efforts fail. She attempts to continue maintaining the original family roles and structure, but this is disrupted more with each episode of his excess. As a result the children start to show increasing emotional disturbance.

Stage 3: The family gives up all attempts to control the addicts' drinking and/or drug use. The children's disturbance becomes more pronounced and attempts to support the addict in his roles as husband and father are abandoned as futile. The wife begins to worry about her own sanity and about her inability to make decisions or correct the situation.

Stage 4: The wife assumes control of the family and sees the husband as a recalcitrant child. Pity and intense protective feelings largely replace her resentment and hostility. The family becomes more stable as it is organized around the mother, minimizing the impact of the disruptive behavior of the husband.

Stage 5: The wife separates from her husband if she can resolve her guilt problems and conflicts around this action.

Stage 6: The wife and children reorganize as a family without the husband and father.

Stage 7: If the husband achieves sobriety, the family usually reorganizes to include a sober father and encounters problems in reinstating him in his previous roles.

Knowledge of common developmental sequences is useful to clergy who do counseling with such families because the counseling approach that can be most helpful depends on what stage of deterioration or reconstruction families are in when counselors become involved. Clergy will usually encounter them in Stages 2, 3, or 7. If they still are in Stage 1, the family will be absorbed, like the CD person is, with attempts to deny that a problem exists. In Stage 2, the family's effort will be to hide the problem from the outside world, coupled with desperate efforts to control the CD's excessive drinking and drug use. Stage 3 is dominated by family disorganization in which a spouse begins to adopt a "What's the use?" attitude. In Stage 4 the wife, mother, or husband (if he is still around) tends to become protective and masochistic in a way that makes the relationships unhealthy for all concerned.

Jackson could include the happy ending of Stage 7 because her study was done in an A.A. wives' group—many of whose husbands were sober. If this stage is missing and the sequence is translated from the language of a social scientist into the parlance of everyday living, one has a picture of stark interpersonal tragedy. The family flounders as it attempts to adjust to its member who lies and is least responsible when responsibility is called for, who is unbearably irritable and egocentric, who embarrasses them in front of friends and spoils their holidays by binges, who spends money for alcohol or drugs that they need for food, and who seems completely oblivious to their welfare or their pleadings.

The picture includes the endless dark spiral of drinking and nagging, drinking and remorse, drinking and broken promises, and more drinking. Spouse's anger and fear pervades the entire picture—fear of violence to themselves or their children, fear that others will find out and bring shame to the family, fear of insanity, and the constant fear that they will return home to find the addict intoxicated or gone. Within such marriages, meaningful communication and satisfying sex disappear like a snowball in the warm sun. Heartbreak hangs over them like a dark cloud. In the midst of this chaos and insecurity, the crowning tragedy for spouses is what is happening to the mental health of their children and teens. In such scenes of sick family despair, well-equipped clergy can sometimes bring small rays of light—the light of hope and help!

In one sense, the crisis of addictions is more difficult for families than the trauma of grief because addictions are unstructured and stigmatized crises. When death—a respectable crisis—strikes, family, friends, and congregations engage in socially prescribed behaviors designed to help the family cope. Alcoholism and drug addictions, in contrast, are stigmatized crises for which there are no socially structured healing responses. Thus, addictions are like mental illness and death by suicide or AIDS. These crises and losses are social deviations that often do not elicit community support for family members, unless they are fortunate enough to get this from an Al-Anon group, or from an understanding minister or congregation. Since most of us do not expect such crises to happen to us or to our families, we are unprepared emotionally for their cruel intrusion. Consequently, families often respond with feelings of humiliation, alienation, self-isolation, and baffled confusion.

Applying the Family Systems Perspective to Addictions and Recovery

One of the most encouraging developments in treating addictions is the success that many alcoholism and drug counselors have reported when they have applied family systems therapies to their work.[3] Among major conjoint family therapies, the theories and methods of Murray Bowen are used frequently by addiction counselors. Here are the key concepts of his approach, many of which also are accepted by other family therapy theoreticians:

- The family is viewed as an operational social system with an identity and family personality that is more than the sum of individual members. Everyone in the family is influenced profoundly by the health or sickness of that organic social system. Healthy or unhealthy changes in one member impact the entire system and everyone in it. For these reasons, families are seen together in therapeutic sessions whenever possible.

• Psychopathologies, including addictions, are understood in terms of family dynamics as being produced by an imbalance between individual autonomy and interdependency. Addictions are one of the common expressions of human dysfunctions, according to Bowen. Recovery and growth also are understood as depending on enabling the entire family system to become healthier so that everyone within it is freer to recover from both addictive and codependent patterns of interaction. Treating CD clients alone may produce abstinence but it ignores the family systems dynamics that tend to maintain addictive patterns. Full recovery must involve changing the family context in which alcohol- and drug-related behaviors are the central organizing principle around which all of family life is increasingly structured.

• The therapist focuses not only on individuals' internal processes but also on the relationship between individual behavior and the interactional field of the family system within which behaviors are expressed. The therapeutic focus often is on communication patterns, verbal and nonverbal, within families. These reflect the structural and interactional patterns governing the family's behavior. A primary therapeutic goal is reducing the blurring of the boundaries separating individuals (called fusion) and the rigidity of boundaries with the outside world that characterizes addicted and other dysfunctional families and leads to their increasing sense of isolation.

Here is how a psychiatric colleague, Peter Steinglass, summarizes Bowen's insightful understanding of alcoholism and its treatment:

Excessive drinking occurs when family anxiety is high, he says. Then the drinking stirs up even higher anxiety in those dependent on the one who drinks; the higher the anxiety, the more other family members react by unconsciously doing more of what they were already doing. This self-feeding process can spiral into a functional collapse [of the family], and the process can become a chronic pattern.

Therapy, then, must be directed initially at the family member or members who have the most resourcefulness, and the most potential for modifying their own functioning. . . . According to Dr. Bowen, when family relationship systems are modified through family therapy [by reducing boundary fusion and rigidity], the alcoholic's dys-function decreases, even though the [most] dysfunctional partner may not have been part of the therapy. . . . Even though "cures" have occurred without any involvement on the part of the alcoholic, he stresses "family therapy with two spouses is one of the high roads to successful results."[4]

Most family therapists who treat addictions insist on the goal of absti-nence for the addicted member. But they agree that the goals of family ther-apy treatment must include more than abstinence. True recovery involves improvement of family functioning, increased flexibility, and use of their potential for growth to develop a new nonaddicted lifestyle that supports their new patterns of interaction and behavior. Several family therapists have reported good results from combining the family therapy approach with Twelve Step principles and participation in A.A. and Al-Anon.

How is this family systems perspective relevant to clergy who counsel with addicted families? Clergy with advanced training in pastoral psy-chotherapy can utilize the theory and methods of conjoint family therapy productively in their therapeutic work with addicted families. Parish cler-gy and other generalists in ministry such as chaplains, can benefit greatly by using the family systems' understanding of families in general, and of addicted families in particular. Those in congregation-centered ministries have unrivaled opportunities to apply family systems principles in many aspects of their caring, counseling, teaching, and spiritual growth work. This is because they have the unique professional advantage of regular access to many family systems and they do this in the context of what hopefully is a family-like religious system—a congregation. Without any need to master the complexities of family therapy theory and methods, clergy can apply systemic insights to their crisis counseling and their referrals to family therapists, as well as their vital ministry of preventive education in the CD dimension of their ministry.

Understanding Codependency and Relationship Addictions

Codependency is a widely used term in current literature describing fam-ily members' most common way of relating to their CD member. The con-cept sheds light on addictive family systems by identifying the relation-ship addictions (called love addictions) from which they suffer and need to recover. Codependents are obsessively dependent on the dependence of addicted members to maintain a sense of their own security, power, and self-esteem. The identifying characteristics of codependents include:

- spending exorbitant time obsessing about the dependent person;
- trying frantically but unsuccessfully to change the addict's dysfunctional behavior, and by so doing, actually increasing that behavior;
- assigning more worth to the dependent addicted person than to themselves, blaming themselves for the addiction, perhaps putting themselves down in order to avoid facing the addict's real situation;
- suffering ongoing harmful consequences from the addicted family member's irresponsible behavior and yet not changing or ending those mutually destructive relationships.

Pastoral theologian/psychologist Robert H. Albers edits the *Journal of Ministry in Addiction and Recovery*, a major resource focusing on the clergy's role in ministering to addicts and their families. In an insightful issue devoted to the psychology, theology, and roles of clergy with codependents, he offers this working definition of codependency:

A primary lifestyle disorder occasioned by adaptation to and being enmeshed with an unhealthy relationship or relationships which result in the loss of a person's sense of self or a group's sense of identity. As family members have adjusted, readjusted, and finally maladjusted to the dysfunctional situation, codependency occurs.

Albers observes that copendency occurs not just in individual family members' relationships with the addicted one and in the collective interaction of their family system, but also in congregations as social systems of shared faith.[5]

Psychologist Charlotte Davis Kasl illuminates the hidden dynamics of codependency succinctly:

The goal of codependent behavior is to find externally the security and power that is lacking internally. The belief system is that one cannot exist on one's own, and one therefore must do whatever it takes to keep a partner and any other symbols of security, such as home, children, and financial support.[6]

Psychologically, those who are addicted to codependency are caught on a nonstop treadmill trying in vain to earn their acceptance by caretaking of others. In theological terms, they are caught in graceless attempts to earn their salvation by their good works.

This crippling interpersonal pattern in addicted families is a vicious, self-feeding cycle that could be described as a "runaway family crisis."

The runaway crisis of their addicted family member, made steadily worse by using addictive chemicals to self-medicate painful effects of previous excessive use, is reciprocally reinforced by the runaway, codependent family crisis. The primary objective of addicted family counseling is helping family members learn how to intentionally interrupt their side of the two interacting runaway crises—the addict's and their own—both of which are made more destructive by their codependent responses.

Getting Inside the Family's Chaotic World

When spouses, parents, or adolescent children of CD victims venture out of hiding, it is important that they experience warm, empathic understanding from clergy and other counselors. The more professionals can feel *with* them in their family agony, the better the chances that they will remain out of hiding and in counseling. Here is a segment of a pastor's first session with Karen, a middle-aged parishioner:

Karen: "I'm not sure I should be here talking about this problem, pastor. But I've tried everything to help John, and nothing seems to help. He says his drinking is nobody else's business, including mine. *(Pause)* It's started to affect our older boy's schoolwork. *(Pause)* I feel I just have to help John, but everything I do seems to backfire and make his drinking worse."

Pastor: "I can sense that it wasn't easy for you to come, but your situation is getting so difficult that you decided that you had to seek some help. I'm glad you came and certainly will help in any way I can."

Karen: "I thought perhaps you could tell me how to approach John so as to help him see what he's doing to himself and his family. If I even mention his drinking, he flares up and stomps out of the room. I don't think he's an alcoholic, but he's been coming home drunk several times a week lately, and he often can't make it to work on Mondays. One of these days his manager is going to get wise to his lame excuses."

Pastor: "It sounds like John's drinking is getting much heavier and may be affecting his work. It must be frustrating that he's so defensive about it that he won't discuss it, no matter how gently you approach the subject."

Karen: "Well, I guess I'm not that gentle when I try to get him to talk about it. I'm so worried and upset that he doesn't seem to care. I thought that things would get better when he changed jobs last fall and got out from under the pressure of his old job. But he seems to be worse. Last night he came in after midnight. First he woke up the children to give them a bawling out for leaving their bicycles where he tripped on one of them. Then he got sick and made a mess right in the middle of the living room. I had to clean that up before the kids got up. He's home sleeping it off today. I can't understand it— he's so different. All he thinks about is himself and liquor.

Pastor: "It's really rough on you and the children when he behaves like he does. And he seems to have changed for the worse?"

Karen: "Yes *(eyes filled with tears)*. His temper is terrible when he's drinking, and he seems to pick on the older boy especially. I try to protect him, and John gets furious. *(Pause)* I keep trying to keep the kids from irritating him, but you know how children are. Whatever I do seems to be the wrong thing."

Pastor: "You're feeling terribly frustrated and like a failure because everything you try seems to make him drink more."

Karen: *(Nods and cries without speaking.)*

Four significant facets of Karen's inner world are evident in her opening statements. First, she communicates feelings about coming without her husband's knowledge and against his wishes. The pastor's response, "It wasn't easy to come," recognized and respected these feelings. This helped her trust him with other painful feelings.

A second important message she communicated was her understanding of what constitutes her problem—her husband's excessive drinking. She also indicated why she came for help now—the crisis the night before. The minister was probably on target in choosing not to follow the lead of her reluctance to apply the label "alcoholic" to her husband, although clarifying the meaning of his addictive behavior will be important in subsequent counseling. Early in the first interview is the time to concentrate on intensive, responsive listening, not the time to do educative counseling.

The third crucial insight that came out is Karen's understanding of the kind of help she needs and wants. Distraught family members seeking clergy's help most often make requests similar to hers: "Do something to help him (or her) with the problem" or "Tell me what to do to help her (or him)." It is hopeful if they ask, in effect, "Help me with the problems created for me and the children by his (or her) drinking or drug use." Karen does not think of herself as needing counseling for her own sake. She cannot recognize, at this point, that her obsession to help her husband makes her do the very things that allow him to excuse his drinking. Because she feels so responsible, ashamed, and guilty, she probably would be threatened by even a hint that what she fears may be partially true—that she is contributing to her husband's problem by her attempts to help him and that she also needs help. Yet, she needs help for herself very much. Whatever personality problems she brought to the marriage (and these may be small or large) have been magnified tremendously by the trauma of trying to survive in an addicted family system. She certainly needs help in coping more constructively with the impact of her husband's behavior, whatever he does or does not do about his drinking. Furthermore, her ability to relate helpfully to her husband also depends on her learning to handle her own inner problems more adequately.

The fourth message Karen revealed is her own painful feelings and experiences connected with the family crisis of alcoholism. In his third and fourth responses, the pastor encouraged her to ventilate these feelings. By so doing, he may have helped her start to move toward becoming aware of her own need for help. Family members often are reluctant to turn in this direction because they are sitting on a volcano of explosive feelings that they fear may erupt embarrassingly and expose them as the weak people they feel they are. This facade of self-sufficiency, however, is a burdensome defense. After a torrent of pent-up resentment, fear, and confusion came gushing forth, one distraught husband said, in effect: "I feel like I have to be strong because she is so weak. I didn't dare let myself go before." The acceptance of the male pastor had enabled him to relax his defenses a little.

Through careful listening and responding, ministers can encourage family members like Karen to discuss their feelings about the private, hopeless hells in which they have been living. This accomplishes four things: (a) rapport is established through significant communication on a feeling level; (b) some relief comes from their mountainous burden of negative, frightening feelings; (c) unburdening may enable them to be freer in coping constructively with their difficult life situation; and (d) through responsive listening, followed by a few questions, counselors gain a tentative picture of the dynamics of the problem.

This diagnostic impression should include informed hunches concerning whether they are dealing with addictive alcoholism or with nonaddictive problem drinking. For example, it may be that John's drinking is mainly a response to the pain from his marriage, job, and inner chaos. If he has not yet become addicted, losing the ability to control his drinking, and if both he and his wife becomes receptive to the pastor's subsequent offer of counseling help, there is a chance that John may eventually return to moderate drinking by healing the source of pain in his life. If John is addicted (as the initial facts about his drinking seem to suggest), changes in his marriage will either not occur or, if they do, they will not reduce his drinking significantly.

As in all counseling, when family members come for help, clergy's first job is to hear what *they* regard as their problem. But, in the process, it is important to respond to their perception of the presenting problems as a bridge to their own emotional and spiritual needs, even if they are not yet aware of needing help. The most difficult counseling issue initially often is to gradually help them move from their self-defined role as "helper" of the addicted to that of "the helper who also needs helping" themselves. By encouraging them to express their painful feelings and reactions to their situation, and responding with empathy, counselors may enable them to become aware of their own needs in the heavy crisis they are in. As they experience a warm, caring counseling relationship, they may come down from what they probably experience as a lonely, precarious pedestal of failing "helper" to accept help for themselves.

As discussed in chapter 13, it is important to ask whether persons who the family believes have substance abuse problems agree with this family diagnosis and, if so, are they interested in getting help with this. If not, do they want help with other problems such as the family conflict? Asking these questions enables counselors to get connected with the "presenting problems," as seen by the family, and also to gain a sense of what may be the addicted family member's motivation to seek help. In forming counseling hunches about absent persons' motivation to seek help, it is wise to remember that family members often are unaware of addicts' hidden feelings, because of the defensiveness and power struggles pervading the system. As described earlier, this is one reason why counselors should do everything possible to talk directly with those alledged to be addicted face-to-face or by phone. On some occasions, I have been surprised to discover some openness to help that had been hidden from family members. When those who are the prime focus of a family's concern begin to sense ministers' genuine, accepting concern for them as persons, they occasionally reveal things that have been buried among the conflicts and power struggles with family members.

The Family Counseling Model: From Crisis to Growth and Empowerment

What types of counseling are most likely to be effective in helping members of addictive families? As indicated earlier, most addiction-related counseling should use short-term, behavior-oriented crisis methods, especially in the early phase of the helping process. When she came, Karen was too distraught by the emotional tornado of shame in which she was living to look deeply within herself or at anything else. To attempt personal therapy or one-sided marriage therapy with the spouses of active addicts is as inappropriate and ill-timed as attempting to discuss redecorating their living rooms with persons whose houses are on fire. The only appropriate goal of pastoral care and counseling with families of those in active addictions is to help them cope constructively and learn how to interrupt the runaway family crisis in which they are deeply entangled.

Let's look again at the dynamics of the self-feeding codependency crisis in which the very things family members do in attempting to control the crisis causes it to intensify. For one thing, families usually isolate themselves increasingly, as the addictions develop, in efforts to protect themselves from the social disapproval they expect from the outside world, including from extended family and congregations. Unfortunately, their increasing social isolation intensifies feelings of lonely alienation and fears of "what they will think if they find out." They thus cut themselves off from potentially supportive, perspective-giving relationships precisely when they need those the most. Supportive adaptive counseling aims at reversing this out-of-control adaptive mechanism that actually has become maladaptive to the family's coping well with their crisis. This requires helping families reduce their shame and isolation, and increase their interpersonal nurture and satisfactions. This may be done by encouraging them to risk reestablishing social relationships—beginning in Twelve Step groups like Al-Anon, Nar-Anon, Codependency Anonymous (Co-Anon), Alateen or Narateen, and then, it is hoped, in a congregation's accepting community of faith.

Supportive and adaptive crisis counseling is based on the premise that there are only certain kinds of insights that people in crisis can use. In the case of Karen, these include understanding the nature of the sickness of alcoholism, the futility of attempts to coerce addicts to stop drinking, and how to mobilize her resources to cope with the practical problems that seem overwhelming. As she learns to handle the acute problems more constructively, her shattered self-confidence will tend to grow stronger. As she mobilizes and uses her latent coping resources, her ability to cope constructively will increase. As one wife put it, "I feel that my head is above water and I can tread water now, even though I'm still stuck in the whirlpool." After Karen has coped with the acute crisis, her pastor should help her revise her erroneous assumption that any improvement in the lives of other family members is totally dependent on John's getting and staying sober.

The acute phase of crisis counseling is more like emotional and cognitive first aid than long-term psychotherapy. As in accidents, immediate first aid sometimes can be lifesaving. When Sally, a women in her midthirties phoned, the pastor sensed that she must arrange to see her at once. In the interview, she learned that Sally's husband, a businessman addicted to both alcohol and cocaine, had become verbally violent with her and their two preteens during two recent episodes of nonstop weekend drinking and "drugging." He had been getting increasingly violent over several weeks. In addition to shouting and swearing at her the day before, he had waved a loaded gun in a threatening manner. Sally was nearly paralyzed by what the minister sensed might be reality-based fear—that he might express his rage in deadly violence or turn it on himself suicidally. The pastor knew that her urgent role was to help Sally face the implications of what she already knew—that she and the children were in a very dangerous situation. As she began to think more clearly, guided by her minister's wise counseling, she weighed the action options that were open to her. She finally decided that moving at least for a while to her sister's home in another city, and getting a lawyer to file for temporary legal separation, were actions that she needed to take without delay.

Disturbed spouses often need such help in making decisions and taking direct action to meet pressing problems. Such crisis counseling often involves drawing on specialized community agencies that complement and supplement what clergy are equipped to bring to the situations. For example, to help families of addicts with dual diagnoses, it is important to know how to contact mental health authorities for a diagnostic interview and possible commitment, and how to help family members understand that commiting their loved one can be a crucial step toward rehabilitation rather than a betrayal.

If there seems to be no immediate danger of violence, it is wise to encourage spouses to postpone decisions about leaving addicted mates until they have had an opportunity to gain a broader perspective on their situation through time and counseling. Unless they are mentally ill, most addicts will control their verbal and physical attacks if they understand that their spouses really mean business when they threaten taking direct action such as leaving or calling the police.

Learning and Facing the Facts: Educative Counseling

If spouses and other family members are to halt their own runaway family crisis, it is essential that they learn basic facts about addictions.

This educative counseling can begin as soon as counselors are reasonably sure that they are dealing with their acute crisis, perhaps during the latter part of the first interview. The family's understanding of addictions provides a solid foundation for reality-based decisions about the necessity of changing their codependent behavior. Educative counseling can be initiated simply by saying, "It may be helpful to you to learn all you can about the problem your relative seems to have."

A primary goal in exposing family members to the facts about alcoholism and other drug addictions is to help them understand that their family members are suffering from an illness *of which they are not the basic cause.* Although the disease concept has considerable shame- and guilt-reducing potential for them, many families initially resist applying it to one of their own. It feels like a blow to their collective self-esteem to accept that a family member has a severe addiction and is not in full control of his or her behavior. The counselor's task is to help them work through their feeling-level resistance to accepting reality. As long as they cling to the hope that "maybe he'll lick it by himself this time," they probably are setting themselves up for another bitter disappointment. When a family accepts that one of their members has a chronic, progressive illness, they will be in a position to insulate themselves to some degree against its most destructive effects on them. It also helps prepare them to relate to the addicted persons in ways that may eventually contribute to their becoming open to help.

Certain kinds of knowledge can be especially helpful to the family. For example, it helps to know that, when addicts are almost unbearably egocentric and lie about their substance abuse, they probably are engaging in desperate attempts to cope with deep feelings of chaos, fear, powerlessness, and worthlessness. As one wife said, "It takes some of the sting out of his obnoxious behavior." Knowledge that symptoms such as blackouts, nameless fears, and secretive drinking or drug use are common among addicts, often has a reassuring effect. To awaken reality-based hope, the fact that chemical addictions usually are incurable in the sense of addicts' recovering the ability to use them in moderation should be presented alongside the fact that they are highly treatable, in the sense of persons recovering constructive lifestyles.

The sickness concept should not be presented too early in the first interview, because this may cut off family members' needed catharsis of resentment and anger toward addicts. The danger that this concept will stimulate parents' or spouses' impulses to be pampering can be minimized by frank discussion of the danger. When a pastor raised the issue of possible overprotection, one wife responded, "After all, if Frank had pneumonia, I would make all kinds of allowances for his actions." To counter this faulty analogy, counselors should point out that alcoholism and other addictions are different from pneumonia in that one of the surest ways to retard addicts' becoming open to help is to overprotect them.

At the close of the first interview, the educational phase of this counseling can be expedited by lending family members an Al-Anon pamphlet or one of the books listed in the bibliography. This may enable new windows of understanding to open in counselees' minds. Family members often return to subsequent sessions with a comment like, "Things are beginning to make sense. I feel as though I have a solid foundation under my feet for the first time."

Making Abundant Use of Twelve Step Programs

Early in counseling relationships with family members, information about A.A. and other nearby treatment resources should be shared so that, if and when the addict becomes open to help, family members will know how to proceed. If they are alert for even minimal openness on addicts' part and know the available helping resources, family members may be keys to their beginning treatment. At an appropriate point, it is well to encourage family members to attend those local Twelve Step groups that are relevant to their own needs. The options include Al-Anon, Nar-Anon, Alateens, open meetings of A.A., and perhaps Adult Children of Alcoholics. Counseling may be needed to help them resolve fears or other resistance to attending such meetings. Their making contact can be expedited by arranging, with their permission, for a stable member of the relevant group to take them to their first meeting.

Becoming involved in Al-Anon and other family-oriented Twelve Step groups, is for them what A.A. or N.A. can be for their addicted family members—a necessary group healing process complementing the healing help of counseling and other treatments. These groups can contribute to healing addicted family systems in these ways:

- They can encourage spouses and other family members to apply the Twelve Steps to their own issues and problems in living.
- They can encourage releasing the addicted person by focusing on their own issues rather than on the problems of the addicts.
- Sharing personal stories by more experienced family members can provide a means of letting go of shame as well as giving wise guidance about daily issues of living with addicts before, during, and after their recovery.

- New friends made in these groups can help family members rebuild their mutual support system after years of living in frightened, shame-saturated isolation. It is heartening to witness the miracle that often happens when spouses of addicts dare to come out of their lonely shell and deal with the explosive feelings that have built up during their solitary self-confinement. Al-Anon friends can give massive emotional support during the dreary days or months or years when addicts are refusing help. They possess insiders' empathy for the feeling of those who have "lived in the same squirrel cage" or "lived with the elephant in the living room."

Al-Anon often helps family members move to a heart-level understanding of their mates' addictions. Experienced members will help them identify the subtle ways in which they are overprotecting the addicted person. By sharing their own experiences they will offer suggestions for handling all sorts of difficult problems. As they learn how to release their addicts, family members will begin to look at themselves with more insight. They will begin to grow personally through the application of the Twelve Steps to their own lives. Practicing these steps often helps them find spiritual resources through awakened relationships with their Higher Power. This provides needed strength for coping with both their spiritual hungers and the practical problems in living, with or without their addicted family member.

Release of Addicted Persons by Family Members

Many addicted people and adult children of alcoholics have intense dependency hungers from having lacked adequate relationships of trustful, loving dependency in childhood. They therefore tend to choose spouses upon whom they can lean heavily and who unwittingly become enablers of their addictions. As suggested earlier, when this occurs, the most salutary thing that concerned families can do—for themselves and also for their addicted family members—is to *release* them. This is a behavioral response that is now commonly called *detachment* in Al-Anon. To the degree that family members do this, their own runaway crisis will be interrupted. A member of Al-Anon put it this way, "When I got out of the driver's seat, it took a terrific load off of me." She told how her determination "to get my husband sober" had become a passion into which she had poured herself. The more she failed, the more frantically and obsessively she tried. Somehow her sense of worth as a person had become bound to her taking responsibility for her husband's sobriety. He sensed this, and it gave him tremendous power over her. Finally, after years of futile struggle, she gave up, accepting that nothing she could do would make her husband get sober unless he decided to do what he must do for sobriety. There is a remarkable parallelism between this kind of letting go by family members and the positive surrender of addicted persons. In a real sense, she "hit bottom" and surrendered her obsession to solve her husband's problem. For the first time in years, she felt a sense of release from his addiction and her first taste of inner serenity.

Facilitating this kind of release or detachment is the most important goal of pastoral care of addicts' families. The process consists of encouraging family members to do three interrelated actions:

1. *Let go of feeling responsible for addicted persons' sobriety and recovery and stop efforts to control their drinking and/or drug use.* This happens when family members recognize the utter futility of their codependent behavior and the painful price such attempts exact from them. When this occurs, they have, in effect, cut the power that they had been giving the addicts by attempting to be responsible for them.

2. *Let go of both angry, punishing attacks and the overprotection that shields addicted persons from the painful consequences of their behavior that often is precisely what they need to experience to hit bottom.* I recall an alcoholic's wife who said to me: "My husband told our minister that he had to join A.A. to figure out what had happened to me in Al-Anon." What had happened was that she had succeeded in releasing her husband and thus detaching herself from feeling responsible for his excessive drinking.[7]

3. *Let go of the assumption that anything they want to do to improve things for themselves and their family must wait until the addicted family member accepts treatment and achieves sobriety.* This assumption is a self-fulfilling belief. As long as it is believed, it is true. When families let go of it and begin to develop their own plans and possibilities they discover its fallacious nature. Releasing this assumption enables spouses and children to develop their own lives and relationships, and fulfill some of their dreams, whether or not the addicted family member ever decides to accept help. The Big Book of A.A. recommends to wives of still-drinking alcoholics:

> Be determined that your husband's drinking is not going to spoil your relation with your children or your friends. They need your companionship and your help. It is possible to have a full and useful life, though your husband continues to drink. We know women who are unafraid, even happy under these conditions. Do not set your heart on reforming your husband.[8]

413

When families succeed in releasing addicted members in these ways, their own well-being is enhanced in several ways. They are insulated emotionally, to some degree, from the destructiveness resulting from addicts' behavior. They interrupt their codependent behavior, gain some detachment from the addictive interpersonal web, and begin to find satisfactions in using more of their own God-given strengths and possibilities.

By changing their side of the interdependent family interaction, family members create what can be change-producing dissonance in that family system. The change in their responses to addicts' drinking and drug behavior may be a kind of shock therapy that creates a crisis in addicts' psychic economy that may result in their becoming accessible to help sooner than they otherwise would.

An insightful portrayal of the codependent dynamics in many alcoholic marriages was in the old movie *Country Girl*. It showed the manner in which each person fed the neurotic needs of the other and, in so doing, produced the mutually harmful, self-perpetuating addiction-codependent cycle. The alcoholic, feeling emotionally starved from childhood, craved mothering. The wife, with a codependently inclined personality, fell naturally into the mothering role. The more she accepted the responsibility for running the family, the more dependent he became, as well as resentful and irresponsible in his drinking. The more irresponsible he became, the more she felt she had to manage everything for the family including his drinking.[9]

The general principle that should guide families is: *Avoid both punishing and pampering.* On the one extreme, some families make the mistake of attempting to coerce the alcoholic by empty threats and recriminations. Addicted people often use such attacks to justify drinking or using even more. Tactics such as pouring liquor down the drain or hiding it from alcoholics are forms of parenting that are no more effective than trying to hide all water from family members with hand-washing compulsions. Addicts often respond to parenting attempts to control their behavior with adolescent rebelliousness expressed in more drinking and/or drug use or violence. It is important to note the difference between punishing, rejecting, judgmental barrages and the carefully planned caring confrontations with reality involved in family interventions described earlier.

At the other extreme is the strategic error of becoming enablers by protecting addicts from the painful consequences of their behavior. As mentined earlier, this has been appropriately called "cruel kindness," meaning that it is motivated in part by caring and kindness but has cruel effects. In such cases, counselors' greatest service is to help family members discover how they are overprotecting or coddling the addict. This involves examining in detail how they responded to a particular drinking or drugging episode. By withdrawing the props they are providing that protect them from reality, former enablers may help their addicts hit bottom and become open to help.

The wives of early members in A.A.'s Big Book, gave this guidance concerning how wives may avoid overprotecting alcoholics:

> Frequently, you have felt obligated to tell your husband's employer and his friends that he was sick, when as a matter of fact he was tight. Avoid answering these inquiries as much as you can. Whenever possible, let your husband explain. . . . Discuss this with him when he is sober and in good spirits. Ask him what you should do if he places you in such a position again.[10]

Encouraging families to walk the middle ground between recrimination and pampering is like inviting them to walk a tightrope. It is possible only to the degree that family members have inwardly released the addicted ones. Often the most important single source of help in walking this tightrope day-by-day is the Al-Anon program and the guidance of its members. Patterns of overprotection often are difficult to interrupt because family members are striving to protect themselves, their children, their family's reputation, and often the family income by protecting the addicted persons. They think: "If we don't take care of him (or her), he (or she) will cause us more embarrassment, heartache, and expense." Release occurs when they see that codependent overprotecting of addicted persons from the painful consequences of their behavior deprives them of incentives to change and thus hurts everyone in the family, especially the children. In this light, releasing then is understood as a necessary act of loving concern and family self-protection rather than of rejection. At this point, families may decide to do an intervention—a responsible releasing of their codependent behavior together.

In the old play "The Pleasure of His Company" by Samuel Taylor and Cornelia Otis Skinner, Mackenzie Savage is asked by his daughter, "You were never very happy with mother, were you?" He replies, "Your mother was a saint who made our home an outpost of heaven. It's why I spent so much time in saloons." The message of this fictional fragment—that behind the alcoholic is a wife who subtly drives him to drink—is a common theme in the folk beliefs of our culture. It is a feeling that many addicts' spouses, as well as the addicts, have somewhere within them.

Certain research findings seemed to confirm this view. They suggest that a common pattern in addicts' marriages is that of dependent, emotionally inadequate males married to controlling but emotionally insecure women who maintained their own minimal sense of adequacy by being married to dysfunctional men. One study of alcoholic's wives showed that when such marriages were ended by death or divorce, some of them married other addicted or dysfunctional men. Some wives do hold tenaciously to the masochistic, controlling postures, even when separating from husbands clearly is in order to protect them and their children from physical and emotional harm. Some wives seem to find personal worth and power when they are, in effect, single parents during their husbands' active addiction. It is understandable that they have ambivalent feelings about their husbands' getting sober. In extreme cases, such wives have been known to sabotage their husbands' attempts to get sober. Others have developed psychosomatic or psychological illnesses after the husband achieved sobriety.

In one such counseling relationship, the wife continued to refuse to consider separating. Her reason was simply: "How would he get along without me? Someone has to take care of him when he's drunk." I remember the parents of an addicted young adult who used a Christian principle—going the second mile—to justify not releasing him. They failed to understand that their self-damaging overprotection was neither healthy spiritually nor helpful to their addicted son.

Being alert to such possibilities does not mean that counselors should use this as a general approach to helping addicts' families. There are as wide differences among addicts, their spouses, and their marriages, as among nonaddicted persons. Many, if not most, of the personality disturbances that have been identified among wives of addicts come directly from the runaway, traumatic crises in which they are caught. When they release their addicted family members or the latter achieve sobriety, their disturbances diminish drastically or disappear.

Let's say that particular spouses (usually wives) do show self-punishing and controlling tendencies that cause overprotective behavior and block detachment for the addicted mate. Searching for the neurotic tendencies that might be satisfied by their spouses' continuing addiction is a strategic error during family crisis counseling. Such family members already suspect that they are somehow responsible for their addicts' substance abuse. For counselors to focus on family members' neurotic problems at this stage tends to block rather than facilitate the all-important emotional release of addicts. It does this by causing family members to feel more guilty and responsible and therefore more self-punishing and controlling. In counseling, it is best to proceed on the assumption that spousal emotional disturbances are mainly the result of the family trauma, until clear evidence emerges of spouses' deeper psychological problems that may need resolution. In any case, it is therapeutically counterproductive to attempt to correct deeper personality problems of either party in the midst of these mutually-reinforcing, dual runaway crises.

Here are some implications of this general approach to counseling families:

First, focusing on why spouses married potential or active addicts is unproductive. Searching for such deeper insights usually intensifies family crises. After release and sobriety have been achieved, continuing, intense family conflicts may point to the need for individual, couple, or family therapy. In such therapeutic contexts, deeper insights may emerge and bring healing at the deeper roots of addicted families' relationships.

Second, it is important to encourage family members to abandon their search for the magic key to curing their addicts' substance abuse, and to give up futile "home treatments" including pleading, nagging, moralizing, making empty threats, and so forth. These are all variations on one ineffective theme that is the opposite of releasing their addicted person.

Third, counselors should emphasize the medical nature of the addictive sickness, pointing out that if their loved ones had diabetes they would not feel responsible for curing them. This can help family members release themselves from emotional entanglement with the addict.

Fourth, it is wise to describe the meaning of *release* or *detachment* as the most potentially healing expression of their love. They need counseling help in talking through and resolving their inappropriate feelings of guilt, shame, and responsibility that block releasing. It may be well to point out that releasing is an inner process and does not necessarily require separating physically, although in some cases it is very difficult without at least a temporary separation.

Fifth, as a part of their releasing and recovery process, family members should be encouraged to begin developing more of their own hopes and dreams. Ideally, this self-empowerment should happen before, during, and after the addicted family member is in recovery. As families face the fact that they cannot transform the addictions of other family members, they should be helped to discover that they *do* have important work to do on their own problems in living and on moving toward the objectives they have been postponing, waiting for the addiction to be solved. In many cases, after family members release themselves and the addicted family member, they spontaneously begin to develop new, more constructive purposes for their lives to replace what has been at their lives' center. Thus they move from recovery into growth and discovery. For traditionally programmed, self-sacrificing wives, developing even a few of their own wishes makes their lives more satisfying and boosts their self-esteem, even though their guilt about doing this for themselves may need attention in counseling. These positive changes help them function more adequately as need-satisfying parents with their children and teens.

Helping Families Before, During, and After Addicts' Treatment

Clergy's important roles with families during the time before addicts become open to help can be summarized as follows:

- Doing crisis and supportive counseling to help families make and implement wise decisions about coping with their difficult situation in the most constructive ways possible.
- Encouraging them to learn as much as possible about both addictions and how the families' dynamics influence the direction of these family illnesses.
- Guiding them as they struggle to release themselves and their addicted family member from the neurotic tangle of their family system.
- Encouraging them to become involved in Twelve Step groups like Al-Anon and Alateens, and Codependency Anonymous (CODA) groups, and linking them with church members who already are active in these groups whenever possible. It is important for counselors to support them in using the Twelve Steps fully as a means of recovering from codependency. This may include taking regular personal inventories, cleaning up any ethical debris in their lives, and reaching out to other families through Twelve Step work.
- Encouraging them to avoid dropping out of church groups they enjoy because of their shame and fear.
- Coaching them in what they can do to encourage their addicted family member to become open to help, as well as in what they should not do.
- Encouraging them to honor and use their own God-given resources as fully as possible.
- Providing spiritual guidance and support to help them renew their spiritual resources for the rigors of coping.
- Encouraging them to obtain, as needed, individual, group, or family therapy in community mental health or addiction treatment programs, including play therapy for disturbed children and teens.

Once clergy have helped families cope with the acute crisis phase of addictions, they have the following crucial roles during what often are times of struggle and disappointment while an addict is in treatment:

- Encouraging family members to continue the helpful disciplines they began during the pretreatment phase.
- Maintaining steady dependable pastoral care relationships with the family.
- Being readily available for additional counseling if slips and other family crises recur, and helping them learn from their crises.
- Helping families change their attitudes and behavior to become part of bridges rather than barriers to recovery for the addicted family member and themselves, particularly during the early stages of treatment.
- Helping family members understand the uphill struggle that addicts will experience, thus enhancing their appreciation of even their little successes and cushioning disappointments when setbacks occur. They can be reminded that, if it took several years for the addictions to develop, it probably will require considerable time for stable, productive sobriety to be achieved. The patience reflected in the A.A. motto "Easy Does It" is good advice for the family as well as their addicted members.
- Encouraging family members with reality-based hope as they participate actively in the family dimension of most treatment programs, and give active supportive to the addicts' participation in their programs. The wives of the first hundred A.A.s wrote to the wives of other alcoholics: "If God can solve the age-old riddle of alcoholism, he can solve your problem, too."[11] Couples who together work at living out their Twelve Step programs often find resources there for resolving marital problems and enhancing their relationships.
- Interpreting to the family, when requested, what is happening in A.A. or other treatment programs, including why their addicted family member is responding as they are. Help them understand why attending frequent meetings, including closed meetings in which non-addicts are not welcome, may be essential, particularly in the early stages of recovery. If new A.A. members display attitudes of superiority, it should be seen as a temporary reaction to lingering feelings of deep inferiority. Spiritual growth by both addicts and their families usually reduces if not eliminates such defensiveness, increasing the potential for spouses to enjoy genuine partnership.
- Helping them realize that attempting to protect the addict from temptation, for example by hiding their own supply of liquor, may backfire by registering as another form of overprotection. Alcohol should never be pushed on recovering addicts, of course, but, if they are to recover, they

must learn how to enjoy living abstinent lives in a society where alcohol is available on every side.

- Recommending other treatment options for addicts and their families if what they try first does not prove effective for them.
- Encouraging them to take advantage of the sustaining, growth-nurturing ministry available in their congregation's corporate worship and life.
- If it becomes evident that a spouse or parent is unwittingly making recovery more difficult for the addict, the minister has the difficult task of helping them become aware of how to quit doing so.[12]
- Linking families with members of a congregation who have had personal experience in their recovery programs. These members can bring depth understanding of a family's struggles, and can be a bridge between churches and Al-Anon.

Clergy continues to have these important roles with addicted family systems after sobriety and recovery have been achieved by them:

- Keeping in regular touch to help them take advantage of the spiritual growth experiences in congregations to which they may become open, having experienced recovery as a family system.
- Helping them understand why the marriage, family, and sexual problems present before addictions or generated during them are not automatically solved by sobriety, as many family members expect. It is well to remember that marital maladjustment can be as much causes as effects of addictions.[13] An insightful discussion of frequent marital problems following sobriety and how they can be met is the chapter of A.A.'s Big Book entitled "The Family Afterward."
- Referring them to pastoral psychotherapists or marriage, family, and child therapists who understand addicted family systems, if serious problems emerge and point to the need for such professional healing skills. It is well to remember that many of the personality problems that make people susceptible to addictions also give rise to marital conflicts and family members' codependency.
- Helping families who have been alienated from organized religions during addictions, reestablishing a relationship with a spiritually enlivening congregation of their choice. The A.A. Big Book (chapter 9) suggests that the readjustments of members can be helped by doing this. The new spiritual and interpersonal wings developed in Twelve Step groups may be strengthened further by flying in a social setting where the majority of members are spiritual searchers who are not chemically addicted. In discussing their experiences in congregations,

early A.A. members reported: The alcoholic "and his family can be a bright spot in such congregations. He may bring new hope and new courage to many a priest, minister, or rabbi."[14] When this happens, clergy find that a vital resource for helping other addicts and their families is very near at hand—in their congregations.

• Inviting recovered family members to help other addicted families who come for counseling. In addition, such family members, along with the recovered addict, should be among those who receive training and participating in the congregation's lay caring team. This will give them opportunities to do Twelve Step work with other families going through the dark valley of addictions, using the healing and learning that they gained in their recovery.[15] Stable recovering addicts and family members can be valuable resource people in a congregation's alcohol and drug educational program.

An invaluble guide for parents confronting the heartbreak of children suffering from addicted diseases is Sally and David B., *Our Children Are Alcoholics: Coping with Children Who Have Addictions.* (Dubuque, Ia.: Islewest Publishing, 1997.) With four addicted children in recovery, they share their parental recovery story and those of a variety of other parents who have learned much from comparable crises in their family systems.

Adding the Missing Dimensions in Codependence

Codependency is a valuable but incomplete concept for use in helping many women and men free and empower themselves. Two significant things are missing in this concept and in much of the A.A. and Al-Anon literature.[16] One is the awareness of the social context of codependency. This, unfortunately, is the normal way that many girls are trained in traditional families and cultures. This serious flaw parallels the limitations for some addicted women in Twelve Step programs, identified by Kasl and other feminist addiction therapists. You will recall that they point out that for addicted women whose self-esteem has been deeply wounded by the widespread male sexism in our society, the road to recovery is not by surrendering their nonexistent pride and admitting powerlessness. Rather it is by discovering their inner power and irreducible worth as human beings.

Kasl's illuminating critique of the negative effects on many women of labeling themselves "codependent" has important implications for counselors who aim at enabling women to develop their full strengths and assets as persons. She emphasizes the need to help women understand their codependency from a cultural perspective and do what they must to extricate

421

themselves from it. Codependency in men, she observes, is fundamentally different from women's simply because our society does not punish men for asserting their power. Many men are dependent on the approval of their boss and on women who provide the love and nurture for which they hunger. What Kasl does not seem to recognize is that such codependency in men is also a result of the hierarchical structures and the one up programming of men in our culture. My view is that both men's and women's codependent behavior results in part from sexist social programming. To help people of both genders free themselves, counselors need to enable them to look at the source—the internalization of oppressive social programming. Kasl holds correctly that codependency groups have been helpful to many women, but they do not empower them fully "because they do not raise consciousness about the politics of patriarchy, which are inseparable from our self-identity, values, and struggles as women."[17] Kasl shows that what is described as codependency fosters in women traits of passivity, compliance, lack of initiative, abandonment of self, and fear of showing power openly.

> These traits are taught and reinforced through institutions of family, education, church, traditional medicine, and mental health practices and philosophy in order to maintain patriarchy, capitalism, and hierarchy.[18]

I would add that the same is true of the codependency fostered in most men except those at the pinnacle of the pecking orders in their society.

The second missing dimension in mainstream codependency thinking is a much needed distinction between codependency understood as symbiotic, unhealthy attachments, and mutually empowering interdependence. Such healthy interdependence occurs when two strong, independent human beings who are capable of standing on their own two feet relate to each other. They enjoy both relating intimately at times and depending on each other in reciprocal, egalitarian ways. The impact of this missing distinction is that many women who accept the label "codependent" uncritically, pathologize their precious ability to give and receive nurture and care for others. Rather than valuing this capacity and seeking to form healthy relationships of interdependence, they tend to think of themselves as sick. Men who reject macho misunderstandings of maleness and who value their ability to nurture and care for others reciprocally in interdependent relationships also should prize this ability.

Mary Elizabeth Moore, a creative Christian educator and former colleague of mine, illuminates with systemic/ecological theology this second missing dimension of mainstream thinking about codependency:

Codependency theory fails to recognize the distinction between codependency, in which one person or social group is defined by the other, and interdependence, in which persons and communities live in relation to one another and with God. Interdependent relationships, if they are to sustain life . . . require an ethic of mutuality—an ethic that calls each to be responsive to the Spirit of Life in oneself and in others, and calls all beings together into solidarity on behalf of the life of the planet.[19]

I agree with the main thrust of Moore's and Kasl's critique of codependency. Kasl concludes her discussion of this with a cogent suggestion that "we proceed further with our collective growth by adopting and adapting the useful parts of the codependency concept, put it in a political framework, and leave the rest behind."[20]

A theology of grace is the key to understanding how pastoral care can facilitate the liberation of family members from codependency. Lutheran pastoral theologian and addiction specialist Robert Albers puts this well:

The invitation to the spiritually hungry codependent is to hear and appropriate a word of grace. To love God, others, oneself and the whole created order for the sake of love itself is a strange, but liberating, message of hope for the codependent.[21]

This kind of grace-full experience is precisely what many recovering people experience in A.A. and other Twelve Step programs. Clergy can use their unique professional integration of theological and psychological understanding of addicts and family members who are still searching for the liberating power of grace in the loving acceptance of the divine Spirit.

It is important to be aware that codependent clergy-congregational relationships are widespread. As in addicted families, such enmeshment produces countless messy problems for both clergy and their congregants. Such clergy will be ineffective in helping codependent families face and resolve their codependence.

Codependency, in summary, is an incomplete but valuable working concept for helping people liberate themselves from enmeshment in dysfunctional systems including addicted families. Emphasizing the two missing dimensions is crucial in counseling, particularly during the growth and discovery phase of counseling after recovery. Traditional codependency thinking must be transformed by adding the explicit goal of healthy interdependency and highlighting its social and political context. Adding these missing dimensions can enhance the concept's usefulness in contributing to the well-being of both genders in addicted families and other families. Doing this will equip both men and women to value interdependence and their own abilities to be both caring and cared about in their relationships. Awareness of the social sources of codependency for both women and men will help clergy and other counselors to deal with social context issues in counseling. This awareness may also help clergy recognize and alter their own codependent interaction with their congregations.

Counseling with Children of Addicted Family Systems

Family life is the most intimate and therefore the most demanding of all human relationships. Addictions, in their advanced stages, crush the interpersonal network of intimate relationships like heavy boots on a delicate spiderweb. In the intricate interdependencies of family systems, the agonies of alcoholism and other addictions are the most devastating. The very qualities that make families healthy and growth-producing—love, tenderness, compassion, forgiveness, open communication, honesty, and emotional maturity in parents—are early casualties of the psychophysical-spiritual illnesses called addictions. In addition, emotional and physical child abuse, including the ultimate violation of incest, and violence between parents are very common in addicted families. (The rate of abuse of women living with alcoholics is estimated to be six times greater than for women in general.) Neonatal crack and alcohol addictions with subsequent developmental and emotional impairments are growing national problems.

It is not surprising, therefore, that the most vulnerable members of addicted family systems, children, often sustain the deepest emotional wounds. In fact, children and youth seldom, if ever, escape without profound psychological and spiritual wounds simply because the abundant, dependable supply of emotional nutrition that human offspring require to grow strong, resilient personalities is not available in most addicted families. The damage sustained by children and youth varies greatly depending on these factors—whether addicts are fathers, mothers, or both; the health of their relationships with nonaddicted parents; the nature of relationships of children with addicted parents; children's ages when the most destructive phases of the addictions began, and when the recovery process began for both the addicted and nonaddicted codependents; the accessibility of other loving adults (such as grandparents), to give needed love, security, and nurture to children; and the social class of the family. On this last point, middle-class, status-seeking families seem to be disturbed the most deeply by parental addictions. In families where the father is addicted and the mother and children receive emotional support from the extended family or friends, wounding of children may be less severe. Where the mother is the addict, damage is often very deep. One husband recalled what his young son said when he found his mother in an alcoholic stupor, "Mommy is dead." Emotionally, she was dead to him, in that she often was nongiving and unavailable to the boy when he needed her. This child's internalization of the husband-wife dysfunction was reflected in these words to his father: "We don't like Mommy, do we?"

It is helpful to counselors to be aware of at least five dynamics in addicted families that are disturbing to children and teenagers:

1. The shifting and reversal of parental roles in unpredictable and confusing ways. When addicted parents are drinking and using, they abdicate their parental roles and these are taken over by the other parent. This overloads and distorts the unique role of that parent—most often the mother. During periods of sobriety, the whole family tries to adjust. When fathers are addicted and there is no other strong, loving male with whom sons can identify, their achieving a firm positive sense of their own emerging maleness is inhibited. The lack of a male figure who is both loving and strong deprives daughters of the developmental opportunity to discover healthy ways of relating to males. When mothers are addicted, the identity problems of both daughters and sons are almost always severe, as mothers are unable to give the dependable caring and nurture that many children get primarily from mothers in our culture.

2. The inconsistent, unpredictable relationship with addicted parents or parent substitutes is also disturbing to children. Many addicts alternate unpredictably between being cold and rejecting to children, and sentimentally overindulgent, for reasons not apparent to children. Children make confused attempts to grasp how to relate to parents to obtain the security, approval, and affection they desperately need, and are continually frustrated by the unpredictable nature of addicted parents' responses.

3. Nonaddicted parents, until they release their addicted mates, usually are unable to relate in very need-satisfying ways with their children because of their own emotional disturbance and deprivation. They are so obsessed with their spouses' drinking and/or drug use, so acutely deprived of having their own needs met in their marriages, that they are painfully frustrated and lonely. Add to all this the chronic emotional chaos in the family, and it becomes clear why effective parenting is extremely difficult for them. A frequent response to the loneliness of living alone with others is to exploit the children by attempting to derive emotional satisfactions and intimacy from

them that they should be receiving from their marital partner. Or, they may use the children as allies in conflicts between spouses. Divisive alliances called "triangulation" in family therapy,"—for example, mother-son versus father-daughter—are frequent and damaging to the mental and emotional health of the children involved.

4. Increased self-isolation of the family causes them to turn in on themselves so that their interaction becomes overloaded and conflict ridden. Studies of the mental and emotional health of family systems have revealed that the best single measure of their health or sickness is the degree of open interaction and mutual support they have with their extended family and friends. Addicted families close their systemic boundaries like a threatened wagon train in the old West forming a tight protective circle. Supportive communication and relationships with friends and community are constricted by this defensive maneuver. Family morale rises and falls with the addict's drinking and drug uses, and children peer relationships often are truncated. Children feel, "I can't bring my friends home because Dad (or Mom) might be drunk and embarrass me in front of them." With their nonaddicted parents, they are shut in the closet of their family's stigmatized secret. The more the family turns in upon itself, the more its problems feed upon themselves and grow.

5. Children of addicts often are deprived of their childhood by the system's demands. They often become an adult child who is forced into adult roles (such as caring for younger siblings or an addicted parent) prematurely. They must do this many years before they have the strength and understanding to bear such adult responsibilities in ways that are not destructive to their own growth and well-being. Some become heroes in their dysfunctional families. They learn early and too well how to be narcissistically self-obsessed stars. Or they may become scapegoats on whom a load of blame is projected by other family members. Or they act out their deep woundedness in antisocial behavior and drug use. Whatever the outcome, they are deeply wounded by developing their personhood in a family system with three unspoken rules that are practiced by everyone—don't feel, don't talk, and don't trust.[22]

What can clergy and other counselors do to help children and teens in addicted families? The most important contribution to their well-being is made by helping their nonaddicted parents come out of hiding, and get involved in Twelve Step groups and release addicted spouses who refuse help. In this way their own emotional and spiritual well-being is enhanced, the overall emotional climate of the home made healthier, and their ability to nurture the wellness of their children increased. If this encourages the addicted parents to enter the recovery process, changes in their behavior can have dramatic healthful effects on all family members, especially children.

In addition, clergy and other counselors can do several things to provide direct help for youth to encourage them to cope constructively with their family crisis. Personal invitations to teenagers to attend local Alateen or Narateen groups, if they are interested, can be arranged. These groups often help teenagers—for whom peer relations are increasingly important—to bond with other adolescents from addicted homes. They often share similar experiences, understand their parents' illness, and apply the Twelve Steps to their own problems of living in addicted homes. The opportunity to talk openly about painful experiences that were formerly family secrets surrounded by feelings of shame has both unburdening and positive bonding effects. Feelings of self-confidence are strengthened gradually by group acceptance. In these and other ways, Alateen groups may bring healing to adolescents much as A.A. and Al-Anon do for their addicted and their nonaddicted parents.

Nonaddicted parents can be instructed and provided with Al-Anon pamphlets that will help them increase their children's and teens' understanding of the addicted parents' sickness. If a family intervention is planned, adolescents should be offered an opportunity to take an active part, if they wish. In addition, clergy should encourage the whole family to stay actively involved in the congregation's educational program and small groups, thus resisting the temptation to retreat into protective but harmful isolation. Mature church school teachers and adult youth group advisors can be enlisted as allies who help surround addicted families with supportive circles of caring and understanding. This must be done, of course, without violating any confidential knowledge that families have entrusted to their clergy about the family's problem.

What should clergy and counselors do if children or teens show symptoms of serious psychological disturbances before, during, or after their parents' recovery? Symptoms can be inward retreats of social self-isolation or outward expressions of aggression, school problems, delinquency, drinking, smoking, and street drug use. When such symptoms appear, the responsible parent or parents should be encouraged and guided in obtaining professional child or teen therapy at the local child guidance or mental health facility. If addicted parents are still drinking or using, they should be made aware of how their behavior may be contributing to their offspring's serious problems. I have known of several cases in which this knowledge helped tip addicts' motivation toward accepting help.

Conjoint family therapy often is the most effective way to help disturbed children by helping the whole addicted family system in which they are enmeshed. They often are the identified patients who express the pain of the whole family system and motivate parents to search for help. In any case, it is very important to involve younger, deeply disturbed family members in whatever therapies or Twelve Step programs are required to heal their wounds. The children of addicted parents, as they enter their teens and young adulthood, contribute at a disproportionately high rate to all forms of chemical dependency and other costly psychosocial problems in our society. Therefore, to help them find healing as children or youth is one of the most significant ways to prevent future addictions and other problems.

Clergy whose relations with their own inner child are open and healthy are able to relate in comfortable, caring ways with children and youth. They can help disturbed children by maintaining supportive and caring pastoral relationships with them. To do this does not require large investments of time, in most cases. What is required is for clergy to express sincere interest in them during brief pastoral conversations characterized by friendliness and affirmations. Such relationships between mentally healthy clergy and children often have qualitative meaning and positive effects, on both sides, that far outweigh the time investment. To the extent that such relationships provide some satisfaction of children's and teens' need for relating with stable, loving adult identity figures, they represent long-range investments in the future mental and spiritual health of these valuable children and youth.

Counseling with Adult Children of Addicted Parents

A forty-one-year-old woman remembers seeing an ad for a conference sponsored by ACoA (Adult Children of Alcoholics). It included a list of the characteristics of such adults which she recognized as a personality profile of herself. She thought, "How did they know about me?" Although she was aware that she had to go, she tenaciously resisted doing so by losing her way, becoming nauseated, and bursting into tears. When she finally arrived she hated being there and had to leave the meeting to throw up. In spite of this she recalls that "it was the first time in my life that I ever felt I belonged in a place. It was the most powerful experience I had ever felt. I didn't know anyone there, yet I felt completely known and part of the group."[23]

A crucial, growing counseling opportunity for clergy and other healing-helping professionals is to provide help for the more than 25 million adult children of addicted parents.[24] Many of these adults still suffer from deep unhealed, hidden wounds coming from having grown up immersed in the emotional chaos and chronic crises of addicted family systems. Many of them are themselves addicts or codependents, married to addicts and other dysfunctional mates, or otherwise suffering from wounded well-being. They are among the millions of the walking wounded who continue to act out the unfinished, unresolved family tragedies from their most formative years. Until they become aware of these unconscious wounds and find healing, they tend to respond to people and events in their adult lives in terms of their dysfunctional early programming. This acting out without awareness distorts their current relationships profoundly—especially those with children, spouses, and authority figures, including clergy.

Many adult children of addicted parents (ACAs) are drawn to organized religion, especially those forms that offer simplistic, authority-centered answers to life's complex tragedies, injustices, and mysteries. They are driven relentlessly by their deep pain and spiritual hunger for faith, security, acceptance, esteem, inner peace, and power. Codependent ACAs, in my experience, seem to be overrepresented among theological students, clergy and lay leaders who move into positions of power and prestige in congregations, as well as in denominational and ecumenical judicatories.

Some who continue to act out their tragic, unconscious childhood dramas contribute disproportionately to the crippling epidemic of sexual and other ethical violations and divisive power struggles within congregations and denominations. Recent religious history provides a plethora of examples of ethical fiascoes by powerful, prominent, and sometimes almost worshiped religious authority figures. They are secret victims of yesterday's tragedies, but they become spiritual tragedies, or tragedies waiting to happen, in religious systems today. It behooves all of us who care about the pathology and health of organized religious systems to implement a deep concern about the widespread impact of these wounded people.

What are some identifying characteristics of ACAs—issues with which they need healing help? The characteristics of their woundedness that become core issues in treatment include: low self-esteem often hidden behind grandiosity that produces a lack of respect for others; distrust of both themselves and others; rigid control of feelings, behavior, and relationships, occasionally alternating with dangerous impulsiveness; ignoring their physical, emotional, and spiritual needs, and the needs of others; being grossly over-responsible or under-responsible; obsessive-compulsive thinking and behavior producing vulnerability to all manner of addictions; using others to gratify their own interests and desires; sneaky codependency often hidden under rigid pseudo-autonomy; paranoid,

defensive fears of anyone who is different; inability to laugh spontaneously and enjoy playfulness, except as expressions of anger or put
down attacks on others; and a lack of healthy faith and values, often disguised by pious religiosity. Most of these problems are extensions of survival strategies ACAs learned in childhood for coping with impossible
family dynamics. But even if these ways worked then, they are grossly
ineffective and dysfunctional in adult relationships.

What are some sources of help for ACAs? The most important and
available resource for helping are the many Twelve Step ACA (or ACoA)
groups that have developed since that movement was organized in 1985.
Because so many adult children are themselves addicted and/or codependent, the huge networks of Twelve Step groups are another important
and widely available resource. Counselors and therapists, including pastoral counselors, have significant roles in providing much needed help for
ACAs. Unfortunately, healing and helping professionals often are not
aware that this may be the hidden issue at the roots of many people's
crises and other presenting problems.

What methods are effective in counseling with ACAs? Even if they are
not obviously addicted or codependent, adult children of addicted families usually have personality characteristics and problems similar to
addicts and codependents. For this reason, the understanding of many of
the spiritually centered methods of helping described throughout this
book can be used effectively in helping them. Furthermore, the self-help
literature for codependents has a wealth of ideas that ACAs can use. For
example, Melody Beattie's *Codependent No More: How to Stop Controlling
Others and Start Caring for Yourself*[25] has practical sections suggesting activities related to "Feeling Your Own Feelings," "How to Have a Love Affair
with Yourself," "Undependence," "Work a Twelve Step Program," and
"Learning to Live and Love Again." In all this, the main points to keep in
mind are that adult children of addicted parents are everywhere, that they
often are not yet aware of their underlying problem, and that their buried
wealth of potentialities for living creative, socially productive lives can be
discovered and developed—if they receive the help they need!

CHAPTER 15

Developing Effective Addiction Treatment and Prevention Programs:

A Strategic Opportunity for Religious Organizations

The experience of recovery from alcohol and drug problems is a gift of God. . . . Pastors and interested lay people in concert with recovering people and community resources can provide a special ministry team for assisting people who suffer from abuse of alcohol and drugs.
—From the mission statement of The Work Group on Alcohol and Drug Concerns of the Texas Conference of Churches

"Almost every study that has examined the relationship between religion and substance abuse has found lower rates among the more religious."
—Harold G. Koenig, M.D., *Is Religion Good for Your Health?: The Effects of Religion on Physical and Mental Health.*

Why should Christians and their congregations become involved in the prevention and treatment of alcohol and drug problems? The basic mission of the Christian life and of congregations is to enable persons to develop life in all its fullness (John 10:10). Therefore, anything that damages or diminishes the wholeness of a single child of God is of concern to those who seek to fulfill this mission. Waldo Beach, a professor of Christian ethics, once defined Christian love aptly as "the ability to read statistics with compassion." Think for a moment of the diminished well-being of one family you know that is afflicted by the dysfunctions of a member's chemical addictions. Then try to imagine the collective pain of five addicted families. Then ten. Then twenty. Long before you multiply one family's suffering by even that modest number, your powers of imagination and empathy probably will be exhausted.

Then take a moment to imagine a city three times the population of New York or Los Angeles. The millions of men and women, children and youth whose lives are diminished, damaged, or destroyed by alcohol and drug problems would constitute such a megacity. It obviously is utterly impossible to imagine the collective load of raw human suffering caused by chemical addictions, not to mention that caused by the millions of behavioral addictions. But what we can and must do is to respond with empathetic Christian caring to some of the wounded who are near us—in our families, churches, and communities.

It is salutary to remember that one of Jesus' challenges to his closest friends as he sent them out on their mission was to be healers wherever they encountered human suffering and brokenness. One of his familiar stories dramatizes the fundamental reason why Christians and their institutions should be involved in helping to prevent and heal addictions. This is his powerful parable about the man who was beaten, robbed, and left terribly wounded beside the road from Jerusalem to Jericho. This moving story provides a model for ministry to battered victims of violence beside today's Jericho roads—including those running through your town and mine. Many of these persons are suffering because of the widespread violence of alcoholism, other chemical addictions, and behavioral addictions.

The spiritual vitality of a congregation is depleted by not reaching out to the rejected victims of individual and social diseases and oppression nearby. Think for a moment about the spiritual price paid by the two busy religious leaders in Jesus' story who chose to walk by without stopping to help. Like them, the spiritual health of clergy and churches today is diminished when they go by on the other side, as they think to themselves, "Let A.A. (or the Salvation Army) take care of these unfortunate victims of addictive violence. Anyway, they probably brought the problem on themselves." Conversely, like the socially rejected Samaritan, Christians and their congregations are spiritually enriched if they interrupt their busyness and get involved.

Being in contact with addicted people and their families, though often difficult and demanding, keeps Christians in touch with the bleeding, infected wounds of sin and sickness—in ourselves as well as in our wounded society. It can provide opportunities to be instruments of God's healing love in the lives of those who are prisoners of addictions, blinded by compulsions, and longing for freedom from their brokenness.

A further reason why Christians and their congregations should be involved in healing and preventing addictions is an often-ignored fact: Both substance and behavior addictions have crucial spiritual and ethical components in both their causes and cures. The meaning of this truth was explored earlier (see chapters 9 and 10), as were the opportunities churches have to make their rich resources of spiritual nurture and ethical guidance readily available to recovering addicts and their families. Many of these persons want and need continuing spiritual nurture beyond the important spiritual help they receive in Twelve Step programs. Wholeness-fostering congregations are like gardens that nurture the spiritual and ethical growth that are keys to whole-person wellness. This vital ministry is sorely needed in both addiction prevention and treatment.

Why have many congregations not developed dynamic alcohol and drug ministries when the need is so great and their role so strategic? Let's be fair. In our chaotic world-in-transition, it isn't easy for congregations to keep their ministries relevant to the places where people are hurting and hoping, cursing and struggling, living and dying. There are numerous other reasons for this neglect. Many of these are derived from erroneous conclusions drawn from half-truths (or less) reflected in assertions such as these: "A.A. is the only answer." "A.A. and the experts in the field can take care of the problem." "The church got overinvolved in Prohibition and that was a fiasco." "Drinking is a personal matter in which the church shouldn't interfere." "Medical experts say that wine is good for your heart." "With all the important problems in our society, why worry about people who drink too much?" "I'm not a teetotaler." "Jesus turned water into wine for a wedding party and Saint Paul told Timothy to drink a little wine for his stomach problems." Overcoming resistances such as these is essential if many more congregations are to develop ministries like those that numerous congregations have demonstrated can make significant contributions to both preventing and treating addictions.

Physician Anderson Spickard challenges congregations to develop such spiritually transforming, healing ministries with addicted people. Drawing on his Christian faith and his long experience as medical director of the Vanderbilt University Institute for the Treatment of Addiction, he declares:

> In my twenty years of medical practice, few experiences have had a resurrection quality equal to that of watching alcoholics and their families leave behind the living death of addiction. Today, while much of the world staggers under the weight of chemical addiction, the church is called upon to be a vessel of this resurrection.[1]

He highlights the potential rewards of such ministry:

> With a small investment of time and effort, any church can equip itself to minister to alcoholics and their families. The rewards of this ministry are enormous. Recovering alcoholics are among the most

spiritually vibrant Christians I know, and the enthusiasm and commitment they bring to their relationship with Christ contribute greatly to the spiritual health of the churches they attend.[2]

In the present global pandemic of addictions, the need for innovative alcohol and drug programs in congregations of all faith groups, church-related schools, and health care institutions has never been greater. The good news is that countless clergy and congregations already are involved in this ministry. Many clergy are now helping alcoholics and their families, providing valuable service in alcoholism and drug education, and working with local Councils on Alcoholism and Drug Dependency. But the vast majority of clergy have hardly scratched the surface of their potential opportunities to lead their people to become "servant churches" in the area of addictions.

Learning from the Past

Let's pause to look back briefly at what some clergy and congregations have done in the past. Lyman Beecher was a distinguished nineteenth-century New England preacher and caring pastor. Around the year 1820, he sat beside the bed of a young parishioner, a chronic alcoholic, as the man died. Reflecting on this experience, he said, "I indulge the hope that God saw it was a constitutional infirmity, like any other disease."[3]

Over the years, many religious leaders have shown enlightened understanding of addictions comparable to the insight articulated more than a century and a half ago by Beecher. Clergy often have had prominent roles in helping alcoholics and their families when few others were involved. As we have seen, the caring ministries of the Salvation Army and rescue missions to low-bottom addicts, and the powerful influence of clergy like Sam Shoemaker in shaping A.A., are striking examples of pioneering ministries. Many clergy from a variety of denominations have led their congregations in developing much-needed caring ministries with alcoholics and their families. An even greater number has developed alcohol and drug education programs aimed at preventing additions. On the other hand, most religious leaders have missed numerous opportunities to help addicts and their families on their recovery journey. Particularly since the disillusionment associated with Prohibition, there has been widespread neglect of alcohol and drug issues in mainstream denominations.

One of the earliest and most noteworthy examples of congregations making remarkable contributions to helping alcoholics was the Emmanuel Movement. Though it no longer exists, it is anything but a mere ecclesiastical museum piece. Its goals, working theology, sickness concept of alcoholism, depth understanding of personality, and some of its methods were many decades ahead of its time and are well worth emulating today. The movement developed the earliest church-sponsored therapeutic clinics integrating the insight of depth psychology and religion to treat a variety of functional illnesses including alcoholism. Twenty-seven years before A.A. began, it considered alcoholism as a disease to be treated like other functional illnesses.[4] It pioneered in treating addictions wholistically using religious resources, medical help, individual and group therapy, hypnosis, social work resources, and home visits by trained volunteers to help addicts and their families and others. Medicine, psychology, and social work were regarded as integral parts of a total religious approach to healing. Many alcoholics sought help and the movement became well known for its success in helping them achieve sobriety.

Launched in 1906 at the Emmanuel Episcopal Church in Boston, the movement was sparked and led by its brilliant rector, Elwood Worcester. He had a Ph.D. in psychology and philosophy from Leipzig where he had studied under Wilhelm Wundt, founder of the first psychological laboratory. Worcester's colleague throughout most of the movement was a clergyman named Samuel McComb who also had extensive graduate study in psychology and philosophy. The spread of the movement was phenomenal with derivative programs developing rapidly in cities across America, as well as a few in England. Ministers of many faith groups set up Emmanuel-type programs and were reported to find new power in their work seeing the approach as a return to the healing practice and faith of the Apostolic Church. Worcester, McComb, and other leaders published numerous books describing the movement's methods.

The movement's theology that undergirded their therapy was positive and person-affirming, centering on the belief that all life is permeated by the divine Spirit. Worcester wrote: "Without this belief man's relations with God become formal and external. The world, robbed of the haunting presence of the indwelling deity, becomes irreligious and profane."[5] Emmanuel workers saw clearly that religion can be employed in ways that promote guilt and neurosis or ways that promote maturity and health. They sought to nurture the latter in those they treated. The general Emmanuel orientation was positive and life-affirming, so much so that moralistic critics labeled it "hedonistic."

In contrast to authority-centered religious approaches, Emmanuel therapy sought to promote patients' freedom and growth by releasing their inner resources. Because this reconstruction of their inner lives dealt with the underlying psychological and spiritual causes of addictions, it often enabled alcoholics to remain abstinent after treatment. No illusions about returning them to social drinking were held by Emmanuel therapists. Addicts and others accepted for treatment were screened medically and psychiatrically. The therapy itself consisted of three elements—what I would call cognitive group therapy in regular "classes," individual analytically oriented therapy sessions (often involving pastoral psychotherapy as well as therapeutic suggestion and self-hypnosis), and a system of social work support and home visits by "friendly visitors." Worcester and McComb wrote that the purpose of these therapeutic visits was "to give to the environment of the patients care similar to that provided for their bodies by the physicians, and for their minds by the clergymen."[6] They also saw these visits as ways to help patients avoid relapses after treatment and "before they acquired full self-reliance."

In 1909, a book was published entitled *The Emmanuel Movement in a New England Town*. Its author, Layman P. Powell, another leader in the Emmanuel Movement, issued this still relevant challenge to churches:

> Whatever plan it followed, it would seem to be a calamity which the church need not add to her many other lost opportunities, to allow the cure and care of the drunkard to fall entirely into the hands of science, which admittedly needs all the help that faith in God can give in dealing with an ill so largely spiritual as the excessive use of alcohol.[7]

The Emmanuel Movement continued through the 1930s, but diminished sharply after Worcester's death in 1940. It is noteworthy that three outstanding nonmedical therapists for alcoholics in this country—Courtney Baylor, Richard Peabody, and Samuel Crocker—were products of the movement. Baylor continued to work at the Emmanuel Church for a time after Worcester died.

Much can be learned today from the Emmanuel approach including its impressive demonstration of how life-affirming theology can help addicted people. It illustrates the way that pastoral psychotherapy can help deal with root psychological and spiritual causes of addictions, and mediate God's grace-full acceptance, thus enhancing both self-acceptance and acceptance of others. It brought healing, not by encouraging surrender to an external deity, but by resolving inner conflict, thus releasing God-given strengths and resources within persons. Most important of all, by its pioneering development of church-sponsored, whole-person healing programs, the Emmanuel Movement should challenge congregations today to establish more holistic healing centers led by pastoral psychotherapists to help burdened people including the addicted.

Preparing for Tomorrow

The overall contributions of many religious leaders in the field of problem drinking and alcoholism has been significant during much of the twentieth century. But as the twenty-first century dawns, it is clear that the growth of addiction problems probably will accelerate even while most congregations, religious schools, and health agencies are far less involved in handling the problem than they might be. The goal of this chapter is to suggest guidelines by which religious institutions can enhance, deepen, and make more effective their ministries in our addictive and addicted society. In earlier chapters you have encountered many suggestions of practical ways that clergy and the people they lead can help prevent and heal addictive diseases. This final chapter will summarize some of these. It will group these under seven overlapping action strategies by which religious institutions can implement a mission to bring healing and growth in the spirit of the Great Physician. Most of these strategies were explored in earlier chapters, so the discussion here will focus on how clergy and religious institutions can implement programs in each of the seven areas. (In addition to congregations, many of the suggestions can be implemented in other religious institutions including schools, hospitals, pastoral counseling, and health-care facilities, as well as in some secular institutions.

First Strategy: Nurturing Spiritual and Ethical Growth

Facilitating spiritual growth, as suggested earlier, is the central and the most unique contribution of clergy and congregations to all dimensions of the problems related to addictions. For this reason, there should be spiritual and ethical healing and nurture in implementing all the other strategies described below. The working theories and methods for doing this were described in depth in chapters 9 and 10.

As Anderson Spickard points out, the spiritual and ethical woundedness of addicts and their families is often catastrophic by the time they seek help.

> Long before a heavy drinker becomes an alcoholic, his relationship with God is badly damaged. Heavy drinking quenches spiritual understanding and often leads the drinker to violate his own moral

principles. . . . A man or woman with perfectly fine family values might drink too much, become euphoric, and climb into bed with a casual acquaintance. When the alcohol wears off, he or she is left with deep feelings of guilt and shame. . . . For the alcoholic, the moral damage never ends. He repeatedly violates his own sense of right and wrong by telling petty lies, cheating at work, hiding bottles, stealing, and verbally or physically abusing other members of his family.[8]

It is no wonder that drinking or using addicts who have been involved in churches usually drop out as their shame and self-hatred increases. Their spirituality loses all its vitality as they sink into the spiritual and ethical quicksand of addictions.

This spiritual and ethical wounding is not limited to adults. Reflecting on his clinical experiences, Spickard describes the devastating blow on children's development:

Children with an addicted parent are severely damaged in their spiritual and moral development, as well as their emotional development. They want to look up to their parents, but are frightened and repulsed by addicted parents' erratic, destructive, often violent drunken behavior. (It is estimated around 80 percent of physical and sexual abuse is by addicted parents.) They feel helpless and controlled by the unpredictable moods and ethically confused by constant moral contradictions, as the family's moral climate disintegrates around them. They often begin to tell lies defensively, as they internalize the addict's lying about many things. Imitating the nonaddicted parent, they learn to use "white lies" in a futile effort to hide the family's shameful problem from their friends.[9]

Think now about how your congregation might implement this first strategy using all its resources and groups that are designed to nurture spiritual and ethical growth throughout the life cycle. As you do so, bear in mind that the emotional-interpersonal-spiritual climate of a congregation is the key factor in determining how effective it is as a place for nurturing spiritual and ethical healing and growth as a central part of its whole-person wellness ministry. Too often churches have failed to create healing/growth-enabling environments that would attract people by translating the good news of the gospel into the language of everyday relationships. In his poem, "The Little Vagabond," English author William

Blake describes his contrasting experiences of what the church and the tavern have to offer in this respect:

> Dear mother, dear mother, the church is cold
> But the ale-house is healthy and pleasant and warm.[10]

In a similar vein, H. L. Mencken once commented that "A prohibitionist is a person you wouldn't want to have a drink with, even if he drank." Whenever religious organizations offer a people-caring climate that is experienced as healthy and pleasant and warm by children, youth, singles, parents, and families, they contribute significantly to healing and preventing human brokenness of all kinds, including addictions, and the basic spiritual message of these institutions comes alive in a redemptive community of shared faith. If you have ever observed people drinking in a public bar you have witnessed an expression of a widespread social and spiritual tragedy. Among those present is a variety of lonely people who, though hungering for human warmth and need-satisfying relationships, are settling for what often is the instant, chemically facilitated pseudointimacy of that setting. Perhaps you have wondered what would need to change in congregations to encourage more of these children of God to come there with their pain and despair. A valuable guide for enabling congregations to be places of healing and wholeness is Gary Gunderson's *Deeply Woven Roots: Improving the Quality of Life in Your Community.*

Second Strategy: Training Resource People for Leadership on Addiction Problems

In the New Testament's understanding of the church, ministry is a function of the entire congregation. Clergy have key roles in empowering the caring ministry of the laity. They should set a tone of concern and help provide inspiration and training for whoever spearheads a congregations' lay ministry. They can provide backup and be available as knowledgeable resource persons, as laity in ministry respond to the needs of addicted individuals and their families. Only as increasing numbers of church leaders catch this vision and accept this challenge, can many more congregations and other religious institutions become the redemptive communities of help and healing for which there is a crying need today.

Effective alcohol and drug programs in churches often are initiated by laypersons or clergy who are motivated by strong concern about the problem. In most cases, one person—a self-starter—decides to get the ball rolling. Frequently such people are moved by knowing addiction problems firsthand from their personal or professional experience. When laypersons are the initiators, it is important for them to confer with their clergy, to seek guidance, support, and possibly active co-leadership from them. Most creative clergy, in my experience, are pleased when informed, concerned laypersons offer to take the initiative in launching such a project. Whether you are a minister or a layperson, you may well be the person to lead the process of establishing a dynamic program in your context.

Whoever takes the initiative, it is important for several people who know a congregation's members well to identify other resource people to join a small, carefully selected, study-action team. Their job is to plan and implement a program designed to meet the high priority alcohol and drug needs in their congregation as well as in their wider community. Team members will need the prayers and continuing support of the congregation's leaders and decision makers. Experience has shown that it is advisable to involve persons such as the following, in addition to a member of the congregation's professional staff:

- A few people with extensive experience in Twelve Step programs including A.A., N.A., Al-Anon, and A.C.A.;
- A physician and/or nurse, and a psychotherapist and/or pastoral counselor, who are experienced in treating addictions and knowledgeable about local treatment resources;
- Teachers (including church school teachers) with expertise in developing effective learning programs for children, teens, and adults;
- Other church members with an interest in the congregation's role in healing and preventing addictions, including those in different age groups, from adolescents to seniors.

Helpful guidelines for selecting and training a congregational addiction team and the role of clergy in the process is found in Trish Merrill's *Committed, Caring Communities: A Congregational Guide for Addiction Ministries*.[11] According to Merrill, the most effective addiction team members are caring, emotionally stable, spiritually growing people who are able to attend rigorous training, maintain confidentiality, and either be active in a Twelve Step group or willing to attend during training. Merrill affirms John Keller's suggestions concerning persons for such teams. They should hold people in high esteem and see them as precious persons created in God's image; start where addicts are, which is often angry at God and turned off to religion; offer them love and time to surrender to the pain, brokenness, and human limitations of their condition; and provide a link with A.A. or Al-Anon.[12] Team members should also be people who have the humility to accept a fact about alcoholics and other addicts expressed well by John Keller: "Spiritually, alcoholics are sick, as all people are to some degree—spiritually sick. They are in need of God's grace but they are not in need of *more* of the grace of God than the rest of us."

To prepare for their task, this core group should have training. A succinct course should cover current knowledge of addictions, early symptoms, treatment options and resources, and biblical attitudes about drinking and drunkenness. This will provide a solid launching pad for beginning an effective program. Members who have this training will eventually be asked to use what they have learned to help equip the congregation with a firm knowledge base so that they will support the program as it develops.

Early in the process of developing a congregational alcohol and drug program, it is wise for someone to discover the various needs, interests, and general knowledge level of the congregation. The questions in such a survey can be organized around the six action strategies outlined below. These issues point up areas in which information can be useful in planning a program that is relevant to the perceived needs of that congregation. If a variety of interests and needs are identified in the area of alcohol and drug issues, they should be prioritized in terms of their importance, urgency, and feasibility as programmatic arenas.

Those who know many of a congregation's members can provide valuable anecdotal information about their interests and needs. But in medium sized to large congregations, it is wise to go beyond this by a more systematic survey involving talking with a cross section of church leaders, teachers, and young people concerning the alcohol and drug issues.

In addition, it is helpful to consult denominational and ecumenical alcohol and drug offices, state programs, and the nearest branch of the National Council on Alcohol and Drug Dependence.[13] Such centers often can provide useful descriptions of what other nearby congregations and other religious organizations have done. In addition, they are sources of valuable resources for alcohol, drug, and addiction education. Other sources for pamphlets, films, video tapes, books, curriculum guides, and teaching materials are denominational social concerns departments. Several mainstream denominations have developed excellent resources in the areas of alcoholism and drug education, community action, and rehabilitation.[14]

How can planners of alcohol and drug programs gain a quick overview of the wide range of possibilities for these ministries in diverse situations? Fortunately, there are several guides and resource manuals that supply this information.[15] Margaret Fuad's description of "Programs in Process—

and Ideas for More" in her guidebook, *Alcohol and the Church: Developing an Effective Ministry,* is an outstanding resource.[16] She describes many effective programs, dividing them helpfully into four categories—ministry by an individual; ministry in and through a congregation; ministry through regional entities or coalitions; and ministry through upper levels of church denominations. The richness of the possibilities is suggested by the fact that ministry by an individual gives almost three dozen models that can be implemented either outside a congregation or within it.

In the planning process, it is important to involve those who may be asked to implement plans so that they can help shape and thus gain ownership of the plans. The sooner they are included in the decision-making, strategy-devising process, the stronger their motivation will be for investing themselves in helping to achieve the objectives of projects.

If focusing on alcohol and drug issues is a new emphasis in a congregation, it is wise to start small and to focus first on a broad educational program. Starting small usually involves concentrating on one high-priority program project at a time, evaluating the outcome carefully, and using that experience to plan the next objective and activity. Key leaders and decision makers in a congregation should be involved as early and fully as possible so that they will gain firsthand knowledge of the nature and importance of these issues in the program of a wholeness-nurturing church. It is important for clergy to give hearty support from the pulpit to alcohol and drug education efforts led by teachers and other laypersons in their congregations.

Third Strategy: Providing Education to Enhance Informed Action

An ongoing, carefully planned alcohol and drug education program is the most significant single contribution that congregations can make to all levels of prevention and treatment. (It is wise to link drug education with alcohol education because many people are concerned about drug problems who are not aware that alcohol is our society's largest drug problem, other than nicotine.) Churches have a superb opportunity to help build a solid foundation of informed concern, enlightened understanding, and healing acceptance of addicted persons and their families. Such a foundation is the only solid basis for any effective program. Taken together, churches, synagogues and temples have the widest educational contact with adults of any institutions in our society—with the exception of public media, especially television. Over one hundred million Americans belong to a congregation. Week after week, millions of adults and young people listen to often-respected spiritual leaders speak on something intimately related to the values that guide their lives. Each week some three million volunteer teachers function in church programs of religious education for children, youth, and adults. Through these channels, the churches have an incredible opportunity to help develop grassroots understanding of all chemical addictions. To take advantage of this opportunity, clergy and congregations' teachers should carry out a sustained, imaginative educational program aimed at reaching all ages from junior high or younger and up with basic facts concerning all the addictions.

Choice of content and methods will be determined, to a large extent, by the objectives of an educational program and the target groups it hopes to reach. The broad aim is to enable an entire congregation to understand addictions and see them as spiritual wholeness concerns in which churches have large stakes. In addition, congregations should have several more limited and strategic target groups. These include: teenagers and preteens who are making decisions about alcohol, nicotine, and other hazardous drugs; parents who are searching for ways to prepare their children to cope constructively with the ubiquitous availability of addictive substances including alcohol; and addicted people and their families who desperately need the help of their faith community. In addition, in most congregations there are employers who have numerous untreated addicted persons among their workers and colleagues; health professionals with addicts among their clients, patients, or colleagues; teachers who struggle to understand and teach disturbed children and youth from addicted families; and opinion molders who through social prestige, political leadership, or involvement in the mass media help to create constructive understanding of community problems. By reaching target groups such as these with an enlightened view of alcohol and other drug problems, clergy can enable key people in the community to think, write, speak, vote, and otherwise act more creatively and responsibly on this network of complex problems.

An essential part of congregational addiction educational programs is to invite learners to reflect on the uses of alcohol and other drugs—their own and that of society—from a Christian ethical perspective. A strategic launching pad for such reflection and discussion is a brief survey of biblical views about wine, drinking, drunkenness, and abstinence. Fortunately Margaret Fuad has done a succinct scholarly review of relevant passages in both Hebrew Scriptures and the New Testament.[17] It is important to emphasize, as she does, the huge differences between biblical times and today. The changes that alter ethical decisions about responsible use and nonuse profoundly include the heavy pressures and lack of community support in contemporary urban society; the lack of unified sanctions controlling dangerous drinking and drug use; the high alcohol content of modern distilled liquor compared with wine; and the lethal dangers posed by using alcohol and drugs in our hi-tech world. Fuad illustrates the last difference with a touch of humor by pointing to the dangers of driving a powerful car versus riding a donkey when under the influence. As she says, donkeys were usually sober.

In thinking about ethical perspectives in alcohol and drug use, it is essential to go beyond biblical passages referring explicitly to alcohol. Ethical reflection should be framed in the broader context of the biblically based understanding of the good life, healing, and God's power to liberate us from all of the countless forms of captivity. On this theme, Jesus read from the scroll of the prophet Isaiah in his hometown synagogue this powerful passage: "The spirit of the Lord is upon me . . . to proclaim release to the captives and recovery of sight to the blind, to let the oppressed go free" (Luke 4:18). The psalmist also affirms God's liberating power in this familiar passage: "I waited patiently for the LORD; he inclined to me and heard my cry. He drew me up from the desolate pit, out of the miry bog, and set my feet upon a rock, making my steps secure. He put a new song in my mouth, a song of praise to our God" (Psalm 40:1-3). It also can be enlightening to view alcohol and drug issues in the light of Christians' responsibilities to implement Jesus' two great commandments—loving God, other people, and ourselves wholeheartedly and effectively. (See Mark 12:30-31.)

Addiction education is most effective when it is integrated into the church's ongoing program of education concerning Christian approaches to social and health problems. In many settings, it is good educational strategy to approach presentations concerning alcoholism and other chemical addictions through the sickness concept and hope-inspiring stories of Twelve Step recoveries.[18] Educationally these provide the best entree to the interest of many persons and the best way of avoiding the widespread resistance among church people to discussing alcohol problems. Because most people are intrigued by the dramatic story of A.A., this is a natural point of departure for discussing the nature, prevention, and treatment of alcoholism and other chemical addictions. Even though most people have at least a superficial knowledge of A.A., their understanding often is incomplete or erroneous. People often listen with rapt attention when evidence is presented that alcoholism and nicotine addiction are life-threatening illnesses to which people expose themselves when they drink or smoke. Many young people today find it nearly impossible to consider that taking a drink is a significant ethical issue, but they can readily grasp the dangers of addictive diseases or a disastrous alcohol-related auto accident. Speakers from A.A., N.A., Al-Anon, and Alateens often make unforgettable impacts on church groups by personalizing drinking problems and recovery from addictions.

Whatever is taught about alcohol, drugs, and addictions should be presented in the context of a positive view of the Christian life as a challenging adventure and a good gift from God, whatever its problems. Emphasis on what churches are *for* is many times more effective than stopping with what they are *against*. Within this frame of reference, informed decisions about many issues of Christian living, including responsible use or nonuse of addictive substances, can best be made. Within an enlightened understanding of addictions and of Christian lifestyles, a clear picture can be formed in learners' minds of their congregation's mission to help persons broken by personal and social sicknesses, including alcoholics and other addicts.

Alcohol, drug, and addiction education in churches, schools, and families should have at least three phases, each with its own objective. The first is head-level understanding. The best information available and the most plausible theories about the nature, causes, prevention, and treatments of chemical addictions should be presented. Special emphasis should be given to knowing the early warning signs of addictions.

Education should always aim at awakening reality-based hope that can be personalized by telling spiritually uplifting A.A. recovery stories of individuals who had been given up as hopeless addicts. These can help show that the hopelessness that still attaches itself to alcoholics and drug addicts in the minds of many people is often inappropriate. Hopeful as well as hopeless expectations tend to be self-fulfilling beliefs. In treating addictions, an old axiom must be reversed to read—"Where there's hope, there's life!" It is crucial, of course, to avoid oversimplifying the enigmatic complexities of addictions, and to avoid painting an overly optimistic picture that ignores the dark realities and unsolved problems that still exist in abundance in the area of addictions.

The objective of phase two of alcohol and drug education is to enable people to move beyond head-level understanding by developing heart understanding of persons suffering from these sicknesses. Achieving this objective involves helping people modify their attitudes and feelings about addicted persons. It also involves increasing compassion toward them and their families, and saying "yes" to them as persons of worth, whatever their slips or continuing problems in living. Relatively little change in basic attitudes occurs in most didactic education. At least two things seem to modify attitudes. First, they are changed in relationships and through experiencing something new that produces cognitive and emotional dissonance because it does not fit learners' old images, feelings, and assumptions. To illustrate, an attitude-altering experience is to ask church school teachers to attend two open meetings of A.A., Al-Anon, or A.C.A. as part of their preparation for teaching about alcohol, alcoholism, and other drug problems.[19] Person-to-person relating to recovering people in Twelve Step groups and hearing their personal stories often does more to lessen punitive attitudes toward alcoholics than any other educational experiences. Such contacts enable teachers to discover that recovering addicts are people—frequently fine, likable people with much more in common with themselves than they had thought.

The second dynamic factor in producing attitudinal change is that it often happens spontaneously when people get involved in constructive action on personal and social problems. For many reasons, church members should be encouraged to do things like serving on local Councils on Alcoholism and Drug Dependence, and volunteering to help in treatment facilities and halfway houses. To do this not only provides needed service but also helps correct relationship-blocking stereotypes concerning chemically dependent people. Involvement in a congregation's own chemical addiction action program can be invaluable for the same reasons.

The ultimate test of a congregation's loving and redemptive concern is its ability to accept the socially unacceptable, including addicted people. The pervasive attitudinal climate of a congregation with respect to addictions and addicts provides either a bridge or a barrier to helping them. If it is to be a bridge, then the icy lumps of judgmentalism that linger in some religious people's psyches will have to be melted by acquiring caring, Christian compassion. Some people must be helped to resolve their fears of addicted persons and their anger toward them. This will enable them to join hands in mutual acceptance as forgiven sinners who also experience areas of unfreedom in their lives. Only then can individual Christians and congregations discover their fuller potentials to become channels of God's healing love.

Blocks to fuller acceptance of others are rooted in a lack of self-acceptance and the resulting inability to accept God's acceptance. In small personal growth and spiritual discovery groups, participants often experience the removal of these inner barriers. Some who suffered from fear of addicted people discover that it is because addicts and other social deviants threaten them psychologically and they turn their anxiety into hostility. Working through to a living experience of grace-full acceptance that does not need to be earned because it is already there in relationships can heal the self-righteousness that keeps many good people cut off from socially rejected people.

Some church people are troubled by the sickness understanding of addictions, believing erroneously that it denies the existence of ethical issues in these problems. This is a serious dilemma for them because the sickness concept is the most effective foundation for either prevention or therapy. Wrestling with the responsibility issues, as discussed in chapter 10, often helps people resolve this dilemma. Addicts are simply people with obsessive-compulsive conditions called addictions. Their behavior, like yours and mine, reflects a complex mixture of compulsiveness and freedom, accountability and drivenness, sin and sickness. A key issue in relating to addicts is how one understands the ethical aspects. To moralize, as we have seen, is utterly futile. But to treat the addicted as persons with the capacity to become more responsible may help to encourage them to move beyond their areas of unfreedom. This approach is close to the heart of effective caring, counseling, and Twelfth Step work.

To maximize their effectiveness in any dimension of the addiction field, clergy, like lay team members, need both head and heart understanding. This informed, empathic understanding is often called a therapeutic or healing attitude toward severely troubled people. The attitude will be reflected in all caring and counseling relationships with them and in the tone of what is said in alcohol and drug education. In short, the ability to implement any of the strategies described in this chapter will be enhanced by the presence of a healing attitude involving both head and heart understanding.

This empathic understanding enables clergy or others to "tune in" to the inner world of feelings and meanings of addicts and their families, as least to some degree. A therapeutic attitude may open the door to the chaotic complexity of their fears and despair, and their haunting feelings of aloneness in a bizarre world that they cannot believe others could possibly comprehend. The healing attitude also involves some warm positive regard for the troubled, seeing them as persons of unconditional worth. With their fragile self-esteem, addicted people usually desperately need positive regard. They hunger, like starving people, for the acceptance they cannot yet give themselves. Because emotional immaturity often causes addicts to behave in ways that are selfish, irresponsible, and impulse-ridden, it may be difficult to remain accepting and nonjudgmental. It sometimes helps me to remind myself that what Longfellow said about enemies is equally applicable to addicts and their families: "If we could read the secret history of our enemies, we should find in each man's life sorrow and suffering enough to disarm all hostility."

Constructive approaches to addictions also can be facilitated by recognizing that they are not isolated problems. Rather they are expressions of the sin and sickness of our society in which all of us are participants. Their problems are a part of the problems in which all of us share in differing degrees and with varying symptoms. This sense of involvement in the cultural sicknesses of which addictions are painful expressions, and an honest recognition of our complicity in the kind of society that produces addictions, are strengths that help overcome distancing from addicts. This was a strength of Lyman Beecher, over a century ago, when he wrote concerning alcoholism, "For verily we all have been guilty in this thing."[20]

The recognition by clergy and other helping persons that they have a basic kinship with addicted persons, helps them accept the addicted without condescension. Deep inside themselves, helping persons must be aware that addicts are not essentially addicts. Rather they are essentially human beings *with* addictions. This affirms their humanity and provides a sense of linkage in helping persons with their shared humanity. To be able to establish this vital link, helping persons must be aware of their own dark side, their own addictions, inner conflicts, dishonesties, anxieties, compulsions, and grandiosities. It is equally important that they be aware of the need for the grace of God in their own lives. I recall the wise words of the late Otis Rice: "More than anything else we need to learn to love the alcoholics. The only way I know to do this is to remember that God loves them, and to remember how much he puts up with in order to love us." The words of Tolstoy come to mind at this point: "Only he who knows his own weakness can be just to the weaknesses of others."

The healing attitude dawns in helping persons as they work with addicted persons when they move beyond, "There but for the grace of God go I" to the deflating awareness, *"There go I!"* This awareness removes the barriers inhibiting the flow of God's healing love in those relationships. But such empathic identification is difficult. To identify with the essential humanness of the despairing threatens our fragile defenses against our own despair. To recognize that addicted persons are much more like us than different from us, shakes the foundation of our defensive self-image. To accept this truth at a deep level requires an inward surrender of subtle feelings of spiritual superiority. A self-aware seminary student of mine once referred to this as "getting off the omnipotence kick." Fortunately, even a partial surrender of one's defensive superiority feelings melts a hole in the icy barrier of pride that keeps people—especially shattered people—at a distance.

Clergy's own spiritual life can help them maintain therapeutic empathy by reminding them that they are only finite, fallible channels through which the healing, growth-producing energies of God's love can, at times, flow. With this awareness, they may be better able to accept that there are many people they cannot help, and many others they can help only in very limited ways, no matter how hard they try. They may even accept that some addicts who improve do so not because of what they do, but in spite of it. This awareness helps avoid the false humility of unproductive self-blame when they fail, even as they look honestly to discover counseling errors that they need not repeat. Their own experiences of growth, reconciliation, and healing sustains their trust in the ultimate power of the divine Spirit.

This faith helps deter them from applying the dead-end label "hopeless" to addicted people they cannot help. The healing attitude includes both a clear awareness of one's limitations and also one's potential effectiveness as an instrument of healing. A certain alcoholic who considered himself an agnostic had been drunk nearly every night for five years. Finally, he came into A.A. When I heard him speak, he had been sober for three-and-a-half years. Here is what he said about how he was helped by a minister:

> "For the first seven months in A.A. I was dry on conceit and ego pride. I had nothing to do with the Higher Power, and no support from the outside. I stayed sober, but it's a hell of a way to stay happy. At the end of that time my wife told me, 'You're just as drunk in your mind as you ever were.' I went to have a talk with a member of the local clergy. That day I saw the grass, the buds, the sky in a way I'd never seen them before. I've never lost the experience I had that day, and I now have a speaking acquaintance with Someone greater than myself."

It is safe to assume that the minister brought something of the precious ingredient called the therapeutic attitude to that relationship. In this I-Thou meeting of two human beings, something wonderful occurred that changed the direction of that alcoholic's existence, turning him toward life, opening his eyes to the world around him, and beginning his relationship with his own Higher Power. What a blessing that clergy can sometimes be instruments in such a life-transforming process!

Fourth Strategy: Implementing Multilevel Prevention

Prevention should be a major focus and objective of congregations' alcohol and drug efforts. Churches have a rich mother lode of largely unmined opportunities to become more effective in preventing addictions. In this country, churches have more regular, face-to-face contacts with more adults than any other institution. This puts a tremendous potential opportunity at their fingertips. Ask yourself, what could occur if a substantial portion of these far flung religious organizations developed innovative, imaginative programs of prevention aimed at everyone from grammar school children through adults in all stages on their life journeys? Chemical addictions, with their gigantic costs in wasted dollars and, more important, wasted lives, could be reduced significantly. Many more people would learn how to protect themselves and their families from this entrapment.

Addiction prevention should be part of congregations' larger strategy for preventing a broad range of interrelated individual, family, and societal problems. The primary preventive method obviously is a comprehensive program of alcohol and drug education and wellness enhancement as described above. Congregations are ideal settings in which to implement many of the recommendations detailed under each of the five levels of prevention described in the second chapter. Here is a summary of ways congregations can prevent addictions. They can:

- Prevent addictions at their roots by enabling parents to learn how to nurture their children's mental and spiritual wellness and thus reduce their receptivity to the seeds of all addictions. (The leaders of the Emmanuel Movement called for churches to offer "preventive psychiatry," which could help parents prevent the "wounds of childhood.") There is no more important mission of churches than to help parents do what they want to do but often cannot—raise children who are physically, mentally, emotionally, and spiritually healthy. To the degree that parents are effective in this, their children will be less likely to use chemicals or addictive behaviors to dull anxieties and compensate for personal feelings of inadequacy. This educational ministry helps fulfill the central purpose of churches—to nurture spiritually centered growth of persons in developing their God-given potentials. It is noteworthy that the words "health," "whole," and "holy" all come from a single Anglo-Saxon root.
- Teach people how to satisfy their need for psychological, sexual, and spiritual highs in nonchemical ways.
- Understand, accept, and teach the sickness concept of both chemical and behavioral addictions as the most viable foundation for prevention and healing.

- Influence public policy decisions so that highly addictive chemicals are not advertised, and are made less attractive and less easily available, particularly to vulnerable people like many adolescents.
- Alert those with family histories of addictions to their high risk because of psychological and probably physiological-genetic factors that increase their vulnerability.
- Educate people concerning the wide range of biochemical addictiveness of different drugs and awaken their resistance to using those that are highly addictive such as nicotine.
- Teach people the early warning signs that signal the onset of addictions and thus increase the possibility that they will seek treatment in the early stages.
- Prevent the advanced stages by encouraging hidden victims and their families to seek help sooner.
- Support family members in using tough love in interventions designed to motivate addicted loved ones to accept treatment.
- Help youth, parents, and families develop healthy spirituality and life-guiding values so that they will be less likely to use chemicals or addictive activities as spiritual shortcuts that turn out to be dead ends.
- Mobilize community attitudes so that unified social sanctions will control excessive, dangerous, and addiction-causing uses of alcohol and other consciousness-changing drugs.
- Use and support community treatment programs, including Twelve Step groups and community preventive education programs.
- Provide congregational support and pastoral guidance during people's accidental and developmental crises and times of loss that may precipitate the onset of addictions.
- Teach children and youth how to distinguish relatively safe and responsible uses of consciousness-changing chemicals from dangerous and irresponsible uses.

Evaluating Abstinence as a Method of Prevention

Although abstaining from all use of beverage alcohol and other recreational drugs seems to have declining support in mainline churches today, it is still the choice of many Christians, especially among those from theologically conservative backgrounds. Let's examine the strengths and limitations of abstinence as a means of enhancing people's general wellness and preventing addictions.

A cogent case can be made for abstinence as the only 100 percent certain way of preventing problem drinking and drug use. Everyone who drinks, smokes, or uses drugs becomes part of what epidemiologists call the "exposed population." People who decide to abstain, detach themselves from the at-risk group, even if they are addiction-vulnerable for psychophysiological or sociocultural reasons. Addiction-prone family members and those highly vulnerable for other reasons are wise to protect themselves in this way.

There are other valid reasons why many people choose abstinence. In our addictive society, choosing not to use dangerous consciousness-altering chemicals can be prudent and ethically wise. Abstinence can be an effective way to model healthier lifestyles for children and youth, as well as those with high addiction vulnerability. Getting high chemically diminishes conscious controls and judgment that can be dangerous in our modern society. It is fortunate that many people prefer experiencing uplift and minivacations from hard reality by nonchemical means such as meditation, prayer, music, sex, exercise, people, or nature. Medical evidence that drinking and drug use, even in moderation, may diminish or jeopardize robust health is another reason for choosing to abstain.[21]

Educationally, it is important to present the benefits of abstinence as one desirable option in a constructive lifestyle and as one option in a multifaceted approach to preventing addictions. If abstinence is presented as the *only* truly responsible and ethical option, several problematic consequences result. It does not provide ethical guidelines for the majority of people in our society who do not accept this absolute position. One-track abstinence teaching does not equip children and youth with what they must learn in order to make constructive decisions in our alcohol and drug saturated society. The majority of American teenagers eventually experiment with alcohol. Many also do so with nicotine and illegal drugs like marijuana. If they have been taught that there are only two kinds of people—the good people who don't and the bad people who do—they lack internalized ethical guidelines required to distinguish between relatively responsible and grossly irresponsible use, if they choose not to abstain. When the total abstinence position is presented in a rigid, morally absolute manner, it invites the "forbidden fruit" responses by teens during the rebellious phase of their search for autonomous identity. Studies of drinking by college students have found that those from rigid abstinence backgrounds, when they defy the taboos they learned in childhood, tend to drink more heavily and get drunk more frequently than do those who grew up in families where adults practiced responsible moderation.

When abstinence is presented as "the only Christian way," people of religious commitment are polarized into two opposing camps—the users and the nonusers. This has serious consequences in terms of preventing addictions. As we have seen, a significant societal cause of proliferating addictions is the absence of broad social sanctions in American life, supported by many diverse groups. What is sorely needed is agreement between users and nonusers, that chemical addictions are genuine, highly treatable illnesses, that driving after using alcohol or drugs is always ethically wrong, as is drunkenness and excessive use of other drugs. Religious individuals and institutions should join their voices and use their collective influence to stimulate the development of such generally accepted preventive attitudes in American life. The abstinence versus moderation polarizing among religious groups wastes valuable time and leadership energy. Those who choose not to drink alcohol or use other drugs, and those who do so responsibly need each other as allies in preventing society's addiction epidemic. They need to agree to disagree without being disagreeable so that they can join hands in providing both effective treatment and prevention.

Parents who choose personal abstinence will help their children most by discussing use/nonuse issues in a matter-of-fact manner, without making it a federal case. Studies have shown that the most important variable influencing teens to use or not use alcohol and drugs, is parental example. What parents try to teach their children on these issues is much less influential than what they actually do. And what parents teach and do is much more important than what children and youth are taught in school or church.

It is important to affirm that churches, through the years, undoubtedly have prevented many addictions by their crisis caring, spiritual nurture, and growth ministries. To the extent that congregations succeed in helping people gain a sense of real belonging in a lonely world, to love and be loved in a violence-plagued society, to find meaning in living and a faith for meeting death constructively, they have prevented people from needing to escape into the pseudospiritual satisfactions that contribute to many addictions. No one can know how many people might have lived and died with untreated addictions but did not because of the faith, fellowship, and spiritual feeding that they found in their congregation. This time-tested preventive ministry can be enhanced immeasurably today and tomorrow. How? It is already happening in congregations that are joining the wisdom of the Christian heritage with the continuing revelations of God's healing truths in the psychosocial sciences, and the healing methods of contemporary counseling and psychotherapy.[22]

Fifth Strategy: Providing Care and Counseling for Addicted Persons

Earlier chapters 11, 12, and 13 have presented many methods by which clergy and other counselors can help addicted people find sanity, sobriety, and continuing spiritual growth. As more and more Twelve Step and other treatment programs have been developed, the roles of clergy and their congregations has gradually been redefined. But the contributions of individual ministers and their churches are still very valuable and much needed. There is a wide variety of needs among addicted people and their families. Some respond to church-sponsored programs who do not do so in Twelve Step programs. Many find stable, maturing sobriety by a combination of Twelve Step and church programs.

Congregations and other religious institutions have numerous unique contributions that they can and should make to the healing and helping processes in addictions. Of their special resources for this task, possessed by no other institutions in our society, one in particular stands out. Helping facilitate spiritual and ethical healing and continuing growth in people's lives is an essential ingredient in both prevention and treatment. This is a ministry that religious organizations are uniquely equipped to provide. In fact, all aspects of a congregation's drug and alcohol programs should be designed to help people move toward greater spiritual and ethical health.

The focus of ministry changes before, during, and after treatment. Before addicted people seek help and achieve stable sobriety, clergy and congregations should focus their efforts on supporting distressed family members. During the early and often tenuous stages of recovery, ministry should focus on encouraging addicts and their families to stay in Twelve Step or other treatment programs, and help them find alternative paths to recovery if what they try first proves to be ineffective. After an addict has achieved reasonably stable sobriety, clergy should stay available to help them rebuild their relationships and live on a firm spiritual and interpersonal foundation. The numerous small spiritual growth groups available in many congregations can be invaluable in this growth phase of recovery.

These illustrations of what churches have done or are doing to help addicted people are presented to stimulate your own creative juices:

- An East Coast church sponsored an experimental program in alcoholic rehabilitation for men on probation because of alcohol-related crimes. The weekly offerings include A.A., mental health and alcoholism speakers, educational films, and discussion of spiritual resources.
- A Southern California church sponsored weekly "Sunday Night with Recovered Alcoholics" for these purposes: to create an occasion and an

atmosphere in which members of the clergy and other professional people could learn more about addictions and observe recovering alcoholics telling their own stories; to give the recovering alcoholics a similar opportunity to listen to professionals who were interested and knowledgeable about addictions; and third, to give recovering alcoholics an opportunity to learn a variety of ways to implement the Eleventh Step, "to seek through prayer and meditation to improve their conscious contact with God." Recovering alcoholics and professional people, in approximately equal numbers, were invited to these meetings.

- On the West Coast a halfway house for alcoholic men was sponsored cooperatively by several churches of one denomination. A church of another denomination sponsored a halfway house for addicted women and their children. In each of these facilities, laypersons within the congregations were trained to serve as volunteers.

- Numerous congregations have invited recovering addicts and their families to join their existing Bible study, prayer, spiritual nurture, and grief recovery groups. Other churches have set up special groups for recovering people and their families. Such groups seem to be most effective when they are co-led by a clergyperson and a spiritually mature layperson who knows the recovery journey firsthand. (Clergy and mental health professionals in those congregations sometimes provide lay growth group leaders with coaching in facilitating small groups.) Such groups are excellent ways of responding to the need expressed by many in Twelve Step programs who reach a certain point in their spiritual growth and then want more resources for continuing this crucial aspect of recovery.

Training a Caring Team

Many congregations greatly strengthen their ministry to burdened people by setting up and training lay caring teams. These are task groups composed of carefully selected people committed to caregiving to burdened people as the primary focus of their lay ministry. Such groups usually function under the guidance of their clergy, supplementing and broadening their pastoral work with the troubled. These teams can be important assets for helping addicted people and their families, particularly if they include stable A.A. and Al-Anon members of both genders, and a health professional who is acquainted with current addiction treatments. A lay caring team should meet regularly for in-service training, and this should include briefings on Twelve Step programs, and on identifying and responding to families in which there are hidden or unhidden addicts. The needs of persons in addicts' family and friends offer many opportunities for lay care-givers, especially if some team members are acquainted with addicted family dynamics firsthand. They can provide ongoing person-to-person spiritual support and practical help that clergy and professional counselors do not have time to provide. Thus, lay caring teams become valuable allies in the ministries of both clergy and the alcohol and drugs study-action group. Depending on their other duties, it may be feasible to ask a lay caring team to be responsible for the functions of the addiction study-action team. But it may be better to have separate teams that often work together, with the latter composed of persons who have special interest in addictions.

Helping Clergy with Their Own Addictions

The fact that addictions can happen to anyone is demonstrated force-fully for many people by the frequency with which clergy and their families become addicted. There are now numerous treatment programs that specialize in helping chemically dependent clergy. Consider the story of one addicted minister. The women at a regular Thursday afternoon closed women's discussion meeting of A.A. went around the table introducing themselves. One said, "My name is Sharon and I am an alcoholic." She is also a United Methodist pastor serving churches during her active addiction and subsequent recovery. Sharon recalls that when she finally admitted the painful truth to herself,

> "powerful words from Deuteronomy flooded my mind: 'I have set before you life and death . . . Therefore, choose life.' God had opened my eyes to the seriousness of my disease. For an alcoholic, drinking is suicide. In my confession, my private moment of truth with God, I was being given a chance and a choice."

Sharon reports that, through her recovery, new understandings of some Bible passages have come to her. She shares one of these:

> "'If any one is in Christ, he is a new creation; the old has passed away, behold the new has come.' As I neared one year of sobriety, I celebrated that newness. Physically and spiritually, I am a new person. No longer abusing my body, the pain and sleeplessness, headaches, and other symptoms of my disease are gone. My hair has a new shine. Inside, I have found strength through weakness. 'When I am weak, then I am strong.' Those words of Paul have new meaning for me."

Sharon R. shared her recovery story in a denominational publication for clergy "because other clergy alcoholics are still drinking and still suffering, and feeling terribly alone."[23]

Many clergy who are not chemically addicted have self-destructive behavioral addiction. Two that are very common are work addiction and codependency. The latter damages the spiritual health and retards the spiritual growth of both themselves and their congregations severely. When clergy are dependent on their parishioners' dependency, they lock themselves and their people into patterns of interaction that keep both from maturing spiritually. Dependent parishioners often alternate between worshiping their ministers and rebelling against their controlling, overprotective leadership. And afflicted clergy hover chronically on the brink of burnout, suffering from the profound loneliness of those who are seduced by dependent people into acting like savior figures.

An astute clergyman named Chilton Knudsen has spelled out "Twelve Steps for Clergy Recovering from Codependence," an adaptation of A.A.'s steps. He rephrases the first step to read, "We admitted we were powerless over our congregations; and that our codependent behavior was making our lives unmanageable."[24] And now the good news! Clergy who recover from codependency or any other addictive behavior usually have new empathy for people still trapped in addictions. They discover with joy, unexpectedly, that they have become more effective as counselors because they have accepted the fact that they are wounded healers!

Sixth Strategy: Caregiving and Counseling for Families with Addicted Members

This dimension of ministry was explored extensively in the previous chapter. The focus of this ministry, like that to the addicted, has both continuity and change before, during, and after sobriety has been achieved by the addicted member. As mentioned above, helping the family usually is the primary focus of ministry before their addicted members become open to treatment. There are three key objectives during this phase: (1) doing everything possible to prevent the family from isolating themselves protectively by withdrawing from what had been meaningful relationships in a congregation and community; (2) encouraging them to become involved in Al-Anon and Alateens; and (3) helping them interrupt their codependent behavior both to protect their own well-being and possibly motivate their addicted family member to accept help. The basic ministry of the first objective—sustaining inclusion in the life of a lively congregation—continues to be invaluable during treatment when family members often need support and understanding of the recovery process, including their own recovery from codependency. After stable sobriety has become a reality, families need a congregation's ongoing sustaining ministry and its spiritual growth nurturance programs, as well as clergy's guidance in readjusting to their new situation.

Here are two concrete examples of how congregations have responded to the needs of addicted families:

- A community center on alcohol and drug problems set up a series of afternoon discussion sessions at a church in a marginal economic area for families of those with addiction problems. Since people from this economically depressed area seldom come to the center for help, it was decided to take the center to them, with the help of the congregation. This illustrates how churches can collaborate with community agencies to make innovative services for addicts and their families available. Churches also are well advised to call on community alcohol and drug agencies in setting up their programs of education, prevention, and treatment.

- Numerous churches have developed special sharing and caring groups for family members of addicts. These serve to complement Al-Anon group meetings by offering Christian resources for coping with and perhaps growing from the stressful experiences of living in an addicted family system. Such groups may offer support to spouses and parents who need to separate from their addicted family member for their own well-being, and are having trouble doing so. These groups have the additional advantage of being held in settings that are already familiar to church members.

Seventh Strategy: Reaching Out to the Community

An essential ministry in all healthy religious organizations is to have active programs for nurturing healing and social, economic, and political justice not only in their local communities, but also in their denominations, nation, and wider world. This is their prophetic mission that helps them to be "the salt of the earth" and "the light of the world." Three ministers expressed these insights in their responses to my original research: "The Church's job, I think, is to shed the searchlight of the gospel on the causes of human misery of which alcoholism is a symptom." A second declared, "We can prevent it by helping people learn how to live in a complex world." A third wrote: "The best preventive measure for alcoholism is developing normal, wholesome personalities in tune with God."

All that clergy and congregations do that diminishes injustice, violence, and environmental degradation, while they enhance justice, peace and caring for God's creation, helps prevent all manner of social pathology including addictions. It does so by contributing to the well-being of persons and their institutions. A great preacher of the early decades of this century, Harry Emerson Fosdick, once observed that persons wrapped up in themselves make very small packages. The same is true of congregations. Outreach to their wider communities enables churches to avoid becoming small, ingrown spiritual cliques narcissistically serving only their own members. This is why outreach in both prophetic action and service to those in need is essential to the spiritual health of congregations. Churches today are challenged to devise imaginative ways of getting more of the millions of their dedicated lay men, women, and youth, directly involved in ministries focusing on many types of personal and social problems, including the addiction pandemic.

As vital responses to their responsibility to their wider communities, clergy and congregations should support the sound prevention and therapeutic addiction programs and agencies that function on local, state, and national levels. Here are some concrete ways that this support has been implemented:

- In their local communities, many clergy and lay people have given support by volunteering time, financial help, and publicity to these programs. Simply visiting community agencies to learn about them and affirm their constructive programs is supportive. One such program is called "Fighting Back." This is a network of prevention programs in numerous cities focusing on school children in grades 4 to 8. It provides guidance, mentoring and nurturing self-esteem aimed at reducing their use of illegal drugs and alcohol, and supports other programs providing youth mentoring for those at risk. Dr. Spickard played a key role in establishing and directing this network.
- One minister tells how he "facilitated some friendly contacts between A.A. and a judge of the municipal court as well as the personnel manager of a large industrial firm."
- Many clergy support Twelve Step programs, the Salvation Army, halfway houses, and comprehensive treatment programs by making referrals after conferring with staff members there.
- Clergy can and should encourage their congregations to use their individual and collective influence to help shape public discourse and political policy to support effective treatment and prevention of chemical addictions. One minister reported, "I did some behind-the-scenes work to get the city welfare association to begin the educational approach to the problem in the community." Another told of working

"to promote consideration of alcoholism as a public health problem with local council of social agencies and state council of social welfare."

- Congregation members have worked to encourage both public schools and community agencies to make current information about addictions and their treatment widely available.
- Many congregations have welcomed A.A., Al-Anon, Alateen, A.C.A., and Nar-Anon groups to use their fellowship halls. This can be a mutually enriching and enlightening experience, particularly if clergy and church members take the initiative in getting acquainted by occasionally attending open meetings and by inviting speakers from these groups to address interested church groups.
- Where basic alcohol and drug education and treatment programs are in short supply in their communities, concerned clergy and their lay leaders often cooperate with other community groups in spearheading efforts that develop these.
- Working through hospital boards to encourage all hospitals to accept alcoholics and drug addicts as they do any other sick patients is an important form of community outreach. It is particularly ironic when church-related hospitals have policies (written or simply understood by admissions staffs) of not accepting addicted persons as patients.
- Mobilizing public support for local and state addiction programs is another important outreach that may prevent budgetary strangulation of needed programs.

Most of the strategies described above for use by local congregations can be adapted advantageously by denominational and ecumenical groups. The need is for greatly increased collaboration by religious groups across denominational, faith, and even national lines. To adapt a familiar slogan, people of religious caring and commitment need to think and act locally but also to think and act globally on this as well as other societal sicknesses. Some leadership has been given by ecumenical bodies such as the National Council of Churches and the World Council of Churches (through the World Health Organization), in designing joint strategies, resources, and action plans. This leadership should be supported by Christians at the grass roots. The need for broad national and international approaches is illustrated by the seductive advertising of alcohol and cigarettes in poor countries as described in chapter 3. As with our country's exporting of violence through huge sales of armaments to poor, developing countries, working to reverse this exporting of ill health should be high on the world mission outreach agenda of concerned clergy and their congregations!

Harbingers of Hope

Since reality-based hope has been a theme in these pages, it seems appropriate to close this chapter and book by highlighting some rays of reality-based hope in the field of religious groups and addictions.

- Twelve Step programs continue to generate widespread hope and help. Anderson Spickard affirms this with this bad news/good news statement: The bad news is that it is difficult to overcome addictions. The good news is that today over three million men, women, and teenagers are sober because, by the grace of God, they are following a rigorous spiritual program of recovery. This program is a comprehensive approach to addiction which neither denies the power of the Holy Spirit nor overlooks the alcoholic's ultimate responsibility for his [sic] own ongoing recovery. All over the world, alcoholics whose lives have been devastated by their drinking are being healed in their bodies, minds, emotions, spirits, and relationships. Equally important, the families of alcoholics—parents, wives, husbands, children—are confronting their own damaged lives and finding healing for their deepest wounds.[25]

I say a ringing "Amen!" to this statement, as I think of the 500,000 Twelve Step recovery groups attended this week by 15 million addicted people in the U.S.A. I extend his hopeful words to all chemical and behavioral addictions.

I invite you to let your mind and spirit be lifted by these other hopeful developments in the addiction pandemic scene:

- The Alateens and A.C.A. (Adult Children of Alcoholics) movement and groups are bringing help to more and more of the millions of childhood and adult victims of addicted family systems.
- Many clergypersons are aware of their strategic opportunities and unique responsibilities in this vast area of human suffering and do a considerable amount of preventative, educational, and counseling work, often with the active support of their congregations. Of course, it must be reemphasized that in a problem area so vast and growing, awakening many others to this challenge is sorely needed.
- Countless clergy have learned much at the major summer schools of alcohol and drug problems. One theological seminary offers a Master of Arts in Alcoholism and Drug Abuse Ministry.[26] Add to this the alcoholism and addiction training programs for clergy and congregations, sponsored by some denominations and by state addiction agencies.[27]
- The publication of the important *Journal of Ministry in Addition and Recovery* to keep clergy and other religiously oriented readers informed in this changing field of ministry. It is edited by Robert H. Albers, a seminary

teacher with graduate training, experience, and expertise in theological and pastoral care issues in this ministry.[28]

- The development of alternative paths to sobriety, recovery, and discovery from a feminist and from explicitly Christian and Jewish as well as secular perspectives.

- The illuminating applications of family systems understandings of addictions to both treatment and prevention.

- The healing of the stigma that has clung to addictions for centuries as more and more people have liberated their minds and hearts by understanding them as very treatable, whole-person sicknesses.

- The growing awareness that healing people, from both their polite and stigmatized addictions, involves helping to heal the social and natural environments upon which all our healing and wholeness ultimately depends. The understanding of some way in which social context factors such as consumerism, injustices, sexism, racism, classism, ageism, and alienation from the earth are among the root causes of many addictions; and the discovery that loving bonding with the earth brings healing energies to all of us, including addicted people and their families. All this has enlarged the recovery challenge, moving it beyond individual and family recovery to include recovery of the church, our society, and our planet.

- The awareness that the century-spanning healing wisdom of our Hebrew and Christian traditions are priceless resources for preventing and healing addictions today. Many centuries before Christ lived, the Hebrew psalmist expressed feelings with which many recovering addicts can identify: "Bless the LORD, O my soul, and do not forget all his benefits—who forgives all your iniquity, who heals all your diseases, who redeems your life from the pit, who crowns you with steadfast love and mercy, who satisfies you with good as long as you live so that your youth is renewed like the eagle's" (Psalm 103:2-5).

I find hope in two other facts:
- The fact that the publisher encouraged me to revise this book and waited as I struggled to rewrite and update it, drawing on the new information that is now available.

- The last but not the least sign of hope is that you have taken time to read this book—to the end! I thank you and pray that you will create ways to bring to fulfillment the hopes generated as you read and reflected on your work with addicted people who are struggling to find healing and wholeness!

Notes

Dedication

1. His department produced a definitive U.S. government report on alcohol and drug problems. He was interviewed on the McNeil/Lehrer News Hour on July 19, 1994.

Appreciation

1. Notes from telephone conversation dated February 10, 1953.

2. In 1965, I received a moving letter from Elinor Roberts, David's widow, part of which I'm sure she would have agreed to have me share here. She said that she had two good visits with Tillich who continued to be (using his own word) "astonishable." About this book she wrote: "My own copy of *Understanding and Counseling* has passed about many times. The response has always echoed mine: This is the most helpful book I know on this subject. I often think how happy Dave would be to know the contribution your book makes and to follow the development of your career." Needless to say, few letters have ever touched me so deeply. I wept again as I experienced more of my unfinished grief work.

3. Anderson Spickard, Jr., M.D. and Barbara Thompson, *Dying for a Drink: What You Should Know About Alcoholism* (Dallas: Word Publishing, 1985), p. 15.

1. Who Are Alcoholics and Drug-Addicted Persons?

1. "Six Sermons on the Nature, Origin, Signs, Evils and Remedy of Intemperance" (New York: American Tract Society, 1827).

2. The American Society of Addictive Medicine uses these diagnostic criteria.

3. It is noteworthy that as long ago as 1955 the World Health Organization Committee on Alcohol and Alcoholism designated alcohol as a drug intermediate (in kind and degree) between *habit-forming drugs* and *addiction-producing drugs*. Later, a WHO committee dropped the distinction between habituating and addictive drugs. Instead, one term, "drug dependence," superseded the distinction with alcoholism identified as one of many forms of drug dependence.

4. "Getting Straight," *Newsweek*, June 4, 1984, p. 63.

5. Estimates of those who suffer dual diagnosis range from 10 to 40 percent of those with chemical dependencies and 25 to 40 percent of those with psychiatric problems.

6. *Alcoholics Anonymous: The Story of How Many Thousands of Men and Women Have Recovered from Alcoholism* (New York: Works Publishing, 1950), p. 43.

7. Robert V. Seliger, "How to Help an Alcoholic: A Brief Medical Summarization with Practical Suggestions and Tests" (Columbus, Ohio: School and College Service, 1951).

8. (New York: Alcoholics Anonymous World Services, Inc., 1976).

9. E. M. Jellinek, *The Disease Concept of Alcoholism* (New Haven: Hillhouse Press, 1960), pp. 36-41.

10. Blythe Sprott, professor of Health Studies at California State University, Los Angeles, has divided Jellinek's Gamma alcoholism into four subtypes: *Chronic addicted* have immediate loss of control. *Progressive addicted* experience gradual loss of control. *Reactive addicted* lose control abruptly following a traumatic episode. *Periodic addicted* (also called *Pseudoepsilon*) have irregular sober periods interspersed with binges.

11. *Quarterly Journal of Studies on Alcohol, (QJSA)*, no. 7 (June, 1946): 8-9.

12. For this descriptive term, I am indebted to the late Harry Tiebout, a psychiatrist who did a great deal of work with alcoholics.

13. Marty Mann, *Marty Mann's New Primer on Alcoholism* (New York: Holt, Rinehart & Winston, 1981), p. 40.

14. Dr. Powell elaborates on this in his book *365 Health Hints* (New York: Simon & Schuster, 1992).

15. Jennifer L. Daw, "Alcohol Problems Across the Generations," *Family Therapy News,* Dec. 1995, p. 19.

16. Rhonda Parks, "Mother and Child Bonding Vital in Curbing Addiction," *Santa Barbara News Press,* March 21, 1992, p. B7.

17. In developing countries where excessive drinking is soaring, it is rarely regarded as a health issue. Alcohol-related problems are seen as something to be tackled after the "real issues" of economic development, dealing with gigantic foreign debts, and conquering infectious diseases.

18. Mark B. Sobell and Linda C. Sobell, *Problem Drinkers* (New York: Guilford Press), p. 3.

19. Most of these cost figures were cited by the *Wellness Letter,* University of California at Berkeley, February 1993, p. 4

20. *Santa Barbara News Press,* June 7, 1995, p. A6.

21. Ibid., September 8, 1993, p. A4.

22. *The Clipsheet,* Methodist Board of Temperance, Washington D.C., July 25, 1955.

23. Alcoholism expert Dwight Anderson once told this poignant story of the tragic cost of alcoholism.

2. Multiple Causes of Addictions, Multiple Levels of Prevention

1. Landis, a faculty member at Columbia University, was an invaluable member of my doctoral dissertation committee there.

2. Henry David Thoreau, *Walden, or Life in the Woods* (New York: Dodd, Mead, & Company, 1946), p. 9.

3. See Wise's classic volume, *Religion in Illness and Health* (New York: Harper and Brothers, 1942), p. 37.

4. Conversation with the Rev. Jim Rhoads, April 27, 1992.

5. "Children of Alcoholic Parents Raised in Foster Homes," in *Alcohol, Science and Society* (New Haven: Journal of Studies on Alcohol, 1945), p. 128.

6. Study cited by Kenneth Blum, et al., "Neurogenetics of Compulsive Disease: Neuronutrients as Adjuncts to Recovery," in Barbara Wallace, ed., *The Chemically Dependent: Phases of Treatment and Recovery* (New York: Brunner/Mazel, 1991), pp. 189-90. A study of adoptees by nonalcoholic parents in the U.S. found that 22.8 percent of sons who had alcoholic biological fathers and 28.1 percent of those whose alcoholic biological mothers were alcohol abusers in their adult lives. This compared with 14.7 percent of the adopted sons who did not have an alcoholic parent and 10.8 percent of daughters of alcoholic mothers became addicted, compared with only 2.8 percent of daughters who had no alcoholic parent.

7. Kenneth Blum and James E. Payne, *Alcohol and the Addictive Brain, New Hope for Alcoholics from Biogenetic Research* (New York: Free Press, 1991).

8. Barbara C. Wallace, ed. *The Chemically Dependent: Phases of Treatment and Recovery* (New York: Brunner/Mazel Publishers, 1992), p. 219.

9. This statement from my notes taken at the Yale Summer School of Alcohol Studies in 1949 has been reinforced in depth by other studies over the years.

10. It is important to remember that, among recovering alcoholics and addicts, relatively few were able to recognize that they were likely candidates before they were trapped in the process of addictions. Some exceptions to this, in my experience, are found among adult children of alcoholic and drug dependent parents who avoid drinking and using because they know they are at high risk if they do.

11. Most addiction researchers do not believe that a unique "alcoholic personality" or other distinctive personality patterns exist that predispose particular people to certain addictions. Most researchers emphasize the wide variety of psychological characteristics of

those addicted to various substances. An overview critique of thirty-seven studies of the personality profiles of chronic alcoholics concluded that evidence did not support the theory that emotionally disturbed people of one type are more likely to become alcoholics than those of other types. The fact that many addicts switch back and forth from alcohol and other drugs, as the supply of one or another becomes inaccessible, seems to belie the existence of specific physiological or psychological predisposing factors. Furthermore, the psychological problems that are common among alcoholics also are common among many non-addicted but disturbed people. It also is important to remember that addicts' psychological hang-ups are shaped by their cultures, and are shared by many of us so-called "normal" folks (including some who write books about addictions).

12. The inherent limitation of my findings is that they were derived from recollections and subjective perceptions rather than from objective measurement of preaddictive familial and psychological dynamics. They therefore must be taken as only suggestive of preaddictive vulnerability-creating factors in the interviewees.

13. The most cogent psychoanalytic explanation of alcoholism suggests that the emotional damage involved probably occurred in the very early life of the person—during the period when the child's primary way of relating to the outside world is oral. During the very early months of life babies not only ingest food but also absorb security and love through their bodies, especially through their mouths. Several addiction authorities have suggested that both alcoholism and food addictions are efforts to regress to the oral stage of human development.

14. This paraphrase is from the book Charlotte and I valued most when our children were young. See Dorothy Walters Baruch, *New Ways in Discipline, You and Your Child Today* (New York: McGraw-Hill Book Co., 1949).

15. David Roberts, *Psychotherapy and a Christian View of Man* (New York: Charles Scribner's Sons, 1950), p. 65.

16. Two interviews were incomplete and two were with siblings.

17. About half mentioned depression and mood swings. Thirty-five described themselves as "the nervous type" (or some equivalent term). Twenty-six complained of chronic insomnia and fatigue. Twenty spoke of "nervous stomach," including nine cases of ulcers, several of which had developed since they had been sober.

18. C. Buhler and D. W. Lefever, *A Rorschach Study on the Psychological Characteristics of Alcoholics* (New Haven: Hillhouse Press, 1948), p. 61.

19. H. W. Main (pseud.), *If a Man Be Mad* (Garden City, N.Y.: Doubleday & Co., 1945), p. 152.

20. Robert Albers, *Shame: A Faith Perspective* (New York: The Haworth Pastoral Press, 1995), p. 81.

21. E. M. Jellinek, *The Disease Concept of Alcoholism* (New Haven: Hilhouse Press, 1960), p. 107.

22. Donald Horton, "The Function of Alcohol in Primitive Societies," *QJSA* 4, no. 2 (1943): 233.

23. J. H. Masserman and K. S. Yum, "An Analysis of the Influence on Experimental Neuroses in Cats," *Psychosomatic Medicine*, no. 6 (1946): 36-52.

24. See Charlotte Kasl, *Many Roads, One Journey: Moving Beyond the 12 Steps* (New York: HarperCollins, 1992), p. 99.

25. Howard Clinebell, *Ecotherapy: Healing Ourselves, Healing the Earth* (Minneapolis: Fortress; Binghamton, N.Y.: Haworth, 1996).

26. Albert J. LaChance, *Greenspirit, Twelve Steps in Ecological Spirituality: An Individual, Cultural, and Planetary Therapy* (Rockport, Mass.: Element Books Ltd., 1991).

27. For elaboration of these dimensions of wellness ministry, see Howard Clinebell's *Counseling for Spiritually Empowered Wholeness: A Hope-Centered Approach* (Binghamton, N.Y.: Haworth, 1994) or *Anchoring Your Well Being: Christian Wholeness in a Fractured World* (Nashville: Upper Room Books, 1997).

28. I heard Jellinek report on this significant study and offer this diagram at the Yale Summer School of Alcohol Studies in 1961 when I was serving on the faculty there.

29. *The Disease Concept of Alcoholism,* pp. 28-29.

30. Karen Horney, *Self-Analysis* (New York: W. W. Norton & Co., 1942), p. 27.

31. I first became aware of this valuable concept when distinguished anthropologist Ruth Benedict lectured at a seminar during my graduate studies at Columbia University. See Benedict, *Patterns of Culture* (New York: Houghton Mifflin Co., 1934).

32. Anne Wilson Schaef, *When Society Becomes an Addict* (San Francisco: Harper & Row, 1987), p. 4.

33. Ibid., pp. 3, 15-16, 37.

34. Ibid.

35. According to Schaef, traditional females have accepted their role, as assigned by the "white male system," to be part of the "female companion system," defined by society and accepted by themselves, as supporters of the "white male system" and its myths. Codependence is simply "basic training for the addictive system."

36. Ibid.

37. From an interview by Anne A. Simpkinson, *Common Boundary,* March/April 1995, p. 24.

38. Ibid., p. 5.

39. This is in spite of the fact that the frequency of use of different drugs fluctuates, particularly in the adolescent subculture as peer pressures cause fads to come and go.

40. The liquor and tobacco mega-industries spend many millions of dollars each year on ads linking their products with attractive, sexy young people, sports heroes, fun and togetherness, being cool, being a macho man or sophisticated woman, and with popular holidays, including Christmas. While I was writing this section, a hopeful breakthrough came as one tobacco company finally confessed that smoking *is* addictive, *does* cause heart problems, cancers, and emphysema, and that tobacco companies do target advertising at young people 14-18.

41. Philosopher Immanuel Kant attributed the low rate of drunkenness among Jews (as well as among clergymen and clergywomen) to their weak social position. Throughout history Jews have been surrounded by hostile and stronger groups so that drunkenness on the part of any individual endangered the group. If a Jew, with pent-up rage against the oppressor, should become intoxicated and vent repressed feeling, the entire Jewish group might suffer. This Kantian explanation is probably the historic reason for strong sanctions against drunkenness.

42. Rabbi Sheldon Zimmerman in Query M. Oltzak and Stuart A. Capans, *Twelve Jewish Steps to Recovery: A Personal Guide to Turning from Alcoholism and Other Addictions* (Woodstock, Vt.: Jewish Lights, 1992), p. 8.

43. Attitudes and practices of the upper classes toward drinking, like other behavior patterns, tend to shift downward in our society. Middle-class groups have tended to be influenced by, and imitate to some degree, the customs of the higher socioeconomic groups into which they, as individuals, would like to move.

44. Inconclusive research has been done exploring various possible physiological X factors including faulty elimination of certain waste products produced in the metabolism of alcohol, lack of vitamins in the brain, or some upsetting of the enzyme balance. In a classic experiment at Yale University, laboratory rats that preferred straight water to water spiked with alcohol were used. After the enzyme system of their livers was disturbed surgically they were found to prefer spiked water, rapidly developing addictions to it that continued even after their enzyme balance was restored.

45. This information was supplemented by a telephone conversation with Les Jones, one of DrinkChoice's founders on March 14, 1997.

46. Quoted by a man suffering from the empty cup affliction in his moving letter to the editor of *Common Boundary* magazine, May/June, 1992, p. 9.

3. Understanding Drug Dependence

1. Some terms need clarification. *Drug dependence,* the term recommended by the World Health Organization's Committee on Addiction-producing Drugs, is an inclusive category.

It encompasses both *drug addiction,* used to mean producing both physiological and psychological dependence, and *drug habituation,* meaning psychological dependence. The distinction between addiction and habituation is far from clear-cut, however. It is often difficult, if not impossible, to distinguish physiological from psychological dependence because the two are inextricably intertwined. Each reinforces the other. It is true, as pointed out earlier, that various drugs possess different degrees of physiological addictiveness—e.g., from opium derivatives, cocaine, and nicotine's high degree to substances like alcohol that have lower degrees of addictiveness.

2. *Wellness Letter,* University of California at Berkeley, February 1997, p. 8.

3. *The A.A. Member and Drug Abuse: A Report from a Group of Doctors in A.A.* (New York: Alcoholics Anonymous World Services, Inc., 1964), p. 7.

4. In spite of the omission of alcohol from war on drugs, and the separate federal funding for alcohol and drug programs, the line separating alcoholics from drug abusers has eroded and treatment has increasingly converged because of polyaddictions.

5. This study was conducted by Harvard's School of Public Health and the University of Maryland Survey Research Center. The editorial was in *The United Methodist Review,* October 4, 1996, p. 6.

6. Shulamith Lala Ashenberg Straussner, ed., *Clinical Work with Substance-Abusing Clients* (New York: The Guilford Press, 1993), p. 7. The examples in this section are from this book.

7. Reported on "CNN Headline News," December 19, 1996.

8. Barry Stimmel, *The Facts About Drug Use: Coping with Drugs and Alcohol in Your Family, at Work, in Your Community* (New York: The Haworth Medical Press, 1993).

9. Much of this information is taken from Straussner, pp. 11-14; and from Stimmel, pp. 11-15.

10. The major tranquilizers are used with psychotic patients on both an outpatient and hospitalized basis to control aggressiveness and anxiety. They include thorazine, resperpine, stelazine, and such. Because they may have unpleasant side effects, they are seldom the drug of choice for those who self-medicate. The early major tranquilizers like thorazine practically revolutionized mental hospital treatment by enabling many mentally ill persons to be released and become accessible to treatment on an outpatient basis. Unfortunately, as countless patients were released from mental hospitals, the extensive network of outpatient mental health facilities that were needed to provide continuing treatment was not created. And, in recent years, drastic downsizing of such facilities has continued, causing thousands of the mentally ill to join the ranks of the homeless wandering the streets, often with no medication or other treatment.

11. Derived from barbituric acid, these drugs were first used medically in the early years of the twentieth century. Under medical supervision, they have value in reducing insomnia and anxiety. Their overuse and risky uses have produced a drug problem with two primary dangers—addictions and overdoses, accidental or intentional. They can cause all degrees of central nervous system depression from mild sedation to coma and death resulting from depression of the breathing control center of the brain.

12. A coroner's report from San Francisco in June 1995 stated that eight people had died and many more became ill when they injected such a combination of heroin and cocaine.

13. It is clear that caution is indicated in using any mood-changing drug to treat alcoholics and other addiction-prone persons. Some alcoholics become hooked on tranquilizers, even though most of these are less addictive than barbiturates.

14. Lauren Neergaard, "CDC: 1 Smoke Kills 7 Minutes of Life," *Santa Barbara News Press,* August 27, 1993, p. A1.

15. Anna Quindlen, "Hypocrisy and the Politics of Smoking," *Santa Barbara News Press,* August 6, 1992, p. A13.

16. In 1955, 42 percent of Americans smoked. In 1996 this has dropped to around 25 percent.

17. *The Johns Hopkins Medical Letter: Health After Fifty Letter,* The Johns Hopkins Medical Institute, October 1996.

18. Straussner, *Clinical Work with Substance-Abusing Clients,* p. 11.

19. "Facts about Barbiturates," Addiction Research Foundation, Toronto, Canada, 1989, p. 1.

20. These findings have already improved treatment of spinal cord injuries, learning disabilities in children, and mental illnesses such as depression, panic attacks, and obsessive-compulsive disorders. Many new drugs with minimal side effects have been developed for treating a variety of mental disorders.

21. Earl Ubell, "Secrets of the Brain," *Parade Magazine,* February 9, 1997, p. 20ff.

22. Anderson Spickard and Barbara R. Thompson, *Dying for a Drink: What You Should Know About Alcoholism* (Dallas: Word Publishing, 1985), p. 15.

23. The clinical picture in treating drug addictions changes continually as fashions in drugs change. Currently, because there is a shortage of treatment facilities for cocaine and heroin abusers, many are referred to treatment centers whose main focus is alcoholism.

24. The down side of this approach is that methadone is itself addictive and withdrawal often is more difficult than with heroin. Furthermore, those receiving methadone often tend to increase their alcohol consumption.

25. These statistics are documented in chapter one of Mary Louise Bringle's, *The God of Thinness: Gluttony and Other Weighty Matters* (Nashville: Abingdon Press, 1992).

26. How can eating disorder be identified? A series of questions developed by Overeaters Anonymous (OA) for self-identification by compulsive overeaters can help people determine if their eating is becoming addictive. According to OA, answering yes to three or more of these questions indicates that a person has a potential problem with compulsive overeating. Here are some of the key questions: Do you eat when you are not hungry? Do you have feelings of guilt and remorse after overeating? Do you eat sensibly in the presence of others and make up for it when you are alone? Do you resent it when people tell you to "use a little will power" and lose weight? Despite evidence to the contrary, have you continued to insist that you can diet successfully on your own whenever you wish? Do you crave food at a definite time of day or night other than mealtimes? Do you eat to escape worries or disappointment and reward yourself with something forbidden to cheer yourself up? Has your physician ever treated you for being overweight? Does your obsession with food make you or others unhappy? Adding two other questions to the O.A. list can help those suffering from anorexia and bulimia identify their eating disorders: Do you still feel "too fat" and continue to eat very little, even when family and close friends worry that you are too thin? Do you sometimes go back and forth between food binges and starvation dieting?

27. Mary Louise Bringle, "Swallowing the Shame: Pastoral Care Issues in Food Abuse," *The Journal of Pastoral Care* 48, no. 2 (Summer 1994), p. 135.

28. Peter de Vries, *Comfort Me with Apples,* cited in Robert Andrews, *Columbia Dictionary of Quotations* (New York: Columbia University Press, 1993), p. 338.

29. In her moving book *The Obsession: Reflections on the Tyranny of Slenderness* (New York: Harper & Row, 1981), Kim Chernin describes her own agonizing struggles to overcome bulimia. She also highlights the tragic story of a patient of existential psychiatrist Ludwig Binswanger, a contemporary of Sigmund Freud. Binswanger called her "Ellen West" in his report of this "mysterious case." Ellen, who grew up in Europe, had "the qualities of which greatness is made: passion and vision, a wild ambition, a powerful social awareness, an overpowering thirst for learning and development, and impassioned love of life, a great gift of expression." Her struggles to develop her creative gifts in her woman's body were stymied by the sexist culture—a culture saturated by fear of women's creative power and full development.

At age twenty, Ellen developed what is now known as bulimia. During extended psychoanalytic treatment, her obsession grew steadily worse. Unfortunately, Binswanger apparently had no awareness of the life-crippling impact of that sexist culture on a passionate, creative young women like Ellen. She hospitalized herself repeatedly for the physical consequences of her obsession and for her depression and sense of failure to control her destructive addiction. When her weight had shrunk to ninety-two pounds, she confessed to her husband that "my thoughts are exclusively concerned with my body, my eating, my laxatives." She told him that she was living her life "only with a view to being able to remain thin," that everything she did was subordinated to that goal. She said that it had a "terrible power" over her and that "all becoming and growing were being choked, because a single idea was filling my entire soul." She added that this all-consuming idea seemed "unspeakably ridiculous" to her. When all attempts to treat her obsession failed, she left the sanitarium, returned to her family feeling completely "incapable of dealing with life."

On her third day at home, she appeared to be utterly transformed. She was in a festive mood. For the first time in thirteen years she ate enough to be really satisfied, including butter, chocolate candy, and Easter eggs. She read poems by Rilke, Tennyson, and Goethe, took a walk with her husband, was amused by reading Mark Twain's essay on Christian Science, and wrote letters to friends. That evening she took a deadly dose of poison and was found dead the following morning. Apparently her festive mood on her last day resulted from having given up her failed struggle with her addiction and deciding to end the agony by ending her life.

30. Like work addiction, I am personally familiar with eating problems. My struggles with compulsive eating are rooted in the food-centered family in which I was raised. Our life orientation was derived in part from the farm culture and values of my parents' background. But it also came from the fact that my mother's traditional social programming limited women's full use of their intelligence and creativity to parent and wife roles. This caused Mom to invest much of her energy and considerable gifts, and gain much of her esteem, from preparing and receiving appreciation for the delicious farm-based meals she prepared for us. The unspoken message was clear—cooking and serving food was a major mode by which she communicated her caring love for her family. In addition, the Great Depression and the ongoing threat of too little money to buy food increased the emotional baggage attached to food in my childhood family. Now, when my self-love, esteem, and security feel shaky, or affirmation from others is less than I desire, I struggle with temptations to mother myself with oral satisfactions by overeating or gulping sweet, fat food I know is unhealthy.

31. For his discussion of this view see *Addiction and Grace* (San Francisco: Harper & Row, 1988), p. 14.

32. Renee Krisko, "Making Friends with Inner Emptiness," *Ground Zero*, Summer/Fall 1989, p. 4.

33. Bringle, pp. 138-42.

34. For a discussion of food as a gift of the earth, see Howard Clinebell, *Ecotherapy: Healing Ourselves, Healing the Earth* (Minneapolis: Fortress; Binghamton, N.Y.: Haworth, 1996), pp. 254-255. For a deeper exploration of this issue see the beautiful photographs and essays in *From the Good Earth: A Celebration of Growing Food Around the World* by Michael Ableman (New York: Harry N. Abrams, 1993). Ableman is an earth-loving farmer, photographer, and author who nurtures a small organic farm near Santa Barbara, California.

35. Anne Platt McGinn, "Preventing Chronic Disease in Developing Countries," *State of the World*, Lester R. Brown, et al. eds. (New York: W. W. Norton, 1997), pp. 71, 73.

36. Ibid., pp. 68-70.

37. Ibid. For a more in-depth exploration of the negative impact of alcohol in developing countries, see Lori Heise, "Trouble Brewing: Alcohol in the Third World," *World Watch*, World Watch Institute, July-August 1991, pp. 11-18.

38. "Drug Use Drops Sharply Over the Last Decade," *Santa Barbara News Press*, Nov. 9, 1997, p. 8.

4. Behavioral or Process Addictions:
Understanding and Helping

1. Reported on "CNN Headline News," August 1, 1992.

2. Lynda W. Warren and Joanne C. Ostrom, "Pack Rats: World Class Savers," *Psychology Today*, February 1988, pp. 58ff.

3. Marline Cimons, "A Travel Addict's Fear of Flying," *Los Angeles Times*, April 4, 1978, part IV, p. 1.

4. "And He's Not Pulling Your Chain," *Santa Barbara News Press*, Dec. 3, 1992, p. A2.

5. I am indebted to the superb wordsmith Ellen Goodman, *Santa Barbara News Press*, Dec. 31, 1996, p. A7. In her annual New Year's Eve media culpas column, she confesses jokingly about her journalistic goofs during the past year. In one column, she told of coining the word "sport-orexic" to describe her "lack of appetite for athletic fodder on TV." Several Greek scholars responded by pointing out that "orex" actually means longing, the opposite of what she had in mind.

6. Michael H. Hodges, "Support Group Gives Non-Fans a Sporting Chance," *The Tennessean*, September 10, 1994, p. D-1.

7. Pastoral counseling pioneer Wayne E. Oates coined the term "workaholic" and wrote a humorous and helpful book on the subject in 1968.

8. *Los Angeles Times*, June 20, 1968, part II, p. 5.

9. Diane Fassel, *Working Ourselves to Death: The High Cost of Workaholism and the Rewards of Recovery* (San Francisco: Harper San Francisco, 1990), pp. 3-4.

10. Ibid. pp. 17-25.

11. These questions are paraphrased from Kenneth R. Pelletier, "Are You (Is He) a Lucky, Happy Workaholic? Or . . . ," *New Woman*, October 1983, p. 114, with several added from my experience. Bryan Robinson, an expert on work addictions, has discovered that adult children of work addicted parents tend to be perfectionistic workaholics who suffer from high levels of anxiety, often accompanied by depression.

12. Psychologist Chellis Glendinning shows the comparable characteristics of substance abuse and this addiction to technology and its products in "Technology, Trauma, and the Wild," *Ecopsychology*, pp. 41ff.

13. Al Gore, *Earth in the Balance: Ecology and the Human Spirit* (New York: Penguin Books, 1992), pp. 220-22.

14. "The All Consuming Self," Theodore Roszak, Mary E. Gomes, Allen D. Kanner, (eds.), *Ecopsychology: Restoring the Earth, Healing the Mind*. San Francisco: Sierra Club Books, 1995, pp. 77ff.

15. *Ecotherapy: Healing Ourselves, Healing the Earth* (Minneapolis: Fortress, 1996).

16. Frederick G. Levine, "Planet in Recovery," *Yoga Journal*, Nov./Dec., 1992, pp. 71ff.

17. Albert LaChance, *Greenspirit: The Twelve Steps of Ecological Spirituality* (Rockport, Mass.: Element, 1991).

18. *Santa Barbara News Press*, Dec. 1, 1996, p. A6.

19. I recommend an insightful manual on pathological gambling—the source of much of the information in this section—by psychologist Martin C. McGurrin, *Pathological Gambling: Conceptual, Diagnostic, and Treatment Issues* (Sarasota, Fla.: Professional Resource, 1992).

20. Ralph Earle and Gregory Crow, *Lonely All the Time: Recognizing, Understanding, and Overcoming Sex Addictions for Addicts and Co-dependents* (New York: Pocket Books, 1989), p. 3.

21. Riane Eisler, *Sacred Pleasure: Sex, Myth, and the Politics of the Body* (San Francisco: Harper San Francisco, 1995), pp. 123-24.

22. Conversation with Erma Pixley shortly before her death in 1979.

23. Leo Booth, *When God Becomes a Drug: Breaking the Chains of Religious Addiction and Abuse* (Los Angeles: Jeremy P. Tarchner, 1991).

24. Adapted from a review of Booth's book, in *Common Boundary*, September/October 1991, p. 27.

25. (Nashville: Abingdon Press, 1966; reprint 1984).

26. Winn, *The Plug-In Drug*, rev. ed. (New York: Viking, 1985).

27. Kimberly S. Young, cited in "On-line Junkie Hooked on His Screen," *Santa Barbara News Press*, June 5, 1995, p. A11.

28. Ibid.

29. From Ann Landers's column, *Santa Barbara News Press*, March 6, 1996, p. B6.

30. "E-mail Alters Students' Social, Academic Lives," *Santa Barbara News Press*, Nov. 11, 1996, p. A1.

31. "On-line Junkie Hooked on His Screen," *Santa Barbara News Press*, June 5, 1995, p. A11.

32. It is estimated that if a person spent only one minute looking at each web page on the World Wide Web, it would take 100 years to see all the pages.

5. Understanding and Helping Those at Special Risk of Addictions

1. David M. Edwards and Mary Allen, "Let's Draw the Line on Underage Drinking—George McGovern," *Treatment Today*, Spring, 1996, pp. 21ff.

2. Ann Landers, "Teenagers Tell of Addictions," *Santa Barbara News Press*, Dec. 16, 1991, p. D2.

3. "A Haven for Sober Students: An Environment for Recovery," *USA Today*, January 18, 1995, p. 5D.

4. Hillary Rodham Clinton, *It Takes a Village: And Other Lessons Children Teach Us* (New York: Simon & Schuster, 1996).

5. Clinton, *It Takes a Village*, p. 165.

6. Paul King, "Treatment for Chemically Dependent Adolescents," *Professional Counselor*, January/February 1988, p. 47.

7. Sharon Diriam, "Drug, Alcohol Abuse a Problem for Elderly," *Santa Barbara News Press*, Nov. 26, 1991, p. B1.

8. "Measuring Alcohol's Effects on You," *Johns Hopkins Medical Letter for Health After Fifty*, April, 1996, pp. 2-3.

9. Ibid.

10. "Elderly Abusing Alcohol, Medicines," *Santa Barbara News Press*, January 14, 1994, p. D5. (This article originally appeared in *Good Houskeeping*.)

11. Soji Kashiwagi, "Addiction and the Asian Family," *Treatment Today, Southern California*, April 1993, p. 30.

12. It is reported that on some tribal reservations, the absence of cultural controls on inebriety and the "we" (as contrasted with "I") culture produces heavy drinking occasions when adults of all ages get very drunk together. When they sober up there is no sense of the guilt or shame like that of people in "I" cultures with strong sanctions against inebriety.

13. Paige St. John, "Find Their Balance: American Indians Battle Alcoholism with Age-Old Spirituality," *San Jose Mercury News*, August 31, 1991, p. 10C.

14. *Manitou* means Great Spirit in Ojibwe. I received this version of the Twelve Steps from Sr. Paula Jacobs who does counseling and social service work with members of the Wisconsin tribe. My extensive efforts to locate the exact source of this version of the steps were unsuccessful.

15. Phone conversation with Enoch Jackson on March 14, 1995. John Bell, my son who has served as a tribal attorney for the Puyallup Tribal Council for two decades, helped me get in touch with Enoch Jackson, who described his use of these methods.

16. For a description of this sweat lodge experience see Howard Clinebell, *Ecotherapy: Healing Ourselves, Healing the Earth* (Minneapolis: Fortress, 1996), pp. 28-29.

17. Ronald J. Dougherty, "Impaired Professionals: The Endangered," *Treatment Today*, Spring 1996, p. 8.

18. Keith Dalton, "Championing Care for Social 'Throwaways,'" *Santa Barbara News Press*, December 4, 1995, p. B1.

19. For an insightful discussion on the social pressures faced by lesbians and bisexual women see Charlotte Davis Kasl, *Women, Sex, and Addiction: A Search for Love and Power* (New York: Harper & Row, 1989), pp. 207-23.

20. Marion Sandmales, "Alcohol Programs for Women," (Bethesda, Md.: National Institute on Alcohol Abuse and Alcoholism, n.d.), pp. 13, 21.

21. Ibid.

22. Louise Erdrich, *Tales of Burning Love* (New York: HarperCollins, 1996), p. 276.

23. The 1992 A.A. Membership Survey found that 35 percent of members were women, 43 percent of whom were under age thirty. Among the 65 percent of members who were men, 57 percent were under thirty.

24. Steven Pratt, "Women Pay a Higher Price for that Second Drink," *Santa Barbara News Press*, December 24, 1996, p. D2.

25. Charlotte Davis Kasl, *Women, Sex, and Addiction: A Search for Love and Power* (New York: Harper & Row, 1989) and *Many Roads, One Journey: Moving Beyond the Twelve Steps* (New York: Harper Collins, 1992).

6. How Religion Helps Low-Bottom Alcoholics and Drug Addicts

1. The U.S. Department of Housing and Urban Development has estimated that as many as six hundred thousand people are homeless in any given night. The fifty major cities are becoming harsher toward them, according to the National Law Center on Homelessness and Poverty, a homeless advocacy group. Half of the cities have laws against sleeping or camping in public places and conduct police sweeps on homeless people. Almost all the cities have more homeless people than emergency shelters and transitional housing spaces. See "Cities Are Becoming Rougher on Homeless People, Report Says," *Santa Barbara News Press*, December 12, 1996, p. A14.

2. I am indebted to him for a telephone interview on December 6, 1996 that provided much of the information about recent changes in Skid Rows and the treatments offered by Salvation Army facilities. In an unpublished article entitled "Homelessness," Dr. Cheydleur cites the following statistics: According to a 1995 study, 45 percent of homeless people were single men and 14 percent were single women, but the homeless also included single mothers with children, impoverished two-parent families, runaway and throw away teenagers and preteens. A Columbia University study found that "at least 5.7 million Americans were homeless for some period between 1985–1990." The homeless population in 1995 was 56 percent African American, 29 percent Caucasian, 12 percent Hispanic, 2 percent Native American, 1 percent Asian, and 21 percent veterans. The deinstitutionalized mentally ill constituted 27 percent of homeless people.

3. Jerry Gray (pseud.), *The Third Strike* (New York and Nashville: Abingdon Press, 1949), p. 11.

4. Robert Straus, "Alcohol and the Homeless Man," *QJSA* 7 (December 1946): 358ff.

5. D. J. Pittman and C. W. Gordon, *Revolving Door: A Study of the Chronic Police Case Inebriate* (New Haven: Yale Center of Alcohol Studies, Publication Division, 1958), p. 145.

6. From an address by the executive director of Men's Service Center and Halfway House, Rochester, N.Y., at the 1966 conference of the Association of Halfway House Alcoholism Programs of North America.

7. Jerry McAuley, *History of a River Thief* (New York: privately published, 1875).

8. Harold W. Maine (pseud.), *If a Man Be Mad* (Garden City, N.J.: Doubleday & Co., 1945), p. 181.

9. This was the strong impression I got from talking to men on the Bowery and from the interviewees who had lived on the Bowery.

10. William Booth, *In Darkest England and the Way Out*. Published in London, International Headquarters of the Salvation Army, 1890.

11. Ibid., p. 48.

12. Ibid., p. 86.

13. William James, *The Varieties of Religious Experience: A Study of Human Nature* (N.Y.: Longmans/Green & Co., 1902), p. 200.

14. From a telephone interview with Captain Cheydleur on December 6 1996.

15. When I visited the Bowery Corps of the S.A. in the early 1950s, the leaders had barred A.A. speakers even though some S.A. facilities welcomed them. This was because, as one of the officers explained: "Some of the A.A. speakers would swear from our platform and say things not in line with our teaching. . . . Here you're either saved or you're not."

16. These steps were presented at the Yale Summer School of Alcohol Studies by Envoy J. Stanley Sheppard of the Salvation Army.

17. Two S.A. centers in California received federal grants years ago that permitted them to augment their professional staffs and expand their rehabilitation programs. A follow-up study of 293 homeless alcoholics treated at the centers was done six months after they had left the centers. Of the one hundred of these who were located, the following improvement in their drinking patterns and employment records had occurred: 23 percent—great improvement; 25 percent—moderate improvement; and 53 percent—no improvement. The fact that nearly half of this group of homeless alcoholics showed significant improvement is impressive indeed.

18. Paul Robb, "Cap'n Tom: The Other Side of Skid Row," *Guideposts,* April, 1951. It is noteworthy that he rejected the offer of a full clinical rehab facility, complete with social workers and a psychiatrist, in favor of the straight evangelistic approach. His success probably indicates the crucial importance of the personality of key leaders, whatever their methods.

19. From a report presented by Major Peter Hofman at a symposium conducted by the Research Council on Problems of Alcohol (undated).

20. "A man may be down but he's never out," attributed to General William Booth, circa 1898, was used by Salvation Army officers in rescue work for many years. It was the inspiration for the song, "Down but Not Out," by composer Erik Leidzen, published by the Army in 1932.

21. Barbara C. Wallace, (ed.), *The Chemically Dependent: Phases of Treatment and Recovery* (New York: Brunner/Mazel, 1992), p. 331.

7. Alcoholics Anonymous: Still Our Greatest Resource

1. M. Scott Peck, *Further Along the Road Less Traveled* (New York: Simon & Schuster, 1993), p. 150.

2. Biographical information on Bill's early life is from my personal interviews, particularly the one on February 10, 1953. Additional biographical data on Bill W. can be found in *Alcoholics Anonymous: The Story of How Many Thousands of Men and Women Have Recovered from Alcoholism* (New York: Alcoholics Anonymous World Service, 1976), pp. 1-16 (also known as the Big Book).

3. The Oxford Group movement, or Buchmanism, first flourished on college campuses (including Oxford in England) and then spread to other areas. It was an attempt to bring vital, first-century Christianity into the lives of people, changing them to live by certain ethical absolutes and motivating them to change others. It stressed the importance of groups in this change process. In 1938 Buchman radically changed the movement into an evangelistic movement aimed at the powerful, affluent, and influential, whom he called the "up and out," and changed the name to Moral Rearmament.

4. W. W. (Bill W.), "The Fellowship of Alcoholics Anonymous," in *Alcohol, Science, and Society* (New Haven, Conn.: Quarterly Journal of Studies on Alcoholism, 1945), p. 462. A comprehensive history of A.A. by the cofounder is contained in *Alcoholics Anonymous Comes of Age* (New York: Harper & Bros., 1957). For an exploration of the origins of A.A. in Akron, the role of Dr. Bob and the spiritual roots in the Oxford Group, see the well-researched books in the bibliography by A.A.'s most dedicated historian, Dick B.

5. Ibid.

6. Ibid.

7. W. G. W., "Alcoholics Anonymous" from a panel discussion on "Chronic Alcoholism as a Medical Problem," *New York State Journal of Medicine,* L (July 15, 1950), 1709.

8. Bill's statement about his vision after the experience was in a letter of appreciation he wrote to Carl Jung on January 23, 1961 and reprinted in the *A.A. Grapevine,* January 1963 edition, p. 5.

9. In the Big Book, Bill states, "I was not an atheist," but in a taped interview with his wife, Lois, toward the end of her life, she said that he had been an atheist "at the beginning." See Dick B., *New Light on Alcoholism* (Corte Madre, Calif.: Good Book Publishing), p. 293, note 26. Bill's statement about his vision after his "hot flash" was in a letter of appre-

ciation he wrote to Carl Jung, January 23, 1961 and was reprinted in the *A.A. Grapevine*, January, 1963, p. 5.

10. W. G. W., "Alcoholics Anonymous," panel discussion.

11. Hunter, *A.A. and M.R.A.*, p. 12.

12. Oscar W. Ritchie, "A Sociohistorical Survey of A.A.," *QJSA* 9 (June, 1948): 122.

13. Dick B., *Dr. Bob's Library* (Wheeling, W.Va.: Bishop of Books, 1992), pp. 5-14.

14. *Dr. Bob and the Good Oldtimers* (New York: Alcoholics Anonymous World Services, 1980), pp. 173-74.

15. I was honored to be invited to be one of the nonalcoholic speakers on the topic, "How A.A. and the Church Can Cooperate."

16. Bill's major writings are in the bibliography of this book.

17. It is important to clarify several points about this description. It is based on an actual meeting that took place in the New York City area—with the exception of the third talk that happens to have been given in a Chicago meeting on the speaker's fifth anniversary in A.A. (Names and places have been altered to protect anonymity.) In spite of the basis in reality, it is impossible to convey on paper the real feeling of being present at an actual A.A. meeting. Neither the talks—of which portions are given—nor the meeting should be taken as representative of A.A. meetings in general. Each of the scores of meetings I have attended and the talk I have heard is a unique entity reflecting the experiences and styles of chairpersons and speakers. Also, meeting practices vary greatly from one section of the country to another.)

18. Adapted from *The Permanent Revolution* by the editors of Fortune, in collaboration with Russell W. Davenport (New York: Prentice-Hall, 1951).

19. *Alcoholics Anonymous*, pp. 83-84. In sharing their experiences after they had taken the moral inventory steps, the early members were describing the rewards that had come to them after they painstakingly went about this unburdening phase of their recovery. This inspiring paragraph is read at times in A.A. meetings to remind newcomers of rewards that others have found, rewards that may come to them.

20. W. G. W., "Alcoholics Anonymous," speaking on a panel discussion.

21. Herbert Fingarette, *Heavy Drinking: The Myth of Alcoholism as a Disease* (Berkeley: University of California Press, 1988), p. 72.

22. Ibid., p. 90.

23. One study resulted in the significant finding that half of a group of alcoholics in a mental hospital were later reported to have achieved sobriety by joining A.A.

24. According to the *1992 Membership Survey* by the A.A. World Services, before coming to A.A., 63 percent of members received some type of treatment or counseling, medical, psychological, or spiritual. Eighty percent of those receiving this said it played an important part in getting them to A.A. (A.A. World Services, Grand Central Station, Box 459, N.Y., NY 10163).

25. *Alcoholics Anonymous* (N.Y.: A.A. World Services, Inc., 1976), p. 564. For an in-depth discussion of the tradition, see Bill W., *Twelve Steps and Twelve Traditions* (New York: Alcoholics Anonymous World Services, 1953).

26. It is noteworthy that, in spite of his own long-term sobriety and his tremendous contributions to the recovery of countless addicted persons, Bill continued to wrestle with depression and his addiction to nicotine until a year before his death. A major contributing cause to his death was emphysema.

27. *1992 Membership Survey*, A.A. World Services.

28. Charles Leerhsen, et al., "Unite and Conquer," *Newsweek*, February 5 1990, pp. 50-55.

29. The mystery regarding the prayer's source was cleared up when Niebuhr's authorship was described in the January, 1950 issue of *The Grapevine*, A.A.'s official monthly publication (pp. 6-7). When Niebuhr was contacted about the prayer, he said: "Of course it may have been spooking around for years, even centuries, but I don't think so. I honestly believe that I wrote it myself."

8. Other Paths to Recovery and Beyond

1. Described by Charoltte Davis Kasl, *Many Roads, One Journey: Moving Beyond the Twelve Steps* (New York: Harper Collins, 1992), p. 166.

2. Jean Kirkpatrick, *Turnabout: New Help for the Woman Alcoholic* (New York: Bantam Books, 1977), p. 161. Kirkpatrick elaborates on these affirmations in chapter 10 of this auto-biographical book.

3. Kasl, *Many Roads,* pp. 162-73.

4. The seven hundred Recovery, Inc. groups begin their two hour meetings by reading from Low's text, *Mental Health Through Will-Training* (New York: Christopher Publishing, 1950). It spells out the principles and methods of this self-help therapy. Then members support one another by sharing accounts of disturbing events and how they coped effectively.

5. Kasl, *Many Roads,* p. XIV.

6. Ibid., pp. 308-27.

7. Ibid., p. 313.

8. Ibid., chapters 10 and 12.

9. Ibid., pp. 19-20.

10. Ibid., pp. 338-39. See chapter 14 for a discussion of these steps.

11. Charlotte Davis Kasl, "The Twelve Step Controversy," *MS,* Nov./Dec., 1990.

12. When I first encountered Kasl's writings, I was pleased to find that her approach includes many parallels with the goals, philosophy, and methodology of *growth counseling*—the spiritually centered, empowerment model of counseling and therapy that has evolved over several decades in my teaching, counseling, and writing. Kasl's emphasis on social context issues that contribute so substantially to individual and family problems parallels insights that have become increasingly important in my own work. The growth counseling approach has proved to be the most effective and therapeutically useful way of helping many people. I regard it as the treatment of choice in working with addicted persons, especially after they have achieved initial sobriety, usually by means of Twelve Step programs. In my view, Kasl's approach and the growth counseling approach are parallel paths for the beyond-healing-to-growing journey.

13. Mark B. Sobell and Linda C. Sobell, *Problem Drinkers: Guided Self-Change Treatment* (New York: Guilford Press, 1993).

14. Ibid.

15. Herbert Fingarette, *Heavy Drinking: The Myth of Alcoholism as a Disease* (Berkeley: Univ. of California Press, 1988).

16. Alcoholics Victorious and Alcoholics for Christ seem to be more theologically conservative than several other explicitly Christian groups.

17. The NACR statistics and statements quoted in this section are from the organization's membership brochure.

18. Ibid.

19. I am indebted to cofounder Bob Bartosch, for providing background information about O.O.

20. Bob Bartosch and Pauline Bartosch, comp., *Overcomers Outreach: A Bridge to Recovery,* (LaHabra: Overcomers Outreach, Inc.; Chicago: Meister, 1994), p. 48.

21. This quotation and some others in this section are from the O.O. brochure.

22. Bob Bartosch and Pauline Bartosch, *Overcomers Outreach.*

23. Ibid., pp. 285-86.

24. Ibid., pp. 291-92.

25. Information about AV is from a telephone interview with Michael Liimatta on December 17, 1996.

26. Information about Alcoholics for Christ is from a telephone interview with their national program coordinator, Brother Jesse Washington, on December 17, 1996, and from a brochure describing their beliefs and program.

27. A significant strength of several of these programs is that they recognize the value of Twelve Step recovery groups, and encourage their members either to attend these groups (as

in the case of O.O.) and/or use their own Christ-centered version of the steps. Another strength is that most of these approaches accept the disease concept of alcoholism, even in its sin-sickness modification. However, it should be noted that according to O.O., some "radical fundamentalist" rejected their movement when they discovered that it believes in the disease concept of addiction and has a Twelve Step program.

9. The Psychosocial Dynamics of Religious Approaches to Alcoholism and Other Drug Addictions

1. This letter was used by Greg Martin (pseud.) as the central theme and part of the title of his insightful book, *Spiritus Contra Spiritum: The Struggles of an Alcoholic Pastor* (Philadelphia: Westminster Press, 1977), p. 11.

2. Paul Tillich, *Shaking of the Foundations* (New York: Charles Scribner's Sons, 1948), p. 170.

3. Paul Tillich, *The Courage to Be* (New Haven: Yale University Press, 1952).

4. Friedrich Nietzsche, *The Works of Friedrich Nietzsche* (New York: Tudor Publishing Company, 1931).

5. Erich Fromm, *Psychoanalysis and Religion* (New Haven: Yale University Press), p. 23.

6. Henry David Thoreau, *Walden: Or Life in the Woods* (New York: Dodd, Mead & Co., 1946), p. 54.

7. Fromm, *Psychoanalysis and Religion*, p. 23.

8. Arnold J. Toynbee, *A Study of History*, Somervell's abridgment (New York: Oxford University Press, 1947), p. 276.

9. Jerry Gray (pseud.), *The Third Strike* (New York; Nashville: Abingdon Press, 1949), p. 32.

10. Thomas Wolfe, *Of Time and the River* (New York: Charles Scribner's Sons, 1935), p. 2.

11. Ibid., p. 281.

12. A powerful lecture at the Yale Summer School of Alcohol Studies, 1949.

13. Thomas Wolfe, *Look Homeward Angel: A Story of Buried Life* (New York: Charles Scribner's Sons, 1947), p. 525.

14. William James, *The Varieties of Religious Experience* pp. 377-78.

15. Terry D. Cooper, "The Psychotherapeutic Evangelism of John Bradshaw," *Pastoral Psychology* 44, no. 2 (1995): 79.

16. Nietzsche, *The Works of Nietzsche*, pp. 172-73. It amazes and humbles me to become aware of how he expressed what became some of the working concepts in my 1996 book, *Ecotherapy: Healing Ourselves, Healing the Earth*.

17. Tillich, *Shaking of the Foundations*, p. 158.

18. James, *Varieties of Religious Experience*, p. 378.

19. Gerald G. May, *Addiction and Grace* (San Francisco: Harper & Row, 1988), as excerpted in *Common Boundary*, Nov./Dec. 1988, p. 28.

20. Ibid., pp. 28-29.

21. Ibid., p. 29.

22. Søren Kierkegaard, *The Concept of Dread*, p. 104.

23. For a more comprehensive discussion of these and other existential needs, see my book, *Well Being: Exploring and Enriching the 7 Dimensions of Life* (Quezon City: Kadena Books, 1995), chapter 2, entitled, "Enriching and Enjoying Your Spiritual Life: Wellspring of Love, Well Being, and Joy."

24. James Christopher, *How to Stay Sober: Recovery Without Religion* (Buffalo, N.Y.: Prometheus Books, 1988), pp. 30, 31.

25. Ibid., p. 29.

26. Ibid., pp. 91, 92.

27. Ibid., p. 105.

28. Ibid., p. 11.

29. Greg Martin, *Spiritus Contra Spiritum* (Philadelphia: Westminster, 1977), p. 183.

30. For a more comprehensive discussion of the role of ultimate or existential anxiety in alcoholism, see Clinebell, "Philosophical-Religious Factors in the Etiology and Treatment of Alcoholism," *Journal of Ministry in Addiction and Recovery* 1, no. 2 (1994): 29-46.

31. Fromm, *Psychoanalysis and Religion*, p. 21.

10. Understanding Ethical Issues in Addiction and Recovery

1. Barney Brantingham, "Why Do the Wrong People Die?" *Santa Barbara News Press*, December 12, 1996, p. B1.

2. An illuminating discussion of the remarkable parallelism between the Pauline-Augustinian concept of original sin and the psychoanalytic concept of neurosis can be found in David Roberts, *Psychotherapy and a Christian View of Man* (New York: Charles Scribner's Sons, 1953), pp. 104-17.

3. Ibid., p. 94.

4. Ibid., p. 95.

5. Marty Mann, in her now classic *Marty Mann's New Primer on Alcoholism* (New York: Holt, Rinehart & Winston, 1981), pp. 202-3, has a cogent answer to the objection that the sickness concept will provide an excuse to drink: "Some people have raised the question as to whether teaching an alcoholic that his drinking is an illness will not give him a heavy weapon to use against those who are trying to persuade him to stop that drinking; saying that he might then be able to shrug the whole thing off with some statement like 'How can I help it—it's a disease, isn't' it?' or 'You must let me do as I please—I'm a sick man and I can't help being like this.' Those who raise the question have forgotten that alcoholics, almost if not entirely without exception, spend their time trying to drink like other people, not to drink alcoholicly. They rarely want to drink the way they inevitably end up drinking."

6. Giorgio Lolli, "On Therapeutic Success," *QJSA* 14 (June, 1953): 238-46.

7. Ibid., p. 241.

8. Ibid.

9. Quoted by Francis W. McPeek in "The Role of Religious Bodies in the Treatment of Inebriety in the United States," *Alcohol, Science and Society* (New Haven: QJSA, 1945), pp. 313-14.

10. Herbert Fingarette, *Heavy Drinking: The Myth of Alcoholism as a Disease* (Berkeley: University of California Press, 1988), p. 129.

11. Giorgio Lolli, "The Addictive Drinker," *QJSA* 10, nos. 3, 4 (December, 1949): 414.

11. Preparation for Counseling Alcoholics and Other Addicted Persons

1. My research on this issue began five decades ago when I did a carefully designed survey of 146 clergy who had attended the Yale Summer School of Alcohol Studies. The findings of that old study are cited in this revision only if they have been confirmed by my subsequent studies or by feedback from participants in numerous clergy workshops on addictions that I have taught since then.

2. In my original research study, clergy who advocated total abstinence and those who favored a return to prohibition had seen an average of only half as many alcoholics each year as those favoring moderation and opposing prohibition. Those advocating no position on these issues had averaged nearly twice the number seen by those holding to the moderation position.

3. D. L. Davies, "Normal Drinking in Recovered Alcohol Addicts," *QJSA* (March, 1962): 94-104.

4. Ibid., p. 103.

5. A summary of the Rand report with strong pro and con responses appeared in the *Los Angeles Times*, August 8, 1996, part VI, p. 5.

6. R. Gordon Bell, "Comments on the Article by D. L. Davies," *QJSA* (June 1963): 322.

7. Mark B. Sobell and Linda C. Sobell, *Individual Behavior Therapy for Alcoholics: Rationale, Procedures, Preliminary Results and Appendix* (California Mental Health Research Monograph no. 13.)

8. Herbert Fingarette, *Heavy Drinking: The Myth of Alcoholism as a Disease* (Berkeley: University of California Press), pp. 126-27.

9. Marty Mann, "The Pastor's Resources in Dealing with Alcoholics," *Pastoral Psychology*, April, 1951.

10. Clergypersons have had prominent roles in helping to start new groups in the past. For instance, the extensive work of A.A. in the St. Louis area grew from the efforts of a minister who shepherded several alcoholics he was trying to help, up to Chicago to have a firsthand experience of A.A. in action. These alcoholics started the first group in St. Louis. It is worth recalling that a minister, Sam Shoemaker, had a major role in the founding and shaping of A.A. It was another minister who gave Bill Wilson the name of Henrietta S., who arranged for his historic meeting with Dr. Bob Smith.

11. In their final, anonymous evaluation of these courses students often rated their attendance at a Twelve Step group as the high point of the course.

12. One of the more outspoken alcoholics I interviewed told of a young minister who tried to use the A.A. group to recruit members for his church. She declared with a touch of humor: "I gave him a piece of my mind. I guess it won't hurt him—he won't get drunk."

13. Barbara C. Wallace, ed., *The Chemically Dependent: Phases of Treatment and Recovery* (New York: Brunner/Mazel, 1992).

14. Antabuse is the American trade name for *tetraethylthiuram disulfide*. The drug is given orally and interferes with the metabolism of alcohol so that even one drink will cause a shock-like toxic reaction. When not taking it, alcoholics often fight the urge to drink countless times each day. When taking it, they have to say no only one time each day—when they decide whether to take the pill. The effects persist for four days, drastically reducing the danger of impulsive drinking. Taking it often abolishes the preoccupation with drinking. It also may relieve the disturbed family who know that the person is at least temporarily safe from alcohol. Some patients get a great lift from discovering that they can live without alcohol. The drug is not a cure and must be taken under the supervision of a physician. A word of caution is in order: In addictions, gullibility springs eternal, fed by desperation and the intense hunger for hope and help. Therefore, it is important to emphasize that Antabuse and other such drugs are not quick cures for alcoholism. Antabuse should never be used secretly as "pills for papa's coffee."

15. The director of this center, Dr. P. Joseph Frawley, describes the approach in *Addiction: Who Is in Control?* (Studio City, Calif.: Schnick Laboratories, 1988).

16. Particularly tragic are addicted people who are assured by psychotherapists that their addictions are merely symptoms of an underlying anxiety or other personality problems. They often continue in psychotherapy for extended periods while their addictive behavior grows steadily more severe.

17. Ruth Fox, "Modified Group Psychotherapy for Alcoholics?" *Postgraduate Medicine* 39 (March 1966): A-134.

18. Alcoholics with schizoid personality problems are unable to feel comfortable with the degree of human closeness that is present in either A.A. groups or group therapy. They may receive more help from a one-to-one relationship with a therapist or counselor who will allow them to keep whatever distance is necessary for them to feel relatively safe. A note of caution is in order about those believed to be mentally ill as well as addicted: Except for addicts with severe mental illnesses, the degree of underlying personality pathology and the type of therapy needed to treat it usually cannot be ascertained accurately until alcoholics and drug addicts have achieved a substantial period of sobriety. Many who appear very sick psychologically while they are drinking and using cope with the demands of reality after they are sober and clean without any therapy beyond Twelve Step programs.

12. Counseling for Recovery and Beyond: Motivating and Beginning the Process

1. These principles are set forth in detail in my textbook, *Basic Types of Pastoral Care and Counseling: Resources for Ministering of Healing and Growth* (Nashville: Abingdon Press, 1966; reprint 1984).

2. Karl Menninger, *The Vital Balance* (New York: Viking, 1963), p. 352.

3. This is Ernst Ticho's apt phrase, quoted by Menninger in *The Vital Balance*, p. 350.

4. Carl G. Jung, *Modern Man in Search of a Soul* (New York: Harcourt, Brace, & World, 1933), p. 234.

5. This was one of E. M. Jellinek's wise gems of advice.

6. Paul Tillich, "The Theology of Pastoral Care," *Clinical Education for Pastoral Ministry*, Ernest E. Bruder and Marian L. Barb, eds. Published by the Advisory Committee on C.P.E., 1958, p. 5.

7. Marty Mann, "The Pastor's Resources in Dealing with the Alcoholic," *Pastoral Psychology*, April 1951, p. 18.

8. Wayne Oates quotes this old gospel hymn in his insightful book, *Religious Factors in Mental Illness* (New York: Association Press, 1951).

9. Having gotten himself in an untenable position, the minister might have salvaged something for the future by saying to Mr. P. that he had come thinking he might want help, but since he was mistaken, he apologized. If he had done this, the door might have been left a bit ajar for Robert to ask for help at some point in the future.

10. Reprinted from M. M. Glatt, "Group Therapy in Alcoholism," *The British Journal of Addiction*, vol. LIX, no. 2 (January, 1958). Used by permission of the author.

11. This probably is due, at least in part, to my personal struggles of coping with diabetes.

12. Feldman presented this at the annual meeting of The National Council of Alcoholism, March, 18, 1955.

13. Vernon E. Johnson, *I'll Quit Tomorrow: A Practical Guide to Alcoholism Treatment* (New York: Harper & Row, 1973). See especially chapter 5, "The Dynamics of Intervention." See also *Intervention: How to Help Someone Who Doesn't Want Help* (Minneapolis: Johnson Institute, 1986).

14. If you wish to read the context of the quotations in this section, you will find this on pages 49-51 in *I'll Quit Tomorrow*.

15. "Alcoholism A Treatable Disease," Revised Edition, The Johnson Institute, 1987, p. 17.

16. Tiebout's innovative writings on surrender, appearing in the *QJSA* include: "Surrender Versus Compliance in Therapy, with Special Reference to Alcoholism," *QJSA* 15 (1953): 58-68; "The Ego Factor in Surrender in Alcoholism," *QJSA* 15 (1954): 610-21; and "Alcoholics Anonymous—An Experiment in Nature," *QJSA* 22 (1961): 52-68. He also published articles on surrender in the *Journal of the American Psychiatric Association* and created critical feedback because his theory went against the mainstream understanding in psychiatry that enhancing self-esteem was crucial in treating alcoholics.

17. Harry Tiebout, *A.A. and the Medical Profession* (New York: A.A. Publishing Company, 1955), p. 24.

18. For an in-depth discussion of this dynamic, see chapter 10, or see "Philosophical-Religious Factors in the Etiology and Treatment of Alcoholism," *Journal of Ministry in Addiction and Recovery* 1, no. 2 (1994): 29-46.

19. David A. Stewart, *Thirst for Freedom* (Toronto: The Mussen Book Co., 1960). See especially chapters 3 and 6.

13. Counseling for Recovery and Beyond: Basic Methods

1. For an elaboration of this model and its methods, see Howard Clinebell, *Basic Types of Pastoral Care and Counseling: Resources for the Ministry of Healing and Growth* (Nashville: Abing-

don Press, Revised Edition 1984), particularly chapter 7, "Supportive Care and Counseling," and chapter 8, "Crisis Care and Counseling." Also see Clinebell, *Counseling for Spiritually Empowered Wholeness: A Hope-Centered Approach* (Binghamton, N.Y.: Haworth Press, 1994).

2. Psychologist David Steward in *Thirst for Freedom: The Inside Story of Drink and Sobriety* (Toronto: Mussen Book Co., 1960), pp. 273-75, describes five stages of sobriety: *Initial sobriety:* physical health regained; preoccupation with sobriety, reduction of guilt and anxiety; increased self-honesty. *Learning sobriety:* loss of freedom (to drink in moderation) accepted; give and take of genuine personal relationships replaces grandiose behavior; regains acceptance of family and friends; sense of humor replaces self-pity; learns to cope with anxious or depressed states. *Accepting sobriety:* loss of desire to drink becomes lasting; thinking, feeling, and ethical perception improves. *Creative sobriety:* freedom from alcohol deeply appreciated; religious desires centered on new way of life; appreciates need for help from others; uses new freedom in other activities. *Pleasurable sobriety:* at peace with oneself and the world; anxiety and shyness diminish in genuine interpersonal relations; enjoys sobriety; rewards of sobriety clearly exceed tough times.

3. William Glasser, *Reality Therapy* (New York: Harper & Row, 1965), p. 60.

4. As mentioned in the A.A. chapter, 63 percent of members in a survey reported that they had received some type of treatment or counseling—medical, psychological, or spiritual— and 80 percent of these said that it had played an important part in getting them in A.A.

5. Bell described this approach in a lecture at the Utah Summer School of Alcohol Studies.

6. See Charlotte Davis Kasl, *Many Roads, One Journey: Moving Beyond the Twelve Steps* (New York: HarperCollins, 1992), especially chapter 12, "Healthy Groups, Dysfunctional Groups: How to Know the Difference."

7. In a study of factors that produce "readiness" for affiliation with A.A., it was discovered that alcoholics with the following characteristics tend to relate well to A.A.: before contact with A.A., they often shared troubles with others; had lost drinking friends; had heard positive things about A.A.; or had no relative or friend who had quit through willpower.

8. See psychiatrist E. Mansell Patterson, "A Critique of Alcoholism Treatment Concepts," *QJSA* 27 (1966): 61-62.

9. As the survey of A.A. members cited earlier discovered, 56 percent of members reported receiving some type of treatment or counseling after coming to A.A. Of those who did, 87 percent said that this help played an important part in their recovery. See "Alcoholics Anonymous 1992 Membership Survey" (New York: A.A. World Services).

10. John E. Keller, *Ministering to Alcoholics* (Minneapolis: Augsburg, 1966), p. 119.

11. Ibid., p. 57.

12. Howard Clinebell, *Well Being: A Personal Plan for Exploring and Enriching the Seven Dimensions of Life* (Quezon City, Philippines: Claretian Publications, republished 1995). Available from Upper Room Books, 1908 Grand Avenue, Nashville, TN 37202.

13. Charles L. Whitfield, *Healing the Child Within: Discovery and Recovery for Adult Children of Dysfunctional Families* (Deerfield Beach, Fla.: Health Communications, 1987).

14. Insoo Kim Berg and Scott D. Miller, *Working with the Problem Drinker: A Solution-Focused Approach* (New York: W. W. Norton, 1992).

15. Clinebell, *Basic Types of Pastoral Care and Counseling.* See chapter 5, "Facilitating Spiritual Wholeness: The Heart of Pastoral Care and Counseling," and chapter 6, "Counseling on Ethical, Value, and Meaning Issues."

16. For a discussion of methods of group care and counseling, see *Basic Types of Pastoral Care and Counseling,* chapter 14.

17. Crawford reported on his careful clinical research on using this method with patients in his 1990 Ph.D. dissertation at the School of Theology in Claremont where I was teaching at the time. It was entitled "Accompanying Individuals Through the First Three Steps of Alcoholics Anonymous."

18. Personal communication from Robin Crawford, September 1990.

19. This classic statement was in an article by Richards entitled, "The Minister and the Bum," *Pastoral Psychology* 6 (May, 1955).

14. Counseling with Families for Recovery: A Systems Approach to Codependency

1. *Al-Anon Faces Alcoholism* (New York: Al-Anon Family Group Headquarters, 1984), contains statements by professionals who work with families of alcoholics and by "those who live with the problem," as well as the working principles and history of Al-Anon. *The Dilemma of the Alcoholic Marriage* (New York: Al-Anon Family Group Headquarters 1971), a guidebook for alcoholic spouses, includes a chapter on applying the Twelve Steps to marriage problems. "The Alcoholic Husband: A Message for Wives" and "The Alcoholic Wife: A Message for Husbands" are A.A. pamphlets aimed at helping readers understand how to get alcoholic mates into A.A. The Big Book of A.A. has a chapter on "The Family Afterward," pp. 122-35.

2. Joan K. Jackson, "Alcoholism as a Family Crisis," *QJSA* 15 (December 1954): 562-86. In spite of the passage of time since Jackson's research, the progression is essentially true today, except that some wives leave addicted husbands sooner.

3. In 1991, a review of the literature on family systems therapy and substance abuse identified some one hundred professional articles reporting successes in using this approach to treatment.

4. Margaret Hindman, "Family Therapy in Alcoholism," *Alcohol Health and Research World* (Washington, D.C.: U.S. Department of Health, Education, and Welfare), Fall 1976, pp. 3-4.

5. Robert H. Albers, "Codependency: Characteristic or Caricature?" *Journal of Ministry in Addiction and Recovery* 2, no. 1 (1995): 1-2.

6. Charlotte Davis Kasl, *Many Roads, One Journey: Moving Beyond the Twelve Steps* (New York: HarperCollins, 1992), p. 266.

7. The first two elements in releasing also apply to clergy and other counselors' behavior in relationship to addicted persons. One minister tells of the hours and hours he spent trying to get and keep an alcoholic parishioner sober. The experience ended in failure and convinced the minister that he had made the mistake of babying the alcoholic—doing things for him that he should have been doing for himself. This conclusion fits with the recognition in A.A. that it is not helpful to pamper or "hold the hands" of a still-drinking alcoholic. Another pastor told of working very closely with an alcoholic: "He recovered, but only after I too had withdrawn my support, and he was forced to return to a hospital for treatment."

8. *Alcoholics Anonymous: The Story of How Many Thousands of Men and Women Have Recovered from Alcoholism* (New York: Alcoholics Anonymous World Service, 1976), p. 111.

9. The psychic economy of many male alcoholics, in my experience, seems to depend on their perceiving their wives or parents as mothering figures. The more they regress into alcoholism, the more they try to keep them in that role. But they also tend to see them less and less as good mothers who nurture and care for them, and more and more as bad mothers who nag, deprive, and try to control them. This seems to such addicts to justify angry and attacking drinking that may help maintain their grandiose illusion of self-sufficiency. The more wives and parents attempt to help them, the more they reinforce the conviction that they are bad, controlling mother figures. When they are able to release the addicts, and thus detach themselves, this neurotic interaction pattern is interrupted. Addicts are deprived of their defensive method of avoiding responsibility for their behavior by blaming their family. Often they will try to force family members back into parenting behavior by acting even more irresponsibly.

10. *Alcoholics Anonymous*, pp. 115-16.

11. Ibid., pp. 129-30.

12. I recall one wife who consistently planned for her husband to do something else on the night when A.A. met in their town, in spite of her conscious eagerness for him to achieve

sobriety. It was not until her unconscious sabotaging was explored and diminished in counseling that she was able to support his participation in A.A.

13. For example, emotionally immature people who find the demands of parenting and being a spouse too heavy, sometimes retreat into addictions to escape the anxiety of adult responsibilities. Their emotional inadequacy and all the attending problems of this are aggravated by their addictions, but the underlying personality problems are still there if their addiction is interrupted.

14. *Alcoholics Anonymous,* p. 129.

15. For a description of how such a pastoral care team that includes such people can be selected and trained, see Howard Clinebell, *Basic Types of Pastoral Care and Counseling: Resources for the Ministry of Healing and Growth* (Nashville: Abingdon Press, 1966; reprint 1984), chapter 16.

16. In Charlotte Davis Kasl's *Many Roads, One Journey* (pp. 267-69) she points out that the traditional codependency literature is full of blame-the-victim statements in many guides and forms. The chapter "To Wives" in A.A.'s Big Book, she says, "is more like a codependency manual (that is, how to be one) than a resource offering any real source of empowerment." For example, its advice includes, "Don't express your anger, don't leave, be as patient, kind and good as Mother Teresa, regardless of the neglect, violence or emotional abuse. It does not say—Be honest, be yourself, find your power, don't be abused, your husband's abuse is not your fault."

17. Ibid., p. 267.

18. Ibid., p. 279.

19. Mary Elizabeth Moore, "Codependence Theory: Heuristic or Reductionistic?" *Journal of Ministry in Addiction and Recovery* 2, no. 1 (1995): 75.

20. Kasl, pp. 288-89.

21. Albers, "Codependency: Characteristic or Caricature?" p. 7.

22. This astute observation was made by Claudia Black, author and leader in the Adult Children of Alcoholics movement

23. Joanne Sanders, "Adult Children of Alcoholics: Out of the Closet to Recovery," *The Common Boundary Between Spirituality and Psychotherapy* 6, no. 3 (May/June 1988): 7.

24. Ibid.

25. Melody Beattie, *Codependent No More: How to Stop Controlling Others and Start Caring for Yourself* (San Francisco: Harper & Row, 1987).

15. Developing Effective Addiction Treatment and Prevention Programs

1. Anderson Spickard and Barbara Thompson, *Dying for a Drink: What You Should Know About Alcoholism* (Dallas: Word Publishing, 1985), p. 16.

2. Ibid., p. 184.

3. Quoted by F. W. McPeek, "The Role of Religious Bodies in the Treatment of Inebriety in the United States in *Alcohol, Science, and Society* (New Haven: Journal of Studies on Alcohol, 1945), p. 142.

4. From insights gained through working in depth with alcoholics, Elwood Worcester arrived at a profound understanding of alcoholism: "The analysis, as a rule, brings to light certain experiences, conflicts, a sense of inferiority, maladjustment to life, and psychic tension, which are frequently the predisposing causes of excessive drinking. Without these few men become habitual drunkards. In reality, drunkenness is a result of failure to integrate personality in a majority of cases. Patients, however darkly, appear to divine this of themselves, and I have heard perhaps fifty men make this remark independently: 'I see now that drinking was only a detail. The real trouble with me was that my whole life and my thought were wrong. This is why I drank.' " *Body, Mind, and Spirit* (Boston: Marshall Jones, 1931) p. 229.

5. Elwood Worcester, *The Living Word* (New York: Moffat, Yard & Co., 1908), pp. 105-6.

6. Samuel McComb and Elwood Worcester, *The Christian Religion as a Healing Power* (New York: Moffat, Yard & Co., 1909), p. 125.

7. Layman P. Powell, *The Emmanuel Movement in a New England Town* (New York: G. P. Putnam & Sons, 1909), p. 126.

8. Spickard and Thompson, *Dying for a Drink*, p. 43.

9. Ibid., pp. 82-83.

10. Quoted in Charles Clapp Jr., *Drinking's Not the Problem: How You Can Help a Potential Alcoholic* (New York: Carowell & Co., 1949), p. 62.

11. Trish Merrill, *Committed, Caring Communities: A Congregational Guide for Addiction Ministries* (Austin: Texas Conference of Churches, 1994), pp. 19-23.

12. Ibid., p. 21. The quote about grace is from John E. Keller, *Ministering to Alcoholics* (Minneapolis: Augsburg Publishing House, 1966), p. 67.

13. The National Council on Alcohol and Drug Dependence has a hotline (800-475-HOPE) that provides automated information about the phone number of an agency within each state that can assist callers in finding local treatment facilities as well as preventive educational materials.

14. For example, the Presbyterian Church (USA) has published an excellent little book by Robin Crawford entitled, *Substance Abuse: A Handbook for Young People.* In language tailored to youth, it discusses both substances and behaviors that are misused and also describes treatment options.

15. Three of these are the books by Margaret A. Faud, Trish Merrill, and Anderson Spickard and Barbara R. Thompson. Faud's and Merrill's books describe a wide variety of alcohol and drug programs that congregations have developed and found to be effective (see annotated bibliography).

16. Margaret Fuad, *Alcohol and the Church: Developing an Effective Ministry* (Pasadena: Hope Publishing, 1992), see chapter 9.

17. Ibid, chapter 5.

18. Exception to this guideline are settings in which the sickness conception are likely to stir up immediate resistance and controversy.

19. A schedule of nearby meetings should be provided and the suggestions be given that no more than two persons attend a given meeting, and that they stay after the meeting to get personally acquainted over coffee with some members.

20. F. W. McPeek, *Alcohol, Science and Society*, p. 406.

21. Malnutrition and gaining weight from empty alcohol calories is one example that undergirds such an ethical perspective. But this view must be balanced by the evidence that very moderate use of red wine apparently has cardio vascular benefits. (Of course, red grape juice seems to have the same benefits.)

22. A recent addition to resources in this wellness ministry is a workbook I wrote, *Anchoring Your Well Being: Christian Wholeness in a Fractured World* (Nashville: Upper Room Books, 1998). It is accompanied by a leader's guide for using it and my book *Well Being* as texts in classes and workshops on Christian wellness.

23. Sharon R., "A Lifeboat for Clergy Alcoholics," *Circuit Rider*, October 1986, pp. 11-12.

24. For all these Twelve Steps see Merrill, *Committed, Caring Communities*, p. 93.

25. Spickard and Thompson, *Dying for a Drink*, pp. 15-16.

26. This pioneering degree program at the Methodist Theological School in Ohio was launched in 1985 with the inspiration and guidance of Paul Nicely, a faculty member with special experience and expertise in the area of addictions. See C. M. Kempton Hewitt, "The MA/ADAM Degree of 1985: An Innovative Theological Curriculum," *Journal of Ministry in Addiction and Recovery* 4, no. 1 (1997): 11-22.

27. The Presbyterian Network on Alcohol and Other Drug Abuse is one such program. Based on her experience in this network, Margaret A. Faud produced *Alcohol and the Church: Developing An Effective Ministry.* The Texas Conference of Churches, with the support of The Texas Commission on Alcohol and Drug Abuse, sponsored ADEPT (Alcohol and Drug Education in Parishes of Texas. Trish Merrill, R.N. led this project and produced *Committed, Car-*

ing Communities: A Congregational Resource Guide for Addiction Ministries. Both of these manuals are valuable resource guides for clergy and congregations.

28. Albers is professor of Pastoral Theology at Luther Seminary, St. Paul, Minneapolis, and a distinguished graduate with a Ph.D. in Pastoral Care and Counseling at Claremont Theological School in California. His dissertation was entitled "The Theological and Psychological Dynamics of Transformation in the Recovery from the Disease of Alcoholism" (Ann Arbor: University Microfilms International, 1982). He also is the author *Shame: A Faith Perspective* (New York: The Haworth Pastoral Press, 1995).

Annotated Guide to Further Resources

A.A. Publications**

Alcoholics Anonymous: The Story of How Many Thousands of Men and Women Have Recovered from Alcoholism. 3rd ed. New York: A. A. World Services, Inc., 1976. Basic text of A.A., published in English and thirty-one other languages, as well as in audio cassettes, braille, Microsoft Windows diskette, and video tapes in American sign language for hearing impaired alcoholics.

Wilson, Bill. *Alcoholics Anonymous Comes of Age*. New York: Harper & Brothers, 1957. The birth and development of A.A. during its first twenty years.

————. *The A.A. Way of Life*. New York: A.A. World Services, 1967.

————. *Twelve Steps and Twelve Traditions*. New York: Harper & Row, 1952. Describes how members recover through the Twelve Steps and how the fellowship functions guided by the Twelve Step traditions.

Other A.A. Books Include:

Dawn of Hope: The Founding of Alcoholics Anonymous. Akron, Ohio: Cinemark, Inc. This is a thirty-minute video documenting the remarkable beginning of A.A. in Akron Ohio. Write to 1761 Karg Dr., Akron, Ohio 44313 or call, 216-867-2116 for more information.

Dr. Bob and The Good Oldtimers is a biography of A.A.'s cofounder.

Pass It On: The Story of Bill Wilson and How the A.A. Message Reached the World is a biography of Bill.

Al-Anon Publications**

In All Our Affairs: Making Crises Work For You. New York: Al-Anon Family Group Headquarters, 1990. Reflections on the Twelve Steps as applied by family members.

Living With an Alcoholic. New York: Al-Anon Family Group Headquarters, 1985. The history and objectives of Al-Anon.

The Dilemma of the Alcoholic Marriage. New York: Al-Anon Family Groups, 1984. Explores the dynamics of the alcoholic marriage.

Other Resources

Ackerman, Robert J. *Let Go and Grow: Recovery for Adult Children.* Pompano Beach, FL: Health Communications, Inc., 1987.

Albers, Robert H. Albers. "Pastoral Care in Recovery from Addiction," in *Handbook for Basic Types of Pastoral Care and Counseling,* Howard W. Stone and William M. Clements, eds. Nashville: Abingdon Press, 1991. Discusses theological foundation for recovery ministry and activating the religious community; *Shame, A Faith Perspective.* N.Y.: The Haworth Pastoral Press, 1995. Explores the psychological and theological dynamics, and resources for gaining freedom from shame; *The Theological and Psychological Dyunamics of Transformation in the Recovery from the Disease of Alcoholism.* Ph.D. dissertation at Claremont Theological School, 1982.

Apthorp, Stephen P. *Alcohol and Substance Abuse: A Handbook for Clergy and Congregations.* 2nd ed. Harrisburg, Pa.: Morehouse Publishing, 1985. Written by the founder of ASAP (Alchohol and Substance Abuse Prevention.)

**B., Dick. *The Akron Genesis of Alcoholics Anonymous,* 1995; *The Good Book and the Big Book: A.A.'s Roots in the Bible,* 1995; *New Light on Alcoholism: The A.A. Legacy from Sam Shoemaker,* 1994. These books were published by Corte Madera, Calif.: Good Book Publishing. *The Oxford Group and Alcoholics Anonymous: An A.A. Good Book Connection.* Seattle: Glen Abbey Books, 1992. *Turning Point, A History of Early A.A.'s Spiritual Roots and Successes.* Paradise Research Publications, Inc., 1997. Carefully researched volumes by the leading historian of A.A.

B., Mel. *New Wine: The Spiritual Roots of the Twelve Step Miracle.* Hazelden Foundation, 1991. An A.A. friend of Bill Wilson, reflects on his leadership & on other people & ideas that shaped the early days of A.A. Emphasizes the spiritual heart of A.A.

**Sally and David B., *Our Children Are Alcoholics: Coping with Children Who Have Addictions.* Dubuque, Ia: Islewest Publishing, 1997. The parents of four addicted children share their own painful learnings, professional information about addicted families, and stories told by other parents of addicted children.

**Bartosch, Bob and Pauline Bartosch, compilers. *Overcomers Outreach: A Bridge to Recovery.* Chicago: Meister Press, 1994. The history and principles of O.O. by the cofounders.

Baumeister, Roy F. *Escaping the Self: Alcoholism, Spirituality, Masochism, and Other Flights from the Burden of Selfhood.* New York: Basic Books, 1991. A psychologist holds that the need underlying the various attempts to escape from the self—including alcoholism—is excessive concern for self-fulfillment and maintaining a positive self-image.

**Beattie, Melody. *Beyond Codependency: And Getting Better All The Time.* New York: Harper/Hazelden, 1989. Describes recovery from codependency.

———. *Codependent No More: How to Stop Controlling Others and Start Caring for Yourself.* New York: Harper/Hazelden, 1987. Describes self-care for codependents.

———. *The Language of Letting Go: Daily Meditations for Codependents.* San Francisco: Harper/Hazelden, 1990. Inspirational reflections for self-care and recovery.

Bell, Peter. *Chemical Dependency and the African-American.* Center City, Minn.: Hazelden.

Bepko, Claudia with Jo Ann Krestan. *The Responsibility Trap.* New York: The Free Press, 1985.

**Berg, Insoo Kim and Scott D. Miller. *Working with the Problem Drinker: A Solution-Focused Approach.* A new paradigm that applies the short-term solution-focused approach to therapy that emphasizes clients' strengths and builds on their solutions to problems.

Bissell, Le Clair and Paul Haberman. *Alcoholism in the Professions.* New York: Oxford University Press, 1984. Discusses alcohol addiction in various professions including the clergy.

**Black, Claudia. *It Will Never Happen To Me!* New York: Ballantine Books, 1981. Children of alcoholics, as youngsters, adolescents, and adults. Used in A.C.O.A. and C.O.A. groups.

**Blum, Kenneth in collaboration with James E. Payne. *Alcohol and the Addictive Brain: New Hope for Alcoholics from Biogenetic Research.* New York: The Free Press, 1991. Gives scientific evidence that alcoholism may be the result of an imbalance in the brain's natural production of neurotransmitters critical to a sense of well-being, an imbalance that may be genetically influenced.

Brisbane, Frances L. and Maxine Womble, eds. *Treatment of Black Alcoholics.* New York: Haworth Pastoral Press, 1985.

Brumbaugh, Alex G. *Transformation and Recovery: A Guide for the Design and Development of Acupuncture-Based Chemical Depenncy Treatment Programs.* Santa Barbara, Calif.: Stillpoint Press, 1993. Written by a therpist who uses acupuncture with alcoholics and drug addicts.

Burns, John and others. *The Answer to Addiction: The Path to Recover from Alcohol, Drug, Food, and Sexual Dependencies.* New Expanded Edition. New York: Crossroad Publishing, 1990. The "answer" is based on surrender to God and to truth, cleansing and amendment of life, helping others; absolute honest, purity, unselfishness, and love; and the Twelve Steps of A.A.

Catanzaro, Ronald J., ed. *Alcoholism: The Total Treatment Approach.* Springfield, Ill.: Charles Thomas, 1968. Includes chapters by many of the pioneers in the alcoholism field including Bill Wilson, Ruth Fox, Ebbe Hoff, and Vernelle Fox. Howard Clinebell's chapter is on "Pastoral Counseling of the Alcoholic and His Family."

**Chernin, Kim. *The Hungry Self: Women, Eating and Identity.* New York: Harper & Row, 1985. A counselor of women with eating disorders shows how they root in women's roles in our sexist society.

Cheydleur, John R., with Ed Forster, eds., *Every Sober Day Is A Miracle,* Wheaton, Ill.: Tyndale House Publishers, Inc., 1996. Ninety-nine inspiring stories of persons who recovered from alcohol and drug addictions, and found spiritual redemption at the 119 Salvation Army Adult Rehabilitation Centers in America.

Clancy, Jo Clancy. *Anger and Addiction: Breaking the Relapse Cycle: A Teaching Guide for Professionals.* Madison, Conn.: Psychosocial Press, 1996. A guide to resolving anger and resentment as a key to recovery.

Clark, Walter Houston. *Chemical Ecstasy: Psychedelic Drugs and Religion.* New York: Sheed & Ward, 1969. A psychologist of religion explores the complex links between psychedelic trips and religious experience.

Clinebell, Howard. "Philosophical-Religious Factors in the Etiology and Treatment of Alcoholism," *Journal of Ministry in Addiction and Recovery* 1, no. 2 (1994): 29ff.

———. "The Role of Religion in the Prevention and Treatment of Addictions: The Growth Counseling Perspective," *Man, Drugs and Society: Current Perspectives.* Proceedings of the first Pan-Pacific Conference on Drugs and Alcohol, Canberra, Australia. (Camberra: Australian Foundation on Alcoholism and Drug Dependence, 1980.

———. *Understanding and Counseling the Alcoholic Through Religion and Psychology.* Nashville: Abingdon Press, 1968. Rev. ed. A revision of the author's doctoral dissertation. ———. *Well-Being: A Personal Plan for Exploring and Enriching the 7 Dimensions of Life.* Quezon City, Philippines: Kadena Books, 1995. All seven dimensions are negatively influenced by addictions. (See chapter 4 for a discussion of "Loving Your Body by Reducing or Eliminating Toxins" and a "Pre-Addiction Checklist." Chapter 9 discusses "The Crisis and Grief of Addictions."

**Christopher, James. *How to Stay Sober: Recovery Without Religion.* Buffalo, N.Y.: Prometheus Books, 1988. The founder of Secular Sobriety Groups describes the approach.

Crawford, Robin C. *Accompanying People through the First Three Steps of Alcoholics Anonymous.* Ph.D. dissertation at Claremont Theological School,

1990. Sets forth an innovative approach to awakening people's spiritual experience.

Daley, Dennis C., Howard Moss, and Frances Campbell, *Dual Disorders: Counseling Clients with Chemical Dependency and Mental Illness*. Center City, Minn. Hazelden, 1987.

Drakeford, John W. *People to People Therapy Self Help Groups: Roots, Principles, and Processes*. New York: Harper & Row, 1978. Traces the roots of self-help groups to John Wesley, Frank Buchman (the Oxford Group), and its most unlikely offshoot, A.A.

Earle, Ralph H. and Marcus R. Earle, with Kevin Osborn., *Sex Addiction: Case Studies and Management*. New York: Bruner/Mazel, 1995. A manual on their multifaceted approach to treatment, which includes an emphasis on the spiritual component in recovery.

————. and Gregory Grow. *Lonely All the Time: Recognizing, Understanding and Overcoming Sex Addictions*. New York: Pocket Books, 1990. A case-enriched approach to understanding and helping persons with sexual addictions.

Eddy, Cristen C. and John L. Ford, eds. *Alcoholism in Women*. Dubuque, Iowa: Kendall Hunt, 1980. Includes chapters on women and men problem drinkers, women on skid row, women employees and alcoholism programs, and femininity in the bottle.

Fasset, Diane. *Working Ourselves to Death: The High Cost of Workaholism and the Rewards of Recovery*. San Francisco: HarperSanFrancisco, 1990. Explores the "killer disease" and what work addicts, families, and organizations can do to help in recovery.

Fein, Rashi. *Alcohol in America: The Price We Pay*. Newport Beach, Calif.: CareInstitute, 1984. A Harvard professor of the economics of medicine overviews the highs costs of the national problems of alcohol abuse and alcoholism.

**Fingarette, Herbert. *Heavy Drinking: The Myth of Alcoholism As a Disease*. Berkeley: Univeristy of California Press, 1988. A specialist in the ethical, legal, and social problems of addictions challenges widely held beliefs about alcoholism.

Finnegan, Dana and Emily McNally. *Counselling Chemically Dependent Gay Men and Lesbians*. Center City, Minn.: Hazelden Press.

Ford, Betty. *The Times of My Life*. New York: Ballantine, 1978. A former first lady tells of her struggles with and recovery from addiction.

Fossum, Merle. *Catching Fire: Men Coming Alive in Recovery*. New York: HarperCollins, 1989. A family therapist illuminates the special problems faced by men in recovery.

Fossum, Merle A. and Marilyn J. Mason. *Facing Shame: Families in Recovery* New York: W.W. Norton, 1986. Staff member of a family therapy institute writes on addictions as reservoirs of family shame, and its treatment.

**Frances, Richard J. and Sheldon I. Miller, eds. *Clinical Textbook of Addictive Disorders*. New York: The Guilford Press, 1991. Chapters by experts on psychoactive substance disorders (alcohol, sedatives, cocaine, tobacco, Opoids, and multiple drug dependencies), diagnostic instruments, a variety of treatment approaches, and the historical and social context of substance disorders.

**Fuad, Margaret A. *Alcohol and the Church: Developing an Effective Ministry*. Pasadena, Calif.: Hope Publishing House, 1992. An insightful discussion of what the Bible says about alcohol and drinking; a study outline on alcohol problems; and 150 practical ideas for setting up an alcohol ministry as a part of the mission of the church. Outstanding bibliography.

Galanter, Marc. *Network Therapy for Alcohol and Drug Abuse: A New Approach in Practice*. New York: Basic Books, 1993. A psychiatrist and research scientist integrate individual psychotherapy with family network therapy and A.A.

Gallant, Donald M. *Alcoholism: A Guide to Diagnosis, Intervention and Treatment*. New York: W.W. Norton, 1987. Includes bibliographies.

Glasser, William. *Positive Addiction*. New York: Harper & Row, 1976. The author of *Reality Therapy* explores getting high and constructive addictions such as running or meditating.

Gomberg, Edith L., Helene R. White, and John A. Carpenter eds. *Alcohol, Science, and Society Revisited*. Ann Arbor: University of Michigan Press, 1982. An updated version of a classic book in the field.

Gunderson, Gary, *Deeply Woven Roots, Improving the Quality of Life in Your Community*. Minneapolis: Fortress Press, 1997. The director of the Interfaith Health Program of the Carter Center shows how to utilize the eight major strengths of congregations to empower ministries of healing and transformation.

**Hester, Reid K. and William R. Miller, eds. *Handbook of Alcoholism Treatment Approaches: Effective Alternatives*. New York: Pergamon Press, 1989. Aiming at "informed eclecticism" in treatment. Overviews evaluation, motivation, primary treatment approaches, and a variety of additional resources including self-help groups, family therapy, psychotropic medication, and community reinforcement.

Hobe, Phyllis. *Lovebound: Recover from an Alcoholic Family*. New York: Penguin, 1991. An A.C.O.A. tells her story of growing up in an alcoholic home and evaluates the various treatment programs she has experienced.

————. *Hope, Faith, and Courage: Stories from the Fellowship of Cocaine Anonymous.* Los Angeles: Cocaine Anonymous World Services, Inc., 1993. The basic book of C.A. with illuminating stories by a variety of people who have found the road to recovery in that program.

Hornick, Edith Lynn. *Teenagers Guide to Living With an Alcoholic Parent.* Center City, Minn.: Hazelden, 1984.

**Jellinek, E. M. *The Disease Concept of Alcoholism.* New Haven, Conn.: College University Press, 1960. A classic exploration of the disease concept.

Joachim, Kitty. *Spirituality and Chemical Dependence: Guidelines for Treatment.* New York: Oxford University Press, 1988.

**————. *Journal of Ministry in Addiction and Recovery.* Binghamton, N.Y.: The Haworth Pastoral Press. The definitive journal on developments in pastoral care of addicted persons, edited by Robert H. Albers.

**Johnson, Vernon E. "God Help Me to Be Me: Spiritual Growth During Recovery." Johnson Institute, 1991.

————. *I'll Quit Tomorrow.* New York: Harper & Row, 1973. Describes the methods of intervention and treatment developed at the Johnson Institute Books.

————. *Intervention: How to Help Someone Who Doesn't Want Help.* Minneapolis: Johnson Institute Books, 1986. A step-by-step guide for families and friends of chemically dependent persons.

Kane, Geofrey P. *Inner-City Alcoholism.* New York: Human Services Press, 1981. From case work studies in the Bronx, discusses Hispanic and African-American alcoholism.

**Kasl, Charlotte Davis. *Many Roads, One Journey: Moving Beyond the Twelve Steps.* New York: HarperCollins, 1992.

————. *Women, Sex, and Addiction: A Search for Love and Power.* New York: Harper & Row, 1989. The writings of a trailbrazing feminist psychologist who has expertise on addiction, codependency, and child abuse.

Kaufman, Edward. *Psychotherapy of Addicted Persons.* New York: Guilford Press, 1994. A psychiatrist who is medical director of a hospital chemical dependency treatment program describes a pragmatic approach that integrates object relations and cognitive-behavioral therapy with family therapy and the Twelve Step movement.

**John Keller. *Ministering To Alcoholics.* Rev. ed. Minneapolis: Augsburg-Fortress, 1991. A classic in the field now updated.

Kinney, Jean. Kinney *Clinical Manual of Substance Abuse.* 2nd ed. St. Louis: Mosby, 1996. A clinical social worker authors a guide for health care professionals. Lists major alcohol and drug organizations, periodicals, and databases.

Kirkpatrick, Jean. *Good-Bye Hangovers, Hello Life*. New York: Atheneum, 1986.

———. *Turnabout: New Help for the Woman Alcoholic*. New York: Bantam Books, 1990. By the founder of Women for Sobriety.

Koenig, Harold G., *Is Religion Good for Your Health? The Effects of Religion on Physical and Mental Health*. New York: The Haworth Press, 1997. Presents the scientific research findings showing that religion can have a negative or a positive impact on health, including addictions.

Krupski, Ann Marie. *Inside the Adolescent Alcoholic*. Center City, Minn.: Hazelden, 1982.

Kurtz, Ernest. *Not God: A History of Alcoholics Anonymous*. Center City, Minn.: Hazelden, 1979. A comprehensive historical account of A.A.

Kus, Robert J., R.N., Ph.D., ed., *Spirituality and Chemical Dependency*. New York: Harrington Park Press, 1995. Edited by a nurse-sociologist who teaches at St. Meinrad School of Theology.

**Mann, Marty. *Marty Mann's New Primer on Alcoholism*. New York: Holt, Rinehart & Winston, 1981.

———. *Marty Mann Answers Your Questions About Drinking and Alcoholism*. New York: Holt, Rinehart & Winston, 1970. By the founder of The National Council on Alcoholism.

Marshall, John Armstrong. *Your Perfect High*. Glendale, Calif.: Happy Eye Enterprises, 1978. Describes right-left brain methods of getting high without alcohol or drugs.

Martin, Greg. *Spiritus Contra Spiritum*. Philadelphia: Westminster, 1977. Insightful autobiography of an alcoholic minister who has come alive in A.A.

Matto, Michele S. *The Twelve Steps in the Bible: A Path to Wholeness for Adult Children*. New York: Paulist Press, 1991. A collection of scriptural reflections on the Twelve Steps for children of alcoholics and other codependents.

**May, Gerald, M.D. *Addiction and Grace*. San Francisco: Harper & Row, 1988. A psychiatrist who holds that everyone suffers from addictions, tells of his awakening to the centrality of grace in recovery from addictions— his own and his patients.

**McConnell, Patty. *Adult Children of Alcoholics: A Workbook for Healing*. San Francisco: Harper & Row, 1986. A guide to recovery from the adult pain and conflicts resulting from growing up in a household filled with denial, confusion, grief, and fear.

**McGurrin, Martin C., Ph.D. *Pathological Gambling: Conceptual, Diagnostic, and Treatment Issues*. Sarasota, Fla.: Professional Resource Press,

1992. Includes a historical overview of gambling, theories of pathological gambling, diagnosis, treatment, and the family's role.

McKenna, Terence. *Food of the Gods: The Search for the Original Tree of Knowledge.* New York: Bantam Books, 1992. A radical history of plants, drugs, and human evolution by an expert on psychodelic experiences.

**McKeever, Bridget Clare, *Hidden Addictions: A Pastoral Response to Abuse of Legal Drugs.* Binghamton, NY: The Haworth Press, 1998. An insightful exploration of the epidemic of addictions to prescribed and over-the-counter drugs, showing the social and spiritual causes, and how to respond in healing ways.

McKeever, Bridget Clave. *A Pastoral Response to Dependency on Prescribed Drugs in Women.* Ph.D. dissertation at Claremont School of Theology, 1983.

Mercadante, Linda, *Victims and Sinners: Spiritual Roots of Addiction and Recovery.* Louisville: Westminster John Knox, 1997. A discussion of the key dynamic of spirituality in the addiction process.

**Merrill, Trish, R.N. *Committed, Caring Communities: A Congregational Guide for Addiction Ministries.* Austin, Texas: Project ADEPT, Texas Conference of Churches, 1994. A valuable, how-to manual for congregational addiction team ministries.

Miller, Peter M. and Marie A. Mastria. *Alternatives to Alcohol Abuse: A Social Learning Model.* Champaign, Ill.: Research Press, 1977. A book for therapists and counselors working with alcoholics, describing methods of assessment, establishing a treatment plan, and using a variety of skill training in that treatment.

Milstead, Robin J. *Empowering Women Alcoholics to Help Themselves and Their Sisters in the Workplace.* Dubuque, Iowa: Kendall/Hunt, 1991. Women, employment and alcohol abuse in the USA.

National Household Survey on Drug Abuse: Main Findings 1990. Rockville, Md.: National Institute on Drug Abuse, Alcohol, and Mental Health Administration, U.S. Department of Health and Human Services. Reports on trends in drug use, 1972–1990; prevalence of use of marijuana, cocaine, hallucinogens, heroin, alcohol, and tobacco.

National Treatment Directory for Alcoholism, Drug Abuse and Other Addiction Problems. Deerfield Beach, Fla.: U.S. Journal on Drug and Alcohol Dependence (updated annually).

Nowinski, Joseph, Ph.D. *Substance Abuse in Adolescents and Young Adults: A Guide to Treatment.* New York: W.W Norton & Co., 1990. A psychologist describes the patterns, causes, and treatment of addictions in adolescents and young adults.

**Oates, Wayne E. *Workaholics: Make Laziness Work For You.* Nashville: Abingdon Press, 1978. A humorous but also serious discussion of laziness—its importance, creative expression, hazards, and being lazy in good conscience.

**Olitzky, Rabbi Kerry M. and Stuart A. Copans. *Twelve Jewish Steps to Recovery*. Woodstock, Vt.: Jewish Light Publishing, 1991. A guide to recovery from a variety of addictions using the rich resources of the Jewish heritage and the Twelve Step approach.

Peele, Stanton. *Diseasing of America: Addiction Treatment Out of Control*. Boston: Houghton Mifflin, 1989. A social psychologist challenges the addiction-as-disease movement, and shows how society can support people in outgrowing or avoiding addictions.

————and Archie Brodsky. *The Truth About Addiction and Recovery: The Life Process Program for Outgrowing Destructive Habits*. New York: Fireside Books, 1992. Claims that addictions are not diseases and not necessarily lifelong problems. Describes a program for overcoming addictions by self-help, coping with stress, and achieving one's goals.

Peluso, Emanuel and Lucy Silvay Peluso. *Women and Drugs*. Minneapolis: CompCare Publishers, 1988.

Pernanen, Kai. *Alcohol in Human Violence*. New York: Guilford Press, 1991. Explores the relation of alcoholism to crime and violence.

Pomerleau, Ovide F. and Cynthia S. Pomerleau. *Breaking the Smoking Habit: A Behavioral Program for Giving Up Cigarettes*. Champaign, Ill.: Research Press, 1977. Describes a program developed at the University of Pennsylvania's Center for Behavioral Medicine.

Ray, Oakley S. *Drugs, Society and Human Behavior*. 5th ed. St. Louis: Times Mirror, Mosby College, 1990. Discusses psychotropic drugs, drug abuse, and neuropsychopharmacology.

Reiners, Ken. *There's More to Life Than Pumpkins: Drugs and Other False Gods*. Wayzata, Minn.: Woodland, 1980. A clergyman who specializes in chemical dependencies and has worked with ghetto and runaway youth, writes this guide to spiritual recovery.

Robertson, Nan. *Getting Better: Inside Alcoholics Anonymous*. New York: William Morrow & Co., 1988. A veteran *New York Times* reporter explores A.A. and the recovery process in depth, including her own moving story.

Roth, Geneen. *Breaking Free From Compulsive Eating*. New York: Signet Book, 1986. The author of *Feeding the Hungry Heart* offers a program to resolve the conflicts at the roots of compulsive eating/dieting.

Sandmaier, Marian. *The Invisible Alcoholics: Women and Alcohol Abuse in America*. New York: McGraw-Hill, 1980. Discusses alcoholic housewives, employed women, minority, teens, lesbians, and skid row women alcoholics.

Scanlon, Walter F. *Alcoholism and Drug Abuse in the Workplace*. New York:

Praeger, 1991. Managing care and costs through employee assistance programs.

**Schaef, Anne Wilson. *Co-Dependence, Misunderstood, Mistreated.* San Francisco: Harper & Row, 1983. A psychotherapist explores codependence.

―――. *When Society Becomes an Addict.* San Francisco: Harper & Row, 1987. Shows how the "white male system" makes the addictive process proliferate in both substance and process addictions.

Seixas, Judith S. and Geraldine Youcha. *Children of Alcoholism: A Survivors Manual.* New York: Harper & Row, 1985.

―――. *Sexaholics Anonymous.* Simi Valley, Calif.: SA Literature, Rev. ed., 1989. "A program of recovery for those who want to stop their sexually self-destructive behavior."

Shoemaker, Samuel M. *Courage to Change: The Christian Roots of the Twelve-Step Movement.* The writings of the clergyman who helped guide Bill Wilson in developing A.A. Compiled and edited by Bill Pittman with Dick B.

**Sobell, Mark B. and Linda C. Sobell. *Problem Drinkers: Guided Self-Change Treatment.* New York: Guilford Press, 1993. A treatment manual for practitioners who work with nonaddicted problem drinkers.

**Spickard, Anderson, M.D. and Barbara R. Thompson. *Dying for a Drink: What You Should Know About Alcoholism.* Dallas: Word Publishing, 1985. A Christian-oriented approach coauthored by the medical director of Vanderbilt University Institute for Treatment of Addictions.

Steiner, Claude. *Games Alcoholics Play: The Analysis of Life Scripts.* New York: Ballantine Books, 1971. A transactional analysis approach to the treatment of alcoholics by a psychologist who rejects the disease concept.

Stewart, David A. *Thirst for Freedom: The Inside Story of Drink and Sobriety.* Toronto: Musson Book, 1960. The frustrated thirst to be yourself is seen as a cause of using alcohol and drugs. The key to sobriety is to satisfy this thirst by empathy, freedom, love, and growth.

**Stimmel, Barry, M.D. and the editors of *Consumer Report. The Facts About Drug Use.* New York: Haworth Medical Press, 1993. An insightful discussion of "Coping with drugs and alcohol in your family, at work, in your community.

**Straussner, Shulamith Lala Ashenberg, ed. *Clinical Work with Substance Abuse Clients.* New York: The Guilford Press, 1993. Overview of treatment of persons addicted to all the major drugs including alcohol and nicotine.

The Twelve Steps for Everyone. Minneapolis: CompCare Publications. Written by recovering people who describe the approach of Emotional Health Anonymous.

U.S. Department of Health and Human Services, National Institute of Alcoholism and Alcohol Abuse, *A Guide to Planning Alcohol-Treatment Programs*. (#017-024-01277-7) Washington, D.C.: Supt. of Documents.

**Vaillant, George E. *A Natural History of Alcoholism*. Cambridge, Mass.: Harvard University Press, 1983.

**Wallace, Barbara C., ed. *The Chemically Dependent: Phases of Treatment and Recovery*. New York: Brunner/Mazel, 1992. An excellent overview of contemporary knowledge and treatment methods by authorities in the addiction field.

Weil, Andrew. *The Natural Mind: An Investigation of Drugs and the Higher Consciousness*. Boston: Houghton Mifflin, 1986.

Wegscheiden-Cruse, Sharon. *Choicemaking: For Co-Dependents, Adult Children and Spirituality Seekers*. Deerfield Beach, Fla.: Health Communications, 1985.

**West, James W., *The Betty Ford Center Book of Answers, Help for those struggling with substance abuse and for the people who love them*. Foreword by Betty Ford. N.Y.: Pocket Books, 1997. An insightful physician, medical director of the outpatient program at the Betty Ford Center, answers a variety of questions asked by readers of his newspaper column.

**Whitfield, Charles L. *Healing the Child Within: Discovery and Recovery for Adult Children of Dysfunctional Families*. Deerfield Beach, Fla.: Health Communications, Inc., 1987. A physician who specializes in treating people with alcohol, drug, and family problems describes the journey of healing the wounded inner child.

Wiseman, Jacqueline P. *Stations of the Lost: The Treatment of Skid Row Alcoholics*. Englewood Cliffs, N.J.: Prentice-Hall, 1983.

Woodruff, C. Roy. *Alcoholism and Christian Experience*. Philadelphia: Westminster, 1968. By the current executive director of the American Association of Pastoral Counselors.

Yates, Alayne. *Compulsive Exercise and the Eating Disorders: Toward an Integrated Theory of Activity*. New York: Brunner/Mazel, 1991. A psychiatrist explores the links between compulsive exercise and eating disorders such as bulimia nervosa, seeing both as activity disorders.

Ziebold, Thomas O. and John Mongeon, eds. *Alcoholism and Homosexuality*. New York: Haworth Press, 1982.

** = cited in this book

Sources of Referral and Other Information

Note: Addresses and phone numbers may have changed. For referrals for any type of substance abuse, contact Drug Help, 1-800-378-4435. The

National Clearing House for Alcohol and Drug Information has a website (www.health.org) that gives information about many of these organizations.

Addiction Connection Website (www.addictioninfo.com)

Addiction Research Foundation of Ontario, 33 Russell St., Toronto, Ont., Canada M5S 251

Adult Children of Alcoholics and Dysfunctional Families, (ACA), World Service Organization, P.O. Box 3216, Torrance, CA 90510 (310-534-1815)

AL-ANON/ALATEEN Family Group Headquarters, 1600 Corporate Landing Parkway, Virginia Beach, VA 23454 (1-800-334-2666)

Alcoholics Anonymous (A.A.), General Service Office, 475 Riverside Dr., N.Y., NY, 10115 (212-870-3400) or P.O. Box 459, Grand Central Station, N.Y., NY 10017

Alcoholics for Christ, 1316 N. Campbell Rd., Royal Oaks, MI 48067

Alcoholics Victorious, 1045 Swift St., North Kansas City, MO 64116, (816-471-8020)

Alcoholism and Substance Program Branch of the Indian Health Service, 5300 Homestead Rd., NE, Albuquerque, NM 87110 (505-248-4121)

Alcohol Treatment Referral Hotline (1-800-ALCOHOL)

American Society of Addiction Medicine (ASAM), 4601 N. Park Ave., Upper Arcade, Suite 101, Chevy Chase, MD 20815 (301-656-3920)

Betty Ford Center, P.O. Box 1560, Rancho Mirage, CA 92270 (619-773-4100)

Brown University's Center for Alcohol and Addiction Studies, Brown University, Box G-BH, Providence, RI 02912 (401-404-1800)

Center for Substance Abuse Prevention (CSAP), Substance and Mental Health Sevices Administration, Rockwall IL, 5600 Fishers Lane, Rm. 900, Rockville, MD 20857 (301-443-0365)

Center for Substance Abuse Treatment (CSAT), Substance and Mental Health Sevices Administration, Rockwall IL, Parklawn Bldg., 6th Fl., Rockville, MD 20857 (301-443-5052) (www.health.org/phone.htm) Referral service (1-800-660-HELP)

The Christopher D. Smithers Foundation, P.O. Box 67, Mill Neck, NY 11765 (516-676-0067)

Codependents Anonymous (CODA), P.O. Box 33577, Phoenix, AZ 85067 (602-977-7991)

Columbia University's Center on Addiction and Substance Abuse (CASA), 152 W. 57th St., 12th Floor, N.Y., NY 10019 (212-841-5200)

Cocaine Anonymous, 9100 Sepulveda Blvd., Suite 216, Los Angeles, CA 90045 (310-216-4444)

Community Anti-Drug Coalitions of America (CADCA), 901 Pitt St., Suite 300, Alexandria, VA 22314 (703-706-0560)

Debtors Anonymous, P.O. Box 400, Grand Central Station, N.Y., NY 10163 (212-642-8220)

Emotions Anonymous, P.O. Box 4245, St. Paul, MN 55104 (612-647-9712)

Families Anonymous, Inc., Box 3475, Culver City, CA 90231 (1-800-736-9805)

Drug Help, 164 W. 74th St., N.Y., NY 10023 1-800-378-4435

Fighting Back, National Program Office, 1107 Oxford House, Nashville, TN 37232 (615-723-5053)

Gamblers Anonymous International Service Office, P. O. Box 17173, Los Angeles, CA 90017 (213-386-8789)

Hazelden Foundation, Box 176, Center City, MN 55012 (800-257-7800) (www.hazelden.org/index.dbrn)

International Council of Alcohol and Addiction, Case Postale 189, 1001 Lausanne, Switzerland (Oll-41-21-320-9865)

Jewish Alcoholic, Chemically Dependent Persons and Significant Others, (JACS) 426 W. 58th St., N.Y., NY 10019 (212-397-4197)

The Johnson Institute, 7205 Ohms Lane, Suite 200, Minneapolis, MN 55439 (1-800-231-5165)

Marijuana Anonymous World Services, P.O. Box 2912, Van Nys, CA 91404 (1-800-766-6779)

Mothers Against Drunk Driving (MADD), 511 E. John Carpenter Freeway, Suite 700, Irving, TX 75062 (1-800-GET-MADD) (www.madd.org)

Nar-Anon Family Group Headquarters, Inc., P.O. Box 2562, Palos Verdes, CA 90274 (310-547-5800)

Narcotics Anonymous, World Service Office, P.O. Box 9999, Van Nuys, CA 91409 (818-773-9999)

National Assn. of Alcoholism and Drug Abuse Counselors (NAADAC), 1911 Fort Meyer Dr., Suite 900, Arlington, VA 22209 (1-800-548-0497)

National Black Alcoholism and Addiction Council, 1101 14th St., NW, Suite 630, Washington, DC 20005 (202-296-2696)

National Clearinghouse for Alcohol and Drug Information (NCADI), P.O. Box 2345, Rockville, MD 20843 (1-800-729-6686) (www.health.org)

National Council on Alcoholism and Drug Dependence (NCADD), 12 W. 21st., NY, NY 10010 (212-206-6770) **NCADD** Referral hopeline (1-800-622-2255) (www.ncadd.org/index.html) Web site has a list of other addiction web sites.

National Institute on Alcohol Abuse and Alcoholism (NIAAA), 6000 Executive Blvd., Bethesda, MD 20892 (301-443-3860) For publications contact NIAAA Distribution Center, P.O. Box 10686, Rockville, MD 20849

National Institute on Drug Abuse (NIDA), 5600 Fishers Lane, Room 10-05, Rockville, MD 20857 (301-443-4577)

National Self-Help Clearinghouse, 25 W. 43rd St., Rm. 20, NY, NY 10036 (212-354-8525)

Overeaters Anonymous, (O.A.) P.O. Box 44020, Rio Rancho, NM 87194 (505-891-2660)

National Association for Christian Recovery, P.O. Box 215, Brea, CA 92822 (714-529-6227)

Overcomers Outreach, Inc., 520 N. Brookhurst Ave, Suite 121, Anaheim, CA 92801 (1-800-310-3001)

Partnership for a Drug-Free America, 405 Lexington Ave., 16th Floor, NY, NY 10174 (212-922-1560)

Rational Recovery Systems, (800-303-CURE)

Rutgers Center of Alcohol Studies, Rutgers, The State University of New Jersey, Busch Campus-Smithers Hall, 607 Allison Rd., Piscataway, NJ 08854 (732-455-2190; fax: 732-445-3500)

Secular Organization for Sobriety (SOS or SAVE OURSELVES), 5521 Grosvenor Blvd., Los Angeles, CA 90066 (310-821-8430)

The Salvation Army (information about addiction programs), William Riley, M.A., The Salvation Army, 440 W. Nyack Rd., P.O. Box C-635, West Nyack, NY 10994 (914-620-7393)

Sexaholics Anonymous, P.O. Box 111910, Nashville, TN 37222 (615-331-6230)

Sex Addicts Anonymous, P.O. Box 70949, Houston, TX 70949 (713-869-4902)

Sex and Love Addicts Anonymous, P.O. Box 650010, West Newton, MA 02165 (617-332-1845)

Treatment Organizations Hotline (NCADD), (1-800-662-HELP)

Students Against Drunk Driving (SADD), P.O. Box 800, Marlboro, MA 01752 (508-481-3568)

Vanderbilt Institute for Treatment of Alcoholics, 4th Flor, Erfoss Bldg., Vanderbilt University Medical Center, Nashville, TN 37232 (615-322-6158)

Women for Sobriety (also Men for Sobriety), P.O. Box 618, Quakertown, PA 18951 (1-800-333-1606)

Index